THE COMPLETE FOOD SUBSTITUTIONS HANDBOOK

INCLUDING OPTIONS FOR LOW-SUGAR, LOW-FAT, LOW-SALT, GLUTEN-FREE, LACTOSE-FREE, SOY-FREE, AND VEGAN

Jean B. MacLeod

MacLeod How-To Books
The Complete Food Substitutions Handbook: Including Options for Low-Sugar, Low-Fat, Low-Salt, Gluten-Free, Lactose-Free, Soy-Free, and Vegan
Copyright © 2018 by Jean B. MacLeod

ISBN-13: 9780997446494
Library of Congress Control Number: 2018913426

For Elizabeth and Pamela,
for which there are no substitutions

A

ABALONE, FARMED, FRESH – 1 pound
- 8 ounces dried abalone/*pao yu*, soaked in water for 3 to 4 hours
- 1 pound French conch, tenderized like fresh abalone
- 1 pound fresh clam meat

ABURAGE *See TOFU, DEEP-FRIED*

AÇAI (South American antioxidant-rich purple berry) – 3.5 ounce-packet frozen pulp/puree
- 1/2 to 3/4 cup dried Chilean wineberries/maqui berries, soaked in liquid for 30 minutes (higher in antioxidants)
- 1 cup fresh or frozen wild blueberries (lower in antioxidants)
- 1 cup fresh, or 1/2 cup dried, blue Oregon grapes/*Mahonia aquifolium/Berberis aquifolium* (lower in antioxidants; much tarter; press fresh berries through a food mill to remove large seeds)
- 1 cup fresh silverberries/*Elaeagnus umbellata* or *E. multiflora* (lower in antioxidants; higher in vitamin C and lycopene; press through a food mill to remove large seeds)

AÇAI JUICE (antioxidant-rich juice) – 1 cup
- 2 tablespoons freeze-dried açai powder mixed with 1 cup water
- 2 tablespoons maqui berry powder mixed with 1 cup water (higher in antioxidants)
- 1 cup 100% blueberry juice, preferably fresh-pressed (lower in antioxidants)
- 2 tablespoons freeze-dried blueberry powder mixed with 1 cup water (lower in antioxidants)

ACHIOTE/ACHUETE *See ANNATTO OIL; ANNATTO SEEDS*

ACHIOTE PASTE/RECADO ROJO (Latin American seasoning and coloring) – 1 tablespoon
- 1 tablespoon Sazon Goya Seasoning
- 2 teaspoons ground annatto seeds or powdered annatto/*bijol* (for coloring; lacks seasoning)
- 1 teaspoon paprika (for coloring only)

ACIDULATED WATER (anti-browning agent for certain cut fruits and vegetables) – 1 cup
- 1 cup water plus 3/4 teaspoon kosher salt (rinse well with fresh water after soaking)
- 1 cup water plus 1 teaspoon distilled white vinegar
- 1 cup water plus 2 teaspoons lemon juice
- 1 cup water plus small pinch ascorbic acid granules, or 1 (250-mg) pure vitamin C pill crushed to a powder
- 1 cup apple juice (for holding prepared apples)

ACITRÓN (Mexican candied cactus pieces) – 4 ounces
- 4 ounces candied pineapple

ACORN SQUASH, FRESH (oval-shaped, orange-fleshed winter squash) – 1 pound
- 1 pound buttercup, butternut, Musquée de Provence, or Rugosa squash

AGAR/AGAR AGAR/KANTEN (gelling agent derived from seaweed) – 2 teaspoons powdered
- 3 tablespoons agar flakes or threads (increase soaking time to 10 to 15 minutes)
- 1 freeze-dried agar bar torn into pieces (increase soaking time to 30 or more minutes)
- 1 (1/4-ounce envelope/1 scant tablespoon) unflavored gelatin powder (follow package directions)
- 4 sheets silver leaf gelatin (follow package directions)
- 2 1/2 teaspoons apple pectin powder (follow package directions)

AGAVE SYRUP/NECTAR, LIGHT OR DARK (honey-like sweetener made from agave cactus plants) – 1 tablespoon
- 4 teaspoons brown rice syrup or coconut nectar
- 1 tablespoon palm honey/syrup, heavy/rich simple syrup, or Swedish light syrup/*ljus sirap*
- 2 teaspoons maple syrup, liquid honey, or barley malt syrup, plus 1 teaspoon water
- 1 tablespoon Jerusalem artichoke syrup (more expensive)

AGAVE SYRUP/NECTAR, LIGHT OR DARK – 1 cup
- 7/8 cup grade A dark, robust maple syrup plus 1 tablespoon water
- 3/4 cup mild-flavored liquid honey, such as acacia or clove, plus 2 tablespoons water
- 1 cup birch syrup
- 1 cup double-strength simple syrup (for drinks) *See SYRUP, SIMPLE/STOCK SYRUP, RICH/DOUBLE STRENGTH*
- 1 cup raw cane double-strength simple syrup made with coarse-grained unrefined sugar, such as turbinado or Demerara (for drinks)

AGRETTI/ROSCANO/SALTWORT, FRESH (Italian leafy green vegetable) – 1 pound
- 1 pound young puntarelle, dark outer leaves of escarole, nasturtium greens, or tender young dandelion greens (less salty tasting)

AGRODULCE (sweet-sour flavoring agent) – 1 cup
Make Your Own Bring 1/2 cup red wine vinegar and 1/2 cup sugar to a boil, stirring to dissolve the sugar. Cool and store in a tightly sealed jar in the refrigerator; it will keep indefinitely.

AGRUMATO-LEMON OIL (Italian citrus oil) *See LEMON-OLIVE OIL*

AISH BALADI (Egyptian flatbread)
- Whole-wheat pita bread

AJI AMARILLO/AJI ESCABECHE, FRESH OR FROZEN (yellow Peruvian chile) – 1
- 1 dried *aji mirasol* chile, soaked in hot water for 15 to 20 minutes
- 1 fresh yellow Hungarian wax/banana chile
- 1 large fresh red jalapeño chile
- 1 canned or jarred whole aji amarillo, rinsed
- 1 tablespoon jarred aji amarillo paste/*pasta de amarillo*
- 1 teaspoon aji mirasol powder/*aji molido*
- 1/4 teaspoon ground cayenne pepper

AJI AMARILLO CHILE POWDER/AJI MOLIDO (Peruvian) – 1 teaspoon
- 1 teaspoon aji amarillo paste/*pasta de amarillo*
- 1 teaspoon hot paprika mixed with 1/2 teaspoon ground turmeric
- 3/4 teaspoon ground cayenne pepper or crushed red pepper flakes

AJI AMARILLO PASTE/PASTA DE AMARILLO (Peruvian condiment) – 1 tablespoon
- 1 tablespoon sambal oelek (for a small amount)

AJI CACHO DE CABRA See GOAT'S HORN PEPPER

AJI DULCE/AJI CACHUCHA (tiny Caribbean sweet peppers) – 6 to 10
- 6 to 10 rocotillo chiles
- 1 fresh Cubanelle pepper
- 1/2 fresh bell pepper

AJI LIMO, FRESH OR FROZEN (spicy Peruvian chile) – 1
- 1 Scotch bonnet or habañero chile
- 1 fresh serrano or jalapeño chile (milder)
- 1 jarred aji limo, drained

AJI PANCA, DRIED (large, mild Peruvian chile) – 1
- 1 dried ancho, guajillo, New Mexico, or aji mirasol chile
- 1 teaspoon aji panca chile powder or aji mirasol chile powder
- 1 tablespoon jarred aji panca paste

AJI ROCOTO/LOCOTO, FRESH OR FROZEN (medium-hot red Peruvian chile) – 1
- 1 fresh Mexican manzano chile
- 2 or 3 fresh red serrano, Tabasco, or Thai chiles (for flavoring; less intense)
- 2 or 3 fresh red jalapeño or Fresno chiles (for stuffing or garnish)
- 2 to 3 rinsed rocoto/locoto peppers in brine (for flavoring)
- 1 tablespoon *aji rocoto* paste (for flavoring)

AJI VERDE (Peruvian condiment) – 1 cup
- 1 cup Mexican tomatillos salsa/*salsa verde* plus 2 tablespoons grated Cotija cheese/*queso añejo* blended until smooth

AJWAIN/AJOWAN/CAROM SEEDS (Indian and Pakistani seasoning) – 1 teaspoon
- 3/4 teaspoon lovage seeds plus 1/4 teaspoon fresh thyme leaves
- 1 packed teaspoon dried thyme leaves, finely crumbled

AKEE/ACKEE (Caribbean fruit) – 2 dozen akees (1 cup edible flesh)
- 1 (18-ounce) can akee, rinsed and drained

ALATOPIPERIGANO (Greek seasoning salt) – 1 tablespoon
- 2 teaspoons dried Greek oregano plus 1 teaspoon sea salt and a few grains of black pepper (stir before using to redistribute)

ALCAPARRADO (Caribbean and Latin American condiment) – 2 tablespoons
- 1 tablespoon each drained and chopped pimiento-stuffed olives and brined capers
- 1 teaspoon each diced green olives, red pimiento, capers, and a touch of garlic

ALEPPO/HALABY CHILE, DRIED/PUL BIBER (Turkish/Middle Eastern) – 1
- 1 dried Marash chile (smokier and spicier)

- 1 dried Antebi chile (milder and fruitier)
- 1 dried Urfa chile/Isot pepper (sweeter and smokier)
- 1 fresh or dried cayenne or serrano chile (more readily available)

ALEPPO/HALABY CHILE POWDER (Turkish/Middle Eastern) – 1 teaspoon

- 1 teaspoon Urfa or ancho chile powder
- 1/2 teaspoon crushed red pepper flakes

ALEPPO/HALABY PEPPER FLAKES (Turkish/Middle Eastern) – 1 teaspoon

- 1 teaspoon Marash pepper flakes/*maras biber* (smokier)
- 1 teaspoon Urfa pepper flakes/*Urfa biber* (darker colored; smokier tasting)
- 3/4 teaspoon Aleppo, Urfa, or ancho chile powder
- 3/4 teaspoon gochugaru chile flakes or powder
- 3/4 teaspoon Hungarian sweet/mild paprika plus 1/4 teaspoon ground cayenne pepper
- 1/2 teaspoon crushed red pepper flakes

ALFALFA SPROUTS See SPROUTS

ALL-PURPOSE FLOUR See FLOUR, ALL-PURPOSE

ALLSPICE, JAMAICAN/PIMENTO BERRIES, DRIED – 1 teaspoon ground

- 1 teaspoon ground Mexican or Central American allspice (larger berries; less aromatic)
- Scant 1/2 teaspoon each ground cloves and cinnamon plus scant 1/4 teaspoon ground nutmeg
- 1/2 teaspoon ground cinnamon plus 1/8 teaspoon ground cloves

ALMOND BUTTER – 1 cup

- 1 cup coconut butter, cashew butter, hazelnut butter, peanut butter, or tahini

Make Your Own Grind 2 cups roasted almonds with 1/2 teaspoon sea salt (optional) in a food processor until reduced to a paste, about 10 minutes, scraping down the sides of the bowl as needed. Transfer to a sterilized jar and store in the refrigerator; it will last for up to 4 weeks.

ALMOND EXTRACT – 1/2 teaspoon
- ⮞ 1 drop bitter almond oil
- ⮞ 1/2 teaspoon amaretto extract
- ⮞ 1 tablespoon almond-flavored liqueur

ALMOND FLOUR See ALMOND MEAL

ALMOND FLOUR, TOASTED – 1 cup
Make Your Own Spread 1 cup almond flour on a baking sheet and toast in a preheated 350°F oven until golden, 6 to 7 minutes.

ALMOND LIQUEUR/ALMOND-FLAVORED SPIRIT (such as amaretto, crème d'amande, or ratafia) – 1 tablespoon for cooking
- ⮞ 1/4 teaspoon almond extract plus 1 tablespoon vodka or water

ALMOND MEAL – 1 cup
- ⮞ 1 cup almond flour/powder (finer texture; more expensive)
- ⮞ 1 cup hazelnut or chestnut flour (finer texture; more expensive)
- ⮞ 1 cup pumpkin seed or sunflower seed meal (denser texture; best for cookies and muffins)

Make Your Own Grind 1 1/2 cups sliced or slivered almonds in a blender or food processor until mealy (add a teaspoon or more of sugar or flour from the recipe to avoid oiliness or freeze the almonds before grinding). Alternatively, grind the almonds in batches in a spice/coffee grinder, then strain and regrind any large pieces. Store, refrigerated, in an airtight container; it will keep for up to 6 months.

ALMOND MILK – 4 cups
- ⮞ 4 cups purified water plus 1/2 cup smooth raw almond butter, processed in a blender or food processor until smooth
- ⮞ 4 cups unsweetened hazelnut, walnut, or soy milk

Make Your Own Soak 1 to 2 cups freshly blanched raw almonds in water to cover for 10 to 12 hours. Drain, rinse, and then blend with

4 cups water until smooth, 3 to 4 minutes. Strain through a nutmilk bag or cheesecloth-lined sieve, pressing firmly on the pulp to extract all the liquid. Keep refrigerated and shake before using. It will keep for up to 5 days. (For thinner milk, increase water to 5 cups; for more nutritious milk, blend the almonds with fresh coconut water.)

ALMOND PASTE – 1 cup
Make Your Own Pulse 1 cup finely ground blanched almonds, 3/4 cup granulated sugar, 2 tablespoons water, and 1/2 teaspoon pure almond extract in a food processor until a paste forms, and then knead until smooth. It will keep, well-wrapped, for up to 1 month in the refrigerator, or up to 1 year in the freezer.

ALMOND SYRUP/ORZATA (Greek) – 1/4 cup
- 1/4 cup orgeat syrup
- 1/4 cup amaretto-coffee flavoring syrup
- 1/4 cup simple syrup (*See SYRUP, SIMPLE*) flavored with 1/8 to 1/4 teaspoon almond extract, plus a few drops of rose water or orange-flower water, if available

ALMONDS, GREEN, FRESH (soft, unripe almonds) – 1 cup for cooking
- 1 cup mature blanched almonds, gently boiled in 4 cups water until softened, about 2 hours (replace water as needed)
- 1 cup mature blanched almonds, soaked for 8 to 12 hours in 2 cups warm water containing 1 teaspoon baking soda

ALMONDS, MARCONA ROASTED (soft flat Spanish almonds) – 1 pound
- 1 pound California blanched almonds, soaked in salted water for 8 to 12 hours; drained, tossed with 1 tablespoon olive oil, then toasted at 300°F until dry, 10 to 15 minutes, stirring halfway through
- 1 pound oven-roasted almonds, such as Blue Diamond

ALMONDS, SWEET – 1 cup shelled
- 1 cup shelled and skinned hazelnuts

ALUM/ALUMINUM POTASSIUM SULPHATE (firming agent for pickles)
- Pickling lime/cal/calcium hydroxide (use as a soak following package directions)
- Pickle Crisp granules/calcium chloride (add to the brine following package directions, usually 0.1 to 0.4 percent diluted in 2 tablespoons purified water, or 1/8 teaspoon added directly to a hot canning jar before filling)
- Freshly washed grape, oak, or sour cherry leaves for naturally fermented pickles (add to the jar, using 1 leaf per 4 or 5 cucumbers)
- Unrefined sea salt (use as the salt ingredient; contains traces of nitrate)

AMARANTH FLOUR – 1 cup
- 1 cup brown rice flour
- 1 cup sorghum flour
- 1 cup light-colored teff flour

AMARANTH GRAIN – 1 cup
- 1 cup quinoa or Bolivian *canahua*
- 1 cup millet (like amaranth, it tastes best when lightly toasted in a dry skillet before adding liquid)

AMARANTH GREENS/CHINESE SPINACH/QUINTONILES/TAMPALA – 1 pound
- 1 pound Swiss chard leaves
- 1 pound small flat-leaf spinach or baby spinach
- 1 pound lamb's quarters
- 1 pound New Zealand spinach/warrigal greens
- 1 pound young pumpkin greens
- 1 pound quinoa greens
- 1 pound orach/mountain spinach

AMARILLO PEPPER See AJI AMARILLO

AMCHUR/AMCHOOR/GROUND MANGO POWDER (Indian souring agent) – 1 teaspoon *See also MANGO, GREEN*
- 1 piece/section of sun-dried amchoor/dried mango (remove before serving if added to curry)
- 1/2 teaspoon tamarind powder
- 1/3 teaspoon powdered citric acid (found in the canning section of the supermarket)
- 1 teaspoon ground sumac or powdered lemon peel
- 1 to 2 teaspoons very finely grated lemon zest (spread it out to dry slightly before using; for sprinkling as a garnish)

AMMONIUM BICARBONATE/AMMONIUM CARBONATE/ HARTSHORN/BAKER'S AMMONIA (leavening agent) – 1 teaspoon finely crushed
- 1 teaspoon cream of tartar
- 1 teaspoon single-acting, aluminum-free baking powder
- 1 1/4 teaspoons baking soda

ANAHEIM CHILE, FRESH (mild green chile) – 1
- 1 fresh New Mexico, poblano, or Hungarian wax chile
- 1 frozen green chile, thawed; or canned whole green chile, drained (half a 4-ounce can)
- 1 fresh bell pepper, Cubanelle pepper, or sweet banana pepper, plus a pinch of New Mexico Hatch green chile powder

ANARDANA *See POMEGRANATE SEEDS, DRIED SOUR*

ANCHO CHILE (dried red poblano chile) – 1
- 1 dried black Urfa chile
- 1 dried choricero pepper
- 1 dried California, guajillo, mulato, pasilla, or New Mexico chile, plus a pinch of sweet smoked paprika
- 1 tablespoon ancho chile powder (or pasilla or New Mexico Hatch chile powder plus a small pinch of mild/sweet smoked paprika)

☞ 1 tablespoon ancho paste
☞ 1/2 teaspoon Urfa chile flakes/*Urfa biber,* or ground cayenne pepper

ANCHO CHILE PASTE *See CHILI PASTE, MILD*

ANCHO CHILE POWDER – 1 tablespoon *See also CHILE POWDER, MILD*
☞ 1 medium ancho chile, dry toasted, stemmed, and ground
☞ 1 tablespoon New Mexico, pasilla, or mild chile molida powder
☞ 1 tablespoon ancho pepper paste
☞ 1 1/2 to 2 tablespoons hot Hungarian paprika

ANCHOVY FILLETS, FRESH – 4 ounces
☞ 4 ounces brined white anchovy fillets/*boccarones*, rinsed and patted dry (softer)
☞ 4 ounces small, fresh sardines, smelt, or sprats/brislings (firmer and meatier)

ANCHOVY FILLETS, OIL PACKED – 2 fillets (1 1/2 teaspoons finely chopped)
☞ 2 to 3 salt-packed anchovy fillets, rinsed, or 1 salt-packed anchovy, rinsed and filleted (firmer texture; soak in water until flexible, 5 to 10 minutes, or 30 minutes to remove salt)
☞ 1 to 1 1/2 teaspoons anchovy paste or extract (contains vinegar and sugar)
☞ 1 or 2 fresh, frozen, or canned smelts
☞ 1/2 teaspoon Asian fish sauce, such as *nam pla* or *nuoc nam*; Filipino anchovy/shrimp sauce/*bagoong isda*; or vegetarian fish sauce/*nuoc mam an chay*
☞ 1 teaspoon Japanese *ayu* fish sauce (less salty)
☞ 1 generous tablespoon drained chopped capers

ANCHOVY PASTE – 1 teaspoon
☞ 1 salt-packed anchovy, rinsed, boned, minced, and mashed to a paste with a little olive oil

- 1 oil-packed anchovy fillet, rinsed, minced and mashed to a paste (or put through a garlic press)
- 1 firmly packed tablespoon finely chopped water-packed tuna
- 1 teaspoon dark miso, such as *inaka* or *hatcho*
- 1 teaspoon Worcestershire sauce plus 1/2 teaspoon powdered kelp or crushed dried dulse flakes
- 1/2 teaspoon sugar-free Asian fish sauce or Italian anchovy syrup/ *colatura di alici*

ANCHOVY SAUCE/MAM NEM (Vietnamese cooking condiment) – 1 tablespoon
- 2 teaspoons anchovy paste plus 1 teaspoon water

ANDOUILLE (Creole/Cajun garlicky smoked pork sausage) – 1 pound
- 1 pound turkey andouille, or vegetarian andouille, such as Soyrizo
- 1 pound Spanish dry-cured chorizo, Portuguese dry-cured chouriço or linguiça, or other spicy ready-to-eat sausage
- 1 pound smoked kielbasa (meat or turkey) plus a small dash of hot pepper sauce such as Tabasco or Crystal

AÑEJO *See COTIJA/QUESO AÑEJO*

ANGELICA STALKS, FRESH – 1 pound
- 1 pound wild angelica/*Angelica atropurpurea* (more bitter)
- 1 pound fresh lovage stalks

ANGLED LOOFAH SQUASH *See CHINESE OKRA*

ANISE EXTRACT – 1 teaspoon
- 1 1/2 tablespoons anise seeds, ground in a mortar or a spice/coffee grinder
- 2 teaspoons ground anise seeds
- 1/8 teaspoon anise oil

ANISE HYSSOP/LICORICE MINT/AGASTACHE FOENICULUM, FRESH – 1 tablespoon chopped
- 1 tablespoon chopped fresh Korean mint/*Agastache rugosa* or young Mexican giant hyssop
- 1 1/2 teaspoons each chopped fresh thyme and mint

ANISE LIQUEUR/ANISE-FLAVORED SPIRIT (such as Absente, arak, Herbsaint, ouzo, pastis, Pernod, Ricard, sambuca, xtabentún, or other unsweetened anise-flavored spirit) – 1 tablespoon for cooking
- 1 tablespoon vodka plus 1 teaspoon ground anise seeds
- 1/2 teaspoon anise extract plus 2 teaspoons water

ANISE SEEDS – 1 teaspoon
- 2 whole star anise pods, crushed or coarsely ground, or 1 1/2 teaspoons broken pieces
- 1/4 teaspoon anise extract
- 1 1/4 teaspoons fennel or caraway seeds

ANNATTO OIL/ACEITE/MANTECA DE ACHIOTE (Latin American coloring agent) – 1/4 cup
- 1/4 cup olive oil plus 1 teaspoon sweet paprika

Make Your Own Slowly heat 1 to 2 tablespoons annatto seeds and 1/4 cup vegetable oil until the oil turns orangey-red and the seeds begin to crackle, 5 to 7 minutes; strain and cool. Store in an airtight container in the refrigerator; it will keep for up to 1 year. (For annatto chili oil, include 1 small crushed dried red chile when heating the seeds and oil.)

ANNATTO SEEDS/ACHIOTE (Latin American and Caribbean coloring agent) – 1 teaspoon
- 1/4 to 1/2 teaspoon liquid annatto (from cheese making suppliers)
- 1/2 teaspoon finely ground annatto seeds or achiote powder/*bijol*
- 3/4 teaspoon achiote paste/*condimento de achiote* (contains oregano and other ingredients), or Yucatan achiote paste/*recado rojo/Achiote recado* (contains garlic and vinegar)

- ☞ 1 teaspoon pesticide-free dried marigold petals, preferably pot marigold/*Calendula officinalis*, steeped in 1 or 2 tablespoons warm water for 5 minutes (use the liquid for color and discard the petals)
- ☞ 1/4 teaspoon sweet California or Hungarian paprika and 1/2 teaspoon ground turmeric, preferably Madras
- ☞ 1/2 teaspoon crumbled azafrán (Mexican saffron) or 1/8 teaspoon pure saffron

ANTHOTIRO/ANTHRÓTYRO (soft white goat's or sheep's milk Greek cheese) – 1 ounce

- ☞ 1 ounce fresh manouri, mizithra, or ricotta, plus a little finely grated feta (for fresh)
- ☞ Aged ricotta salata, aged mizithra, Pecorino Romano, or Parmesan (for aged)

APPELSTROOP (Dutch dark thick apple syrup) – 1 cup

- ☞ 4 cups fresh apple juice, simmered until reduced to 1 cup, 45 to 60 minutes
- ☞ 1 cup *keukenstroop*, molasses, or strong honey

APPENZELLER (Swiss semihard cheese) – 1 ounce

- ☞ 1 ounce Abondance, Gruyère, Emmental, Fontina d'Aosta, Vacherin Fribourgeois, or Raclette

APPLE BRANDY/APPLEJACK (such as Calvados or Laird's) – 2 tablespoons

- ☞ 1 tablespoon each apple juice concentrate and brandy
- ☞ 2 tablespoons hard cider

APPLE CIDER – 1 cup

- ☞ 3/4 cup apple juice and 1/4 cup unsweetened applesauce

APPLE PIE SPICE – 1 tablespoon

- ☞ 2 teaspoons ground cinnamon, 1/2 teaspoon ground nutmeg, and 1/2 teaspoon ground ginger (or a pinch of allspice)

APPLES, FRESH – 1 pound
- 1 pound pears or Asian pears (add lemon juice for tartness)
- 1 pound quinces (tarter flavor; for cooking and jam; rich in pectin)
- 1 pound crab apples or unsprayed hawthorne fruits/thorn apples/ *Crataegus* species (use for cooking, especially combined with other fruits for jams and sauces; tarter flavor; rich in pectin)

APRICOTS, FRESH – 1 pound
- 1 pound fresh peaches or nectarines
- 1 pound fresh apriums (yellowish-white hybrid; three-quarters apricot and one-quarter plum)
- 1 pound fresh plumcots (clingstone hybrid; one-half plum and one-half apricot)
- 1 cup dried apricots, soaked in boiling water 1 hour, then drained and blotted dry
- 1 cup dried quandongs, soaked in boiling water until softened (tarter flavor; use for jams, pies, or sauces)
- 1 pound ripe wild plums/*Prunus americana*, scalded and peeled (light orange-yellow flesh; similar in taste to apricots but stronger; use in jam)

ARALIA/TARA NO ME/DUREUP (Japanese and Korean angelica tree buds) – 1 pound
- 1 pound young asparagus

ARAME, DRIED (Japanese mild shredded seaweed) – 1 ounce
- 1 ounce wakame (soak for 15 to 20 minutes; cut out the center rib, then slice the rest into thin ribbons)
- 1 ounce kiri kombu/long narrow kombu strands (soak for 10 minutes)
- 1 ounce alaria (saltier; soak for 30 minutes)
- 1 ounce hijiki (stronger tasting; soak for 10 minutes)

ÁRBOL CHILE See DE ÁRBOL CHILE

ARBORIO RICE See RICE, ARBORIO

AREPA (South American thick corn cake) – 1
- 1 chalupa, gordita, sope, or thick homemade corn tortilla

AREPA FLOUR/MASAREPA/HARINA PAN (Latin American precooked white cornmeal) – 1 cup
- 1 cup masa harina
- 1 cup quick-cooking corn grits
- 1 cup extra-fine-grind cornmeal, preferably white

ARGAN OIL (Moroccan golden-colored unrefined oil) – 1 cup
- 1/2 cup each extra-virgin olive oil and peanut oil
- 1 cup peanut oil, hazelnut oil, or walnut oil

ARONIA BERRY/BLACK CHOKEBERRY, FRESH OR FROZEN – 1 cup
- 1 cup fresh or frozen cranberries or blueberries (fewer antioxidants)

ARONIA/CHOKEBERRY JUICE, FRESH OR FROZEN – 1 cup
- 1 cup cranberry or pomegranate juice

ARROPE (Spanish grape syrup) See GRAPE MOLASSES/MUST SYRUP

ARROWHEAD ROOT/CI GU/CHI GU, FRESH (Chinese vegetable) – I pound
- 1 pound small red or yellow boiling potatoes

ARROWROOT POWDER (thickening agent producing a clear appearance) – 2 teaspoons
- 1 tablespoon tapioca starch; or 2 1/2 teaspoons small tapioca pearls, ground until powdery (will have a clear appearance)
- 1 1/2 tablespoons kudzu powder (will have a clear appearance)
- 1 1/2 tablespoons low- or no-sugar needed fruit pectin (will have a clear appearance)
- 1 1/2 teaspoons cornstarch (will have a cloudy, translucent appearance)
- 1 1/4 teaspoons potato starch (will have a cloudy, translucent appearance; do not boil)

- 2 teaspoons coconut flour (will have a cloudy, translucent appearance and slightly sweet taste)
- 1 tablespoon all-purpose or quick-mixing flour (cook at least 3 minutes after thickened; will have an opaque appearance)

ARTICHOKE HEARTS, COOKED – 1 cup
- 1 cup thawed frozen artichoke hearts
- 1 cup drained and rinsed canned artichoke hearts
- 1 cup cooked fresh hearts of palm, or drained and rinsed canned hearts of palm
- 1 cup cooked organic milk thistle flower heads/*Silybum marianum* (harvest in summer; prepare and boil or steam until tender)
- 1 cup cooked organic burdock flower stems/*Arctium lappa* (cut before flowering; peel and boil in salted water)
- 1 cup cooked organic sunflower buds/*Helianthus annuus* (cut before flowering; prepare and steam like artichokes)

ARTICHOKES, BABY – 1 cup
- 1 cup quartered artichoke hearts

ARUGULA/ITALIAN CRESS/ROCKET/ROCKETTE – 8 ounces
- 8 ounces wild arugula/rocket/*Rucola selvatica* (smaller leaves; more pungent flavor)
- 8 ounces tender sprigs of watercress, garden cress/peppercress, or upland cress
- 8 ounces agretti, young dandelion greens, baby puntarelle greens, young purslane leaves, daikon greens, or young fresh radish leaves, especially French Breakfast or White Icicle
- 8 ounces young mustard greens, torn into pieces, center ribs discarded
- 8 ounces fresh chile pepper leaves
- 8 ounces leaves from young fresh broccoli rabe or Chinese broccoli
- 8 ounces upper stem leaves of wild mustard/*Brassica rapa* or black mustard/*Brassica nigra*
- 8 ounces young oxeye daisy leaves/*Chrysanthemum leucanthemum*

ASADERO/QUESO OAXACA/QUESO MENONITA/CHIHUAHUA (Mexican stretched-curd cheese) – 1 ounce
- ⊨ 1 ounce young *caciocavallo*, Monterey Jack, Muenster, whole-milk mozzarella, scamorza, or fresh Carmody or Teleme

ASAFETIDA/ASAFOETIDA/HING/PERUNKAYA (pungent Indian seasoning) – 1 teaspoon ground lump asafetida
- ⊨ 1 teaspoon yellow asafetida powder (milder; contains turmeric)
- ⊨ 1/2 teaspoon each onion and garlic powder

ASAM GELUGOR/ASAM KEPING (Malaysian acid fruit) See KOKUM

ASCORBIC ACID CRYSTALS (water-soluble vitamin C; used for preventing browning of certain fruits and vegetables) – 1 teaspoon (3,000 milligrams)
- ⊨ 6 (500-mg) ascorbic acid tablets (granulated vitamin C), crushed to a powder with a spoon or dissolved in water
- ⊨ 1 tablespoon citric acid powder (found in the canning section of the supermarket)

ASCORBIC ACID POWDER (vitamin C powder for strengthening gluten in whole-grain bread dough) – 1/8 teaspoon
- ⊨ 1 tablespoon lemon juice

ASHTAR (Lebanese clotted cream) See CREAM, CLOTTED

ASIAGO, AGED/ASIAGO D'ALLEVO (Italian sharp, dry cheese) – 1 ounce
- ⊨ 1 ounce Dry Jack, aged Montasio, Grana Padano, domestic Parmesan, Piave, or Romano

ASIAGO/ASIAGO PRESSATO (Italian tangy, semisoft cheese) – 1 ounce
- ⊨ 1 ounce Bra Tenero, *caciocavallo*, domestic fontina, provolone, scamorza, or Trugole

ASIAN BASIL *See BASIL, HOLY; BASIL, THAI*

ASIAN CELERY *See CHINESE CELERY*

ASIAN DIPPING SAUCE – 1/4 cup
Make Your Own Stir together 2 tablespoons each soy sauce and un-seasoned rice vinegar, 1 teaspoon finely minced green onion, and a little grated fresh ginger.

ASIAN FISH PASTE, FERMENTED/PRESERVED FISH/PADEK/PRAHOK/ MAM CA SAC (Southeast Asian salty solid flavoring agent) – 1 teaspoon
- 1 teaspoon fermented shrimp paste: Filipino *bagoong,* Thai *kapi,* Indonesian *trassi/terasi* (more pungent), or Burmese *ngapi*
- 1 1/2 teaspoons French or Italian anchovy paste
- 1 whole salt-packed anchovy, deboned and mashed
- 2 oil-packed anchovies, rinsed and mashed
- 2 teaspoons Asian fish sauce
- 1 tablespoon Japanese red *inaka* miso or brown *hatcho* miso

ASIAN FISH SAUCE *See FISH SAUCE; FISH SAUCE, VEGETARIAN*

ASIAN LETTUCE *See CHINESE LEAF LETTUCE*

ASIAN PEAR/KOREAN PEAR/JAPANESE PEAR/NASHI/NAJU PAE – 1 medium
- 2 crisp pears, such as Bosc

ASIAN SAUSAGE *See CHINESE SAUSAGE*

ASPARAGUS – 1 pound
- 1 pound stalks from broccoli, bok choy, or choy sum (peel and slice vertically, if necessary, then steam or sauté until tender)
- 1 pound Good King Henry shoots and flower buds

- ☞ 1 pound annual sow thistle/*Sonchus oleraceus* thick upper stems or young tender stalks, peeled (tastes like a cross between asparagus and artichoke hearts)
- ☞ 1 pound Solomon's seal/*Polygonatum commutatum*, young shoots peeled; unfurled leaves discarded (tastes like asparagus only sharper)

ATE (Mexican concentrated fruit paste) *See GUAVA PASTE; QUINCE PASTE*

ATTA/PATENT DURA FLOUR/CHAPATI FLOUR (Indian extra-fine soft whole-wheat flour) – 1 cup *See also BESAN; MAIDA; URAD DAL FLOUR*
- ☞ 1 cup whole-wheat pastry flour, sifted
- ☞ 1/2 cup each white whole-wheat flour and maida (Indian soft white flour), sifted
- ☞ 2/3 cup all-purpose flour and 1/3 cup finely ground whole-wheat flour, sifted before measuring to remove any coarse flakes

AUBERGINE *See EGGPLANT*

AVOCADO LEAF/HOJA DE AGUACATE, FRESH OR DRIED (Latin American seasoning and food wrapper) – 1 leaf (for seasoning)
- ☞ 1 scant teaspoon ground avocado leaf
- ☞ 1 fresh or dried hoja santa/yerba santa leaf
- ☞ 1 dried California bay leaf
- ☞ 1 small piece fresh fennel frond
- ☞ 1 teaspoon fennel seeds

B

BABA GHANOUSH (Middle Eastern spread or dip) – about 1 1/4 cups
Make Your Own Peel 1 medium cooked eggplant (about 1 pound, preferably grilled) then process with 1 or 2 medium garlic cloves, 1 or 2 tablespoons each lemon juice and olive oil, and 2 tablespoons tahini in a blender or food processor until smooth, and then season with salt.

BACON BITS – 1/4 cup
- 1/4 cup imitation (vegan) bacon bits, such as Bacuns
- 1/4 cup crumbled smoked tempeh
- 1/4 cup dry-roasted tamari sunflower seeds
- Kiri kombu/sea vegetable, fried in 350°F oil until crisp, 1 to 2 minutes, and then crumbled (measure after crumbling)

BACON, CURED PORK – 2 ounces (1 thick slice or 2 to 3 medium/ thin slices)
- 2 to 3 slices lower-sodium pork or turkey bacon (less salt) or uncured bacon (less nitrates)
- 2 ounces bacon ends (less expensive)
- 2 to 3 small slices smoked ham or Canadian bacon (less fat; drier)
- 2 to 3 slices *pancetta affumicata*
- 2 to 3 slices plain slab pancetta/*tesa*, rigatino pancetta, or *prosciutto crudo* (unsmoked)
- 2 to 3 slices duck prosciutto or duck pastrami (less fat; drier)
- 1 thick slice smoky tempeh bacon, such as Fakin' Bacon; soy bacon, such as Lightlife Smart Bacon; coconut bacon, such as Phoney Baloney, or any smoke-seasoned prebaked tofu (less fat; moister)
- 3 or more applewood smoked dulse strips, baked at 250°F until lightly toasted, 4 to 7 minutes; or fried in an oiled skillet over medium heat until crisp, 15 to 20 seconds each side.

☞ Chicken skin from a cooked chicken, seasoned with salt and fried in a dry skillet over medium heat until crispy, or baked in a pre-heated 350°F oven until brown and crisp

☞ 2 to 3 tablespoons real bacon bits, coconut bacon pieces, or any imitation vegan bacon-flavored bits (for flavoring)

☞ Bacon fat or vegan bacon fat, such as Magic Vegan Bacon Grease (for flavoring)

☞ Sprinkling of bacon salt (for flavoring only; reduce the salt in the recipe accordingly)

BAGEL CHIPS
Make Your Own Cut bagels into very thin slices, spread them out on a baking sheet, and dry in a preheated 275°F oven until brown and crisp, 15 to 20 minutes (or bake at 450°F for 5 to 7 minutes). Store in an airtight container for up to 2 weeks.

BAGOONG (Filipino seasoning) See SHRIMP PASTE, FERMENTED

BAHARAT (Middle Eastern spice blend) – 1 tablespoon
☞ 1/2 teaspoon each ground cloves, ground cumin (preferably roasted), paprika, ground black pepper, and ground cinnamon (or allspice)

☞ 1 teaspoon each ground coriander and cumin plus 1/2 teaspoon each ground cinnamon and paprika

☞ 1 tablespoon garam masala or *ras el hanout* spice blend

BAKER'S AMMONIA See AMMONIUM BICARBONATE

BAKER'S CARAMEL/CARAMEL COLOR (dry, powdered non-sweet coloring agent) – 1 teaspoon
☞ 1 teaspoon gravy browner, such as Gravy Master or Kitchen Bouquet

☞ 1 tablespoon extra-strong coffee

Make Your Own Melt 1/4 cup granulated sugar over low heat, stirring constantly, until very dark brown, about 3 minutes; cool completely, about 10 minutes, before slowly stirring in 1/4 cup hot water. Use 1

to 2 teaspoons in place of baker's caramel. Store in a tightly covered container at room temperature; it will keep for up to 3 months.

BAKER'S CHEESE *See FARMER CHEESE*

BAKEWELL CREAM (New England pyrophosphate leavening agent usually combined with baking soda) – 1 teaspoon
- ⮞ 1 teaspoon cream of tartar (to replace 1 teaspoon bakewell cream)
- ⮞ 1 teaspoon baking powder (reduce the baking soda in the recipe by 1/2 teaspoon)

BAKING MIX/ALL-PURPOSE BISCUIT MIX – 4 3/4 cups
Make Your Own Pulse 2 cups all-purpose flour and 2 cups cake flour (or 4 cups pastry or all-purpose flour), 2 tablespoons baking powder, 2 teaspoons fine sea salt, and 2/3 cup chilled nonhydrogenated solid vegetable shortening in a food processor until combined. It will keep, tightly sealed, for up to 2 months.

BAKING MIX/ALL-PURPOSE BISCUIT MIX, QUICK AND EASY – 1 cup
Make Your Own Whisk together 1 cup all-purpose flour, 1 1/2 teaspoons baking powder, and 1/2 teaspoon salt, then cut in 2 tablespoons chilled vegetable shortening.

BAKING POWDER, DOUBLE ACTING (leavening agent) – 1 teaspoon
- ⮞ 1 1/4 teaspoons sodium-free baking powder containing monocalcium phosphate, potato starch, and potassium bicarbonate, such as Hain's Featherweight
- ⮞ 1/2 teaspoon cream of tartar and 1/4 teaspoon baking soda (bake the batter immediately after mixing; not for batter being refrigerated or frozen before baking)
- ⮞ 1/4 teaspoon baking soda plus 1/2 cup well-shaken buttermilk to replace sweet milk or other fluid called for in the recipe (bake the batter immediately after mixing; not for batter being refrigerated or frozen before baking)
- ⮞ 1 teaspoon baker's ammonia/ammonium bicarbonate (for super-crisp cookies and crackers only)

☞ Beat egg whites separately and fold them into the batter (for recipes using eggs and baking powder).

BAKING SODA/SODIUM BICARBONATE (leavening agent) – 1/4 teaspoon
- ☞ 1/4 teaspoon potassium bicarbonate for a low-sodium alternative (add toward the end of mixing and avoid overbeating)
- ☞ 1/2 teaspoon calcium carbonate–based baking soda, such as En-erg-G (for a sodium-free alternative)
- ☞ 1 teaspoon double-acting baking powder plus replace buttermilk or other acidic liquid in the recipe with sweet milk

BALACHAN/BLACHAN See SHRIMP PASTE, FERMENTED

BALSAMIC GLAZE/CRÈMA DE BALSAMICO – 1/4 cup
Make Your Own Simmer 1 cup balsamic vinegar gently until syrupy and reduced to 1/4 cup, about 15 minutes. This will keep in the refrigerator for up to 1 month.

BALSAMIC GLAZE, SWEET – 1/4 cup
Make Your Own Gently simmer 1/2 cup balsamic vinegar and 1 1/2 teaspoons granulated sugar until reduced to 1/4 cup, 7 to 10 minutes. Store, refrigerated, for up to 1 month.

BALSAMIC VINEGAR – 1 tablespoon
- ☞ 1 tablespoon Chianti or red wine vinegar, preferably aged, plus 1/8 teaspoon sugar or honey
- ☞ 1 tablespoon Chinese aged black-rice vinegar, preferably Chinkiang
- ☞ 1 tablespoon white balsamic vinegar (milder; less sweet and syrupy)
- ☞ 1 tablespoon apple balsamic vinegar (less sweet)
- ☞ 4 teaspoons cranberry juice

BALSAMIC VINEGAR, AGED/ACETO BALSAMICO TRADIZIONALE (Italian grape-based) – 1 tablespoon
- ☞ 1 tablespoon Italian grape-based balsamic aged in wood less than 12 years/condimento balsamico

- 1 tablespoon Italian vinegar-based balsamic/*Aceto Balsamico di Modena* or *Industriale*
- 1 tablespoon reduced nonartisinal balsamic vinegar (Simmer 1 cup non-artisinal balsamic until syrupy and reduced by one-half or more, then measure.)
- 1 tablespoon Italian apple balsamic vinegar, such as Lucini
- 1 tablespoon Greek grape Corinthian vinegar (fruitier flavored)

BALSAMIC VINEGAR, WHITE (Italian mild, unaged grape-based) – 1 tablespoon
- 1 tablespoon Moscatel vinegar
- 1 tablespoon white wine vinegar or unseasoned rice vinegar plus 1/8 to 1/4 teaspoon sugar

BAMBOO LEAVES See WRAPPERS FOR FOOD, NONEDIBLE

BAMBOO SHOOTS, DRIED/MANG KO – 3 to 4 ounces (3-to-4-inch-wide strips)
- 9 to 12 ounces fresh or canned bamboo shoots (less meaty; reduce the cooking time)

BAMBOO SHOOTS, FRESH – 1 pound (1 large or 3 to 4 small)
- 8 ounces canned whole bamboo shoots, drained and rinsed (To remove the tinny taste, blanch the bamboo shoots in boiling water for 1 minute, and then rinse with cold water.)
- 8 ounces refrigerated vacuum-packed trimmed bamboo shoots
- 2 cups fresh peeled water chestnuts (about 10) or 1 (8-ounce) can water chestnuts, drained and rinsed
- 8 ounces jícama, peeled and cut into pieces
- 8 ounces tender fresh broccoli stems, cut into pieces

BANANA BLOSSOM/BUD/JANTUNG PISANG/HUAPLI/BAP CHUOI (Southeast Asian vegetable) – 1 pound (1 medium)
- 1 (19-ounce) can banana blossom in brine *(puso ng saging)*, drained and rinsed

☞ 1 large artichoke, trimmed, halved lengthwise, and choke re-moved (for cooking; lacks color)
☞ 3 red Belgium endives, halved lengthwise (for salads and garnish)
☞ 1 pound crisp red cabbage leaves, finely shredded (for salads and garnish; for color, not taste)

BANANA CHILE PEPPER, FRESH – 1
☞ 1 fresh Cubanelle, Nardello, or Corno di Toro pepper
☞ 1 fresh yellow bell, Hungarian wax, or Marconi pepper

BANANA FLOUR/PISANG STARCH (Filipino plantain flour) – 1 tablespoon for thickening
☞ 2 teaspoons arrowroot powder
☞ 1 tablespoon superfine sweet rice flour/glutinous rice flour, such as Mochiko or Erawan brand

BANANA LEAF, FROZEN (food wrapper) See also WRAPPERS FOR FOOD, NONEDIBLE
☞ Fresh or dried corn husks (smaller)
☞ Foil lined with large lettuce leaves or other tender leaves
☞ Parchment paper (lacks aroma)

BANANA SAUCE/TAMIS ANCHANG (Filipino condiment) – 1 tablespoon
☞ 1 tablespoon ketchup

BANYULS (French fortified wine) – 2 tablespoons
☞ 1 tablespoon each syrah and ruby port
☞ 2 tablespoons tawny port, Madeira, or dry vermouth

BANYULS VINEGAR/VINAIGRE de BANYULS (French aged wine vinegar) – 1 tablespoon
☞ 1 tablespoon aged sherry or balsamic vinegar
☞ 1 tablespoon red wine vinegar

BAOBAB LEAF POWDER *See KUKA/BAOBAB LEAF POWDER*

BARBARI BREAD (Iranian oblong flatbread) – 1 pound
- ⮞ 1 pound thin foccacia (thicker)
- ⮞ 1 pound sangak, taftoon, soft lavash, piadina, or pocketless pita bread/*pide* (thinner and softer)

BARBECUE SAUCE – 1 cup
- ⮞ 1 cup tomato sauce plus 1 tablespoon (or more) smoky seasoning blend, barbecue spice blend, rib and chicken rub, steak seasoning, or Cajun seasoning
- ⮞ 1 cup ketchup plus 2 teaspoons Worcestershire sauce
- ⮞ 1 cup Chinese hoisin, chee hou, or char siu barbecue sauce

Make Your Own Stir together 1 cup ketchup, 1/4 teaspoon (or more) liquid smoke or hickory smoke powder (optional), 1 or 2 tablespoons molasses or brown sugar, and a pinch of garlic powder. For hot barbecue sauce add 1 teaspoon hot pepper sauce; for smoky hot sauce add 2 to 3 teaspoons liquid from canned chipotles in adobo; for thinner sauce add 1 to 2 tablespoons cider or rice vinegar or red wine (regular or nonalcoholic).

BARBECUE SEASONING/DRY RUB – 1/3 cup
Make Your Own Stir together 1 tablespoon each paprika, brown sugar, kosher salt, and ground black pepper. If desired, add 1/2 teaspoon onion or garlic powder or 1 tablespoon of one of the following: dried crumbled sage, dried oregano, ground cumin, dried thyme leaves, mustard powder, mild chile powder, or Cajun seasoning.

BARBERRIES, DRIED/ZERESHK (Persian sour cooking fruit) – 1 cup
- ⮞ 1 cup coarsely chopped dried cranberries or sour/tart cherries
- ⮞ 1 cup dried currants (red or Zante)

BARLEY FLOUR – 1 cup
- ⮞ 2/3 cup whole hulled/pot barley, whole hull-less barley, or pearl barley, ground in batches in a spice/coffee grinder until powdery

(For Tibetan roasted barley flour/*tsampa,* or Ecuadorian toasted barley flour/*máchica,* toast the barley in a dry skillet until golden, about 4 minutes, then cool before grinding.)
- 1 cup whole-wheat, whole spelt, or light/white rye flour

BARLEY MALT SYRUP, PLAIN/MOOL YUTI (non-diastatic liquid grain sweetener) – 1 tablespoon
- 1 tablespoon non-diastatic barley malt powder
- 2 teaspoons diastatic barley malt powder
- 1 tablespoon wheat malt syrup
- 1 tablespoon Chinese brown rice syrup/*yinnie*
- 1 tablespoon honey
- 1 tablespoon dark brown sugar
- 2 teaspoons mild unsulphured molasses

BARLEY RUSKS/PAXIMADIA/PAXIMATHIA (Cretan and Greek rusk bread)
- Italian wheat or barley rusks/*friselle* or Dutch dry rusks/*beschuit*
- Zwieback
- Friganies (for crushing)

Make Your Own Place 1/2- or 1-inch-thick slices of barley, whole-wheat, or country bread (or halved Kaiser rolls or ciabatta) on a baking sheet and dry in the oven with the pilot light on (or on the lowest setting) until golden and dry, 2 or more hours. Let cool in the oven overnight, then store airtight.

BARLEY TEA See KOREAN ROASTED BARLEY TEA/BORICHA

BARLEY, PEARL – 1 cup uncooked
- 1 cup whole hulled/pot barley or whole hull-less barley (longer cooking time; chewier; more nutritious; reduce the cooking time by soaking the barley in cool water 8 to 10 hours in the refrigerator, then cook it in the soaking water)
- 1 cup uncooked 10-Minute Barley, barley flakes, cracked barley grit, or fine-grain barley grits (less cooking time)

- 1 cup uncooked pearled, semi-pearled, or 10-Minute farro (slightly nuttier flavor; less cooking time)
- 1 cup uncooked sprouted brown rice, or small- or medium-grain brown rice (gluten-free)
- 1 cup uncooked hulled Job's tears/*hato mugi* (large pearl barley; more expensive)

BAROLO WINE VINEGAR, AGED – 1 tablespoon
- 1 tablespoon red wine vinegar or raspberry vinegar

BAR SUGAR *See SUGAR, SUPERFINE*

BASIL SALT
Make Your Own Layer fresh basil leaves in kosher salt in a small container (make sure the salt completely covers the leaves); seal and leave several days for the salt to develop flavor.
Or
Pulse 1 or 2 cups fresh basil leaves and 1/2 cup kosher salt in a food processor until combined; spread on a baking sheet and dry at 160°F, 30 to 40 minutes, stirring halfway through. Cool, then pulse again to a fine powder. (For a coarser product, dry the leaves first, pulverize to a powder, then stir into the salt.)

BASIL, AFRICAN BLUE – 1 tablespoon chopped fresh leaves
- 1 tablespoon chopped fresh Thai basil or anise hyssop (less camphor taste)

BASIL, HOLY/BAI KAPHRAO/BAI KRAPAU/BAI GRAPAO/TULSI – 1 tablespoon chopped fresh leaves
- 1 1/2 teaspoons chopped fresh mint and small-leafed Mediterranean basil (if using in a cooked dish, add at the last minute)
- 1 tablespoon chopped fresh spice/Peruvian basil, Thai basil, or anise/licorice basil
- 1 teaspoon jarred holy basil paste or holy basil seasoning

BASIL, SWEET/MEDITERRANEAN/GENOVESE – 1 tablespoon chopped fresh leaves for seasoning
- 1 scant tablespoon Greek basil (smaller leaves and softer stems; stronger flavor)
- 1 teaspoon sweet dried Mediterranean basil leaf, crumbled
- 3/4 teaspoon sweet dried California, French, Italian, Peruvian/spice, or opal basil
- 1 to 2 tablespoons chopped lettuce leaf basil (milder flavor)
- 1 teaspoon dried Italian seasoning or dried crushed thyme leaves
- 2 to 3 teaspoons finely chopped fresh mint leaves
- Scant 1/2 teaspoon basil pesto (for marinara sauce)

BASIL, SWEET/MEDITERRANEAN/GENOVESE – 1 cup chopped fresh leaves, for pesto
- 1 cup coarsely chopped arugula, flat-leaf parsley leaves, cilantro stems and leaves, radish tops, stemmed baby spinach, shiso leaves, or any peppery green

BASIL, THAI/ASIAN BASIL/SIAM QUEEN/BAI HORAPA – 1 tablespoon chopped fresh leaves
- 1 tablespoon chopped fresh Holy basil or anise basil/licorice basil
- 1 1/2 teaspoons chopped small fresh regular/sweet basil leaves and small fresh mint leaves

BASMATI RICE See RICE, BASMATI AGED WHITE

BASTURMA/PASTIRMA (Middle Eastern highly seasoned air-dried beef) – 1 pound
- 1 pound Italian bresaola

BAY LEAF POWDER – 1 teaspoon
- 8 to 10 dried Turkish bay leaves, stem and spines removed, pulverized in a spice/coffee grinder (add a little raw rice, if necessary, to help the grinding process)

BAY LEAF, CALIFORNIA DRIED – 1

- ⇨ 2 dried Turkish bay leaves
- ⇨ 1 very small fresh bay leaf (or part of a larger one)
- ⇨ 1/4 teaspoon crushed dried bay leaf
- ⇨ Scant 1/8 teaspoon bay leaf powder/ground dried bay leaf
- ⇨ 2 fresh bayberry leaves/*Myrica pensylvania* (milder flavor)

BAY LEAF, INDIAN *See CASSIA LEAF/CINNAMON LEAF/TEJ PATTA*

BAY LEAF, TURKISH, DRIED – 1

- ⇨ 1/2 dried California bay leaf (best for quick-cooking dishes)
- ⇨ 1/8 teaspoon Turkish bay leaf powder
- ⇨ 1 or 2 fresh bayberry leaves/*Myrica pensylvanica*

BEANS, CANNED – 1 (14.5 – 15.5-ounce) can

- ⇨ 1/2 to 3/4 cup dried beans, soaked and cooked
- ⇨ 1 1/2 cups instant beans plus 2 cups boiling water, covered and left for 5 minutes

BEANS, DRIED – 1 pound (2 to 2 3/4 cups)

- ⇨ 58 ounces canned beans (four 14.5-ounce cans), drained and rinsed

BEANS, FERMENTED, SALTED BLACK *See FERMENTED BLACK BEANS*

BEANS, REFRIED (Mexican) – 1 cup

- ⇨ 1 cup cooked black beans or pinto beans, mashed with 1/4 cup cooking liquid
- ⇨ 1 cup canned black beans or pinto beans, drained and pureed with 1/4 cup water

BEAUFORT (French semihard cheese) – 1 ounce

- ⇨ 1 ounce Gruyère, Comté, Fontina D'Aosta, Pleasant Ridge Reserve, Tarantaise, or Vacherin Fribourgeois

BEAU MONDE SEASONING – 1 teaspoon
- 1/2 teaspoon each onion powder and celery salt
- 1 teaspoon seasoning salt

BEAUMONT (French semisoft cheese) – 1 ounce
- 1 ounce Muenster, Reblochon, Saint-Nectaire, Tamié, or Taleggio

BEE BALM/BERGAMOT (mint-family herb) – 1 tablespoon chopped fresh leaves
- 1 tablespoon chopped fresh oregano

BEECH MUSHROOMS/BROWN BEECH/PIOPPINI/SHIMEJI – 7 ounces
- 7 ounces golden enoki, oyster, or small cremini mushrooms

BEEF BOTTOM ROUND – 2 pounds
- 2 pounds rump roast

BEEF BRISKET, WHOLE – 1 1/2 pounds
- 1 1/2 pounds beef plate or shank

BEEF DENVER STEAK (underblade chuck steak) – 8 ounces
- 8 ounces top sirloin steak
- 8 ounces Sierra or Vegas strip steak

BEEF FLANK STEAK/LONDON BROIL – 1 pound
- 1 pound hanger steaks or skirt steak/fajita steak with center membrane removed
- 1 pound flap meat or sirloin steak tips
- 1 pound boneless short rib steak, sliced in half horizontally

BEEF FLAT IRON/TOP BLADE STEAK – 8 ounces
- 8 ounces Vegas strip steak, petite tender, or top sirloin steak

BEEF, GROUND *See MEAT, GROUND*

BEEF HANGER STEAK/ONGLET – 8 ounces

- ⇨ 8 ounces top sirloin steak
- ⇨ 8 ounces skirt steak, preferably outside skirt
- ⇨ 8 ounces flank steak

BEEF RIB-EYE STEAK/SPENCER STEAK/DELMONICO STEAK – 8 ounces

- ⇨ 8 ounces T-bone steak or strip steak
- ⇨ 8 ounces top sirloin or sirloin flap/bavette, or hanger steak (chewier)

BEEF RUMP ROAST – 2 pounds

- ⇨ 2 pounds bottom round

BEEF, SHABU-SHABU (thinly sliced meat for shabu shabu) – 1 pound

- ⇨ 1 pound beef strip loin or rib eye, sliced paper-thin across the grain (partly freeze the meat to make it easier to slice)

BEEF SHANK, CROSS CUT – 1 pound

- ⇨ 1 pound boneless short ribs (reduce the cooking time by half)

BEEF SHORT RIBS, BONELESS – 1 pound

- ⇨ 1 1/3 pounds chuck roast, trimmed of fat and sinew and cut across the grain into 1 by 2-inch thick pieces

BEEF SIRLOIN TIP ROAST/ROUND TIP ROAST – 1 pound

- ⇨ 1 pound boneless chuck roast or top blade roast (increase the cooking time)

BEEF SKIRT STEAK/FAJITA STEAK/PHILADELPHIA STEAK – 8 ounces

- ⇨ 8 ounces sirloin steak tips/flap meat/bavette
- ⇨ 8 ounces flank steak

BEEF STEAK, AGED – 1 pound

Make Your Own Wrap 1 pound regular supermarket rib-eye, strip, or similar tender steak loosely in cheesecloth, place on a cooling rack set in a rimmed baking sheet, and place in the coldest area of the refrigerator until slightly dried out, 3 to 4 days (change the cheese-cloth if it gets saturated and bring the steak to room temperature before cooking). Alternatively, salt the steak, using 1 tablespoon per pound, and refrigerate, uncovered, up to 3 days.

BEEF STRIP STEAK/KANSAS CITY STRIP/NEW YORK STRIP/SIRLOIN STRIP/TOP LOIN/SHORT LOIN/SHELL – 1 pound
⇛ 1 pound rib-eye steak or T-bone steak

BEEF SUBSTITUTE See MEAT SUBSTITUTE

BEEF, SUKIYAKI (thinly sliced meat for sukiyaki) – 1 pound
⇛ 1 pound rib-eye, strip loin, or sirloin sliced paper-thin against the grain (partly freeze the meat first to make it easier to cut)
⇛ 1 pound Korean bulgogi beef

BEEF T-BONE STEAK – 1 pound
⇛ 1 (1-inch-thick) rib-eye steak (about 1 pound)
⇛ 1 pound bone-in strip steak/loin steak

BEEF TENDERLOIN – 1 pound
⇛ 1 pound rib-eye steak, or strip steak/top loin
⇛ 2 (8-ounce) shoulder petite tender steaks (petite chuck tender/bistro filet/teres major)

BEEF TOP SIRLOIN STEAK/CENTER CUT ROAST/BONELESS SHELL SIRLOIN – 8 ounces
⇛ 8 ounces sirloin tip steak/round tip steak, or flatiron/top blade steak
⇛ 8 ounces top round steak (less expensive)

BEEF TRI-TIP ROAST – 1 pound
⇛ 1 pound sirloin tip roast/round tip

BEER – 1 cup, for cooking
⇛ 1 cup porter, stout, or other slightly bitter dark ale (for braised meat dishes)

- 1 cup light beer (3% alcohol), low-alcohol beer (less than 2% alcohol), near beer (0.5% alcohol), or nonalcoholic beer (lowest in calories)
- 1 cup gluten-free beer, such as Bard's, Green's, New Grist, or Redbridge; or vegan lager beer
- 1 cup hard cider (gluten-free)
- 1 cup wine (regular or nonalcoholic)
- 1 cup beef or chicken stock
- Small amount beer extract powder (for rubs and blends)

BEET/BEETROOT, RED – 1 pound
- 1 pound golden beets (sweeter) or striped beets/Chioggias (much milder; stripes fade in cooking)
- 14 to 15 ounces canned cooked beets or packaged roasted beets

BEET GREENS – 1 pound
- 1 pound amaranth greens/Chinese spinach, Swiss chard, quinoa leaves, lamb's quarters, or spinach

BELGIAN ENDIVE/WITLOOF/CHICON – 1 pound
- 1 pound chicory, baby mustard greens, arugula, endigia, or puntarelle
- 1 pound Treviso or Chioggia radicchio (maroon color; more bitter; use Chioggia's cup-shaped leaves as edible containers)

BELIMBING/SOUR FINGER CARAMBOLA/BELIMBING WULUH (Southeast Asian fresh or dried sour green fruit) – 4 ounces
- 4 ounces fresh or dried kabosu, sudachi, yuzu, or rhubarb stems

BELL PEPPER See PEPPER, BELL

BEL PAESE (Italian semisoft cheese) – 1 ounce
- 1 ounce Butterkäse, chantelle, Italico, Monterey Jack, Muenster, or mozzarella

BENCH MATE See ITALIAN LEAVENING

BENGALI FIVE-SPICE MIX/PANCH PHORON (Bengali seasoning) – 1/3 cup
  Make Your Own Combine 1 tablespoon each black cumin seeds, fenugreek seeds, black or brown mustard seeds, nigella seeds, and fennel seeds; store in an airtight container in a cool, dry place.

BENITADE SPROUTS (Japanese maroon-colored garnish) – 1 cup
  ▸ 1 cup alfalfa sprouts (for the taste)
  ▸ 1 cup finely shredded red cabbage (for the color)

BERBERE (Ethiopian spice blend) – 1 tablespoon
  ▸ 1 tablespoon harissa powder or peri peri seasoning (for powder blend)
  ▸ 1 tablespoon harissa (for paste blend)
  ▸ 2 teaspoons hot or bittersweet/semi-hot paprika plus 1 teaspoon Chinese chili garlic sauce (for paste blend)

BERMUDA HOT PEPPER SHERRY See SHERRY PEPPER SAUCE

BESAN/GRAM FLOUR/CHANNA FLOUR (Indian chickpea flour) – 1 cup See also CHICKPEA FLOUR; CHICKPEA FLOUR, TOASTED
  ▸ 1 cup coarse chickpea flour/*jada besan*, ground to a powder
  ▸ 1 cup stone-ground garbanzo bean flour or garbanzo–fava bean flour blend
  ▸ 1 cup Italian chickpea flour/*farine de ceci*, such as Bartolini or Lucini Italia (finer texture)
  ▸ 2/3 cup fine-grind cornmeal plus 1/3 cup all-purpose flour (for coating fried chicken or seafood)
  Make Your Own Toast 3/4 cup dried chickpeas/Bengal gram in a dry skillet over medium heat for 3 minutes, stirring constantly. Cool, grind to a powder in a spice/coffee grinder, then sieve to remove the husks.

BESCHUIT (Dutch dry rusk) – 1
  ▸ 1 Holland rusk or zwieback

BESSARA (Moroccan dip) – 1 cup
- 1 cup hummus, preferably with sweet red peppers

BETEL LEAF See *WILD PEPPER LEAF*

BEYAZ PEYNIR (Turkish soft brined cheese) – 1 ounce
- 1 ounce mild feta, soaked in cool water to remove excess salt

BHUT JOLOKIA/NAGA VIPER/GHOST CHILE/COBRA CHILE (Northeast Indian hot chile) – 1
- Carolina Reaper, Trinidad Moruga Scorpion, or Scorpion Butch T chile (hotter)
- Infinity chile (much hotter)
- Red Savina chile (hotter cultivar of the habañero)
- Habañero, Scotch bonnet, or goat chile (fruitier tasting)
- Ghost pepper powder (plain or smoked)

BIBER SALÇASI/ACI BIBER See *RED PEPPER PASTE, HOT*

BICARBONATE OF SODA/BREAD SODA See *BAKING SODA*

BILTONG (South African air-dried meat strips) – 1 pound
- 1 pound Swiss Bundnerfleisch, Italian bresaola, or moist beef jerky

BIRCH SYRUP – 1 cup
- 1 cup maple syrup
- 1 1/3 cups brown sugar plus 1/4 cup water

BIRD'S EYE CHILE, FRESH OR DRIED (Southeast Asian medium hot chile) – 3
- 3 fresh or dried de árbol, pequín, puya, or tepín chiles
- 1/2 fresh Scotch bonnet or habañero chile (hotter)
- 1 fresh red serrano, cayenne, or jalapeño chile
- 1 teaspoon Thai red pepper flakes or chile de árbol pepper flakes or powder

☞ 1 teaspoon sambal oelek or other hot chili paste; reduce the salt in the recipe accordingly

BISCUIT MIX *See BAKING MIX/ALL-PURPOSE BISCUIT MIX*

BISCUITS, QUICK – 6 small (for topping a potpie)
Make Your Own Stir 1 cup sour cream (or 3/4 cup heavy cream) into 1 cup self-rising flour and 1 teaspoon sugar until just mixed. Pat into a rectangle, divide into 6 squares, and bake on an ungreased baking sheet in a preheated 475°F oven until golden brown, 10 to 15 minutes. *See FLOUR, SELF-RISING*
Or
Stir 1/2 cup soymilk or almond milk and 1/4 cup extra-virgin olive oil into 1 cup self-rising flour and 1 teaspoon sugar until just mixed. Spoon dough in 6 places onto an ungreased baking sheet and bake in a preheated 450°F oven until golden brown, 10 to 12 minutes.

BITTER ALMOND OIL *See OIL OF BITTER ALMONDS*

BITTER MELON/BALSAM PEAR/KU GUA/KARELA *See SQUASH, ASIAN*

BITTER ORANGE *See ORANGE, SOUR/BITTER/SEVILLE*

BITTERS (aromatic flavoring agent, such as Angostura or Peychaud's) – 1/4 teaspoon
☞ 1/2 teaspoon Worcestershire sauce (regular or vegetarian)

BLACHAN/BLACAN/BALACHAN *See SHRIMP PASTE, FERMENTED*

BLACK BEAN GARLIC SAUCE (Chinese salty cooking condiment) – 1/3 cup
☞ 2 tablespoons each rinsed salted black beans, light soy sauce, and rice wine plus 1 minced garlic clove, mashed to a coarse paste

BLACK BEAN SAUCE/PASTE/DOU CHI JIANG (Chinese salty cooking condiment) – 1 tablespoon
- 1 tablespoon Chinese fermented black beans, rinsed, mashed, and then combined with 1 teaspoon soy sauce
- 1 tablespoon Japanese dark miso, such as *hatcho*, or Korean soybean paste/*doenjang*

BLACK BEANS, FERMENTED SALTED See FERMENTED BLACK BEANS

BLACKBERRIES – 1 cup
- 1 cup boysenberries (purplish-red; larger and slightly sweeter; cross between blackberry, loganberry, and raspberry)
- 1 cup nectarberries (larger and sweeter; cross between blackberry and boysenberry)
- 1 cup loganberries (purplish-red; sweeter and tarter; cross between Pacific dewberry and raspberry)
- 1 cup tayberries (bright deep purple; sweeter; cross between blackberry and raspberry)
- 1 cup marionberries (dark red to black; larger and sweeter; cross between Chelahem blackberry and olallieberry)
- 1 cup olallieberries (dark purple; larger and sweeter; cross between youngberry and loganberry)
- 1 cup youngberries (dark red; smaller and tarter; cross between blackberry, raspberry, and dewberry)
- 1 cup dewberries (smaller and juicier) or Pacific/California dewberries (larger)
- 1 cup raspberries (preferably black caps; smaller, softer, and sweeter)
- 1 cup mulberries, black or red/*Morus nigra/M. rubra* (purplish-black; larger, denser, and less tart)
- 1 cup cloudberries/*Rubus chamaemorus* (amber; smaller, juicier, and tarter)

BLACK CABBAGE/TUSCAN KALE/CAVOLO NERO/LACINATO See KALE, TUSCAN

BLACK CURRANT JUICE – 1 cup
  ⊳ 1 cup 100% pure pomegranate juice

BLACK CURRANT VINEGAR – 1 tablespoon
  ⊳ 1 tablespoon red wine vinegar plus a few drops of black currant liqueur, such as crème de cassis
  ⊳ 1 tablespoon raspberry vinegar

BLACK CURRANTS See CURRANTS

BLACKENING SEASONING (New Orleans spice rub) – 3 tablespoons
  ⊳ 2 teaspoons salt plus 1 teaspoon each garlic powder, ground black pepper, hot paprika, onion powder, dried thyme leaves, dried oregano, and ground cayenne pepper to taste

BLACK FOOD COLORING – few drops
  ⊳ Few drops squid or cuttlefish ink

BLACK MINT See HUACATAY

BLACK PUDDING See BLOOD SAUSAGE

BLACK RICE VINEGAR See CHINESE BLACK RICE VINEGAR

BLACK SUGAR See JAPANESE BLACK SUGAR

BLACK TRUMPET/HORN OF PLENTY MUSHROOMS – 1 pound
  ⊳ 3 ounces dried black trumpet mushrooms soaked in warm water until softened, 30 to 40 minutes
  ⊳ 1 pound fresh golden chanterelle/*girolle* (added to a dish at the last second), or hedgehog/*pied de mouton* mushrooms

BLEU DE BRESSE See BLUE CHEESE, DOUBLE- OR TRIPLE-CRÈME

BLEWIT/BLUE FOOT MUSHROOMS, FRESH – 1 pound
- ⊨ 1 pound fresh matsutake, or shiitake mushrooms
- ⊨ 3 ounces dried shiitake mushrooms, soaked in warm water until softened, 30 to 40 minutes

BLINI BATTER (Russian crepe batter) – 1 cup
- ⊨ 1 cup prepared Buckwheat pancake mix (add a little extra liquid)

BLOOD SAUSAGE – 1 pound
- ⊨ 1 pound British or Irish black pudding
- ⊨ 1 pound Cajun boudin rouge
- ⊨ 1 pound French boudin noir
- ⊨ 1 pound German Blutworst or Schwartenmagen
- ⊨ 1 pound Portuguese morcela or chouriço nero
- ⊨ 1 pound Spanish morcilla
- ⊨ 1 pound French or German Schwarzwurst (spicy)

BLUEBERRIES, CULTIVATED, AND WILD BLUEBERRIES/VACCINIUM OVALIFOLIUM – 1 cup
- ⊨ 1 cup bilberries/whortleberries/*Vaccinium myrtillus* (dark blue or black; smaller and tarter)
- ⊨ 1 cup cascade/blue bilberries/*Vaccinium deliciosum* (smaller and juicier)
- ⊨ 1 cup black huckleberries/*Vaccinium membranaceum* (thicker skin; tarter; crunchier seeds)
- ⊨ 1 cup haskap berries/honeyberries/Lonicera caerulea(blue-purple; smaller and tarter; seedless)
- ⊨ 1 cup salal berries/*Gaultheria shallon* (dark blue; seedy and juicy; blueberry/blackberry taste)
- ⊨ 1 cup juneberries/serviceberries/sarvisberries/*Amelanchier alnifolia* (purple-black; harder seeds; some berries more tart than others; cook to soften the seeds before adding to muffin batter)
- ⊨ 1 cup black crowberries/*Empetrum nigrum* (tart with several seeds; freeze overnight to improve flavor; use in cooking)

BLUE CHEESE, DOUBLE- OR TRIPLE-CRÈME – 1 ounce

- ✏ 1 ounce Bleu de Bresse, Bavarian Blue, Bavarian Red, Blue Brie, Blue Castello, Blue de Bresse, Cambozola, Cremo, Duet, Gorgonzola dolce, Montbriac/Rochebaron, Oreganzola, Portella, or Saga Blue
- ✏ 1 ounce regular blue cheese plus 1 teaspoon butter

BLUE CHEESE, MEDIUM – 1 ounce

- ✏ 1 ounce Adalost, Azul, Barkham blue, Beenleigh Blue, Berkshire Blue, Bleu d'Auvergne, Bleu des Causses, Bleu de Gex, Blue Cheshire, Blue Wensleydale, Cashel Blue, Castelmagno, Caveman Blue, Danish Blue/Danablu, Devon Blue, Exmoor Blue, Fourme d'Ambert, Maytag Blue, Moncenisio, Mycella, Nauvoo, Point Reyes Original Blue, Rogue River Blue, Saint Agur, Shropshire Blue/orange, Stagnola Blu, Stella Blue, Strichelton, Valdeón, or Vinny
- ✏ 1 ounce blue cheese powder (for flavor without moisture)

BLUE CHEESE, MILD – 1 ounce

- ✏ 1 ounce Bayley Hazen Blue, Blue Brie, Dolcelatte/Gorgonzola dolce, or Erbo

BLUE CHEESE, STRONG – 1 ounce

- ✏ 1 ounce Cabrales, Gorgonzola Picante, Picon, Stilton, or Roquefort

BOCCONCINI (1- to 2-ounce fresh mozzarella balls) – 8 ounces See also CILIEGINE

- ✏ 2 *ovolini* (4-ounce fresh mozzarella balls), cut into quarters
- ✏ 8 ounces fresh mozzarella/*fior di latte*, cut into 1-inch cubes

BOK CHOY/WHITE MUSTARD CABBAGE/CHINESE WHITE CABBAGE/PAK CHOY – 1 pound

- ✏ 1 pound choy sum, Swiss chard, Savoy cabbage, napa cabbage, firm-ribbed loose-leaf lettuce, or leggy stalks of romaine lettuce
- ✏ 1 pound baby bok choy (sweeter; less fibrous)
- ✏ 1 pound celery stalks (for stir-fries)

BOLDO/BOLDINA LEAF/HOJA DE BOLDO, DRIED (South American seasoning) – 1 leaf
- 1 small fresh or dried California bay leaf

BOMBAY DUCK/BOMBIL (Indian sun-dried salted fish) – 1 pound
- 1 pound salt cod

BONIATO/BATATA/CAMOTE (Caribbean ivory-fleshed sweet potato) – 1 medium (1 pound)
- 1 pound white or yellow-fleshed cush-cush yam/*mapuey*
- 1 pound starchy white potato, such as russet
- 1 pound dry sweet potatoes or Asian sweet potatoes

BONITO FLAKES/SKIPJACK TUNA, DRIED See FISH FLAKES, DRIED

BORAGE/BORRAJA (European green herb)
- Kirby cucumber spears or wedges (for garnishing drinks)
- Small celery sprigs with leaves (for garnishing drinks)
- Fresh thyme or salad burnet (for flavoring food)
- Celery leaves and nasturtium leaves, stems, and blossoms (for adorning salads)

BOTTARGA DI MUGGINE (salt-cured, dried gray mullet roe) – 1 ounce See also CAVIAR, BLACK
- 1/2 ounce powdered dried mullet bottarga (milder)
- 1 ounce tuna bottarga/*bottarga di tonno* (stronger flavor and moister texture; harder to grate so thinly shave with a knife)
- 1 ounce Japanese salt-cured, dried mullet roe/*karasumi* (softer texture)
- 1 ounce Spanish salt-cured, dried tuna loin/*majama* (moister; less expensive)
- 1 ounce Chinese dried scallop/*con poy* (expensive flavoring agent)

BOUILLON – 1 cup
- 1 beef bouillon cube, 1 teaspoon beef bouillon granules, or 1 envelope instant broth, dissolved in 1 cup boiling water

☞ 1 seasoning packet from a 3-ounce-package beef-flavored ramen noodles dissolved in 1 cup boiling water

☞ 4 teaspoons dark miso (or 5 teaspoons light) added to 1 cup very hot (not boiling) water a little at a time and stirred until smooth

☞ 1 porcini-flavored bouillon cube or 1 teaspoon wild mushroom bouillon granules dissolved in 1 cup boiling water

☞ 1 cup water plus a little soy sauce for flavor

BOUILLON CUBE, BEEF – 1

☞ 4 teaspoons Japanese dark miso, such as *hatcho*; Korean soybean paste/*doenjang*; or tamari

BOUKOVO PEPPER FLAKES (Greek) – 1 teaspoon

☞ 1/2 to 3/4 teaspoon hot Spanish paprika or chipotle chile powder

BOUQUET GARNI (seasoning herbs tied in a bundle) – 1

☞ 3 sprigs fresh parsley, 1 small sprig fresh thyme, and 1 small fresh bay leaf, tied together with kitchen twine or a leftover tea bag string

☞ 1 teaspoon dried parsley, 1/2 teaspoon dried thyme, and 1 whole or crumbled bay leaf, wrapped in a 6-inch square of cheesecloth or placed in a reusable muslin tea bag or metal tea infuser

☞ 1 bay leaf (in a pinch)

BOURSAULT (triple-crème cheese) – 1 ounce

☞ 1 ounce Brie, Bouche d'affinois, Brillat-Savarin, Delice de Bourogne, Excelsior, Explorateur, Largo, La Tur, Lucullus, Mt. Tam, Italian Piedmont, Pierre Robert, or Saint-André

BOURSIN (seasoned triple-crème cheese) – 1 ounce

☞ 1 ounce Alouette, Rondelé, or Tartare

☞ 1 ounce herbed cream cheese plus a little butter

☞ 1 ounce creamed cream cheese plus a little white wine, minced garlic, dried thyme, and coarsely ground black pepper

BOYSENBERRIES – 1 cup
- 1 cup nectarberries (larger and sweeter; cross between blackberry and boysenberry)
- 1 cup loganberries (redder color; cross between blackberry and red raspberry)
- 1 cup blackberries (tarter; larger seeds)
- 1 cup olallieberries (larger and sweeter; cross between a loganberry and youngberry)

BRAN See OAT BRAN; RICE BRAN; WHEAT BRAN, UNPROCESSED/ MILLERS BRAN

BRANDY – 1 tablespoon for cooking
- 1 tablespoon rum, hard cider, unsweetened apple juice, or brewed coffee
- 1/2 teaspoon imitation brandy, rum, or bourbon extract plus 2 1/2 teaspoons vodka or water

BRANDY EXTRACT – 1 teaspoon
- 2 tablespoons brandy or rum; reduce the liquid in the recipe by 2 tablespoons

BRATWURST (German pork and veal sausage) – 1 pound
- 1 pound Bockwurst, Weisswurst, or French boudin blanc

Make Your Own Knead together vigorously 1 pound ground pork (25 to 30% fat), 1 tablespoon bratwurst sausage seasoning, 2 tablespoons finely minced onion, and 3 to 4 tablespoons ice water, then cover and refrigerate for 24 hours before cooking.

BRAZIL NUT MILK – 4 cups
Make Your Own Soak 1 cup raw Brazil nuts in water to cover 4 hours. Drain, rinse, then blend with 4 cups water until smooth, about 4 minutes; strain through a nutmilk bag or cheesecloth-lined sieve, pressing firmly on the pulp to extract all the liquid. Keep refrigerated and shake before using; it should keep for up to 5 days.

BREAD, QUICK, NON-SWEET – 1 pound
- 1 pound beer bread, Irish soda bread, salt-raised bread, Swedish quick rye bread, or various non-yeast flatbreads
- 1 pound biscuits, buttermilk or sour cream muffins, cornbread, or spoon bread

BREAD, STALE (dried bread for breadcrumbs, pudding, strata, or stuffing) – 1 pound
- 1 pound fresh bread slices, spread on a tray or baking sheet and left to dry at room temperature, 6 to 8 hours
- 1 pound fresh bread slices, baked at 250°F until slightly dried, 15 to 20 minutes, or longer for thoroughly dried

BREADCRUMBS, DRY (breading and binding agent) – 1 cup
- 1 1/4 cups packaged dry poultry stuffing cubes, crushed in a paper or plastic bag with a rolling pin, or pulsed in a blender or food processor
- 1 or 2 day-old hard roll(s) or French bread grated, crushed, or ground
- 1 cup golden flaxseed meal, oat bran, matzo meal, quinoa flakes, or yellow pea flour or peasemeal
- 3/4 to 1 1/4 cups unsalted pretzels, breadsticks, plain Melba toast, matzo, pita chips, cornflakes, puffed brown rice, low-sodium tortilla chips, or Japanese rice crackers, pulsed in a food processor, or coarsely crushed in a paper bag to measure 1 cup
- 1 cup ground roasted peanuts (for Southeast Asian–themed foods)

Make Your Own Dry 3 or 4 slices of bread in a preheated 300°F oven until crisp, 10 to 15 minutes. Cool, then crush or grind. Alternatively, tear the bread into small pieces and microwave on High for 2 to 3 minutes, stirring after 1 minute, then cool and crush.

BREADCRUMBS, FRESH (filler/binding agent) – 1 cup
- 1 cup coarsely grated frozen bread or rolls (grate on the large holes of a box grater; for sliced bread, grate 3 or 4 halved pieces at a time)
- 1 cup unsweetened cornbread or corn muffin crumbs

- ⇨ 1 cup instant mashed potato flakes, coarsely ground in a blender
- ⇨ 1 cup rolled oats, coarsely ground in a blender
- ⇨ 1 cup quick-cooking/instant couscous, soaked in water 5 minutes; or fine-ground bulgur (grind #1), simmered 5 minutes

BREADCRUMBS, ITALIAN-STYLE SEASONED – 1 heaping cup
- ⇨ 3/4 cup dry breadcrumbs plus 2 tablespoons grated Parmesan cheese, 1 tablespoon dried parsley, and 1 tablespoon Italian seasoning
- ⇨ 1 1/4 cups seasoned croutons or seasoned Melba toast, crushed into crumbs

BREADCRUMBS, JAPANESE-STYLE See PANKO

BREADFRUIT – 1 medium (about 2 pounds)
- ⇨ 1 (26-ounce) can breadfruit in brine, drained and rinsed
- ⇨ 2 (20-ounce) cans young/green jackfruit in brine, drained and rinsed
- ⇨ 2 pounds waxy boiling potatoes

BREADING/COATING MIX – 1 generous cup
- ⇨ 1 cup flour, dry breadcrumbs, or ground toasted oats, plus 2 to 3 tablespoons grated Parmesan cheese and 1/2 teaspoon each salt, paprika, and crushed dried herbs (optional)
- ⇨ 3 ounces (about 26) savory or cheese crackers, crushed or ground
- ⇨ 4 ounces (2 cups) canned fried onions plus a pinch of salt (optional), crushed or ground
- ⇨ 2 cups whole-grain flake or bran cereal, finely crushed
- ⇨ 3 to 4 cups cornflakes (4 ounces), lightly crushed
- ⇨ 2 to 3 cups flavored croutons, spicy tortilla chips, flavored pita chips, fish-shape crackers, or nonsalted light-colored potato chips, crushed or ground and then measured
- ⇨ 1 cup packaged biscuit mix plus 1 tablespoon seasoning dry rub or spice blend, such as Italian, Cajun, Creole, Poultry, Greek, or herbes de Provence

BREADING/COATING MIX, GLUTEN-FREE – 1 cup (about)
- 1 cup rice or potato flour seasoned with grated Parmesan (or nutritional yeast), garlic salt, paprika, and dried parsley (Alternatively, replace some of the rice or potato flour with whole-grain soy flour, which inhibits fat absorption.)
- 1 cup finely ground fresh gluten-free bread crumbs, toasted in a preheated 425°F oven until golden brown, 5 to 7 minutes, then seasoned with grated Parmesan, 1 scant teaspoon cornstarch, plus a pinch each of onion powder and Italian seasoning
- 1 cup almond meal, coconut flour, golden flaxseed meal, finely chopped walnuts or hazelnuts, fine cornmeal, rice bran, or instant mashed potato flakes
- 3 cups cornflakes or plain potato chips, or 2 cups puffed/crisped rice or corn cereal, crushed with a rolling pin
- 2 cups cold unsalted plain popcorn (preferably hot-air popped), ground in small batches in a blender or food processor until powdery
- 1 or 2 puffed rice cakes (white or brown), broken up and ground in a blender or food processor
- 1 1/2 to 2 cups gluten-free corn chips, pulsed in a food processor until the mixture resembles coarse meal

BRESAOLA/SALAA COME BRISA (Italian air-dried beef) – 1 pound
- 1 pound Swiss air-dried beef/*viande des Grisons* or *bünderfleisch*, French *brési,* Greek *pastourma,* South African *biltong,* or Turkish *basţurma*

BRIE (French soft-ripened smooth cheese) – 1 ounce
- 1 ounce American-style Brie (firmer, longer lasting) or Appalachian (thicker; square-shaped)
- 1 ounce Bouche d'affinois, Camembert, Coulommiers, Caprice des Dieux (double-crème), Crema Dania (double-crème), Dunbarra, Humboldt Fog (chèvre), Le Petit Créme, Le Fougerus, or Sharpham

BRIK PASTRY/FEUILLES DE BRIK/MALSUSQA/WARKA/OUARKA (North African and Middle Eastern tissue-thin sheets of pastry dough) – 1 pound
- ☞ 1 pound thawed frozen phyllo/filo dough or strudel dough brushed with oil (for baking; less sturdy)
- ☞ 1 pound country-style phyllo dough/*horiatiko* (thicker and easier to work with)
- ☞ 8 ounces frozen puff pastry sheets, brushed with oil (for baking; not for frying)
- ☞ 1 pound fresh or thawed frozen yufka dough, lumpia wrappers, or rice-flour spring-roll wrappers (for frying)

BRILLAT-SAVARIN *See BOURSAULT (triple-crème-cheese)*

BRINE SOLUTION, SALTWATER (flavoring agent for pork and poultry) – 1 quart
- ☞ 1/4 cup kosher salt (or 2 tablespoons table salt) dissolved in 1 quart cold water (for plain brine)
- ☞ 1/2 cup kosher salt (or 1/4 cup table salt) and 1/4 cup granulated sugar dissolved in 1 quart cold water (for sweetened brine)
- ☞ 1 to 4 tablespoons kosher salt (for poultry dry brine; rub salt evenly over the bird, including cavity and under breast skin; refrigerate, lightly covered, at least 24 hours before roasting)

BRINZA/BRYNDZA (Romanian brine-cured cheese) – 1 ounce
- ☞ 1 ounce feta, ricotta salata, or fresh ricotta for young bryndza (soak feta in cold water a few hours to remove some of the saltiness)

BROCCIO/BROCCIU CHEESE (unsalted sheep's-milk cheese) – 1 ounce
- ☞ 1 ounce thick whole-milk ricotta, drained for 2 to 3 hours in a dampened cheesecloth-lined sieve

BROCCOLI – 1 pound
- ☞ 1 pound broccoli di cicco (smaller florets; firmer texture)

☞ 1 pound broccoflower (lighter color; milder flavor; firmer texture)

☞ 1 pound Romanesco broccoli (chartreuse color; sweeter flavor; firmer texture)

☞ 1 pound cauliflower (white color; firmer texture)

BROCCOLINI/BABY BROCCOLI/ASPARATION – 1 pound

☞ 1 pound thin-stemmed Chinese broccoli or baby Chinese broccoli/ *gai lan miew*

☞ 1 pound regular broccoli stalks sliced lengthwise

☞ 1 pound thin asparagus

BROCCOLI RABE/BROCCOLI RAAB/RAPINI – 1 pound

☞ 1 pound domestic spigarello (leafier, milder flavor, more delicate)

☞ 1 pound Chinese broccoli (thicker stems; milder flavor)

☞ 1 1/2 pounds escarole (dark outer leaves), Chinese mustard greens/*amsoy,* mustard greens, dandelion greens, purple mizuna, puntarelle, or turnip greens

☞ 1 pound wild mustard flower bud stems/*Brassica rapa* or *B.nigra*

BROTH, BEEF – 1 cup

☞ 1/2 cup each consommé and water

☞ 1 cup boiling water plus one of the following: 1 reduced-sodium bouillon cube, 1 envelope instant broth or granules, or 3/4 teaspoon beef soup base or gluten-free beef-flavored base (use half the amount for light meat or light broth)

☞ 2 teaspoons tamari or soy sauce added to 1 cup water

☞ 1 tablespoon noodle soup base, such as Kikkoman brand, added to 1 cup water

☞ 1 seasoning packet from a 3-ounce-package beef-flavored ramen noodles dissolved in 1 cup boiling water

☞ 2 teaspoons Maggi Seasoning added to 1 cup water

☞ 3/4 teaspoon beef extract or concentrated beef broth, such as Bovril, Better than Bouillon Beef Base, or Home Again, dissolved in 1 cup boiling water

BROTH, CHICKEN – 1 cup
- 1 cup canned or boxed reduced-sodium chicken broth, no-salt chicken stock, "no-chicken" broth/chicken-flavored vegetarian broth, plus 1/8 teaspoon unflavored gelatin powder or agar powder dissolved in cold broth or stock before heating
- 1 cup boiling water plus 1 reduced-sodium chicken bouillon cube, or 1 envelope instant chicken broth or granules, or 1/2 to 3/4 teaspoon chicken extract or soup base, or 2 teaspoons vegetarian-based chicken broth powder

BROTH, CHICKEN OR BEEF, FAT-FREE – 1 can
- 1 can regular broth, refrigerated in the container for 8 to 12 hours (or in the freezer for 20 to 30 minutes) before removing solidified fat from the top

BROTH, LIGHT MEAT/BROWN VEAL TYPE – 1 cup
- 2/3 cup chicken broth plus 1/3 cup beef broth

BROTH, VEGETABLE – 1 cup
- 1 cup boiling water plus one of the following: instant vegetable broth package, vegetable bouillon cube, no-salt vegan vegetable cube, or 1/2 to 3/4 teaspoon powdered or jarred vegetable or mushroom soup base
- 1 cup bean or vegetable cooking water (water left from cooking beans or mild-tasting vegetables)
- 1 cup mushroom soaking water (from dried mushrooms rehydrated with boiling water)

BROWN RICE See RICE, BROWN

BROWN RICE FLOUR See FLOUR, RICE, BROWN

BROWN RICE MILK See RICE MILK

BROWN RICE SYRUP/YINNIE (Chinese naturally processed sweetener) – 1 cup See also JAPANESE BLACK SUGAR SYRUP
- ☞ 3/4 cup mild-flavored liquid honey or maple syrup plus 2 tablespoons water
- ☞ 1 cup agave syrup/nectar or coconut nectar

BROWN RICE VINEGAR See JAPANESE BROWN RICE VINEGAR/ GENMAIZU

BROWN SAUCE, BOTTLED (British condiment) – 1 tablespoon
- ☞ 1 tablespoon HP sauce, A-1 sauce, steak sauce, or gluten-free brown sauce, such as Granovita
- ☞ 1 1/2 teaspoons each Worcestershire sauce and ketchup

BROWN SUGAR See SUGAR, DARK BROWN; SUGAR, LIGHT BROWN

BROWN SUGAR SYRUP/KURO MITSU (Japanese sweetener) – 1 cup
- ☞ 1 1/3 cups (firmly packed) brown sugar, a pinch of salt, and 1/2 cup boiling water, simmered until syrupy and reduced to 1 cup

BRUSSELS SPROUTS – 1 pound
- ☞ 1 pound Kalettes (milder and sweeter; cross between Brussels sprouts and kale)
- ☞ 1 pound broccoli florets (milder; faster cooking)
- ☞ 1 pound cut-up green cabbage (milder; faster cooking)

BUCKWHEAT FLOUR See FLOUR, BUCKWHEAT

BUCKWHEAT GROATS See KASHA

BUDDHA'S HAND/FINGERED CITRON – 1
- ☞ 1 fresh etrog citron or pomelo
- ☞ 2 large thick-skinned lemons

BULGUR, COARSE-GROUND (grind #3 or #4) – 1 cup

- ⇨ 1 cup cracked wheat or cracked farro
- ⇨ 1 cup red wheat berries or whole-grain farro, chopped in a blender or food processor 15 to 20 seconds, then sifted to remove any smaller particles
- ⇨ 1 cup buckwheat groats, medium-grain kasha/roasted buckwheat groats, or quick-cooking brown rice (for gluten-free)

BULGUR, FINE- OR MEDIUM-GRIND (grind #1 or #2) – 1 cup

- ⇨ 1 cup bulgur from a box of wheat salad mix (reserve the seasoning packet for another use)
- ⇨ 1 cup coarse-ground bulgur (grind #3), ground in a spice/coffee grinder until fine or medium fine
- ⇨ 1 cup whole-wheat couscous or barley couscous/*balboula*
- ⇨ 1 cup fine-grain barley grits (lightly toasted in a dry skillet, then cooked following package directions)
- ⇨ 1 cup light quinoa, prewashed or well rinsed; or Bolivian *canahua* (lightly toasted in a dry skillet before cooking; gluten-free)
- ⇨ 1 cup grated white cauliflower (grated on the large holes of a box grater or pulsed briefly in a food processor)

BULLWHIP KELP, DRIED (brown algae) – 1 ounce

- ⇨ 1 ounce dried wakame or alaria/winged kelp

BURDOCK ROOT/GOBO/VETOING (Japanese root vegetable) – 2 ounces (6-inch piece/1/2 cup scraped and sliced)

- ⇨ 1/2 cup thawed frozen burdock strips or canned burdock pieces, rinsed in cold water
- ⇨ 1/3 cup dried shaved burdock root/*gobo*, soaked in warm water until softened
- ⇨ 1/2 cup wild burdock root/lesser burdock/*Arctium minus*
- ⇨ 1/2 cup peeled and sliced white salsify/oyster plant or black salsify/scorzonera (less sweet)

 1 medium parsnip or White Satin carrot, peeled and sliced on the bias (sweeter)

BURICOTTA (fresh mozzarella sacks filled with ricotta) – 8 ounces
 8 ounces fresh ricotta

BURRATA (fresh mozzarella sacks filled with cream and mozzarella shreds/stracciatella) – 8 ounces
 8 ounces *burrino/provole* (fresh mozzarella sacks filled with butter)
 8 ounces *buricotta* (fresh mozzarella sacks filled with ricotta)
 8 ounces fresh cow's milk mozzarella/*fior di latte*

BUTIFARRA/BOTIFARRA, WHITE (Catalonian veal sausage) – 1 pound
 1 pound mild chicken sausage

BUTTER REPLACEMENT, FAT-FREE – 1/2 cup, for baking
 1/2 cup thick, unsweetened applesauce, well drained (for spice cake)
 1/2 cup prune puree (for chocolate cake)
 1/2 cup mashed bananas (for muffins)

BUTTER, BRITTANY (cooking butter containing sea salt crystals) – 2 ounces (1/4 cup)
 2 ounces softened unsalted European-style butter plus 2 teaspoons coarse sea salt, thoroughly combined

BUTTER, CLARIFIED – 4 ounces (1/2 cup)
 1/2 cup pure ghee/*usli ghee*, vegetable-oil ghee/*vanaspati ghee*, light sesame oil, macadamia nut oil, or refined coconut oil
 1/2 cup nonhydrogenated solid vegetable shortening (or rendered leaf lard) plus a few drops toasted sesame oil (or hazelnut oil) for the taste
 5 ounces unsalted butter (lower smoke point; be careful not to overheat)

Make Your Own Slowly heat 5 ounces unsalted butter in a small saucepan until melted (or microwave for 2 minutes on High in a loosely covered large microwave-safe bowl); let sit until the milk solids settle, about 30 minutes, then gently pour the butter into a container, and leave the milky residue behind.

BUTTER, CULTURED – 4 ounces
- Homemade butter made with 1 cup heavy cream (not ultra-pasteurized) and 1/2 cup crème fraîche instead of all heavy cream

BUTTER, EUROPEAN-STYLE/HIGH FAT (82 to 84% butterfat) – 4 ounces (1/2 cup)
- 1/2 cup plus 2 teaspoons North American–style butter; reduce the liquid in the recipe by 1 tablespoon

BUTTER, FRESH – 8 ounces (1 cup/2 sticks)
- 8 ounces (1 cup) canned butter, such as Red Feather (expensive)
- 4 ounces (1 cup) powdered butter plus 1 cup water
- 8 ounces (2 sticks) vegan margarine containing 80% fat, such as Earth Balance (reduce the salt in the recipe by 1/2 teaspoon if the recipe calls for unsalted butter)
- 6 ounces (3/4 cup) plus 2 tablespoons butter-flavored shortening, or nonhydrogenated vegetable shortening, such as organic palm shortening, or lard, preferably rendered leaf lard (for pie crusts and biscuits)
- 5 ounces (3/4 cup) plus 2 tablespoons chicken fat (for sautéing aromatics, roasting root vegetables, and frying eggs)
- 8 ounces (1 cup) European-style/high fat butter (for buttercream, croissants, puff pastry, or shortbread; increase the baking time for all-butter pie crust; for cookies, reduce the butter by 2 teaspoons if critical to the recipe)
- 18 ounces (1 1/2 cups) pure whipped butter (for cakes and cookies that require creaming the butter and sugar together)
- 5 1/2 ounces (3/4 cup) plus 2 tablespoons refined coconut oil (for drop cookies, brownies, muffins, and sweet breads)

- 5 3/4 ounces (3/4 cup) plus 2 tablespoons coconut butter (for frostings)
- 6 fluid ounces (3/4 cup) mild olive oil, macadamia nut oil, or cold-pressed canola or safflower oil plus 1/4 cup water (for drop cookies not cutout cookies, brownies, muffins, and sweet breads)
- 7.7 ounces (1 cup) unsalted soy butter (does not melt but can be used for pastry)
- 1 cup pureed avocado (for sweet breads and brownies; reduce the oven temperature by 25% and increase the baking time)
- 1/2 cup mild-tasting vegetable oil plus 1/2 cup thick unsweetened applesauce that has been drained for 15 minutes (for lowfat quick breads; avoid overmixing and reduce the baking time slightly)

Make Your Own Blend or whip 2 cups heavy cream (not ultra-pasteurized) until butter forms, 5 to 8 minutes; strain, rinse in cold water until clear, then knead or press to extract the remaining buttermilk; store, refrigerated, up to 3 weeks.

BUTTER, PRUNE See PRUNE PURÉE/PRUNE BUTTER

BUTTER, REDUCED-FAT SOFT SPREAD – 1 pound
Make Your Own Beat 8 ounces (1 cup/2 sticks) room-temperature butter until creamy, then slowly beat in 1 cup chilled evaporated milk. Transfer to an airtight container and keep refrigerated.

BUTTER, SALTED – 8 ounces (1 cup/2 sticks)
- 8 ounces unsalted butter plus increase salt in the recipe by 1/2 teaspoon

BUTTER, SOFT SPREAD – 1 cup
Make Your Own Beat 4 ounces (1/2 cup/1 stick) unsalted butter until creamy, then slowly beat in 1/2 cup grapeseed or canola oil; pour into an airtight container and keep refrigerated. Alternatively, pulse the oil and butter in a blender, then pour into a container; it will harden when chilled. (Light or mild-tasting olive oil can be used,

but extra-virgin olive oil can turn bitter when whipped; for salted spread, use salted butter plus 1/4 teaspoon fine sea salt.)

BUTTER, WHIPPED – 1 cup
▷ 2/3 cup firm butter, beaten until light and fluffy

BUTTER-FLAVORED GRANULES – 1 tablespoon
▷ 4 tablespoons (2 ounces/1/4 cup/1/2 stick) salted or unsalted butter

BUTTERMILK STARTER CULTURE, DIRECT SET – 1 packet (1/2 teaspoon)
▷ 1/4 cup cultured buttermilk

BUTTERMILK, CULTURED (2% butterfat) – 1 cup
▷ 1/4 cup buttermilk powder added to dry ingredients, plus 1 cup water as liquid component (less acidic than fresh; less efficient for yeast dough)
▷ 1 cup minus 1 tablespoon room-temperature lowfat milk plus 1 tablespoon distilled white vinegar or cider vinegar (or lemon juice), left 10 minutes until thickened (for baking)
▷ 1 cup lowfat milk (or 1/2 cup each full-fat milk and water) plus 1 1/2 teaspoons cream of tartar (mix cream of tartar with dry ingredients before adding milk)
▷ 1 (8-ounce) bottle cow or goat yogurt drink
▷ 1 cup kefir (slightly alcoholic due to fermentation)
▷ 1 cup Bulgarian buttermilk (thicker and more tart)
▷ 1/2 cup plain full-fat yogurt whisked with 1/2 cup water until smooth
▷ 1/2 cup plain lowfat yogurt whisked with 1/2 cup lowfat milk until smooth
▷ 2/3 cup plain nonfat yogurt whisked with 1/3 cup full-fat or lowfat milk until smooth
▷ 1 cup plain homemade yogurt (thicker)
▷ 1 cup whey (thinner)

BUTTERMILK, EUROPEAN-STYLE – *1 cup*
- ⇨ 3/4 cup cultured buttermilk whisked with 1/4 cup plain full-fat yogurt until smooth

BUTTERMILK, LACTOSE FREE – *1 cup, for baking*
- ⇨ 1 cup soy, rice, or almond milk plus 2 teaspoons lemon juice (or cider vinegar) left until slightly thickened, about 10 minutes (if using rice milk, reduce the amount in recipes by up to 25%; rice-based buttermilk will be thin)
- ⇨ 1 cup plain dairy-free yogurt plus 1 tablespoon lemon juice (or distilled white or cider vinegar) left, undisturbed, 5 to 10 minutes
- ⇨ 1 cup water plus 1 tablespoon lemon juice or vinegar

BUTTERNUT SQUASH, FRESH OR FROZEN – *1 cup cooked*
- ⇨ 1 cup canned butternut squash puree
- ⇨ 1 cup cooked acorn, buttercup, Rugosa, or Musquée de Provence squash
- ⇨ 1 cup cooked delicata squash (sweeter with tender edible skin)
- ⇨ 1 cup cooked fresh or canned pumpkin or sweet potato (moister and sweeter)

BZAR (Middle Eastern seasoning mix) – *1 teaspoon*
- ⇨ 1 teaspoon garam masala spice blend

C

CABBAGE (ballhead, savoy, napa) – 1 pound
- 1 pound miniature Chinese cabbage/Tenderheart (for single servings)
- 1 pound Brussels sprouts: whole, sliced, or shaved leaves (for cooking, salads, and slaw)
- 1 pound celery root (for slaw)

CABBAGE LEAVES – 1 pound, for stuffing
- 1 pound fresh, tender, unsprayed fig leaves, stemmed and blanched until softened
- 1 pound fresh, jarred, or canned grape leaves, blanched until softened
- 1 pound fresh greens (kale, kohlrabi, mustard, turnip, Swiss chard), stemmed, deribbed if necessary (or the rib shaved until even with the leaf), then blanched until softened
- 1 pound bok choy outer leaves, steamed until tender, 3 to 5 minutes, then trimmed
- 1 pound Boston or looseleaf lettuce leaves, trimmed
- 1 pound older nasturtium leaves, blanched for 60 seconds (more delicate texture; for brief cooking only)

CABERNET SAUVIGNON VINEGAR – 1 tablespoon
- 1 tablespoon Zinfandel vinegar or other mellow red wine vinegar
- 1 tablespoon sherry vinegar
- 1 to 2 tablespoons red wine (regular or nonalcoholic)

CACAHUAZINTLE MAIZE, DRIED (Mexican corn grain) – 1 pound
- 1 pound white or yellow stone-ground dent corn

CACAO NIBS *See COCOA NIBS/CHOCOLATE NIBS*

CACAO POWDER, RAW (unprocessed cocoa) – 1/4 cup
- 1/4 cup cocoa nibs, pulverized to a fine powder
- 3 to 4 tablespoons natural cocoa powder (less potent)

CACHAÇA/AGUARDENTE/PINGA (Brazilian clear sugarcane alcohol) – 2 tablespoons
- 2 tablespoons white (light) rum

CACHUCHA CHILE PEPPER, FRESH (Cuban) *See AJI DULCE*

CACIOCAVALLO (Southern Italian cow's milk cheese) – 1 ounce
- 1 ounce scamorza or Italian provolone

CACIOCAVALLO, SMOKED – 1 ounce
- 1 ounce smoked mozzarella/*mozzarella affumicata*, smoked provolone, or smoked scamorza
- 1 ounce Polish Kurplanka (lightly smoked with garlic)

CACTUS LEAF *See NOPALE/PRICKLY PEAR CACTUS*

CAJETA (Mexican caramelized goat's-milk) – 1 cup *See also CARAMEL PASTE*
- 1 cup dulce de leche/*doce de leite* or other thick caramel sauce (milder taste)

CAJUN SEASONING – 1 tablespoon
- 1/2 teaspoon each ground black pepper, white pepper, ground cayenne pepper, garlic powder, onion powder, and paprika. Or, in place of white pepper, use dried thyme or increase paprika to 1 teaspoon.
- 1 tablespoon Creole seasoning

CAKE GLAZE – 1 cup *See also FRUIT GLAZE*
- 1 cup store-bought frosting plus a little liquid (water, milk, cream) heated in a small pan over low heat, stirring constantly, until liquid enough to pour

CALABAZA SQUASH/WEST INDIAN PUMPKIN/GIRAUMON – 1 pound
- 1 pound acorn, golden acorn, buttercup, butternut, baby Hubbard, Carnival, kabocha, Potimarron, or Red Kuri squash
- 1 pound Fairytail or sugar pumpkin squash

CALABRESE RED PEPPER POWDER, SWEET/PEPE ROSSA (Italian seasoning) – 1 tablespoon
- 1 tablespoon mild/sweet Spanish paprika

CALABRIAN BOMB (Italian spicy condiment paste) – 1 tablespoon
- 1 tablespoon Calabrese sweet pepper paste
- 1 tablespoon spicy red chili paste, such as harissa or sambal oelek

CALABRIAN CHILE/PEPERONCINO (Italian hot chile) – 1
- 1 oil-packed Calabrian chile
- 1 fresh red cayenne or Thai chile

CALABRIAN CHILI PASTE/SILAFUNGHI HOT CHILI SAUCE – 1 generous tablespoon
- 1 tablespoon minced jarred roasted red pepper, 1/2 teaspoon each olive oil and lemon juice, plus 1/4 teaspoon each crushed red pepper flakes and smoked Spanish paprika

CALABRIAN RED PEPPER POWDER, HOT (Italian seasoning powder) – 1 tablespoon
- 1 tablespoon Calabrese red pepper flakes or ground cayenne pepper

CALAMANSI *See CALAMONDIN*

C

C

C

CALAMINT See NEPITELLA

CALAMONDIN/KALAMANSI/LIMAU KETSURI (Southeast Asian citrus fruit) – 1
- 3 large kumquats or mandarinquats
- 2 or 3 fully ripe (yellowing) Key limes
- 1 small blood orange or sour Valencia orange

CALAMONDIN JUICE – 1 tablespoon
- 2 teaspoons lemon or lime juice plus 1 teaspoon tangerine or mandarin juice (or orange juice)

CALCIUM CHLORIDE (firming agent for pickles)
- Pickling lime/cal/calcium hydroxide (add to brine following package directions)
- Freshly washed grape, cherry, or oak leaves for naturally fermented pickles (use 1 leaf per 4 or 5 cucumbers to improve texture)

CALÇOT (Catalan grilling onion) – 5 ounces (1 bunch)
- 5 ounces fat scallions or green onions
- 5 ounces baby leeks or thin regular leeks cut in half lengthwise (milder)

CALLALOO/TARO LEAF/DASHEEN LEAF/ARVI LEAF/PATRA (West African and Caribbean leafy vegetable) – 1 pound See also MALANGA LEAVES
- 8 to 10 ounces canned callaloo greens, drained and rinsed
- 1 pound frozen cassava leaves
- 1 pound mature spinach, Swiss chard, turnip greens, mustard greens, or collard greens

CALTROP STARCH See WATER CHESTNUT POWDER

CAMBODIAN FISH SAUCE/TUK TREY See FISH SAUCE

CAMEMBERT (French soft-ripened smooth cheese) – 1 ounce
- ⇨ 1 ounce Brie, Capricorn Goat, Chaource, Cooleeney, Coulommiers, Eskdale, Green Hill, Le Coutances, Roucoulons, Saint-Killian, Timboon, or Tunsworth

CAMPARI (Italian bittersweet apéritif) – 2 tablespoons
- ⇨ 2 tablespoons Aperol or Fernet Branca

CANADIAN BACON/BACK BACON (cured pork loin) – 1 pound
- ⇨ 1 pound lean smoked ham or Irish bacon

CANAPÉ BASES, PLANT-BASED (small edible containers for holding food tidbits) *See also CRUDITÉS*
- ⇨ Radish rounds (daikon, jicama, or black radish, peeled and sliced crosswise into thin rounds, crisped in very cold water, then blotted dry)
- ⇨ Lettuce cups (cup-shaped leaves of Chiogga radicchio, or small inner leaves of butter or Baby Gem lettuce)
- ⇨ Belgian endive spears (small trimmed endives, cored and separated)
- ⇨ Cucumber cups (3/4-inch-thick cucumber slices hollowed out leaving the bottom intact; or halved lengthwise, hollowed out, and cut into small boat-like pieces; remove a thin strip from the underside to stabilize)
- ⇨ Baby potato disks (small waxy potatoes cut into 1/3-inch slices and steamed until cooked through, 10 to 12 minutes; or small boiled new potatoes hollowed out)
- ⇨ Carrot coins (thinly sliced raw chubby carrots)
- ⇨ Brussels sprouts cups (large outer leaves from Brussels sprouts blanched for 1 minute, shocked in ice water, then drained and patted dry)
- ⇨ Miniature pattypan or baby yellow squash cups (squash tops removed, flesh and seeds scooped out, then steamed until tender; or baked at 350°F until soft, about 15 minutes, and then tops removed and flesh and seeds scooped out)

- Cherry tomato cups (flesh scooped out, inside lightly salted, inverted on a rack for 10 minutes, and then rinsed)
- Small zucchini or yellow squash boats (sliced in half lengthwise, blanched 30 seconds, refreshed in ice water, then flesh scooped out)
- Zucchini or yellow squash cups (thick slices with centers scooped out, blanched until slightly softened, then rinsed in cold water and patted dry)
- Mini bell pepper halves (cored and thin slice cut from the bottom to stabilize)
- Snow pea purses/boats (thread removed, blanched 30 seconds, refreshed in ice water, then slit open and peas removed)
- Sweet potato slices (small potatoes boiled until just soft; cooled, peeled, and cut into 1/2-inch slices)
- Apple half-moons (1/8-inch-thick inner slices dipped in acidified water, then dried)
- Vegetable wafers (small turnips or yellow beets shaved on a mandoline, then crisped in ice water 1 or 2 hours in the refrigerator)

CANAPÉ BASES, STARCH-BASED (small edible platforms for holding hot or cold toppings)

- Sturdy flat commercial chips (bagel, black bean, cassava, gluten-free, lentil, multigrain, pita, rice, tortilla, vegetable)
- Mini buckwheat blini/*oladyi/binchiki*, thin silver-dollar pancakes, mini oatcakes, thin mini cornmeal cakes, thin mini biscuit halves, or tiny pastry shells
- Lavash crisps (pieces of crisp lavash, recrisped in the oven or microwave, then cooled and broken into pieces)
- Mini poppadoms (plain uncooked mini poppadoms/pappadams, toasted or fried until blistered and crisp)
- Polenta rounds (chilled prepared polenta cut into rounds, lightly coated with melted butter or cooking spray, and broiled or fried until lightly browned, about 5 minutes each side)
- Polenta cups (warm prepared polenta spooned into greased mini muffin cups, an indentation made in the top center of each cup, then chilled until set)

- Pumpernickel/rye triangles (pumpernickel or rye cocktail bread cut into triangles; or unsliced pumpkin or rye bread thinly sliced, then cut into triangles)
- Egg bread squares (1/4-inch-thick brioche slices cut into 2-inch squares and fried in butter)
- French bread crisps (thinly sliced French flute or ficelle baked in a preheated 400°F oven until crisp, 4 to 5 minutes, then cooled)
- Crostini (day-old baguettes cut in 1/2-inch-thick slices, brushed with olive oil, then baked at 350°F until lightly golden, about 10 minutes)
- Bread cups (thin slices of crustless bread cut into rounds, brushed lightly with olive oil, pressed into mini muffin cups, and baked in a preheated 350°F oven until crisp, about 10 minutes; for crunchier croustades, thinly roll out the bread)
- Mini toasts (thinly sliced crustless bread brushed lightly with olive oil, cut into 1- to 1 1/2-inch squares, and baked at 400°F until golden, about 5 minutes)
- Biscuit bowls (thinly rolled out biscuit dough pressed over the back of mini muffin cups to form bowl shapes; baked at 450°F until lightly browned, 7 to 9 minutes; cooled on the cups; then removed)
- Wonton cups (small wonton wrappers pressed into greased mini muffin pans (or draped over inverted muffin cups), sprayed with cooking spray and baked at 350°F until brown and crisp, 4 to 6 minutes)
- Mini pizzette (thinly rolled out pizzette dough cut into small rounds and baked at 400°F until lightly browned, about 10 minutes)
- Phyllo shells (frozen prepared mini shells baked in a preheated 350°F oven until crisp, 3 to 5 minutes or buttered phyllo sheets cut into 2-inch squares, layered in greased mini muffin pans and baked at 350°F until crisp, 6 to 8 minutes)
- Puff pastry squares (puff pastry cut into small squares, brushed with olive oil, and baked at 375°F for 15 minutes)
- Whole-wheat crackers (whole-wheat pie dough rolled thin, cut into rounds, squares, or diamonds and baked at 375°F until golden brown, about 15 minutes)

- Pâte à choux cases (pâte à choux dough thinly spread in greased mini muffin cups and baked at 350°F until golden brown, about 14 minutes; or small baked cream puff shells, halved and hollowed out)
- Waffle rounds (frozen mini waffles toasted in the oven to a golden brown)

CANARY BEANS/CANARIO-PERUANO/MAYACOBA (Peruvian small yellow beans) – 1 cup
- 1 cup Tuscany Zolfino beans/*fagioli zolfino*
- 1 cup cannellini, Great Northern, or navy beans

CANDIED FRUIT/GLACÉ FRUIT – 1 cup
- 1 cup Italian spiced fruits/*mostarda di Cremona,* drained from the syrup
- 1 cup dried apricots, blueberries, cherries, cranberries, dates, figs, nectarines, peaches, pears, persimmons, or pineapple chunks (chopped if large)

CANDLENUT/KEMIRI/BUAH KERAS (Southeast Asian thickening agent) – 1/2 ounce (4 to 5 nuts)
- 1/2 ounce unsalted, unroasted macadamia nuts (5 or 6), or 1/2 ounce medium unsalted cashews (9 or 10)

CANELA See CINNAMON, GROUND (Ceylon, Sri Lanka, Mexican, canela)

CANE SUGAR, RAW/UNREFINED See SUGAR, DEMERARA; SUGAR, TURBINADO CANE

CANE SYRUP/INVERT SYRUP (Caribbean and Creole strong-flavored sweetener) – 1 cup
- 1 1/4 cups granulated sugar and 1/3 cup water simmered over medium heat until syrupy
- 1 cup plain barley malt syrup or dark corn syrup
- 1/2 cup each molasses and light-colored corn syrup

CANE SYRUP/INVERT SYRUP, DARK (dark, very strong-flavored sweetener) – 1 cup
- 1 cup sorghum syrup, unsulphured molasses, or treacle

CANE VINEGAR, DARK/SUKANG ILOKO (Caribbean and Southeast Asian dark sugarcane vinegar) – tablespoon
- 1 tablespoon sherry vinegar, cider vinegar, or brown rice vinegar

CANE VINEGAR, WHITE/SUKANG MAASIM (Filipino mild, all-purpose sugarcane vinegar) – 1 tablespoon
- 1 tablespoon unseasoned rice vinegar or rice wine vinegar
- 1 scant tablespoon distilled white vinegar

CANISTEL/EGG FRUIT See LÚCUMA PULP

CANNELLINI BEANS/WHITE KIDNEY BEANS (Italian white beans) – 1 cup
- 1 cup heirloom cassoulet beans, such as Rancho Gordo brand
- 1 cup Emergo beans, Great Northern beans, navy beans, or soissons
- 1 cup Tuscany Zolfino beans/fagioli zolfino (pale yellow in color)

CANNELLONI SHELLS, DRIED (Italian large pasta tubes) – 8 ounces
- 8 ounces dried manicotti shells/wrappers
- 8 ounces no-boil, flat lasagna noodles, softened in simmering water until pliable, 3 to 5 minutes, then cut to size, if necessary
- 10 ounces fresh (8-inch square) wheat-flour spring roll or lumpia wrappers, softened individually in simmering water until pliable, then cut to size
- 10 ounces fresh pasta, cut to size
- 12 to 14 homemade crespelle, or homemade or store-bought crepes (more delicate)

CANOLA OIL/RAPESEED OIL (neutral-flavored oil) – 1 cup
- 1 cup grapeseed, safflower or sunflower oil

CANTAL (French semihard cheese) – 1 ounce
- 1 ounce sharp Cheddar or Laguiole

CAPE GOOSEBERRIES/CHINESE LANTERNS/GOLDEN BERRIES/ GROUND CHERRIES – 1 cup fresh or dried
- 1 cup gooseberries (for fresh; more tart)
- 1 cup dried cranberries (for dried)

CAPELLINI PASTA See PASTA, THIN STRAND OR ROD

CAPERS/CAPER BUDS, BRINED – 1 tablespoon (12 to 15 large; or 24 or 30 small; or 45 to 50 petite nonpareils)
- 9 to 12 large salt-packed capers, soaked in cold water 20 or more minutes then drained; if very salty, soak in 3 or 4 changes of water or for 2 hours in warm water (less firm)
- 1/4 cup brined caperberries, stemmed and rinsed (larger, starchier, milder flavor; best for garnish)
- 2 tablespoons tubed caper paste
- 1 to 2 tablespoons chopped green olives or dill pickles
- 2 tablespoons pickled green nasturtium buds, pickled green coriander seed, or pickled young marsh mallow buds (*Althaea officinalis*)

CAPICOLA/COPPA (Italian dry-cured pork shoulder) – 1 pound
- 1 pound prosciutto, bresaola, or any dry-cured or country-style ham

CAPPUCCINO PASTE (flavoring agent for frozen desserts and pastries) – 1 tablespoon
- 1 tablespoon espresso or coffee paste
- 3 1/2 tablespoons instant espresso powder mixed with enough heavy cream to form a thick paste

CARAMBOLA, SOUR COOKING TYPE/BILIMBI See BELIMBING

CARAMBOLA/STAR FRUIT/BABACO (Southeast Asian tart-sweet fruit) – 1 medium (2/3 cup sliced)
- 2 green or gold kiwi fruit, peeled and sliced
- 4 or 5 kiwi berries/cocktail kiwi, sliced (no peeling required)

CARAMEL COLORING See BAKER'S CARAMEL/CARAMEL COLORING

CARAMEL PASTE/DULCE DE LECHE/DOCE DE LEITE/AREQUIPE/ MANJAR – 1 cup
Make Your Own Heat 1 (14-ounce) can sweetened condensed milk, uncovered, in a double boiler over low heat until golden, 2 to 3 hours, replacing water as needed (it will thicken on cooling).
Or
Simmer 1 cup firmly packed dark brown sugar, 1/3 cup butter, and 1/4 cup heavy cream (or evaporated milk) until slightly thickened; remove from heat and add 1 teaspoon vanilla extract.

CARAMEL SYRUP/NUOC MAU (Vietnamese sweetener) – 1 teaspoon
- 1 1/2 teaspoons granulated sugar

CARAWAY SEEDS – 1 tablespoon
- 1 tablespoon anise, fennel, or dill seeds

CARDAMOM PODS, BLACK/BROWN/CHA KOH/TSAO-KO; THAO QUA – 1 tablespoon
- 1 tablespoon Chinese cardamom/*Amomum globosum* (less expensive; more pungent)
- 2 or 3 whole cloves

CARDAMOM PODS, GREEN OR WHITE – 1 tablespoon
- 1 teaspoon ground cardamom
- 1 tablespoon Ethiopian koreima/*Aframomum korarima* (less expensive; more camphor overtones)

CARDAMOM SEEDS, GREEN OR WHITE, GROUND – 1 teaspoon
- Seeds from 6 to 8 green or white cardamom pods, finely ground with a mortar and pestle
- 1 or 2 drops Elaichi essence (Indian cardamom seed essence)
- 3 drops cardamom extract
- 3/4 teaspoon ground cinnamon plus 1/4 teaspoon finely grated lemon zest
- 1/2 teaspoon each ground cloves and nutmeg (or cinnamon)

CARDOON/CARDONI (GLOBE ARTICHOKE) – 1 pound
- 1/2 each celery stalks and artichoke hearts
- 1 pound thick upper stem of annual sow thistle/*Sonchus oleraceus*

CARMODY CHEESE (Northern California Jersey milk cheese) – 1 ounce
- 1 ounce Monterey Jack or young Teleme cheese

CARNE SÊCA/CHARQUE/CHARKI/CARNE DE SOL (South American dried salted beef) – 4 ounces
- 4 ounces Cuban tasajo, Cajun tasso, or Mexican cecina
- 4 ounces spicy salted beef jerky

CAROB SYRUP/MOLASSES/HARNUP PEKMEZI (Middle Eastern sweetener) *See DATE MOLASSES*

CAROM SEEDS *See AJWAIN*

CARRAGEENAN/IRISH MOSS (thickening agent) – 1 tablespoon
- 1 tablespoon gelatin
- 1 teaspoon powdered agar/kanten

CARROTS (orange, yellow, white, or purple) – 1 pound
- 1 pound parsnips or turnips (for a vegetable dish)
- 1 pound golden beets or young tender parsnips (for a carrot cake)

CARROTS, BABY (Thumbelina or Little Finger) – 1 pound
☞ 1 pound baby-cut carrots, or regular size carrots cut into 1/2 by 1 1/2-inch pieces

CASHEW BUTTER – 1 cup
☞ 1 cup smooth, natural peanut butter (less sweet)
Make Your Own Process 2 cups whole roasted, unsalted cashews and 1/4 teaspoon sea salt in a food processor until reduced to a paste, 6 to 10 minutes, scraping down the sides of the bowl and adding a little oil if needed. Store in a sterilized jar in the refrigerator; it will last for up to 4 weeks.

CASHEW CREAM – 1 to 1 1/4 cups
Make Your Own Soak 1 cup whole raw unsalted cashews in 2 cups water for 4 to 8 hours; drain and rinse, then blend with 1/2 cup water until completely smooth; strain if necessary. For a faster procedure, soak 1 cup cashew pieces in 1/2 cup boiling water 30 minutes. For a thicker, richer cream use 1/3 cup water and 1/4 cup refined coconut oil. For a thinner, pourable cream use 1 1/2 cups water. Store, refrigerated, for up to 4 days, or freeze for up to 6 months.
Or
Soak 1/3 cup whole raw unsalted cashews in 2/3 cup water for 4 to 8 hours; drain and rinse, then blend with 2/3 cup unsweetened soy milk until completely smooth; strain if necessary. Store, refrigerated, for up to 4 days or freeze for up to 6 months.

CASHEW MILK – 3 to 4 cups
Make Your Own Soak 1 cup whole raw unsalted cashews in water to cover for 4 to 8 hours; drain and rinse, then blend with 4 cups warm water until smooth, 3 to 4 minutes. Strain in a nutmilk bag or cheesecloth-lined sieve, pressing firmly on the pulp to extract all the liquid. Store in a sterilized jar in the refrigerator; it should keep for up to 4 days; shake before using.

CASHEWS – 1 cup
- 1 cup macadamia nuts or pine nuts
- 1 cup almonds (less soft)

CASHEWS, FRESH – 1 cup
- 1 cup raw cashews soaked in 2 cups cold water for 10 to 12 hours

CASHEW VINEGAR/GOAN VINEGAR – 1 tablespoon
- 1 tablespoon cider vinegar

CASSAREEP (Caribbean thick black cassava sweetener) – 1 cup
- 1 cup blackstrap molasses or *yacón* syrup

CASSAVA See YUCA ROOT

CASSAVA FLOUR/YUCA MEAL/MANIOC MEAL See GARI/GARRI

CASSAVA LEAVES See MALANGA LEAVES/CALLALOO

CASSIA See CINNAMON, GROUND

CASSIA BARK See CINNAMON STICK, INDONESIAN

CASSIA LEAF/CINNAMON LEAF/TEJ PATTA (Indian flavoring agent) – 1 dried leaf
- 1 whole clove or small pinch ground cloves
- 1 small dried Turkish bay leaf and a few grains cassia cinnamon

CATALAN RED CHILE, DRIED (Spanish medium-hot chile) – 1
- 1 dried red California, New Mexico, or guajillo chile
- 2 dried ñora chiles
- 1 tablespoon crushed red pepper flakes

CATUPIRY CHEESE (Brazilian fresh creamy cheese) – 1 ounce
- 1 ounce mascarpone

CAUL, PORK/CRÉPINE (lace-like fatty membrane) – 4 ounces
- ☞ 4 ounces thinly sliced back fat or pork belly
- ☞ 4 ounces thinly sliced bacon, boiled for 5 minutes to reduce the salt content
- ☞ Plastic wrap (for lining paté molds)

CAULIFLOWER – 1 pound
- ☞ 1 pound broccoflower or Romanesco broccoli (green color; nuttier flavor)

CAVIAR, BLACK/GRAY/BROWN STURGEON ROE (beluga, osetra/ oscietre, sevruga) – 1 ounce
- ☞ 1 ounce bowfin/*choupique*, pike/*piluga,* American sturgeon/*transmontanus*, American hackleback, lumpfish, or paddlefish/spoonbill roe
- ☞ 1 ounce smoked golden herring roe/*avruga*
- ☞ 1 ounce pressed caviar (paste made from eggs that have been damaged)
- ☞ 1 ounce black vegetarian caviar, such as Cavi-art (derived from seaweed)

CAVIAR, RED/ORANGE/CORAL/SALMON ROE/IKURA – 1 ounce
- ☞ 1 ounce capelin/*masago,* carp or red mullet/*tarama,* codfish/*tarako,* flying fish/*tobiko*, scallop, smelt/*ebikko,* steelhead, or French trout roe
- ☞ 1 ounce whitefish/American Golden Caviar roe (yellow-gold), sea urchin/*uni* (rich gold to light yellow), or herring roe/*kazunoko* (pink/yellow)
- ☞ 1 ounce salted Alaskan pollock roe/*momojiko* (red), or flavored with chile power/*mentaiko* (deep red)
- ☞ 1 ounce red vegetarian caviar, such as Cavi-art, derived from seaweed

CAYENNE CHILE, FRESH (green or red) – 1
- ☞ 1 to 3 fresh green or red serrano or Thai chiles, depending on size

☞ 1/4 to 1/2 teaspoon ground cayenne pepper or paste

CAYENNE PEPPER, GROUND/GROUND RED PEPPER – 1/2 teaspoon
☞ 1/2 teaspoon Aleppo, de árbol, or Thai chile powder
☞ 1/2 teaspoon hot paprika
☞ 3/4 teaspoon crushed red pepper flakes
☞ 3 to 4 drops hot pepper sauce, such as Tabasco or Crystal

CELERIAC See CELERY ROOT/CELERIAC

CELERY – 1 medium stalk
☞ 2 tablespoons dried celery flakes, softened in 1/3 cup warm water for 5 minutes
☞ 1 or 2 lovage stalks, smallage stalks/cutting celery, or Chinese celery stalks, depending upon size (stronger flavor)
☞ 1 raw fennel stalk (especially baby fennel), Swiss chard stalk, or mature tatsoi stalk (for cooking; crunchy but a different flavor)
☞ 1 crisp apple, pared, cored and chopped (for chicken or tuna salad; crunchy but a different flavor; sprinkle with lemon juice or toss with mayonnaise before adding other ingredients; or use a Cortland apple, which doesn't brown when cut)

CELERY FLAKES
☞ Celery leaves, dried in a preheated 200°F oven until brittle, then coarsely crushed

CELERY ROOT/CELERIAC/KNOB CELERY – 1 pound (1 medium root peeled and chopped)
☞ 2 or 3 large outer stalks of celery, trimmed and chopped (milder flavor)
☞ 2 cups chopped rutabaga or parsnips plus 1/4 teaspoon crushed celery seed (or use a pinch of celery salt and reduce the salt in the recipe accordingly)

CELERY SALT – 1 tablespoon
Make Your Own Grind 1 1/2 teaspoons whole celery seeds in a coffee/spice grinder (or use 1 teaspoon ground celery seed) and mix with 2 teaspoons salt; cover and let sit for a few days to develop flavor.

CELERY SEEDS – 1 teaspoon
- 1/2 teaspoon ground celery seed
- 3/4 teaspoon celery salt, and reduce the salt in the recipe by 1/2 teaspoon
- 1 tablespoon finely minced celery leaves
- 1 teaspoon dill seeds

CELERY SOUP, CANNED CREAM OF (for recipes) – (10.5 ounce can)
- 1 cup thick homemade white sauce plus 2 to 3 tablespoons finely chopped sautéed celery and 1/2 teaspoon celery salt; stir until combined

***CELERY, WILD/SMALLAGE** See CHINESE CELERY*

***CELLOPHANE NOODLES** See NOODLES, CELLOPHANE*

CELTUCE/STEM LETTUCE/CHINESE LETTUCE/WHO SUN/A-CHOY – 8 ounces
- 8 ounces celery or thin peeled broccoli stems (for stems)
- 8 ounces Romaine lettuce (for tops)

***CÈPES** See PORCINI MUSHROOMS/KING BOLETES/CÈPES*

CHAI SEASONING/YOGI TEA (Thai and Indian spice mix for tea) – 2 teaspoons
- 1 teaspoon ground cardamom plus 1/4 teaspoon each ground allspice, ground cinnamon, ground ginger, and ground nutmeg
- 1-inch cinnamon stick, 2 green cardamom pods, and 3 whole cloves

CHALLAH (Jewish egg-rich bread) – 1 pound
- ☞ 1 pound brioche, Hawaiian bread, Mexican *pan de yema*, Portuguese sweet bread/*pao duce*, or other egg-rich bread

CHAMOMILE FLOWERS, DRIED – 1 tablespoon
- ☞ 2 chamomile tea bags
- ☞ 2 tablespoons finely chopped fresh chamomile leaves

CHAMPAGNE – 1 cup
- ☞ 1 cup cava, Asti spumante, Franciacorta, moscato, prosecco, Sekt, or other sparkling white wine
- ☞ 1 cup rosé wine
- ☞ 1 cup pale sparkling cider, such as Martinelli's
- ☞ 1 cup sparkling white grape juice (for cold dishes)
- ☞ 1 cup Muscadet or any dry, high-acid white wine (for cooked dishes)

CHANCACA (Latin American unrefined sugar) See PILONCILLO/ PANELA/PANOCHA

CHANTERELLE MUSHROOMS/GIROLLES – 1 pound
- ☞ 3 ounces dried chanterelle mushrooms soaked in warm water until softened, about 30 minutes
- ☞ 1 pound fresh hedgehog or king oyster/royal trumpet mushrooms

CHAPATI/CHAPATTI (Indian unleavened whole-wheat bread) – 1
- ☞ 1 whole-wheat tortilla or pita bread

CHAPATI FLOUR See ATTA/PATENT DURA FLOUR/CHAPATI FLOUR

CHARDONNAY VINEGAR – 1 tablespoon
- ☞ 1 tablespoon champagne vinegar or white wine vinegar

CHARD/SWISS CHARD/SILVER BEET/SEAKALE BEET – 1 pound
- ☞ 1 pound amaranth greens
- ☞ 1 pound mature spinach

- ☞ 1 pound beet greens
- ☞ 1 pound bok choy
- ☞ 1 pound lamb's quarters
- ☞ 1 pound quinoa greens
- ☞ 1 pound Good King Henry leaves
- ☞ 1 pound young nettle tops (Use gloves when handling raw nettles; cooking removes their sting.)
- ☞ 1 pound young orach
- ☞ 1 pound young turnip greens

CHAROLI NUTS/CHIRONGI/CALUMPANG (Indian sweetmeat garnish) – 1 ounce
- ☞ 1 ounce slivered blanched almonds
- ☞ 1 ounce chopped unsalted pistachios or hazelnuts

CHAR SIU SAUCE See CHINESE BARBECUE SAUCE

CHAURICE (Creole/Cajun spicy fresh pork sausage) – 1 pound
- ☞ 1 pound Mexican fresh chorizo

CHAYA LEAF (Mexican and Central American large leafy green) – 1 pound
- ☞ 8 ounces each mature spinach and arugula
- ☞ 1 pound Swiss chard

CHAYOTE/MIRLITON/CHRISTOPHENE/PEPPINELLA/CHOKO/XUXU – 1 pound
- ☞ 1 pound bottle gourd, calabash/cucuzza, or winter melon
- ☞ 1 pound Kirby cucumber, zucchini, or yellow squash

CHEDDAR (British semifirm cheese) – 1 ounce
- ☞ 1 ounce Cheshire (mild and crumbly), Dunlop (soft), Lancashire (soft and crumbly), Leicester (moist), Orkney (soft), or Wensleydale (crumbly)
- ☞ 1 ounce French Cantal (crumbly) or Laguiole (crumbly and sharp)

☞ 1 ounce North American Colby or Monterey Jack (soft and mild)

☞ 1 ounce vegan cheese such as Daiya or Follow Your Heart

CHEDDAR, SHARP SHREDDED – 1 cup for cooking
- ☞ 1 cup shredded mild cheddar cheese, 1/4 teaspoon Worcester-shire sauce (or a pinch of ground cayenne pepper), and 1/8 tea-spoon mustard powder
- ☞ 1 cup canned sharp white cheddar cheese, such as Cougar Gold (for convenience)
- ☞ 1 cup freeze-dried cheddar cheese, rehydrated
- ☞ 1 cup cheddar cheese powder (for sprinkling on pasta and salads; does not melt)

CHEE HOU SAUCE/CHU HOU PASTE (Chinese braising sauce) – 1/4 cup
- ☞ 1/4 cup hoisin sauce diluted with a little rice vinegar

CHEESE, BLUE See BLUE CHEESE, DOUBLE- OR TRIPLE-CRÈME; BLUE CHEESE, MEDIUM; BLUE CHEESE, MILD; BLUE CHEESE, STRONG

CHEESE CURDS (firm, chewy unprocessed cheddar lumps) – 1 cup
- ☞ 1 cup kasseri cheese cubes
- ☞ 1 cup fresh salted mozzarella, cut into small pieces

CHEESE, DOUBLE-CRÈME See PETIT SUISSE

CHEESE, FRYING See HALLOUMI/HALUMI

CHEESE, MELTING (soft or semifirm cheese; used for pizza, lasagna, sauces, and fondues) – 1 ounce
- ☞ 1 ounce American, mild Cheddar, Colby, Edam, Emmental, fon-tina, Gruyère, Gouda, Havarti, Jarlsberg, Manchego, Monterey Jack, mozzarella, or provolone

CHEESE, NON-MELTING (acid-coagulated cheeses; used for crostini, pasta, and salads) – 4 ounces
- 4 ounces Cotija, feta, fresh goat cheese, paneer, or queso blanco/fresco/*queso pana freir*

CHEESE, PIZZA BLEND, SHREDDED – 1 cup
- 1/2 cup each shredded cheddar and mozzarella cheese
- 1 cup coarsely grated brown rice mochi (dairy- and gluten-free)

CHEESE POWDER – 1 cup
- 1 cup nutritional yeast powder

Make Your Own Spread 1 1/2 cups grated cheddar cheese on parchment paper-lined trays and dry in a dehydrator at high setting until the oil is released, 8 to 12 hours. Drain on paper towels until cool, then pulse in a blender or food processor until powdery. Store in a tightly sealed container; it will keep for up to 1 year in the refrigerator.

CHEESE, PUNGENT – 1 ounce
- 1 ounce Backstein, Bierkäse/Brick, Èpoisses, Handkäse, Herve, Langres, Liederkranz, Limburger, Livarot, Maroilles, Mignot, Red Hawk, Romadur, or Winnimere

CHEESE SAUCE – 1 cup
- 2/3 cup condensed cheese soup, 1/3 cup milk, plus a few drops hot pepper sauce, whisked together and heated

Make your own: Whisk together 1/2 cup condensed cream of mushroom soup and 1/2 cup milk; bring to a boil, then remove from the heat and stir in 2/3 cup shredded cheese until the cheese is melted.

CHEESE, SMOKED – 1 ounce
- 1 ounce smoked *caciocavallo*, medium cheddar, Gouda, Gruyère, Jarlsburg, provolone, scamorza, or Swiss
- 1 ounce Greek Metsovone
- 1 ounce Spanish Idiazabal or San Simon
- 1 ounce Polish Kurplaka (contains garlic)

CHEESE, SWISS-TYPE See EMMENTAL

CHEESE, TRIPLE-CRÈME See BOUSAULT; BLUE CHEESE, DOUBLE- OR TRIPLE-CRÈME

CHEESE, TRIPLE-CRÈME, SEASONED See BOURSIN

CHENNA (Indian fresh cheese) – 1 cup
  ☞ 1 cup ricotta cheese or dry-curd cottage cheese

CHERIMOYA/CUSTARD APPLE, FRESH (sweet tropical fruit) – 1
  ☞ 8 ounces thawed frozen cherimoya pulp
  ☞ 1 fresh atemoya, soursop/guanabana, sweetsop, or mango

CHERRIES, GLACÉ – 1 cup
  ☞ 1 cup dried cherries, soaked in heavy syrup for a day or two

CHERRIES, MARASCHINO, JARRED – 1 cup cherries plus 1 cup liquid
  Make Your Own Combine 1 cup fresh pitted cherries, 1 cup vodka, 1/2 cup granulated sugar, and 1/2 teaspoon pure almond extract in a sterilized jar and place in a cool, dark place for 5 to 6 days, shaking the jar daily. Store, refrigerated, for up to 4 months.

CHERRIES, SOUR/TART, FRESH OR FROZEN (Aleppo, Amarelle, Morello, Montmorency, or Early Richmond) – 1 pound (2 cups pitted)
  ☞ 1 (24-ounce jar) Morello cherries, drained, or 1 (14- to 16-ounce) can sour cherries, drained
  ☞ 1 cup dried pitted Montmorency cherries, soaked in 1 cup boiling water until softened, about 30 minutes (or 6 to 8 hours in cool water)
  ☞ 2 cups pitted wild black sweet cherries/*Prunus serotina*, purple black sandcherries/*Prunus pumila*, red Nanking cherries/*Prunus tomentosa*, or crimson chokecherries/*Prunus virginiana* (smaller; more astringent; best for jams, jellies, syrup, and drying)

☞ 2 cups pitted dark red cornelian cherries/cornels/*Cornus mas* (huge pits and extremely tart; best for jam, jelly, syrup, or fruit leather)
☞ 2 cups pitted acerola/Barbados cherry/West Indian cherry (reduce the sugar in the recipe by one-third; best for preserves and cakes)
☞ 2 1/2 cups pitted fresh sweet cherries or thawed frozen sweet cherries (reduce the sugar in the recipe by one-third; best for cakes, pies, and sauce)
☞ 2 cups pitted Surinam cherries/Brazilian cherry *pitanga*/*Eugenia uniflora* (for jams and jellies)

CHERRIES, SWEET, FRESH (Bing, Lambert, Royal Anne, Stella) – 1 pound
☞ 1 pound acerola/Barbados cherry/West Indian cherry

CHERRY EXTRACT – 1 teaspoon
☞ 2 to 3 tablespoons cherry juice or liquid from jarred maraschino cherries (sweeter; reduce the liquid in the recipe by 2 to 3 tablespoons)

CHERRY LIQUEUR/CHERRY-FLAVORED SPIRIT (such as Cherry Heering, Cherry Marnier, Cherry Rocher, Cusenier Heering, or Kirschenliqueur) – 2 tablespoons
☞ 2 tablespoons crème de cerise or crème de griotte
☞ 2 tablespoons cherry schnapps or kirsch (less sweet)
☞ 1/2 to 1 teaspoon cherry extract plus 2 tablespoons vodka or water

CHERVIL/CICELY/SWEET CICELY, FRESH – 8 sprigs (1 tablespoon finely chopped leaves)
☞ 1 teaspoon dried crumbled chervil leaf
☞ 2 teaspoons chopped fresh flat-leaf parsley plus 1 teaspoon chopped fresh tarragon
☞ 1/2 teaspoon dried parsley plus 1/4 teaspoon dried tarragon
☞ 1 tablespoon finely chopped fennel fronds

CHESAPEAKE BAY SEASONING – 1 teaspoon
- 1 teaspoon shrimp boil seasoning

CHESTNUT FLOUR – I cup (3 3/4 ounces)
- 3/4 to 7/8 cup dried chestnuts, cut up and ground in small batches in a spice/coffee grinder
- 1 cup acorn meal/oaknut flour (cold-leached, dried, roasted, ground edible acorns, preferably white or black oak)

CHESTNUT MUSHROOMS/BROWN CAP – 8 ounces
- 8 ounces fresh cremini or white cap/button mushrooms
- 4 ounces canned sliced cremini or portobello mushrooms

CHESTNUT PURÉE/PUREE DE MARRONS, CANNED – 1 cup
- 1 cup cooked and mashed Japanese white-fleshed sweet potatoes/satsuma-imo

Make Your Own Cover 8 ounces (1 1/4 cups) shelled and peeled chestnuts with water and simmer until very tender, about 1 hour. Drain and process in a food processor or blender until very smooth, adding a tablespoon or two of water if necessary.

CHESTNUTS, FRESH SHELLED – 1 cup
- 1 cup frozen, canned, or packaged chestnuts
- 1/2 cup (3 ounces) dried chestnuts, soaked in 1 cup hot water for 4 hours or in cold water for 8 to 12 hours
- 1 cup shelled hazelnuts, macadamia nuts, or chufa nuts
- 1 cup large cooked chickpeas or drained and rinsed canned chickpeas
- 1 cup breadfruit seeds
- 1 cup shelled, leached, and dried acorns, preferably white oak or valley oak

CHÈVRE (soft fresh goat cheese) – 4 ounces See also GOAT CHEESE, AGED
- 2 ounces crumbled feta and 2 ounces softened cream cheese, beaten until smooth then chilled

⮞ 4 ounces natural cream cheese (no added gum) or regular cream cheese, softened
⮞ 4 ounces *fromage blanc/fromage fraise*

CHÈVRE STARTER CULTURE, DIRECT-SET – 1 packet
⮞ 1 packet direct-set *fromage blanc* starter culture
⮞ 1/4 teaspoon mesophilic starter culture plus 1 drop liquid rennet, diluted in 1 or 2 tablespoons cool nonchlorinated water

CHHANA/CHHENA (Indian soft fresh cheese) – 4 ounces *See also* PANEER/PANIR
⮞ 4 ounces drained ricotta cheese (drained 8 to 12 hours in a dampened, cheesecloth-lined sieve set over a bowl in the refrigerator)
⮞ 4 ounces paneer (firmer texture)

CHIA SEEDS/SALBA SEEDS – 2 tablespoons
⮞ 1 1/2 tablespoons chia powder or 2 tablespoons ground flaxseed/ flaxseed meal (sprouted or regular)
⮞ 2 tablespoons sesame seeds (lacks omega-3s and gelatinous property)

CHICHARRÓN (Mexican and Spanish twice-fried pork skin) – 8 ounces
⮞ 8 ounces crispy pork rind/crackling

CHICKEN CUTLETS – 1 pound
⮞ 4 (4-ounce) boneless, skinless, chicken breasts, fat and tender removed, gently pounded to 1/2-inch thickness between two pieces of plastic wrap coated with cooking spray
⮞ 2 (8-ounce) packages tempeh, halved lengthwise
⮞ 1 (14-ounce) package firm tofu, drained and pressed under a heavy weight for 1 to 2 hours, then cut into slices

CHICKEN DEMI-GLACE *See POULTRY GLAZE/GLACE DE VOLAILLE*

CHICKEN OF THE WOODS/SULFUR SHELF MUSHROOMS, FRESH – 1 pound

- 1 pound fresh porcini, portobello, or shiitake mushrooms
- 3 ounces dried porcini, portobello, or shiitake mushrooms, soaked in warm water until softened, 30 to 40 minutes

CHICKEN OR TURKEY, GROUND OR SHREDDED – 1 pound See also MEAT, GROUND

- 1 (18-ounce) package chicken-style seitan, chopped
- 16 ounces textured vegetable protein, reconstituted in chicken-flavored broth
- 1 (20-ounce) can young/green jackfruit in brine, drained, rinsed, and shredded
- 1 pound firm or extra-firm tofu weighted to extract the liquid, about 1 hour, then blotted dry and crumbled (Alternatively, blanch the tofu for 1 minute, drain, squeeze dry, and then crumble.)
- 1 pound freeze-dried tofu/*koyadofu*, softened in hot water 2 to 3 minutes, then squeezed dry and chopped; or firm tofu, frozen for 8 to 10 hours, thawed in hot water, about 10 minutes, then pressed dry and chopped

CHICKEN SOUP, CANNED CREAM OF– 1 (10.5-ounce) can for recipes

- 1 can Gluten-free Condensed Cream of Chicken Soup, such as Great Value
- 1 cup thick homemade white sauce plus 1 teaspoon chicken bouillon granules or crumbled bouillon cube
- 1 (8-ounce) package cream cheese, 1/2 cup water, and 1/2 teaspoon chicken soup base, thoroughly combined

CHICKPEA FLOUR/GARBANZO FLOUR/FARINA DE CECI (20% protein) – 1 cup

- 1 cup Indian *besan*/channa dal flour/gram flour (darker; less finely ground)
- 1 1/8 cups dried chickpeas ground in batches in a spice/coffee grinder until reduced to a powder; sift, then regrind any remaining particles

☞ 1 cup cold-leached acorn flour, preferably white oak

CHICKPEA FLOUR/GARBANZO FLOUR, TOASTED (South Asian thickening agent) – 1 cup
☞ 1 cup toasted rice powder

Make Your Own Toast 1 cup chickpea flour in a dry heavy skillet over medium heat until golden, about 10 minutes, stirring constantly; or roast on a baking sheet in a preheated 350°F oven until golden, 12 to 15 minutes, stirring once. Store, tightly sealed, in a cool, dark place.

CHICKPEA PANCAKE/SOCCA/FARINATA/CECINA/PANELLE/CHILA (Provençal flatbread) – 1 large
Make Your Own Stir together 1 cup chickpea flour, 1 cup water, 2 tablespoons olive oil, and 1/2 teaspoon kosher or sea salt until very smooth. Cover and let sit for 2 hours. Pour into a large preheated cast-iron skillet containing 1 tablespoon olive oil and bake in a preheated 450°F oven for 8 to 10 minutes.

CHICKPEAS/GARBANZOS, DRIED – 1 cup
☞ 2 cups thawed frozen green garbanzos (smaller; higher in protein)
☞ 1 cup dried Italian thin-skinned chickpeas/*ceci flora* (smaller; thinner skinned; more tender)
☞ 1 cup dried Indian *kala chana,* or black organic kabuli chickpeas (smaller; brownish-black; thick-skinned)
☞ 1 cup dried Turkish skinned chickpeas (less flavorful; saves time)
☞ 1 cup dried tan or white tepary beans (larger)

CHICORY See BELGIAN ENDIVE; CURLY ENDIVE; ESCAROLE; FRISÉE; RADICCHIO

CHICOS/HORNOS CHICOS (Mexican and South American sweet dried corn) – 1 cup
☞ 1 cup dried sweet corn, cracked into bits

CHIHUAHUA/MENONITO *See ASADERO/QUESO OAXACA*

CHILACAYOTE (Central American and Mexican summer squash) *See ZUCCHINI*

CHILEAN SEA BASS (moderately oily fish; overfished and on the endangered list) – 1 pound
  ⊫ 1 pound black cod/sablefish/sable or other sustainable fatty fish (more than 6% fat by weight)

CHILE DE ÁRBOL *See DE ÁRBOL CHILE*

CHILE DULCE, FRESH (Yucatan mild chile) – 1
  ⊫ 1 fresh bell pepper

CHILE JELLY *See JALAPEÑO JELLY*

CHILE OIL *See CHILI OIL, CHINESE; CHILI OIL, ITALIAN*

CHILE PASTE *See CHILI PASTE, MILD; CHILI PASTE, HOT; CHILI PASTE WITH GARLIC*

CHILE POWDER, HOT – 1/4 cup (about)
  Make Your Own Toast 1 ounce (2/3 to 1 cup) hot dried red chiles (cayenne, de árbol, japonés pequín, or tepín/chiltepin) in a dry skillet over medium-high heat, stirring constantly, until crispy and fragrant, 3 to 5 minutes. Cool, then grind until powdery in a food processor or spice/coffee grinder. (Let the dust settle before removing the lid and avoid inhaling the fumes.) Store in an airtight container in a cool, dry place; it will keep for up to 3 months.

CHILE POWDER, MILD – 1/2 cup (about) *See also CHILI POWDER/ CHILI CON CARNE SEASONING*
  Make Your Own Toast 6 mild dried chiles (ancho, New Mexico, mulato, or pasilla) in a dry skillet over medium heat until fragrant, 2 to

3 minutes per side (or in a preheated 350°F oven until fragrant and puffed, 5 to 6 minutes). Cool, remove stems and seeds, then grind until powdery. Store in an airtight container in a cool, dry place; it will keep for up to 3 months. (Wear plastic gloves when handling chiles, and avoid inhaling the fumes.)

CHILE SAUCE *See CHILI BEAN SAUCE; CHILI GARLIC SAUCE; CHILI SAUCE; CHILI SAUCE, ASIAN*

CHILE SECO (smoky-flavored Yucatan chile) *See ANCHO CHILE*

CHILHUACLE CHILE, DRIED (large black, red or yellow Oaxaca chile) – 1
- 1 dried guajillo or ancho chile

CHILI BEAN SAUCE/TOBAN JIANG/DOUBAN JIANG (Chinese condiment) – 2 generous tablespoons
- 2 tablespoons black bean sauce (or black bean and garlic sauce) plus a little chili oil, hot pepper sauce, or chopped hot chile
- 1 tablespoon chili bean paste mixed with 1 crushed garlic clove and 2 teaspoons each soy sauce and rice vinegar

CHILI GARLIC SAUCE/LA JIAO JIANG (Chinese condiment) – 1 tablespoon
- 1 tablespoon Chinese chili sauce or sambal oelek, plus minced fresh garlic
- 1 teaspoon crushed red pepper flakes plus few grains granulated garlic
- 2 teaspoons Chinese chili oil

Make Your Own Process in a food processor 5 (3-inch) fresh, chopped, seeded red chiles, 3 garlic cloves, and 2 tablespoons seasoned rice vinegar. Store, refrigerated, for up to 1 week.

CHILI OIL, CHINESE/DAU OT/LA JIAO YOU (dipping sauce and cooking condiment) – 1 teaspoon
- 1 teaspoon Asian sesame oil (or peanut oil) plus 1/8 teaspoon ground cayenne pepper or hot chile powder

➤ 1/8 teaspoon (or more) crushed red pepper flakes or hot sauce, such as Tabasco or Crystal

➤ 1 teaspoon Thai or Malaysian chili oil (more pungent)

Make Your Own Slowly heat 1/2 cup peanut or sesame oil and 1/4 cup crushed red pepper flakes until the oil becomes a shade darker, about 5 minutes (or microwave in a 2-cup glass measuring jug for 1 minute). Let sit, covered, for 24 hours, then strain through a fine-mesh sieve; discard the pepper flakes and store the oil for up to 6 months in the refrigerator. Makes about 1/2 cup.

CHILI OIL, ITALIAN/OLIO PEPERONCINO/OLIO SANTA (bean soup condiment) – 1/4 cup

Make Your Own Combine 1/4 cup olive oil and 1 to 2 tablespoons crushed red pepper flakes (or ground medium-hot dried chile) and gently heat until infused, 3 to 4 minutes, stirring occasionally. Use within 2 or 3 days.

CHILI PASTE WITH GARLIC – 1/4 cup (about)

Make Your Own Stem, peel, seed, and chop 1 fresh mild chile (New Mexico, Anaheim, or poblano), then soften in hot water to cover for about 20 minutes before draining and pureeing with 2 or 3 garlic cloves. (Wear plastic gloves when handling chiles and avoid touching your face.)

CHILI PASTE, HOT – 1/4 cup (about) See also SAMBAL OELEK

Make Your Own Toast 1/2 cup dried hot chiles (bird's eye, pequín, or tepín) in a preheated 300°F oven until plump, about 5 minutes. Bring to a boil with 1/2 cup water, 1 tablespoon rice vinegar, and 1/2 teaspoon salt; cool, stem, then process to a paste. (Wear plastic gloves when handling the chiles and avoid touching your face.)

CHILI PASTE, MILD (cooking condiment) – 1/4 cup

Make Your Own Stem, seed, and chop fresh or dried mild chiles, such as ancho, New Mexico, mulato, or pasilla; simmer in water to cover until very soft, about 15 minutes. Drain, cool, then process to a paste with some of the soaking water. Alternatively, soak the seeded chiles in boiling water until softened, about 20 minutes, and then scrape the pulp off the skin with a knife. (Wear plastic gloves when handling the chiles and avoid touching your face.)

CHILI POWDER/CHILI CON CARNE SEASONING – 1/4 cup
⇨ 3 tablespoons mild chile powder, such as ancho or New Mexico, seasoned with 1 teaspoon ground cumin, 1 teaspoon dried oregano (preferably Mexican), 1/2 teaspoon garlic powder, and 1/2 teaspoon onion powder (Add ground cayenne pepper to taste for medium-hot chili, and cayenne and crushed red pepper flakes for extra-hot chili.)

CHILI SAUCE (tomato-based condiment) – 1 cup
⇨ 1 cup ketchup plus red hot-pepper sauce, such as Tabasco, to taste
Make Your Own Stir together 3/4 cup tomato sauce, 2 tablespoons firmly packed brown sugar (or 1/4 cup granulated sugar), 2 to 3 tablespoons cider or malt vinegar, and 1/4 teaspoon ground allspice (optional) until the sugar dissolves.

CHILI SAUCE, ASIAN – 1 teaspoon See also CHILI PASTE, HOT; CHILI SAUCE
⇨ 1 teaspoon Chinese chili sauce/*la jiao jiang*, Indonesian *sambal oelek*, Japanese chile yuzu paste/*yuzu koshu*, Thai *Sriracha*, or Vietnamese *tuong ot toi*
⇨ 1 teaspoon hot pepper sauce, such as Tabasco or Crystal

CHILI SESAME OIL, HOT See CHILI OIL, CHINESE

CHILI SOY SAUCE – 1 cup
⇨ 3/4 cup light soy sauce, and 3 tablespoons Chinese chili sauce
⇨ 3/4 cup light soy sauce, 1/4 cup deveined and seeded minced fresh chiles, plus sugar to taste (Wear plastic gloves when handling chiles and avoid touching your face.)

CHILI THREADS, DRIED RED See KOREAN CHILI THREADS

CHILI VINEGAR, INDIAN – 1 cup
Make Your Own Chop 5 or 6 hot dried red chiles and place in a sterilized jar with 1 cup cider vinegar. Cover and let sit in a cool, dark place for 7 to 10 days, shaking the bottle occasionally. Strain and discard the chiles. Store in an airtight container in a cool, dry place; it will keep for up to 6 months.

CHILOPITAS (Greek egg pasta) – 1 pound
- 1 pound *evriste* (made with flour and water)
- 1 pound *hilopites* (dried egg pasta)
- 1 pound Italian tagliatelle (or gluten-free tagliatelle), cut into pieces

CHILTEPIN CHILE POWDER – 1 teaspoon
- 1 teaspoon Thai or piri-piri powder or ground cayenne pepper

CHIMAYO RED CHILE POWDER – 1 tablespoon
- 1 tablespoon New Mexico or ancho chile powder (less flowery aroma)

CHIMICHURRI SAUCE (Argentinean condiment) – 3/4 cup
- 1/4 to 1/2 teaspoon ground cayenne pepper or hot pepper sauce, such as Tabasco or Crystal, stirred into 3/4 cup parsley pesto

Make Your Own Process 1 packed cup flat-leaf parsley, 1/3 cup olive oil, 2 to 3 tablespoons red wine vinegar, 2 or 3 garlic cloves, and 1/4 teaspoon each kosher salt, dried oregano (optional), and cayenne to a paste in a food processor or blender. Let sit for 1 hour to develop the flavor before using.

CHINESE ARTICHOKE See CROSNES/CHINESE ARTICHOKE/CHOROGI

CHINESE BABY BROCCOLI/GAI LAN MIEW – 1 pound
- 1 pound regular Chinese broccoli with stems thinly sliced

CHINESE BARBECUE SAUCE/CHAR SIU CHIANG – 1 cup
- 1 cup oyster sauce

☞ 1 cup Chinese vegetarian barbecue sauce, such as AGV brand

CHINESE BLACK BEAN GARLIC SAUCE See BLACK BEAN GARLIC SAUCE

CHINESE BLACK BEAN SAUCE See BLACK BEAN SAUCE

CHINESE BLACK BEANS, FERMENTED See FERMENTED BLACK BEANS

CHINESE BLACK FUNGUS See CLOUD EAR/BLACK TREE FUNGUS

CHINESE BLACK MUSHROOMS, DRIED/GAN XIANG GU See SHIITAKE MUSHROOMS

CHINESE BLACK RICE VINEGAR/CHINKIANG/SHANXI/HEI MI CU – 1 tablespoon
- ☞ 1 1/2 teaspoons each non-aged balsamic vinegar and red wine vinegar
- ☞ 1 tablespoon cider or unseasoned red rice vinegar plus 1 or 2 drops Worcestershire sauce

CHINESE BROCCOLI/CHINESE KALE/GAI LAN/JIE LAN/KAI LAN – 1 pound
- ☞ 1 pound Chinese baby broccoli/*gai lan miew* (smaller, slimmer stemmed)
- ☞ 1 pound broccoli raab/rabe, or *yau choy/yai tsoi* (stronger flavor)
- ☞ 1 pound broccolini, or stalks of regular broccoli sliced lengthwise
- ☞ 1 pound field mustard flower bud stems/*Brassica rapa*

CHINESE CABBAGE/CELERY CABBAGE See NAPA CABBAGE

CHINESE CELERY/ASIAN CELERY/PARCEL/QIN CAI/KUN CHOY/KAN TSAI/SERI-NA – 1 cup chopped
- ☞ 1 cup chopped lovage stalks and leaves
- ☞ 1 cup chopped celery hearts (or thin, tender celery stalks and tops) plus some flat-leaf parsley
- ☞ 1 cup Mitsuba, or celery leaves plus a little chopped flat-leaf parsley (to replace Chinese celery leaves)

CHINESE CHEE HOU/CHOU HEE SAUCE See CHEE HOU SAUCE

CHINESE CHILI BEAN PASTE See SICHUAN CHILI BEAN PASTE

CHINESE CHILI BEAN SAUCE See CHILI BEAN SAUCE

CHINESE CHILI FLAKES/LA JIAO MIAN – 1 tablespoon
- 1 tablespoon Korean coarse chile flakes/*gochugaru*
- 1 1/2 teaspoons Italian crushed red pepper flakes

CHINESE CHILI, DRIED/GAN LA JIAO – 1/4 cup
- 1/4 cup cayenne, de árbol, or Thai chiles

CHINESE CHILI-GARLIC SAUCE See CHILI-GARLIC SAUCE

CHINESE CHILI OIL See CHILI OIL, CHINESE

CHINESE CHIVES/CHINESE LEEK See GARLIC CHIVES

CHINESE COOKING WINE/LIAO JIU See CHINESE YELLOW RICE COOKING WINE

CHINESE CURRY POWDER – 1 teaspoon
- 1 teaspoon mild Madras curry powder
- 1/4 teaspoon each ground turmeric, cardamom, ginger, and cumin

CHINESE DATES See JUJUBES/NATSUME

CHINESE DIPPING SAUCE– 1 cup
- 1/2 cup each soy sauce and brown rice vinegar plus 1 teaspoon grated fresh ginger

Make Your Own Stir together 1/2 cup soy sauce, 1/4 cup water, 2 tablespoons seasoned rice vinegar, and 2 teaspoons sugar until the sugar dissolves. Add 2 tablespoons thinly sliced scallions or green onions, if desired.

CHINESE DRIED SCALLOP/CON POY (flavoring agent) – 1 ounce
- ⇨ 1 ounce tuna bottarga/*bottarga di tonno*

CHINESE DUCK SAUCE *See PLUM SAUCE*

CHINESE EGG NOODLES/CHOW MEIN NOODLES/MIAN TIAO, FRESH – 1 pound *See also CHINESE WHEAT NOODLES*
- ⇨ 1 pound fresh Chinese wheat noodles or ramen noodles
- ⇨ 12 ounces dried spaghetti or fettuccine (longer cooking time)

CHINESE FERMENTED BLACK BEANS *See FERMENTED BLACK BEANS*

CHINESE FISH SAUCE/FISH MIST/YUE LO *See FISH SAUCE*

CHINESE FIVE-SPICE POWDER – 1 teaspoon
- ⇨ 1/8 teaspoon each ground cinnamon, ground cloves, ground ginger, ground Sichuan pepper (or freshly ground black or white pepper), and ground star anise (or crushed anise or fennel seed)
- ⇨ 1 whole ground star anise (or 1/2 teaspoon star anise powder) plus a dash of ground white pepper or ginger
- ⇨ 1/2 teaspoon anise or fennel seeds, crushed, plus a dash of ground white pepper or ginger

CHINESE FLOWERING QUINCE *See FLOWERING QUINCE*

CHINESE GARLIC STEMS/SUAN TAI – 4 ounces
- ⇨ 4 ounces garlic chives, or garlic scapes (curly garlic shoots)
- ⇨ 4 ounces green onions plus a little chopped garlic
- ⇨ 4 ounces unsprayed wild garlic greens/shoots/onion grass/*Allium vineale*

CHINESE GINGER *See KRACHAI*

CHINESE HAM (Yunnan or Jinhua) – 1 pound
☞ 1 pound smoky Serrano ham, or dry-cured and smoked country-style ham, such as Smithfield

CHINESE HOISIN SAUCE *See HOISIN SAUCE*

CHINESE HOT PEPPER OIL *See CHILI OIL, CHINESE*

CHINESE HOT RED CHILE *See CHINESE CHILI, DRIED*

CHINESE KALE *See CHINESE BROCCOLI*

CHINESE KEYS *See FINGERROOT*

CHINESE LANTERN *See CAPE GOOSEBERRIES*

CHINESE LEAF LETTUCE/PAK KAD/SANG CHOY – 1 pound
☞ 1 pound Romaine/cos lettuce

CHINESE MU SHU SAUCE *See MU SHU/MOO SHU SAUCE*

CHINESE MUSTARD *See MUSTARD, CHINESE*

**CHINESE MUSTARD CABBAGE/MUSTARD GREENS/GAI CHOY/
TAKANA – 1 pound**
☞ 1 pound mustard greens; turnip greens; or escarole, especially the dark outer leaves
☞ 1 pound Japanese mustard spinach/*Komatsu-na* (smaller, darker-colored leaves)
☞ 1 pound Chinese spinach/*yin choy* or mature curly-leaf spinach/Savoy (milder flavor)

CHINESE NOODLES *See CHINESE EGG NOODLES; CHINESE WHEAT NOODLES*

CHINESE OKRA/ANGLED LOOFAH SQUASH/SILK SQUASH/SING GWA/HECHIMA, FRESH – 1 pound (2 medium)
- 1 pound young sponge gourd or medium zucchini (peeling unnecessary)
- 1 large English/hothouse cucumber (peeled and any seeds removed)

CHINESE PANCAKES See MU SHU PANCAKES

CHINESE PARSLEY/FRESH CORIANDER See CILANTRO

CHINESE PICKLED GARLIC – 1 cup
Make Your Own Separate and peel the cloves from 5 heads (about 8 ounces) of garlic. Heat with 1/2 cup unseasoned rice vinegar, 1 tablespoon sugar, and 1/2 teaspoon salt until boiling; let cool. Refrigerate in a covered jar for at least 1 month before using.

CHINESE PRESERVED CABBAGE/SALTED MUSTARD CABBAGE/SALTED TIEN JING CABBAGE/KIAM CHYE/TUNG CHAI – 1 tablespoon
- 1 tablespoon salt-packed capers, rinsed in cold water and patted dry
- 1 tablespoon sauerkraut or napa cabbage kimchi (milder)

CHINESE PRESERVING MELON See SQUASH, ASIAN

CHINESE RADISH See DAIKON

CHINESE RED DATES See JUJUBES/NATSUME

CHINESE RED RICE POWDER/HONG QU FEN (coloring agent) – 1 tablespoon
- 1 tablespoon red rice (labeled red yeast rice) ground to a fine powder in a spice/coffee grinder

CHINESE RED RICE VINEGAR/DA HONG ZHE CU (vinegar dipping/ condiment sauce) – 1 tablespoon
- 1 tablespoon Japanese rice vinegar (milder)

- 1 tablespoon red wine vinegar sweetened with a little sugar
- 1 tablespoon Chinese black rice vinegar or cider vinegar

CHINESE RICE WINE/HUANG JIN/CHIEW *See SHAOXING*

CHINESE SAUSAGE/LAP CHEONG (thin cured sweet seasoned sausage) – 1 pound
- 1 pound Spanish dry-cured chorizo
- 1 pound Portuguese dry-cured chouriço or linguiça
- 1 pound Italian pepperoni or dry salami

CHINESE SESAME PASTE *See SESAME PASTE*

CHINESE SHANXI VINEGAR *See CHINESE BLACK RICE VINEGAR*

CHINESE SHRIMP PASTE/XIA JIANG *See SHRIMP PASTE, FERMENTED*

CHINESE SHRIMP SAUCE/BALICHAO *See SHRIMP SAUCE, FERMENTED*

CHINESE SOY SAUCE *See SOY SAUCE, CHINESE DARK; SOY SAUCE, CHINESE DOUBLE DARK; SOY SAUCE, CHINESE LIGHT*

CHINESE SPINACH/YIN CHOY/RAU TIO *See AMARANTH GREENS*

CHINESE STEAMED BUNS/BAO – 1 dozen
- 1 dozen unbaked refrigerated biscuits, such as Pillsbury buttermilk, flattened slightly, folded in half, and steamed until doubled in size, about 10 minutes

CHINESE SUGAR *See SUGAR, BROWN ROCK; SUGAR, YELLOW ROCK*

CHINESE SWEET-AND-SOUR SAUCE – 1/2 cup
- 1/2 cup Italian sweet and sour sauce/*agrodolce*
Make Your Own Simmer 1/4 cup each plum jam and apricot (or peach) jam with 3 to 4 tablespoons cider vinegar until slightly

thickened, about 10 minutes, or microwave on High for 4 minutes; let cool. (The sauce will thicken further as it cools.)

CHINESE SWEET BEAN PASTE/SAUCE *See SICHUAN SWEET BEAN PASTE*

CHINESE VEGETABLE MARROW *See SQUASH, ASIAN*

CHINESE WATERCRESS/ONG TOY – 4 ounces
- 4 ounces watercress, garden/pepper cress, or upland cress

CHINESE WATER DUMPLING WRAPPERS/SIU KOW – 1 pound
- 1 pound wonton wrappers *See also WRAPPERS FOR FOOD, PRE-PARED EDIBLE*

CHINESE WHEAT NOODLES/SHANDONG LA MIAN/HOKKIEEN MEE, FRESH – 1 pound *See also CHINESE EGG NOODLES; NOODLES, CELLOPHANE*
- 1 pound fresh Chinese egg noodles or fresh-frozen ramen noodles
- 12 ounces dried thin Japanese wheat noodles/*hiyamugi/somen*, Korean thin wheat noodles/*somyun/gougsou*, or Filipino fine white wheat noodles/*miswa*
- 12 ounces dried spaghettini or vermicelli

CHINESE WHITE RICE VINEGAR/CLEAR RICE VINEGAR/BAI MI CU – 1/2 cup
- 1/3 cup distilled white vinegar or cider vinegar plus 3 tablespoons water

CHINESE WOLFBERRY *See GOJI BERRY/WOLFBERRY*

CHINESE YELLOW/BROWN BEAN SAUCE/HUGAN CHI JIANG – 1 tablespoon
- 1 tablespoon canned, salted yellow beans, rinsed briefly in a fine sieve, then mashed with a fork

☞ 1 tablespoon Japanese all-purpose light miso, such as *shinshu*

CHINESE YELLOW RICE COOKING WINE/MICHIU/MI JIU – 1 tablespoon
☞ 1 tablespoon pure yellow rice wine/*huang jiu,* such as Shaoxing, plus a few grains of salt
☞ 1 tablespoon glutinous yellow rice wine/*gnow mei dew*
☞ 1 tablespoon sake, dry vermouth, Latin American *vino seco*, or medium dry sherry, such as amontillado

CHIPOLATA (tiny spicy sausages) – 8 ounces
☞ 8 ounces hot links or kielbasa, cut in half crosswise then lengthwise

CHIPOTLE CHILE POWDER – 1 teaspoon
☞ 2 teaspoons pureed chipotle chile from canned chipotle chiles in adobo
☞ 1 teaspoon Urfa chile powder or 1 1/4 teaspoons Urfa pepper flakes
☞ 1 1/2 teaspoons Aleppo chile powder, or 1 tablespoon ancho chile powder plus a touch of hickory smoke powder (or a drop of liquid smoke)
☞ 1 teaspoon crushed red pepper flakes or ground cayenne pepper, plus a touch of hickory smoke powder (or a drop of liquid smoke)
☞ 1/2 teaspoon Spanish hot paprika
☞ Chipotle-flavored mini bouillon cube (add a small section to soups, chili, or stews; reduce the salt in the recipe accordingly)

CHIPOTLE HOT PEPPER SAUCE – 1 tablespoon
☞ Hot pepper sauce, such as Tabasco or Frank's RedHot, plus a few drops of liquid smoke
☞ Liquid from canned or jarred chipotles in adobo, thinned if necessary

CHIPOTLE MORA/MORITA/CHIPOTLE COLORADO (smoked-dried jalapeño chile) – 1
☞ 1 small dried chipotle meco chile

- 1 large dried, smoked serrano
- 1 small dried *pasilla de Oaxaca*
- 1 de árbol or cascabel chile (spicy but not smoked)
- 1 large canned chipotle in adobo, rinsed and dried (not for a concentrated seasoning paste)
- 1/2 teaspoon chipotle chile powder, morita chile powder, smoked red aji chile powder, Chilean *merkén*, or Spanish hot paprika
- 1/4 teaspoon chipotle hot pepper sauce, such as Tabasco or Texas Pete

CHIPOTLE PASTE/PUREE – 1 tablespoon
- 2 or 3 drained chipotles in adobo, pureed until smooth
- 1 tablespoon ketchup plus 1 teaspoon hot chili sauce, such as Sriracha, and a pinch of smoked paprika

CHIPS *See BAGEL CHIPS; COLLARD CHIPS; CHOCOLATE CHIPS; COCONUT CHIPS; KALE CHIPS; NORI CHIPS; PITA CHIPS; ROOT VEGETABLE CHIPS; TORTILLA CHIPS*

CHIVE OIL – 1/2 cup
Make Your Own Blanch 1 bunch chives in boiling water for 30 seconds, then dip in ice water; squeeze dry and process in a food processor or blender with 1/2 cup oil and a pinch of salt until combined, about 2 minutes. Store in the refrigerator.

CHIVES, FRESH, FROZEN, OR FREEZE DRIED – 4 ounces
- 4 ounces green parts of scallions or green onions, smashed and cut lengthwise into ribbons
- 4 ounces garlic chives or Chinese garlic stems (more garlicky tasting)
- 4 ounces garlic leaves, slivered (cut leaves sparingly when the plants are no more than 8 inches tall)
- 4 ounces Egyptian walking onion leaves, slivered
- 4 ounces unsprayed wild garlic foliage/shoots/*Allium vineale*

CHOCOLATE CHIPS OR FÈVES, BITTERSWEET OR SEMISWEET (41 to 63% cacao) – 1 cup
- 6 ounces thin chocolate bars (semisweet or bittersweet; regular or dairy-free) cut or broken into pieces a little larger than chocolate chips (will not hold their shape when baked)
- 1 cup carob chips (less flavorful; not for melting)
- 1 cup cocoa nibs (for extra-dark/bittersweet mini chips)
- 2 ounces unsweetened chocolate plus 1/2 cup granulated sugar and 2 tablespoons shortening or vegetable oil (for melting)
- 2/3 cup natural unsweetened cocoa powder, 6 tablespoons granulated sugar, and 3 tablespoons shortening or vegetable oil (for melting)

CHOCOLATE CRUMB CRUST See CRUMB CRUST, CHOCOLATE

CHOCOLATE FUDGE TOPPING – 3/4 to 1 cup
Make Your Own Combine 1/2 cup each unsweetened cocoa powder, sugar, and boiling water, plus a pinch of salt; stir over low heat until smooth, about 2 minutes. The sauce hardens upon standing. (For a thinner sauce, use 1/3 cup cocoa powder.)
Or
Heat 1/2 cup heavy cream or evaporated milk and 2 tablespoons corn syrup just until boiling, then pour over 2/3 cup chocolate chips and stir until smooth.

CHOCOLATE LIQUEUR/CHOCOLATE-FLAVORED SPIRIT (such as Godiva, Haagen Dazs, Lejay-Lagoute, or Mozart) – 1 tablespoon for cooking
- 1 tablespoon crème de cacao or chocolate syrup (reduce the sugar in the recipe by 1 1/2 teaspoons)

CHOCOLATE MINT SAUCE – 1 cup
- 1/4 cup heavy cream (or soy or coconut creamer) stirred into 8 ounces chopped and melted chocolate peppermint creams (serve warm)

CHOCOLATE NIBS *See COCOA NIBS/CHOCOLATE NIBS*

CHOCOLATE SHELL (thin coating for cold or frozen items) – 1/2 cup
Make Your Own Melt 3 tablespoons refined coconut oil (or firm rendered leaf lard) and 3 ounces chopped dark chocolate (or 1/2 cup semisweet chocolate chips) in the microwave until smooth, stirring every 20 seconds. Let cool to room temperature, about 10 minutes. Dip frozen fruit using a toothpick or pour over ice cream. (For a thinner shell, increase the fat to 1/4 cup; for a thicker shell, increase the chocolate up to 8 ounces.)

CHOCOLATE SYRUP – 3/4 cup (about)
- Simmer 1/2 cup water, 1/4 cup granulated sugar, 1/3 cup unsweetened cocoa powder, and a pinch of sea salt for 3 or 4 minutes. Remove from the heat and add 1/2 teaspoon vanilla; store in a lidded jar in the refrigerator. (For a sweeter syrup, increase the sugar to up to 1 cup.)

CHOCOLATE, BITTERSWEET (50 to 67% cacao) – 1 ounce
- 3 tablespoons natural unsweetened cocoa powder plus 1 tablespoon granulated sugar and 1 1/2 teaspoons shortening or vegetable oil
- 2/3 ounce unsweetened chocolate plus 2 teaspoons granulated sugar

CHOCOLATE, BITTERSWEET (50 to 67% cacao) – 4 ounces
- 4 ounces dark chocolate, such as Hershey's Special Dark
- 3 ounces semisweet chocolate plus 1 ounce unsweetened chocolate
- 3 ounces bittersweet chocolate (70 to 75% cacao) plus 2 tablespoons granulated sugar

CHOCOLATE, COUVERTURE (high-gloss coating/dipping chocolate)
– 4 ounces callets or buttons
- 1 ounce finely chopped or grated dark chocolate added to 3 ounces barely melted dark chocolate and stirred until melted and smooth (use immediately)

☞ 1 tablespoon neutral-tasting vegetable oil added to 3 ounces barely melted dark chocolate and stirred until smooth (use immediately and consume within 3 days)

CHOCOLATE, GERMAN'S SWEET (48% cacao) – 1 ounce
☞ 1 ounce semisweet chocolate plus 1 1/2 teaspoons granulated sugar
☞ 1/2 ounce unsweetened chocolate plus 4 teaspoons granulated sugar
☞ 3 tablespoons natural unsweetened cocoa powder plus 4 teaspoons granulated sugar and 1 tablespoon shortening or vegetable oil

CHOCOLATE, MEXICAN (such as Ibarra or Abuelita) – 2 ounces
☞ 1 ounce chilled baking chocolate broken into pieces plus 1 tablespoon each granulated sugar and ground almonds, and 1 teaspoon ground Ceylon/Mexican cinnamon, ground in a blender or spice/coffee grinder until fine
☞ 1/3 cup bittersweet chocolate chips (or 2 ounces bittersweet bar chocolate), 1 teaspoon ground Ceylon/Mexican cinnamon, and 1 or 2 drops almond extract
☞ 3 tablespoons natural unsweetened cocoa (for moles calling for chocolate)

CHOCOLATE, MILK – 6 ounces
☞ 5 ounces semisweet or bittersweet chocolate, 2 ounces whole milk powder, and 3 tablespoons granulated sugar

CHOCOLATE, SEMISWEET (35 to 60% cacao) – 1 ounce
☞ 1/2 ounce unsweetened chocolate and 1 tablespoon granulated sugar
☞ 3/4 ounce bittersweet chocolate (70% cacao) and 1 1/2 teaspoons granulated sugar
☞ 1 1/2 tablespoons unsweetened cocoa powder, 3 1/2 teaspoons granulated sugar, and 1 tablespoon shortening or vegetable oil

CHOCOLATE, SWEET See CHOCOLATE, GERMAN'S SWEET

CHOCOLATE, TEMPERED *See CHOCOLATE, COUVERTURE*

CHOCOLATE, UNSWEETENED (99 to 100% cacao; 50 to 60% butterfat) – 1 ounce
- ☞ 3 tablespoons natural unsweetened cocoa powder plus 1 tablespoon shortening or vegetable oil
- ☞ 3 tablespoons natural unsweetened high fat (22 to 24%) cocoa powder plus 2 teaspoons shortening or butter
- ☞ 2 1/2 ounces semisweet chocolate; reduce the sugar in the recipe by 3 tablespoons and the shortening or butter by 1 1/2 tablespoons
- ☞ 3 tablespoons toasted carob powder plus 2 tablespoons water or milk; reduce the sugar in the recipe by 2 tablespoons (less flavorful)

CHOCOLATE, UNSWEETENED (99 to 100% cacao; 50 to 60% butterfat) – 4 ounces
- ☞ 6 1/2 ounces bittersweet chocolate (70% cacao); reduce the butter or shortening in the recipe by 1 tablespoon and the sugar by 1/4 cup

CHOCOLATE, UNSWEETENED (99 to 100% cacao; 50 to 60% butterfat) – 8 ounces
- ☞ 5 ounces natural unsweetened high fat cocoa powder plus 3 tablespoons shortening or vegetable oil
- ☞ 4 1/2 ounces natural unsweetened cocoa powder plus 3 1/2 tablespoons shortening or vegetable oil

CHOKECHERRIES – 1 cup
- ☞ 1 cup red currants
- ☞ 1 cup small sour cherries

CHORICERO PEPPER, DRIED (Spanish mild red pepper) – 1
- ☞ 1 dried ñora/murican pepper
- ☞ 1 dried ancho chile
- ☞ 1 1/2 teaspoons Choricero powder or smoked mild/sweet Spanish paprika/*Pimentón de la Vera Dulce*

CHORIZO DE BILBAO (Filipino spicy cured sausage) – 1 pound
- 1 pound Csabai or Gyulai Hungarian smoked sausage
- 1 pound spicy smoked kielbasa

CHORIZO, COOKING (Spanish or Mexican spicy fresh sausage) – 1 pound
- 1 pound Creole/Cajun chaurice
- 1 pound Italian hot sausage or other spicy fresh pork or beef sausage
- 1 pound vegan chorizo or Italian-style vegan sausage

CHORIZO, DRY-CURED (Spanish spicy pork sausage) – 1 pound
- 1 pound Portuguese linguiça or chouriço (has less paprika)
- 1 pound smoked kielbasa (meat or turkey)
- 1 pound soppressata or other well-seasoned meaty salami

CHOURIÇO (Portuguese dry-cured sausage) – 1 pound
- 1 pound linguiça or dry-cured Spanish chorizo (not fresh or cooking chorizo)
- 1 pound smoked kielbasa (meat or turkey) or other spicy ready-to-eat sausage

CHRISTOPHENE/CHRISTOPHINE See CHAYOTE

CHRYSANTHEMUM LEAVES, EDIBLE/GARLAND CHRYSANTHEMUM / SHUNGIKU/TUNG HO/SUKGOT (Japanese, Chinese, Korean slightly bitter greens) – 1 pound
- 1 pound mature arugula, young dandelion leaves, watercress, or escarole

CHUFA/TIGER NUTS (small tubers) – 1 cup
- 1 cup almonds or chestnuts

CIABATTA (Italian wide, oval-shaped bread) – 1 loaf
- 1 focaccia, plain fougasse, *pain rustique*, or prebaked pizza crust, such as Boboli or Mama Mary's

☞ 2 ciabattini (ciabatta rolls)

CICELY, SWEET *See CHERVIL*

CICERCHIA BEANS (Umbrian dried beans) – 1 cup
☞ 1 cup chickpeas or black-eyed peas

CICI FLOUR *See CHICKPEA FLOUR*

CIDER BRANDY *See APPLE BRANDY/APPLEJACK*

CIDER MOLASSES – 1 cup
☞ 2 quarts unfiltered apple cider, gently boiled over medium heat until reduced to 1 cup, 40 to 50 minutes, stirring occasionally (store, refrigerated, for up to 1 month)

CIDER VINEGAR/APPLE CIDER VINEGAR – 1 tablespoon
☞ 1 tablespoon white wine vinegar or unseasoned rice vinegar
☞ 1 tablespoon distilled colorless malt vinegar or distilled white vinegar (for pickling and preserving)
☞ 1 tablespoon vinegar powder (for barbecue spice rubs)

CIDER, APPLE *See CIDER, SWEET APPLE*

CIDER, BOILED (thick, pourable syrup) – 1 cup (12 ounces)
☞ 3 cups apple cider, boiled, uncovered, over moderate heat until reduced to 1 cup
☞ 1 cup thawed frozen apple juice concentrate

CIDER, HARD/CIDRE/SAGARDOA – 1 cup
☞ 7/8 cup sweet apple cider plus 2 tablespoons bourbon
☞ 1 cup dry apple wine or dry white wine

CIDER, MEDIUM-HARD – 1 cup
☞ 7/8 cup dry hard cider plus 2 tablespoons apple juice

☞ 2/3 cup organic apple juice plus 1/3 cup apple cider vinegar
☞ 1 cup lambic beer or ale (not light ale)

CIDER, SWEET APPLE – 1 cup
☞ 1 tablespoon boiled cider mixed with 3/4 cup water
☞ 1 cup cold-pressed apple juice (less tangy)
☞ 1 or 2 teaspoons cider vinegar added to 1 cup apple juice
☞ 1 cup pear cider/perry

CILANTRO/FRESH CORIANDER LEAVES – 1 tablespoon chopped leaves
☞ 1 teaspoon dried broken leaf cilantro
☞ 1 tablespoon chopped fresh sawleaf herb/*culantro*
☞ 1 tablespoon chopped Italian flat-leaf parsley leaves, 1/8 teaspoon sage, and 1/8 teaspoon finely grated lime or lemon zest
☞ 1 tablespoon chopped Italian flat-leaf parsley sprigs (for color)
☞ Small piece cilantro-flavored mini bouillon cube (for soups or stews; reduce the salt in the recipe accordingly)
☞ 1 to 2 tablespoons cilantro cooking base/*recaito* (for soups or stews; reduce the salt and seasoning accordingly)

CILANTRO ROOT See CORIANDER ROOT

CILANTRO, MICRO – 1 ounce
☞ 1 ounce cilantro leaves, amaranth sprouts, or watercress

CILIEGINE, FRESH (1/3-ounce cherry-sized mozzarella balls) – 4 ounces
☞ 1 *ovolini* (4-ounce fresh mozzarella ball), cut into 12 pieces using the small end of a double melon baller or a demitasse spoon
☞ 2 *bocconcini* (2-ounce golf-ball-size mozzarella balls), cut into 12 (1/2-inch) cubes

CINNAMON OIL – 2 drops
☞ 1/2 teaspoon cinnamon extract
☞ 1 1/2 to 2 teaspoons ground cassia cinnamon

CINNAMON STICK, INDONESIAN KORINTJE – 1 (3- or 4-inch) stick
- ⇨ 1 (5-inch) soft Ceylon cinnamon stick/canela
- ⇨ 2 teaspoons ground cinnamon (to replace a smashed/crushed cinnamon stick used in cooking)
- ⇨ 1/4 teaspoon ground cinnamon (to replace a whole cinnamon stick removed after cooking)
- ⇨ 1 tablespoon cinnamon chunks (to flavor coffee, mulled wine, or cider)

CINNAMON SUGAR – 1 cup
- ⇨ 3 to 4 tablespoons ground cinnamon thoroughly mixed with 3/4 cup granulated sugar
- ⇨ 2 or 3 cinnamon sticks buried in a jar containing 1 cup sugar and then left for a few weeks

CINNAMON SYRUP – 1 cup
- ⇨ 4 or 5 whole cinnamon sticks added to 1 cup heated heavy syrup (See SYRUP, SIMPLE) and simmered 1 or 2 minutes; strain and cool before using (for more intense flavor, let the mixture sit a few hours before straining)

CINNAMON, GROUND (Ceylon, Sri Lanka, Mexican, canela) – 1 teaspoon
- ⇨ 1-inch Ceylon/Sri Lanka cinnamon stick, crumbled or grated with a Microplane grater
- ⇨ 2/3 teaspoon Indonesia/Korintje or China cassia cinnamon
- ⇨ 1/4 to 1/2 teaspoon Vietnamese/Saigon cassia cinnamon

CINNAMON, GROUND (Indonesian, Korintje, Padang, cassia) – 1 teaspoon
- ⇨ 1 1/2 teaspoons pure Ceylon/Sri Lanka cinnamon/canela
- ⇨ 1/4 teaspoon cinnamon extract
- ⇨ 1/2 teaspoon ground allspice plus scant 1/8 teaspoon ground nutmeg
- ⇨ 1/4 teaspoon ground cardamom plus 1/8 teaspoon ground nutmeg

☞ 1 teaspoon apple or pumpkin pie spice

CINNAMON, GROUND (Vietnamese/Saigon, cassia, Cinnamomum loureiroi) – 1 teaspoon
☞ 1 1/4 teaspoons Indonesia/Korintje or China/Tung Hing cassia cinnamon
☞ 2 teaspoons pure Ceylon/Sri Lanka cinnamon/canela

CINNAMON, SOFT-QUILL See CINNAMON, GROUND (Ceylon, Sri Lanka, Mexican, canela)

CIRUELA CHILE, DRIED (El Salvadorian chile) – 1
☞ 1 dried pasilla or mulato chile

CITRIC ACID/CITRIC SALT (tart flavoring and anti-discoloration agent for fruits and vegetables) – 1 tablespoon powdered
☞ 1 heaping tablespoon citric acid crystals (lemon salt/sour salt), finely crushed and then measured to equal 1 tablespoon (found in the canning section of supermarkets)
☞ 1 tablespoon tartaric acid (found at wine supply stores)
☞ 1 teaspoon ascorbic acid powder (found in drugstores)
☞ Six (500-mg) ascorbic acid vitamin C tablets, crushed to a powder or dissolved in water
☞ 3/4 cup bottled lemon juice, such as ReaLemon
☞ 1 1/2 cups distilled white vinegar (5% acidity)

CITRON/YUJA (Asian large tart citrus) – 1 fruit
☞ 1 large lemon (juice and zest only; not the white pith)

CITRON SALT/CITRUS SALT – 1 cup
Make Your Own Thoroughly combine 1 cup coarse sea salt or flake salt and 3 tablespoons freshly grated citron zest (or lemon zest), spread on a baking sheet, then dry in a preheated 200°F oven, about 1 hour; cool completely. Store in an airtight container. Alternatively, let sit at room temperature until completely dry, 8 to 12 hours.

CITRUS OIL, PURE (lemon, lime, orange, or tangerine) – 1/2 teaspoon
- 1 1/2 teaspoons pure citrus extract
- 3 or 4 teaspoons finely grated citrus zest from a scrubbed fruit, preferably organic (Place the whole fruit in the freezer until partly hardened, about 30 minutes, before grating.)

CITRUS PEPPER See LEMON PEPPER

CITRUS SUGAR – 1 cup
Make Your Own Process 1 cup granulated sugar and 2 to 4 tablespoons finely grated zest (lemon, lime, or tangerine) in a blender or food processor until combined, 30 to 40 seconds, or in a spice/coffee grinder in batches. Alternatively, bury thin strips of zest in the sugar and store airtight at room temperature for at least 1 week before opening.

CITRUS SYRUP – 1 cup
Make Your Own Remove 8 to 10 strips of lemon, yuzu, or lime peel (scrub the fruit first) with a vegetable peeler and scrape away any white pith. Simmer with 1 cup heavy syrup (See SYRUP, SIMPLE) 1 to 2 minutes; strain and cool before using.

CITRUS ZEST, DRIED See LEMON PEEL, DRIED; ORANGE PEEL, DRIED GRANULATED; TANGERINE/MANDARIN PEEL, DRIED

CLAMATO JUICE – 1 cup for cooking
- 2/3 cup tomato juice and 1/3 third cup bottled clam juice

CLAM JUICE – 1 cup for cooking
- 20 to 30 shrimp shells and heads, sautéed in 1 or 2 teaspoons vegetable oil until bright orange (optional), simmered with 2 cups water for 30 minutes, and strained
- 1 cup bottled/jarred clam juice (or 1/2 cup juice from canned clams and 1/2 cup water)
- 1 cup boxed clam cooking stock
- 1/2 teaspoon bonito-flavored seasoning/soup stock, such as *hondashi* or *dashi-no-moto*, dissolved in 1 cup hot water

- ⊯ 1/2 to 3/4 teaspoon concentrated seafood base dissolved in 1 cup hot water
- ⊯ 3/4 to 1 teaspoon clam flavored soup stock granules, such as Dashida, dissolved in 1 cup hot water.

CLAMS, LITTLENECK, FRESH – 1 pound
- ⊯ 1 pound countneck clams, Manila/asai clams, or New Zealand cockles (smaller; use more)
- ⊯ 1 pound topneck clams, cherrystone clams, or Mahogany clams (larger; use less)
- ⊯ 1 pound Prince Edward Island/black mussels (more delicate)
- ⊯ 5 ounces shelled brine-packed canned clams, rinsed

CLAMS, MANILA – 1 pound
- ⊯ 1 pound Littleneck, Mahogany, or cherrystone clams (larger; heat slightly longer to open)
- ⊯ 1 pound New Zealand cockles (smaller)

CLEARJEL (modified cornstarch thickener) – 1 tablespoon
- ⊯ 1 tablespoon arrowroot powder, cornstarch, potato starch, or rice starch
- ⊯ 1 tablespoon quick-cooking tapioca softened in the liquid/mixture for 10 to 15 minutes before cooking
- ⊯ 1 1/2 to 2 tablespoons all-purpose flour, potato flour, tapioca flour/starch, or a proprietary thickener such as King Arthur Flour Pie Filling Enhancer

CLOTTED CREAM See CREAM, CLOTTED/DEVONSHIRE CREAM

CLOUD EAR/BLACK TREE FUNGUS/HED HUNA/YUN'ER/WUN YEE (dried Asian mushrooms) – 1/2 ounce (1/4 to 1/3 cup)
- ⊯ 1/2 ounce dried wood ear fungus/mook yee/hei mu er/kikurage (larger, thicker, tougher; increase the cooking time)
- ⊯ 1/2 ounce dried silver ear/white fungus/sit gnee/yin'er/nam trang (white to pale gold)

⇨ 1/2 ounce small dried shiitake mushrooms (triple the soaking time)

CLOVES, GROUND – 1 teaspoon
⇨ 1 1/4 teaspoons whole cloves ground in a spice/coffee grinder
⇨ 1/3 teaspoon each ground allspice, cinnamon, and nutmeg
⇨ 1 teaspoon ground allspice

COCKLES, NEW ZEALAND – 1 pound (about 24)
⇨ 1 pound littleneck or Manila/*asari* clams (larger)

COCKTAIL SAUCE (sauce for shrimp cocktail) – 1 cup
Make Your Own Stir 2/3 cup ketchup or ketchup-based chili sauce, such as Heinz; 1/4 to 1/3 cup strained bottled horseradish (or 1 tablespoon wasabi paste); and a few dashes of hot pepper sauce until combined. Alternatively, in place of the horseradish, increase the hot pepper sauce and add a dash of lemon juice plus a few drops of Worcestershire sauce.

COCKTAIL WIENERS/FRANKFURTERS – 1 dozen
⇨ 3 regular size hot dogs, preferably all-beef or kosher, cut in half crosswise, then lengthwise

COCO de MOLLANS – 1 cup
⇨ 1 cup cannellini or navy beans

COCOA BUTTER – 1 ounce
⇨ 4 teaspoons unsalted butter, palm oil, grapeseed oil, or other neutral-tasting oil

COCOA MIX/HOT CHOCOLATE POWDER – 1 2/3 cups
Make Your Own Whisk together 1 1/2 cups nonfat dry milk powder, 1/2 cup unsweetened cocoa powder (natural or Dutch-process), and 1/2 cup sugar. Add 1/4 cup mix to 3/4 cups hot water. Makes 10 servings. Store in an airtight container; it will keep for up to 6 months.

COCOA NIBS/CHOCOLATE NIBS (roasted shelled cocoa beans) – 4 ounces (1 cup)
- 1 cup finely chopped bittersweet chocolate, preferably 70% cacao

COCOA POWDER/ DOUBLE-DUTCH DARK (ALKALIZED), UNSWEETENED (such as King Arthur) – 1 cup
- 1/2 cup each Dutch-process and black cocoa

COCOA POWDER, DUTCH-PROCESS (ALKALIZED), UNSWEETENED (such as Callebaut, Droste, Pernigotti, Valrhona, or Hershey's European Style or Special Dark) – 3 tablespoons
- 3 tablespoons natural unsweetened cocoa powder, preferably high fat, plus 1/8 teaspoon baking soda
- 3 tablespoons natural unsweetened cocoa powder (for recipes not requiring baking powder or baking soda, such as brownies)
- 1 ounce unsweetened chocolate plus 1/8 teaspoon baking soda; reduce the fat in the recipe by 1 tablespoon

COCOA POWDER, DUTCH-PROCESS (ALKALIZED), UNSWEETENED – 1 cup
- 1 cup natural unsweetened cocoa powder, preferably high fat, plus 1/2 teaspoon baking soda
- 1 cup natural unsweetened cocoa powder (for recipes not requiring baking powder or baking soda, such as brownies)
- 1 cup all-purpose baking cocoa, such as King Arthur, or black cocoa (for more intense color)

COCOA POWDER, NATURAL (NONALKALIZED), UNSWEETENED (10 to 12% cocoa butter, such as Baker's, Hershey's, Ghirardelli, or Nestlé) – 3 tablespoons
- 3 tablespoons European or Dutch-process cocoa powder plus 1/8 teaspoon cream of tartar (or 1/8 teaspoon lemon juice or vinegar added to the liquid in the recipe)
- 3 tablespoons Dutch-process cocoa powder and omit the baking soda from the recipe (milder flavor)

- 1 ounce unsweetened chocolate; reduce the fat in the recipe by 1 tablespoon
- 2 ounces semisweet chocolate; reduce the fat in the recipe by 1 tablespoon and the sugar by 3 tablespoons
- 4 tablespoons toasted carob powder; reduce the sugar in the recipe by 1 tablespoon and increase the fat by 1 tablespoon (less flavorful)

COCOA POWDER, NATURAL (NONALKALIZED), UNSWEETENED (10 to 12% cocoa butter) – 1 cup
- 1 cup high fat cocoa powder (22 to 24% cocoa butter)
- 1 cup European or Dutch-process cocoa powder; substitute baking powder for baking soda and double the amount

COCONUT BUTTER/CREAMED COCONUT – 1 cup for cooking
- 1 cup vegetable shortening or unsalted butter (lacks coconut flavor)

Make Your Own Process 4 cups dried unsweetened flaked or desiccated coconut in a food processor or high-speed blender until reduced to a paste, 15 to 20 minutes, scraping down the sides of the bowl as needed. Store in a lidded jar at room temperature up to 2 months.

COCONUT CHIPS
Make Your Own Slice fresh coconut into wafer-thin strips, sprinkle with salt (optional), spread out on baking pans, and bake at 325°F until crisp, 25 to 30 minutes, rotating the pans and flipping the chips halfway through. Cool and store in an airtight container. (Freezing the whole coconut overnight makes shelling it easier.)

COCONUT CREAM, UNSWEETENED – 1/2 cup
- 1/2 cup thick liquid that rises to the top of canned or homemade coconut milk after chilling it several hours
- 1/2 cup light cream or whipping cream plus 1/4 teaspoon coconut extract

COCONUT MILK BEVERAGE, BOXED – 1 cup for drinking or cooking
- 1/4 cup canned coconut milk mixed with 3/4 cup water

C

☞ 1 cup hemp milk

COCONUT MILK, FRESH – 1 cup
☞ 3 tablespoons canned cream of coconut plus enough water to make 1 cup

COCONUT MILK, FULL-FAT CANNED (53 to 55 % coconut extract) – 1 cup for cooking
☞ 1/4 cup (one-third of a packet) concentrated coconut cream mixed with 3/4 cup water
☞ 1/2 cup unsweetened coconut cream mixed with 1/2 cup water (whisk or stir the coconut milk before measuring)
☞ 1 cup coconut powder mixed with 1 cup water
☞ 1 cup half-and-half plus 1/2 teaspoon coconut extract (optional)
☞ 1 cup thin cauliflower puree plus 1/2 teaspoon coconut extract

Make Your Own Pour 1 1/4 cups boiling water over 1 cup packed fresh or frozen grated/shredded coconut (or unsweetened dried coconut); cool to room temperature. Process in a high-powered blender until smooth, about 2 minutes, then strain in a nutmilk bag or cheesecloth-lined sieve, pressing on the pulp to extract all the liquid. For light/lite coconut milk that resists curdling when heated, pour 1 cup water through the same puréed coconut and press again; to prevent full-fat coconut milk from curdling, add a scant 1/8 teaspoon baking soda before heating.

COCONUT MILK, LIGHT/LITE CANNED – 1 cup
☞ 1 cup of the second pressing of fresh grated coconut after making homemade coconut milk
☞ 1 cup lowfat or nonfat milk plus 1/2 teaspoon coconut extract
☞ 7/8 cup fresh coconut water plus 2 tablespoons full-fat sour cream or regular coconut milk
☞ 3/4 cup canned or homemade coconut milk mixed with 1/4 cup water

➺ 1/2 cup canned or homemade coconut milk mixed with 1/2 cup soymilk

➺ 1/3 cup unsweetened coconut cream mixed with 2/3 cup water

➺ 1 cup prepared potato milk, such as DariFree; or lactose-free milk, such as Lactaid (for coconut-free cooking; not for whipped topping)

COCONUT NECTAR/PALM SYRUP/EVAPORATED COCONUT SAP/ KITHUL TREACLE (thick, dark sweetener) – 1 cup

➺ 1 cup dark agave syrup/nectar, birch syrup, brown rice syrup, maple syrup, or *yacón* syrup

➺ 3/4 cup liquid honey plus 2 tablespoons water

COCONUT OIL, REFINED – 1 cup

➺ 1 cup firm rendered leaf lard

➺ 1 cup solid shortening

➺ 1 cup liquid and pourable coconut oil, or neutral-flavored vegetable oil, such as canola

COCONUT PALM SUGAR, GRANULATED See PALM SUGAR, LIGHT

COCONUT SUGAR, POWDERED – 1 cup

➺ 1/2 cup each confectioners' sugar and coconut milk powder, sifted together until thoroughly combined

COCONUT SYRUP, LIGHT – 1 cup See also COCONUT NECTAR

➺ 1 tablespoon coconut extract added to 1 cup simple syrup (*See SYRUP, SIMPLE*)

COCONUT VINEGAR/SUKANG TUBA/NAM SOM MAPLOW (Filipino low-acidity vinegar) – 1/3 cup

➺ 1/3 cup organic coconut vinegar (sold in health food stores)

➺ 1/3 cup white sugarcane vinegar/*sukang maasim*

➺ 3 tablespoons cider vinegar plus 2 tablespoons water

➺ 1/4 cup rice vinegar plus 1 tablespoon water

COCONUT WATER/JUICE – 1 1/2 cups (contents of one young, fresh coconut)

- 1/2 cup canned coconut milk blended with 1 cup plain water
- 1 cup young coconut meat and 1/2 cup coconut water, pureed in a high-speed blender until smooth (add more coconut meat or water as necessary)

COCONUT WHIPPED CREAM – 1 cup

Make Your Own Beat 1 cup top layer of cream from coconut milk, 1 1/2 teaspoons sugar, 1/2 teaspoon vanilla, and a pinch of salt in a chilled bowl on low speed until small bubbles form, about 30 seconds. Increase the speed to high and beat until the mixture thickens and forms light peaks, about 2 minutes. Use immediately.

COCONUT, COLORED – 1 cup

Make Your Own Shake 1 cup flaked or shredded coconut with 3 or 4 drops food coloring, in a tightly closed jar or sealable plastic bag until the color is evenly distributed. (Alternatively, use a pinch of powdered food coloring in place of the liquid.)

COCONUT, DRY DESICCATED/MACAROON TYPE – 1 cup

- 1 1/3 cups unsweetened flaked coconut, ground in a blender or food processor until fine
- 1 1/4 cups unsweetened shredded coconut, ground in a blender or food processor until fine

COCONUT, FRESH GRATED – 1 cup

- 1 1/3 cups frozen flaked coconut (squeeze out excess water from thawed frozen coconut and pat dry)
- 3/4 to 7/8 cup flaked or shredded unsweetened dried coconut, soaked in warm water 1 hour, using enough to barely cover the coconut; strain if necessary and pat dry (Alternatively, steam the coconut 30 minutes over simmering water.)
- 1 1/4 cups flaked or shredded unsweetened dried coconut; reduce the sugar in the recipe by 2 tablespoons

COCONUT, SWEETENED – 1 cup
☞ 1 cup unsweetened coconut; increase the sugar in the recipe by 1 tablespoon

COCONUT, TOASTED SHREDDED – 1 cup
Make Your Own Spread 1 cup shredded or flaked coconut (sweetened or unsweetened) in a single layer on an ungreased baking sheet and bake at 325°F until golden, 5 to 8 minutes, stirring halfway through. Alternatively, microwave on High for 2 to 3 minutes, stirring every 30 seconds, or toast in a dry skillet over low heat, stirring frequently, 4 to 7 minutes if dry or 10 to 15 minutes if fresh. Store, tightly sealed, at room temperature for up to a month.

COCONUT, UNSWEETENED SHREDDED – 1 cup
☞ 1 cup sweetened coconut, rinsed and strained with water until the sugar is gone, 2 to 4 times
☞ 1 cup sweetened coconut; reduce sugar in the recipe by 1 tablespoon
☞ 1 cup unsweetened reduced-fat coconut (40% less fat)

COCOZELLE SQUASH – 1 pound
☞ 1 pound zucchini

COFFEE-BASED CREAM LIQUEUR (such as Bailey's) – 2 tablespoons for cooking
☞ 1 tablespoon strong coffee, 1 1/2 teaspoons each heavy cream and whiskey, and 1 scant teaspoon sugar, preferably vanilla
☞ 2 tablespoons *crème de noyaux* (almond-flavored), or Tiramisu liqueur (chocolate-, coffee-, and almond-flavored)
☞ Few drops Irish cream flavoring; increase the liquid in the recipe by 2 tablespoons

COFFEE BEANS – 1 pound
☞ 1 pound roasted or malted barley, carob, rice, wheat germ, or other grain coffee, such as Cafix, Guayaki, Postum, Roma, or Teeccino

- ☞ 1 pound roasted dandelion root coffee, such as Dandy Blend, or homemade (Dry large dandelion roots from old dandelion plants on a rack at room temperature for 1 to 2 weeks or in a 120°F dehydrator for 8 hours, then roast in a preheated 325°F oven until dark brown and brittle, 30 to 90 minutes. Cool, then grind.)
- ☞ 1 pound soy coffee (Soak 1 pound soybeans in water to cover for 8 to 12 hours in the refrigerator, then drain. Spread in a single layer on a baking sheet and roast in a preheated 300°F oven until dark brown, 45 to 60 minutes. Grind while hot.)

COFFEE CONCENTRATE – 1 scant cup
Make Your Own Combine 4 ounces (1 1/4 cups) regular-grind coffee with 2 cups cold water, cover, and let sit for 12 hours before straining; store in a small bottle in the refrigerator.

COFFEE CREAMER – 1 tablespoon
- ☞ 1 tablespoon instant dry milk powder
- ☞ 1 tablespoon nonfat dry milk powder combined with 1 tablespoon nonfat milk (for lowfat creamer)
- ☞ 1 tablespoon sweetened condensed milk (for sweetened coffee)
- ☞ 1 tablespoon canned or homemade coconut milk (for a vegan alternative)
- ☞ 1 tablespoon almond creamer, coconut creamer, or soy creamer (for a vegan alternative)

COFFEE ESSENCE – 1/3 cup
Make Your Own Bring 1/4 cup finely ground French roast or espresso roast and 1/2 cup water just to a boil, stir a few times, then cover and let steep for 3 to 4 minutes. Strain through a paper coffee filter or paper towel, then cool. Store, refrigerated, for up to 1 month.

COFFEE EXTRACT – 1 tablespoon
- ☞ 1 1/2 teaspoons instant espresso powder, such as Medaglia d'Oro, or 1 3/4 espresso granules dissolved in 1 tablespoon warm water; cool before using

- 2 teaspoons instant coffee granules dissolved in 1 tablespoon boiling water; cool before using
- 1 tablespoon coffee-flavored syrup; reduce the sugar in the recipe by 1 or more teaspoons

COFFEE LIQUEUR/COFFEE-FLAVORED SPIRIT (such as Kahlúa, Crème de Café, Tia Maria, or Pasha) – 1 tablespoon for cooking
- 1 tablespoon chocolate-, hazelnut-, or almond-flavored liqueur
- 1/2 teaspoon freeze-dried instant coffee dissolved in 1 tablespoon vodka or hot water
- 1/4 teaspoon chocolate extract and 1/4 to 1/2 teaspoon instant coffee dissolved in 1 tablespoon vodka or hot water
- 1 tablespoon mocha-flavored espresso drink

COFFEE PASTE – 1 tablespoon
- 1 tablespoon instant coffee dissolved in 1 tablespoon hot water

COFFEE, CHICORY – 1 pound
- 1 pound dark-roasted regular coffee, such as French roast or Italian roast

Make Your Own 1 pound scrubbed and sliced chicory taproot (*Cichorium intybus*) roasted on a baking sheet in a preheated 250°F oven until fragrant, dark-brown throughout, and brittle when snapped, 2 to 4 hours. Cool and then grind. Keep tightly sealed at room temperature.

COFFEE, STRONG BREWED OR DOUBLE STRENGTH – 1 cup for flavoring
- The first cup from a pot of drip coffee
- 1 tablespoon instant espresso powder dissolved in 1 cup hot water
- 4 teaspoons freeze-dried instant coffee granules dissolved in 1 cup hot water

COGNAC (French brandy) – 2 tablespoons See also BRANDY
- 2 tablespoons Armagnac

COLATURA DI ALICI (Italian anchovy sauce/syrup) – 1 tablespoon
☞ 1 tablespoon Asian fish sauce (such as *nam pla* or *nuoc nam*)

COLESLAW DRESSING – 1/4 cup
Make Your Own Whisk together 2 tablespoons mayonnaise, 1 tablespoon each sour cream (or plain yogurt) and white wine vinegar (or cider vinegar), and 1 teaspoon granulated sugar.

COLLARD CHIPS
Make Your Own Rub collard greens with olive oil, season with salt if desired, then tear into 3-inch pieces. Spread in a single layer on a baking sheet, and bake at 300°F until crisp, about 15 minutes. Store in an airtight container; they will keep for up to 3 days.

COLLARD GREENS – 1 pound
☞ 1 pound flat-leaf kale, kohlrabi greens, mustard greens, Swiss chard, or turnip greens
☞ 1 pound broad-leaf plantain leaves/*Plantago major* or annual sow thistle leaves/*Sanchus oleraceus*

COLTSFOOT, SWEET/BUTTERBUR/FUKINOTO (Japanese stalk vegetable) – 1 pound
☞ 1 pound canned coltsfoot stalks packed in water
☞ 1 pound thick celery stalks

COMTÉ (French semihard, Gruyère-type cheese) – 1 ounce
☞ 1 ounce Beaufort, Bergkäse, Emmental, Fontina d'Aosta, Jarlsberg, Swiss Gruyère

CONCH (large sea mollusk) – 8 ounces conch meat
☞ 8 ounces abalone, tenderized like conch
☞ 8 ounces fresh clam meat (add at the last minute and cook until tender)

CONDENSED MILK, DAIRY-FREE SWEETENED – 1 cup (about)

- ⇨ 1 can full-fat coconut milk and 1/2 cup granulated sugar, simmered until the sugar is dissolved and the mixture is thick and reduced by one-quarter to one-half, about 1 hour
- ⇨ 1 cup vegan evaporated milk and 1 1/2 cups granulated sugar, slowly heated until the sugar is dissolved and the mixture is thick *See EVAPORATED MILK, VEGAN*

CONDENSED MILK, SWEETENED – 14-ounce can

- ⇨ 1 cup instant nonfat dry milk powder, 3/4 cups granulated sugar, 1/2 cup boiling water, and 3 tablespoons melted unsalted butter, whipped in a blender or by hand until smooth
- ⇨ 1 cup evaporated milk and 1 1/4 cups granulated sugar, slowly heated until the sugar is dissolved

CONFECTIONERS' SUGAR *See SUGAR, CONFECTIONERS'*

CONSOMMÉ – 1 cup

- ⇨ 1 cup canned or boxed beef broth plus 1 1/2 teaspoons unflavored gelatin powder (dissolve the gelatin in the broth before heating)

CONSOMMÉ, DOUBLE – 1 cup

- ⇨ 2 cups consommé, gently boiled in a large pan until reduced to 1 cup, 5 to 10 minutes

COOKING SPRAY/NONSTICK COOKING SPRAY (oil and lecithin-based propellant used to apply a light, nonstick coating to cooking and baking pans)

- ⇨ Equal parts canola, or other vegetable oil, and liquid lecithin (Combine in a food-grade pump/spray bottle; for nonstick pans or a soy-free spray, omit the lecithin and use oil only.)
- ⇨ Canola oil, coconut oil, or olive oil (Spread thin with a pastry brush or paper towel, then wipe off the residue; a thin film will remain.

Use 1/4 teaspoon for the equivalent of a 1- to 2-second spray, or 1 teaspoon for a 10- to 15-second spray.)

COPPA *See CAPICOLA*

CORIANDER LEAVES *See CILANTRO/FRESH CORIANDER LEAVES*

CORIANDER ROOT/RAK PAK CHI/PAK CHEE MET (Thai) – 3 to 4 medium (1 tablespoon chopped)
- 3 tablespoons chopped cilantro stems

CORIANDER SEED, DRIED (European and Indian) – 1 tablespoon (1/8 ounce)
- 1 to 1 1/2 teaspoons ground coriander
- 2 tablespoons fresh green coriander seeds
- 1 tablespoon caraway or fennel seeds
- 1 1/2 teaspoons black cardamom seeds or cumin seeds

CORN FLOUR, WHOLE KERNEL (white or yellow finely ground cornmeal; not cornstarch or UK cornflour) – 1 cup
- 1 1/4 cups freeze-dried corn kernels (or cornmeal), ground to a fine powder in a blender or spice/coffee grinder

CORN GRITS – 1 cup
- 1 cup hominy grits, barley grits, buckwheat grits, millet grits, rice grits, or soy grits or granules
- 1 1/3 cups whole-grain barley or dried corn, ground in a blender or in small batches in a spice/coffee grinder
- 1 cup coarse-ground polenta cornmeal, preferably stone-ground; or stone-ground cornmeal/maize meal (increase the liquid and cooking time)

CORN HUSKS *See WRAPPERS FOR FOOD, NONEDIBLE*

CORN, CREAM-STYLE/CREAM OF CORN – 1 cup
- ☞ 1 cup canned corn with liquid, pureed in a blender until nearly creamy, 3 or 4 seconds

CORNELL UNIVERSITY FORMULA *See FLOUR, CORNELL (UNIVERSITY) FORMULA*

CORNFLAKE CRUMBS – 1 cup
- ☞ 4 cups cornflakes, ground in a food processor until fine, 8 to 10 seconds

CORNICHONS (small French pickles) – 1/4 cup
- ☞ 1/4 cup Mexican fresh sour gherkins, brined gherkins, or other sour brined pickles, cut small
- ☞ 1/4 cup drained pickle relish (for chopped or minced cornichons)

CORNMEAL (for crumb coating/breading chicken and seafood) – 1 cup
- ☞ 1 cup dry corn muffin mix
- ☞ 1 cup fine dried breadcrumbs
- ☞ 1 cup oat bran
- ☞ 1 cup almond meal
- ☞ 1 cup finely ground crisp whole-grain crackers or corn or pita chips

CORNMEAL (for dusting pizza pans and peels) – 2 tablespoons
- ☞ 1 tablespoon coarse-ground semolina or grits
- ☞ 1 tablespoon wheat farina or dry regular Cream of Wheat
- ☞ 1 tablespoon oatmeal
- ☞ 1 tablespoon wheat bran

CORNMEAL, PRECOOKED, INSTANT *See AREPA FLOUR; MASA HARINA*

CORNMEAL, SELF-RISING – 1 cup
- ☞ 1 cup cornbread mix

Make Your Own Whisk together 3/4 cup fine-ground cornmeal, 1/4 cup all-purpose flour, 1/2 teaspoon baking powder, and 1/4 teaspoon each baking soda and salt.

CORNMEAL, STONE-GROUND – 1 cup *See also BREADING/COATING MIX, GLUTEN-FREE*
- 1 cup regular milled (steel-ground) cornmeal, preferably coarse-ground
- 1 cup polenta or corn grits
- 1/3 cup each almond flour, rice flour, and rice bran (for baking)

CORN SMUT *See HUITLACOCHE*

CORNSTARCH (for baking or gluten-free flour component) – 1 cup
- 7/8 cup potato starch
- 1 cup tapioca starch or arrowroot powder

CORNSTARCH (for coating/dredging or batter) – 1 cup
- 1 cup arrowroot powder
- 1 cup potato flour
- 1 cup chickpea flour
- 1 cup water chestnut flour
- 1 cup kudzu powder
- 1 cup matzo meal
- 1 cup sweet rice flour/glutinous rice flour, or brown rice flour

CORNSTARCH (for thickening) – 1 tablespoon
- 1 tablespoon waxy modified cornstarch, such as instant ClearJel (semi-translucent appearance; does not separate when frozen)
- 1 tablespoon sweet rice flour/glutinous rice flour/mochiko (opaque appearance; does not separate when frozen)
- 2 to 3 tablespoons all-purpose or quick-mixing flour (cook for 5 or more minutes after thickening to remove floury taste; opaque appearance; separates when frozen)
- 4 teaspoons arrowroot powder (clear appearance; separates when frozen; not for dairy-based sauces)

- 2 tablespoons tapioca starch, or 5 teaspoons small-pearl or quick-cooking tapioca ground in a spice/coffee grinder until powdery, about 30 seconds (clear appearance; does not separate when frozen)
- 2 teaspoons potato starch (do not let boil; semi-opaque appearance; separates when frozen)
- 1 1/2 to 2 teaspoons coconut flour (good for thickening coconut milk–based dishes)

CORN SYRUP, DARK – 1 cup
- 3/4 cup light corn syrup plus 1/4 cup unsulphured molasses
- 1 cup pure cane syrup, such as Steen's, or golden syrup, such as Lyle's (sweeter and thicker)
- 1 cup brown rice syrup/bran rice syrup
- 1 1/4 cups firmly packed brown sugar dissolved in 1/4 cup hot water (or the liquid called for in the recipe) and simmered until syrupy and reduced to 1 cup, about 5 minutes

CORN SYRUP, LIGHT-COLORED (not "lite") – 1 cup
- 1 cup liquid glucose
- 1 1/4 cups granulated sugar dissolved in 1/3 cup water (or the liquid called for in the recipe) and simmered until syrupy and reduced to 1 cup, 5 to 7 minutes

COSTEÑO CHILE, DRIED (hot Oaxacan chile) – 1
- 1 dried chile de árbol or cayenne chile

COTIJA/QUESO AÑEJO (Mexican sharp white grating cheese) – 1 ounce
- 1 ounce aged Asiago, aged ricotta salata, dry feta, dry Jack, Romano, or domestic Parmesan

COTTAGE CHEESE – 1 cup
- 1 cup ricotta, chenna, or pot cheese
- 1 cup lactose-free cottage cheese, such as Lactaid

COTTAGE CHEESE, DRY – *1 cup*
- 1 cup baker's cheese, hoop cheese, or dry ricotta
- 1 cup large-curd cottage cheese, drained for 1 hour in a fine-mesh sieve set over a bowl in the refrigerator

COURGETTES *See ZUCCHINI*

COUSCOUS, PEARL/MOGHRABIYEH/MUHAMMAS (Israeli/Lebanese large-grain semolina) – *1 cup*
- 1 cup toasted Sardinian pasta/*fregula*
- 1 cup Middle Eastern spherical pasta/*moghrabieh* (larger)
- 1 cup Greek pasta/*keskasune*, Italian pasta/orzo, Jewish egg pasta/farfel (smaller)

COUSCOUS, QUICK COOKING/INSTANT (Moroccan granular semolina) – *1 cup*
- 1 cup hand-rolled, whole-wheat, or quick-cooking barley couscous (darker, richer tasting; longer cooking time)
- 1 cup fine-ground bulgur (grind #1), shaken in a fine-mesh sieve to remove any starch
- 1 cup barley grits (or pearled or cracked barley, coarsely ground in a spice/coffee grinder or blender, then sifted to remove any starch)
- 1 cup instant rice, quick-cooking rice, or broken rice (gluten-free)
- 1 cup light prewashed quinoa or Bolivian *canahua* (gluten-free)
- 1 cup amaranth seed/grain (gluten-free; takes longer to cook; to help seeds stay separate, toast them briefly in a dry skillet before adding liquid)
- 1 cup millet (gluten-free; takes longer to cook; tastes best when lightly toasted in a dry skillet before adding liquid)
- 1 cup white grated cauliflower (trimmed cauliflower grated on the large holes of a box grater, shaved with a sharp knife, or pulsed briefly in a food processor to the couscous-size stage)

CRAB APPLES (small tart apples high in pectin) – *1 pound*
- 1 pound hawthorne fruits/thorn apples/*Crataegus monogyna* (smaller)

CRAB BOIL SEASONING – 1 (3-ounce) packet
- 2 1/2 tablespoons Old Bay seasoning (regular or low-sodium) or Zatarain's seasoning
- 1 to 2 tablespoons pickling spice

CRAB, GUMBO (cleaned, hard-shell blues for flavoring) – 1 pound
- Raw hard-shell crabs, cleaned and cut in half

CRABMEAT, JUMBO LUMP/PREMIUM, FRESH – 1 pound
- 1 pound backfin lump (smaller pieces; most delicate); backfin (broken lump and small pieces); or claw meat (darker color; stronger flavor; less expensive)
- 1 pound canned pasteurized "special" crabmeat (softer; small pieces)
- 1 pound shrimp or lobster (firmer)
- 1 pound formed fish/imitation crabmeat/crab sticks/surimi (less flavorful)

CRACKED WHEAT See WHEAT, CRACKED

CRACKER CRUMBS – 1 cup
- 1 1/4 cups unseasoned fine breadcrumbs, regular or gluten-free
- 1 cup gluten-free cracker crumbs, such as Mary's Gone Crackers

CRACKER CRUST See CRUMB CRUST, CHOCOLATE; CRUMB CRUST, SAVORY; CRUMB CRUST, SWEET

CRACKERS, WATER – 1 dozen
Make Your Own Mix together 2/3 cup flour, 1/4 teaspoon salt, scant 1/4 cup water, and 1 tablespoon vegetable oil, then roll out as thin as possible. Bake on a baking sheet at 350°F until light brown and crisp, about 30 minutes, flipping the crackers halfway through. Cool on a wire rack and store in an airtight container.

CRANBERRIES, DRIED UNSWEETENED – *1 cup*

- 1 cup sweetened dried cranberries; reduce the sugar in the recipe by 2 tablespoons
- 1 cup raisins or sultanas/golden raisins
- 1 cup dried blueberries, bilberries, or cherries
- 1 cup dried barberries/*Berberis vulgaris*, Oregon grape berries/*Mahonia aquifolium*, juneberries or serviceberries/*Amelanchiers* (for cooking)

CRANBERRIES, FRESH OR FROZEN – *1 cup*

- 1 cup lingonberries/mountain cranberries/cowberries/*Vaccinium vitis-idaea* (smaller)
- 1 cup squashberries/*Viburnum edule* (remove large flat seeds before or after cooking)
- 1 cup sea buckthorn berries/*Hippophae rhamnoides* (deep yellow to bright orange; sweeter after freezing)
- 1 cup bilberries/blaeberries/whortleberries/*Vaccinium myrtillus* (sweeter)
- 1 cup barberries, fresh or dried (soak dried berries in water 30 minutes)
- 1 cup red currants (smaller and sweeter)
- 1 cup blueberries (smaller and sweeter)
- 1 cup red chokeberries/*Aronia arbutifolia* (more astringent; higher in pectin and antioxidants; use for sorbets, jam, jelly, or juice)
- 1 cup red oval silverberries/*Elaeagnus umbellate* or *E. multiflora* (sweeter; high in vitamin C and lycopene; large seed; use raw, or for fruit soup or jelly)

CRANBERRY BEAN/BORLOTTI BEAN, FRESH – *1 pound unshelled*

- 1 pound fresh Tongue of Fire beans
- 1/3 to 1/2 cup dried cranberry beans, Anasazi beans, red or pink kidney beans, or pinto beans

CRANBERRY LIQUEUR/CRANBERRY-FLAVORED SPIRIT (such as DeKuyper, Boggs, or Flag Hill) – *1 tablespoon for cooking*

- 1 tablespoon cranberry syrup (sweeter)

☞ 1/2 teaspoons cranberry extract plus 1 tablespoon water
☞ 1 tablespoon raspberry liqueur

CRANBERRY VINEGAR – 1 tablespoon
☞ 1 tablespoon raspberry vinegar or other red fruity vinegar

CRAYFISH/CRAWFISH TAIL MEAT, COOKED – 1 cup
☞ 1 cup cooked and chopped shrimp, crabmeat, or lobster meat

CRAYFISH/CRAWFISH, DRIED -1 ounce
☞ 1 ounce fermented fish powder/*pla ra*
☞ 1 ounce smoked dried shrimps
☞ 1 tablespoon Thai fish sauce/*nam pla*

CREAM CHEESE (38% butterfat) – 1 cup (8 ounces)
☞ 1 cup Neufchâtel cheese (23% butterfat; more moisture)
☞ 1 cup reduced-fat cream cheese (16.5 to 20% butterfat; more sodium)
☞ 1 cup fat-free cream cheese (nearly twice as much sodium; separates when heated)
☞ 1 cup fresh goat cheese/chèvre or thick fromage blanc (softer texture)
☞ 1 cup soy cream cheese or tofu cream cheese
☞ 2 to 3 cups plain yogurt, Greek yogurt, quark, skyr, or labneh, drained for 12 to 24 hours in a sieve lined with dampened cheesecloth (or 2 basket-style paper coffee filters) and set over a bowl in the refrigerator (cover the sieve with a plate or plastic wrap)
☞ 1 1/2 cups lowfat cottage cheese, 2 tablespoons butter, and 1 tablespoon milk blended until smooth, then drained for 8 to 12 hours in a sieve lined with dampened cheesecloth and set over a bowl in the refrigerator (cover the sieve with a plate, cloth, or plastic wrap)
☞ 2 sticks (8 ounces) vegan margarine, such as Earth Balance, plus liquid cream cheese flavoring (for cakes, cookies, fillings, or frostings)

C

CREAM CHEESE, CREOLE – 8 ounces
- 1 teaspoon lemon juice stirred into 8 ounces softened cream cheese
- 8 ounces fromage blanc

CREAM CHEESE, DOUBLE (60% butterfat) *See PETIT SUISSE*

CREAM CHEESE, WHIPPED (27.9% butterfat) – 1/2 cup
- 1 (3-ounce) package room-temperature cream cheese, beaten until light and fluffy (unlike whipped cream cheese, will not separate in cooking)

CREAM, CLOTTED/DEVONSHIRE CREAM (English cream containing 55 to 75% butterfat) – 1 cup
- 1/2 cup heavy cream slowly beaten into 3 ounces (1/3 cup) softened cream cheese until smooth
- 1 cup mascarpone

Make Your Own Pour 4 cups heavy cream (not ultra-pasteurized) into a wide ovenproof bowl or pot and set in a preheated 175°F oven for 8 hours. Cool; cover and refrigerate for 8 to 12 hours, then remove the thick top layer of cream (use the remaining loose cream as heavy cream).

CREAM, DOUBLE/CRÈME DOUBLE (European cream containing 48% butterfat) – 1 cup
- 1 1/2 cups heavy whipping cream, gently boiled in a large pan until reduced to 1 cup, about 20 minutes (Whisk the cream for a few seconds every couple of minutes, and be careful it doesn't boil over.)
- 1 cup canned double cream, such as Nestlé Double Cream
- 1 1/2 cups crème fraiche, drained overnight in a sieve lined with dampened cheesecloth (or 2 basket-type paper coffee filters) set over a bowl in the refrigerator (cover the sieve with a plate or plastic wrap)

CREAM, HEAVY (35 to 40% butterfat) – 1 cup *See also CASHEW CREAM*
- 1 cup refrigerated or shelf-stable whipping cream (30 to 35% butterfat)

- 1 (8-ounce) carton unsweetened coconut cream, or 1 cup thick cream that rises to the top of canned or homemade coconut milk after chilling several hours (for cooking and whipping)
- 2/3 cup undiluted icy-cold evaporated milk (for whipping)
- 1 cup undiluted evaporated milk (for cooking)
- 3 tablespoons powdered heavy cream mixed with 1 cup water
- 2/3 cup whole milk or soy milk plus 1/3 cup melted unsalted butter, vegan butter/margarine, or coconut oil (for cooking)
- 1 cup dairy-free alternative, such as Mimic Crème, So Delicious Creamer, or Silk or Mocha brand soy creamer
- 1 cup brown rice cream (for cooking)
- 1 cup raw cashews, soaked in water to cover for 8 to 10 hours, drained, then pulverized in a blender with 1/2 cup water

CREAM, LIGHT/SINGLE CREAM (18 to 30% butterfat) – 1 cup
- 1 cup canned table cream, all-purpose light cream, or Mexican *media* cream, such as Nestlé
- 1/2 cup whipping cream and 1/2 cup whole milk (18% butterfat)
- 1/2 cup heavy cream and 1/2 cup half-and-half (25% butterfat)
- 3 tablespoons melted unsalted butter and enough whole milk to make 1 cup (for cooking)
- 1 cup canned or homemade coconut milk (dairy- and casein-free)
- 1 cup coconut milk creamer (nonfat and dairy-free)

CREAM OF COCONUT (cocktail ingredient, such as Coco López) – 1 cup
- 1 cup unsweetened coconut cream, whisked before measuring, plus 1/3 cup confectioners' sugar
- 1 cup sweetened condensed milk plus 1/2 teaspoon coconut extract

CREAM OF COCONUT, UNSWEETENED – 1 cup
Make Your Own Heat 2 cups shredded or flaked coconut with 1 (12-ounce) can evaporated milk until small bubbles appear around the edge, 6 to 7 minutes. Cool, then cover and refrigerate for 8 to 12 hours; strain in a cheesecloth-lined sieve, pressing firmly to extract

all the liquid, then keep refrigerated. It will stay, tightly sealed, for up to 2 weeks.

CREAM OF TARTAR (potassium hydrogen tartrate/potassium bitartrate) – 1/4 teaspoon
- 1/2 teaspoon distilled white vinegar (for stabilizing egg whites)
- 1/4 teaspoon xanthan gum (for stabilizing egg whites)
- 3/4 teaspoon distilled white vinegar or lemon juice (for acidifying liquids)
- 1/8 to 1/4 teaspoon tartaric acid (for acidifying liquids)
- Few drops distilled white vinegar (for preventing cooked sugar from crystallizing)

CREAM OF WHEAT – 1 cup
- 1 cup whole-grain brown rice farina

CREAM SAUCE – 1 1/2 cups
- 1 (10 5-ounce) can condensed cream of mushroom, cream of chicken, or cream of celery soup whisked with 1/3 to 1/2 cup milk. (Use regular or gluten-free soup)
- 1 (12-ounce) package silken tofu, pureed to a creamy consistency with a little soymilk, then seasoned to taste
- 2 to 3 cups tender steamed cauliflower florets, pureed to a creamy consistency with a little water, then seasoned to taste

CREAM SHERRY – 1 cup
- 4 teaspoons dark brown sugar stirred into 1 cup dry sherry (for recipes only)

CREAM, SOUR See SOUR CREAM

CREAM, WHIPPED – 1 cup (chill bowl and beaters at least 20 minutes before whipping)
- 1/2 cup ice water, 1/2 cup instant dried milk powder, and 1 tablespoon lemon juice beaten at high speed until stiff (For nonfat dry milk

powder, use 1/3 cup ice water instead of 1/2 cup; whip until slightly thickened and then add the lemon juice and continue whipping.)
- 1 cup chilled crème fraîche whipped until fluffy; will not increase in volume (For sweetened crème, add 1 tablespoon superfine sugar, then refrigerate for at least 15 minutes before whipping; it will keep for up to 3 days.)
- 1 (8-ounce) can thick cream, such as Nestle
- 1/2 cup liquid nondairy whipped topping, such as MimicCreme Healthy Top, whipped for 3 to 5 minutes
- 1 ounce powdered nondairy whipped topping mix prepared following package directions
- 4 ounces frozen nondairy whipped topping, such as Cool Whip or Cool Whip Lite, thawed
- 1/2 to 3/4 cup solid coconut fat, whipped until fluffy (Use the fat that rises to the top of canned, full-fat unsweetened coconut milk and do not overwhip; keep chilled; will melt at room temperature. For sweetened cream, add 2 to 3 teaspoons confectioners' sugar before whipping.)

CREAM, WHIPPED, LIGHT – 1 cup
- 1/2 cup chilled heavy cream and 1/4 cup chilled plain Greek yogurt, whipped until stiff (Add sugar if desired.)

CREAM, WHIPPED, NONDAIRY See DAIRY-FREE TOPPING

CREAM, WHIPPED, STABILIZER – 1 cup cream (2 cups whipped)
- 1 tablespoon dry milk powder (or 2 tablespoons nonfat dry milk powder), sprinkled over the cream before whipping
- 1/4 cup heavy cream mixed with 1 teaspoon cornstarch and heated until thickened; cooled to room temperature; then whipped into 3/4 cup heavy cream just as it begins to thicken (For sweetened whipped cream, add 1 or 2 tablespoons confectioners' sugar when heating the cream and cornstarch.)
- 1/2 teaspoon unflavored gelatin powder softened in 1 tablespoon cold water 2 to 3 minutes, heated in the microwave 10 seconds,

then cooled to room temperature; stir it into semi-whipped cream, then resume whipping

☞ 1 cut-up marshmallow, softened in the microwave a few seconds, then whisked a little at a time into the cold whipped cream (or use 1/4 cup marshmallow crème)

☞ 1/2 cup crème fraiche, folded into semi-whipped cream

☞ 1 or 2 tablespoons melted and cooled apple jelly used in place of sugar (the pectin acts as a stabilizer)

☞ 1 tablespoon, or 1 (10-gram) packet, stabilizing powder, such as Whip it or Whip Cream Aid, added before whipping; slightly decrease the amount of sugar

☞ 1/2 teaspoon waxy modified cornstarch, such as Instant ClearJel, mixed with the sugar before adding to the cream

☞ Drain the whipped cream, for at least 2 hours, in a fine-mesh sieve set over a bowl in the refrigerator and covered with plastic wrap.

CREAMER, COFFEE See COFFEE CREAMER

CRÈMA MEXICANA/MEXICAN CRÈMA – 1 cup
☞ 1 cup crème fraîche (richer; less salty)
☞ 1 cup *crema Salvadoreña*, *crema Centroamericana*, or *crema Hondureña* (darker-hued and tangier)
☞ 3/4 cup sour cream thinned with 1/4 milk or water plus salt to taste, about 1/8 teaspoon
☞ 1 cup heavy cream (for cooking)

CRÈME FRAÎCHE (French cultured cream with 48% butterfat) – 1 cup (8 ounces)
☞ 1 cup Mexican *crema/crema Mexicana* (will separate if boiled)
☞ 1 cup double cream (less tart; will not separate if boiled)
☞ 1 cup sour cream and 2 tablespoons heavy cream whisked together (will separate if boiled)
☞ 1 cup *labna* (more sour; will not separate if boiled)

Make Your Own Combine 1 tablespoon buttermilk or crème fraîche with 1 cup heavy cream, then lightly cover and leave in a warm spot until thickened, about 24 hours. Refrigerate, well covered, for up to 7 days (it will continue to thicken).
Or
Whisk together 1/2 cup heavy cream and 1/2 cup sour cream, cover lightly and leave at room temperature until thickened, 2 to 4 hours or longer. Refrigerate, well covered, for at least 4 hours before using. It will keep for up to 1 week refrigerated (it might separate if boiled).

CRÈME FRAÎCHE DIRECT-SET STARTER CULTURE – 1 packet (1/2 teaspoon)
- 1/3 cup buttermilk (for making crème fraîche)
- 1/2 teaspoon citric acid, or 1/8 to 1/4 teaspoon tartaric acid, dissolved in 1 to 2 tablespoons cool water (for making mascarpone)

CRÈME FRAÎCHE, LOW-FAT – 1 cup (8 ounces)
- Nonfat or 2% Greek-style yogurt, whisked until smooth
- 1/2 cup fat-free cream cheese (or fat-free sour cream), 1/2 cup 1% milk, and 1/4 teaspoon sugar whisked together, lightly covered, and left at room temperature until thickened, about 8 hours

Make Your Own Whisk together 1/2 cup evaporated nonfat milk, 1/2 cup plain low-fat yogurt, and 1 teaspoon lemon juice; lightly cover and leave at room temperature until thickened, about 8 hours. Will keep in the refrigerator for up to 1 week; whisk before using (might separate if boiled).

CREMINI/BABY BELLA MUSHROOMS/ITALIAN BROWN – 8 ounces
- 1 pound white cap/button or baby portobello/portobellini mushrooms
- 4 to 5 ounces canned mushrooms, drained

CREOLE MUSTARD See MUSTARD, CREOLE

CREOLE SEASONING – 1/4 cup *See also CAJUN SEASONING*
- 2 tablespoons salt, 1 tablespoon cayenne, and 1 teaspoon each ground white pepper, ground black pepper, and garlic powder

CREOLE SEASONING, SALT-FREE – 2 tablespoons
- 1 teaspoon each ground black (or white) pepper, ground cayenne pepper, garlic powder, onion powder, and paprika

CRESCENZA/CRESCENZA STRACCHINO (Italian rich, creamy fresh cheese) – 8 ounces
- 8 ounces mascarpone or cream cheese

CRESS (watercress, curly cress/peppergrass, upland/land cress) – 4 ounces
- 4 ounces young agretti, nasturtium leaves and stems, arugula, young radish greens, purslane leaves and tender stems, or young dandelion greens

CROSNES/CHINESE ARTICHOKE/CHOROGI (small crunchy tubers) – 1 pound (2 cups)
- 1 pound chopped sunchokes/Jerusalem artichokes, salsify, artichoke hearts, or young burdock root (Place the cut vegetables in acidulated water to keep them from discoloring.)

CROSTINI (Italian little toasts) – 8 ounces
- 8 ounces little bruschettas (thin slices of baguette cut on an angle, drizzled with olive oil, and grilled until crisp on both sides; cool on a wire rack)
- 8 ounces crispy poppadom or lavash pieces (crunchy lavash or poppadoms crisped in the oven or microwave, then broken into pieces)
- 8 ounces Melba toasts, whole-wheat or rice crackers, or round bagel or tortilla chips

CROUTONS (garnishes for soup or salad) – 1 cup
- ⇨ 1 cup Chinese fried chow mein noodles, such as LaChoy
- ⇨ 1 cup croutons from a package of herb seasoned stuffing mix, such as Pepperidge Farm (for seasoned croutons)
- ⇨ 1 cup baked chips (pita, bagel, or tortilla) or crostini, broken into pieces
- ⇨ 1 cup Indian *sev* (small crispy chickpea noodles)
- ⇨ 1 cup Southeast Asian *krupuk* (small shrimp and fish chips) fried and drained with larger ones broken into pieces
- ⇨ 1 cup crumbled curly chucka soba toasted in a skillet with a little oil, or noodles from a 3-ounce packet of instant ramen noodles crumbled and toasted (use the seasoning packet as a soup base, or to intensify a soup)
- ⇨ 1 cup crumbled wonton crisps *See WONTON CRISPS*

Make Your Own Cut firm-textured bread into 1/2-inch cubes, toss with a little olive oil or melted butter, and sprinkle with salt and dried herbs (such as oregano and basil), if desired. Spread out on a baking sheet and dry in a preheated 300°F oven until golden and crunchy, 15 to 20 minutes (or microwave in a single layer on High, 3 to 4 minutes; they will crisp as they cool).

Or

Cut cornbread into 3/4-inch cubes, spread out on an ungreased baking sheet, and bake in a preheated 300°F oven until crisp and lightly browned, 30 to 40 minutes.

CROWN DAISY LEAVES/SOOTGAT *See CHRYSANTHEMUM LEAVES, EDIBLE*

CRUDITÉS (crisp raw vegetables cut into bite-size pieces; usually served with a dipping sauce) *See also CANAPÉ BASES*
- ⇨ Baby bok choy; Belgian endive; carrots (red, yellow, purple, white); cauliflower; peeled celery; seedless cucumber; cherry tomatoes (red and yellow); fennel bulb; jicama; kohlrabi (green and purple); cultivated mushrooms; peppers (green, yellow, red); radishes (black, red, white, watermelon); red cabbage; romaine

lettuce hearts or Little Gem lettuce, small peeled rutabaga; sun-chokes/Jerusalem artichokes (preferably knobless); Hakurei or To-kyo Market turnips; water chestnuts; young water spinach sprigs/shoots, or young zucchini (sliced into bite-sized pieces; broken into florets; or cut into strips, wedges, or spears)
☞ Young lotus root (drop into acidulated water immediately after peeling and slicing), or jarred lotus rootlets
☞ Young asparagus segments, peeled cauliflower and broccoli stems, haricots verts, sugar snap peas (strings removed), snow peas, broccoli florets, or very young snap beans (blanched in boiling water for 20 to 30 seconds, then freshened in ice water)

CRUMB CRUST, CHOCOLATE – 8- or 9-inch

Make Your Own Crush 9 ounces chocolate wafers (about 30) to crumbs, then process with 1/2 cup melted chocolate chips and 1 tablespoon oil or melted butter in a food processor until combined. Press against the bottom and sides of a pie pan and freeze until set, about 15 minutes.

CRUMB CRUST, SAVORY – 8- or 9-inch

Make Your Own Mix 3 tablespoons melted butter thoroughly into 1 1/3 cups savory cracker crumbs (or finely grated crusty French bread). Press against the bottom and sides of a quiche dish or pie pan and bake in a preheated 350°F oven for 10 minutes; cool to room temperature before adding a filling.

CRUMB CRUST, SWEET – 8- or 9-inch

Make Your Own Mix 3 to 4 tablespoons melted butter or canola oil thoroughly into 1 1/2 to 2 cups cookie crumbs (graham crackers, di-gestive biscuits, ginger or chocolate snaps, or Maria cookies). Press against bottom and sides of a greased Pyrex pie pan. Microwave on High for 2 minutes, or bake in a preheated 350°F oven for 10 to 12 minutes. Cool to room temperature before adding a filling; the crust becomes firm as it cools. (For a salty-sweet crust, substitute crushed salted pretzels. For a fat-free crust, substitute 1 egg white for the fat and coat the pan with cooking spray.)

CRUMBS See BREADCRUMBS; CRACKER CRUMBS; GRAHAM
CRACKER CRUMBS; MATZO FARFEL; PANKO

CUBANELLE PEPPER, FRESH (Italian sweet frying pepper) – 1
- 1 fresh Gypsy, Nardello, Corno di Toro, Marconi, Black Hungarian, Romanian, or Hungarian wax/banana pepper
- 1 fresh bell pepper, peeled

CUBEB BERRIES/TAILED PEPPER (Indonesian seasoning) – 1 teaspoon
- 1/2 teaspoon allspice berries

CUCUMBER, ENGLISH/HOTHOUSE – 1 medium
- 2 medium Armenian or Korean cucumbers
- 4 medium Persian cucumbers
- 4 to 5 tender-skinned Kirby cucumbers (peel if not soft skinned)
- 2 medium American/garden cucumbers, peeled and seeded
- 4 small, slender zucchini (less crisp; less sweet)
- 8 to 10 (3- to 4-inch long) peeled cattail shoot centers/hearts/ *Typha latifolia* (white and milder)

CUCUMBER VINEGAR – 1 tablespoon
- 1 tablespoon champagne vinegar

CUCUZZA/CALABASH – 1 pound
- 1 pound chayote/mirliton, winter melon/wax gourd section, or fat zucchini

CUCUZZA TENDRILS/VINES/TENERUMI (Sicilian) – 4 ounces
- 4 ounces tender young cucumber, pumpkin, or zucchini vine tendrils

CUITLACOCHE See HUITLACOCHE

**CULANTRO/SAW-LEAF HERB/RECAO/NGO GAI/PAK CHI FARANG
(Latin American and Southeast Asian seasoning) – 1 fresh leaf**
- 1 teaspoon each fresh minced cilantro, mint, and basil leaves

☞ 1 large sprig fresh cilantro or 1 scant tablespoon minced (less robust)

CUMARI CHILE (hot, pea-size yellow Brazilian chile) – 2 or 3
☞ 1 habañero or Scotch Bonnet chile

CUMIN SEEDS, AMBER OR WHITE/SHAH JEERA – 1 teaspoon whole seeds
☞ 1 1/2 to 2 teaspoons packaged preground cumin or roasted cumin (in place of 1 teaspoon whole seeds toasted and ground)
☞ 1 teaspoon chili or taco seasoning (adds other flavors)
☞ 1/2 teaspoon ground coriander or caraway (for adding to curry or chile powder mix)

CUMIN SEEDS, BLACK/KALA JEERA (Kashmir, Pakistan and Iranian seasoning) – 1 teaspoon
☞ 1 teaspoon amber or white cumin seeds
☞ 1/2 teaspoon toasted ground cumin seeds (less sweet)
☞ 1/2 teaspoon caraway seeds

CURD CHEESE *See FARMER CHEESE*

CURLY ENDIVE – 1 pound
☞ 1 pound purple-red-tipped endive/*Quattro stagioni,* chicory, young arugula, baby mustard greens, endigia, or young puntarelle
☞ 1 pound frisée (lighter color; less bitter), escarole (inner heart), Chioggia radicchio (burgundy-colored leaves), or small leaves of tatsoi (less bitter; slightly sweet)

CURRANTS, BLACK, FRESH OR FROZEN – 1 cup *See also CURRANTS, RED*
☞ 1 cup red currants (smaller; less tart; more fragile)
☞ 1 cup fully ripe elderberries/*Sambucus nigra* (blue-black; sour; low in pectin)
☞ 1 cup ripe European barberries/*Berberis vulagris* (pink-red; tart with a smooth texture; or Japanese barberries/*Berberis thumbergii* (bright red; bitter with a mealy texture)

☞ 1 cup crowberries/*Empetrum nigrum* (blue-black with several seeds; freezing overnight improves flavor)

☞ 1 cup rowanberries/*Sorbus aucuparia* (red; sour; high in pectin; freezing overnight reduces bitterness; best combined with other fruit for jam or jelly; toxic when raw)

☞ 1/4 to 1/3 cup thawed frozen black-currant puree

CURRANTS, DRIED (dried black Corinth or Zante grapes) – 1 cup

☞ 1 cup Uvette raisins (tiny, sweet Italian raisins)

☞ 1 cup black or crimson raisins, coarsely chopped or snipped (freeze the raisins to make them easier to chop)

☞ 1 cup dried barberries (less sweet)

☞ 1 heaping cup dried cherries, sweetened dried cranberries, dried figs, dates, or prunes, cut into tiny pieces (Coat the knife blade with a thin film of cooking spray to make the fruit easier to chop.)

CURRANTS, RED, FRESH OR FROZEN – 1 cup See also CURRANTS, BLACK

☞ 1 cup white currants (smaller and sweeter)

☞ 1 cup bilberries/*Vaccinium myrtillus* (purple-black; sweet and juicy)

☞ 1 cup blueberries (purple; sweet)

☞ 1 cup ripe Hinnomaki gooseberries (red or yellow; tart) or Captivator gooseberries (red; sweet)

☞ 1 cup fully ripe autumnberries/autumn-olives/*Elaegnus umbellata* (red and juicy with soft seeds)

CURRY LEAF/DAUN KARI/KARI PATTA/KARAPINCHA/KITHA NEEM/ BAI KAREE (South Asian seasoning) – 1 fresh sprig (8 to 12 leaves)

☞ 12 to 16 dried or semidried curry leaves (check for aroma; dried leaves can have little flavor)

☞ 1 teaspoon curry leaf/*Kari patta* powder

☞ 2 dried salam leaves/*daun salam*

☞ 2 to 3 dried bay leaves

☞ 1 tablespoon chopped fresh cilantro leaves (grassier flavor)

CURRY OIL (Indian seasoning) – 1/2 cup

Make Your Own Gently heat 1/2 cup peanut or vegetable oil and 1 tablespoon mild Indian curry powder or paste for 15 minutes (do not let the oil get too hot). Cool, then strain through a small cloth-lined sieve; store, refrigerated, for up to 3 months. Or, rather than heating the oil, dry-toast the curry powder, then mix to a paste with 1 tablespoon of the oil; add the rest of the oil and shake to mix thoroughly; leave at room temperature for 8 to 12 hours, then strain.

CURRY POWDER, JAMAICAN – 1 tablespoon

☞ 1 tablespoon Madras curry powder plus 1/4 teaspoon each ground allspice and star anise

CURRY POWDER, JAPANESE – 1 tablespoon

☞ 1 tablespoon Indian-style spice blend, such as S&B Oriental Curry Powder

CURRY POWDER, MADRAS – 1 tablespoon

☞ 1 tablespoon sweet or mild curry powder plus 1/16 teaspoon ground cayenne pepper

CURRY POWDER/SEASONING, VINDALOO – 1 tablespoon

☞ 2 teaspoons mild/regular sweet curry powder, 3/4 teaspoon hot paprika, and 1/4 teaspoon ground black pepper
☞ 1 tablespoon Madras curry powder plus 1/2 to 1 teaspoon crushed red pepper flakes

CURRY POWDER, STANDARD/REGULAR BLEND – 1 tablespoon, or to taste

☞ 1 tablespoon Columbo curry powder (West Indian; mild)
☞ 1 tablespoon Maharajah-style curry powder, sweet curry powder, Korma curry paste, Tikka masala paste, Patak's paste, or tandoori powder or paste (Indian; mild)
☞ 1 tablespoon Vadouvan curry blend (French-Indian; delicate and mild; flavored with shallots and garlic)

- 1 tablespoon Mussaman/Masaman curry blend (Southern Thai; mild; similar to Malaysian and Indian but with a nuttier flavor)
- 1 tablespoon Madras curry powder (classic all-purpose curry powder, spicier and less bitter than most commercial versions; sometimes contains chickpea flour for less heat)
- 1 tablespoon hot Madras curry powder (regular Madras curry powder plus a pinch of ground cayenne pepper)
- 1 tablespoon Muchi curry powder (Indian southwest coast; hot and spicy)
- 2 tablespoons Thai kari/yellow curry paste or Thai Massaman/matsaman curry paste (mild sweet/spicy)
- 2 tablespoons Thai Panang curry paste (mellow and moderately hot; contains lemongrass and chiles)
- 2 teaspoons Thai red curry paste (medium-hot)
- 2 teaspoons Thai green or hot Madras green curry paste
- 1 1/2 to 2 teaspoons Vindaloo curry paste or powder/seasoning (Indian; spicy/tangy and hot)
- 4 teaspoons garam masala (Indian; warm spice blend; add at the end of cooking to heighten the flavor)

CUSTARD POWDER (British sweet sauce mix) – 2 tablespoons
- 2 tablespoons dry vanilla pudding mix (not instant)
- 2 tablespoons vegan vanilla pudding mix, such as Dr. Oetker Organics
- 2 tablespoons cornstarch, 1/4 teaspoon vanilla powder (or extract), plus scant 1/8 teaspoon turmeric, preferably Madras (for the color only)

CUSTARD POWDER, INSTANT – 1/4 cup
- 1/4 cup instant vanilla pudding mix

CUSTARD SAUCE/POURING CUSTARD – 1 cup
- 1 cup vanilla pudding prepared with 1 1/2 to 2 times the quantity of milk called for in the recipe

CUTTLEFISH, FRESH – 1 pound
- 1 pound fresh squid or octopus (less tender)
- 8 to 12 ounces Chinese dried squid/*qian you yu/gawn yo yue* soaked in water with a little baking soda until softened (for using cooked; baking soda tenderizes the squid)

D

DAIDAI JUICE (Japanese bitter citrus souring agent) – 1 tablespoon
- 1 tablespoon lemon or lime juice

DAIKON/ASIAN WHITE RADISH/MOOLI/LUOPO – 1 pound
- 1 pound Korean radish/*mu* or jícama (sweeter)
- 1 pound white icicle radish, red radish, or crisp, young turnip (for using raw or pickled)
- 1 pound Japanese giant turnip/*kabura* (for using cooked or pickled)
- 5 to 6 ounces sliced or shredded dried daikon/*kiriboshi daikon*, soaked in lukewarm water for 30 to 60 minutes, then squeezed dry (for using cooked or pickled)

DAIKON GREENS/YOUNG DAIKON LEAVES/MU CHONG – 8 ounces
- 8 ounces watercress, broadleaf cress, curly cress, or arugula

DAIKON LEAF/MATURE DAIKON LEAVES/SHEN LI HON (Taiwan) – 1 bunch
- 1 bunch Taiwan lettuce/*a choy*, mustard greens, or turnip greens

DAIKON SPROUTS/KAIWARE – 4 ounces
- 4 ounces sunflower sprouts
- 4 ounces pea or chickpea shoots

DAIRY-FREE TOPPING – 1 cup
- 1 cup soy- or rice-based topping, such as Soyatoo
- 1 cup coconut-based topping, such as heavy coconut cream or CocoWhip
- 3/4 cup liquid soy-dairy creamer, such as Silk, and 2 1/2 tablespoons confectioners' sugar, beaten at high speed until soft peaks form

▷ 3/4 cup chilled unsweetened coconut cream (or thoroughly chilled cream from the top of no-emulsion-added canned coconut milk) plus 1 1/2 teaspoons sugar and a pinch of salt, beaten at high speed until fluffily

▷ 1 cup almond cream (1 1/3 cups soaked almonds blended with 1/3 cup water until creamy)

▷ 1 cup plain soy or coconut yogurt, sweetened with vanilla liquid stevia (thinner)

DAL/DHAL (small, split dried Indian pulses) – 1 cup

▷ 1 cup yellow split peas or yellow lentils for Bengal gram, *channa dal, matar dal, tur/toor dal,* or *moong dal* (less creamy; requires longer cooking time and a bit more water)

▷ 1 cup red/salmon lentils (for *arhar dal, tuvar dal,* or *masoor/masur dal*)

▷ 1 cup Beluga lentils (for *mash* or *urd/urad/urid dal*)

▷ 1 cup coarsely ground chickpeas (for *channa dal*)

DANDELION GREENS/LEAVES, CULTIVATED – 8 ounces

▷ 8 ounces wild young dandelion leaves/*Taraxacum officinale*

▷ 8 ounces arugula, escarole, watercress, or nasturtium leaves

▷ 8 ounces young, tender wild chicory leaves/*Cichorium intybus*)

▷ 8 ounces young cat's ear leaves/*Hypochaeris radicata* (fuzzy texture; best boiled or blended in a smoothie)

▷ 8 ounces orange greens (handful of orange seeds scatted in the spring on pesticide-free ground and harvested when finger-length)

DASHEEN *See TARO ROOT*

DASHI/ICHIBAN DASHI/NIBAN DASHI (Japanese cooking stock) – 1 cup

▷ 1/4 teaspoon instant dashi granules, such as *hon-dashi* or *dashi-no-moto*, dissolved in 1 cup hot water (*hon-dashi* contains salt; *dashi-no-moto* contains salt, and some contain MSG)

▷ 1/3 teaspoon liquid dashi concentrate, such as *katsuo dashi, tsuyu no moto,* or *shiro dashi,* dissolved in 1 cup hot water (contains a little salt)

☞ 1/3 teaspoon white soy sauce/*shiro shoyu* dissolved in 1 cup hot water

☞ 1 cup kelp stock (10 grams/1/3 ounce kombu soaked in 1 cup cold water for 8 to 12 hours)

☞ 1/2 cup each light vegetable and seafood stock

☞ 1 cup low-sodium or diluted chicken broth (if the recipe contains chicken)

DASHI CONCENTRATE/SHIRI DASHI – 1 tablespoon

☞ 1 tablespoon white soy sauce/*shir shoyu*

DASHI, VEGETARIAN/KOMBU DASHI/SHOJIN DASHI (Japanese cooking stock) – 1 cup

☞ 2 to 3 small squares of kombu/kelp and 1 dried shiitake mushroom soaked in 1 cup cold water for 30 to 60 minutes, then simmered for 10 to 15 minutes

☞ 1 cup low-sodium vegetable stock

DATE HONEY/SILAN/DEVASH (Israeli sweetener) *See DATE MOLASSES*

DATE MOLASSES/DATE SYRUP/DIBIS TAMAR (Middle Eastern thick sweetener) – 1 cup

☞ 1 cup Middle Eastern grape syrup (*dibs/pekmez*) or carob syrup (*harnup pekmezi*)

☞ 1 cup Italian grape syrup (*vino cotto*) or fig syrup (*miele di fichi/ cotto di fichi*)

☞ 2/3 cup strong-flavored dark honey, such as buckwheat, chestnut, linden, or sage

☞ 1 cup grade A dark, robust pure maple syrup

☞ 1/2 cup dark molasses or treacle plus 1/2 cup light-colored corn syrup

Make Your Own Simmer 8 ounces fresh pitted Medjool dates in 2 cups water until the mixture is thick and syrupy, about 1 hour;

let cool then process in a blender or food processor until smooth. Store, refrigerated, for up to 2 weeks.

DATE-PALM JAGGERY, LIQUID/JHOLA GUR (Indian sweetener) – 1/4 cup
- 1/4 cup coconut nectar or maple syrup
- 1/4 cup grated cane jaggery or other palm sugar
- 1/4 cup dark brown or maple sugar, moistened to a coarse paste with 1 teaspoon light molasses

DATE PASTE (thick natural sweetener) – 1 1/2 cups
Make Your Own Soak 1 pound fresh pitted Medjool dates in 1 cup warm water for 8 to 10 hours; then process to a smooth paste in a blender or food processor. Store, refrigerated, for up to 2 weeks.
Or
Simmer 1 pound chopped pitted dates with 1/2 cup water gently until the water evaporates and the dates become a soft paste. Store, refrigerated, for up to 2 weeks

DATE SUGAR (dehydrated ground dates) – 1 cup
- 1 1/3 cups light brown sugar
- 1 cup granulated sugar

DATE SYRUP See DATE MOLASSES

DATES, SEMI-SOFT (Deglet Noor, Thoori, Zahidi) – 1 cup
- 1 cup figs, prunes, or jumbo Thompson seedless raisins

DATES, SOFT (Barhi, Halawi, Hadrawi, Medjool) – 1 cup
- 1 cup semi-soft dates, soaked in boiling water until softened, about 60 minutes; drained; and blotted dry
- 3/4 cup date paste (for smoothies)

DATIL PEPPER (small hot yellow chile) – 1
- 1 red habañero or Scotch bonnet chile

DE ÁRBOL CHILE/BIRD'S BEAK CHILE/RAT'S-TAIL CHILE (small red chile) – 1

- ☞ 1 dried Thai, cayenne, or serrano chile
- ☞ 1/4 teaspoon Thai, de árbol, or other crushed red chile/pepper flakes
- ☞ 1/8 teaspoon Thai or de árbol chile powder, or ground cayenne pepper
- ☞ 1/2 teaspoon sambal oelek

DELICATA/BOHEMIAN SQUASH (small yellow-fleshed winter squash) – 1 pound

- ☞ 1 pound sweet dumpling squash (stronger flavor; peeling unnecessary when small)
- ☞ 1 1/4 pounds butternut, buttercup, or autumn cup squash (less moist; peeling necessary)
- ☞ 1 pound sweet potatoes or 2 pounds mini pumpkins (peeling necessary)

DELI RYE FLAVOR (flavoring agent for rye bread) – 1/2 teaspoon

- ☞ 1 tablespoon caraway seeds, ground in a spice/coffee grinder; reduce the flour in the recipe by 1 tablespoon
- ☞ 1 tablespoon cider vinegar added to the starter liquid; or 1 tablespoon dill pickle brine (from a jar of pickles) added to the recipe's liquid ingredients; reduce the liquid in the recipe by 1 tablespoon (To further enhance the loaf's flavor, toast the rye flour on a parchment-lined baking sheet in a preheated 350°F oven for about 15 minutes, stirring every 5 minutes.)

DENDÊ /RED PALM OIL See PALM OIL, RED

DESSERT SHELLS (small pastry cases for holding cold or frozen dessert items) – 1 dozen

- ☞ 1 dozen chocolate cups (Paint cupcake liners with melted dark chocolate, chill until firm, then gently peel the paper off.)

- ⮊ 1 dozen chocolate shells (Line the inside of small scallop shells tightly with foil, then paint the foil with melted dark chocolate to form a smooth, thick coating. Chill until firm, then gently peel the foil off and repair any cracks.)
- ⮊ 1 dozen wafer cups (Press freshly baked wafer cookies, such as brandy snaps, lace cookies, or tuiles, over inverted custard cups, juice glasses, or muffin cups while still warm, and then remove when cool.)
- ⮊ 1 dozen gyoza cups (Brush gyoza wrappers on both sides with 1 to 2 teaspoons each water, honey, and vegetable oil. Press each wrapper into a muffin cup and bake at 375°F until golden, about 12 minutes. Cool and remove.)
- ⮊ 2 dozen wonton cups (Brush wonton wrappers with melted butter and press into muffin cups (or over inverted cups), then bake at 375°F until golden brown, 7 to 9 minutes.)
- ⮊ 1 dozen marshmallow–crisped rice cups (Mold freshly made crisped rice treat mixture over inverted muffin cups or tart shells; remove when cool.)
- ⮊ 1 dozen thin, hollowed out shortcakes
- ⮊ 1 dozen flat-bottomed ice cream wafer cones

DEXTROSE (finely textured glucose) – 1 tablespoon See also
GLUCOSE/GLUCOSE SYUP
- ⮊ 2 teaspoons granulated cane sugar

DHANIA JEERA POWDER (Indian spice blend) – 1 tablespoon
- ⮊ 2 teaspoons roasted ground coriander and 1 teaspoon roasted ground cumin

DIASTATIC MALT POWDER See MALT POWDER, DIASTATIC

DIBS (Middle Eastern thick sweet syrup) See GRAPE MOLASSES

DIGESTIVE/WHEATMEAL BISCUITS (British wheatmeal cookies) – 1 pound
- ⮊ 1 cup graham crackers (sweeter)

DILL, FRESH – 1 tablespoon minced
- 1 teaspoon dried dill weed or dill seeds (or more to taste)
- 1/2 teaspoon dill pollen
- 1 1/2 teaspoons each chopped fresh tarragon and fresh Italian or curly parsley
- Fresh fennel fronds/leafy tops (for decoration)

DILL POLLEN – 1 tablespoon
- Dried dill blossoms (shake out the pollen to measure 1 tablespoon); or dry dill flower heads upside down in a paper bag (the pollen will fall out)
- 1 1/2 tablespoons dried dill seeds, finely ground with a mortar and pestle or a spice/coffee grinder

DILL SEED – 1 tablespoon
- 2 to 3 fresh flowering dill heads
- 3 to 4 fresh dill fronds
- 1/2 teaspoon dill pollen
- 2 teaspoons caraway seeds plus 1/2 teaspoon celery salt; reduce the salt in the recipe by 1/2 teaspoon
- 1 1/2 teaspoons each caraway seeds and celery seeds

DIPPING SAUCE See ASIAN DIPPING SAUCE; CHINESE DIPPING SAUCE; KOREAN SESAME PASTE DIPPING SAUCE; PEANUT DIPPING SAUCE; TEMPURA DIPPING SAUCE; THAI DIPPING SAUCE; VIETNAMESE DIPPING SAUCE

DISTILLED WHITE VINEGAR – 1 tablespoon for flavoring
- 1 tablespoon lemon or lime juice
- 1 1/2 tablespoons dry white wine or dry vermouth
- 1 to 2 teaspoons vinegar powder (use dry in cooking or spice rubs)
- 1 tablespoon mango powder (for curries and chutneys)
- 1 1/2 teaspoons tamarind concentrate (for curries and chutneys)

DISTILLED WHITE VINEGAR – 1 cup for pickling and preserving
- 1 cup cider vinegar, white wine vinegar, colorless malt vinegar, or any vinegar with at least 5% acidity level
- 1 tablespoon citric acid powder dissolved in 1 cup boiled water (approximates 6% acidity level)

DOENJANG See KOREAN SOYBEAN PASTE

DOLCE DE LEITE See CARAMEL PASTE

DOUGHNUTS – 1 dozen
Make Your Own Using a 1-inch round cutter, punch a hole from the middle of 1 dozen biscuits from tubed refrigerated biscuit dough. Fry, a few at a time, in 350°F oil until golden, 2 to 3 minutes each side; drain on paper towels, then toss with cinnamon sugar. (Fry the doughnut holes about 1 minute per side.)

DOUGLAS FIR NEEDLES (aromatic base for oven roasting)
- Douglas fir organic hydrosol (food-safe essential oil) sprayed very lightly on food right before serving

DRY RUB See BARBECUE SEASONING/DRY RUB

DUBLIN BAY PRAWNS/LANGOUSTINES/ NORWAY LOBSTERS/ SCAMPI – 1 pound
- 1 pound super-colossal/extra-jumbo (U-12) shrimp
- 1 pound crayfish/crawfish
- 1 pound spiny rock lobster or small Maine lobster
- 1 pound monkfish tail meat, cut in pieces

DUCK EGG, LARGE – 1 (about 3 ounces)
- 1 extra-large or jumbo hen egg, or 2 medium hen eggs

DUCK FAT, RENDERED – 1 tablespoon
- 1 tablespoon rendered goose fat, pork fat, tallow, or leaf lard

☞ 1 tablespoon fruity olive oil, or 1 1/2 teaspoons each olive oil and unsalted butter

DUCK, LONG ISLAND/PEKING – 1 pound
☞ 1 pound female Muscovy duck (darker and tastier meat)
☞ 1 pound farm-raised Mallard, or wild duck (richer-tasting and less fatty)
☞ 1 pound gosling/goose
☞ 1 pound squab

DUCK SAUCE/SUÀN MÉI JIÀNG (Chinese condiment) – 1/4 cup
☞ 1/4 cup plum sauce thinned with a little orange juice See PLUM SAUCE

DULCE DE LECHE See CARAMEL PASTE

DULSE POWDER (red seaweed thickening agent) – 1/4 cup
☞ 2 (6-inch) dulse sheets, or 1/2 cup tightly packed dulse flakes, crumbled and ground to a powder

DUMPLING DOUGH – 8 ounces
☞ 8 ounces refrigerated buttermilk biscuit dough

DUTCH DARK APPLE SYRUP See APPELSTROOP

DUTCH DARK THICK SYRUP See KEUKENSTROOP

DUTCH THICK SWEET SYRUP See STROOP

DYES, NATURAL FOOD See FOOD COLORING, NATURAL

E

EDAM (Dutch semifirm cheese) 1 ounce
- 1 ounce Edamer, Cheedham, Emek, Fontina D'Aosta, Gilboa, Gouda, Mimolette, Molbo, or Tulare Cannonball

EDAMAME, FRESH OR FROZEN (young green soybeans) – 1 pound
- 1 pound fresh chickpeas in the pod (steam or boil the 1-inch pods, then eat the single chickpea like edamame)
- 1 pound young fresh garden peas in the pod (steam or boil, then eat the peas like edamame)
- 1 pound smaller, younger fava beans in the pod (steam or grill, then eat the beans like edamame)

EDAMAME, SHELLED AND COOKED, FRESH OR FROZEN – 8 ounces
- 8 ounces blanched and peeled small fava beans
- 8 ounces cooked baby lima beans
- 8 ounces cooked green peas
- 8 ounces chopped cooked green beans

EGGPLANT/AUBERGINE, PURPLE GLOBE – 1 pound (1 medium)
- 1 pound (3 to 4) Italian, Chinese, or Japanese eggplants (milder; tenderer; less seedy)
- 1 pound (5 to 10) Fairy Tale eggplants
- 1 pound portobello mushroom caps (scrape off the gills with a table knife)
- 1 pound large zucchini (more watery)

EGGPLANT, THAI PEA/MAKHUA PHUONG (pea-size green eggplants) – 1 pound
- 1 pound Thai green apple eggplants/makhua khum (golf-ball size)

cut into pieces (soak in acidulated water before adding to the dish)
⮞ 1 pound frozen peas (added toward the end of cooking)

EGGPLANT, WHITE – 1 pound
⮞ 1 pound Japanese eggplants

EGG REPLACER, POWDERED – 2 teaspoons (mixed with 3 tablespoons water for baking)
⮞ 3 tablespoons liquid egg substitute
⮞ 1/4 cup liquid pasteurized egg
⮞ 1 whole fresh egg
⮞ 2 fresh egg whites

EGG ROLL WRAPPERS – 1 pound
⮞ 1 pound lumpia wrappers
⮞ 1 pound wonton or gyoza wrappers (smaller)
⮞ 1 pound empanada wrappers (round)
⮞ 1 pound thin fresh pasta sheets, cut to size
⮞ 1 pound Vietnamese spring roll wrappers, rice paper, or fresh or dried bean curd skins/yuba sheets, cut to size (thinner, more delicate; gluten-free)

Make Your Own Beat together 1 cup all-purpose flour, 2 cups water, and 2 eggs. Spoon 1 tablespoon batter at a time into a 6-inch non-stick skillet, spreading it out, and cook over medium-low heat until set on both sides, making thin flexible pale pancakes. Cover with a damp cloth until ready to use.

EGG SUBSTITUTE, LIQUID – 3 tablespoons
⮞ 1 egg white, lightly beaten
⮞ 2 teaspoons powdered egg replacer mixed with 3 tablespoons water

EGG WASH (solution brushed on pastry to seal edges, or add sheen, or help toppings adhere) – 2 tablespoons
⮞ 2 tablespoons undiluted evaporated milk
⮞ 1 tablespoons tapioca starch mixed with 2 tablespoons cold water

- 1 tablespoon potato starch mixed with 2 tablespoons warm water
- 1 tablespoon cornstarch mixed with 2 tablespoons cold water
- 1- or 2-second spritz of egg-free finishing spray, such as Quick Shine or Bake Sheen

EGG WHITE, LARGE FRESH – 1 (1 ounce/2 tablespoons/1 fluid ounce)

- 2 tablespoons (1 ounce) thawed frozen egg white
- 3 tablespoons pasteurized liquid egg whites, such as AllWhites or Whippin Whites; or pasteurized packaged organic, kosher egg whites, such as Eggology (ideal for uncooked or lightly cooked preparations; takes longer to whip into foam or peaks)
- 1 tablespoon 100% dried/dehydrated packaged egg whites, such as Just Whites, dissolved in 2 tablespoons warm water (whips up faster than fresh whites)
- 1 tablespoon meringue powder dissolved in 2 tablespoons water (contains a small amount of sugar)
- 1 tablespoon plain agar powder whisked with 2 tablespoons water, chilled for 15 minutes, then whisked again before using
- 2 tablespoons aquafaba (liquid from canned chickpeas)
- 2 teaspoons ground golden flaxseed or white chia seeds soaked in 2 tablespoons water until slightly thickened, 5 to 10 minutes (for sealing the edges of dough or helping toppings adhere) *See also EGG WASH*

EGG WHITE, PASTEURIZED LIQUID – 3 tablespoons

- 1 fresh egg white (for cooking, baking, and Italian meringue topping)

EGG, WHOLE LARGE FRESH – 1 (1.6 ounces/3 1/4 tablespoons/1 1/2 fluid ounces)

- 3 1/2 tablespoons thawed frozen whole egg
- 2 egg whites plus 1 teaspoon vegetable oil
- 1 egg white, 1 teaspoon vegetable oil, and 4 teaspoons water (for pancakes and moist cookies increase oil in the recipe to 1 tablespoon and omit the water)

- 2 large egg yolks plus 1 tablespoon cold water (omit the water for sauces, custards, or cream pie fillings)
- 3 tablespoons liquid egg replacement, such as Better'n Eggs or Eggbeaters
- 2 teaspoons powdered egg replacement, such as Ener-G Egg Replacer, plus 2 tablespoons water (for cookies)
- 2 1/2 tablespoons freeze-dried egg powder (powdered whole eggs) plus 2 1/2 tablespoons warm water for baking, or 4 tablespoons for scrambling (stir until smooth, or add egg powder to dry ingredients and water to other liquid called for in the recipe; use right away)
- 3 tablespoons aquafaba (liquid from canned chickpeas)
- 1/4 cup (2 ounces) soft silken tofu, blotted dry and puréed until smooth (increase baking powder by 1/4 teaspoon and increase the cooking time slightly; best for brownies, coffee cakes, and quick breads)
- 2 ounces plain yogurt (whole or low-fat) mixed with 1/2 teaspoon vegetable oil (increase the cooking time slightly; best for coffee cakes, quick breads, and muffins)
- 1 tablespoon golden flaxseed meal, chia seeds, or hulled hemp seeds soaked in 3 tablespoons hot water until slightly thickened, 10 to 15 minutes, stirring occasionally (or microwaved on High until mixture bubbles and thickens slightly); cooled to room temperature; (increase baking powder in the recipe by 1/8 teaspoon; best for brownies, cookies, coffee cakes, and quick breads)
- 3 tablespoons undiluted evaporated milk, cream, or soymilk creamers (for egg wash, glazing, breading)
- 2 tablespoons creamy style salad dressing, mayonnaise, or plain yogurt whisked with 1/2 tablespoon each vegetable oil and water (for breading)
- 2 tablespoons tapioca starch plus 1 tablespoon water (for sealing the edges of dough or helping toppings adhere)

EGG, WHOLE LARGE – 1 (for cakes mostly, not including chiffon, sponge, or angel food cakes)
- 2 tablespoons mayonnaise (best for chocolate cake)

⮞ 1 teaspoon baking powder and 1 teaspoon cider or distilled vinegar (add baking powder to dry ingredients and vinegar to liquid; add at the last minute and bake immediately after mixing; to take the place of one egg only)

EGG, WHOLE LARGE, EQUIVALENTS
⮞ 1 large = 1 jumbo, 1 extra-large, 1 medium, 2 small
⮞ 2 large = 2 jumbo, 2 extra-large, 2 medium, 3 small
⮞ 3 large = 2 jumbo, 3 extra-large, 3 medium, 4 small
⮞ 4 large = 3 jumbo, 4 extra-large, 5 medium, 5 small
⮞ 5 large = 4 jumbo, 4 extra-large, 6 medium, 7 small
⮞ 6 large = 5 jumbo, 5 extra-large, 7 medium, 8 small

EGG YOLK, LARGE – 1 (0.6 ounce/1 1/4 tablespoons/1/2 fluid ounce)
⮞ 1 1/2 tablespoons thawed frozen egg yolk
⮞ 1 large whole egg as a substitute for 2 egg yolks
⮞ 1 1/2 teaspoons powdered non-egg product, such as Ener-G Egg Replacer, plus 1 tablespoon water
⮞ 2 tablespoons pasteurized liquid egg, such as Eggbeaters
⮞ 1 tablespoon Dijon mustard or mild liquid honey (for a vinaigrette emulsion)
⮞ 1 tablespoon aquafaba (canned chickpea liquid)
⮞ 1/4 teaspoon xanthan gum (for a vinaigrette emulsion)

EGGS, PASTEURIZED – 1 dozen
⮞ 1 dozen whole fresh eggs submerged in hot tap water (140°F) for 3 minutes before cracking and using (if not using immediately, chill them in ice water)

EGUSI SEED/EPUSI (West African flavoring and thickening agent) – 1 tablespoon
⮞ 1 tablespoon raw hull-less squash seeds or shelled pumpkin seeds (for shelled seeds)
⮞ 1 tablespoon Tahini/sesame paste, or mashed navy or pinto beans (for egusi paste)

☞ 2 teaspoons finely ground raw pumpkin or sesame seeds (for egu-si powder)

ELBOW MACARONI *See PASTA, TUBULAR, SHORT DRIED*

ELDERBERRY SYRUP – 1 tablespoon
☞ 1 tablespoon aged balsamic vinegar

EMERGO BEANS/SWEET WHITE RUNNER BEANS, DRIED – 1 cup
☞ 1 cup dried lima or cannellini beans (smaller)

EMMENTAL (Swiss semihard cheese) – 1 ounce:
☞ 1 ounce Beaufort, Bergkäse, Comté, Danbo, Erkentaler, Fontina Val d'Aosta, Gruyère, Hoch Ybrig, Jarlsberg, Maasdam, Mountaineer, Murbodner, Samsoe, Svenbo, Tarentaise, Texelaar, Vacherin Fribourgeois, or reduced-fat, lower-sodium Swiss-type cheese (such as Alpine Lace)
☞ 1 ounce Baby Swiss cheese (milder)

EMMER WHEAT *See FARRO*

EMPANADA DOUGH DISKS, FROZEN *See WRAPPERS FOR FOOD, PREPARED EDIBLE*

ENCHILADA SAUCE – 1 cup
☞ 1 (8-ounce) can tomato sauce (or 1 cup tomato puree) plus 2 teaspoons chili powder/seasoning

ENDIVE *See BELGIAN ENDIVE; CURLY ENDIVE*

ENGLISH PUDDING SPICE/BRITISH MIXED SPICE *See MIXED SPICE, SWEET*

ENO FRUIT SALT POWDER (Indian leavening agent) – 1 teaspoon
☞ 1 teaspoon baking soda

ENOKI MUSHROOMS/SNOW PUFF/ENOKITAKE – 1 bunch (6 ounces)
- 4 ounces canned enoki mushrooms, drained
- 6 to 7 ounces fresh oyster/shimeji or white cap/button mushrooms

EPAZOTE, FRESH (Mexican seasoning herb) – 1 sprig or 1 tablespoon chopped
- 2 frozen epazote sprigs (leaves only)
- 1 to 2 teaspoons dried epazote leaves, crumbled
- 3 fresh cilantro sprigs, and 1 small sprig fresh oregano (5 or 6 leaves)
- 1 tablespoon chopped fresh oregano leaves, or 1 teaspoon dried, preferably Mexican
- 1-inch piece of kombu/kelp (for digestive properties only)

ERBETTE (Italian tender, chard-like salad green) – 1 pound
- 1 pound baby spinach or loose-leaf lettuce

ESCAROLE – 1 pound
- 1 pound Belgian endive/witloof, curly endive, young dandelion greens, young mustard greens, or other spicy greens

ESPELETTE PEPPER See PIMENT d'ESPELETTE

ESPRESSO, BREWED – 1 (5-ounce) cup
- 4 tablespoons finely ground French roast coffee added to 6 ounces boiling water, steeped 5 minutes, then strained through a coffee filter or paper towel–lined funnel (Alternatively, brew regular coffee double (or triple) strength.)
- 2 to 4 teaspoons instant espresso granules or powder dissolved in 5 ounces boiling water

ESPRESSO EXTRACT OR POWDER – 1 teaspoon
- 1 1/2 teaspoons freeze-dried instant coffee finely ground to a powder

ETROG CITRON (Israeli large pithy yellow citrus) – 1
⇨ 1 fresh Buddha's hand/fingered citron, or pomelo
⇨ 1 or 2 large thick-skinned lemons (smaller and juicier)

EVAPORATED CANE JUICE (golden unrefined sugar crystals) See SUGAR, TURBINADO CANE

EVAPORATED MILK (6.6% butterfat) – 1 cup
⇨ 1 cup fat-free evaporated milk (0.5% butterfat)
⇨ 2 1/4 cups whole milk, simmered in a medium pan until reduced to 1 cup, about 20 minutes (be careful it does not boil over)
⇨ 1/2 cup powdered whole milk blended with 2/3 cup water
⇨ 1 cup half-and-half or light cream

EVAPORATED MILK, VEGAN – 1 cup
⇨ 1/2 cup soymilk powder blended with enough water to make 1 cup

EXPANDEX (modified tapioca food starch) – 1 teaspoon
⇨ 1 teaspoon xanthan gum
⇨ 1 1/4 teaspoons guar gum

F

FABES (Spanish extra-large white kidney beans) – 1 cup cooked dried beans
- 1 cup drained jarred fabes
- 1 cup cooked frozen butter beans
- 1 cup cooked dried butter beans or cannellini beans

FARINA, WHEAT *See SEMOLINA*

FARINHA *See GARI/GARRI/MANIOC MEAL/CASSAVA FLOUR/YUCA MEAL*

FARMER CHEESE/BAKER'S CHEESE/HOOP CHEESE/TOPFEN – 8 ounces
- 9 ounces large-curd dry cottage cheese, drained for 1 hour in a fine-mesh sieve set over a bowl in the refrigerator
- 10 ounces small-curd dry cottage cheese (not creamy) rubbed through a coarse-mesh sieve, or drained in a dampened cheese-cloth–lined sieve set over a bowl in the refrigerator

FAROFA/TOASTED YUCA FLOUR (Brazilian condiment) – 1 cup
- 1 cup coarse gari/toasted manioc meal/*farinha torrada*, sautéed with 3 tablespoons butter or oil until golden and fragrant, 2 to 4 minutes
- 1 cup finely ground whole-wheat breadcrumbs, toasted in a dry skillet until fragrant
- 1 cup coarse almond flour, toasted in a dry skillet until a few shades darker

FARRO/EMMER WHEAT, CRACKED – 1 cup
- 1 1/4 cups whole-grain farro chopped in a blender or food processor to a cracked wheat or steel-cut oats stage, 15 to 20 seconds; sift to remove any smaller particles

FARRO/EMMER WHEAT, WHOLE-GRAIN/FARRO MEDIO (Tuscan wheat grain similar to spelt) – 1 cup
- 1 cup semi-pearled farro, pearled farro, or cracked farro
- 2 cups pre-cooked, 10-minute farro, such as Arden Farms or Trader Joe's
- 1 cup cracked wheat or bulgur (less cooking time)
- 1 cup spelt berries, hulled/pot barley, wheat berries, Kamut berries, or triticale berries (longer cooking time)

FATBACK (fresh unsalted pork fat) – 4-ounces (1 cup finely chopped)
- 4 ounces fat trimmed from a pork roast (package and freeze until needed)
- 4 ounces Italian lardo, soaked in water to cover for 8 to 10 hours, then rinsed and blotted dry
- 4 ounces salt pork, slab bacon, or thick presliced bacon, blanched in boiling water for 40 to 60 seconds, then rinsed and blotted dry

FAVA BEANS/BROAD BEANS, FRESH YOUNG – 1 pound (1 to 1 1/2 cups shelled)
- 1 (15-ounce) can small fava beans, drained and rinsed
- 1 to 1 1/2 cups double-peeled frozen fava beans
- 1 to 1 1/2 cups fresh or frozen baby lima beans
- 1 pound small-seeded favas (faba/field beans; much starchier)
- 1/3 to 1/2 cup skinless dried favas or chickpeas cooked following package directions

FAVA LEAVES See SPINACH; CHARD

FEIJOA/PINEAPPLE GUAVA – 1 medium
- 1 medium kiwi fruit

FENNEL, BULB/FLORENCE FENNEL/FINOCCHIO – 1 pound
- 1 pound chopped celery cooked with a few crushed fennel seeds
- 1 pound scraped and chopped udo

FENNEL FRONDS/LEAFY TOPS/GREENS – 1 cup
- 1 cup bronze fennel fronds (milder aroma and flavor)
- 1 cup wild fennel fronds/*Foeniculum vulgare*
- 1/3 cup dried fennel fronds/*Alholva* soaked in warm water until softened
- 1 cup fresh dill, chervil leaves, or parsley

FENNEL POLLEN/FINOCCHIETTO (Italian and Sicilian seasoning) – 1 tablespoon
- Dried wild fennel blossoms (shake out the pollen to measure 1 tablespoon), or fennel flower heads placed upside down in a paper bag to dry (the pollen will fall out)
- 2 teaspoons dried fennel seeds, lightly toasted in a dry skillet and then ground with a mortar and pestle or a spice/coffee grinder

FENNEL SEEDS, DRIED – 1 teaspoon whole seeds
- 1 scant teaspoon mature wild black fennel seeds/*Foeniculum vulgare* (more intense flavor)
- 1 1/2 teaspoons fresh green fennel seeds or 1 tablespoon minced fresh fennel leaves
- 1/2 teaspoon ground fennel seeds
- 1 scant teaspoon anise seeds
- 3/4 teaspoon caraway or dill seeds

FENNEL STALKS – 4 ounces
- 4 ounces thinly sliced fennel bulb or Swiss chard stems plus 1 to 2 teaspoons crushed fennel seeds

FENNEL, WILD/FOENICULUM VULGARE (Sicilian seasoning) – 1 cup chopped fronds (1 small bunch)
- 1 cup regular chopped fennel fronds plus 1 or 2 fennel seeds

☞ 1 cup chopped dill plus 2 teaspoons ground fennel seeds
☞ 1 finely chopped fennel bulb plus 1/3 cup snipped fresh dill

FENUGREEK LEAVES/METHI KA SAAG /METHI BHAJI/SHANBALILEH/ KASURI METHI, FRESH OR FROZEN (Indian and Pakistani seasoning) – 1 cup

☞ 1 cup fresh Chinese celery leaves, regular celery leaves, chrysan-themum greens/*Chrysanthemum coronariumi,* baby arugula, tat-soi, or watercress (for salad)
☞ 1 cup fresh curry leaves or baby spinach leaves (for cooked dishes; different flavor)

FENUGREEK LEAVES, DRIED/KASURI METHI (Indian and Pakistani seasoning) – 1 tablespoon

☞ 1 teaspoon fenugreek powder; or a small pinch ground roasted fenugreek seeds (for curries; sprinkle over the dish just before serving)

FENUGREEK POWDER (Indian and Pakistani seasoning) – 1 teaspoon

☞ 1 tablespoon dried fenugreek leaves crushed through a medi-um-mesh sieve; discard stem pieces

FENUGREEK SEEDS/METHI KA BEEJ/METHI DANA (Indian curry flavoring) – 1 tablespoon whole seeds

☞ 1 3/4 tablespoons ground fenugreek seeds
☞ 2 teaspoons brown mustard seeds and 1 teaspoon celery seeds

FERMENTED BLACK BEANS/FERMENTED BLACK SOYBEANS/DOW SEE/DOUCHI (Chinese seasoning) – 1 tablespoon

☞ 1 1/2 tablespoons fermented black bean paste/*douchi jiang*
☞ 1 to 2 tablespoons Japanese dark miso, such as inaka or hatcho
☞ 1 to 2 tablespoons mashed salt-packed capers
☞ 2 to 3 tablespoons dark soy sauce (usually labeled all-purpose)

FERMENTED BLACK GARLIC – 1 whole head/bulb (1/2 ounce)
- 1 well-roasted whole garlic head/bulb plus a little balsamic vinegar or molasses
- 1 to 1 1/2 teaspoons fermented black garlic powder plus 2 to 2 1/2 teaspoon water

FERMENTED DRIED LOCUST BEAN/NETETOU/SUMBALA (Senegalese seasoning) – 1 tablespoon
- 1 tablespoon Chinese fermented black beans/*dow see*

FERMENTED SOYBEAN PASTE/TUA NAO PBUH/TAO JIAO (South Asian flavoring agent) – 1 tablespoon *See also MISO*
- 1 1/2 teaspoons Japanese dark miso, such as *hatcho*, or Korean soybean paste/*doenjang*
- 2 teaspoons Chinese black bean sauce/*douchi jiang* or fermented soybeans/*douchi*

FERMENTED SOYBEAN SAUCE/SALTED SOYBEANS/TAUCHEO/TAUEO (Indonesian and Malaysian seasoning) – 1 tablespoon
- 1 tablespoon Thai soybean paste/fermented soybeans/*tao jiao*

FERMENTED TOASTED SOYBEAN DISK/TUA NAO KHAAP (South Asian seasoning) – 1 tablespoon chopped or crumbled disk
- 1 tablespoon toasted chickpea flour plus 1 teaspoon Japanese brown miso paste
- 2 tablespoons Thai soybean paste/fermented soybean/*tao jiao*

FIDDLEHEAD FERNS/OSTRICH FERNS/KOSARI/WARABI/ZENMAI (young, unfurled ostrich sprouts) – 1 pound fresh or frozen
- 1 pound pencil-thin fresh asparagus or haricots verts, blanched in boiling water until crisp-tender, then refreshed in ice water

FIDEOS (thin pasta pieces or coiled nests) – 1 pound *See PASTA, THIN STRAND OR ROD*
- 1 pound angel hair, capellini, fedelini, or thin spaghettini broken into 1/2- to 1-inch lengths

FIG LEAVES (food wrappers) – 1 dozen *See also WRAPPERS FOR FOOD, VEGETABLE*
- ␥ 1 dozen grape leaves (fresh, jarred, or canned)

FIGS, DRIED – 1 pound
- ␥ 1 pound pitted dried dates or prunes
- ␥ 1 pound dried apricots or mulberries

FIGS, FRESH SMYRNA/CALIMYRNA – 1 pound
- ␥ 1 pound fresh Kadota or Sierra figs
- ␥ 1 pound fresh Brown Turkey or Black Mission figs (reduce the amount of sugar called for in the recipe)
- ␥ 1 cup dried Calimyrna figs, soaked in boiling hot water until softened, about 15 minutes
- ␥ 1 pound pitted prunes plumped in cool water, if necessary (reduce the amount of sugar called for in the recipe)

FIG SYRUP/MIELE DI FICHI/COTTO DI FICHI (Italian dark, thick sweetener) – 3/4 cup
- ␥ 3/4 cup grape molasses/*mosto cotto* or dark strong-tasting honey
Make Your Own Stem and halve 1 pound dried figs. Simmer in 4 cups water until soft and reduced by half. Strain, then simmer the syrup until thickened and dark.

FIG VINEGAR/BLACK FIG VINEGAR – 1/4 cup
- ␥ 1/4 cup balsamic vinegar

FILÉ POWDER/GUMBO FILÉ/POWDERED SASSAFRAS LEAVES (thickening and flavoring agent) – 1 tablespoon
- ␥ 1/2 to 1 teaspoon each ground anise seeds, ground cloves, and ground ginger (for flavoring only)
- ␥ 2 cups sliced fresh okra; or 1 (10-ounce) package sliced frozen okra, or whole frozen okra cut into 1/4-inch rounds (cook okra in gumbo for thickening, adding frozen okra without thawing)

☞ 1 or more tablespoons mallow powder (tender young mallow leaves/*Malva neglecta* dried then ground to a powder; add at the end for thickening)
☞ 2 teaspoons cornstarch or potato starch mixed with 1 tablespoon cold water (add at the end for thickening only)

FILIPINO DIPPING SAUCE/TOYOMANSI See SOY SAUCE, FILIPINO KALAMANSI/TOYOMANSI

FILO See PHYLLO/FILO

FINES HERBES (French seasoning blend) – 1 heaping tablespoon
☞ 1 teaspoon each finely chopped fresh parsley, chives, and chervil, plus 1/4 teaspoon chopped French tarragon

FINGER LIME See LIME, AUSTRALIAN FINGER, PULP/JUICE VESICLES

FINGERROOT/CHINESE KEYS/CHINESE GINGER/KRACHAI, FRESH (Southeast Asian seasoning) – 1-inch piece (1 tablespoon peeled and finely chopped)
☞ 2 teaspoons brined fingerroot slivers, well drained and rinsed
☞ 1 1/2 tablespoons jarred galanga/*Ka Chai* (rinse to remove brine, then finely chop)
☞ 1 tablespoon finely chopped fresh greater galangal
☞ 1 1/2 teaspoons kencur powder (ground *Kaempferia galanga*)
☞ 2 scant teaspoons finely chopped fresh young ginger

FINNAN HADDOCK/FINNAN HADDIE (Scottish cold-smoked haddock) – 1 pound
☞ 1 pound Glasgow pales (smaller lightly smoked version)
☞ 1 pound Arbroath smokies/pinwiddies (hot smoked, ready-to-eat smaller version; split when ready to serve)
☞ 1 pound brined smoked cod

☞ 1 pound cold-smoked bluefish, mackerel, pollock, sturgeon, or whiting

FISH BATTER MIX – 2/3 cup
Make Your Own Mix 1 cup self-rising flour with 3/4 cup cold water until almost smooth but with a few lumps.
Or
Mix 1 cup cake or pastry flour, 1/2 teaspoon kosher salt, and 8 to 10 ounces chilled light beer/pale lager, or club soda until almost smooth but with a few lumps.

FISH, FATTY (more than 6% of fat by weight) – 1 pound
☞ 1 pound Arctic char, bonito, black cod/sablefish/sable, herring, mackerel, pilchard, pompano, salmon, sardine, shad, smelt, sturgeon, trout (rainbow and lake), yellowtail, or whitebait

FISH FLAKES, DRIED/KATSUOBUSHI (Japanese dried bonito/ skipjack tuna flakes) – 1 loosely packed cup See also DASHI
☞ 1 cup dried mackerel flakes/*sababushi* (for soups and stocks; less expensive)
☞ 1 cup bonito thread shavings/*ito-kezuri katsuo* (for garnish on salads and tofu)
☞ 1 cup dried baby sardines or anchovies/*iniko/niboshi*, dry-roasted until very crisp, 20 minutes, then cooled and ground (stronger tasting; use according to taste)
☞ 1 cup ready-to-use dried baby anchovies or tiny whitebait/*ikan teri/ikan bilis/jiang yu zi*, rinsed and lightly pounded (stronger; use according to taste)
☞ 1 *ikan bilis* stock cube, or part thereof (for soups and stocks)

FISH FRY MIX – 1 cup
☞ 1/2 cup yellow cornmeal mixed with 1/2 cup yellow corn flour (fine-ground yellow cornmeal ground to a powder in a blender, or in small batches in a spice/coffee grinder)

FISH, LEAN (less than 2% fat by weight; some belong to the same, or related species, but identified or known by different names) – 1 pound

▸ 1 pound branzino/Mediterranean sea bass, barramundi, bass (white sea and black sea), Cape capensis, brill, catfish, char, cod (scrod), croaker/drum, cusk, flatfish, flounder, fluke, grouper, haddock, hake, halibut (Atlantic, California, Pacific), John Dory, moi, monkfish tail, orange roughy, perch, pike, pickerel, plaice, pollock/coley, porgy/sea bream/dorade, redfish/red drum, red snapper, rockfish, sand dab, sculpin, sea bass, shark, skate, sole (Dover, lemon, petrale, Rex), tautog/blackfish, tilapia, tilefish, turbot, walleye, or whiting

FISH MINT/FISH SCALE MINT/RAU DIEP CA/VAP CA (Vietnamese seasoning) – 1 ounce

▸ 1 ounce fresh spearmint, young sorrel, lemon basil, or Thai basil
▸ 1 ounce unsprayed variegated chameleon plant/*Houttuynia cordata* (use the top leaves)

FISH, MODERATELY FATTY (between 2% and 6% fat by weight) – 1 pound

▸ 1 pound barracuda, bluefish, carp, mahimahi/dorado, mullet, striped bass, swordfish, tuna, yellowtail, and whitefish

FISH PASTE, FERMENTED *See ASIAN FISH PASTE, FERMENTED*

FISH SAUCE/NAM PLA/NUOC NAM/PATIS/SHOTTSURU/TUK TREY (Southeast Asian salty liquid seasoning) – 1 tablespoon

▸ 1 tablespoon Vietnamese vegetarian fish sauce/*nuoc mam an chay*
▸ 1 tablespoon Japanese *ayu* sweet fish sauce (more delicate) or *ishiri* fermented squid sauce (stronger flavor)
▸ 1 tablespoon Italian anchovy sauce/syrup/*colatura di alici*, or Vietnamese anchovy sauce/*mam nem*
▸ 2 to 3 teaspoons Thai unfiltered fish sauce/*pla ra* or *pla ra* powder (stronger flavor)

- 2 teaspoons anchovy paste mixed with 1/2 teaspoon soy sauce or Maggi Seasoning
- 1 1/2 teaspoons each Golden Mountain Seasoning sauce and soy sauce
- 1 tablespoon soy sauce and 1 finely minced anchovy fillet
- 2 tablespoons white or Thai soy sauce
- 1/4 teaspoon salt (or to taste)

FISH SAUCE, VEGETARIAN – 1/4 cup
- 1/4 cup coconut aminos plus 1 teaspoon sea salt

Make Your Own Break 1 small dried shiitake mushroom into pieces and combine with 1/2 cup water plus 1 1/2 teaspoons each sea salt and soy sauce. Simmer until reduced by half. Strain, cool, and store refrigerated for up to 3 weeks.

FISH STOCK See STOCK, FISH/FUMET

FISH, WHOLE – 1 (8 ounces to 3 pounds)
- 1 Arctic char, barramundi, branzino/Mediterranean bass, black bass, butterfish/pomfret, carp, small catfish, dorade/porgy/sea bream, flounder, gray mullet (striped and silver), grouper, herring, lake perch, mackerel, plaice, pompano/yellowtail, rainbow trout, rockfish, sea bass, scrod, snapper, striped bass, golden or black tilapia

FIVE-SPICE MIX, INDIAN See BENGALI FIVE-SPICE MIX

FIVE-SPICE POWDER, CHINESE See CHINESE FIVE-SPICE POWDER

FLAVOR ENHANCERS See UMAMI

FLAX OIL – 1 cup
- 1 cup hemp oil

FLAXSEED MEAL/FLAX MEAL – 1 cup for baking
- 3/4 cup chia seed meal/chia powder

☞ 1 cup walnut meal (lacks gelatinous property)

☞ 1 cup almond meal, pecan meal, pumpkin seed meal, sesame seed meal, or sunflower seed meal (lacks omega-3s and gelatinous property)

FLAXSEEDS (brown or golden) – 1 cup

☞ 1 cup chia, salba, or hemp seeds

☞ 1 cup sesame seeds (lacks omega-3s and gelatinous property)

FLEUR DE SEL DE GUÉRANDE (fine-grained finishing salt from Brittany) – 1 teaspoon

☞ 1 teaspoon French *fleur de sel de Camargue* (from the Mediterranean coast) or *fleur de sel Ile de Ré* (from the Atlantic coast)

☞ 1 1/2 teaspoons crystalline-flake sea salt, such as Maldon, Cornish, or Halen Môn (finishing salt)

☞ 1 teaspoon coarse-grain moist French sea salt/*sel gris Marin/sel gris de Guérande,* moist Baja sea salt, Korean sea salt, or Maine sea salt

☞ 3/4 teaspoon finely ground refined sea salt such as Baja, Atlantic, or Mediterranean

FLOUR, ALL-PURPOSE BLEACHED OR UNBLEACHED (9.5 to 11.7% protein) – 1 cup unsifted for baking

☞ 1 cup plus 3 tablespoons cake flour (for cakes, biscuits, or rich short pastry; not for quick breads or cookies)

☞ 1 cup plus 1 tablespoon unbleached pastry flour (for cakes, biscuits, quick breads, or regular pastry)

☞ 1 cup instantized/quick-mixing flour, such as Wondra (for sponge-type cakes, flaky pastry, puff pastry, crepes, or breading)

☞ 1 cup bread flour (for strudel, phyllo, or yeast-raised breads; increase the liquid and kneading time as needed)

☞ 1 cup self-rising flour (for biscuits and pancakes; omit any baking powder, baking soda, or salt in the recipe)

☞ 1 cup gluten-free all-purpose flour blend (for cakes and quick breads; will have a drier consistency; best used with buttermilk or yogurt)

☞ 1/2 cup finely ground whole-wheat flour (or whole-wheat flour ground fine in a blender, then sifted to remove any coarse particles) plus 1/2 cup cake flour (for cookies, full-bodied cakes, and quick breads; avoid overmixing)

▻ 1 cup Italian-style *Tipo 00* flour (for lighter pasta, cakes, or Italian flatbreads; more finely milled)

▻ 1 cup light spelt flour or sprouted spelt flour (if using sprouted flour, increase the baking powder in the recipe by 1/4 teaspoon, reduce the liquid in the recipe by 1 tablespoon and avoid overmixing)

▻ 1 cup whole-wheat pastry flour or soft winter whole-wheat flour with 9 to 11% protein; (for heartier, full-bodied cakes, quick breads, cookies, or pastry; increase the liquid in the recipe by 2 tablespoons)

▻ 1/2 cup whole-wheat pastry flour and 1/2 cup light buckwheat flour (for pancakes, waffles, blintzes, crepes, or pasta; increase the liquid in the recipe by 2 tablespoons and avoid overmixing)

▻ 1 cup commercial premixed flour blend, such as Williams Sonoma Cup4Cup or Bob's Red Mill 1 to 1 Baking Flour (for gluten-free applications)

▻ 1 cup white rice flour or superfine brown rice flour; or half rice flour and half chestnut or chickpea flour (for crepes, pancakes, or fritters; increase the liquid in the recipe by 1 to 2 tablespoons)

▻ 3/4 cup almond flour, 1/4 cup golden flaxseed meal, and 1 tablespoon coconut flour; separate the eggs, then fold the beaten whites into the batter (for muffins and cookies; for savory applications, replace the coconut flour with chickpea flour)

FLOUR, ALL-PURPOSE – 1 cup for coating dredging, dusting, and kneading

▻ 1 cup brown or white rice flour, white rye flour, or premade gluten-free flour blend (for dusting bread-kneading surfaces, bannetons, and peels; rice and rye flour absorb less moisture)

▻ 1 cup grits, wheat farina, semolina, Cream of Wheat, or cornmeal (for dusting pizza-kneading surfaces and peels; absorbs less moisture and adds crunch to the dough)

▻ 1 cup cornstarch, white or brown rice flour, or water chestnut flour (for dredging/coating; produces a thin crisp, coating, and fries up lighter)

- 1 cup corn flour/finely ground yellow or white cornmeal, or rice flakes/flaked rice (for dredging/coating fish; produces a thin crunchy coating)
- 1 cup tapioca flour/starch (for flouring cake pans)
- Vegetable oil (for kneading bread on a countertop or for rolling out pizza dough; doing so will prevent too much flour being absorbed)

FLOUR, ALL-PURPOSE – 1 tablespoon for thickening
- 2 tablespoons browned all-purpose flour or rice flour (Brown the flour in a dry skillet over medium heat or on a pie pan in the oven.)
- 1 tablespoon quick-mixing flour, such as Wondra, cake flour, pastry flour, or oat flour
- 1 1/4 to 1 1/2 tablespoons biscuit or pancake mix
- 1 tablespoon *besan*/chickpea flour or cashew butter (for curries)
- 1 tablespoon finely ground brown or white rice flour, or regular rice flour ground until fine (especially for roux)
- 1 1/2 teaspoons sweet rice flour/glutinous rice flour (does not separate when frozen)
- 1 1/2 teaspoons cornstarch (boil no longer than 1 minute)
- 1 1/4 teaspoons potato starch (cook until just thickened)
- 2 teaspoons arrowroot powder (clear appearance for puddings, delicate sauces, pie filling, and glazes; stir until just thickened)
- 1 tablespoon tapioca flour/starch, or 2 1/2 teaspoons small-pearl tapioca, ground until fine (clear appearance; does not separate when frozen)
- 1 teaspoon instant mashed potato flakes (whisk in to avoid clumping)

FLOUR, AMARANTH See AMARANTH FLOUR

FLOUR, BREAD, UNBLEACHED/BRITISH-TYPE STRONG/GERMAN-TYPE 813/CANADIAN-TYPE ALL-PURPOSE (12 to 13.5% protein) – 1 cup unsifted
- 1 cup high-protein all-purpose flour, such as King Arthur unbleached all-purpose flour with 11.7% protein

- ☞ 1 cup plus 1 1/2 tablespoons national brand unbleached all-purpose flour, such as Gold Medal or Pillsbury with 10.5% protein; or 1 cup all-purpose flour plus 1 1/2 teaspoons vital wheat gluten, or 1 tablespoon wheat germ
- ☞ 1 cup French-style flour with 11.5% protein, or European-style/artisan flour with 11.7% protein (for French and other European breads)
- ☞ 1 cup Indian-style finely milled soft whole-wheat flour (atta/chapati flour) or Italian-type (*Tipo 00* flour) (for ultrathin pizza and flatbreads; reduce the liquid in the recipe by 20%)
- ☞ 1 cup finely ground whole-wheat flour; white whole-wheat flour; or regular whole-wheat flour ground in a blender until fine (add 1 1/2 teaspoons vital wheat gluten, increase the kneading time and increase the liquid in the recipe as required)
- ☞ 1 cup plus 2 tablespoons coarsely ground whole-wheat, wheat meal, or graham flour (add 1 1/2 teaspoons vital wheat gluten, increase the kneading time, and increase the liquid in the recipe as required, usually about 2 tablespoons)

FLOUR, BRITISH-TYPE PLAIN UNBLEACHED *See FLOUR, SOFT WINTER WHEAT*

FLOUR, BRITISH-TYPE SOFT FLOUR *See FLOUR, CAKE*

FLOUR, BRITISH-TYPE STRONG UNBLEACHED *See FLOUR, BREAD, UNBLEACHED*

FLOUR, BUCKWHEAT (13 to 15% protein) – 1 cup:
- ☞ 1 1/4 cups white, untoasted buckwheat groats (hulled seeds) or buckwheat grits, ground in a high-powered blender until powdery or in small batches in a spice/coffee grinder
- ☞ 1/2 cup each whole-wheat flour and all-purpose flour (contains gluten)

FLOUR, CAKE/BRITISH SOFT FLOUR/ARGENTINE HARINA 0000 (6 to 7% protein) – 1 cup sifted

Tip: Aerate the substitute flour with a whisk or sieve, lifting it above the bowl to add as much air as possible

☞ 3/4 cup sifted bleached all-purpose flour and 2 tablespoons cornstarch or potato starch

☞ 1 cup sifted soft Southern wheat flour with low protein content, such as White Lily all-purpose or Southern Biscuit flour with 7 to 8% protein

☞ 1 cup unbleached (unbromated) cake flour blend, such as King Arthur with 9.4% protein (contains malted barley flour)

☞ 3/4 cup plus 3 tablespoons pastry flour

☞ 3/4 cup plus 2 tablespoons sifted bleached all-purpose flour, such as Pillsbury or Gold Medal

☞ 3/4 cup potato starch and 1/4 cup matzo cake meal (for Passover)

FLOUR, CLEAR (extra fine whole-wheat flour with 11.5% protein) – 1 cup

☞ 1 cup whole-wheat flour previously sifted through a fine-mesh sieve to remove the bran

☞ 3/4 cup plus 2 tablespoons unbleached bread flour and 2 tablespoons whole-wheat flour

FLOUR, CORNELL (UNIVERSITY) FORMULA (enriched flour for added protein) – 1 cup

Make Your Own Whisk together 3/4 cup plus 2 tablespoons bread flour, 1 tablespoon full-fat soy flour, 1 tablespoon nonfat milk powder, and 1 teaspoon wheat germ until thoroughly combined.

FLOUR, CRACKED WHEAT – 1 cup

☞ 1 cup cracked wheat cereal (for bread recipes when combined with other flour)

FLOUR, DURUM (13.5% to 14% protein) – 1 cup

☞ 1 cup finely milled semolina flour

☞ 1 cup wheat farina or regular Cream of Wheat, ground in a high-powered blender until extra fine or in batches in a spice/coffee grinder

FLOUR, FRENCH-TYPE 55, MEDIUM PROTEIN, HIGH-ASH BREAD FLOUR (11.5% protein) – 1 cup
- ⇨ 3/4 cup unbleached all-purpose flour plus 1/3 cup unbleached bread flour

FLOUR, GERMAN-TYPE 550 UNBLEACHED *See FLOUR, ALL-PURPOSE BLEACHED OR UNBLEACHED*

FLOUR, GERMAN-TYPE 813 UNBLEACHED *See FLOUR, BREAD UNBLEACHED*

FLOUR, GERMAN-TYPE 1050 *See FLOUR, HIGH-GLUTEN, UNBLEACHED*

FLOUR, GLUTEN (14.5 protein; best for bread machines) – 1 cup unsifted
- ⇨ 1 cup unsifted bread flour plus 2 teaspoons vital wheat gluten; decrease liquid as necessary
- ⇨ 1 cup unsifted Very Strong Canadian Bread Flour/red spring wheat flour (14.8% protein; sold in Britain)

FLOUR, GLUTEN-FREE *See GLUTEN-FREE GRAINS, FLOURS, STARCHES*

FLOUR, GLUTINOUS/SWEET RICE *See RICE FLOUR, SWEET/ GLUTINOUS*

FLOUR, GRAHAM/WHEATMEAL (14% protein) – 1 cup
- ⇨ 3/4 cup whole-wheat flour (preferably stone-ground) plus 1/3 cup unprocessed wheat bran
- ⇨ 1 cup coarsely ground whole-wheat flour (preferably stone-ground) or 1 cup plus 2 tablespoons regular whole-wheat flour
- ⇨ 3/4 cup unbleached all-purpose flour, 2 tablespoons whole-wheat flour, and 2 tablespoons wheat germ

FLOUR, HIGH-EXTRACTION – 1 cup
- ⇨ 3/4 cup whole-wheat flour and 1/4 cup bread flour

FLOUR, HIGH-GLUTEN, UNBLEACHED/GERMAN-TYPE 1050 (14% protein) – 1 cup

☞ 1 cup unbleached all-purpose flour plus 1 1/2 teaspoons vital wheat gluten; increase the flour in the recipe as needed

☞ 1 cup unbleached bread flour; increase the flour in the recipe as needed

FLOUR, HIGH-PROTEIN, UNBLEACHED (14 1/2% protein) *See FLOUR, HIGH-GLUTEN*

FLOUR, IRISH WHOLEMEAL/WHOLE-WHEAT (9 to 11% protein) – 1 cup

☞ 1 cup King Arthur Irish-style wholemeal flour

☞ 2/3 cup whole-wheat pastry flour and 1/3 cup wheat flakes coarsely ground in a food processor

FLOUR, ITALIAN TIPO 00/GRANO TENERO (8 to 8.5% protein) – 1 cup *See also FLOUR, PIZZA*

☞ 1 cup Argentinean soft wheat 000 flour, such as *Favorita* or *Blanca Flor*

☞ 1 cup King Arthur Italian-style flour (8% protein)

☞ 1/2 cup each unbleached all-purpose flour and cake flour (for pizza)

☞ 2/3 cup all-purpose flour and I/3 cup fine semolina flour (for pasta)

☞ 1 cup bleached all-purpose flour, such as Gold Medal (10.5% protein)

FLOUR, JAPANESE SOFT/WEAK/HAKURIKI-KO *See JAPANESE SOFT FLOUR*

FLOUR, MESQUITE (11 to 17% protein) – 1 cup

☞ 1 cup pure buckwheat flour

☞ 1 cup coconut flour (less nutty tasting)

FLOUR, MILLET (12.8% protein) – 1 cup
- 2/3 cup organic hulled millet, ground in a high-powered blender until powdery or in small batches in a spice/coffee grinder
- 1 cup light-colored teff flour or quinoa flour
- 1 cup superfine brown rice flour
- 1 cup Kamut flour (contains gluten)

FLOUR, MUNG BEAN See MUNG BEAN FLOUR/STARCH/POWDER

FLOUR, NUT (almond, hazelnut, pecan, walnut) – 1 cup See also PISTACHIO FLOUR
- 3/4 cups whole nuts, ground at low speed in a blender or in small batches in a spice/coffee grinder (For baking, include a teaspoon of sugar or flour from the recipe to avoid oiliness.)

FLOUR, OAT BRAN See OAT BRAN FLOUR

FLOUR, OAT, WHOLE-GRAIN See OAT FLOUR, WHOLE GRAIN

FLOUR, PASTA See PASTA FLOUR

FLOUR, PASTRY, UNBLEACHED (soft red winter wheat flour; 7.5 to 9.5% protein) – 1 cup See also FLOUR, WHOLE-WHEAT PASTRY
- 2/3 cup soft white wheat berries, ground until powdery in a high-powered blender, or in small batches in a spice/coffee grinder
- 1 cup all-purpose Southern-milled soft flour, such as While Lily; or 3/4 cup plus 3 tablespoons national brand bleached all-purpose flour, such as Pillsbury or Gold Medal (for most applications)
- 2/3 cup bleached all-purpose flour and 1/3 cup cake flour (for most applications)
- 3/4 cup plus 2 tablespoons quick-mixing flour, such as Wondra (for sponge-type cakes, puff pastry, flaky pastry, and crepes)
- 1/2 cup plus 2 tablespoons cake flour and 6 tablespoons bread flour (for pastry, cookies, biscuits, pancakes, and waffles)

- 3/4 cup plus 2 tablespoons bleached all-purpose flour and 2 tablespoons cornstarch or potato starch (for cookies, pastry, quick breads, pancakes, and waffles)
- 1 cup pastry blend, such as King Arthur Perfect Pastry Blend (for pastry)
- 1 cup Canadian cake and pastry flour
- 1 cup Italian *Tipo 00* flour
- 1 cup Argentinean or Uruguayan finely ground 000 flour

FLOUR, PATENT *See FLOUR, BREAD*

FLOUR, PIZZA (Caputo pizza flour, Alimonti organic pasta flour; 12 to 13% protein) – 1 cup *See also FLOUR, ITALIAN TIPO 00*
- 1 cup pizza flour blend, such as King Arthur
- 3/4 cup plus 2 tablespoons unbleached all-purpose flour and 2 tablespoons semolina flour

FLOUR, PLAIN (British all-purpose flour with 9 to 10% protein) *See FLOUR, SOFT WINTER WHEAT*

FLOUR, POPCORN (1% protein) – 1 cup
- 2 cups cold unsalted plain popcorn (preferably hot-air popped), ground in small batches in a blender or food processor until powdery

FLOUR, POTATO (15% protein) – 1/4 cup
- 1/2 cup dry potato flakes/instant mashed potatoes, such as Hungry Jack

FLOUR, PUMPERNICKEL/RYE MEAL/WHOLE-RYE FLOUR (8 to 13% protein) – 1 cup
- 1 cup coarsely ground stone-milled dark rye flour
- 3/4 cup plus 3 tablespoons medium rye flour and 2 tablespoons wheat bran

FLOUR, QUINOA *See QUINOA FLOUR*

FLOUR, RICE, BROWN (7% protein) – 1 cup
- 3/4 cup short-grain American-grown brown rice, ground until fine in a grain mill, or in small batches in a spice/coffee grinder, then sieved
- 1 cup superfine brown rice flour (less grainy)
- 1 cup stone-ground garbanzo bean flour, garbanzo–fava bean flour blend such as Authentic Foods Garfava Flour, or Indian *besan*/gram or urad dal flour
- 1 cup premade gluten-free flour blend, preferably brown rice–based

FLOUR, RICE, WHITE, SUPERFINE OR ASIAN (5 to 5.8% protein) – 1 cup
- 3/4 cup plus 2 tablespoons short- or medium-grain American-grown and packaged white rice, or dry Cream of Rice cereal, ground in small batches in a spice/coffee grinder until fine
- 1 cup oat flour (for shortbread)

FLOUR, RYE, WHITE/LIGHT (8.3% protein) – 1 cup
- 1 1/4 cups rye flakes, ground in batches in a spice/coffee grinder until powdery
- 1 cup pastry flour mixed with 1/4 teaspoon powdered rye flavoring

FLOUR, SELF-RAISING UNBLEACHED (British self-rising flour; 8 to 9% protein) – 1 cup
- 1 cup U.S. unbleached self-rising flour; reduce the salt in the recipe by 1/2 teaspoon
- 1 cup pastry flour plus 1 teaspoon baking powder, thoroughly combined with a whisk or electric mixer on low

FLOUR, SELF-RISING, UNBLEACHED (U.S. self-rising flour; 8.5% to 9% protein) – 1 cup
- 1 cup pastry flour, 1 1/2 teaspoons baking powder, and 1/2 teaspoon salt, thoroughly combined with a whisk or electric mixer on low

- 1 cup all-purpose Southern milled flour, such as White Lily, Martha White, or Southern Biscuit; 1 teaspoon baking powder; 1/2 teaspoon salt; and 1/4 teaspoon baking soda (especially for recipes using buttermilk)
- 3/4 cup plus 2 tablespoons bleached all-purpose flour, 2 tablespoons cornstarch or potato starch, 1 teaspoon baking soda, and 2 teaspoons cream of tartar (for recipes specifying buttermilk when regular milk is being substituted)

FLOUR, SELF-RISING SOFT/CAKE (7 to 8% protein) – 1 cup
- 1/2 cup plus 2 tablespoons all-purpose flour, 1/3 cup cornstarch, 1 teaspoon baking powder, and 1/2 teaspoon salt, thoroughly combined with a whisk or electric mixer on low
- 1 cup cake flour plus 1 1/4 teaspoons baking powder

FLOUR, SEMOLINA, FINE-GRIND (13 to 16% protein) – 1 cup
- 1 cup extra-fancy pasta flour or farina-grade silky fine flour

FLOUR, SOFT WINTER WHEAT ALL-PURPOSE/SOUTHERN U.S. MILLED/ UNBLEACHED BRITISH-TYPE PLAIN (7.5 to 9.5% protein) – 1 cup
- 1 cup unbleached all-purpose Southern milled flour, such as White Lily or Martha White
- 1 cup unbleached pastry flour (8% protein), or unbleached cake flour blend, such as King Arthur with 9.4% protein
- 1 cup Italian-type 000 flour (8.5% protein)
- 2/3 cup national brand bleached all-purpose flour, such as Pillsbury or Gold Medal, and 1/3 cup bleached cake flour, thoroughly combined
- 3/4 cup national brand bleached all-purpose flour and 3 tablespoons cornstarch or potato starch, thoroughly combined

FLOUR, SORGHUM (11% protein) See SORGHUM FLOUR

FLOUR, SOY, FULL FAT (26 to 35% protein; 20 to 24 grams fat) – 1 cup

- 1 cup defatted soy flour (7 grams fat)
- 1 cup garbanzo/chickpea/*besan* flour or garbanzo-fava bean flour blend, such as Authentic Foods Garfava Flour (increase the liquid in the recipe by 2 tablespoons per cup of flour; baked goods will be slightly denser)

FLOUR, SPELT WHOLE GRAIN (13 to 15% protein) – 1 cup

- 1 1/4 cups rolled spelt flakes, ground in batches in a spice/coffee grinder until fine, then sifted to remove any coarse bran
- 1 cup white or light spelt flour; reduce the liquid in the recipe as required
- 1 cup whole-wheat flour (more bitter)

FLOUR, SPROUTED WHEAT (13.5% protein) – 1 cup

- 1 cup panocha flour/*harina para panocha*
- 1 cup finely milled whole-wheat flour

Make Your Own Sprout 3/4 cup soft white wheat berries. Drain, then arrange the berries on dehydrator sheets and dry in a dehydrator set at 95°F to 112°F until hard, 12 to 24 hours. Grind in batches in a grain mill, high-powered blender, or spice/coffee grinder until powdery, then sift if necessary.

FLOUR, STRONG (British hard wheat flour; 11 to 12% protein) See FLOUR, BREAD

FLOUR, SUPERFINE See FLOUR, CAKE

FLOUR, TEFF (14 to 15% protein) – 1 cup

- 1 scant cup whole-grain teff, ground until powdery in a high-powered blender, or in batches in a spice/coffee grinder
- 1 cup finely ground millet flour (or 2/3 cup organic millet ground until powdery in a high-powered blender, or in batches in a spice/coffee grinder)

☞ 1 cup sorghum flour or superfine brown rice flour

FLOUR, WHEATMEAL *See FLOUR, GRAHAM*

FLOUR, WHITE LILY ALL-PURPOSE – 1 cup
  ☞ 1/2 cup all-purpose flour and 1/2 cup cake flour

FLOUR, WHITE WHOLE-WHEAT (13% protein) – 1 cup
  ☞ 1 cup whole-wheat pastry flour
  ☞ 1 cup spelt flour

**FLOUR, WHOLE-WHEAT/BRITISH WHOLEMEAL FLOUR/GERMAN–
TYPE 1600 FLOUR (14 to 14.4% protein) – 1 cup**
  ☞ 1/2 to 2/3 cup hard red winter wheat berries ground until pow-
    dery in a high-powered blender or in batches in a spice/coffee
    grinder; measure after grinding and increase liquid in the recipe
    slightly
  ☞ 1 cup white whole-wheat flour (13% protein; lighter color, milder
    tasting; reduce the liquid in the recipe slightly)
  ☞ 3/4 cup plus 2 tablespoons unbleached all-purpose flour and 2
    tablespoon wheat germ
  ☞ 2/3 cup unbleached all-purpose flour and 1/3 cup raw/unpro-
    cessed bran flakes (or 1/4 cup pulverized plain bran cereal; reduce
    the sugar in the recipe by 1 tablespoon)
  ☞ 3/4 cup plus 3 tablespoons unbleached all-purpose flour, 2 table-
    spoons wheat bran, and 1 teaspoon wheat germ
  ☞ 1 cup whole-spelt flour (lower in gluten)
  ☞ 1 cup einkorn flour (lower in gluten and less dense; reduce the
    liquid by one-third)
  ☞ 1 cup sprouted wheat flour or stone-ground whole-wheat flour
    (increase the liquid in the recipe as required)
  ☞ 1 cup graham, Kamut, or 12-grain flour (increase the liquid in the
    recipe as needed)

FLOUR, WHOLE-WHEAT BREAD (13 to 14% protein) – 1 cup

- 1 cup very finely ground whole-wheat flour plus 2 teaspoons vital wheat gluten
- 1 cup unbleached hard spring white flour with a high protein count, such as Wheat Montana Prairie Gold (for a sweeter, lighter, less dense loaf)
- 1 cup Hovis Granary Bread Flour or King Arthur Irish-Style Flour (coarser grind; for British wholemeal)

FLOUR, WHOLE-WHEAT CAKE (7 to 8% protein) – 1 cup

- 3/4 cup fine-grain whole-wheat flour (sifted to remove any coarse bran) plus 2 tablespoons cornstarch or potato starch
- 3/4 cup plus 3 tablespoons whole-wheat pastry flour

FLOUR, WHOLE-WHEAT PASTRY (9% protein) – 1 cup

- 1/2 to 2/3 cup soft white wheat berries, ground until powdery in a high-powered blender, or in batches in a spice/coffee grinder; increase the liquid in the recipe slightly
- 1/2 cup whole-wheat flour and 1/2 cup all-purpose flour (sift to discard any coarse bran)
- 1 cup gluten-free all-purpose flour

FLOUR, WHOLE-WHEAT SELF-RISING (9% protein) – 1 cup

- 1 cup whole-wheat flour plus 1 teaspoon baking powder

FLOWERING QUINCE (Chinese or Japanese firm, sour fruit) – 1 pound

- 1 pound green Mexican papaya

FLOWERS/BLOSSOMS/PETALS, FRESH EDIBLE – 1 cup for salads and garnish

- 1 cup non-sprayed, pesticide-free anise hyssop, apple, arugula, basil (including African blue basil), bachelor's buttons/cornflower, bee balm, begonia, bergamot, bok choy, borage, broccoli, cabbage,

calendula, chervil, chickweed, chicory, flowering chive, miner's lettuce/claytonia, clover, collards, crowder peas, daisy, dandelion, daylily, dill, elderflower, fava, fennel, French marigold, geranium, hibiscus, hollyhock, kale, lavender, leek, lemon, lovage, pot marigold, marjoram, Mexican tarragon/Mexican mint marigold, mustard greens, nasturtium, onion, orange, oregano, pansy, parsley, peach, peas, perilla, pineapple, plum, primrose, radish, sage, stock, squash, thyme, turnip, viola, violet, or sweet woodruff
- 1 cup rose petals (rugosa and pink damask especially; cut off the white part at the base of each petal, as it is bitter)

FOCACCIA (Italian flat savory bread) – 8 ounces
- 8 ounces fougasse or prebaked pizza crust, such as Boboli or Mama Mary's

FONTINA (domestic mild cheese) – 1 ounce
- 1 ounce Monterey Jack, Muenster, provolone, or mozzarella

FONTINA VAL D'AOSTA (Italian semifirm cheese) – 1 ounce
- 1 ounce Fontina Valbella, Fontal, Fontinella, Raclette, Emmental, Gruyère, Morbia, Vacherin Fribourgeois, or high-quality provolone

FOOD COLORING, NATURAL
- **Blue:** crushed and strained fresh or canned blueberries, Concord grape juice, thawed frozen grape juice concentrate, or concentrated water from boiled red cabbage
- **Black:** squid or cuttlefish ink, purchased or extracted from the ink sacs of fresh squid or cuttlefish
- **Dark brown:** caramelized sugar or baker's caramel/powdered caramel color, or strong brewed coffee, or instant or freeze-dried coffee mixed with a little hot water
- **Green:** spinach powder or matcha (green tea powder) dissolved in a little hot water; or fresh green vegetation (basil, coltsfoot, kale, spinach, parsley, watercress, or trimmed pandan leaves), pureed and then squeezed in cheesecloth to extract the liquid

> ⊱ **Orange:** achiote/Bijol powder, annatto seeds soaked in a little hot water (use the water and discard the seeds), or concentrated water from boiled yellow onion skins
> ⊱ **Pink/red/violet:** thawed frozen cranberry juice concentrate; sumac berries soaked in cold water a few hours; beet powder mixed with hot water (or sliced beets dried, then ground in a spice/coffee grinder); or juiced raw red beets especially Bull's Blood; or beets pureed, then squeezed in cheesecloth (Wear plastic gloves; 1 pound raw beets will yield 1/4 scant cup juice; the juice can be concentrated by gently boiling until reduced to 1 tablespoon.)
> ⊱ **Purple:** fresh elderberries, cooked and then strained
> ⊱ **Yellow:** thawed frozen orange juice concentrate, marigold flowers, or turmeric powder
> ⊱ **Yellow/orange:** carrot juice, or half ground turmeric and half mild paprika

FOOD COLORING FOR PASTA
> ⊱ **Pink:** 2 teaspoons tomato paste or 1 tablespoon cooked pureed beet per beaten egg
> ⊱ **Green:** 1/4 cup thawed and pureed frozen chopped spinach per beaten egg
> ⊱ **Gold:** Pinch of ground saffron or turmeric, added to the flour

FOOD WRAPPERS See WRAPPERS FOR FOOD, PREPARED EDIBLE; WRAPPERS FOR FOOD, NONEDIBLE; WRAPPERS FOR FOOD, VEGETABLE-BASED

FRA DIAVOLO SAUCE (Italian chile-spiced tomato sauce) – 1 cup
> ⊱ 1 cup marinara sauce plus crushed red pepper flakes or ground cayenne pepper to taste

FREEKEH (Middle Eastern roasted green wheat See WHEAT, FRESH/GREEN, ROASTED

FREGOLA SARDA/FREGOLONE/FREGULA See PASTA, FREGOLA

FRENCH FOUR-SPICE MIX *See QUATRE-ÉPICES*

FRESNO CHILE, FRESH – 1
- 1 fresh red jalapeño chile or Holland/Dutch chile

FRISÉE (blanched curly endive) – 1 pound
- 1 pound curly endive, escarole (inner heart), small leaves of tatsoi, or Verona radicchio (burgundy-colored leaves)

FROMAGE BLANC/FROMAGE FRAIS (French soft fresh cheese) – 1 cup
- 1 cup quark or yogurt cheese
- 1/2 cup each cream cheese and plain Greek-style yogurt, mixed until smooth
- 1 1/4 cups small-curd cottage cheese, drained for 30 minutes in a dampened, cheesecloth-lined sieve, then processed with 3 tablespoons sour cream until perfectly smooth
- 1/2 cup each fresh mild goat cheese, such as Montrachet, and sour cream, mixed until smooth

FROMAGE BLANC/FROMAGE FRAIS, NONFAT – 1 cup
- 2/3 cup nonfat cottage cheese and 1/3 cup nonfat sour cream, blended or processed until perfectly smooth

FROMAGE BLANC DIRECT-SET STARTER CULTURE – 1 packet
- 1 packet direct-set chèvre starter culture
- 1/4 teaspoon direct-set mesophilic starter culture plus 1 drop liquid animal rennet diluted in 1 or 2 tablespoons cool nonchlorinated water (stir in the mesophilic starter and then the rennet mix)

FRUCTOSE/LEVULOSE – 1 cup
- 1 1/2 cups superfine sugar (or 1 1/2 cups plus 1 tablespoon granulated sugar pulverized in a blender or food processor until fine-textured, 20 to 30 seconds)

FRUIT FRESH (anti-darkening agent for fruit and vegetables) – 1/4 teaspoon

- 1/4 teaspoon citric acid or 1/8 teaspoon ascorbic acid
- 1 tablespoon lemon juice

FRUIT GLAZE (apricot, cherry, raspberry, strawberry, or red currant) – 1/2 cup

Make Your Own Combine 1/2 cup (6 ounces) jelly (or jam or preserves) and 2 tablespoons water (or citrus juice or fruit-flavored liqueur) and heat over low heat, or microwave on High until bubbling. Strain to remove seeds, if necessary, pressing hard on the solids. (For a thinner glaze add 1 or 2 more tablespoons liquid; for a thicker glaze cook, stirring frequently, until glaze is very sticky; use while warm.)

FRUIT SWEET (liquid fruit juice concentrate) – 1 cup

- 12 ounces thawed frozen white grape or apple juice concentrate, gently boiled in a large pan until reduced to 1 cup, about 10 minutes (or microwaved on High in a 4-cup glass measuring cup, about 12 minutes)

FRUIT VINEGAR – 1 cup

Make Your Own Heat 1 cup vinegar (cider, wine, or unseasoned rice vinegar) and pour over 1/2 cup fresh cleaned fruit in a sterilized jar. Cool, then cover and let steep in a cool, dark place for 2 weeks. Strain and discard the fruit.

FÛL/FUL MEDAMES (Egyptian small round fava beans) – 1 (15-ounce) can

- 1/2 cup small dried fava beans/*ful hammam*, broad white beans, or black-eyed peas, soaked in cold water for 8 to 10 hours, then simmered in salted water until softened

FURIKAKE (Japanese sesame and seaweed condiment for rice) – 1 tablespoon
- 1 tablespoon dried nori shreds with sesame seed/*nori komi furikake*
- 1 tablespoon flaked or shredded green nori/*ao-nori*
- 1 tablespoon toasted black sesame seeds/*kura goma*
- 1 tablespoon powdered purple shiso leaves and sea salt/*yukari/ shiso yukari/shiso furikake*
- 1 tablespoon toasted sesame seed and sea salt/*gomashio;*
- 1 tablespoon dried nori, alaria/winged kelp, or dulse, toasted then crushed by hand

FUSHIMI PEPPER, FRESH/FUSHIMI-TOGARASHI (Japanese mild chile pepper) – 1 or 2
- 2 or 3 Spanish padrón peppers
- 3 or 4 Japanese shishito peppers
- 1 Anaheim chile or Cubanelle pepper, cut into strips

FUZZY MELON/HAIRY MELON/MOW GWA/JIT GWA *See SQUASH, ASIAN*

G

GALANGAL, GREATER (Southeast Asian seasoning root) – 1 1/2-inch slice fresh or frozen (1 tablespoon peeled and finely chopped)
- 4 teaspoons chopped pickled galangal/*kha*
- 3 or more (1/8-inch) slices dried galangal root/galanga soaked in hot water 30 minutes, then squeezed dry
- 1 tablespoon galangal paste
- 1 1/2 teaspoons (or more) Indonesian Laos powder (dried ground galangal root; less flavorful)
- 1-inch piece fresh young ginger (or 2 or 3 teaspoons finely chopped) plus a few grains of ground black pepper, or a few drops of lemon juice, or a small pinch of finely chopped lemongrass
- 1 (2-inch) piece mature ginger, or 1 1/2 to 2 tablespoons peeled and finely chopped ginger (less pungent)

GANACHE, VEGAN – 3/4 cup
Make Your Own Heat 1/4 cup nondairy liquid creamer (such as coconut or soy) and 2 tablespoons vegan margarine to boiling, then pour over 4 ounces vegan chocolate chips; gently stir until the chips are melted, and the mixture is smooth. Alternatively, use 1/4 cup canned coconut milk in place of the creamer and omit the margarine.

GANDANA (Afghan leek-like vegetable) *See LEEK, LARGE*

GARAM MASALA (Indian all-purpose aromatic seasoning) – 1 tablespoon
- 1 teaspoon mild/sweet curry powder
- 1/2 teaspoon each ground toasted coriander and cumin

G

GARI/GARRI/MANIOC MEAL/YUCA MEAL *(African and Caribbean fermented, roasted, and ground cassava) – 1 cup*
- 1 cup Brazilian toasted cassava flour/*farinha de mandioca torrado*
- 1 cup cocoyam *fufu* flour, plantain flour, garbanzo flour, or garbanzo–fava bean flour blend, such as Authentic Foods Garfava Flour
- 1 cup tapioca flour/starch; or small tapioca pearls, ground fine then measured (for fine grade and smooth grade; less flavorful)
- 1 cup wheat farina or dry regular Cream of Wheat (for the rough grade; less flavorful)
- 1 cup finely ground whole-wheat breadcrumbs or coarse almond meal (for making farofa)

GARLIC, BLACK FERMENTED *See FERMENTED BLACK GARLIC*

GARLIC BUTTER *– 4 ounces (1/2 cup)*
Make Your Own Stir 2 finely minced or grated garlic cloves (or 1 teaspoon or more liquid garlic seasoning or instant garlic) into 1/2 cup (1 stick) room-temperature butter. Let sit for a few minutes to develop flavor. It will keep, well sealed and refrigerated, for up to 1 week.

GARLIC CHIVES, JAPANESE/CHINESE CHIVES *– 1 ounce (1/4 cup finely chopped)*
- 1 or 2 sliced garlic leaves (harvest the leaves when plants are no more than 8 inches tall)
- 1/4 cup snipped Western chives or thinly sliced scallion or green onion greens plus 1 scant teaspoon minced garlic

GARLIC, FRESH *– 1 medium clove (1 teaspoon minced or pressed)*
- 1 thawed frozen garlic cube, such as Dorot, crushed
- 1 tablespoon green fresh garlic/wet garlic (milder and juicier)
- 1 tablespoon finely minced garlic chives
- 1/2 teaspoon garlic juice, garlic flakes, or instant garlic
- 1 teaspoon garlic paste from a tube, or jarred minced garlic
- 1/4 teaspoon granulated garlic, or dried minced garlic softened in 1 teaspoon water, about 10 minutes

- 1/8 teaspoon garlic powder
- 1/2 teaspoon garlic salt; reduce the salt in the recipe by 1/2 teaspoon
- 1 small shallot or 1 medium shallot lobe, finely minced (1 tablespoon)
- 1/2 medium clove (or 1/2 teaspoon minced) wild/meadow garlic or field/crow garlic
- 1 to 2 teaspoons garlic vinegar (if compatible)

GARLIC, GREEN/YOUNG GARLIC – 2 stalks minced (white and tender green parts only)

- 2 stalks garlic chives, garlic scapes (curly garlic shoots), or Chinese garlic stems
- 3 scallions (white and tender green parts only)
- 2 garlic cloves blanched in boiling water 1 minute, then minced

GARLIC MAYONNAISE/AÏOLI/ALLIOLI (Provençal condiment) – 1/2 cup

Make Your Own Crush 2 to 3 cloves of garlic to a smooth paste with 1/8 teaspoon sea salt, then combine with 1/2 cup mayonnaise and 1 to 3 teaspoons lemon juice. (Alternatively, blend all ingredients until smooth.) Let sit, covered, for 1 hour to develop flavor.

GARLIC OIL (Asian cooking condiment) – 1/4 cup

Make Your Own Crush 2 large garlic cloves and cook in 1/4 cup peanut oil over low heat, stirring occasionally, until light brown, 4 to 5 minutes. (Do not let the garlic become too dark or it will be bitter.) Cool and strain, discarding the garlic. Use immediately, or refrigerate in a small sterilized jar for up to 1 week.

GARLIC PASTE/PUREE, ROASTED – 1/4 cup

Make Your Own Toast unpeeled garlic cloves from 2 large garlic heads in a dry skillet over medium heat for 7 or 8 minutes, then squeeze through a garlic press (remove the peels in the press as needed). Or roast the unpeeled garlic, tightly wrapped in foil, in a preheated 425°F oven for 35 to 45 minutes (slice 1/2 inch from the top of the garlic heads and drizzle with 1 teaspoon olive oil before roasting).

GARLIC PEPPER – 1 tablespoon, ground
- 2 teaspoons black or white peppercorns and 1/8 to 1/2 teaspoon (or more) dried garlic flakes, ground in a pepper mill or spice/coffee grinder (mild garlic flavor)
- 1 1/2 teaspoons each coarse ground black pepper and garlic powder (strong garlic flavor)

GARLIC, PICKLED See CHINESE PICKLED GARLIC

GARLIC POWDER (pulverized dehydrated garlic) – 1/8 teaspoon
- 1/2 teaspoon garlic salt; reduce the salt in the recipe by 1/2 teaspoon
- 1/2 teaspoon instant minced garlic, jarred minced garlic, or garlic flakes
- 1/2 teaspoon garlic juice
- 1 teaspoon garlic paste (or 1 garlic clove mashed to a paste with kosher salt; reduce the salt in the recipe accordingly)
- 1 fresh garlic clove, minced

GARLIC SALT – 4 teaspoons
- 1 small peeled garlic clove pounded together with 1 tablespoon kosher salt or coarse sea salt (spread on a saucer to dry if not using immediately)
- 1 piece dried-out garlic scape pulsed in a spice/coffee grinder with 1 tablespoon kosher salt or coarse sea salt
- 1 teaspoon granulated garlic mixed with 1 tablespoon kosher salt or coarse sea salt
- 1/2 teaspoon garlic powder and 1/2 teaspoon dried crumbled parsley flakes mixed with 1 tablespoon kosher salt or coarse sea salt

GARLIC SHOOTS, YOUNG GREEN/GARLIC SCAPES – 1 cup
- 1 cup thinly sliced young scallions, green garlic/young garlic, or garlic chives
- 2/3 cup finely chopped chives plus scant 1/3 cup finely chopped garlic

☞ 1/2 cup chopped garlic

GARLIC VINEGAR – 1/2 cup
Make Your Own Combine 1 or 2 peeled and halved garlic cloves with 1/2 cup cider vinegar and heat just to the boiling point. Cover and let sit for 24 hours or more in a cool, dark place; then remove the garlic and store in the refrigerator.

GARLIC YOGURT SAUCE (Greek and Turkish) – 1 cup
Make Your Own Stir 1 to 2 teaspoons crushed garlic into 1 cup plain Greek-style yogurt (or 1 1/2 cups plain regular low-fat or full-fat yogurt drained several hours in a dampened, cheesecloth-lined sieve). Season with salt, then refrigerate for 1 or 2 hours to develop the flavor. For added flavor, stir in 1 to 2 tablespoons minced fresh cilantro or spearmint leaves along with the garlic.

GELATIN, FLAVORED – 1 (3-ounce) package
Make Your Own Whisk 1 packet (1/4 ounce or 1 scant tablespoon) unflavored gelatin powder into 1/4 cup cold fruit juice and let sit until dissolved, 3 to 5 minutes. Microwave for 40 seconds on High, then add 1 3/4 cups more juice and stir until combined. Cool; then chill until set. (For more intense flavor add a little sugar and lemon juice before heating.)

GELATIN, GRANULATED/POWDERED UNFLAVORED – 1 packet (1/4 ounce/1 scant tablespoon)
☞ 4 to 6 sheets leaf gelatin, depending upon size and grade (usually 4 sheets for silver grade or 225 bloom strength)

☞ 4 teaspoons (.375 ounce) unflavored vegan gelatin powder (a blend of vegetable gums and tapioca starch; not for highly acidic ingredients)

☞ 1 scant tablespoon kosher gelatin (made from fish or all-beef gelatin)

☞ 2 1/2 teaspoons apple pectin powder (use following the package directions; reduce sugar as necessary)

➺ 2 teaspoons agar powder (use 2 1/2 teaspoons for acidic ingredients, such as citrus fruit, lemon juice, vinegar, or wine)
➺ 2 tablespoons agar flakes, or 1 bar (increase the amount for acidic ingredients)

GELATIN SHEETS/LEAVES, SILVER GRADE – 4 sheets
➺ 1 package (1/4 ounce/1 scant tablespoon granulated/powdered unflavored gelatin), such as Knox, prepared according to the package directions

GHEE/USLI GHEE (Indian-style clarified butter with a higher smoke point than regular clarified butter) – 1 tablespoon
➺ 1 tablespoon vegetable ghee/*vanaspati*
➺ 1 tablespoon refined or virgin coconut oil
➺ 1 tablespoon extra-virgin macadamia oil
➺ 1 tablespoon clarified butter (lower smoke point)
➺ 2 teaspoons unsalted butter plus 1 teaspoon corn or sunflower oil (lower smoke point)

GHOST CHILE See BHUT JOLOKIA/NAGA VIPER

GIANDUJA (chocolate-hazelnut spread, such as Nutella or Noccioata) – 1 cup
➺ 3 ounces melted chocolate (milk or bittersweet) stirred into 1/2 cup room-temperature nut butter, preferably hazelnut
➺ 1 cup low-carb vegan chocolate-hazelnut spread

GINGELLY/GINGILI/TIL OIL (Indian and Burmese cooking oil) – 1 cup
➺ 3/4 cup untoasted sesame oil and 1/4 cup toasted sesame oil
➺ 2/3 cup vegetable oil and 1/3 cup toasted sesame oil

GINGER, CRYSTALLIZED/PRESERVED – 1/3 cup
➺ 2 tablespoons grated fresh ginger; add 3 1/2 tablespoons granulated sugar to the recipe
➺ 1/4 teaspoon powdered ginger

GINGER, DRIED
Make Your Own Cut peeled knobs of ginger into 1/8-inch slices; dry in a dehydrator at 115°F until completely dry, 4 to 8 hours, rotating the trays a few times. Let cool, and then grate.

GINGER EXTRACT – 1 cup
Make Your Own Add 1 teaspoon finely grated lemon zest and 2 tablespoons finely grated fresh ginger to 1 cup brandy or whiskey; seal tightly and leave in a cool place for 10 days, shaking the bottle daily. Strain through a cloth-lined funnel or sieve, and store tightly covered.

GINGER FLOWER/TORCH GINGER/BAO JIANG/BUNGA KANTAN (Southeast Asian seasoning) – 1 cup
- 1 cup ginger bud/*myoga* or fresh young/spring ginger

GINGER, FRESH MATURE TROPICAL – 1-inch peeled segment (1 tablespoon minced or coarsely grated)
- 4 teaspoons fresh or frozen minced young stem ginger (no peeling required)
- 4 teaspoons thawed frozen grated ginger (Flash-freeze teaspoon-size portions of grated ginger, then transfer to a small freezer bag when frozen; will keep for up to 1 year.)
- 1 tablespoon bottled ginger puree/paste
- 1 1/2 teaspoons dried cracked ginger, freeze-dried minced ginger, or dried ginger slices broken into pieces (for marinades, stock, soup, and pickling)
- 1/2 teaspoon ginger juice (for curries, marinades, and stir-fries)
- 2 teaspoons minced or grated fresh galangal (stronger flavor; has pine notes)
- 1/4 to 1/2 teaspoon powdered ginger plus few drops lemon or lime juice (for soups, curries, fruit, and baking)
- 1 tablespoon minced or ground fresh wild ginger rhizome/*Asarum canadense*

GINGER, FRESH YOUNG/SPRING – 2-inch segment

- 1 (1-inch) piece regular ginger, peeled and soaked in salted water 5 minutes (about 1/8 teaspoon salt), then rinsed and dried (harsher, less delicate)
- 1 (2-inch) piece regular ginger, peeled and sliced or julienned, then rinsed repeatedly in cold water until the water runs clear (harsher, less delicate)

GINGER-GARLIC PASTE/ADRAK LEHSUN KA PASTE (Indian seasoning) – 1/2 (scant) cup

Make Your Own Process 1/3 cup coarsely chopped fresh ginger, 1/3 cup coarsely chopped fresh garlic, and 1 tablespoon water in a blender or food processor to a fine paste. Store in a sterilized jar in the refrigerator; it will keep for up to 1 month.

GINGER, GROUND DRIED/POWDERED – 1 teaspoon

- 1 tablespoon grated fresh ginger (freeze ginger for 30 minutes, then use a rasp-type grater)
- 2 tablespoons dried uncrystallized ginger, minced (or 1/4 cup crystallized ginger rinsed to remove sugar, then minced; reduce the sugar in the recipe by 2 tablespoons)
- 1 teaspoon ginger juice (grate fresh ginger, then squeeze to extract the juice; add to liquid ingredients)
- 1/4 teaspoon crumbled or ground mace and 3/4 teaspoon finely grated lemon zest

GINGER JELLY – 1/2 cup

- 1/2 cup apple jelly and 2 to 3 teaspoons ginger juice, gently heated together until the jelly melts; cover, and refrigerate overnight to develop the flavor. (For jam, replace the ginger juice with 3 tablespoons minced uncrystallized ginger and add 1/2 teaspoon ground ginger.) Store in the refrigerator; it will keep for 3 to 4 days.

GINGER JUICE – 1 tablespoon (or more)

Make Your Own Peel a 1 1/2- to 2-inch piece of fresh ginger (about 1 1/2 to 2 ounces), finely grate it, and then press through a garlic press, tea strainer, fine-mesh sieve, or cheesecloth. (Freezing and thawing the ginger will produce more juice.)

GINGER JUICE – 6 tablespoons to 1 scant cup
Make Your Own Wash 1 pound unpeeled fresh ginger then chop or thinly slice (should yield 2 1/2 to 3 cups). Process in a blender or food processor for 3 to 5 minutes, then strain in a cheesecloth-lined sieve, pressing on solids to extract all the liquid. It will keep in the refrigerator for up to 1 week, or freeze for more extended storage.

GINGER LIQUEUR/GINGER-FLAVORED SPIRIT (such as Domaine de Canton) – 1 tablespoon for cooking
☞ 1/4 teaspoon ginger juice plus 2 1/2 teaspoons vodka or water

GINGER MARMALADE – 1/2 cup
☞ 1/2 cup orange or lemon marmalade, 1/2 to 1 teaspoon ground ginger, and 2 to 3 teaspoons grated fresh ginger stirred together (Cover and leave at room temperature overnight to develop the flavor; then keep refrigerated.)

GINGER PASTE/PISSA ADRAK/AADA BATA (Indian seasoning) – 1/3 cup
☞ 4 ounces scrubbed fresh ginger grated on a rasp-type grater
Make Your Own Process 1/2 cup peeled chopped ginger and a pinch of salt in a food processor until reduced to a paste, adding a little water if necessary. (Cut the ginger lengthwise first, then against the grain.)

GINGER, PICKLED/GARI/AMAZU SHOGA/BENI SHOGA (Japanese sushi accompaniment) – 1 cup
☞ 1 cup matchstick-size pieces of red bell pepper, 1/2 cup rice wine vinegar, and 3 tablespoons granulated sugar, marinated for 12 hours, then drained
Make Your Own Bring to a boil 1 cup peeled and very thinly sliced fresh ginger (about 4 ounces), 1/2 cup unseasoned rice vinegar, and 1/4 cup granulated sugar (or less if desired); cool, then transfer to a jar. Cover, and refrigerate for 3 or 4 days before using. It will keep in

the refrigerator for up to 12 months. (For *beni shoga,* shred rather than slice the ginger and add a little beet juice or a drop of food coloring; for *amazu shoga* use the young tender ginger shoot, which turns pink automatically.)

GINGER, POWDERED *See GINGER, GROUND DRIED/POWDERED*

GINGER SOY SAUCE – 1 cup
  ▷ 1 cup light soy sauce and 1 tablespoon ginger juice

GINGER, STEM, PRESERVED IN SYRUP – 2 tablespoons
  ▷ 2 teaspoons thinly sliced soft/uncrystallized ginger; or crystallized ginger, rinsed (for ginger)
  ▷ 2 tablespoons ginger syrup (for syrup)

GINGER SYRUP – 1 cup
  ▷ 1 cup syrup from jarred preserved stem ginger (for 1 tablespoon, mix 1 teaspoon honey with 1 tablespoon ginger juice)
Make Your Own Bring to a boil 1/3 cup thinly sliced unpeeled ginger, 1/2 cup firmly packed brown sugar, and 1 cup water, then simmer until reduced and syrupy, about 10 minutes. Cool then strain; store, refrigerated, for up to 1 month. (For more intense flavor, let the syrup sit for 45 to 60 minutes before straining.)
Or
Add 2/3 cup peeled and sliced fresh ginger to 1 cup heated heavy syrup (*See SYRUP, SIMPLE*); cool then steep, covered, for 2 days before straining. Store, refrigerated, for up to 1 month.

GINGER VINEGAR – 1 cup
Make Your Own Bring 1 cup cider vinegar, 1/4 cup peeled sliced fresh ginger, and 1 to 2 teaspoons sugar to a boil; cool, covered, then steep in a cool, dark place for 10 days, then strain. It will keep in the refrigerator for up to 3 months.

GINKGO NUTS, FRESH (Japanese and Korean) – 1 dozen shelled and blanched for cooking
- ☞ 1 (3.5-ounce) package gingko nuts, shelled and peeled
- ☞ 1 dozen canned ginkgo nuts, rinsed
- ☞ 1 dozen fresh wild ginkgo nuts/*Ginkgo biloba*, baked for 1 hour at 300°F, then shelled and any remaining skin rubbed off
- ☞ 1/4 cup shelled green peas (lacks bitterness)

GINSENG ROOT, AGED/PANAX (Chinese seasoning and medicinal agent) – 1 ounce (2 tablespoons minced)
- ☞ 1 ounce fine side roots, stem bits, shavings, or sun-dried white ginseng (less expensive)
- ☞ 1 ounce dried precut bellflower root/vine/codonopsis/*doraji/ dang shen* (for soups and other cooked dishes; not as strong but less expensive; soak root overnight then squeeze dry)
- ☞ 2 ginseng-root tea bags (for fresh minced or dried ground ginseng)

GLACE DE VIANDE See MEAT GLAZE

GLASSWORT/SALICORNIA/MARSH SAMPHIRE/SEA BEAN (salt marsh plant) – 1 pound
- ☞ 1 pound sea purslane (reddish color)
- ☞ 1 pound young green beans, haricots verts, or pencil-thin young asparagus, cut into pieces, blanched in salted water for 10 seconds, then salted

GLAZE See BALSAMIC GLAZE; CAKE GLAZE; FRUIT GLAZE; MEAT GLAZE; POULTRY GLAZE

GLUCOSE/GLUCOSE SYRUP/DEXTROGLUCOSE – 1 cup
- ☞ 3/4 cup light-colored (not "lite") corn syrup brought to a full boil, cooled completely, then mixed with 1/3 cup unheated corn syrup
- ☞ 1 cup light-colored (not "lite") corn syrup

GLUTEN-FREE GRAINS, FLOURS, STARCHES

☞ Acorn flour; almond meal; amaranth grain, flour, and flakes; arrowroot powder; brown rice flour and flakes; buckwheat flour, groats, and Cream of Buckwheat (if label reads 100% buckwheat); *canahua* grain; carob; cassava/*gari* flour; chestnut flour; chickpea/garbanzo/*besan* flour; coconut flour; corn flour; cornmeal; cornstarch; garbanzo and fava bean flour blend; glutinous rice and glutinous/sweet rice flour (despite the name, does not contain gluten); lentil flour; lupin flour; mesquite flour; hulled millet and millet flour; Montina flour (Indian ricegrass); oats and oat flour (if label reads gluten-free, such as Bob's Red Mill); potato flour and starch; quinoa flakes, flour, and grain; rice flour and rice bran/polish; sago and sago flour; sorghum flour; soy flour; tapioca and tapioca starch; teff berries and teff whole-grain flour; water chestnut flour; or yuca flour/starch

GLUTINOUS RICE FLOUR *See RICE FLOUR, SWEET*

GOAT – 1 pound
☞ 1 pound lamb

GOAT CHEESE, AGED – 1 ounce
☞ 1 ounce Etude, goat Gouda, Manchego, or Roncal

GOAT CHEESE, FRESH *See CHÈVRE*

GOAT'S HORN CHILE PEPPER/AJI CACHO DE CABRA (dried Chilean pepper) – 1
☞ 1 dried guajillo, puya/pulla, or New Mexico chile
☞ 1 1/2 teaspoons New Mexico or guajillo chile powder
☞ 1/2 teaspoon ground cayenne pepper

GOAT'S MILK, PASTEURIZED FULL-FAT – 1 gallon (for cheese making)
☞ 1 gallon full-fat cow's milk plus 1/4 teaspoon lipase powder (dissolve lipase in 1/4 cup cool water and let stand for 20 minutes)

☞ 1 gallon sheep's milk

GOCHUGARU/KOCHUKARU See *KOREAN CHILI FLAKES*

GOCHUJANG/KOCHUJANG/KOCHUCHANG See *KOREAN CHILI BEAN PASTE*

GOJI BERRY/WOLFBERRY, DRIED (Chinese flavoring) – 1 cup
☞ 2 cups homegrown fresh goji berries
☞ 1 cup dried jujubes (Chinese red dates)
☞ 1 cup dried Chilean wineberries/maqui berries
☞ 1 cup dried cranberries, barberries, or mulberries
☞ 2 to 3 tablespoons goji berry powder (for drinks and smoothies)

GOLDEN MOUNTAIN SAUCE/TUONG GIA VI (Thai seasoning sauce) – 1 tablespoon
☞ 1 tablespoon Maggi Seasoning, Healthy Boy Stir Fry Seasoning Sauce, or soy sauce

GOLDEN NEEDLES See *LILY BUDS*

GOLDEN SYRUP/LIGHT TREACLE (British pure cane sugar syrup with a butterscotch flavor) – 1 cup
☞ 1 cup Swedish light syrup/*ljus sirap*, coconut syrup, or Steen's pure cane syrup
☞ 3/4 cup light-colored (not "lite") corn syrup and 1/3 cup dark corn syrup, simmered, uncovered, until syrupy and reduced to 1 cup, about 5 minutes
☞ 2/3 cup light-colored corn syrup plus 1/3 cup light unsulphured molasses or grade A golden, delicate maple syrup, heated until combined
☞ 1/2 cup each dark corn syrup and light, mild-flavored honey, heated until combined

GOMASHIO/GOMASIO See *SESAME SALT*

GOOSE FAT, RENDERED – 1 tablespoon
- ▷ 1 tablespoon rendered duck fat, pork fat, tallow, or leaf lard
- ▷ 1 tablespoon fruity olive oil, or 1 1/2 teaspoons each oil and unsalted butter

GOOSEBERRIES, GREEN, FRESH OR FROZEN – 1 cup
- ▷ 1 cup smooth-skinned pink dessert gooseberries (reduce the sugar and cooking time)
- ▷ 1 cup red or white currants (smaller; reduce the sugar and cooking time)
- ▷ 1 cup dark red Worcesterberries/*Ribes divaricatum* or purple-black Jostaberries/*Ribes nidigrolaria* (blackcurrant and gooseberry hybrids; smaller and sweeter; reduce the sugar and cooking time)
- ▷ 1 cup coarsely chopped rhubarb (less sweet; increase the sugar)

GORAKA/GAMBODGE (Sri Lankan souring agent) – 4 dried segments ground to a pulp (1 tablespoon)
- ▷ 1 tablespoon tamarind concentrate
- ▷ 1 tablespoon bitter orange juice, lemon juice, or lime juice

GORGONZOLA – 1 ounce See BLUE CHEESE, STRONG

GOUDA, AGED (Dutch hard cheese) – 1 ounce
- ▷ 1 ounce aged Edam, Beemster Classic, aged Boerenkaas, Coolea, Doddington, aged Mimolette, Parmigiano-Reggiano, Parmesan, or Romano

GOUDA, SMOKED – 1 ounce
- ▷ 1 ounce smoked medium cheddar or smoked Irish Blarney

GOUDA, YOUNG (Dutch semisoft mild cheese) – 1 ounce
- ▷ 1 ounce Baby Bel, Baby Samsoe, Blarney Castle, Boerenkaas, Doolin, Dutch Farmstead, Edam, Kartano, Kleinkase, Lamb Chopper, Penbryn, Roomkaas (double-crème Gouda), or Tybo

GOURD (angle/luffa, bottle, turban, wax/winter gourd) *See* SQUASH, ASIAN

GOURD STRIPS, DRIED/KAMPYO (Japanese long, thin food wrappers) – 1 dozen
- 1 dozen fresh chives, dipped into boiling water for 1 or 2 seconds, rinsed in cold water, then patted dry
- 12 long strips of cucumber peel, sliced lengthwise into thin ribbons, dipped into boiling water until softened, then patted dry

GRAHAM CRACKER CRUMBS – 1 1/4 cups packed crumbs for an 8- or 9-inch crust
- 1 package graham crackers (11 double crackers 4 7/8 x 2 3/8 inches), crushed or processed to a fine or coarse crumb
- 1 1/4 cups crushed animal crackers, arrowroot cookies, digestive biscuits, or Maria cookies
- 1 1/4 cups crushed gingersnaps, shortbread cookies/Lorna Doones, or vanilla wafers (for a crumb crust, reduce the fat and sugar in the recipe)
- 1 cup finely ground Honey Nut Chex or Cinnamon Rice Chex
- 1 1/2 cups crushed fruit-free granola (for a crumb crust, reduce the fat and sugar in the recipe)
- 1 1/4 cups crushed pretzel crumbs and scant 1/4 cup sweetened flaked coconut
- 1 1/4 cups pecan or walnut meal (for a crumb crust, use softened butter and reduce it to 1 1/2 tablespoons)

GRAIN ALCOHOL/NEUTRAL SPIRITS (151 to 190 proof alcohol) – 1 cup
- 1 cup 100-proof vodka
- 1 cup grappa (for a fruit liqueur base)

GRAINS OF PARADISE/GUINEA PEPPER/MELEGUETA (West African seasoning) – 1 tablespoon ground
- 2 teaspoons each cardamom seeds (from black cardamom pods) and black peppercorns, ground in a mortar or spice/coffee grinder

(Alternatively, use 1 1/2 teaspoons each ground cardamom and ground black pepper.)

GRAM FLOUR See BESAN

GRANA PADANO (Italian hard cheese) – 1 ounce
- Aged Asiago, Parmesan, Pecorino Romano, Sbrinz, or domestic Romano

GRANO (Italian whole durum wheat) See WHEAT BERRIES, RED WHOLE

GRAPEFRUIT – 1 pound
- 1 pound Mandelo/cocktail grapefruit (pomelo and Fru mandarin hybrid; sweeter and smaller)
- 1 pound Melogold, Oroblanco, pomelo, or Ugli/uniq fruit (for white grapefruit; milder)
- 1 pound Minneola tangelo (for pink or red grapefruit; grapefruit and mandarin cross; sweeter)

GRAPE LEAVES – 1 (16-ounce) jar (40 to 56 leaves)
- 40 tender fresh, unsprayed grape or fig leaves, washed, stemmed, and softened in boiling water until limp, 30 to 60 seconds; then rinsed in cold water and drained (pick unsprayed pale green leaves in the spring–the young ones at the very end of the vines)
- 20 to 30 large green chard or Savoy cabbage leaves, softened in boiling water until limp, about 30 seconds, then drained, de-ribbed, and halved
- Older nasturtium leaves blanched for 60 seconds (for brief cooking only; peppery tasting; more delicate texture)
- Fresh cherry or oak leaves (for pickle firming application)

GRAPE MOLASSES/MUST SYRUP/DIBS/MOSTARDA/PEKMEZ/ PETIMÉSI (Italian, Spanish, and Middle Eastern thick syrup) – 1/4 cup See also VIN COTTO
- 3/4 cup unsweetened grape juice or prune juice, gently boiled until syrupy and reduced to 1/4 cup, about 10 minutes (Stir constantly and skim the foam as necessary.)
- 1/4 cup thick fig syrup/*miele di fichi/melazzo di fichi*
- 3 tablespoons lemon juice and 4 teaspoons dark molasses (or strong-tasting honey) warmed in the microwave a few seconds, then cooled
- 3 tablespoons dark, strong-tasting/bitter honey thinned with 1 tablespoon warm water
- 1/4 cup sweet, heavy wine, such as Greek Mavrodaphne
- 2 to 3 tablespoons aged balsamic vinegar

GRAPES, RED TABLE – 1 cup
- 1 cup deep red to deep-purple wild fox grapes/*Vitis labrusca* or southern fox grapes/Muscardine or scuppernong/*Vitis rotundifolia* (more seeds and sour tougher skin)

GRAPPA (Italian clear distilled spirit) – 2 tablespoons
- 2 tablespoons Chilean or Peruvian pisco, French marc, Portuguese bagaciera, Spanish aguardiente, or very dry vermouth, such as Noilly Prat

GRASS PEA/CICERCHIE (Italian yellow legume) – 1 pound dried
- 1 pound dried chickpeas

GRAVIERA (Greek semihard cheese) – 1 ounce
- 1 ounce *kasseri, kefalotyri,* or Gruyère

GRAVLAX (Swedish dill-seasoned, salt-cured salmon) – 1 pound
- 1 pound cold-smoked salmon or lox, plus fresh dill as a garnish

GRAVY BROWNING – 1 teaspoon
- ⊯ 1/2 teaspoon powdered caramel color *See BAKER'S CARAMEL*
- ⊯ 1/2 teaspoon sugar added to the fat before adding flour, then cooked several minutes to a rich brown color
- ⊯ 1 teaspoon instant coffee granules or unsweetened cocoa powder, preferably Dutch processed, dissolved in 1 tablespoon of liquid, then stirred into the sauce
- ⊯ Few drops soy sauce; omit or reduce the salt in the recipe accordingly
- ⊯ Toast the flour used in making the gravy but use twice as much (toast the flour in a dry skillet until brown)
- ⊯ Onion slices, caramelized until golden (will also add flavor to the gravy)
- ⊯ Unpeeled, washed onions when making beef stock/broth (peels will color it a rich brown)

GRAVY THICKENER *See THICKENER FOR GRAVY OR SAUCE*

GREATER GALANGAL/GALANGA *See GALANGAL, GREATER*

GREEK HONEY/MELI (wildflower and herbs/Attiki, or thyme/ Hymettus) – 1 cup
- ⊯ 1 cup Italian wildflower honey/*millefiori*
- ⊯ 1 cup unfiltered, aromatic honey, such as pine tree or sunflower
- ⊯ 1 cup grape must syrup/*petimezi*

GREEK OREGANO/RIGANI *See OREGANO, GREEK*

GREEK SEASONING – 1 tablespoon
- ⊯ 1 teaspoon dried Greek (or Mediterranean) oregano plus 1/2 teaspoon each dried marjoram, garlic powder, ground black pepper, and finely grated lemon zest
- ⊯ 1 teaspoon dried oregano and 2 teaspoons lemon pepper

GREEK SWEET WINE (Mavrodaphne, Samos, Muscat) – 1/4 cup for cooking
- 1/4 cup Madeira

GREEK VINEGAR, AGED RED WINE – 2 tablespoons
- 1 tablespoon each balsamic vinegar and red wine vinegar

GREEK VINEGAR, SWEET – 1 tablespoon
- 1 tablespoon aged sherry vinegar

GREEN BEANS – 1 pound
- 1 pound Chinese yard-long beans or asparagus beans, cut into 3-inch lengths
- 1 pound nopales, shaved and cut into strips

GREEN GARLIC See GARLIC SHOOTS, YOUNG GREEN

GREEN TEA ICE CREAM See ICE CREAM, GREEN TEA

GREENS, ASIAN BLEND – 1 pound
- 1 pound Chinese spinach/amaranth, Chinese mustard greens, garland chrysanthemum, mizuna, and/or tatsoi

GREENS, BABY COOKING – 1 pound
- 1 pound baby arugula, frilly-leafed collards, organic mixed kales, mustard, spinach, and/or tatsoi

GREENS, BABY SALAD – 1 pound
- 1 pound baby arugula, baby Forellenschluss, Littte Gem, mâche, baby Lollo Rossa, baby oak-leaf (red and green), Deer Tongue, Salanova, small Boston, tatsoi, and/or Winter Density lettuce

GREENS, BITTER BLEND – 1 pound
- 1 pound young agretti, arugula, chicory, curly endive, dandelion greens, escarole (dark outer leaves), mustard greens, purslane leaves, parsnip greens, turnip greens, and/or watercress

GREENS, SOUTHERN BLEND – 1 pound
- 1 pound collard greens, mustard greens, turnip greens, and/or curly green kale

GRITS See CORN GRITS; HOMINY GRITS

GRITS, QUICK-COOKING – 1 cup
- 1 1/3 cups regular hominy grits, corn grits, or samp, finely ground in a blender or in small batches in a spice/coffee grinder
- 1 cup instant grits (reduce the cooking time to 5 minutes)

GROUNDNUT OIL/PEANUT OIL – 1 cup
- 1 cup corn oil

GROUND RED PEPPER See CAYENNE PEPPER, GROUND

GRUYÈRE (Swiss semihard to hard cheese) – 1 ounce See also EMMENTAL
- 1 ounce Comté, Appenzeller, Beaufort, Emmental, Fontina d'Aosta, Groviera, Heidi Gruyère, Hoch Ybrig, Le Brouère, L'etivaz, Pleasant Ridge Reserve, or St. Claire

GUAJILLO CHILE (Mexican and Guatemalan reddish-brown, moderately hot chile) – 1
- 1 dried New Mexico or puya/pulla chile
- 2 teaspoons guajillo or New Mexico chile powder

GUANCIALE (Italian salt-cured pork jowl) – 4 ounces
- 4 ounces jowciale or pancetta (saltier and leaner)
- 4 ounces lean salt pork

☞ 4 ounces unsmoked bacon, blanched in boiling water for 1 or 2 minutes, then rinsed and blotted dry

GUANCIALE, SMOKED – 4 ounces
☞ 3 ounces regular guanciale or pancetta and 1 ounce (1 or 2 slices) traditional bacon

GUAQUE/HUAQUE CHILE See GUAJILLO CHILE

GUAR GUM (thickening and emulsifying agent made from guar beans) – 1 teaspoon
☞ 1 teaspoon xanthan gum
☞ 2 teaspoons powdered unflavored gelatin or agar powder (softened in water)
☞ 1 teaspoon golden flax meal (ground golden flaxseed)
☞ 1 teaspoon Expandex (especially for yeast baking)
☞ 2 tablespoons potato flour
☞ 2 teaspoons psyllium powder (use 5 teaspoons for drop cookies)

GUASCAS/GALINSOGA/QUICKWEED, DRIED (wild Columbian herb) – 1 tablespoon
☞ 1 teaspoon dried Mexico oregano plus 2 teaspoons chopped fresh cilantro

GUAVA PASTE/ATE/GOIABADA (Latin American and Portuguese condiment) – 4 ounces
☞ 4 ounces quince paste/membrillo; jellied quince paste/pâte de coing, plumbrillo, or any tart Mexican fruit paste/ate
☞ 4 ounces strawberry or raspberry paste (Cook 6 to 7 ounces strawberry or seedless raspberry jam until very thick and reduced by at least one-third, then transfer to a shallow greased dish and chill until firm.)

GUAVA PUREE – 1 cup
☞ 1/2 to 2/3 cups guava paste and 1/2 cup water, pureed in a blender until smooth

GUINDILLA CHILE, DRIED – 1
- 1/2 teaspoon crushed red pepper flakes

GUINDILLA CHILES, JARRED – 1/4 cup
- 1/4 cup pepperoncini pickled in brine, or any small brined mild green chiles

GUM ARABIC/ACACIA GUM (natural thickening and emulsifying agent) – 1 teaspoon
- 1 teaspoon xanthan gum
- 1 teaspoon guar gum,
- 1 to 2 teaspoons instant ClearJel used following package directions

GVINA LEVANA (Israeli soft white cheese) – 1 cup *See also QUARK*
- 1 cup fromage blanc, plain full-fat quark, or plain full-fat Greek-style yogurt

GYOZA DIPPING SAUCE *See ASIAN DIPPING SAUCE*

H

HABAÑERO CHILE, FRESH OR DRIED – 1
- 1 to 2 fresh Manzano/Rocoto chiles
- 1 fresh red Zavory habañero pepper (much milder; 100 Scoville units)
- 1 fresh red Caribbean habañero (twice as hot; 450,000 Scoville units)
- 1 fresh red Caribbean Savina, Fatali, or Scotch bonnet chile (more aggressive)
- 1 fresh orange malagueta chile (milder)
- 2 to 3 fresh jalapeño or serrano chiles (milder; lacks fruity aroma)
- 1/8 teaspoon red Caribbean habañero powder
- 1/2 teaspoon habañero pepper sauce

HAJIKAMI (Japanese sweet pickled young ginger) See GINGER, PICKLED

HALABY CHILE See ALEPPO/HALABY CHILE

HALF-AND-HALF (10.5 to 12% butterfat) – 1 cup
- 3/4 cup whole milk and 1/4 cup heavy cream
- 2/3 cup nonfat or lowfat milk and 1/3 cup heavy cream
- 1/2 cup light cream and 1/2 cup whole milk
- 1 1/2 tablespoons melted unsalted butter plus enough whole milk to make 1 cup (for baking)
- 1 cup evaporated milk (for baking)
- 1 cup nondairy liquid creamer, such as Silk, So Delicious, or Organic Valley

HALLABONG JUICE (Korean citrus fruit) – 1 tablespoon
- 1 1/2 teaspoons each orange and tangerine juice

HALLOUMI/HALUMI (firm salty frying cheese) – 1 ounce
- 1 ounce aged provolone, paneer, mozzarella, queso blanco, queso fresco, *queso pana freir,* or scamorza

HALOUMI/JUBNA (Greek and Middle Eastern salt-brined goat-sheep-milk cheese) – 1 ounce
- 1 ounce Middle Eastern *nabulsi*, Greek feta, or Russian *suluguni*

HAM, BRINE-CURED/WET-CURED – 1 pound
- 1 pound Canadian bacon
- 1 pound canned ham, or canned seasoned pork product, such as Spam
- 1 pound fresh smoked dark meat turkey or turkey salami

HAM, DRY-CURED See CHINESE HAM; IBÉRICO HAM; PROSCIUTTO DI PARMA; SPECK; WESTPHALIAN HAM

HAM HOCK, SMOKED – 1 small meaty hock for seasoning
- 1 meaty ham bone, or ham rind
- 4 ounces meaty salt pork, rinsed if crusted with salt
- 3 ounces smoked prosciutto or speck scraps or rind
- 1 or 2 smoked sausages
- 2 1/2 to 4 ounces smoked ham, or nitrate-free turkey ham or bacon
- 2 1/2 to 4 ounces smoked pork shoulder butt or smoked pork shank
- 4 ounces smoked pork neck bones
- 1 smoked turkey wing, drumstick, thigh, or neck
- 2-ounce end piece of *prosciutto crudo*
- Parmesan rind (has a rich, slightly smoky flavor)
- 3/4 teaspoon ham soup base, such as Better than Bouillon, or ham concentrate, such as Goya
- 1/4 cup lightly packed smoked dulse (sea vegetable) or smoked dulse flakes, heated in a dry skillet until brown and crunchy, about

5 minutes, stirring several times; add during the last five minutes of cooking
- ⮞ 1 or 2 teaspoons smoked salt or a smoky seasoning blend; reduce the salt in the recipe accordingly
- ⮞ 2 or 3 drops liquid smoke (for aroma only)

HAM STOCK – 1 cup for soup base
- ⮞ 1 cup water from cooking a ham or corned-beef brisket (spicier)

HARICOTS VERTS/FILET BEANS/FAGIOLINI, FRESH (thin, tender French green beans) – 1 pound
- ⮞ 1 pound young or slender small green beans, or tender green beans halved lengthwise

HARINILLA (Mexican blue dried powdered masa) See MASA HARINA

HARISSA (Moroccan thick spicy chili paste) – 1 tablespoon
- ⮞ 1 tablespoon berbere seasoning, harissa powder, or peri peri seasoning (add to oil to make a paste, or use dry for seasoning)
- ⮞ 1 tablespoon tabil or berbere paste
- ⮞ 1 tablespoon hot chili paste, such as sambal oelek, plus 1 or 2 teaspoons vegetable oil, 1 crushed garlic clove, and 1/2 teaspoon each toasted ground cumin and coriander

HATCH CHILE (New Mexico's green mild chile) – 1 fresh or frozen
- ⮞ 1 fresh green Anaheim or California chile

HATCHO MISO (Japanese dark brown, soybean-based miso) – 1 tablespoon
- ⮞ 1 tablespoon red miso/*inaka miso/sendai miso*
- ⮞ 1 tablespoon *akadashi miso* (*hatcho* and *saikyo* miso blend; less pungent)

HATO MUGI See JOB'S TEARS

HAVARTI (Danish semisoft mild cheese) – 1 ounce
⇨ 1 ounce Tilsit, Butterkäse, Esrom, Monterey Jack, St. George, or Tetilla

HAZELNUT BUTTER See NUT BUTTER

HAZELNUT MEAL/FLOUR – 1 cup
⇨ 3/4 cup raw skinless hazelnuts ground in a food processor with 1 to 2 tablespoons flour (for meal)
⇨ 3/4 to 7/8 cup raw skinless hazelnuts ground in batches in a spice/coffee grinder until powdery; sift, then regrind any large particles (for flour)

HAZELNUT MILK – 4 cups
Make Your Own Soak 1 cup hazelnuts in water to cover for 8 to 10 hours. Drain, rinse, then process with 4 cups warm water in a blender until smooth, 2 to 4 minutes. Strain through a nutmilk bag or cheesecloth-lined sieve, pressing firmly on the pulp to extract all the liquid. Store in the refrigerator, and shake before using.

HAZELNUT OIL, ROASTED (finishing oil) – 1 cup
⇨ 1 cup roasted walnut oil or extra-virgin olive oil

HAZELNUT PASTE/PASTA DI NOCCIOLA – 1 cup
⇨ 1 cup pistachio paste/*pasta di pistachio*, or creamy-type almond butter
Make Your Own Toast and skin 1 1/2 cups hazelnuts, then process in a high-speed blender to a smooth paste (or add 1 tablespoon neutral-tasting vegetable oil and process in a food processor or regular blender to a smooth paste).

HAZELNUTS – 1 cup shelled nuts
⇨ 1 cup shelled beechnuts or almonds

HEARTS OF PALM/PALMITOS, CANNED OR JARRED – *1 cup*
- 1 cup canned or jarred artichoke hearts, rinsed and blotted dry
- 1 cup cooked white asparagus

HEDGEHOG MUSHROOMS/PIEDS DE MOUTON – *1 pound*
- 1 pound golden or white chanterelle mushrooms

HEMP MILK – *4 cups*
Make Your Own Soak 1 cup raw hulled hemp seeds (hemp hearts) in water to cover for 4 hours. Drain and process with 4 cups water in a blender until smooth, 2 to 4 minutes. Strain through a nutmilk bag or cheesecloth-lined sieve, pressing firmly on the pulp to extract all the liquid. Keep refrigerated and shake before using. (For hemp seeds in the shell, soak for 8 to 12 hours; for a nuttier flavor, toast the hemp seeds in a dry skillet until crisp, stirring constantly.)

HEMP SEEDS (raw or toasted) – *1/4 cup*
- 1/4 cup sunflower seeds (raw or toasted)
- 3 to 4 tablespoons plain hemp powder/hemp protein powder (for smoothies)

HEMPSEED BUTTER – *1 cup*
Make Your Own Toast 1 1/2 cups hemp seeds in a dry skillet until fragrant, 3 to 4 minutes, then process in a blender. Add 2 to 3 tablespoons grapeseed oil, and continue to process to a coarse paste. Put in a small lidded jar and store in the refrigerator.

HEMPSEED OIL – *1 cup*
- 1 cup walnut or flaxseed oil

HEN OF THE WOODS/MAITAKE MUSHROOMS – *1 pound*
- 1 pound shiitake or oyster/shimeji mushrooms

HERB BOUQUET *See BOUQUET GARNI*

HERBES DE PROVENCE (Provençal seasoning mix) – 1 teaspoon

- ☞ 1/4 teaspoon each dried basil, dried marjoram, dried rosemary, and dried thyme, plus a small pinch lavender if available (or desired)
- ☞ 1/2 teaspoon each dried thyme and dried basil
- ☞ 3/4 teaspoon Italian seasoning

HERBS, FRESH, HOME-DRIED (lavender, marjoram, mint, oregano, rosemary, sage, tarragon, thyme)

- ☞ Microwave (Place washed and dried leaves in a single layer between plain paper towels and microwave on High until fully dry and brittle, 1 to 3 minutes, depending upon the amount and moisture content.)
- ☞ Air-dry (Place sprigs in a single layer on a wire cooling rack or paper and cover with cheesecloth; or hang a bundle of sprigs upside down in a mesh produce bag, or paper bag punctured with air holes. Leave in a warm, dry, airy, preferably dark place for 7 to 10 days. Strip the leaves when dry.)

HERBS, FRESH, HOME-FROZEN (basil, borage, chives, cilantro, dill, garden cress, lemon balm, lemongrass, marjoram, mint, parsley, savory, young sorrel, kaffir lime leaves)

- ☞ Put chopped herbs in ice cube trays with a little water or olive oil and freeze until solid. Transfer the frozen cubes to freezer bags. To use oil-based cubes, toss 1 or 2 cubes into the pan; for water-based, place in a fine-mesh sieve until the ice melts, then use immediately.
- ☞ Flash-freeze herbs until stiff, about 2 hours, then wrap flat in foil to freeze; or freeze directly in a freezer bag that lies flat.
- ☞ Blanch herb leaves in boiling water until brightly colored, about 10 seconds, freshen in ice water, then process in a blender or food processor to a smooth paste. Drain in a small cheesecloth-lined sieve for 1 to 2 hours, then freeze in ice cube trays and transfer to freezer bags when frozen.

HERBS, FRESH, PRESERVED IN SALT

Make Your Own Layer fresh herbs in a glass container between 1/2-inch layers of kosher salt, beginning and ending with salt. Make sure the salt covers the leaves completely and is removed before using the herbs. (The leaves will keep their green color for up to 6 months.)

HIBISCUS FLOWERS, DRIED/ROSELLE/FLOR DE JAMAICA/BISAAP (Caribbean, Spanish, and African seasoning) – 1 ounce (1 cup)
- 1 ounce dried white hibiscus flowers/*bisaap blanc* (less tart)
- 15 hibiscus tea bags (remove leaves from the bags)

HIBISCUS FLOWERS, FRESH – 1 cup
- 1/4 cup dried hibiscus flowers

HIBISCUS LEAVES /INDIAN SORREL/KRACHIAP/PULINCHA KIRA/ RATA BILINCHA (tangy Asian vegetable) See SORREL, COMMON GARDEN

HICKORY SMOKED SALT See SALT, SMOKED SEA

HIJIKI/HIZIKI (Japanese sun-dried black strand seaweed) – 1 ounce
- 1 ounce refrigerated *mozuku* (lighter flavor; stringy shreds; soak for 10 minutes or add directly to the soup)
- 1 ounce arame (milder and less salty, longer thinner strands; soak for 5 minutes; less cooking time)
- 1 ounce kiri kombu (stronger flavor; long narrow strips; soak for 10 minutes)
- 1 ounce wakame (soak for 10 to 20 minutes; cut out the tough center rib, then slice the rest into thin ribbons)

HILOPITES See CHILOPITAS

HING See ASAFETIDA

HOG PLUM/MAKAWK (Southeast Asian souring agent) – 1 pound peeled
- 12 ounces tomatillos, green or unripe cherry tomatoes, or gooseberries

HOISIN SAUCE/HÓI SÌN JÌANG (Chinese thick, sweet cooking condiment) – 1/4 cup
- ⮞ 1/4 cup Chee hou sauce plus 1 or 2 teaspoons brown sugar or dark-bodied honey
- ⮞ 2 tablespoons each oyster sauce and thick tomato sauce

Make Your Own Whisk together 2 tablespoons thick barbecue sauce, 1 tablespoon each molasses and dark soy sauce, and 1/2 teaspoon Chinese five-spice powder.

HOJA SANTA/HIERBA SANTA/ACUYO/MOMO (Mexican seasoning) – 1 fresh leaf See also WRAPPERS FOR FOOD, VEGETABLE
- ⮞ 2 dried *hoja santa* leaves
- ⮞ 2 Mexican avocado leaves, toasted
- ⮞ 1/2 cup chopped green fennel fronds/leafy tops plus a pinch of ground black pepper
- ⮞ 1/2 teaspoon freshly ground anise seed
- ⮞ 1 tablespoon dried Mexican oregano leaf or dried Mexican or French tarragon

HOKKAIDO/POTIMARON/RED KURI (Japanese squash) – 1 pound
- ⮞ 1 pound Baby Red Hubbard, Fairytale, Sugar, or pie pumpkin (for Orange Hokkaido)
- ⮞ 1 pound buttercup, butternut, Carnival, or acorn squash (for Green Hokkaido)

HOLLANDAISE SAUCE, QUICK – 3/4 cup
- ⮞ 1/2 cup mayonnaise thinned with 1 or 2 tablespoons water, then gently heated until warm (do not let boil)
- ⮞ 1/2 cup sour cream, 2 tablespoons mayonnaise, 1 tablespoon lemon juice, and 1/4 teaspoon salt, gently heated until warm (do not let boil)

HOLLAND/DUTCH/FINGER CHILES, FRESH – 1
- ⮞ 1 red jalapeño or red Fresno chile

HOLY BASIL *See BASIL, HOLY*

HOMINY GRITS – 1 cup *See also GRITS, QUICK-COOKING*
- 1 heaping cup samp (broken hominy), processed briefly to the desired consistency
- 1 cup polenta

HOMINY, WHOLE DRIED/MAIZE CACAHUACINTLE – 1 cup
- 1 cup samp/broken hominy (shorter cooking time)
- 1 cup chicos, or large white dried corn kernels
- 2 (29-ounce) cans or 4 (14-ounce) cans cooked hominy, drained and rinsed

HONEY–1 cup
- 1 cup light agave syrup/nectar
- 1 cup Coconut Nectar
- 1 cup rice-based nectar, such as Just Like Honey
- 1 cup Yacon root syrup (deeper flavor; not for baking)
- 1 cup Italian pine syrup/*mugolio* (expensive; not for cooking)
- 1 1/2 cups firmly packed light or dark brown sugar (or 1 1/4 cups granulated sugar) plus 1/4 cup liquid (for baking, use 1/4 cup more of the liquid called for in the recipe plus 1/2 teaspoon cream of tartar)
- 3/4 cup unsulphured molasses or dark corn syrup plus 1/2 cup granulated sugar (for baking, increase liquid in the recipe by 2 tablespoons)
- 1 cup granulated honey crystals/honey powder, dehydrated maple syrup, or molasses powder (for dry rubs and sprinkling over cereal)

HONEY, AVOCADO – 1 cup
- 1 cup strongly flavored dark honey, such as buckwheat, chestnut, manuka, or pine

HONEY, BITTER/SAVORY HONEY/MIELE AMARO (Sardinian) – 1 cup
- 1 cup robust or strongly flavored honey, such as avocado, buckwheat, chestnut, manuka, or pine

HONEY BUTTER – 4 ounces (1/2 cup/1 stick)

▷ 1 or 2 tablespoons honey stirred into 4 ounces room-temperature butter (for more honey taste, beat together 1/3 cup honey and 1/2 cup butter until creamy)

HONEY, CHESTNUT (Italian) – 1 cup

▷ 1 cup strong, earthy honey, such as Sardinian, buckwheat, pine, or eucalyptus

HONEY, LAVENDER (French) – 1 cup

▷ 1 cup wildflower, orange blossom, or any mild, fragrant honey

HONEY, LYCHEE (Asian) – 1 cup

▷ 1 cup clover; or a mild, golden, fragrant honey

HONEY, MILD – 1 cup

▷ 1 cup acacia, alfalfa, blueberry, clover, grapefruit blossom, linden blossom, or orange blossom honey
▷ 1 cup Tupelo honey (sweeter)

HONEY MUSTARD – 1/4 cup

▷ 2 tablespoons each Dijon mustard and honey

HONEY MUSTARD SAUCE – 1/2 cup

Make Your Own Stir together 1/3 cup mayonnaise, 1 or 2 tablespoons Dijon or American mustard, and 1 or 2 tablespoons honey until combined. Refrigerate for 3 or 4 hours for the flavors to meld.
Or
Stir together 1/3 cup yellow mustard and 2 1/2 tablespoons honey until smooth; season with salt and pepper.

HONEY, THYME, WILD/HYMETTUS (Greek) – 1 cup

▷ 1 cup flavorful dark honey, such as berry, chestnut, or wildflower

HONEY, TIGLI (Tuscan) – 1 cup
☞ 1 cup linden, lavender, or acacia honey

HONEY VINEGAR/CHESTNUT HONEY VINEGAR – 1 cup
☞ 1 cup champagne vinegar and 2 tablespoons honey, gently heated until the honey melts (for 1 tablespoon substitute apple cider vinegar)

HONTAKA CHILE, FRESH OR DRIED – 1
☞ 1 fresh or dried Thai or cayenne chile
☞ 1 teaspoon crushed red pepper flakes

HOOP CHEESE *See FARMER CHEESE*

HOP MARJORAM/CRETAN DITTANY (Cretian and Greek herb) *See MARJORAM, FRESH*

HORCHATA (Spanish chufa nut beverage) – 1 cup
☞ 1 cup rice or almond milk, flavored with cinnamon and vanilla to taste

HORENSO (Japanese spinach) *See SPINACH*

HORNCHEN (dried German pasta) *See PASTA, TUBULAR*

HORN OF PLENTY MUSHROOM *See BLACK TRUMPET/HORN OF PLENTY MUSHROOM*

HORSERADISH, BOTTLED – 2 tablespoons
☞ 1 tablespoon dried horseradish powder (or horseradish flakes), mixed with 1 tablespoon each vinegar and water then left, covered, for 10 to 15 minutes to develop the flavor

HORSERADISH CREAM – 2/3 cup (about)

Make Your Own Fold 2 to 3 tablespoons (or more) strained bottled horseradish (or grated fresh horseradish root) into 1/2 cup sour cream, crème fraîche, or full-fat yogurt. Refrigerate for at least 30 minutes to develop the flavor.

Or

Whisk 1/4 cup heavy cream until softly whipped (should equal 1/2 cup), then fold in 1/2 cup strained bottled horseradish plus 1/2 teaspoon salt. Refrigerate for at least 30 minutes to develop the flavor.

HORSERADISH, FRESH – 1 tablespoon grated (from a peeled 1/2-inch segment)

- 2 tablespoons drained bottled horseradish
- 1 to 2 teaspoons dried horseradish powder, or horseradish flakes, mixed with 1/2 to 1 tablespoon water then left, covered, 10 to 15 minutes to develop the flavor
- 1 tablespoon wasabi paste (or 1 tablespoon wasabi powder mixed with 2 teaspoons cold water then left, covered, 10 minutes to develop the flavor
- 1 tablespoon grated black radish (the more pungent the better)
- 1 tablespoon grated toothwort rootstock/*Dentaria*, or garlic mustard taproot/*Alliaria petiolata*

HORSERADISH LEAVES/MALUNGGAY (Indian and Filipino vegetable) – 8 ounces

- 8 ounces baby spinach, mizuna, or tatsoi

HORTA/KHÓRTA (wild or cultivated leafy Greek greens) – 1 pound

- 1 pound young agretti, amaranth greens, beet greens, chicory, curly endive, dandelion greens, escarole (dark outer leaves), kale, milk thistle, stinging nettle, orach/mountain spinach, purslane leaves, radish tops, watercress, wood sorrel, or end-of-season lettuces going to seed

HOSRUM (Lebanese) See VERJUICE

HOT DOG BUNS – 1 dozen
☞ 1 dozen 2 1/2-inch-wide pieces of ciabatta, focaccia, or baguette, cut to hot-dog length and split horizontally (Hollow out the baguette if necessary, reserving the torn bread for fresh breadcrumbs.)

HOT PEPPER OIL See CHILI OIL, CHINESE; CHILI OIL, ITALIAN

HOT PEPPER SAUCE – 1 teaspoon
☞ 1 teaspoon Louisiana-style hot sauce, harissa, sambal oelek, Sriracha, or chili paste
☞ 1/4 teaspoon ground cayenne pepper
☞ 3/4 to 1 teaspoon crushed red pepper flakes, Korean chili powder/*kochukaru*, or hot Hungarian paprika

HOT PEPPER SAUCE– 1 cup
Make Your Own Combine 1 cup stemmed hot fresh chiles, 1 cup heated distilled white (or cider) vinegar, and 1 teaspoon salt in a narrow, sterilized jar; cap tightly and let steep for at least 4 weeks. Strain to remove the chiles, or leave as is and replenish the vinegar a few more times; keep refrigerated. Alternatively, liquefy the ingredients in a blender or food processor and then steep. (Wear plastic gloves when handling the chiles.)

HUACATAY/BLACK MINT/TAGETES GRAVEOLENS, FRESH OR FROZEN (Peruvian seasoning) – 1 tablespoon chopped
☞ 1 tablespoon huacatay powder (ground dried huacatay) or jarred paste
☞ 1 1/2 teaspoons each chopped fresh cilantro (or tarragon) and mint leaves
☞ 1 tablespoon chopped fresh cilantro

HUAUNZONTLE (Mexican vegetable) – 1 pound
☞ 1 pound Broccolini or Chinese broccoli

HUCKLEBERRIES, FRESH OR FROZEN – 1 cup
- ☞ 1 cup blueberries (sweeter; softer seeds)
- ☞ 1 cup bilberries/whortleberries/*Vaccinium myrtillus* (dark blue or black; smaller and tarter)
- ☞ 1 cup salal berries/*Gaultheria shallon* (dark blue; seedy and juicy; blueberry/blackberry taste)
- ☞ 1 cup Juneberries/serviceberries/sarvisberries/*Amelanchier alnifolia* (purple-black; some berries more tart than others; cook to soften the seeds before adding to muffin batter)
- ☞ 1 cup black crowberries/*Empetrum nigrum* (tarter; freeze overnight to improve flavor; use in cooking)

HUITLACOCHE/CUITLACOCHE/BLACK CORN FUNGUS/CORN SMUT, FRESH OR FROZEN (Mexican seasoning) – 4 ounces
- ☞ 1 to 2 tablespoons canned huitlacoche puree
- ☞ 4 ounces black trumpet/horn of plenty mushrooms
- ☞ 4 ounces morel mushrooms

HUMMUS (Middle Eastern dip) – 2 cups
Make Your Own Drain and rinse 1 (15-ounce) can room-temperature garbanzo beans; process with 2 to 3 tablespoons each fresh lemon juice, tahini, and olive oil and 1 minced garlic clove in a blender or food processor until smooth. (Add water if necessary and season with salt, cumin, or more lemon juice, if desired.) Alternatively, use cannellini or Fordhook lima beans, adding more garlic and olive oil and omitting the tahini. Another alternative is replacing beans with 1 cup roasted garbanzo/chickpea flour mixed with 2/3 cup cold water then cooking it for a few minutes.

HUNGARIAN WAX PEPPER, FRESH – 1
- ☞ 1 fresh Cubanelle, Corno di Toro, Nardello, or Marconi pepper
- ☞ 1 fresh guero chile
- ☞ 1 fresh yellow bell pepper, peeled

HYSSOP/HYSSOPUS OFFICINALIS, FRESH (European seasoning) – 1 tablespoon chopped
 ⇨ 1 1/2 teaspoons each chopped fresh mint and sage

HYSSOP, SYRIAN/ORIGANUM SYRIACUM (Middle Eastern seasoning) – 1 tablespoon dried
 ⇨ 2 teaspoons dried thyme and 1 teaspoon dried marjoram

I

IBÉRICO HAM/JAMÓN IBÉRICO/JAMÓN DE PATA NEGRA (Spanish artisanal salted and dry-cured ham) – 1 pound
- 1 pound Serrano ham or prosciutto di Parma

ICE CREAM, BANANA SOFT-SERVE– 1 to 1 1/2 cups
Make Your Own Cut up 2 to 4 frozen bananas. Process with 1/2 cup yogurt, cream, or milk in a blender or food processor until smooth, 1 to 3 minutes. Serve immediately. (Adding 1 tablespoon dry milk powder makes it creamier; adding 1 teaspoon honey makes it sweeter; omitting yogurt, cream, or milk makes it smoother and dairy-free.)

ICE CREAM CHOCOLATE SHELL *See CHOCOLATE SHELL*

ICE CREAM CONES, MINIATURE – 1 dozen
- 1 dozen freshly-baked wafer cookies, such as brandy snaps, lace cookies, or tuiles, quickly formed into cone shapes while still hot (Insert the point of each cone into the neck of a bottle to hold its shape until it cools completely.)

ICE CREAM, GREEN TEA – 1 pint
- 1 scant teaspoon green tea powder/*matcha,* diluted with 1 teaspoon water, then stirred into 2 cups softened vanilla ice cream (Cover tightly and freeze until hard.)

ICE CREAM, SOFT-SERVE – 1 quart
- 1/2 cup heavy cream whipped until stiff with 1 tablespoon sugar, then combined with 3 cups softened vanilla ice cream (Freeze in a large freezer bag until semifirm, 4 to 6 hours, then knead the bag until the mixture is uniformly soft, about 30 seconds.)

ICE CREAM, RUM RAISIN – 1 quart
☞ 1/2 cup raisins and 1/4 cup dark rum brought to a simmer; cooled completely, then chopped and folded into 1 quart softened vanilla ice cream (Repack into its container and freeze overnight before serving.)

ICE CREAM, VANILLA – 1 quart
Make Your Own Whip 2 cups heavy cream until stiff, then fold into 1 cup sweetened condensed milk and 1 or 2 teaspoons vanilla extract. Freeze in a covered container until firm, 6 to 8 hours. (For a sweeter product, use more condensed milk; for less sweet, use less.)

IDIAPPAM/IDIAPPA, DRIED (South Indian and Sri Lankan thin rice noodles) – 1 pound
☞ 1 pound dried Thai rice sticks/*sen yai/phat*, Chinese rice vermicelli/*mi fen/mai fun,* Vietnamese rice noodles/*banh pho kho,* or Filipino rice stick noodles/*pancit bihon*

IDIAZÁBAL (Spanish lightly smoked sheep's milk cheese) – 1 ounce
☞ 1 ounce Spanish San Simon cheese, smoked medium cheddar, smoked Gouda, smoked Irish Blarney, or smoked provolone

INDIAN DRIED RED CHILE/BEGDI/GUNTUR – 1
☞ 1 dried Kashmiri chile *See also KASHMIRI CHILE*

INDIAN FIVE-SPICE MIX *See BENGALI FIVE-SPICE MIX*

INDONESIAN FISH SAUCE/KECAP IKAN/KETJAP IKAN *See FISH SAUCE*

INDONESIAN SOY SAUCE *See KECAP ASIN; KECAP MANIS*

INDONESIAN VINEGAR/CUKA – 1 tablespoon
☞ 1 tablespoon distilled colorless malt vinegar or rice vinegar

INJERA (Ethiopian teff-fermented flatbread with a spongy texture) – 3 large

⮞ 3 Indian dosas or pita breads (lacks sour flavor)

Make Your Own Stir together 1 cup light-colored teff flour, 1/2 teaspoon salt, and 1 1/4 cups water, cover and let sit for 8 to 12 hours at room temperature. Cook in a nonstick skillet (or seasoned cast-iron skillet) over moderately high heat until holes barely start to form, 20 to 30 seconds, then cover and cook until the injera is firm, about 1 minute.

Or

Stir together 1 cup sourdough or buckwheat pancake mix, 1/4 teaspoon baking soda, 9 ounces club soda, and 1 or 2 teaspoons lemon juice. Cook immediately on one side only, partly covered, until spongy and holes appear on the surface, about 1 minute.

INVERT SUGAR SYRUP/TREMOLINE – 1 cup

⮞ 1 cup pure cane syrup, such as Steen's, or golden syrup, such as Lyle's

⮞ 1 1/4 cups granulated sugar, 1/3 cup water, and 1/2 teaspoon lemon juice, simmered until syrupy and reduced to 1 cup, 7 to 8 minutes (will thicken as it cools)

ITALIAN LEAVENING (Bench Mate, Pane Angel, or Rebecchi) – 1 teaspoon

⮞ 1/2 teaspoon each baking powder and baking soda; add 1/2 teaspoon vanilla extract to the recipe

ITALIAN SAUSAGE, BULK – 1 pound

⮞ 1 pound ground pork or turkey (25 to 30% fat), 1 tablespoon Italian sausage seasoning or pizza seasoning, and 2 tablespoons chilled red wine or ice water, thoroughly combined (For hot sausage, add 1/8 teaspoon ground cayenne pepper and 1/2 teaspoon crushed red pepper flakes to the meat. For a more developed flavor, cover and refrigerate for 24 hours before cooking.)

ITALIAN SEASONING – 1 teaspoon
- ☞ 1/4 teaspoon each dried basil, dried marjoram, dried Mediterranean oregano, and dried thyme plus 1/8 teaspoon crushed dried rosemary (optional)
- ☞ 1 1/2 tablespoons chopped fresh Italian-type herbs (basil, thyme, or oregano)

ITALIAN SQUASH *See ZUCCHINI*

J

JABOTICABA/BRAZILIAN GRAPE – 1 pound
- 1 pound large purple grapes, or small Damson plums

JACK CHEESE (North American semisoft, cheddar-type or hard cheese) – 1 ounce
- 1 ounce Asadero/*queso Oaxaca*, Caciotta, Havarti, Muenster, or fresh Teleme (for Monterey and Sonoma)
- 1 ounce aged Asiago, Parmesan, or Romano (for dry Jack)
- 1 ounce high-temperature pepper Jack cheese (the non-melting variety for sausage making; contains peppers)

JACKFRUIT/JAKFRUIT/NANGKAI, FRESH OR FROZEN (Southeast Asian fruit and vegetable) – 1-pound section
- 2 (20-ounce) cans jackfruit in brine, drained and rinsed (for mature, yellow fruit) or drained young (green) jackfruit in brine (for young green fruit)
- 1 large Hawaiian papaya, or 1-pound piece of peeled and seeded Mexican papaya (for mature, yellow fruit)
- 1 (1-pound section) winter melon or breadfruit, 2 medium chayote squash, 1 or 2 unripe plantains, or 3 medium boiling potatoes (for young green fruit)

JAGGERY/PALM SUGAR/GUR (Indian dark, unrefined sugar) – 1 cup grated, shaved, granulated, or jarred
- 1 cup grated or crushed Mexican unrefined sugar/*piloncillo/panela* or *panocha/panucha*
- 1 cup crushed/grated Indonesian palm sugar/*gula jawa* or Malaysian palm sugar/*gula melaka*
- 1 cup dark muscovado/Barbados sugar

▷ 1 cup dark brown unrefined cane sugar, such as Natural Molasses
▷ 3/4 cup granulated sugar plus 5 tablespoons molasses
▷ 1 cup dark brown or maple sugar moistened to a coarse paste with 1 tablespoon light molasses (for jarred palm sugar)

JALAPEÑO CHILE – 1
▷ 1 fresh Fresno, Holland/Dutch, serrano, or cayenne chile
▷ 1/2 fresh NuMex Jalmundo (jumbo-size jalapeño)
▷ 1 canned jalapeño chile, rinsed and blotted dry
▷ 1 teaspoon dried green jalapeño flakes added toward the end of cooking (or softened in 1 tablespoon warm water for 5 to 10 minutes)
▷ 1/2 teaspoon jalapeño chile powder
▷ 1/4 teaspoon ground cayenne pepper
▷ Jalapeño salt for seasoning; reduce the salt in the recipe accordingly

JALAPEÑO JELLY – 1 generous cup
Make Your Own Boil 1/4 cup distilled white vinegar, 1/4 cup granulated sugar, and 1 seeded and finely chopped jalapeño until reduced to a few tablespoons, 3 to 4 minutes. Add 1 cup apple jelly and simmer, stirring, until the jelly melts; cool, then stir before transferring to a lidded jar. Store in the refrigerator for up to 4 months.

JAMAICA See HIBISCUS FLOWERS, DRIED

JAMAICAN JERK SEASONING (dry spice blend) – 1 tablespoon
▷ 2 teaspoons chili seasoning and 1/2 teaspoon each dried thyme and ground allspice (for food)
▷ 2 to 3 tablespoons allspice berries, softened in warm water, then sprinkled over hot barbecue coals (for imparting an aroma while food is being grilled)

JAPANESE BLACK SUGAR/KUROZATO/KURO SATO (dark unrefined sugar) – 1 cup chopped
▷ 1 cup chopped or shaved Mexican unrefined sugar/piloncillo/panela

- 1 cup Indian palm sugar/jaggery/*gur* or Indonesian palm sugar/ *gula jawa*
- 1 cup firmly packed dark brown sugar plus 1 tablespoon unsulphured molasses
- 1 cup dark brown molasses unrefined cane sugar, such as Billington's

JAPANESE BLACK VINEGAR/AGED RICE VINEGAR/KUROZU – 1 tablespoon
- 1 tablespoon balsamic vinegar or good-quality sherry vinegar

JAPANESE BLACK SUGAR SYRUP/KUROMITSU – 1 cup
- 1 cup dark corn syrup or blackstrap molasses

JAPANESE BROWN RICE VINEGAR/GENMAIZU – 1 tablespoon
- 2 teaspoons cider or balsamic vinegar and 1 teaspoon water
- 1 tablespoon unseasoned rice wine vinegar

JAPANESE CHILI OIL/RAYU – 1 teaspoon
- 1 teaspoon toasted sesame oil and 1/2 teaspoon Japanese spice mixture *shichimi togarashi*
- Chinese chili oil

JAPANESE CHILI POWDER/ICHIMI TOGARASHI – 1 teaspoon
- 3/4 teaspoon Chinese ground red pepper
- 1/2 teaspoon Hungarian or Spanish mild paprika, or ground cayenne pepper

JAPANESE CHIVES/BUNCHING ONION/ASATSUKI – 1 tablespoon
- 1 tablespoon finely snipped green part of scallions or green onions
- 1 tablespoon finely snipped sprouted tips of yellow or white onion

JAPANESE CITRUS FRUIT See SUDACHI; YUZU

JAPANESE CUCUMBER/KYURI – 1
- 1 Lebanese/Persian cucumber
- 2 tender-skinned Kirby or pickling cucumbers
- 1/2 English/hothouse cucumber

JAPANESE CURRY POWDER – 1 tablespoon
- 1 tablespoon mild, sweet-flavored curry powder, such as S&B Oriental Curry Powder
- 1 tablespoon mild Madras curry powder (spicier)

JAPANESE DAIKON AND RED PEPPER CONDIMENT/GARNISH/ MOMIJI OROSHI – 1/4 cup
- 1/2 teaspoon red chili yuzu paste/*yuzu koshu* mixed with 1/4 cup grated drained daikon (adds citrus flavor)
- 1/4 cup grated daikon/*daikon oroshi* (lacks heat)

JAPANESE DIPPING SAUCE See ASIAN DIPPING SAUCE; PONZU SAUCE, QUICK; TEMPURA DIPPING SAUCE

JAPANESE EGGPLANT/NASU – 1 (about 6 ounces)
- 1 slender Asian/Indian or Persian eggplant
- 3 or 4 Thai green eggplants (not pea/baby eggplants)
- 1/4 globe eggplant, peeled and cut into strips

JAPANESE FERN SPROUTS/WARABI – 1 pound
- 1 pound baby asparagus or very thin asparagus spears
- 1 pound Chinese yard-long beans

JAPANESE FIELD POTATOES/SATOIMO – 1 pound (about 8)
- 1 pound small taro roots/dasheen (best when served immediately upon cooking)
- 1 pound small baby white potatoes (use small sweet potatoes for Japanese pale-fleshed sweet potatoes/*satsuma-imo*)

JAPANESE FISH SAUCE/SHOTTSURU/ISHIRI/ISHIRU – 1 teaspoon
- ☞ 1 teaspoon Japanese fermented sweet fish sauce/*ayu* (more mellow)
- ☞ 1 teaspoon Thai fish sauce/*nam pla*, Vietnamese fish sauce/*nuoc nam*, Filipino fish sauce/ *patis*, or any Asian fermented fish sauce
- ☞ 1 to 2 teaspoons anchovy paste or finely chopped anchovies

JAPANESE GOMA PASTE See SESAME PASTE

JAPANESE GREEN ONION/LONG ONION/WELSH ONION/TOKYO NEGI/NAGA NEGI – 1 regular stalk
- ☞ 2 or 3 Mexican onions or large thick scallions

JAPANESE GREEN PEPPER/AOTOGARASHI See SHISHITO PEPPER

JAPANESE HORSERADISH See WASABI/HON WASABI; WASABI, POWDERED; WASABI, PREPARED

JAPANESE HOT RED CHILE/SANTAKA/TOGARASHI JAPONES/ TAKANOTSUME, FRESH OR DRIED – 1
- ☞ 1 fresh cayenne, japonés, serrano, or Thai chile
- ☞ 1 dried de árbol, cayenne, serrano, or Thai chile
- ☞ 1 teaspoon ground Japanese chile/*ichimi togarashi*
- ☞ 1 teaspoon ground cayenne pepper; or red pepper flakes, crushed fine
- ☞ 1 1/4 teaspoons seven-spice seasoning/*shichimi togarashi*

JAPANESE KOBE BEEF – 1 pound
- ☞ 1 pound American Wagyu or Washugyu (Kobe-style beef; cross between Japanese Black Wagyu and American Black Angus)
- ☞ 1 pound American prime beef
- ☞ 1 pound Italian Chianina or French Charolais beef

JAPANESE KUROBUTA PORK – 1 pound
- ☞ 1 pound American Berkshire, Berkshire-Duroc blend, Duroc, or Red Wattle pork

JAPANESE MAYONNAISE/TOMAGO-NO-MOTO – 1/4 cup
- ☞ 1 tablespoon Kewpie brand or any light, creamy mayonnaise
- ☞ 1 tablespoon Western-style mayonnaise, 1/2 teaspoon rice vinegar, and 1/8 teaspoon superfine sugar, stirred until the sugar dissolves

JAPANESE MOUNTAIN YAMS/YAMAIMO – 1 pound
- ☞ 1 pound red skinned yams, such as Garnet or Jewel (less gelatinous)

JAPANESE MUSTARD/KARASHI See MUSTARD, JAPANESE

JAPANESE NIHAIZU SAUCE BASE See NIHAIZU

JAPANESE NOODLES, BEAN THREAD/BEAN VERMICELLI/ HARUSAME/SAIFUN – 8 ounces
- ☞ 8 ounces *itokonnyaku* noodles, rinsed and drained (brownish colored; thicker; more gelatinous)
- ☞ 8 ounces *shirataki* noodles, rinsed and drained (white colored; thinner; more gelatinous)
- ☞ 8 ounces agar-agar noodles/*yang fen*, rinsed and drained (transparent; thinner; more gelatinous)
- ☞ 8 ounces Chinese mung bean noodles/*fen si,* Korean sweet potato vermicelli/*dang myun,* Thai cellophane noodles/*woon sen,* or Vietnamese cellophane noodles/*bun tau*

JAPANESE NOODLES, BUCKWHEAT/SOBA/CHA SOBA, FRESH OR DRIED – 1 pound
- ☞ 1 pound fresh or dried 100% buckwheat flour noodles/*juwari soba,*
- ☞ 1 pound fresh or dried 80% buckwheat flour and 20% wheat flour noodles/*nippachi soba* (milder)
- ☞ 1 pound fresh or dried whole-grain buckwheat noodles/*hikigurumi soba* (darker, with a rougher texture)
- ☞ 1 pound fresh or dried Korean buckwheat noodles/*naeng myun*
- ☞ 1 pound fresh or dried buckwheat and mountain yam soba noodles/*yamaimo soba* (paler and chewier)
- ☞ 1 pound dried Kamut or spelt soba noodles, such as Eden Organic

☞ 1 pound dried whole-wheat or brown rice vermicelli (add salt to the cooking water)

JAPANESE NOODLES, THICK WHEAT/UDON, FRESH OR FROZEN – 18 ounces (2 packages)
☞ 14 ounces dried udon noodles, *sanuki* udon noodles (thicker and chewier), or *inaniwa* udon noodles (thinner; more delicate)
☞ 18 ounces fresh or 14 ounces dried *kishimen/himokawa* noodles (thicker and wider)
☞ 14 ounces dried linguine noodles

JAPANESE NOODLES, THIN WHEAT/SOMEN/TAMAGO SOMEN, DRIED – 14 ounces
☞ 14 ounces dried *hiyamugi* noodles, Filipino *miswa* noodles, or Indian *misoa* noodles
☞ 14 ounces dried angel hair, spaghettini, or vermicelli pasta

JAPANESE NOODLES, THIN WHEAT EGG/RAMEN, FRESH – 1 pound
☞ 1 pound Chinese lo mein or chow mein noodles
☞ 1 pound spaghetti, spaghettini, or vermicelli pasta

JAPANESE OKINAWA POTATOES (purple sweet potatoes) – 1 pound
☞ 1 pound Hawaiian Molokai sweet potatoes, or other purple sweet potatoes, such as Stokes
☞ 1 pound white sweet potatoes/*Ipomoea batatas* (less starchy and colorful)

JAPANESE OKONOMIYAKI SAUCE See OKONOMIYAKI SAUCE

JAPANESE PICKLED CABBAGE/QUICK PICKLES/TSUKEMONO/SHIO ZUKE – 3 cups
Make Your Own Toss 4 cups coarsely shredded napa cabbage with 2 teaspoons coarse salt in a freezer bag; press out the air, seal, and refrigerate for 2 to 3 days, turning the bag daily. Drain, rinse with water, then squeeze out the water. For quick pickling, refrigerate the

cabbage until limp and reduced to nearly half, 2 to 24 hours. For instant pickling, rub the cabbage vigorously with salt until tender and reduced to half, about 10 minutes, then squeeze out excess water.

JAPANESE PLUM, SALT-PICKLED *See UMEBOSHI; UMEBOSHI PASTE*

JAPANESE PLUM WINE *See PLUM WINE*

JAPANESE PONZU SAUCE *See PONZU SAUCE*

JAPANESE POTATO *See JAPANESE FIELD POTATOES; JAPANESE MOUNTAIN YAMS; JAPANESE OKINAWA POTATOES; JAPANESE PRAWN POTATOES*

JAPANESE PRAWN POTATOES/EBI-IMO – 1 pound
- 1 pound Japanese field potatoes/*sato-imo* (coarser texture)

JAPANESE PURPLE SWEET POTATO VINEGAR/BENIMOSU – 1 tablespoon
- 1 tablespoon sherry vinegar or balsamic vinegar

JAPANESE RADISH *See DAIKON/ASIAN WHITE RADISH*

JAPANESE RAPE BLOSSOMS/FLOWERING TOPS/NANOHANA – 1 pound
- 1 pound thin broccoli raab/*rapini*

JAPANESE RICE – *See RICE, JAPANESE SHORT-GRAIN*

JAPANESE RICE VINEGAR, PURE/JUNMAI ZU/GENMAI MOCHIGOME ZU/JUN-YOMEZU – 1 tablespoon *See also JAPANESE BLACK VINEGAR*
- 1 tablespoon light yellow rice vinegar/*komezu* (made with rice plus other grains)
- 1 tablespoon brown rice vinegar/*genmaizu* (darker color)

⊳ 1 tablespoon distilled rice vinegar/*kokumotsu-su* or part synthetic rice vinegar/*gohseisu* (lower cost grain vinegars)
⊳ 1 tablespoon organic rice wine vinegar, such as Ka-Me brand
⊳ 2 teaspoon Chinese white rice vinegar (or cider vinegar) plus 1/4 teaspoon water (sharper flavor)

JAPANESE RICE VINEGAR, SEASONED/AWASEZU/SUSHIZU/YAMABUKUSU – 1 cup

⊳ 1 cup white rice vinegar plus 1 tablespoon sugar and 1 teaspoon salt; alternatively, use 2 tablespoons sugar and omit the salt

JAPANESE RICE WINE/CHŎNGJU – 2 tablespoons See also SAKÉ

⊳ 2 tablespoons dry white vermouth

JAPANESE SEA SALT/ARAJIO (coarse natural sea salt) – 1 tablespoon

⊳ 1 teaspoon coarse grain moist French sea salt/*sel gris Marin/sel gris de Guérande*

JAPANESE SEASONED SOUP BASE/MEMMI – 1 generous tablespoon

⊳ 1 tablespoon Japanese soy sauce, 1 teaspoon unseasoned rice vinegar, 1/2 teaspoon sugar, and 1/4 teaspoon Asian fish sauce
⊳ 1 to 2 tablespoons Japanese light or dark soy sauce

JAPANESE SEAWEED MOZUKU See MOZUKU

JAPANESE SESAME SEED PASTE/NERI-GOMA See SESAME PASTE

JAPANESE SEVEN-SPICE SEASONING/SHICHIMI TOGARASHI/NANAMI TOGARASHI – 1 teaspoon

⊳ 3/4 teaspoon ground Japanese chile/*ichimi togarashi* or Chinese ground red pepper (for heat only; lacks flavor)

JAPANESE SOBA DIPPING SAUCE/SOBA-TSUYU See TEMPURA DIPPING SAUCE

JAPANESE SOBA FLOUR/KISOBA (100% pure buckwheat flour) – 1 cup
- ☞ 1 cup fine buckwheat flour or stone-ground buckwheat flour, such as Cold Mountain

JAPANESE SOFT FLOUR/HAKURIK-KO (for cakes and batter) – 1 cup
- ☞ 1 cup cornstarch

JAPANESE SOYA BEAN FLOUR/KINA-KO See FLOUR, SOY, FULL-FAT

JAPANESE SOY SAUCE/SHOYU See SOY SAUCE, JAPANESE

JAPANESE SQUASH See HOKKAIDO; KABOCHA

JAPANESE SUSHI VINEGAR/KASUZU – 1 cup
- ☞ 1 cup Japanese seasoned rice vinegar/*awasezu/sushizu*
- ☞ 1 cup red sushi vinegar/*kasuzu/akazu*

JAPANESE SU WATER See ACIDULATED WATER

JAPANESE SWEET POTATO See JAPANESE MOUNTAIN YAM

JAPANESE SWEET RICE WINE See MIRIN

JAPANESE SWEET VINEGAR SEASONING SAUCE/AMAZU – 1/2 cup
Make Your Own Gently heat 1/2 cup rice vinegar, 3 tablespoons granulated sugar, and 1 1/4 teaspoons sea salt until the sugar dissolves; cool to room temperature.
Or
Gently heat 1/4 cup each rice vinegar and water, and 1 1/2 tablespoons granulated sugar until the sugar dissolves; cool to room temperature (for sunomono or cucumber salad).

JAPANESE TEMPURA BATTER See TEMPURA BATTER

JAPANESE TEMPURA DIPPING SAUCE See TEMPURA DIPPING SAUCE

JAPANESE TEMPURA FLOUR See TEMPURA FLOUR

JAPANESE TERIYAKI SAUCE See TERIYAKI SAUCE

JAPANESE TONKATSU SAUCE See TONKATSU SAUCE

JAPANESE TORIGARA BASE (WEIHA) See TORIGARA BASE (WEIHA)

JAPANESE YAKITORI SAUCE See YAKITORI SAUCE

JAPANESE YUKARI SHISO SALT – 1 tablespoon
- 1 tablespoon matcha salt (powdered green tea salt)
- 1 tablespoon seasoning for rice/furikake See also FURIKAKE

JAPONÉS CHILE/HONTAKA/SANTAKA, FRESH – 1
- 1 fresh or dried serrano, cayenne, or Thai chile
- 1 or 2 dried de árbol chiles
- 1/2 to 1 teaspoon crushed red pepper flakes

JARLSBERG (Norwegian semihard, Emmental-type cheese) – 1 ounce
- 1 ounce Emmental, Gruyère, Comté, Danbo, Fontina D'Aosta, or domestic Swiss

JASMINE RICE See RICE, THAI JASMINE

JBANE/JBEN (Moroccan fresh or matured goat cheese) – 1 ounce
- 1 ounce mild domestic goat cheese/chèvre

JERUSALEM ARTICHOKE See SUNCHOKE

JIBNEH ARABIEH (Middle Eastern mild brined cheese) – 1 ounce
- 1 ounce ackawi (soak to remove salt if necessary), Greek feta, fresh mozzarella, queso fresco, or haloumi

JICAMA/YAMBEAN/BANGKWANG (Malaysian and Latin American crisp root vegetable) – 1 pound
- ⮞ 1 pound fresh or canned water chestnuts (well-rinsed or blanched in boiling water if canned)
- ⮞ 1 pound daikon, white icicle radishes, crosnes, or small young or salad turnips

JOB'S TEARS/HATO MUGI/COIX LACRYMA–JOBI (Japanese whole-grain barley) – 1 pound
- ⮞ 1 pound whole-grain/pot or pearl barley (smaller; slightly different flavor)

JOCOQUE/LABIN/LABNE (Mexican fermented cream) – 1 cup
- ⮞ 1/2 cup buttermilk stirred into 1/2 cup Mexican crèma or sour cream

JUANITA PEPPER See PEPPADEW/PIQUANTÉ PEPPER, JARRED

JUBNA BAYDĀ'/JIBNI BEIDA (Syrian white cheese) See HALOUMI

JUJUBES/NATSUME (Chinese red dates) – 1 cup
- ⮞ 1 cup canned jujubes, drained (for fresh)
- ⮞ 1 cup hard crisp apple chunks (for fresh)
- ⮞ 1/2 cup dried jujubes, softened in cold water 30 minutes (for fresh)
- ⮞ 1 cup dried goji berries/wolfberries (for dried)
- ⮞ 1 cup up dried dates, dried figs, or dried plums/prunes (for dried)

JUNIPER BERRIES, DRIED – 1 teaspoon (8 crushed)
- ⮞ 8 to 10 wild fresh juniper berries/*Juniperus communis* (soft and easily bruised)
- ⮞ 8 or 9 dried black myrtle berries/*Myrtus communis* crushed and seeded (juniper-, rosemary-, and pine-tasting); or 1 or 2 teaspoons chopped fresh myrtle leaves (more juniper-tasting), added toward the end of cooking
- ⮞ 2 to 3 teaspoons gin, stirred in during the last 5 minutes of cooking

K

KABOCHA/NAN GUA (Japanese small, orange flesh winter squash) – 1 pound
☞ 1 pound autumn cup, buttercup, butternut, large acorn, golden nugget, or baby Hubbard (contains more moisture)

KABOSU (Japanese acidic citrus fruit) – 1
☞ 2 Key limes or 1 Persian lime

KABURA (giant Japanese turnip) – 1 pound
☞ 1 pound daikon radish

KADAYIF See KATAIFI

KAFFIR LIME JUICE (Southeast Asian) – 1 tablespoon
☞ 1 tablespoon sour, unripe Persian lime juice

KAFFIR LIME LEAF/WILD LIME LEAF/BAI MAKRUT/JERUK PURUT, FRESH (Southeast Asian) – 1 leaf
☞ 2 thawed frozen kaffir leaves, or 4 reconstituted dried leaves
☞ 1/4 teaspoon kaffir lime leaf powder/bai maikrut
☞ 1 young, fresh organic lemon or lime leaf
☞ 3/4-inch strip of kaffir or lime zest; or 1/4 to 1/2 teaspoon finely grated kaffir or lime zest (added toward the end of cooking)

KAFFIR LIME LEAF POWDER/KAFFIR POWDER – 1 teaspoon
☞ 4 or 5 dried kaffir lime leaves, chopped, then ground to a fine powder

KAFFIR LIME ZEST, FRESH, FROZEN, OR BRINED – 1 teaspoon finely grated
☞ 2 teaspoons dried zest soaked in water to rehydrate (discard soaking water)

▷ 1 to 2 tablespoons shredded kaffir lime leaves
▷ 1 1/2 teaspoons finely grated fresh citron or Persian lime zest

KAHLÚA *See COFFEE LIQUEUR*

KAKDI MAGAZ (Indian dried cucumber seeds) – 1 tablespoon
▷ 1 tablespoon Chinese dried melon seeds/*qwa tze*, or other dried melon seeds, such as cantaloupe or honeydew

KALA JEERA *See CUMIN SEEDS, BLACK*

KALAMANSI *See CALAMONDIN*

KALAMATA VINEGAR (Greek vinegar from sun-dried grapes) – 1 tablespoon
▷ 1 tablespoon balsamic vinegar

KALE CHIPS
Make Your Own Rub stemmed kale leaves with olive oil and spread in a single layer on a baking sheet. Bake in a preheated 375°F oven until crisp, 10 to 15 minutes; cool and break into pieces. Alternatively, microwave 2-inch pieces in a single layer for about 3 minutes.

KALE, CURLY OR RUSSIAN RED – 1 pound
▷ 1 pound Tuscan kale/lacinato (sweeter and milder; preferred for salad and grilling)
▷ 1 pound Kalettes (cross between kale and Brussels sprouts)
▷ 1 pound collard greens, especially baby or frilly-leafed; green chard; turnip greens; or sweet potato greens

KALE, TUSCAN/BLACK CABBAGE/CAVOLO NERO/LACINATO – 1 pound
▷ 1 pound Portuguese cabbage/*couve galega* (for salads or cooking)
▷ 1 pound broccoli leaves (for salads or cooking)

☞ 1 pound Russian Red kale (less tender; soften trimmed leaves for salad by massaging them with olive oil and a little salt, or with vinaigrette)
☞ Curly leaf kale or Swiss chard (for cooking)
☞ Collard greens (for chips), or very thinly sliced (for salad or cooking)
☞ Mild wild greens: green amaranth, lamb's quarters, mallow leaves, miner's lettuce/claytonia, portulaca, Siberian miner's lettuce, or fresh picked grape leaves (for smoothies)

KALONJI *See NIGELLA SEEDS*

KAMUT/KHORASAN WHEAT KERNELS – 1 cup
☞ 1 cup organic wheat berries (much smaller)

KANTEN *See AGAR*

KANZURI (Japanese fermented chili paste) – 1 teaspoon
☞ 1 teaspoon green yuzu chili paste/*yuzu koshu*
☞ 1 or 2 drops chili oil

KAPI/GAPI (Thai seasoning) *See SHRIMP PASTE, FERMENTED*

KASHA (whole roasted buckwheat groats) 1 cup
☞ 1 cup uncooked buckwheat groats, toasted in a dry skillet over medium heat, stirring frequently, until lightly browned and fragrant, 6 to 8 minutes (or on a baking sheet in a preheated 350°F oven until lightly browned, about 10 minutes)
☞ 1 cup buckwheat grits or barley grits, toasted in a dry skillet over medium heat, stirring frequently, until golden and fragrant, 3 to 4 minutes

KASHKAVAL (Bulgarian stretched-curd cheese) – 1 ounce
☞ 1 ounce *caciocavallo*, gilead, *hajdú*, Muenster, provolone, or scamorza (for young)
☞ 1 ounces aged Asiago, dry Jack, kefalotyri, Parmesan, or Romano (for aged)

KASHMIRI CHILE/LAL MIRCH/HARI MIRCH, FRESH OR DRIED (Indian) – 1

⇨ 1 California chile or peeled deep red bell pepper, plus a pinch of mild paprika for extra color

⇨ 1 teaspoon Kashmiri chili powder or medium-hot Hungarian paprika

KASHMIRI CHILE POWDER/DEGHI MIRCH (Indian) – 1 teaspoon

⇨ 1/2 teaspoon California or New Mexico chile powder and 1/2 teaspoon mild paprika

⇨ 1 teaspoon medium-hot Hungarian paprika

KASSERI/KASERI/KASAR (firm Greek cheese) – 1 ounce

⇨ I ounce *kashkaval*, *kefalotyri*, Asiago, Pecorino Romano, Turkish *kasar*, or Parmesan

KATAIFI/KADAYFI/KNAFEH/KONAFA (Greek and Middle Eastern threadlike pastry) – 1 pound

⇨ 1 pound phyllo pastry, shredded or cut into thin strips

⇨ 1 pound regular Shredded Wheat cereal, crushed

KATAKURIKO (Japanese starch thickener) *See POTATO STARCH*

KATSUOBUSHI *See FISH FLAKES, DRIED*

KAYMAK/KAÏMAK/SER (Middle Eastern water buffalo cream) – 1/4 cup *See also CREAM, CLOTTED/DEVONSHIRE CREAM*

⇨ 1/4 cup top thick layer from creamline yogurt, such as Brown Cow

⇨ 1/4 cup softened natural cream cheese (no gum added) lightened with a little heavy cream

⇨ 1/4 cup clotted cream, thick crème fraîche, or mascarpone

KECAP ASIN (Indonesian soy sauce) – 1 tablespoon

⇨ 1 tablespoon Chinese light soy sauce or Maggi Seasoning

KECAP MANIS/KETJAP MANIS (Indonesian sweet, thick soy sauce) – 1/3 cup
- 1/3 cup Thai sweet black soy sauce/*see-eu wan*
- 1/3 cup Chinese double dark/double black sweet soy sauce/*yewn she jiang*
- 3 tablespoons Chinese dark soy sauce or Japanese tamari, 2 packed tablespoons palm or dark brown sugar plus a pinch of garlic powder and star anise (if available), gently heated until sugar melts (or microwaved on High for 20 seconds); stir to mix
- 1/4 cup Maggi Seasoning plus 1 1/2 tablespoons unsulphured molasses

KEFALOTIRI/KEPHALOTÝRI (hard, sharp-tasting Greek cheese) – 1 ounce
- 1 ounce *kefalograviera*, aged *kasseri*, or aged *mizithra/myzithra*
- 1 ounce Grana Padano, Pecorino Romano, or Parmesan cheese

KEFIR (Russian fermented dairy beverage) – 1 cup
- 1 cup kumiss (thicker and more alcoholic)
- 1 cup Rejuvelac (strained liquid from fermented grains; thinner; less alcoholic)
- 1 cup tart liquid yogurt, or 3/4 cup plain yogurt whisked with 1/4 cup milk (nonalcoholic)

KEFIR STARTER CULTURE – 1 (5-gram) packet
- 1 teaspoon milk kefir grains (strained grains; can be used indefinitely)
- 3 tablespoons prepared kefir

KELP, POWDER/GROUND KELP GRANULES (powdered seaweed) – 1 tablespoon
- 1 tablespoon dulse powder or granules
- 2 tablespoon dulse flakes

KELP STOCK See DASHI, VEGETARIAN/KOMBU DASHI; KOMBU STOCK

KENARI NUTS (Southeast Asian) – 1 cup
⊳ 1 cup almonds

KETCHUP – 1 cup
Make Your Own Combine 1 (8-ounce) can tomato sauce, 1/3 cup granulated or brown sugar, 2 tablespoons malt or cider vinegar, and 1/8 teaspoon ground cloves (optional) in a small saucepan and boil gently until thickened.

KEUKENSTROOP (Dutch thick dark syrup) – 1 cup
⊳ 1 cup molasses, treacle, golden syrup, coconut honey, or strong traditional honey
⊳ 1 cup Appelstroop (milder and fruitier tasting)

KEWRA/KEORA/KEVDA ESSENCE (Indian and Sri Lankan flavoring agent) – 1 or 2 drops
⊳ 1/2 or 1 teaspoon kewra (screwpine) water or rose water
⊳ 1/2 teaspoon pandan powder or paste (will add green color)
⊳ 1 or 2 drops food-grade pure rose extract/essence
⊳ 1/4 to 1/2 teaspoon Tahitian vanilla extract
⊳ 1- or 2-inch section Tahitian vanilla bean, split lengthwise and seeds scraped out (use the bean and the seeds)

KEY LIME JUICE See LIME JUICE, KEY

KHICHIYA (Indian popped rice) – 1 cup
⊳ 1 cup crisped rice cereal, such as Rice Crispies (regular or gluten-free)

KHOA/KHOYA/MAWA (East Indian unsweetened solid condensed milk) – 1 cup crumbled
⊳ 5 cups full-fat milk heated until reduced to 1 cup, stirring constantly, about 30 minutes
⊳ 3/4 cup full-fat dried milk powder

KIDNEY BEANS, RED OR PINK – *1 pound*
- 1 pound cannellini, cranberry/borlotti, Italian Rose, Great Northern, navy, pinto, or Tongues of Fire beans

KIKURAGE *See CLOUD EAR/BLACK TREE FUNGUS*

KIMCHI/KIMCHEE/BAECHU KIMCHI (Korean pickled napa cabbage) – *1 cup*
- 1 cup vegan kimchi, such as Trader Joe's
- 1 cup rinsed and drained sauerkraut plus 1 or 2 teaspoons Korean chile bean paste, such as *gochujang or taeyangcho*, stirred until combined

KIMCHI PASTE/GOCHUJANG/TAEYANGCHO *See KOREAN CHILI BEAN PASTE*

KING OYSTER/ROYAL TRUMPET MUSHROOMS – *8 ounces*
- 8 ounces fresh white chanterelle, shiitake or matsutake mushrooms
- 4 ounces canned oyster, matsutake, or straw mushrooms

KINOME/PRICKLY ASH LEAF SPRIGS, FRESH (Japanese garnish) – *2 tablespoons*
- 2 tablespoons small sprigs of watercress, flat-leaf parsley, cilantro, or mint (for the color)

KIPPERS (British split, brined, cold-smoked herrings) – *1 pound*
- 1 pound red herring/hard smoked herring (brined and heavily cold smoked; requires soaking)
- 1 pound bloaters (lightly cold smoked whole herrings)
- 1 pound buckling (whole hot smoked, ready-to-eat herrings)
- 1 pound Arbroath smokies (hot smoked, ready-to-eat haddock or whiting)

KIRMIZI BIBER (Turkish red chili powder) – *1 teaspoon*
- 1 teaspoon Aleppo chile powder

- ▷ 3/4 teaspoon crushed red pepper flakes plus 1/8 teaspoon paprika
- ▷ 1/2 teaspoon mild chile powder, such as ancho, California, or New Mexico, plus a pinch of paprika
- ▷ 1 teaspoon paprika

KIWI FRUIT – 8 ounces
- ▷ 8 ounces yellow or pink pitaya/dragonfruit (crunchier seeds)
- ▷ 8 ounces carambola/starfruit (yellow color)
- ▷ 8 ounces prickly pear/cactus pear/tuna (singe the prickles, if any, or remove with a rough cloth)

KLUWAK NUTS/BUAH KELUCK (Indonesian seasoning) – 1 cup prepared
- ▷ 1 cup fresh shelled chestnuts

KOBE BEEF See JAPANESE KOBE BEEF

KOCHUJANG See KOREAN CHILI BEAN PASTE

KOCHUKARU See KOREAN CHILI FLAKES

KOHLRABI/CABBAGE TURNIP – 1 pound (2 medium bulbs, including greens)
- ▷ 2 or 3 turnips (1 pound, including greens)

KOHLRABI GREENS – 1 pound
- ▷ 1 pound turnip greens, curly green kale, green chard, or collard greens

KOKUM/COCUM/BIRUND AAMSOL/PULAM PALLI (Indian and Malaysian souring agent) – 1-inch by 1/2-inch dried slice
- ▷ 1 dried tamarind slice/asam gelugor/asam jawa
- ▷ 1 tablespoon tamarind pulp or paste/asam jara
- ▷ 1 tablespoon green mango powder/amchur (add toward the end of cooking)

- 1 1/2 tablespoons fresh lemon or lime juice (use 1/2 teaspoon for each segment or broken piece)

KOMBU/DRIED KELP/KONBU/DASHIMA/HAI DAI (dried edible seaweed) – 1/2 ounce
- 1/2 ounce wakame, winged kelp, or sea girdle/finger kombu (milder flavor)
- 1/2 ounce whole leaf digitata kelp/oarweed (tougher; sweeter flavor)
- 1/2 ounce dulse, digitata, or wakame flakes/granules (for dashi/stock, or added at the beginning for cooking grains or beans)

KOMBU CRISPS
Make Your Own Break 4 or 5 strips of kombu into 1-inch pieces and fry in 350°F oil until crisp, 1 to 2 minutes.

KOMBU POWDER (Japanese condiment)
Make Your Own Cut dried kombu into small pieces and toast in a dry skillet, stirring constantly, until very crisp, about 5 minutes. Crumble or grind to a coarse powder with a mortar and pestle (or rolling pin).

KOMBU STOCK/KOMBU DASHI-JIRU (Japanese) – 1 cup See also
DASHI, VEGETARIAN
- 1-inch strip (1/8 ounce) dried kiri kombu/kelp (or kombu strands/natto kombu), soaked in 1 cup cold water 8 to 12 hours, then strained (discard the kombu)
- 1 1/2 teaspoons dulse flakes brought just to boiling in 1 cup water (or water from soaking dried mushrooms); removed from heat; cooled 5 minutes, then strained
- 1 teaspoon powdered kombu dissolved in 1 cup hot water

KOREAN BLACK BEAN PASTE See BLACK BEAN SAUCE/PASTE

KOREAN CABBAGE See NAPA CABBAGE

KOREAN CHILI BEAN PASTE/RED PEPPER PASTE/HOT PEPPER PASTE/GOCHUJANG – 1 tablespoon

- 1 tablespoon Chinese or Szechuan chili bean paste/*dou ban jiang* plus 1 teaspoon molasses
- 1 tablespoon Japanese red miso/*inaka/sendai* plus 1/2 teaspoon each corn syrup (or sugar) and ground cayenne pepper
- 1/2 tablespoon each Japanese white miso/*shiro/saikyo* and Asian red chili sauce, such as sambal oelek, plus 1/2 teaspoon molasses

KOREAN CHILI FLAKES/COARSE RED PEPPER POWDER/KOCHUKARU – 1 teaspoon

- 1 teaspoon Chinese coarsely ground chile/*la jiao mian*
- 1 teaspoon mild chile powder, such as ancho, California or New Mexico (for chile powder)
- 3/4 teaspoon crushed red pepper flakes (for chile flakes)

KOREAN CHILI THREADS/SILGOCHU

- Mild, red, deseeded chiles, flattened and wrapped in a damp paper towel; left an hour to soften, then rolled and sliced into 2- to 3-inch-long threads

KOREAN DIPPING SAUCE – 3 tablespoons See also KOREAN SESAME PASTE DIPPING SAUCE

- 1 tablespoon unseasoned rice vinegar and 2 tablespoons reduced-sodium soy sauce, stirred until combined

KOREAN DRIED LAVA SEAWEED/GIM See NORI

KOREAN FERMENTED BEAN AND CHILI SAUCE/SSÄMJANG – 3 tablespoons

- 1 tablespoon soybean paste/*doenjang* stirred into 2 tablespoons chili bean paste/*gochujang/taeyangcho*

KOREAN FERMENTED BEAN PASTE/DOENJANG See KOREAN SOYBEAN PASTE

KOREAN FISH SAUCE/SAENGSEON SAUCE *See FISH SAUCE*

***KOREAN GRAIN SYRUP/MALT SYRUP/JOCHEONG/ CHOCHONG/
MUL YUT – 1 cup***
- 1 cup light-colored corn syrup

KOREAN GREEN PEPPER/KOCHU – 1
- 1 large green jalapeño chile
- 1 peeled green bell pepper or Anaheim chile (for mild green pepper)

KOREAN LEEK/DAEPA – 1
- 1 large scallion or green/spring onion

KOREAN MUSHROOMS/PYOGA *See SHIITAKE MUSHROOMS*

***KOREAN NOODLES, BUCKWHEAT AND SWEET POTATO STARCH/
NAENG MYUN – 8 ounces***
- 8 ounces buckwheat noodles/*soba/memil guksu*, green tea soba/
  cha soba, or thin soba/*ki soba*
- 8 ounces Italian whole-wheat spaghetti, spaghettini, or vermicelli

***KOREAN NOODLES, SWEET POTATO OR MUNG BEAN STARCH/DANG
MYUN – 8 ounces***
- 8 ounces Chinese cellophane/bean thread noodles/*fen si/sei fun*
- 8 ounces Japanese bean thread vermicelli/*harusame*
- 8 ounces Thai clear transparent noodles/*wun sen*
- 8 ounces Vietnamese mung bean noodles/*bun tau*
- 8 ounces Filipino cellophane noodles/*sotánghon*

***KOREAN NOODLES, THICK WHEAT/NAMA/JAJAN MYUN, DRIED – 8
ounces***
- 8 ounces dried Japanese udon noodles, Chinese water noodles/
  main fun, ramen noodles/*chukka soba*, or spaghetti

KOREAN NOODLES, THIN WHEAT/SOMYUN/GOUGSOU, DRIED – 8 ounces
- 8 ounces dried Japanese *somen* or *hiyamugi* noodles, Filipino *miswa* noodles, or Indian *misoa* noodles
- 8 ounces dried angel hair pasta, spaghettini, or fine vermicelli

KOREAN PEAR *See ASIAN PEAR*

KOREAN PICKLED CABBAGE/KIMCHI *See KIMCHI*

KOREAN RADISH/MU *See DAIKON*

KOREAN RED PEPPER FLAKES *See KOREAN CHILI FLAKES*

KOREAN RED PEPPER THREADS *See KOREAN CHILI THREADS*

KOREAN RICE *See RICE, KOREAN*

KOREAN RICE VINEGAR *See RICE VINEGAR*

KOREAN RICE WINE/CHUNG-JU/YAKJU – 1/4 cup
- 1/4 cup Chinese yellow rice wine/*Shaoxing/Shao Hsing*, or medium dry sherry, such as amontillado

KOREAN RICE WINE, SWEET COOKING/SOJU – 1 tablespoon
- 1 tablespoon Japanese sweet rice cooking wine/*mirin*
- 1 tablespoon Chinese yellow rice cooking wine/*michiu/mi jiu*
- 1/2 teaspoon sugar or honey dissolved in 1 tablespoon white wine, saké, vermouth, sherry, or water

KOREAN ROASTED BARLEY TEA/BORICHA – 1/4 cup
Make Your Own Toast 1/4 cup pearl barley in a dry skillet over medium heat, stirring occasionally, until brown and fragrant, 10 to 15 minutes. Cool, then add to boiling water and simmer until infused to desired color/strength; serve hot or cold.

KOREAN SESAME PASTE DIPPING SAUCE/SSAMJANG – 1/4 cup
Make Your Own Toast 1/4 cup hulled (white) sesame seeds in a dry skillet over medium heat, stirring constantly, until golden brown, about 2 minutes. Immediately pour onto a plate to prevent over-browning. Crush the seeds to a paste with 1 tablespoon soy sauce, 1 tablespoon unseasoned rice vinegar, and 1 1/2 teaspoons sugar.

KOREAN SHRIMP, SALTED/FERMENTED MINI/SAEUJEOT/SAEWOO-JEOT – 1 tablespoon
  ☞ 1 tablespoon dried shrimp
  ☞ 1 tablespoon Asian fish sauce
  ☞ 2 teaspoons Asian fermented shrimp paste

KOREAN SOLAR SALT (coarse, crunchy salt) – 1 tablespoon
  ☞ 1 tablespoon kosher salt

KOREAN SOYBEAN PASTE/DOENJANG – 1 tablespoon
  ☞ 1 tablespoon Japanese red miso/*inaka/sendai* or brown miso/*hatcho* (less salty; smoother texture)

KOREAN SOY SAUCE See SOY SAUCE, KOREAN

KOREAN UNPOLISHED RICE VINEGAR See RICE VINEGAR, KOREAN UNPOLISHED

KOREAN WATERCRESS/MINARI – 1 cup
  ☞ 1 cup fresh garden cress stems or flat-leaf parsley stems

KOSHER SALT See SALT, KOSHER

KOUSKOUSI (Greek rice-shaped pasta) See PASTA, TINY SHAPED

KRACHAI See FINGERROOT

KREPLACH WRAPPERS See WONTON WRAPPERS

KRITHARAKI (small Greek oblong-shaped pasta) *See PASTA, TINY SHAPED*

KUDAMPULI/GARCIA CAMBOGIA *See KOKUM; TAMARIND CONCENTRATE*

KUDZU/KUZU ROOT STARCH/KO FEN/GOK FUN (Asian thickening agent) – 1 tablespoon powder
- 1 1/2 teaspoons arrowroot powder (Remove from the heat as soon as it reaches a boil.)

KUKA/BAOBAB LEAF POWDER (West African thickening agent) – 1 tablespoon
- 1 tablespoon filé/sassafras leaf powder (added at the end of cooking)
- 2 cups sliced fresh okra; or 1 (10-ounce) package sliced frozen okra, or whole frozen okra cut into 1/4-inch rounds (cooked with the stew)

KUMATO, FRESH (European brownish-green tomato) – 1 pound
- 1 pound vine-ripened, sweet, meaty-textured tomatoes

KUMQUATS, FRESH (tiny citrus fruit with sweet edible skin and tart flesh) – 2 or 3
- 2 or 3 preserved kumquats, rinsed and drained
- 2 or 3 fresh orangequats or mandarinquats (or, for a different flavor, lemonquats or limequats)
- 1 fresh calamondin/*kalamansi* (mandarin orange and kumquat hybrid; juicier)
- 2 to 3 tablespoons grated orange zest (for 2 or 3 minced kumquats in cooking)

KURPIANKA (lightly smoked Polish cheese with garlic) – 1 ounce
- 1 ounce smoked *caciocavallo*, smoked Gouda, smoked mozzarella, smoked provolone, or smoked scamorza (lacks garlic flavor)

KUZU ROOT STARCH *See KUDZU/KUZU ROOT STARCH*

KYOHO GRAPES (Japanese) – 1 pound
  ☞ 1 pound Concord grapes

KYONA (Japanese mustard green) *See MIZUNA, EARLY*

L

LABNA/LABNEH/LABNI/LABAN (Middle Eastern thick yogurt/ yogurt cheese) – 8 ounces (1 cup)

▷ 1 cup thick Greek yogurt

Make Your Own Stir 1/2 teaspoon kosher salt into 2 cups plain full-fat yogurt, preferably Greek-style (without pectin or additives). Transfer to a fine sieve lined with dampened cheesecloth set over a bowl and drain in the refrigerator for 1 to 3 days. (For low-fat labna, replace full-fat yogurt with low-fat and omit the salt; it will be less smooth.)

LADYFINGERS/SPONGE FINGERS/SAVOIARDI (Italian) – 8 ounces

▷ 8 ounces pound cake, sponge cake, or génoise, cut into 3-inch by 1-inch fingers and baked at 350°F until dry and crisp, 10 to 15 minutes; cool before using (For American ladyfingers, bake cake slices until barely crisp, 7 to 10 minutes.)

▷ 8 ounces Champagne biscuits, or vanilla wafers

LAFFA (Middle Eastern large doughy flatbread) – 1 pound

▷ 1 pound naan, large pita bread, or 12- to 14-inch ready-to-eat pizza shell

LAKSA LEAF See VIETNAMESE MINT

LAKSA NOODLES/LEI FUN, FRESH (Singaporean and Malaysian) – 1 pound

▷ 8 ounces dried Filipino pancit noodles, or other thick white rice noodles, prepared according to the package directions

▷ 8 to 12 ounces dried Shanghai noodles or spaghetti *grossi* (contains wheat), prepared according to the package directions

LACUMA PULP, FRESH OR FROZEN (Peruvian fruit puree) – 1/2 cup
- 3/4 cup lucuma powder mixed with 3/4 cup cool water and left to thicken for 2 to 3 hours

LALU (African leavening agent from dried crushed seeds of the baobab tree) – 1 tablespoon
- 1 1/2 teaspoons baking powder

LAMB'S QUARTERS/WILD SPINACH/PIGWEED/GOOSEFOOT/ QUELITES – 1 pound
- 1 pound spinach See also SPINACH; SWISS CHARD

LANGOUSTE/SPINY LOBSTER/ROCK LOBSTER/ARAGOSTA See LOBSTER, MAINE

LANGOUSTINES See DUBLIN BAY PRAWNS

LAOS POWDER (ground galangal root) – 1 teaspoon See also GALANGAL, GREATER
- 1/2 inch (2 teaspoons) peeled and finely minced galangal (fresh, frozen, or brined)
- 1 or 2 small (1/8-inch) slices dried galangal root/*galanga* (add whole to soup or stock without soaking)
- 1 1/2 teaspoons grated fresh ginger plus a few grains of ground black pepper, or a few drops of lemon juice

LARD, FRESH (rendered pork fat) – 1 cup
- 1 cup beef tallow (rendered beef fat)
- 3/4 cup nonhydrogenated solid vegetable shortening plus 1/4 cup chilled strained bacon drippings
- 1 cup plus 1 1/2 tablespoons supermarket lard or nonhydrogenated solid vegetable shortening
- 1 cup clarified unsalted butter
- 1 cup plus 3 tablespoons unsalted butter (for biscuits and pastry dough; reduce liquid accordingly)

☞ 1 cup peanut oil plus 1 teaspoon clarified/strained bacon drippings (for frying)

☞ 1 cup clarified/strained bacon, poultry, or meat fat/drippings; or mild virgin olive oil (for sautéing/shallow frying, not deep fat frying)

Make Your Own Grind or finely chop 12 ounces semifrozen unsalted pork fatback (or fat trimmed from pork shoulder without any traces of meat). Melt in a large, heavy skillet in a preheated 200°F to 225°F oven (or with 1/4 cup water on the lowest possible stovetop setting) for 1 to 1 1/2 hours. Strain in a cheesecloth-lined sieve and cool until solid (it will be softer than leaf lard rendered from kidney fat).

LARDO (Italian salt-cured seasoned fatback) – 8 ounces
☞ 8 ounces thinly sliced pancetta (for wrapping)

☞ 8 ounces salt pork or slab bacon (for cooked dishes)

LASAGNA/LASAGNETTE NOODLES, DRIED WHEAT – 1 pound
☞ 1 pound no-boil lasagna sheets; increase the liquid in the recipe by 25% (For a more delicate texture, boil no-boil noodles for 3 minutes; use a fish poacher or oval pan to keep the noodles flat and drain them on a wire rack.)

☞ 1 pound dried brown rice lasagna noodles

☞ 1 pound dried 1 1/2-inch-wide pappardelle, mafalde, or other wide flat pasta, laid side by side

☞ 1 pound dried rombi/short ribbon pasta, laid side by side (for individual lasagnas)

LASAGNA/LASAGNETTE NOODLES, NO-BOIL – 1 pound
☞ 1 pound fresh lasagna noodles or pasta sheets (Boil a few at a time in salted water, until barely al dente, about 2 minutes for noodles or 3 for sheets.)

☞ 12 ounces regular dry lasagna noodles (Boil a few at a time in salted water, until barely al dente.)

☞ 1 pound fresh or thawed frozen wonton wrapper strips (wonton wrappers cut into 1/2- to 1-inch strips; for small, individual lasagnas)

- 1 pound summer squash or zucchini, sliced 1/4 inch thick lengthwise and steamed or blanched until just tender (for gluten-free lasagna)
- 4 matzo sheets (use an 8-inch square baking dish)

LASSI (Indian yogurt drink) – 1 cup
- 1/2 cup each plain yogurt and water blended until smooth, then poured over ice (For a thicker consistency, increase the yogurt.)

LAVASH, CRISP (Armenian flatbread) – 1 pound
- 1 pound matzo

LAVASH, SOFT (Armenian flatbread) – 1 (10 1/2 by 9-inch) segment
- Flour tortilla (10-inch size), large pocketless pita bread/*pide*, or pita bread split into two halves (for thin lavash)

LAVENDER, FRENCH OR ENGLISH – 1 tablespoon dried culinary flowers
- 3 to 4 tablespoons pesticide-free fresh lavender buds (*Lavandula augustafolia* or *L. xintermedia*), stripped from stems and flower heads
- 1/2 teaspoon lavender extract
- 1 or 2 tablespoons lavender-flavored liqueur, such as *parfait amour* (for a dish containing liquid)

LAVENDER SUGAR (French) – 1 cup
Make Your Own Pulse 1 cup granulated sugar and 2 teaspoon dried lavender blossoms/culinary lavender buds in a food processor until the lavender is finely chopped; store airtight at room temperature. Alternatively, store bruised or coarsely chopped buds in a tightly sealed container with 1 cup granulated or superfine sugar until the sugar is flavored, 2 to 3 weeks, shaking the container periodically, then sift to remove the buds.

LAVENDER SYRUP – 1/2 cup
Make Your Own Add 1 tablespoon dried lavender blossoms/culinary lavender buds to 1/2 cup hot simple syrup (*See SYRUP, SIMPLE*) and cool for about 30 minutes. Strain and refrigerate for up to 1 week.

LEBANESE CLOTTED CREAM/ASHTAR See CREAM, CLOTTED

LEBANESE FOUR-SPICE MIX/MIXED SPICE – 1 teaspoon
 ☞ 1 teaspoon pumpkin pie spice or apple pie spice

LEBANESE MOUNTAIN BREAD See MARQŪQ

LEBANESE PEPPER MIX – 1 scant tablespoon
 ☞ 1 teaspoon each ground allspice and ground black pepper plus 1/2 teaspoon ground white pepper

LEBANESE SPICY BEEF SAUSAGE/SOUJOUK/SUJUK/YERSHIG – 1 pound
 ☞ 1 pound pepperoni or spicy salami

LEBAN YOGURT (Middle Eastern thick yogurt) See LABNA

LEBNEH See LABNA

LEEK, LARGE – 1 trimmed (1 cup sliced)
 ☞ 3 pencil-thin French baby leeks
 ☞ 1/2 cup sliced shallots (sweeter flavor)
 ☞ 1 cup sliced scallions/green onions, white part only
 ☞ 1 cup sliced ramp bulbs/wild leeks/*Allium tricoccum* (stronger flavor)
 ☞ 1 cup mild/sweet onion slices, soaked in cool water for 1 hour, then drained (stronger flavor)

LEEKS, BABY – 1 bundle
 ☞ 2 regular-size leeks

LEFSE (Norwegian round thin flatbread) – 1
 ☞ 1 thin flour tortilla

LEKVAR See PRUNE PUREE

LEMON AGRUMATO OIL See LEMON OLIVE OIL

LEMON BALM/SWEET BALM, FRESH – 2 tablespoons chopped (10 to 12 leaves)
- 4 teaspoons chopped fresh spearmint, Moroccan mint, or apple mint and 2 teaspoons chopped fresh lemon basil or lemon verbena
- 1 peppermint tea bag plus 1/4 teaspoon lemon zest (for tisane)
- 1 trimmed lemongrass stalk, cut into pieces and crushed with the side of a knife
- Spearmint or applemint (for garnishes and fruit salads)

LEMON BASIL/KEMANGIE, FRESH – 1 ounce
- 1 ounce fresh Thai lemon basil/green holy basil/*Bai manglak*
- 1 ounce fresh lime basil (darker leaves; lime aroma)
- 1 ounce fresh sweet basil (Italian, French, or California) plus a little lemon balm or lemon zest

LEMON CURD (for cake filling) – 1 cup
- 1 cup lemon pudding, thinned with a little fresh lemon juice

LEMON, DAQ (Turkish, small juicy, thin-skinned lemon) – 1
- 1/2 Meyer lemon

LEMON EXTRACT – 1 teaspoon
- 1/8 teaspoon lemon oil, such as Boyajian
- 2 to 3 teaspoons finely grated lemon zest from a scrubbed lemon, preferably organic

Make Your Own Combine 3 tablespoons lemon zest from well-scrubbed organic lemons with 1/2 cup vodka and let steep in a small, dark-colored bottle for 14 or more days in a cool, dark cupboard. Shake the bottle from time to time, then strain and store in the refrigerator. Use 1 generous teaspoon for 1 teaspoon extract.

LEMONGRASS, FRESH – 3- to 5-inch trimmed bottom third of inner core/1 to 3 tablespoons finely chopped
- 2 tablespoons frozen lemongrass slices (if home-frozen, slice thinly while frozen)

- 1 to 1 1/2 tablespoons crumbled or shredded freeze-dried lemongrass soaked in 1 to 1 1/2 tablespoons water until softened, 15 to 20 minutes
- 2 teaspoons oil-packed lemongrass, blotted dry
- 1 teaspoon sereh/serai powder (lemongrass powder)
- 2 or 3 teaspoons lemongrass paste/puree
- 2 tablespoons chopped lemon leaves or lemon verbena leaves (added at the last moment)
- 2 teaspoons chopped lemon balm or lemon myrtle leaves (added at the last moment)
- 2 (1-inch) strips lemon peel (white pith scraped away) blanched in boiling water 2 or 3 seconds, then blotted dry
- 1 teaspoon finely grated lemon zest

LEMON JUICE, EUREKA/LISBON – 1 tablespoon

- 1 tablespoon Meyer lemon juice; reduce the sugar in the recipe by 1/4 teaspoon
- 2 teaspoons freshly squeezed lime juice
- 1 teaspoon lemon juice powder (for baking, increase the liquid by 1 tablespoon)
- 1/4 teaspoon citric acid powder mixed with 1 tablespoon warm water
- 1/2 teaspoon finely grated lemon zest from a scrubbed lemon, preferably organic; reduce the liquid in the recipe by 1 tablespoon
- 1 tablespoon white wine (only if lemon flavor is not needed)
- 1 1/2 teaspoons distilled white vinegar or cider vinegar (only if lemon flavor is not needed)
- Tiny drop of acid phosphate (for cocktails and sodas only if lemon flavor is not needed)

LEMON JUICE, MEYER – 1/4 cup

- 2 tablespoons each regular lemon juice and orange or tangerine juice
- 3 tablespoons regular lemon juice, 1 tablespoon orange juice, and 1/8 teaspoon sugar

LEMON JUICE POWDER – 1 tablespoon
- 2 tablespoons lemon zest
- 1 tablespoon lemon juice (reduce the liquid in the recipe by 1 scant tablespoon)

LEMON, MEYER (cross between a lemon and a mandarin) – 1
- 1 large, thin-skinned regular Eureka lemon (more acidic)

LEMON OIL (American flavoring agent) – 1/8 teaspoon
- 1/8 teaspoon food-grade lemon essential oil
- 1/2 teaspoon lemon extract
- 1 1/2 teaspoons finely grated lemon zest from a scrubbed lemon, preferably organic
- 1/4 cup coarsely grated lemon zest from a scrubbed lemon, preferably organic, squeezed in a piece of cheesecloth

LEMON OIL/DAU CHANH (Asian flavoring agent) – 1/3 cup
Make Your Own Combine 1/3 cup vegetable oil with 1 tablespoon lemon zest from a well-scrubbed lemon (preferably organic) and heat slowly until small bubbles appear, 7 to 10 minutes. Cool and strain; store, tightly covered, in the refrigerator.

LEMON OLIVE OIL/AGRUMATO OIL (Italian flavoring agent) – 1/2 cup
Make Your Own Combine 1/2 cup extra-virgin olive oil with 1 tablespoon lemon zest from a well-scrubbed lemon (preferably organic) and heat to 250°F. Cover and let sit for a day or two to develop the flavor, then strain. (Alternatively, use 2 teaspoons natural lemon flavor, such as Simply Organic, in place of the lemon zest.)

LEMON OMANI (Middle Eastern dried lime powder) See LIME, DRIED

LEMON PEEL, DRIED See also LEMON ZEST
Make Your Own Finely grate lemon zest from well-scrubbed lemons (preferably organic). Spread in a single layer and dry at room temperature for 1 to 2 days; or in a preheated 200°F oven until crisp, about 20 minutes; or in a microwave on High for 1 to 1 1/2 minutes,

stirring every 30 seconds. Use it as is, or crush to a powder just before using.

LEMON PEPPER SEASONING, DRIED – 1/2 cup (about)
➢ 1 tablespoon ground, dried lemon peel (*See LEMON POWDER*), 1 tablespoon coarse salt, 6 tablespoons ground black pepper, and 1 teaspoon garlic powder. For salt-free lemon pepper, use 1 teaspoon onion powder in place of salt

LEMON PEPPER SEASONING, FRESH – 1 tablespoon (about)
➢ 1/2 teaspoon finely grated lemon zest, 2 teaspoons coarsely ground black pepper, and 1/4 teaspoon coarse salt

LEMON, PICKLED See PICKLED LEMONS

LEMON POWDER
➢ Dried lemon peel crushed to a powder *See LEMON PEEL, DRIED*

LEMON PUDDING – 1 cup
➢ 1 cup vanilla pudding plus 1/2 teaspoon lemon extract, or to taste

LEMON, PRESERVED See PRESERVED LEMON

LEMON SALT See CITRIC ACID; CITRON SALT

LEMON SEASONING SALT – 1/3 cup
Make Your Own Grind 2 tablespoons dried lemon peel in a spice/coffee grinder until very fine, then mix with 1/4 cup kosher or coarse sea salt. (Alternatively, use 1/4 cup finely grated fresh lemon zest in place of the dried peel; dry the salt mixture in a preheated 200°F oven, then cool before storing.) Keep in an airtight container for up to 3 months.

LEMON SUGAR – 1 cup
Make Your Own Trim the pith from strips of lemon zest (preferably organic); then bury the strips in 1 cup granulated sugar; store airtight in a cool dry place for 2 weeks before using.

LEMON SUGAR, SUPERFINE – 1 cup See also *VANILLA SUGAR*
Make Your Own Mix 2 tablespoons finely grated lemon zest (from well-scrubbed lemons, preferably organic) with 1 cup granulated sugar. Spread on a baking pan, and dry in a preheated 200°F oven for 20 minutes, stirring occasionally. Cool, then grind in a blender or food processor until fine, 30 to 40 seconds. Store, tightly covered, at room temperature.

LEMON THYME See *THYME, LEMON, FRESH*

LEMON VERBENA, FRESH – 2 tablespoons coarsely chopped (2 to 4 leaves)
- 1/2 to 1 teaspoon dried lemon verbena
- 1 lemon verbena herbal tea bag
- 2 to 4 sprigs lemon thyme
- 1 fresh lemongrass stalk, trimmed, flattened, and cut into 2-inch pieces (tie together with twine to make removal easier)
- 2 teaspoons shredded lemon zest
- Light spritz of verbena hydrosol (food-safe essential oil) applied to the dish just before serving

LEMON ZEST – 1 teaspoon (zest from one-third of a medium Eureka lemon)
- 1 teaspoon grated Buddha's hand citron (more aromatic)
- l/2 (scant) teaspoon lemon extract
- 1/3 teaspoon dried minced lemon peel, softened for 15 minutes in 1 teaspoon water (or other liquid from the recipe)
- 1/4 (generous) teaspoon lemon juice powder (powdered lemon peel)
- 1 1/2 teaspoons frozen lemon peel (Freeze the peel in strips, then finely mince before using; for a non-organic lemon, dunk it into boiling water and firmly wipe off the wax before freezing.)
- 1/16 to 1/8 teaspoon lemon oil, such as Boyajian (double the amount for a cooked dish)

☞ 2 teaspoons grated or minced candied lemon peel (Rinse to remove sugar before grating or reduce sugar in the recipe by 1/2 teaspoon; for easier grating or mincing, pulse with the flour or sugar called for in the recipe.)
☞ 1 teaspoon finely grated lime zest

LEMON ZEST – 1 tablespoon (zest from 1 medium Eureka lemon)
☞ Triple amounts indicated for *LEMON ZEST – 1 teaspoon*

LEMON ZEST, MEYER – 1 tablespoon
☞ 2 teaspoons regular lemon zest and 1 teaspoon tangerine or orange zest

LENGKUAS (Indonesian and Malaysian seasoning) *See GALANGAL, GREATER*

LENTIL FLOUR – 1 cup
☞ 1 1/4 cups washed and thoroughly dried lentils, ground to a powder in a food processor, or in batches in a spice/coffee grinder

LENTILS, BLACK BELUGA – 1 cup
☞ 1 cup green Eston lentils
☞ 1 cup Spanish Pardina lentils
☞ 1 cup French dark green lentils/*lentilles du Puy*

LENTILS, CANARY/YELLOW/SUTTER'S GOLD – 1 cup
☞ 1 cup yellow split peas
☞ 1 cup yellow split and husked mung beans/*moong dal;* or split pigeon peas/*toor dal* (firmer)
☞ 3/4 cup lentil flour or whole yellow pea flour (for soup)

LENTILS, GREEN – 1 cup
☞ 1 cup French dark green lentils/*lentilles du Puy*
☞ 1 cup German brown lentils

LENTILS, FRENCH GREEN/LENTILLES DU PUY – 1 cup
- 1 cup Spanish Pardina lentils
- 1 cup Italian Castelluccio or Colfiorito lentils
- 1 cup beluga lentils

LENTILS, RED CHIEF/EGYPTIAN – 1 cup
- 1 cup canary or crimson/petite crimson lentils
- 1 cup German brown or regular olive-green lentils (longer cooking time)
- 1 cup split red lentils/*masoor dahl/masar dal* (less cooking time)

LENTILS, SPANISH BROWN/PARDINA – 1 cup
- 1 cup beluga lentils
- 1 cup French dark green lentils/*lentilles du Puy*

LETTUCE – 1 pound
- 1 pound regular or baby spinach, New Zealand spinach, or young orach
- 1 pound Chinese spinach, or wild green amaranth leaves/*Amaranthus retroflexus*
- 1 pound mâche/lamb's lettuce/*Valerianella locusta*
- 1 pound miner's lettuce/*Claytonia perfoliata*
- 1 pound tender chickweed tops/*Stellaria media*
- 1 pound lamb's quarters/*Chenopodium album*

LICORICE/LIQUORICE ROOT POWDER/GLYRRHIZA GLABRA (flavoring agent) – 1 tablespoon
- 1 or 2 licorice root tea bags, ground in a spice/coffee grinder until powdery
- 1 tablespoon anise seed or dried star anise, ground in a spice/coffee grinder until powdery

LILY BUDS/GOLDEN NEEDLES/GUM JUM/JIN ZHEN/CAI KIM CHAM/ WONCHURI, DRIED (Asian seasoning and garnish)
- Yellow, unopened daylily flower buds (*Hemerocallis fulva*), dried in a warm, airy place until brittle, about 7 days (To rehydrate, soak in warm water 30 minutes, then trim off the fibrous end bit.)

☞ Finely shredded green cabbage (for texture; lacks taste)

LILY BULB/TIGER LILY BULB/LILIUM TIGRINUM/BOCK HUP/YURINE/BAI HE, FRESH OR VACUUM PACKED (Asian vegetable) – 1/2 cup chopped
☞ 1/2 cup chopped canned bamboo shoots, rinsed and drained
☞ 1/2 cup small salad turnips, such as Hakurei or Tokyo Market
☞ 1/2 cup chopped white-fleshed sweet potatoes, such as Cuba, boniato, or yampi

LIMA BEANS, FRESH OR FROZEN – 1 cup shelled
☞ 1 cup soaked and cooked dried lima or navy beans
☞ 1 cup fresh or frozen shelled green soybeans/edamame/mukimame
☞ 1 cup fresh or frozen shelled and peeled fava beans
☞ 1 cup fresh shelled young hyacinth beans (green seim variety/Dolichos lablab)

LIMBURGER (strong-smelling, ripened cheese) – 1 ounce
☞ 1 ounce Backstein, Bierkäse/brick, Handkäse/Harzer Käse, Herve, Liederkranz, Mamirolle, Old Heidelberg, or Romadur

LIME, AUSTRALIAN FINGER/DOOJA LIME, PULP/JUICE VESICLES – 1 tablespoon
☞ 1 1/2 teaspoons each lemon juice and lime juice
☞ 1 tablespoon Meyer lemon juice

LIME, BEARSS SEEDLESS – 1
☞ 1 Meyer lemon (sweeter)
☞ 2 Persian limes (more acidic)

LIME, BITTER/LIMA/CITRUS LIMETTA (Yucatecan seasoning) – 1
☞ 1/2 Seville orange
☞ 1 Persian lime plus a little grapefruit zest

LIME CITRUS OIL/PURE LIME OIL – 1/8 teaspoon
☞ 1/8 teaspoon food-grade lime essential oil

- ⮞ 1/2 teaspoon lime extract
- ⮞ 1 teaspoon finely grated lime zest

LIME, DRIED/BLACK LEMON/OMANI LIME/LOOMI BASRA/LIMOO AMANI (Persian and Middle Eastern souring agent) – 1

- ⮞ 2 teaspoons ground lemon omani/*limon molido* or dried lime powder
- ⮞ 1 tablespoon lime or lemon juice (stirred in when the dish is finished cooking)

Make Your Own Boil 1 Persian lime in salted water for a few minutes, then dry on a rack in a warm sunny spot until light and hollow, about 14 days. Alternatively, dry the lime in a preheated 170°F oven until hard and hollow-sounding.

LIME JUICE, KAFFIR See KAFFIR LIME JUICE

LIME JUICE, KEY – 1/2 cup

- ⮞ 1/2 cup Persian lime juice plus 1 teaspoon finely grated lime zest
- ⮞ 1/4 cup Persian lime juice and 1/4 cup lemon juice
- ⮞ 1/2 cup bottled Key lime juice, such as Floribbean, Nellie and Joe's, or Rose's

LIME JUICE, PERSIAN/TAHITI – 1/2 cup

- ⮞ 2/3 cup lemon juice

LIME JUICE POWDER – 1

- ⮞ 2 tablespoons lemon zest
- ⮞ 1 tablespoon lemon juice (reduce the liquid in the recipe by 1 scant tablespoon)

LIME, KAFFIR See KAFFIR LIME

LIME, PERSIAN – 1

- ⮞ 2 Key limes
- ⮞ 1 Eureka/Lisbon lemon, or 1/2 Meyer lemon

LIME POWDER/LIMU OMANI/LIMON MOLIDO (Persian seasoning) – 2 teaspoons

- ☞ 1 home-dried lime, cracked into pieces, seeds removed, then ground until fine *See LIME, DRIED/BLACK LEMON*
- ☞ 1 preserved lime or whole dried lime soaked 15 minutes before adding to dish, then discarded before serving

Make Your Own Grate 2 to 3 tablespoons zest from well-scrubbed limes (preferably organic). Place on a plain paper towel and microwave on High, tossing every 30 seconds, until dry, 1 to 1 1/2 minutes. Cool, then finely crush or grind to a powder.

LIME, RANGPUR, JUICE – 1 tablespoon

- ☞ 2 teaspoons Key or Persian lime juice and 1 teaspoon tangerine juice

LIME, RANGPUR, ZEST – 1 teaspoon

- ☞ 1 teaspoon Key lime, tangerine, or tangelo zest

LIME, SWEET/LIMO/NARAN-KAI/SOM KLEANG (mild-tasting citrus fruit) – 1

- ☞ 1 Meyer lemon

LIME, THAI/MANAO

- ☞ Key lime (for zest)
- ☞ Key lime juice plus a dash of Meyer lemon juice (for juice)

LIME ZEST – 1 teaspoon

- ☞ 1 teaspoon limequat, lemon, or orange zest
- ☞ 1/3 teaspoon dried lime peel, softened in 2 teaspoons water for 15 minutes
- ☞ 1/2 teaspoon lime extract
- ☞ 1/8 teaspoon lime citrus oil

LINGONBERRIES, FRESH OR FROZEN (Scandinavian tart berries) – 1 cup

- ☞ 1 cup fresh or frozen cranberries, halved

⊫ 1 cup highbush cranberries/*Viburnum trilobum*, large flat seeds removed before cooking
⊫ 1 cup red or black currents

LINGUIÇA (Portuguese dry-cured sausage) – 1 pound
⊫ 1 pound Spanish dry-cured chorizo, andouille, hot links, or other dry-cured or fully cooked sausage

LIQUID FRUIT JUICE CONCENTRATE – 1 cup *See also FRUIT SWEET*
⊫ 1 cup white grape juice concentrate or apple juice concentrate

LIQUID SMOKE (seasoning to replicate the flavor of food prepared in a smoker, grill, or wood-burning oven)
⊫ Bottled mesquite spray (for a light misting at the end of cooking)
⊫ Smoky ham powder (Dry thin pieces of lean country-style ham on a baking sheet in a preheated 200°F oven until crisp, about 1 hour; cool and grind to a powder in a spice/coffee grinder. Store, tightly sealed, at room temperature.)
⊫ Lapsang Souchong or Scottish breakfast tea (strongly brewed and added to marinades or liquid ingredients; or finely ground and added to cooking ingredients)
⊫ Smoked salt (plain or seasoned), or smoked black pepper (for recipes calling for salt, seasoning salt, or pepper)
⊫ Smoked olive oil, such as hickory-and-pecan-wood-smoked or Spanish-pine-cone-smoked (for a light smoky finishing touch)
⊫ Smoke-dried tomatoes (for recipes calling for tomatoes)
⊫ Smoked paprika, hot or mild (for recipes calling for paprika)
⊫ Smoked mozzarella/*mozzarella affumicata* or other smoked cheese (for pizza)
⊫ Dried dark morel or black shiitake mushrooms (for recipes calling for mushrooms)
⊫ Homemade cold-smoked butter (for recipes calling for sautéed onions, or a mirepoix)
⊫ Canned smoked oysters (for shellfish chowder recipes calling for salt pork or bacon)

☞ Chipotle chile powder or paste, or chipotle chile crushed or finely ground, or liquid from canned chipotle in adobo (for recipes calling for heat as well as smoke flavor)

LJUS SIRAP (Swedish light syrup) *See GOLDEN SYRUP/LIGHT TREACLE*

LOBSTER, MAINE – 1 pound
    ☞ 1 pound rock lobster tails (stringier and less sweet)
    ☞ 1 pound lobster "culls" (lobsters that have lost a claw; less expensive)
    ☞ 1 pound prawns (Dublin Bay prawns/langoustines, Italian *scampi*, King prawns, or rock shrimp)
    ☞ 1 pound super-colossal/extra-jumbo (U-12) shrimp, California/Santa Barbara spot prawns (shrimp), or tiger prawns (kuruma shrimp)
    ☞ 1 or more pounds signal crayfish
    ☞ 1 pound crab or imitation crab meat/*surimi* (less firm)

LOBSTER STOCK – 1 cup
    ☞ 1/4 cup lobster concentrated sauce base/*glace* mixed with 3/4 cup water
    ☞ 1 cup boxed clam cooking stock
    ☞ 1/2 to 3/4 teaspoon seafood soup base dissolved in 1 cup hot water

LONGANIZA (thin Yucatan cured sausage) – 1 pound
    ☞ 1 pound firm Mexican chorizo, or smoked sausage

LONG PEPPER, INDONESIAN/INDIAN/DIPPLI/PIPPALI/TIEU LOP (Indian and Southeast Asian seasoning) – 1 tablespoon
    ☞ 1 tablespoon dried Tasmanian pepperberries or Szechuan peppercorns (red colored)
    ☞ 1 tablespoon white peppercorns or 2 teaspoons black peppercorns

LOQUATS, FRESH (small sweet-sour yellow fruits) – 1 pound
    ☞ 1 (15-ounce) can loquats, drained
    ☞ 1 pound fresh acerola or apricots

*LOTUS LEAVES, MATURE/DRIED See WRAPPERS FOR FOOD,
NONEDIBLE*

*LOTUS ROOT/ŎU/RENKON/HASU/LEEN NGOW (crisp Asian
vegetable) – 1 (5-inch) section/7 to 8 ounces/1 cup peeled and sliced*
- ⯈ 1 cup sliced frozen lotus roots; or canned lotus roots, drained and well rinsed
- ⯈ 1 cup sliced fresh lotus stems/*ngo sen*
- ⯈ 1 cup sliced canned lotus root, rinsed under cold water (light gray in color; best in a soy sauce–based dish)
- ⯈ 1/2 cup sliced, unbleached, dried lotus root soaked in cool water for 2 hours (or 20 minutes in hot water) then drained
- ⯈ 1 cup peeled and sliced fresh water chestnuts (blanch for 5 minutes to make peeling easier)
- ⯈ 1 cup scrubbed and sliced Chinese artichokes/crosnes or young Jerusalem artichokes/sunchokes

*LOTUS ROOT FLOUR/OU FEN (Chinese thickening and dredging
agent) – 1 tablespoon*
- ⯈ 1 tablespoon cornstarch, kudzu powder, or water chestnut flour

*LOTUS ROOTLETS/STEMS/NGO SEN (Southeast Asian vegetable) – 1
cup*
- ⯈ 1 cup jarred brined lotus rootlets, rinsed under cold water
- ⯈ 1 cup thinly sliced peeled lotus root

*LOTUS SEEDS, DRIED/LIEN TZU/LIEN JEE/MED BUA (Chinese and
Southeast Asian) – 1 cup*
- ⯈ 1 cup canned lotus seeds or canned whole hominy, drained and rinsed

*LOVAGE/CÉLERI BÂTARD – 8 ounces (2 cups chopped stalks and
leaves)*
- ⯈ 8 ounces celery heart (1 cup leaves and 3 inner stalks) plus 1/2 teaspoon celery seeds (use 4 tablespoons chopped celery heart leaves for one fresh lovage stalk)

- 4 ounces each chopped celery leaves and flat-leaf parsley sprigs and leaves
- 8 ounces Chinese celery stalks and leaves

LOVAGE SEEDS – 1 tablespoon
- 1 tablespoon celery seeds or ajwain/ajowan seeds

LÚCUMA/LÚCMO (Peruvian yellow-fleshed, starchy fruit)
- White sapote or sapodilla (juicier texture)
- Frozen lúcuma puree
- Lúcuma powder flour/*pouteria lúcuma* (for baking; use following the package directions, usually 2 parts powder to 1-part liquid)

LUGANEGA/LUCANICA (Italian thin coiled pork sausage) – 1 pound
- 1 pound mild fresh Italian sausage

LUMPIA WRAPPERS (Filipino fresh pastry wrappers) – 8 wrappers
- 8 spring roll wrappers
- 8 Shanghai-style egg roll wrappers
- 8 ounces rice paper/wafer paper or phyllo pastry cut to size (thinner, more delicate)

Make Your Own Whisk together 2/3 cup cornstarch, 1 egg, 1/2 cup plus 2 tablespoons water, and a pinch of salt until smooth; let sit for 15 minutes. Working with a scant 2 tablespoons batter at a time, cook in a preheated, lightly oiled nonstick skillet, about 1 minute on the first side and 30 seconds on the second side.

LUPIN/LUPINE/LUPINI BEANS, FRESH (Italian large white beans) – 1 cup
- 1 1/2 cups jarred pickled lupins
- 1 cup fresh mature fava beans, shelled and peeled (about 1 pound unshelled)
- 1/2 cup dried skinless fava beans/*habas* soaked in cool water for 8 to 10 hours
- 1 cup fresh or thawed frozen Fordhook lima beans/broad beans

LYCHEE/LITCHI PUREE – 1/4 cup
- ☞ 8 canned litchis pulsed in a blender until smooth

LYCHEES/LITCHIS, FRESH – 1 bunch (about 20), peeled and seeded
- ☞ 2 ounces dried lychees softened in warm water
- ☞ 1 (20-ounce) can lychees/litchis, rambutans, or longans, drained
- ☞ 20 fresh or frozen pulasans, rambutans, or longans, peeled and seeded
- ☞ 20 large fresh grapes, such as Red Globe, Tokay, or Muscat, seeded and peeled

LYE MICROBEADS/PELLETS, FOOD-GRADE/SODIUM HYDROXIDE (alkali for pretzel wash) – 1 ounce (2 tablespoons)
- ☞ 2 tablespoons sodium carbonate (Make the sodium carbonate by drying 1 1/3 cups baking soda/sodium bicarbonate for 2 hours on a foil-lined baking sheet in a preheated 250°F oven.)
- ☞ 1/4 cup baking soda/sodium bicarbonate

LYLE'S SYRUP *See GOLDEN SYRUP/LIGHT TREACLE*

M

MACADAMIA NUTS – 1 pound
- 1 pound Brazil nuts, hazelnuts, beechnuts, cashews, or almonds

MACAPUNO COCONUT STRINGS (Filipino jarred sweet coconut in syrup) – 1 cup
- 1 cup coarsely shredded young coconut tossed with a little heavy syrup

MACE – 1 mace blade (1 teaspoon crumbled/flakes)
- 1/2 teaspoon ground mace
- 1 scant teaspoon freshly grated nutmeg, or 1/2 teaspoon fine-ground nutmeg
- 1/2 teaspoon ground allspice

MÁCHE/LAMB'S LETTUCE/CORN SALAD/VALERIANA/VALÉRIANELLE/KYONA – 4 ounces
- 4 ounces baby arugula, baby spinach, mixed baby kales, young mizuna, tatsoi, or young chickweed tips/*Stellaria media*
- 4 ounces Bibb, Boston, or Panisse lettuce, torn into pieces

MACKEREL – 1 pound See FISH, FATTY

MADAN/GARCINIA (Southeast Asian small sour, crisp fruit) – 1
- 1 unripe green plum or nectarine

MADEIRA (Portuguese fortified wine) – 2 tablespoons
- 1 tablespoon Banyuls, semi-dry Marsala, port, dry sherry, or dry vermouth

MAENGLUK BASIL SEEDS/HOT E (Thai-Chinese gelatinous seeds) 1 cup
- ☞ 1 cup tiny tapioca pearls, cooked until tender

MAGGI SEASONING (Swiss-made vegetable-based liquid seasoning) – 1 tablespoon
- ☞ 1 tablespoon Golden Mountain Seasoning sauce/*tuong gia vi* (contains MSG)
- ☞ 1 1/2 teaspoons each Worcestershire sauce and Chinese dark soy sauce (or Thai sweet soy sauce or mushroom soy sauce)
- ☞ 1 tablespoon Japanese tamari
- ☞ 1 (or more) teaspoons Marmite or Vegemite

MAGUEY LEAVES (for wrapping) *See WRAPPERS FOR FOOD, NONEDIBLE*

MAHLAB/MAHLEB (Turkish and Middle Eastern baking spice) – 1 teaspoon powdered or crushed
- ☞ 1 teaspoon ground Chinese almonds or ground fennel seeds
- ☞ 1 drop each almond extract and cherry extract

MAHLEPI (Greek aromatic spice) – 1 teaspoon ground seeds
- ☞ 1 teaspoon ground cardamom

MAHÓN CHEESE (Spanish semisoft cheese) – 1 ounce
- ☞ 1 ounce Gouda, Baby Bel, Boerenkaas, Doolin, Dutch Farmstead, or Edam

MAIDA/MAITHA FLOUR/NAAN FLOUR (Indian all-purpose soft white flour) – 1 cup
- ☞ 2/3 cup unbleached all-purpose flour and 1/3 cup pastry flour
- ☞ 1 cup pastry flour

MAITAKE MUSHROOMS *See HEN OF THE WOODS/MIATAKE*

MALABAR SPINACH/CEYLON SPINACH/BASELLA ALBA/LO KUI/ MONG TOI/SAAN CHOY/PUI SHAAG – 1 pound

- ⊨ 1 pound sweet potato leaves/*Ipomoea batata* (not regular potato leaves, which are poisonous)
- ⊨ 1 pound tender young mallow leaves/*Malva neglecta*
- ⊨ 1 pound mature spinach, Chinese spinach, or green chard (no mucilaginous properties)
- ⊨ 2 teaspoons filé powder/dried sassafras leaves (for mucilaginous agent; add it to dish after removing from heat)

MALAGA (large Italian seedless raisins) – 1 cup

- ⊨ 1 cup Muscat raisins
- ⊨ 1 cup Lexia or Chilean flame raisins

MALAGUETA/MALEGUATA CHILES, FRESH (Brazilian) – 1 ounce

- ⊨ 1 ounce fresh malaguetinha (tiny malagueta chiles)
- ⊨ 1 ounce fresh serrano, Thai, finger hot/Korean, or red cayenne chiles
- ⊨ 1 ounce fresh jalapeño chiles (for less heat)
- ⊨ 1 ounce pickled malagueta or cumari chiles, rinsed
- ⊨ 1 or 2 teaspoons hot pepper sauce

MALAGUETA CHILES, PICKLED (Brazilian) – 1 ounce

- ⊨ 1/2 ounce pickled jarred or canned jalapeño chiles

MALAI (Indian clotted cream) See CREAM, CLOTTED

MALANGA/YAUTIA/TANNIA/NEW COCOYAM/OCUMO (African and Caribbean starchy staple) – 1 pound peeled and trimmed (about 2 medium)

- ⊨ 16 ounces frozen malanga
- ⊨ 1 pound peeled and trimmed fresh taro root/cocoyam, yuca root/ cassava, boniato/*batata,* or waxy boiling potatoes

MALANGA LEAVES/CALLALOO (African and Caribbean leafy vegetable) – 1 pound
- ☞ 1 pound callaloo/taro leaves (cooked at least 45 minutes)
- ☞ 12 to 14 ounces canned callaloo greens, drained (no cooking involved)
- ☞ 1 pound mustard greens, turnip greens, collard greens, kohlrabi greens, or curly kale (shorter cooking time)

MALDIVE FISH/UMBALAKADA (Sri Lankan cooking condiment) – 1 tablespoon pounded, flaked or powdered
- ☞ 1 tablespoon coarsely chopped dried shrimp, or 1 1/2 tablespoons shrimp powder/floss
- ☞ 1 or 2 tablespoons bonito flakes/*katsuobushi,* crumbled to a powder
- ☞ 1 tablespoon flaked or crumbled dried cod

MALTED MILK POWDER – 1 tablespoon
- ☞ 1 tablespoon non-diastatic malt powder

MALT EXTRACT, DRIED (brewing base component) – 2 tablespoons
- ☞ 2 tablespoon sorghum extract/syrup (for gluten-free ale/beer)

MALTED WHEAT FLAKES (yeast bread flavoring) – 1 tablespoon
- ☞ 1 tablespoon Maltex wheat cereal

MALTOSE/MALT SUGAR – 1 cup
- ☞ 3/4 cup rice bran syrup, corn syrup, golden syrup, or clear honey (increase the liquid in the recipe by 1/4 cup if necessary)

MALT POWDER, DIASTATIC (amylase enzyme dough improver) – 1 tablespoon
- ☞ 1 tablespoon sprouted wheat flour/wheat malt (sprouted wheat berries dried in a 120°F oven until brittle, then ground; use 1/4 teaspoon per large loaf)
- ☞ 1/4 cup sprouted wheat berries, pureed in a blender with part of the liquid called for in the recipe (use 1/4 cup per large loaf)

MALT POWDER, NON-DIASTATIC (flavoring agent and sweetener) – 1 tablespoon
- ☞ 1 tablespoon packed light/golden brown sugar (for pretzel, bagel, pancake, or waffle batter)
- ☞ 1 tablespoon barley malt syrup/plain malt syrup or honey (for boiling water bath for bagels)
- ☞ 1 tablespoon granulated sugar, honey, or agave syrup/nectar (for yeast or flatbread dough)

MALT SUGAR See MALTOSE

MALT SYRUP, BARLEY, NON-DIASTATIC See BARLEY MALT SYRUP, PLAIN

MALT VINEGAR – 1 tablespoon
- ☞ 1 tablespoon distilled colorless malt vinegar (for pickling and preserving)
- ☞ 1 tablespoon cider vinegar or white wine vinegar
- ☞ 1 tablespoon vinegar powder (used dry in cooking or spice rubs)

MANCHEGO (Spanish sheep milk semihard to hard cheese) – 1 ounce
- ☞ 1 ounce Castellano (tangier and moister), Roncal (stronger and firmer), queso de Huerte, Zamorano, Malvern, aged Emmental, or sharp cheddar (for *curado)*
- ☞ 1 ounce aged Asiago, dry Jack, Grana Padano, or Pecorino Romano (for *viejo)*

MANDARIN ORANGES, CANNED NO SUGAR ADDED – 8 ounces
- ☞ 8 to 10 ounces fresh Satsumas, small Pixies, clementines, or Kishu mandarins, sectioned, seeded if necessary, and microwaved on High until softened, 20 to 30 seconds

MANGO CHUNKS, FROZEN – 1 pound
- ☞ 3 pounds fresh mangos, pitted, peeled and chopped

MANGO, GREEN/KACHA AM, FRESH OR FROZEN (Indian and Southeast Asian souring and tenderizing agent) – 1 medium (1 pound) *See also AMCHUR*
- 1/3 cup *amchur* slices (sun-dried green mango) soaked in hot water until softened, 30 to 60 minutes
- 1 hard green unripe yellow/eating mango plus a few drops lime juice (wear plastic gloves when handling raw green mango)
- 1/4 of a green papaya
- 1 large unpeeled green tart cooking apple, such as Granny Smith or Bramley's Seedling, soaked in acidulated water after cutting, then patted dry

MANGO POWDER, GREEN *See AMCHUR*

MANGO PUREE, FROZEN – 1 cup
- 1 cup canned Alphonso mango pulp (or Kesar variety for Indian dishes)
- 2 fresh ripe Alphonso or Ataulfo mangos, peeled and pureed

MANGO, RIPE, FRESH – 1 cup sliced
- 1 cup thawed frozen mango chunks or halves
- 1 cup drained canned mango chunks
- 1/2 cup unsweetened dried mango slices soaked in warm water until softened, about 4 hours
- 1 cup canned Alphonso mango pulp (for desserts and drinks)
- 1 cup sliced Hawaiian papaya or very sweet cantaloupe

MANICOTTI SHELLS/TUBES/WRAPPERS, DRIED – 8 ounces
- 8 ounces no-boil, flat lasagna noodles, softened in a baking dish of just-boiled water until pliable, about 5 minutes
- 8 to 10 ounces wheat-flour spring roll or lumpia wrappers, softened individually in simmering water until pliable
- 10 ounces fresh pasta sheets cut to size, or fresh lasagna noodles cut in half

☞ 12 to 14 homemade crespelle, or homemade or store-bought crepes (more delicate)

MANIOC *See YUCA ROOT*

MANOURI/MANOORI (Greek soft white cheese) – 1 ounce
☞ 1 ounce soft, mild feta soaked in cool water 1 or 2 hours to reduce saltiness
☞ 1 ounce mizithra/myzithra/anari (less fat)
☞ 1 ounce natural cream cheese (without thickeners)

MANTI DOUGH (Turkish pasta dough for making stuffed dumpling squares/tiny raviolis) – 1 pound
☞ 1 pound Italian fresh pasta for ravioli/*pasta all'uovo*, or store-bought sheet of fresh pasta/*la sfoglia*
☞ 1 pound fresh or thawed frozen wonton wrappers
☞ 1 pound fresh or thawed frozen gyoza/potsticker wrappers (thicker)
☞ 1 pound store-bought or homemade crepes or thin pancakes

MANTOU (fluffy, steamed Chinese buns made with wheat flour) *See CHINESE STEAMED BUNS*

MANZANO CHILE, FRESH (small red Mexican and Ecuadorian chile) – 1 *See also AJI ROCOTO*
☞ 1 fresh aji rocoto or cayenne chile

MAPLE SUGAR CRYSTALS *See SUGAR, MAPLE*

MAPLE SYRUP – 1 cup *See also PANCAKE SYRUP*
☞ 1 cup gluten-free, sugar-free maple syrup
☞ 1 cup agave syrup/nectar, birch syrup, brown rice syrup, or Swedish light syrup/*ljus sirap*
☞ 1 1/4 cups barley malt syrup (reduce the liquid in the recipe by 1/4 cup)

- 3/4 cup plus 2 tablespoons honey thinned with 2 tablespoons apple juice
- 1/2 cup finely grated maple sugar (increase the liquid in the recipe by 1/4 cup)
- Simmer 2 cups dark brown sugar and 1 cup water until syrupy, then cool. Add 1 teaspoon maple extract and leave for 24 hours to develop the flavor. Store, refrigerated, for up to 6 months.

MARASCHINO LIQUEUR/MARASCHINO-FLAVORED SPIRIT (such as Luxardo or Maraska) – 2 tablespoons
- 2 tablespoons cherry liqueur or bottled maraschino cherry juice

MARAS RED PEPPER FLAKES (Turkish) – 1 teaspoon:
- 1 teaspoon mild or hot Turkish, Hungarian, or Spanish paprika
- 1 teaspoon Aleppo or Urfa pepper flakes
- 3/4 teaspoon Aleppo or Urfa chile powder

MARCONA ROASTED ALMONDS See ALMONDS, MARCONA ROASTED

MARINADE FOR MEAT OR POULTRY – 1/2 cup
- 1/2 cup bottled salad dressing, light vinaigrette, or seasoned yogurt or buttermilk

MARINA DI CHIOGGIA (large Italian greenish-gray turban squash) – 1 pound
- 1 pound hubbard or Jarrahdale squash

MARJORAM, FRESH – 3 sprigs or 1 tablespoon finely chopped
- 1 teaspoon dried marjoram, crumbled
- 1 1/2 teaspoons chopped fresh oregano or 1/2 teaspoon dried oregano
- 2 to 3 teaspoons fresh thyme, or 1 scant teaspoon dried thyme
- 1 tablespoon chopped fresh basil
- 1/2 teaspoon dried basil, and 1/4 teaspoon dried Mediterranean oregano

➼ 1 teaspoon dried Italian seasoning

MARMITE (British yeast extract) – 1 tablespoon
➼ 1 tablespoon Vegemite (less salty)

MARQŪQ/SHRAK TANNOUR BREAD/LAVASH/LEBANESE MOUNTAIN BREAD (very thin Middle Eastern flatbread) – 2
➼ 1 pita bread split into two halves

MARROW (British vegetable) – 1 pound See also ZUCCHINI
➼ 1 pound Italian trombone squash/*tromboncino/rampicante* (less watery)
➼ 1 pound large zucchini or bottle gourd

MARSALA, COOKING (Sicilian fortified wine) – 2 tablespoons
➼ 1 tablespoon each sweet vermouth and dry sherry
➼ 2 tablespoons Madeira or dry sherry, such as Dry Sack
➼ 2 tablespoons white wine (or white grape juice) and 1/2 teaspoon brandy

MARSALA, SWEET COOKING (Sicilian fortified wine) – 2 tablespoons
➼ 1 tablespoon dry Marsala sweetened with a little sugar

MARSHMALLOW CRÈME – 1 (7-ounce) jar
➼ 1 (16-ounce) package marshmallows melted with 2 1/2 tablespoons light-colored corn syrup until smooth (Melt the marshmallows in the microwave on High, about 1 1/2 minutes, stirring every 45 seconds; or in a double boiler over simmering water. For 1 cup of crème, use 16 large marshmallows and 2 teaspoons light corn syrup.)
➼ 7 ounces Ricemellow (brown rice vegan crème alternative)

MARSHMALLOWS, MINIATURE – 1 cup (1 1/2 ounces)
➼ 10 to 11 regular-size marshmallows, cut into pieces with kitchen shears (dust the shears with cornstarch or flour)

MARZIPAN – 10 ounces (1 1/4 cups)
- 1 cup (9 to 10 ounces) almond paste, 1/2 cup powdered sugar, and 1 tablespoon light-colored corn syrup (not Lite), kneaded together until combined

MASA, FRESH (Mexican nixtamalized corn dough for tamales) – 1 pound (2 cups)
- 1 3/4 cups tamal flour/*masa harina* (dried, coarse-ground masa flour for tamales) mixed with 1 cup plus 2 tablespoons hot water, then cooled
- 2 cups whole cooked fresh hominy or rinsed and well-drained canned hominy, ground or mashed until pliable
- 2 3/4 cups nixtamal/half-cooked hominy, thoroughly rinsed and ground in a food processor

MASA, FRESH (Mexican nixtamalized corn dough for tortillas) – 1 pound (2 cups)
- 1 3/4 cups tortilla flour/masa flour (precooked cornmeal/fine-ground dried masa harina for tortillas) mixed with 1 cup plus 2 tablespoons hot water, then cooled

MASA HARINA/MASECA (Mexican instant corn masa flour) – 1 3/4 cups for making tortillas or tamales
- 2 cups fine ground fresh masa (for making tortillas)
- 2 cups coarse-ground fresh masa (for making tamales)

MASA HARINA/MASECA (Mexican instant corn masa flour) – 2 tablespoons for thickening
- 2 tablespoons corn muffin mix
- 2 tablespoons pulverized corn chips
- 1 small corn tortilla (or part of a larger one) blended to a smooth paste with the recipe's liquid ingredients

MASAREPA *See AREPA FLOUR*

MASCARPONE (Italian double or triple cream cheese) – 1 cup
- 3/4 cup natural cream cheese (no gum added), 1/4 cup heavy cream, and 1 1/2 tablespoons sour cream, blended together until smooth
- 1/2 cup softened natural cream cheese and 1/2 cup sour cream, blended until smooth
- 1 cup crème fraîche
- 1/2 cup ricotta and 1/2 cup heavy (or whipping) cream, beaten until very smooth
- 1 cup ultra-smooth ricotta cheese, such as SorrentoVelvety Smooth Ricotta

Make Your Own Heat 1 1/2 cups light cream (or 3/4 cup each heavy cream and half-and-half) to 185°F and stir in 2 teaspoons fresh lemon juice. Let sit off the heat for 20 minutes. Line a sieve with dampened cheesecloth and set it over a bowl; transfer the mixture to the sieve, place in the refrigerator, and let drain for 12 to 24 hours.

MATCHA/MACCHA/HIKI-CHA (Japanese culinary-grade green tea powder)
- Japanese new crop green tea/*Sincha*, ground, pressed through a fine-mesh sieve, then spread on parchment paper to dry, about 1 hour (less colorful)
- Food coloring powder (for baking; use following package directions)

MATSUTAKE/JAPANESE PINE MUSHROOMS – 8 ounces
- 8 ounces fresh blewit/blue foot, oyster, or shiitake mushrooms
- 4 ounces canned matsutake or nameko mushrooms, drained

MATSUTAKE POWDER – 1 tablespoon
- 1 tablespoon porcini powder (or dried porcini mushrooms ground in a spice/coffee grinder)

MATZO (Jewish unleavened bread) – 8 ounces
- 2 cups all-purpose flour and 1/2 cup water mixed together until smooth; rolled thin and immediately baked at 500°F for 10 minutes
- 8 ounces crisp lavash

MATZO CAKE MEAL (finely powdered matzo) – 1 cup
- 1 cup finely ground matzo meal (or 4 ounces unsalted matzo broken up and pulverized to a powder)
- 1 1/4 cups sifted cake flour (sifted before measuring)

MATZO CAKE MEAL, GLUTEN-FREE (tapioca, potato starch, plus egg products) – 1 cup
- 1 cup potato starch

MATZO FARFEL (crumbled matzo) – 1 cup
- 1 1/2 matzo sheets, crushed to the consistency of fine breadcrumbs

MATZO MEAL, FINE GRIND (crushed matzo) – 1 cup
- 4 ounces (3 pieces) unsalted matzo or 4 1/2 matzo crackers, finely ground in a blender or food processor
- 2 cups matzo farfel ground fine
- 1 cup finely ground water cracker crumbs

MAYONNAISE – 1 cup
- 1 cup canola or olive oil whisked very gradually into 1/4 cup store-bought mayonnaise, along with a little lemon juice. Season with salt and more lemon juice if required
- 3/4 cup silken tofu, 1 tablespoon each unseasoned rice vinegar, lemon juice, and canola or olive oil, plus 1/2 teaspoon Dijon mustard, blended until smooth, then seasoned to taste with salt
- 1 cup creamed cottage cheese, processed in a blender until very smooth, then seasoned to taste with salt and lemon juice
- 1 cup plain Greek-style yogurt seasoned with 1 tablespoon Dijon mustard
- 1/2 cup plain yogurt or sour cream mixed with 1/2 cup mayonnaise, then seasoned to taste with salt and lemon juice (for reduced-fat mayonnaise)
- 1 cup dairy- and egg-free mayonnaise, such as Mindful Mayo, Nayonaise, or Vegenaise

MAYONNAISE, FLAVORED/MAYONNAISE-BASED SAUCE – 1/2 cup (about)

1/2 cup mayonnaise (or 1/4 cup mayonnaise and 1/4 cup sour cream) plus any of the following:

- 2 tablespoons Dijon or whole-grain mustard
- 1 1/2 tablespoons black olive paste or tapenade
- 1 tablespoon strained bottled horseradish or wasabi paste
- 1 tablespoon wasabi powder, 1 tablespoon lemon juice, and 1/4 teaspoon salt
- 1 canned or jarred chipotle in adobo, seeded and finely chopped, 1/2 teaspoon adobo sauce, and 2 (or more) garlic cloves mashed to a paste with a pinch of salt
- 2 teaspoons dark *hatcho* miso, or 1 to 2 tablespoons white *shiro* miso
- 1 tablespoon curry powder, toasted in a dry skillet over medium heat for 20 to 30 seconds
- 1 tablespoon Chinese chili-garlic sauce plus fresh lime juice to taste
- 1 tablespoon hot chili sauce, such as Sriracha
- 2 tablespoons pesto or pistou
- 2 tablespoons each fresh lemon juice and extra-fine capers

MEALIE (South African dry-type corn) – 1 cup

- 1 cup canned whole hominy, rinsed and dried

MEALIE MEAL/MIELIE MEAL/PUTU/UGALI (South African staple starch) – 1 cup

- 1 cup white cornmeal, preferably stone-ground

MEAT GLAZE/GLACE DE VIANDE – 1/4 cup

- 1 quart fat-free unsalted beef stock gently boiled, uncovered, in a wide-bottomed pan until syrupy and reduced to 1/4 cup; cool and refrigerate, tightly covered; will keep for up to 1 month
- 1/4 cup stock base paste or meat extract, such as Bovril, or yeast extract, such as Marmite, or Vegemite; use a small amount to flavor sauces and reduce the salt in the recipe accordingly

MEAT, GROUND – 1 pound *See also CHICKEN OR TURKEY, GROUND OR SHREDDED*

- ⊵ 1 pound ground turkey plus 2 tablespoons olive oil to keep the turkey juicy and moist
- ⊵ 1 pound frozen ground-beef–style soy crumbles, such as Boca, Morningstar, or Yves
- ⊵ 1 pound textured vegetable protein, reconstituted with 7/8 cup beef-flavored broth
- ⊵ 1 pound portobello mushrooms, gills removed and coarsely grated
- ⊵ 1 pound low-fat five-grain tempeh, or other tempeh variety, crumbled into small pieces
- ⊵ 1 pound extra-firm tofu weighted to expel the liquid, 30 to 60 minutes, then blotted dry and crumbled
- ⊵ 1 pound freeze-dried tofu/*koyadofu* softened in hot water for 2 to 3 minutes; drained and squeezed to expel the liquid, then crumbled, grated, or finely chopped (or firm tofu, frozen overnight, thawed in boiling-hot water 10 minutes, then squeezed dry, rinsed, and crumbled)

MEAT SUBSTITUTE – 1 pound

- ⊵ 1 pound beef-style seitan
- ⊵ 1 pound tempeh (plain, hickory smoked, or savory; freeze for 1 hour to make slicing easier)
- ⊵ 1 pound Organic Savory Flavor Tofu/baked bean curd (spicy marinated or smoked)
- ⊵ 1 pound extra-firm tofu weighted to expel the liquid, 30 to 60 minutes; blotted dry, sliced and seasoned, then fried in a lightly greased skillet over medium heat until golden, 2 to 3 minutes each side. (For a bacon taste, use pork chop seasoning; for a crispier coating, dust with cornstarch or rice flour before frying; for a chewier texture, freeze overnight, then thaw at room temperature before frying)
- ⊵ 1 pound King Oyster/royal trumpet or portobello mushrooms, whole, sliced, or diced

☞ 1 pound Asian eggplant (or peeled globe eggplant), sliced or diced

MEDLAR/AZGIL (small brown fruit) – 1 soft bletted medlar
☞ 1 green unripe medlar, frozen until hard, then left at room temperature until bletted (freezing and thawing hastens bletting)
☞ 1/4 cup apple butter plus a very tiny pinch of ground cinnamon

MELBA TOAST – 1 ounce
☞ 1 ounce bagel chips
☞ 1 ounce pumpernickel triangles, small cocktail rye bread rounds, or very thinly sliced white sandwich bread cut into quarters and dried (Dry on a baking sheet in a preheated 275°F oven until crisp, 30 or more minutes, turning halfway through. Placing an inverted cooling rack over the bread will help keep it flat during baking and cooling.)
☞ 1 ounce crisp lavash or poppadoms crisped in the oven or microwave, cooled, then broken into pieces

MELEGUETA PEPPER See GRAINS OF PARADISE

MELINJO/BELLINJO NUTS (Indonesian soup addition) – 1/4 cup
☞ 1/4 cup raw peanuts

MELOKHIA/JEW'S MALLOW/MELOUKHIA/MALOKHEI/ MOLOKHIYA/MULŪKHIYYA (Middle Eastern slightly gelatinous vegetable) – 1 pound fresh
☞ 1 (14-ounce) package frozen chopped molokhia leaves (to avoid overcooking, add to simmering dish in its frozen state)
☞ 1 (27-ounce) can melokhei, well drained
☞ 3 ounces dried meloukhia leaves, softened in warm water until doubled in bulk, about 30 minutes
☞ 1 pound Malabar spinach/Ceylon spinach
☞ 1 pound young wild mallow leaves/Malva neglecta, trimmed and chopped

☞ 1 pound mature spinach or Swiss chard, plus a pinch of filé pow-der and a few drops of lemon juice stirred in after cooking

MELON, GREEN/CREAM/WHITE-COLORED FLESH – 1 pound
☞ 1 pound Boule d'Or, Canary, Casaba, Eden's Gem, Galia, Green Nutmeg, honeyball, honeydew, Kharbouza, kiwano (horned Mel-on), Ogen, Piel de Sapo, Santa Claus (Christmas), Sharlyn, Sprite, Spanish, or Temptation melon

MELON, ORANGE/SALMON/YELLOW-COLORED FLESH – 1 pound
☞ 1 pound Ambrosia, cantaloupe, Cavaillon, Charentais, Crane, Crenshaw, Minnesota Midget, Orange-fleshed Honeydew, Pan-cha, or Persian melon
☞ 1 pound Yellow Crimson, Cream of Saskatchewan, or Tendersweet watermelon

MEMBRILLO/COTOGNATA See QUINCE PASTE

MERGUEZ (Moroccan highly-spiced beef or lamb sausage) – 1 pound
☞ 1 pound Andouille, chorizo, or spicy kielbasa
☞ 1 pound hot Italian sausage (chicken, turkey, or pork)

MERINGUE POWDER – 1 tablespoon
☞ 1 tablespoon dried/powdered egg white
☞ 1 large fresh egg white or 2 to 3 tablespoons thawed frozen egg white

MERKÉN, NATURAL (Chilean smoked chile spice blend) – 1 tablespoon
☞ 2 teaspoons hot smoked paprika or ancho chile powder plus a pinch of salt

MESCLUN/GOURMET SALAD MIX/SPRING MIX/MISTICANZA/ SALATINA – 8 ounces
☞ 8 ounce mixture of young/baby leaves (arugula/rocket, baby green and red romaine, chervil, curly endive, young dandelion greens, escarole (pale inner leaves), frisée, garden cress, Little Gem or Winter Density lettuce, lollo biondo, lollo rosso, máche,

young mizuna, nasturtium leaves and blossoms, panisse lettuce, oak leaf lettuce, radicchio, sorrel, or tatsoi

MESQUITE POWDER – 1 tablespoon
☞ 1 tablespoon carob powder

METHI See FENUGREEK LEAVES

METSOVONE/KAPNISTO METSOVONE (Greek semihard smoked cheese) – 1 ounce
☞ 1 ounce smoked Irish Blarney, Gouda, cheddar, Dunlop, Jarlsberg, or other semihard smoked cheese

MEXICAN SEASONING MIX/SPICE BLEND – 1 tablespoon
☞ 2 teaspoons mild chile powder, such as ancho, California, or New Mexico; 1 teaspoon ground cumin; and 1/8 teaspoon garlic powder

M'HAMSA (Tunisian hand-rolled, large-grain toasty semolina) – 1 cup
☞ 1 cup Israeli or Lebanese couscous, toasted before boiling

MICROGREENS (young leaves and stems of salad greens) – 1 cup
☞ 1 cup young leaves of any of the following: amaranth (mild), broccoli (hot, spicy), Bull's Blood beets (mild), buckwheat (delicate, sweet), cabbage (mild), celery (sweet), chamomile (mild), chard (mild), chervil (anise flavor), cilantro (strong flavor), cress (peppery), fennel (anise flavor), kale (mild), mustard (mild to hot and spicy), or radish (spicy, mustard-like)
☞ 1 cup tiny heirloom lettuce, such as Petite Verde Crystal, Petite Emerald Crystal, or Petite Ruby Crystal (larger leaves)
☞ 1 cup unsprayed moneywort/creeping jenny/Lysimachia nummularia
☞ 1 cup mixed sprouts

MILK, ALMOND See ALMOND MILK

MILK, CASHEW See CASHEW MILK

MILK, CLABBERED – 1 cup
 ☞ 1 cup buttermilk *See BUTTERMILK*

MILK, COCONUT See COCONUT MILK

MILK, CONDENSED See CONDENSED MILK, SWEETENED

MILK, EVAPORATED See EVAPORATED MILK

MILK, HEMP See HEMP MILK

MILK, LOW-FAT/1% (102 to 140 calories; 8.2 to 10 g protein; 2.4 to 5 g fat; 3 g saturated fat; 14 g carbs; 13 g sugars; 31 to 35% DV calcium) – 8 ounces (1 cup)
 ☞ 1 cup nonfat milk plus 1 to 2 teaspoons unsalted butter or unsalted stick margarine
 ☞ 1/2 cup each nonfat milk and whole milk
 ☞ 1 cup seven-grain milk (140 calories; 2 to 3 g protein; 2 to 2.5 g fat; 0 g saturated fat; 27 to 28 g carbs; 16 g sugars; 35% DV calcium)
 ☞ 1 cup almond milk (30 to 60 calories; 1 g protein; 2 to 3 g fat; 0g saturated fat; <1 to 8 g carbs; 0 to 7 g sugars; 20% to 45% DV calcium)
 ☞ 1 cup camel's milk (110 calories; 5 g protein; 4.5 g fat; 3 g saturated fat; 15 mg cholesterol; 30% DV calcium)
 ☞ 1 cup cashew milk (25 calories; <1 g protein; 2 g fat; 0 g saturated fat; 1 g carbs; 0 g sugars; 45% DV calcium)
 ☞ 1 cup coconut milk beverage (45 to 80 calories; 0 to 1 g protein; 4.5 to 5 g fat; 0 g saturated fat; 1 g carbs; 1g sugars; 10 to 45% DV calcium)
 ☞ 1 cup flax milk (50 to 60 calories; 2 to 5 g protein; 2.5 g fat; 0 g saturated fat; 2 g carbs; 0 g sugars; 30% DV calcium)
 ☞ 1 cup hazelnut milk (110 calories; 2 g protein; 3.5 g fat; 0 g saturated fat; 18 to 19 g carbs; 14 g sugars; 30% DV calcium)

☞ 1 cup hemp milk (70 to 140 calories; 2 to 3 g protein; 0.5 to 6 g fat; 0 to 0.5 g saturated fat; 1 to 9 g carbs; 6 g sugars; 30 to 50% DV calcium)

☞ 1 cup oat milk (130 calories; 4 g protein; 0 to 2.5 g fat; 0 g saturated fat; 24 g carbs; 19 g sugars; 35% DV calcium

☞ 1 cup potato milk (70 calories; 0 g protein; 0g fat; 0 g saturated fat; 20 g carbs; 2 g sugars; 30% DV calcium)

☞ 1 cup rice milk (90 to 130 calories; 1 g protein; 2 to 2.5 g fat; 0 g saturated fat; 23 to 27 g carbs; 10 g sugars; 30% DV calcium)

☞ 1 cup soymilk (80 to 110 calories; 4 to 7 g protein; 1.5 to 4.5g fat; 0.5 g saturated fat; 3 g carbs; 1 g sugars; 20 to 45% DV calcium)

☞ 1 cup sunflower milk (70 to 80 calories; 2 g protein; 3.5 to 4 g total fat; 0.5 g saturated fat; 4 to 10 g carbs; 6 g sugars; 8% DV calcium)

☞ 1 cup water (for cookies, muffins, pancakes, waffles)

MILK, NONFAT/SKIM (<0.5% butterfat) – 1 cup

☞ 1/3 cup instant nonfat dried milk powder and 3/4 cup water

☞ 1/4 cup regular nonfat dried milk powder (or soymilk powder) and 1 cup water

☞ 1/2 cup fat-free evaporated milk and 1/2 cup water

☞ 1 cup fat-free evaporated milk (use undiluted for lowfat but full-bodied sauces)

☞ 1 cup potato milk

☞ 1 cup seltzer or sparkling water (for extra-light pancakes and batter)

MILK, NUT See ALMOND MILK; CASHEW MILK; COCONUT MILK; HAZELNUT MILK; WALNUT MILK

MILK, OAT See OAT MILK

MILK, POTATO See POTATO MILK

MILK, QUINOA See QUINOA MILK, UNSWEETENED

MILK, RICE See RICE MILK/RICE DRINK

MILK, SEED See HEMP MILK; SUNFLOWER MILK

MILK, SOUR -- 1 cup for baking
- 1 cup milk and 3/4 teaspoon baking soda
- 1 cup milk and 1 tablespoon distilled white vinegar

MILK, SOY See SOY MILK

MILK, SUNFLOWER See SUNFLOWER MILK

MILK, WHOLE (3.5% butterfat) – 1 cup
- 1/4 cup dried whole milk powder and 7/8 cup water
- 1/3 cup instant nonfat dried milk powder, 3/4 cup water, and 2 1/2 teaspoons melted unsalted butter or stick margarine
- 3/4 cup plus 3 tablespoons nonfat milk and 2 1/2 teaspoons melted unsalted butter
- 1/2 cup plus 2 tablespoons nonfat milk and 6 tablespoons half-and-half
- 3/4 cup plus 2 tablespoons nonfat milk and 2 tablespoons heavy cream
- 1 cup low-fat/1% milk and 2 teaspoons melted unsalted butter
- 2/3 cup low-fat/1% milk and 1/3 cup half-and-half
- 3/4 cup reduced fat/2% milk and 1/4 cup half-and-half
- 1 cup reduced fat/2% milk and 1 1/2 teaspoons melted unsalted butter
- 1/2 cup each full-fat evaporated milk and water
- 1/2 cup each thick cashew cream and water
- 1 cup full-fat unsweetened soy milk or reconstituted soy milk powder (avoid using with acidic ingredients such as lemon juice, chocolate, or wine, or letting it boil; doing so will cause it to curdle)
- 1 cup buttermilk (for baking, add 1/2 teaspoon baking soda and reduce any baking powder in the recipe by 2 teaspoons)

☞ 1 cup sparkling or seltzer water; or 1 cup plain water plus 1 egg yolk (for pancakes, waffles, fritters, or batter mix; makes them extra-light)

☞ 1 cup silken tofu puréed with 1 or 2 tablespoons water until completely smooth (for salad dressings, dips, cream soups)

MILLET GRITS – 1 cup
☞ 1 cup hulled millet, ground in batches in a spice/coffee grinder until it's the consistency of coarse grits

MILLET, HULLED – 1 cup
☞ 1 cup sorghum (tastes best when lightly toasted in a dry skillet before cooking)

☞ 1 cup kasha/roasted buckwheat groats, whole grain teff, rice, or prewashed light quinoa

☞ 1 cup whole-wheat or semolina couscous, or medium-grind bulgur #2 (less cooking time; contains gluten)

MINT EXTRACT – 1 teaspoon
☞ 4 drops oil of peppermint (for chocolate and candies)

☞ 1 cup fresh mint leaves (for infusing and then straining)

MINT, FRESH (peppermint, spearmint) – 1 tablespoon minced leaves
☞ 1 tablespoon fresh, young minced leaves of wild mint/*Yerba buena,* wild spearmint/*Mentha spicata*, wild Tuscan mint/*Nepitella,* catmint/catnip/*Nepeta cataria*, or mountain mint/*Pycnanthemum* (more bitter)

☞ 1/2 to 1 teaspoon dried peppermint from a mint tea bag

☞ 1 tablespoon whole-leaf dried spearmint leaves, pressed through a fine-mesh sieve to make 1 teaspoon

☞ 1/2 teaspoon Indian sun-dried mint powder/*pudina*

☞ 1/4 teaspoon mint extract (for desserts and confections)

☞ 1 drop oil of peppermint (for chocolate and candies)

☞ 1 tablespoon chopped fresh mint basil or Thai basil (for savory dishes)

☞ 1 crushed peppermint candy, such as Altoids (for desserts, confections, and lamb jus)

MINT OIL (Turkish seasoning and condiment) – 1/3 cup
Make Your Own Gently heat 1 tablespoon crushed dried peppermint leaves and 1/3 cup olive oil over very low heat for 10 minutes. Cool, and then strain through a fine-mesh sieve; it will keep refrigerated in an airtight container for up to 5 days.

MINT SAUCE (British condiment for lamb) – 2/3 cup (about)
Make Your Own Stir together 1/2 cup chopped fresh spearmint leaves (or 1 or 2 tablespoons crumbled dried leaves), 1 tablespoon sugar, and 1/4 cup boiling water, then add 1/4 cup malt vinegar. Let sit at room temperature for an hour or more to develop the flavor.

MINT SUGAR (beverage flavoring) – 1/4 cup
Make Your Own Grind 2 tablespoons firmly packed fresh spearmint leaves with 2 tablespoons granulated sugar until fine in a spice/coffee grinder. Cover and let sit for 10 or more minutes to develop the flavor.

MINT SYRUP (beverage flavoring) – 1 cup
Make Your Own Heat 1 cup water, 1 cup sugar, and 1/4 cup finely chopped fresh spearmint leaves to boiling, stirring occasionally, then simmer, uncovered, for 5 minutes. Cool and strain. Store, refrigerated, for up to 1 month

MINUTINA (delicate salad ingredient) – 1 pound
☞ 1 pound mizuna/early spider mustard (stronger flavor)

☞ 1 pound tender raw spinach leaves, tightly rolled and cut into thin strings

***MIRIN/HON-MIRIN (Japanese sweetened rice cooking wine
containing 14% alcohol, or 8% if sold in the United States) – 1
tablespoon***
- 1 tablespoon *aji no haha mirin* (more like sake; contains 10% alcohol)
- 1 tablespoon *shin-mirin* or *mirin-fuhmi*) (synthetic mirin; contains 1% alcohol)
- 1 1/2 tablespoons *aji-mirin* (contains sweetener and salt)
- 2 tablespoons each saké and granulated sugar gently simmered until the sugar dissolves, and the liquid is reduced by half
- 1 teaspoon sugar dissolved in 1 tablespoon saké or sweet sherry
- 2 teaspoons sugar (or 1 teaspoon honey) dissolved in 1 tablespoon unseasoned rice wine vinegar, white wine, vermouth, or hot water

***MISO, DARK/KURO/MUGI/ INAKA/SENDAI/ HATCHO (Japanese red
or dark brown fermented soybean-based paste) – 1 tablespoon***
- 1/2 teaspoon beef bouillon (stock) granules or 1/2 beef bouillon cube
- 2 teaspoons Chinese fermented black beans/*dow see,* rinsed
- 1 tablespoon fermented soybean paste: Chinese *dou jiang,* Korean *doenjang,* or Filipino *tausi*
- 1 teaspoon Japanese organic whole-bean soy sauce/*marudaizu shoyu,* organic tamari, or other thick soy sauce

***MISO, LIGHT/SHIRO/SHINSHU/SAIKYO (Japanese mild white or
yellow fermented soybean-based paste) – 1 tablespoon***
- 1 tablespoon (or more) low-sodium saikyo miso (contains 5% salt)
- 1 tablespoon *awase* miso (a mixture of white and red miso)
- 1 tablespoon Chinese yellow soybean paste, Vietnamese *tuong ot,* or Thai *tao jiaw*
- 1 1/2 teaspoons anchovy paste and 1/2 teaspoon tahini or sesame paste
- 1/2 scant teaspoon coarse sea salt

MISO, GLUTEN-FREE – 1 tablespoon
- 1 tablespoon rice *kome* miso, brown rice *genmai* miso, garbanzo bean miso, soybean *hatcho* miso, or golden millet miso

MISO, SOY-FREE – 1 tablespoon
- 1 tablespoon azuki miso, chickpea miso, or sweet brown rice miso

MITSUBA/JAPANESE PARSLEY/JAPANESE CHERVIL/TREFOIL, FRESH – 1 tablespoon chopped leaves
- 2 teaspoons chopped fresh Italian flat-leaf parsley and 1 teaspoon chopped fresh celery leaves (for seasoning)
- 1 tablespoon chopped fresh cilantro or parsley (for garnish)
- 1 tablespoon watercress sprigs or daikon sprouts/*kaiware* (for garnish)
- 1 tablespoon chervil, or young stems and leafy tops of honewort/wild chervil/*Cryptotaenia canadensis*

MIYOGA See MYOGA/GINGER BUD

MIYUK (Korean sun-dried kelp) See KOMBU; SEAWEED

MIXED SPICE, SWEET (British spice blend) – 4 teaspoons
- 1 teaspoon each ground allspice, cloves, and coriander plus 1/2 teaspoon each grated nutmeg and ground Ceylon cinnamon
- 4 teaspoons pumpkin pie spice

MIZITHRA/MEZITHRA/MYZITHRA/ANÁRI (Greek sheep or goat's milk cheese) – 1 ounce
- 1/2 ounce each baker's/farmer/hoop cheese and whole-milk ricotta (to replace fresh)
- 1 to 2 ounces small-curd cottage cheese drained and pressed through a fine sieve (to replace fresh)
- Manouri (tangier; to replace fresh)
- Aged ricotta salata, aged Kefalotyri, Pecorino Romano, or Parmesan (to replace aged variety)

MIZUAME See RICE MALT SYRUP

MIZUNA, EARLY/SPIDER MUSTARD/KYONA/SIU CAI (Japanese mustard greens) – 1 ounce (1 cup)
- 1 cup Kyona (wider leaves; stronger peppery flavor)
- 1 cup mibuna (long, slender leaves; stronger mustard flavor)
- 1 cup baby arugula, baby mustard greens, young horseradish leaves, or tatsoi
- 1 cup mustard spinach/*komatsuna,* trimmed and torn into bite-size pieces (milder flavor)
- 1 cup minutina/*Erba stella* leaves cut into 1 1/2- to 2-inch lengths (milder flavor)

MOJO SAUCE (Cuban and Latin American condiment) – 1/3 cup (about)
Make Your Own Crush 4 minced garlic cloves to a paste with 1/2 teaspoon salt; then combine with 2 tablespoons olive oil, 1/2 teaspoon crumbled dried oregano (or ground cumin), and 1/3 cup sour orange juice. (Alternatively, use 1/4 cup lemon juice and 1 1/2 tablespoons orange juice in place of the sour orange juice.)

MOLASSES, DARK/REGULAR UNSULPHERED – 1 cup
- 1 cup cane syrup, dark honey, dark corn syrup, dark treacle, palm syrup/kithul treacle, or very dark, strong maple syrup

MOLASSES, LIGHT/MILD UNSULPHERED – 1 cup
- 1 cup yacon syrup, sorghum syrup, or Swedish dark syrup/*mörk sirap*
- 1/2 cup dark molasses and 1/2 cup light-colored corn syrup
- 3/4 cup dark brown sugar dissolved in 1/4 cup hot water (or other liquid in the recipe)

MOLASSES, MIDDLE EASTERN See DATE MOLASSES; GRAPE MOLASSES; POMEGRANATE MOLASSES

MOLASSES VINEGAR (dark, heavy vinegar) – 1 tablespoon
- 1 tablespoon balsamic vinegar

MOLE NEGRO SAUCE (Oaxacan-style sauce) – 8 ounces
- 1/4 cup black mole paste/*mole negro* mixed with 3/4 cup beef broth
- 8 ounces brown poblano sauce
- 1/4 cup poblano paste/*mole poblano* mixed with 3/4 cup beef broth

MOLOKHIA See MELOUKHIA

MONGETES, DRIED (Spanish small white beans) – 1 pound
- 1 pound dried Navy beans
- 1 pound small dried cannellini beans (larger)

MONGOLIAN FIVE-SPICE POWDER See CHINESE FIVE-SPICE POWDER

MONTEREY CHEESE See JACK CHEESE

MORA BERRY/RUBUS GLAUCUS (South American) See BLACKBERRIES

MORA CHILE See CHIPOTLE MORA

MORCILLA See BLOOD SAUSAGE

MOREL MUSHROOMS/MERKEL/MORCHELLA, FRESH – 8 ounces
- 3/4 ounce dried morel mushrooms, thoroughly rinsed, soaked in warm water until softened, 20 to 30 minutes, then lifted out of the water and squeezed dry
- 8 ounces fresh shiitake mushroom caps (freeze the stems and use to flavor stock)
- 8 ounces fresh portobello mushrooms, gills removed and sliced

MORITA CHILE See CHIPOTLE MORA

MORNING GLORY GREENS/CHINESE WATER MORNING GLORY See WATER SPINACH

MOSCATEL VINEGAR (Spanish) – 1 tablespoon
- 1 tablespoon white balsamic vinegar, champagne vinegar, or white wine vinegar

MOSTO COTTO/SABA/SAPA See GRAPE MOLASSES

MOUSSERON/FRENCH MEADOW MUSHROOMS, FRESH – 8 ounces
- 8 ounces fresh white cap/button, cremini, or small portobello mushrooms
- 4 ounces canned mushrooms, rinsed

MOZUKU (Japanese seaweed) – 8 ounces fresh
- 7 ounces water-packed mozuku, drained and rinsed
- 4 ounces dried mozuku, soaked in water for 1 hour, rinsed, and then scalded with hot water

MOZZARELLA, BUFFALO/MOZZARELLA DI BUFALA, FRESH – 8-ounce ball
- 8 ounces fresh cow's milk mozzarella/*fior di latte* (lower fat content; easier to melt)
- 8 ounces fresh mozzarella nuggets (*bocconcini*, *ciliegini*, or mozzarella pearls)
- 8 ounces smoked mozzarella/*mozzarella affumicata*
- 8 ounces firm low-moisture mozzarella (for cooking and pizza topping)
- 8 ounces fresh asadero/*queso Oaxaca*, or soft fresh goat cheese (for eating)

MOZZARELLA, FIRM LOW-MOISTURE – 1 ounce See also
BOCCONCINI
- 1 ounce scamorza, young *caciocavallo*, *provola*, provolone, asadero/*queso Oaxaca*, Bel Paese, or string cheese
- 1 ounce almond mozzarella (low-fat alternative for cooking)

MOZZARELLA SHEETS – 8 ounces
- Fresh, frozen, or dried bean curd skins/yuba sheets (soak dried sheets 5 to 6 minutes in cold water until softened, then blot dry)

MOZZARELLA, SMOKED/MOZZARELLA AFFUMICATA – *8 ounces*

- 8 ounces fresh mozzarella smoked on the rack of a stovetop smoker until light brown on the outside, about 5 minutes; remove before it starts to melt, then let cool. (Alternatively use diced high-temp mozzarella, made specifically to withstand high smoking temperatures without melting.)
- 8 ounces firm, low-moisture mozzarella smoked in an outdoor smoker or wood-burning oven (Place a pan of ice water slightly smaller than the smoking rack between the smoke box and the cheese and smoke for an hour or so.)
- 8 ounces smoked *caciocavallo*, smoked scamorza, or smoked provolone

MUENSTER (North American semisoft mild cheese) – *1 ounce*

- 1 ounce French *Munster* (more pungent), domestic fontina, Havarti, Monterey Jack, or Tilsit

MULATO CHILE (type of dried poblano) *See ANCHO CHILE*

MULBERRIES, PERSIAN BLACK, FRESH – *1 cup*

- 1 cup fresh, fully ripe Chinese white mulberries (milder; sometimes seedless)
- 1 cup fresh fully ripe white mulberries from the weeping mulberry plant (bland; best for drying)
- 1 cup fresh blackberries, boysenberries, loganberries, or olallieberries
- 1 cup fresh, fully ripe (purple) red mulberries

MULBERRIES, WHITE, DRIED – *1 cup*

- 1 cup red or black mulberries (larger and tarter)
- 1 cup golden raisins/sultanas or chopped dried figs

MULFALFAL (Middle Eastern pasta) – *1 pound*

- 1 pound Greek orzo, or Italian soup pasta

MUNG BEAN FLOUR/STARCH/POWDER/TEPUNG HOEN KWE (smooth Asian thickening and cooking flour) – 1 tablespoon

- ☞ 1 1/2 tablespoons mung beans ground until fine in a spice/coffee grinder, then sifted and measured (for thickening)
- ☞ 1 tablespoon brown or white rice flour (for pastries)
- ☞ 1 tablespoon arrowroot powder, sweet rice flour/glutinous rice flour, or cornstarch (for thickening)

MUNG BEAN SPROUTS – 1 cup (2 ounces)

- ☞ 1 cup regular bean sprouts or sunflower sprouts (smaller, less crunchy)
- ☞ 1 cup Chinese pea sprouts (more delicate)
- ☞ 1 cup soybean sprouts (stronger flavored)
- ☞ 1 cup snow peas trimmed and julienned
- ☞ 1 cup celtuce stems peeled and thinly sliced

MUNG BEANS, DRIED – 1 pound

- ☞ 1 pound dried Spanish verdina beans
- ☞ 1 pound small dried flageolets or pigeon peas (larger)

MUNSTER (French semisoft pungent cheese) – 1 ounce See also MUENSTER (North American semisoft mild cheese)

- ☞ 1 ounce Chaumes, Chimay, Époisses, Langres, Lingot d'Or, Livarot, Robiola Lombardia, Stinking Bishop, or Taleggio

MUSCATEL SWEET WHITE WINE VINEGAR – 1 tablespoon

- ☞ 1 tablespoon sherry vinegar, champagne vinegar, or seasoned rice vinegar

MUSCOVADO SUGAR See SUGAR, MUSCOVADO

MUSHROOM BROTH – 1 quart

- ☞ 1 quart reduced-sodium vegetable broth plus 4 to 8 ounces cut-up mushrooms (portobello, cremini, shiitake) simmered partly covered for 20 to 25 minutes, then strained

☞ 2 to 3 teaspoons mushroom base added to 1 quart boiling water

MUSHROOM ESSENCE – 1/3 to 1/2 cup

☞ 1 pound fresh porcini or shiitake mushrooms frozen, thawed, and squeezed to extract the liquid (reserve the juiced mushrooms for another use)
☞ 1 pound fresh porcini or shiitake mushrooms and 2 cups water cooked for 15 minutes in a covered saucepan; strained, then gently boiled until reduced to one-quarter the volume

MUSHROOM POWDER/POWDERED MUSHROOMS – 2 tablespoons
See also PORCINI POWDER

☞ 6 tablespoons crumbled dried mushrooms, ground in a spice/coffee grinder or blender until powdery
☞ 8 ounces fresh mushrooms
☞ 1 (4-ounce) can whole or sliced mushrooms, drained

MUSHROOM POWDER, WILD – 1 teaspoon

☞ 1 teaspoon ground dried mushrooms (mushrooms ground to a powder in a spice/coffee grinder)

MUSHROOM SALT/BOT NEM (Vietnamese seasoning) – 1 teaspoon

☞ 1/2 teaspoon kosher salt (less flavor)

MUSHROOM SOUP, CANNED CREAM OF– (10.5-ounce can) for recipes

☞ 1 cup thick homemade white sauce plus 1/2 cup chopped sautéed mushrooms (or 2 tablespoons mushroom powder)
☞ 8 ounces reduced-fat cream cheese stirred into 1/2 cup chopped sautéed mushrooms until smooth
☞ 1 (2-ounce) package gluten-free cream of mushroom soup mix, combined with water according to directions

MUSHROOM SOY SAUCE See SOY SAUCE, MUSHROOM

MUSHROOMS, DRIED – 3 ounces

▷ 1 pound fresh mushrooms
▷ 10 ounces canned mushrooms, drained

Make Your Own Slice 1 pound fresh mushrooms, spread in a single layer on a baking sheet, and dry at 170°F until and crisp, about 2 hours, flipping halfway through. Keep well wrapped in a cool, dark place, or freeze for up to 12 months.

MUSHROOMS, FRESH – 1 pound

▷ 3 ounces dried mushrooms soaked in 1 1/2 cups warm water until softened, about 30 minutes; strained through a fine-mesh sieve, then dried on a paper or cloth towel (For shiitake mushrooms, use boiling-hot water for soaking or soak 8 hours for the deepest flavor.)
▷ 1 (8- to 10-ounce) can mushrooms, drained
▷ 1 porcini-flavored bouillon cube, or 1 teaspoon wild mushroom bouillon granules, dissolved in 1 cup boiling water (for flavor only; reduce the salt in the recipe by 1 teaspoon)

MUSHROOMS, POWDERED See MUSHROOM POWDER

MUSHROOMS, WILD – 1 pound

▷ 14 ounces cultivated mushrooms plus 1/2 ounce dried porcini or shiitake mushrooms soaked in 2/3 cup warm water until softened, 30 to 40 minutes (Strain the soaking water and use in the recipe if liquid is called for, or reserve for another use.)

MU SHU/MOO SHU SAUCE (Chinese condiment) – 1 tablespoon

▷ 1 tablespoon hoisin sauce

MU SHU PANCAKES/PEKING DOILIES/BAO BING (small, thin Chinese pancakes)

▷ Very thin 5 1/2-inch flour tortillas (Brush or spray the tortillas with oil, preferably Asian sesame oil; sandwich into pairs, oiled sides together; wrap in foil, and heat in a preheated 350°F oven until warm, 10 to 15 minutes. Peel the pancakes apart to serve.)

MU SHU SKINS, FROZEN (Chinese wheat flour wrappers) – 1 dozen

☞ 1 dozen small, thin flour tortillas; small crepes; or small, paper-thin pancakes

MUSSELS, BLACK – 1 pound

☞ 1 pound small plump oysters, such as Wellfleet or Olympia
☞ 1 pound littleneck or cherrystone clams
☞ 1 pound New Zealand cockles

MUSTARD, CHINESE/PAI-CHIEH – 1 tablespoon

Make Your Own Stir together 1 tablespoon mustard powder (Chinese *gai lat* or European Colman's) and 1 tablespoon cool water to form a paste. Cover and let sit for 15 minutes to develop the flavor.

MUSTARD, CREOLE – 1 tablespoon

☞ 1 tablespoon horseradish mustard
☞ 1 tablespoon whole-grain Dijon mustard plus a little horseradish or a dash of hot pepper sauce

MUSTARD, ENGLISH – 1 tablespoon

Make Your Own Stir together 1 tablespoon mustard powder (such as Colman's) and 2 1/2 teaspoons cold water (or flat beer) to form a paste. Cover and let sit for 15 minutes to mellow and develop the flavor.

MUSTARD, FLAVORED – 1/2 cup

☞ 1/2 cup prepared mustard plus one or more of the following: fresh or strained bottled horseradish; ground or cracked peppercorns; chile powder or minced fresh chile; grated fresh ginger; honey; or minced herbs such as tarragon, chives, parley, or cilantro

MUSTARD GREENS, FRESH – 1 pound

☞ 1 pound arugula, broccoli rabe, escarole (dark outer leaves), purple mizuna, daikon or other radish greens, turnip greens, garland chrysanthemum, or Texsel greens/Abyssianian mustard/*Brassica carinata*

- 1 pound collard greens, kohlrabi greens, parsnip greens, or purple pak choy (milder flavor)
- 1 pound field mustard/wild mustard leaves/*Brassica rapa* or *B. nigra* (smaller leaves; spicier flavor)
- 1 pound garlic mustard leaves/*Alliaria petiolata,* stringy stems discarded (garlic flavor)
- 1 pound wild pennycress leaves/*Thlaspi arvense* (smaller leaves; spicier flavor)

MUSTARD GREENS, SOUR PICKLED/DURA CHUA/PHAK DONG/PAKK GADD DORNG (Southeast Asian condiment) – 1/2 cup
- 1 chopped kosher dill pickle

MUSTARD, JAPANESE/NERIGARASHI – 1 tablespoon
- 1 tablespoon Chinese or English prepared hot mustard

Make Your Own Stir together 2 teaspoons Japanese powdered mustard/*konakarashii* (or Chinese or English mustard powder) and 1 tablespoon cold water to form a paste. Cover and let sit for 15 minutes to mellow and develop the flavor.

MUSTARD MAYONNAISE – 1 cup
- 1 cup mayonnaise plus 2 (or more) teaspoons prepared mustard, according to taste

MUSTARD OIL/MUSTARD SEED OIL/SHORSHER TEL (Indian seasoning) – 1 tablespoon
- 1 tablespoon vegetable oil plus 1/4 teaspoon dry mustard (add the powder when adding the recipe's liquid)

MUSTARD POWDER – 1 teaspoon
- 1 1/2 teaspoons yellow mustard seeds, ground with a mortar and pestle or a spice/coffee grinder until powdery
- 1 tablespoon prepared mustard; reduce the liquid called for in the recipe by 1 teaspoon (for wet mixtures)

MUSTARD, PREPARED – 1 tablespoon

Make Your Own Stir together 1 tablespoon mustard powder, 1 teaspoon vinegar, 1 teaspoon cool water, and 1/4 to 1 teaspoon sugar or honey (optional) until smooth. Cover and let sit for 30 minutes to mellow and develop the flavor.

- 1/8 teaspoon (0.5 gram) xanthan gum (used as a vinaigrette emulsifier)
- 3/4 teaspoon mustard powder (used as a vinaigrette emulsifier)
- 1 tablespoon paprika paste or mayonnaise (used as a vinaigrette emulsifier)

MUSTARD, RUSSIAN/SAREPTSKAJA – 1 tablespoon

Make Your Own Stir together1 tablespoon mustard powder, 1 teaspoon sugar, 1/2 teaspoon ground black pepper, and 2 teaspoons hot water to form a paste. Cover and let sit for 15 minutes to mellow and develop the flavor.

MUSTARD SEEDS, BLACK – 1 tablespoon

- 4 teaspoons brown mustard seeds (less pungent)

MUSTARD SEEDS, YELLOW – 1 teaspoon

- 3/4 teaspoon mustard powder
- 1 tablespoon prepared mustard; reduce the liquid in the recipe by 1 teaspoon (for wet mixtures)

MYOGA/GINGER BUD/ZINGIBER MIOGA (Japanese and Korean seasoning) – 1 tablespoon shredded

- 1 tablespoon minced young ginger with a pinch of minced lemongrass
- 1 tablespoon minced scallions with a pinch of grated fresh ginger
- 1 tablespoon shredded pickled ginger, rinsed

MYRTLE (Corsican and Sardinian seasoning) – 1 teaspoon

- 1 teaspoon crushed juniper berries

MYZITHRA See MIZITHRA

N

NAARTJIE (South African citrus fruit) – 1
  ⇨ 1 tangerine

NAARTJIE PEEL, DRIED See TANGERINE/MANDARIN PEEL, DRIED

NAGA VIPER CHILE See BHUT JOLOKIA

NAGAIMO (Japanese gelatinous white-fleshed tuber) – 1 ounce for thickening (2 tablespoons grated)
  ⇨ 1 tablespoon cornstarch mixed with 1 tablespoon liquid

NAMEKO MUSHROOMS, FRESH – 1 pound
  ⇨ 10 ounces canned or jarred nameko mushrooms, drained
  ⇨ 3 ounces dried nameko or shiitake mushrooms, soaked in warm water until softened, 30 to 45 minutes
  ⇨ 1 pound fresh shiitake mushrooms, stems discarded

NAM PLA See THAI FISH SAUCE

NAM PRIK (Thai dipping sauce) – 1/4 cup
  ⇨ 2 tablespoons fresh lime juice, 1 tablespoon each sugar and Thai fish sauce (*nam* pla *or pla ra*), 1 teaspoon chopped cilantro, and 1 small minced garlic clove (For chili dipping sauce, add 1 or 2 tablespoons minced or sliced fresh Thai chile.)

NAN/NAAN (Indian white-flour or whole-wheat flatbread) – 1
  ⇨ 1 pita bread or flour tortilla

NAN/NAAN FLOUR See MAIDA

NAPA CABBAGE/CHINESE CABBAGE/CHINESE LEAVES/CELERY CABBAGE/DA BAI CAI/WONG NGA BAK/BAECHU/HAKUSAI – 1 pound
- 1 pound Tenderheart cabbage or Savoy cabbage
- 1 pound bok choy, choy sum, green chard, frilly-leafed collard greens, or curly green kale (for cooked dishes)
- 1 pound torn or shredded romaine lettuce, or plain-leaved Russian kale massaged with salt and olive oil (for salads and cold dishes)

NARANJA AGRIA See ORANGE, SOUR/BITTER/SEVILLE/NARANJA AGRIA

NARANJILLA/LULO JUICE, FROZEN (Ecuadorian fruit juice) – 1 (14-ounce) package
- Pulp from 2 pounds thawed frozen naranjillas (about 8 large fruits), blended with 1 cup water and strained
- 14 ounces passion fruit juice

NARANJILLA/LULO PUREE, FROZEN (Ecuadorian fruit puree) – 1 (7-ounce) package
- Pulp from 6 thawed frozen naranjillas, lightly mashed
- 1 cup frozen passion fruit puree/*maracuyá*

NASTURTIUM BLOSSOMS/INDIAN CRESS (peppery salad ingredient) – 1 cup
- 1 cup calendulas, marigolds, pansies, or other colorful edible, un-sprayed blossoms (for flowers)
- 1 cup watercress, broadleaf cress, garden peppercress, arugula, or a combination of watercress and spinach (for stems and leaves)

NATTO (Japanese fermented soybean condiment) – 1/4 cup
- 1/4 cup fermented black beans or bean paste (less pungent)

NAVY BEANS, DRIED – 1 pound
- 1 pound dried Great Northern beans, marrow beans, pea beans, cannellini beans, or baby white lima beans/butter beans

NDUJA (Italian soft, spreadable, red spicy sausage) – 1 pound
- ☞ 1 pound soft spicy salami
- ☞ 1 pound diced and pureed calabrese sausage or pepperoni

NEBRODINI MUSHROOMS, FRESH – 8 ounces
- ☞ 8 ounces fresh King oyster/royal trumpet mushrooms

NEEM LEAF *See CURRY LEAF*

NEPITELLA/CALAMINT/WILD TUSCAN MINT/CALAMINTHA NEPETA, FRESH (Italian seasoning) – 1 tablespoon chopped
- ☞ 2 teaspoons chopped fresh marjoram or oregano and 1 teaspoon chopped fresh mint

NETETOU *See FERMENTED DRIED LOCUST BEAN*

NEUFCHÂTEL (French soft unripened cheese) – 1 ounce
- ☞ 1 ounce 1/3-less-fat cream cheese or reduced-fat cream cheese

NEW MEXICO CHILE/CHILE COLORADO, FRESH, FROZEN, DRIED – 1
- ☞ 1 dried guajillo or pulla/puya chile (for dried)
- ☞ 1 Anaheim or poblano chile (for fresh or frozen)
- ☞ 1 1/2 teaspoons New Mexico or guajillo chile powder (for fresh or dried)
- ☞ 3/4 teaspoon each Hungarian sweet and hot paprika (for fresh or dried)
- ☞ 1/2 to 3/4 teaspoon ground cayenne pepper (for fresh or dried)

NEW MEXICO CHILE POWDER – 1/3 cup (about)
- ☞ 2 1/2 tablespoons each Hungarian sweet and hot paprika

Make Your Own Toast 3 medium dried New Mexico chiles (about 3/4 ounce) in a preheated 350°F oven until puffed, about 6 minutes. Cool, remove the stems and seeds, and process in a food processor to a powder. (Wear plastic gloves, avoid inhaling the fumes, and wear a mask if available.)

NIGARI/MAGNESIUM CHLORIDE, LIQUID (tofu coagulant/firming agent) – 1 teaspoon
- 3/4 teaspoon (tightly packed) refined crystalline or granulated nigari/calcium chloride
- 3/4 teaspoon food-grade gypsum/calcium sulfate
- 3/4 teaspoon Epsom salt/magnesium sulfate
- 2 tablespoons distilled white vinegar, apple cider vinegar, or lemon juice

NIGELLA SEEDS/KALONJI/KALIJEERA/CHARNUSHKA (Indian and Middle Eastern seasoning) – 1 teaspoon
- 1 teaspoon ajwain/ajowan seeds, black cumin seeds, black sesame seeds, caraway seeds, or cracked black pepper (for garnish, not taste)

NIGER OIL (Ethiopian) – 1 tablespoon
- 1 tablespoon melted ghee, or browned clarified butter

NIHAIZU (Japanese base for dressings and marinades) – 1/4 cup
- 2 tablespoons rice vinegar and Japanese soy sauce; or equal parts rice vinegar, soy sauce, and dashi

NIXTAMAL (Mexican lime-treated corn) – 1 cup
- 1 cup canned whole hominy, rinsed and dried

NOODLES See CHINESE EGG NOODLES; CHINESE WHEAT NOODLES; JAPANESE NOODLES; KOREAN NOODLES; PASTA; THAI NOODLES; VIETNAMESE NOODLES

NOODLES, CELLOPHANE/BEAN THREAD/FEN SI/HARUSAME/SAIFUN/SOTANGHON/DANGMYUN/WUN SEN/BUN TAU – 8 ounces
- 8 ounces fresh, precooked *shirataki* noodles, rinsed and drained
- 8 ounces kelp noodles, rinsed and drained

‣ 8 ounces fresh raw squash noodles (cut from a spiral slicer; or cut into long flat strips, then stacked and cut into noodle-like ribbons)

‣ 8 ounces fresh (or 4 ounces dried) rice noodles, rice sticks, or rice vermicelli, prepared according to the package directions

NOODLES, EGG – 8 ounces for soup

‣ 8 ounces fresh strand pasta, such as linguine, *bavettine*, or fettuccine

‣ 8 ounces fresh or thawed frozen spring roll wrappers, cut into thin slices (add to soup at the end of cooking)

‣ 8 ounces Japanese egg sheets/paper-thin homemade omelets, cut into 1/2-inch strips (add to soup just before serving)

NOODLES, RAMEN, FRESH – 1 (5-ounce) package See also JAPANESE NOODLES, THIN WHEAT EGG

‣ 5 ounces fresh Chinese egg noodles (lo mein or chow mein noodles)

‣ 1 (3-ounce) package dried ramen noodles/*chukka soba/chukamen*

‣ 5 ounces fresh Italian capellini or vermicelli

‣ 5 ounces fresh shirataki noodles or rice angel hair (gluten-free)

NOODLES, THICK, FLAT WHEAT, FRESH – 1 pound

‣ 1 pound fresh *pici*, pappardelle, lasagna noodles, or other thick pasta, cut into segments

‣ 1 pound fresh or thawed frozen wonton or gyoza wrappers, sliced into ribbons

NOODLES, THIN, FLAT RICE, SEMI-DRIED – 8 ounces See also THAI NOODLES

‣ 6 ounces thin dried rice noodles, soaked an extra 10 minutes

‣ 8 ounces dried wheat noodles, cooked according to the package directions

NOODLES, VEGETABLE-BASED – 1 cup

‣ 1 cup cooked spaghetti squash strands

‣ 1 cup dried vegetable noodles, such as Hungryroot

Make Your Own Trim and peel firm raw vegetables, such as butternut squash, cucumbers, jícama, rutabagas, parsnips, hearts of palm, sweet potatoes, or yellow squash. Using a spiral slicer set on the thin noodle setting, a julienne peeler, or a vegetable peeler, cut the vegetables into long, paper-thin ribbons. Blanch for 1 minute in boiling salted water, then rinse with cold water; or sautée until barely wilted, 2 to 4 minutes.

NOPALE/PRICKLY PEAR CACTUS (Mexican succulent vegetable) – 1 nopale (1/3 cup shaved and sliced) *See also PRICKLY PEAR*
- 1/3 cup canned or jarred nopalitos, rinsed with cool water (less flavor)
- 1/3 cup tender fresh green beans or strips of peeled green bell pepper

NOPALITOS (Mexican canned or bottled nopale) – 1 (15-ounce) can
- 1 pound (3 to 4) fresh nopalitos trimmed, cut crosswise into 1/4-inch strips and cooked in boiling water until tender, about 2 minutes
- 1 pound canned or cooked green beans

ÑORA PEPPERS, DRIED (Spanish smoked peppers) – 2 or 3
- 2 or 3 dried choricero peppers
- 1 dried ancho chile
- 1 1/2 teaspoons smoked mild/sweet Spanish paprika

NORI/DRIED PURPLE LAVER/HOSHI-NORI/KIM (thin seaweed sheets of dried compressed laver for wrapping sushi and rice balls) – 4 sheets
- 4 sheets pretoasted nori sheets/*yakinori*
- 4 thin, tender blades of rehydrated wakame, giant kelp, or bullwhip kelp
- 4 sheets rice paper/wafer paper
- 8 paper-thin sheets of daikon radish
- 2 soybean wrappers/paper/*mamenori* (thin, pliable soybean sheet; cut whole sheet in half)

- 4 paper-thin fried egg sheets/sweet crepes/*usa yaki tamago* (use 3 eggs, 1/4 teaspoon salt, and 1 teaspoon sugar for 4 (8-inch) crepes)
- Silicone mat, plastic wrap, dampened cotton dishtowel or linen napkin (for forming sushi rolls/*nori-maki* without nori sheets or other edible wrappers)

NORI CHIPS

Make Your Own Brush nori sheets lightly with olive oil, sprinkle lightly with salt, then bake in a preheated 300°F oven until crisp, 15 to 20 minutes. Cool and break into bite-size pieces.

NORI FLAKES, SHREDS, OR POWDER/AO NORI/AO-NORIKO (Japanese seaweed seasoning and garnish for salads and raw vegetables)

- Nori or wakame sheets, shredded and toasted in a dry skillet for 1 minute, then crushed or ground in a spice/coffee grinder
- Roasted and seasoned nori/*ajitsuke-nori*, or nori with sesame seeds/*nori komi furikake*, shredded
- Powdered sea lettuce/green laver powder
- Buckwhip kelp, lightly crushed

NORWAY LOBSTER/LOBSTERETTE See DUBLIN BAY PRAWNS

NUOC CHAM See VIETNAMESE SWEET-AND-SOUR DIPPING SAUCE

NUOC NAM See VIETNAMESE FISH SAUCE

NUT BUTTER, PURE (no added fat) – 1 cup

Make Your Own Toast 2 cups nuts on a baking sheet in a preheated 350°F oven until fragrant, 7 to 10 minutes, stirring halfway through. Transfer the warm nuts to a food processor or high-powered blender and process until reduced to a paste. Cool, then put in a lidded jar and store in the refrigerator. *See also ALMOND BUTTER; CASHEW BUTTER; COCONUT BUTTER; HEMPSEED BUTTER; PEANUT BUTTER; PECAN BUTTER; SOY NUT BUTTER; SUNFLOWER SEED BUTTER*

NUTELLA *See GIANDUJA*

NUT-FLAVORED LIQUEUR (such as Frangelico, Nocciole, or Noisette) – 1 tablespoon for cooking
- 1/4 teaspoon almond, hazelnut, or walnut extract, plus 3/4 tablespoon vodka or water

NUT FLOUR *See FLOUR, NUT*

NUTMEG, EAST INDIAN – 1 teaspoon fine ground
- 2 teaspoons freshly grated East Indian nutmeg
- 1 1/3 teaspoons freshly grated Grenadian West Indian nutmeg
- 2/3 teaspoon fine ground Grenadian West Indian nutmeg
- 3/4 teaspoon crumbled mace blade, or 1/2 teaspoon ground mace
- 1 teaspoon ground allspice
- 1/2 teaspoon ground cinnamon
- 1 teaspoon apple pie spice or pumpkin pie spice

NUTMEG, GRENADIAN WEST INDIAN – 1 teaspoon fine ground
- 2 teaspoons freshly grated Grenadian nutmeg
- 1 tablespoon freshly grated East Indian nutmeg
- 1 1/3 teaspoons fine ground East Indian nutmeg

NUT MILK *See ALMOND MILK; CASHEW MILK; COCONUT MILK; HAZELNUT MILK; WALNUT MILK*

NUTRITIONAL YEAST *See YEAST, NUTRITIONAL*

NUTS – 1 cup for snacking
- 1 cup roasted chickpeas or soybeans

NUTS, CHOPPED – 1 cup for baking
- 1 cup toasted rolled oats (Toast old-fashioned oats on a baking sheet in a preheated 400°F oven until golden, 15 to 20 minutes,

stirring halfway through; or in a large skillet over medium heat for 4 to 5 minutes, stirring frequently; or in a microwave on High for 3 to 5 minutes, stirring every minute. Cool before using.)

☞ 1 cup chopped pretzels

☞ 1 cup coarsely crushed thick unflavored potato chips

☞ 1 cup crisped rice cereal, crushed cornflakes, or whole grain wheat and barley cereal, such as Grape-Nuts

☞ 1 cup toasted pumpkin or sunflower seed kernels (Toast raw kernels in a dry skillet over medium heat, stirring frequently, until golden and fragrant, about 5 minutes; cool before using.)

☞ 1 cup coarsely ground hot-leached acorns

☞ Browned butter/*beurre noisette* (for the flavor only; use in place of the butter specified in the recipe)

NUTS, UNSALTED – 1 cup

☞ 1 cup salted nuts blanched in boiling water for 1 or 2 minutes (or rinsed in a colander under cool water), then dried on a baking sheet in a preheated 300°F oven for 4 or 5 minutes; or in a dry skillet over low heat, shaking the pan constantly; or on a paper or cloth towel at room temperature, 1 or 2 hours

O

OAT BRAN – 1 cup
- 1 cup rice bran
- 1 1/2 cups wheat bran
- 1 scant cup toasted wheat germ
- 1 cup plain instant oatmeal (adds salt)

OAT BRAN FLOUR (16% protein) – 1 cup
- 1 cup oat bran, ground until fine in a blender or food processor, or in batches in a spice/coffee grinder

OAT FLOUR (17% protein) – 1 cup
- 1 1/4 cups old-fashioned rolled oats (regular or certified gluten-free), ground to a fine powder in a blender or food processor, or in batches in a spice/coffee grinder

OAT MILK – 1 quart
Make Your Own Soak 1 cup oat groats in water to cover 8 to 10 hours. Drain, then blend with 2 cups fresh water until smooth, 2 to 3 minutes; let steep 30 to 45 minutes. Strain through a cheesecloth-lined sieve, pressing firmly on the pulp to extract all the liquid. Add 2 cups more water; keep refrigerated for up to 3 days. Shake before using. (For 1 pint use 1 cup old-fashioned rolled oats and 1 1/2 cups water and blend until smooth; will keep refrigerated for up to 3 days.)

OATS, INSTANT – 2/3 cup (1 serving)
Make Your Own Spread 4 cups old-fashioned rolled oats on a baking sheet and toast in a preheated 350° F oven until lightly colored, about 15 minutes. Cool, pulse in a food processor until coarsely chopped,

then combine with 1/4 cup light brown sugar, 1/2 teaspoon ground cinnamon, and 1/4 teaspoon sea salt. Store in a tightly sealed container for up to 2 weeks. Makes 4 cups (6 servings). For 1 serving, stir 2/3 cup oats into 2/3 cup boiling water and let sit for 2 to 3 minutes.

OATS, OLD-FASHIONED ROLLED – 1 cup
- 1 cup steel-cut or stone-cut oats, soaked overnight in boiling water to reduce the cooking time to 10 minutes; or cooked in a pressure cooker to reduce the cooking time to 8 minutes; or cooked in a rice cooker for cook-and-hold convenience
- 1 cup quick-cooking rolled oats
- 1 cup rolled barley flakes, quinoa flakes, buckwheat flakes, rye flakes, Kamut flakes, spelt flakes, triticale flakes, or whole-wheat flakes (for cooked cereal and baking)
- 2/3 cup all-purpose flour (for baking)

OATS, QUICK-COOKING – 1 cup
- 1 cup plus 2 tablespoons old-fashioned or thick-cut rolled oats, pulsed briefly in a food processor

OATS, STEEL-CUT/PIN HEAD/IRISH (for cooked cereal) – 1 cup
- 1 1/4 cups whole oat groats, coarsely ground in a blender or food processor (Alternatively, leave groats whole and increase the cooking time by 20 to 25 minutes; or soak them for 8 to 12 hours, refrigerated, for a shorter cooking time and creamier oats.)
- 1 cup quick-cooking steel-cut oats (cooks in 5 or 10 minutes depending upon the brand)
- 1 cup stone-cut Scottish oatmeal, or jumbo/extra thick-cut rolled oats, such as Bob's Red Mill or Silver Palate
- 1 cup stone-ground Kamut, whole-grain cracked rye, whole-grain cracked wheat, barley grits, or triticale cereal
- 1 cup millet (overcook slightly, or coarsely grind and soak for 8 to 12 hours before cooking)

OAXACA CHEESE See ASADERO/QUESO OAXACA

OIL, ALMOND See OIL, NUT

OIL, CURRY See CURRY OIL

OIL, LEMON See LEMON OIL; LEMON OLIVE OIL

OIL, MILD/NEUTRAL TASTING – 1 cup
- 1 cup canola or safflower oil

OIL, NUT (almond, hazelnut, macadamia, pecan, pine, pistachio, walnut) – 1 cup
- 1 cup poppy seed oil or Butternut squash seed oil
- 1 cup mild-tasting extra-virgin olive oil

OIL OF BITTER ALMONDS – 1 drop
- 1/2 teaspoon almond extract

OIL OF PEPPERMINT – 1 drop
- 1/8 to 1/4 teaspoon mint extract
- 1 tablespoon chopped fresh peppermint
- 1 teaspoon dried cut-leaf peppermint, or leaves from a peppermint tea bag

OIL, VEGETABLE – 1 cup for baking
- 1 1/4 cups nonhydrogenated solid vegetable shortening
- 1 cup mayonnaise (not reduced-fat or fat-free)
- 1/2 cup thick unsweetened applesauce, drained for 15 minutes, and 1/2 cup well-shaken buttermilk (for recipes where oil is the only liquid)

OIL, VEGETABLE – 1 cup for deep frying
- 1 cup canola, grapeseed, palm, peanut, rice bran, safflower, sunflower, soybean, or other neutral-tasting vegetable oil with a high smoke point

OIL, VEGETABLE – 1 tablespoon for salads and finishing

☞ 1 tablespoon unrefined almond, argan, avocado, flaxseed (cold-pressed), grapeseed, hazelnut, macadamia, olive (extra-virgin, preferably less than 3 months old/olio nuovo), pecan, pine nut, pistachio, pumpkin seed, rice bran, sesame (cold-pressed), Butternut squash seed, sunflower, or walnut oil

OIL, VEGETABLE – 1 tablespoon for shallow frying/sautéing

☞ 1 tablespoon neutral-tasting vegetable oil *See OIL, VEGETABLE – 1 cup for deep frying*

☞ 1 tablespoon refined almond oil, refined avocado oil, butter (dairy, coconut, or soy-based), ghee, margarine, macadamia nut oil, palm kernel oil, sesame oil, or nonhydrogenated solid vegetable shortening)

☞ 1 tablespoon rendered beef fat/tallow or pork fat

☞ 1 tablespoon chicken, duck, or goose fat drippings

☞ 2 teaspoons bacon fat and 1 teaspoon olive oil

☞ 1 tablespoon chicken, mushroom, or vegetable broth (regular, fat-free, or reduced-sodium)

OKONOMIYAKI SAUCE (Japanese condiment) – 1 tablespoon

☞ 1 tablespoon tonkatsu sauce or yakisoba sauce

OKRA, DRIED/BAMIES/BAMYA (Middle Eastern non-gelatinous vegetable) – 1 pound

☞ 1 pound fresh, thawed frozen, or canned okra, soaked in vinegar water for 8 hours before cooking to remove the gelatinous quality (Use 1 cup vinegar to 4 cups water.)

OKRA, FRESH (gelatinous vegetable often used as a thickening agent in soups and stews) – 1 pound

☞ 1 pound purslane leaves, cut into pieces and thick stems discarded

☞ 1 pound nopale/cactus paddles, shaved and sliced

☞ 1 to 2 pounds young common mallow leaves or stems/*Malva neglecta,* or young Malabar spinach leaves/*Basella alba* (for thickening)

☞ 1 tablespoon (or more) filé powder/dried sassafras leaves (for thickening; add to the dish just before or after removing from the heat)

OLD BAY SEASONING (seafood seasoning mix) – 1 tablespoon
☞ 1 tablespoon crab boil spice mix
☞ 1 tablespoon Cajun seasoning
☞ 1 teaspoon celery salt, 1/2 teaspoon paprika, 1/2 teaspoon ground coriander, and a scant teaspoon each of ground cayenne pepper and ground cinnamon

OLIVE OIL, EXTRA-VIRGIN, COLD PRESSED (free oleic acid no more than 0.8%) – 1 cup
☞ 1 cup unrefined avocado oil
☞ 1 cup virgin olive oil (higher in acidity)

OLIVE OIL, REGULAR/MILD/PURE (free oleic acid no more than 3%) – 1 cup
☞ 1 cup green olives or pits added to 1 cup canola oil and left, covered, 2 or 3 days for the oil to develop flavor (Use immediately or store it, tightly covered, in the refrigerator for no more than a few days.)
☞ 3/4 cup canola oil, or other neutral tasting oil, plus 1/4 cup extra-virgin olive oil

OLIVE PASTE, BLACK/KALAMATA OLIVE SPREAD/OLIVADA – 1/2 cup
Make Your Own Pulse in a food processor 1 cup brine-cured pitted black olives, such as Gaeta, Alfonso, or Kalamata, and 2 tablespoons (or more) extra-virgin olive oil until reduced to a paste. Transfer to a small jar, top with a thin layer of olive oil and store, tightly covered, in the refrigerator; it will last up to a few weeks.

OLIVE POWDER, KALAMATA – 1 cup (about)
Make Your Own Spread 2 cups pitted Kalamata olives on a parchment-lined baking sheet and dry in a preheated 200°F oven until hard and crisp, about 8 hours. Alternatively, microwave the olives on High at 2-minute intervals. Cool, then grind in a spice/coffee grinder. Store, tightly covered, in the refrigerator.

OLIVES, BLACK, BRINE- OR OIL-CURED

⮞ Alphonso/Alfonso (Chile), Amphissa/Ámfissa (Greece), Arbequina (Spain), Beldi (Italy), Belladi (Italy) black Cerignola/*Bella di Cerignola* (Italy) Castellammare (Italy) Cerignola (Italy), Elítses (Greece), Farga Aragon (Spain), Gaeta (Italy), Kalamata (Greece/Italy), Koroneiki (Greece), Leccino (Italy), Ligurian (Italy), Lugano (Italy), black Manzanilla (Spain), Maonias (Greece), Mission (California), Moroccan (Morocco), Niçoise (France), Nyons (France), Pendolino (Italy), Picual (Spain), Ponentine (Italy), Royal (Greece), Salona (Greece), San Remo (Italy), Saracena/Minuta (Sicily), Souri (Israel), Taggiasca/Taggiasche (Italy), Throumbe (Greece)

OLIVES, BLACK, DRY-CURED/SALT-CURED

⮞ Aleppo (Syria), Castellammare (Italy), Gaeta (Italy), Gemlik (Turkey), Moroccan (North Africa), Niçoise (France), Nyons (France), Tanchy (France), Thassos throumba (Greece)

OLIVES, GREEN AND LIGHT-COLORED, BRINE-CURED

⮞ Agrinion/Agriniou (Greece), Aleppo (Syria), Arauco (Spain), Arbequina (Spain), Ascoli (Italy), Ascolana (Italy), Atalánda (Greece), Atalanta pitted (Greece), Barnea (Israel), Baresane (Italy), Barouni (Italy), Calabrese (Italy), Chemiali (Morocco), Cypriot (Cyprus), Domat (Turkey), Frantoio (Tuscany), Graber (California), Halkidiki/Mount Athos (Greece), Hojiblanca (Spain), Kura (Middle East), Lindsay (California), Lucques (France), Manzanilla (Spain), Moraiolo (Italy), Moroccan red (North Africa), Nabali (Israel), Naphlion/Náfplion (Greece), Nocellara (Italy), Paternò (Sicily), Picudo (Spain), Picholine (France), Picudo (Spain), Royal (Greece), Servillana (Spain), Sevillano Queen (California), Sicilian Queen (Sicily), Tsakiste (Greece)
⮞ Brine-cured caper berries

OLIVES, GREEN-BRINED, EXTRA-LARGE, MILD

⮞ Italian Green Cerignola/*Bella di Cerignola*, Spanish Gordal/Spanish Queen, or Californian Sevillano Queen

OLIVES, GREEN, LYE-TREATED, VERY MILD
➼ Castelvetrano/*Nocellara del Belice* (Sicily)

OLIVES, OIL-CURED
Make Your Own Place black or green unpitted olives in a small jar and cover with olive oil. Store, tightly covered, in the refrigerator; they will last up to a month.

ONION FLAKES – 1 tablespoon
➼ 1 teaspoon onion powder
➼ 1 teaspoon onion salt; reduce the salt in the recipe by 1 teaspoon
➼ 3/4 teaspoon liquid onion seasoning
➼ 1/2 cup finely chopped fresh onion

ONION JUICE – 1 tablespoon
➼ 1 medium fresh onion squeezed through a garlic press, or grated on large holes of a box grater then pressed through a fine-mesh sieve

ONION POWDER – 1 teaspoon
➼ 2 1/2 tablespoons jarred minced onion
➼ 1/2 cup chopped fresh onion
➼ 1 tablespoon dried minced onion, onion flakes, or instant minced onion
➼ 1 teaspoon onion salt; reduce the salt in the recipe by 1 teaspoon

ONION SALT – 1 tablespoon
➼ 1 teaspoon onion powder mixed with 2 teaspoons kosher or coarse sea salt

ONIONS, CIPOLLINI/CIPOLLA/BORETTANE (Italian small squat onions) – 1 pound
➼ 1 pound small red torpedo onions or white silverskin/boiling onions (ping pong ball size)
➼ 1 pound very small (1 1/2-inch in diameter) sweet white onions, such as Vidalia or Walla Walla

- 1 pound large shallots
- 1 pound wild garlic bulbs/*Allium vineale* (stronger flavor; tougher texture)

ONIONS, FRIED, CANNED – 1 cup for casserole topping

- 1 cup Vietnamese packaged fried shallots/*Hahn Phi/chiên hahn huong*
- 1 cup crushed onion-flavored soy crisps

ONION SOUP – 2 cups

- 1 (15-ounce) can beef broth plus 3 tablespoons dried onions, simmered until the onions are soft

ONION SOUP MIX, DRY – 2 scant tablespoons (1/4 packet soup mix)

- 1 teaspoon instant beef bouillon granules (or crumbled bouillon cube), mixed with 1 tablespoon instant minced onion and a pinch of parsley flakes (optional)

ONIONS, PEARL/PICKING, FRESH OR FROZEN – 1 pound

- 1 pound fresh boiling onions, or small cipollini onions cut into quarters

ONION, STORAGE, MEDIUM – (1 cup chopped) See also ONION, STORAGE, SMALL

- 1 medium chopped leek (white and light green parts only; faster cooking)
- 3 to 5 chopped shallots, depending upon size, or 3 1/2 ounces frozen diced shallots
- 1 1/2 cups chopped sweet onions, such as Granex, Maui, Oso, Vidalia, or Walla Walla; or Italian cippolini onions (moister)
- 1/3 cup jarred minced onion
- 3 to 4 tablespoons dried minced onion, softened in 3/4 cup warm water for 15 to 20 minutes
- 1 1/2 to 2 teaspoons onion juice

ONION, STORAGE, SMALL – (1/3 to 1/2 cup chopped) *See also* ONION, STORAGE, MEDIUM
- 1 teaspoon onion powder or liquid onion seasoning
- 1 tablespoon dry onion flakes softened in warm water 15 minutes
- 2 tablespoons dried minced onion softened in 1/3 cup warm water 10 to 15 minutes
- 1 onion-flavored mini bouillon cube (or part thereof) added to the cooking liquid; reduce salt in the recipe accordingly

ONION, SWEET (Oso, Vidalia, Walla Walla, Maui) – 1 cup sliced or chopped
- 1 cup sliced or chopped regular/storage onion, soaked in cold water for 30 or more minutes, then blotted dry

ORACH/MOUNTAIN SPINACH – 8 ounces
- 8 ounces baby spinach, mâche, lamb's-quarters, Bibb or Boston lettuce, or any tender salad greens (for young leaves)
- 8 ounces mature spinach, green or rainbow chard, or beet greens (for mature cooking leaves)

ORANGE BITTERS (such as Fee Brothers, Pomeranzen, Regan's, or Angostura Orange) – 1 dash
- 1/16 teaspoon orange extract

ORANGE, BLOOD (thin-skinned orange with deep red interior) – 1
- 1 small Ruby Red pink grapefruit (tarter)
- 1 Cara Cara orange, or another naval-type orange (a little sweeter)

ORANGE, BLOOD, JUICE – 1 cup
- 1 cup Florida orange juice plus 1 tablespoon grenadine
- 3/4 cup plus 2 tablespoons Florida orange juice and 2 tablespoons unsweetened pomegranate juice

ORANGE BLOSSOM WATER *See ORANGE FLOWER WATER*

ORANGE, CARA CARA (low-acidity, sweet navel orange with deep-pink flesh) – 1

☞ 1 fully ripe navel orange; or sweet blood orange, preferably Tarocco

ORANGE CITRUS OIL/PURE ORANGE OIL – 1/8 teaspoon

☞ 1/2 teaspoon orange extract
☞ 1 or 2 teaspoons finely grated orange zest

ORANGE EXTRACT – 1 teaspoon

☞ 1 teaspoon dried granulated orange peel or orange juice powder
☞ 1 tablespoon finely grated orange zest from a well-scrubbed orange, preferably organic
☞ 2 teaspoons grated candied orange peel (Rinse to remove the sugar before grating or reduce the sugar in the recipe; for easier grating, pulse with the flour called for in the recipe.)
☞ 1/4 cup orange juice; reduce the liquid in the recipe by 1/4 cup

ORANGE FLOWER WATER/ORANGE BLOSSOM WATER – 1 tablespoon

☞ 1/2 teaspoon orange extract
☞ 1/16 to 1/8 teaspoon orange citrus oil, such as Boyajian (double the amount for a cooked dish)
☞ 2 teaspoons finely grated orange zest
☞ 1/3 teaspoon Sicilian flower essence/*Fiori di Sicilia* (has vanilla and orange aroma)

Make Your Own Steep 2 teaspoons crushed or minced dried orange peel (preferably sour) for 2 days in 1 cup sweet, nonsparkling white wine. Strain through a fine-mesh sieve; discard the peel. Store in a covered jar in the refrigerator. Makes 1 cup. Use the amount called for in the recipe.

ORANGE JUICE CONCENTRATE – 2 tablespoons

Make Your Own: 1 cup fresh orange juice, gently boiled, uncovered, until reduced to 2 tablespoons, 10 to 12 minutes, or microwaved on High in a 4-cup glass measuring cup coated with cooking spray, until reduced to 2 tablespoons

ORANGE JUICE, FRESH – 1 cup
☞ 1/4 cup frozen orange juice concentrate mixed with 3/4 cup water
☞ 2 cups brewed orange herbal tea; reduce the liquid in the recipe by 1 cup

ORANGE JUICE POWDER – 1 tablespoon
☞ 2 tablespoons orange zest
☞ 1/2 teaspoon orange extract

ORANGE LIQUEUR/ORANGE-FLAVORED SPIRIT (such as Bauchant, Citrónge, Cointreau, Curaçao, Gran Torres, Grand Marnier, Leopold Bros., or triple sec) – 1 tablespoon for cooking
☞ 1/2 teaspoon orange extract and 2 1/2 teaspoons water
☞ 1 1/2 teaspoons frozen orange juice concentrate and 1 1/2 teaspoons water
☞ 1 tablespoon fresh orange juice and 1/2 teaspoon finely grated orange zest (or 1/4 teaspoon orange extract)
☞ 1 teaspoon finely grated orange zest

ORANGE PEEL, DRIED GRANULATED – 1 tablespoon
☞ Strips of orange peel (removed with a paring knife or vegetable peeler and any white pith scraped away) dried at room temperature for 3 to 7 days, or in the microwave on High for 2 to 3 minutes; crushed or ground as needed
☞ 1 tablespoon finely grated fresh orange zest
☞ 2 teaspoons grated candied orange peel; remove sugar in the recipe by 1/2 teaspoon
☞ 1/2 teaspoon orange extract

ORANGE, SOUR/BITTER/SEVILLE/NARANJA AGRIA (high-acid orange) – 1
☞ 1 calamondin/*kalamansi*, or 3 kumquats

ORANGE, SOUR/BITTER/SEVILLE/NARAJIA AGRIA, JUICE – 1 tablespoon
- Juice of 3 large kumquats
- 1 teaspoon each lemon juice, grapefruit juice, and sweet orange juice
- 1 1/2 teaspoons each lime or lemon juice and sweet orange juice
- 2 teaspoons sweet orange juice and 1 teaspoon distilled white vinegar (for savory dishes only)
- 1 tablespoon verjuice (for savory dishes only)

ORANGE, SOUR/BITTER, ZEST – 1 tablespoon
- 2 teaspoons grated orange zest, and 1 teaspoon grated lemon zest
- 1 tablespoon grated lime zest

ORANGE ZEST – 1 tablespoon
- 1 teaspoon dried minced orange peel, softened for 15 minutes in 1 tablespoon water
- 1 tablespoon tangerine or kumquat zest
- 1 1/2 teaspoons orange extract
- 2 tablespoons fresh orange juice
- 1/2 teaspoon orange citrus oil, such as Boyajian (Double the amount for a cooked dish.)
- 1 tablespoon grated or minced candied lemon peel (Rinse to remove the sugar before grating or reduce the sugar in the recipe by 1/2 teaspoon; for easier grating or mincing, pulse with the flour or sugar called for in the recipe.)

OREGANO, CUBAN/INDIAN BORAGE/SPANISH THYME (Caribbean seasoning) – 1 tablespoon fresh or dried
- 1 tablespoon fresh or dried sage

OREGANO, GREEK/RIGANI/ORIGANUM HERACLEOTICUM, FRESH – 1 tablespoon chopped
- 2 to 3 teaspoons cultivated dried rigani, crumbled

☞ 2 tablespoons dried Italian oregano, preferably wild mountain, crumbled (milder)

OREGANO, MEDITERRANEAN, FRESH – 3 sprigs (1 tablespoon chopped)
- ☞ 1 teaspoon crumbled dried Mediterranean oregano (Italian, Sicilian, Turkish)
- ☞ 1/2 teaspoon powdered Mediterranean oregano
- ☞ 1 scant tablespoon chopped fresh Mexican oregano, or 1 scant teaspoon dried (more pungent)
- ☞ 1 1/2 tablespoons chopped fresh sweet marjoram, or 1 1/2 teaspoons dried (milder and more delicate; add towards the end of cooking)
- ☞ 2 teaspoons chopped fresh thyme, or 1/2 teaspoon dried
- ☞ 1 teaspoon dried Italian or Greek seasoning
- ☞ 3 tablespoons chopped fresh bee balm/*Monarda didyma*

OREGANO, MEXICAN/OAXACAN/PUERTO RICAN, DRIED – 1 sprig (1 teaspoon broken leaf, crumbled)
- ☞ Scant 1/2 teaspoon powdered (ground) Mexican oregano
- ☞ 1 tablespoon fresh Greek or Spanish oregano
- ☞ 1 tablespoon chopped fresh pot/Sicilian marjoram, or 1 teaspoon dried
- ☞ 1/2 teaspoon each dried Mediterranean oregano and dried marjoram

ORGEAT SYRUP (cocktail flavoring) – 1/4 cup
- ☞ 1/4 cup almond syrup/Greek orzata syrup
- ☞ 1/4 cup amaretto-coffee flavoring syrup
- ☞ 1/4 cup simple syrup (*See SYRUP, SIMPLE*) flavored with 1/4 teaspoon almond extract, plus a few drops of rose water or orange-flower water, if available

OROBLANCO (large grapefruit hybrid) – 1
- ☞ 1 small pummelo

> ⊯ 1 large cocktail grapefruit/Ugli fruit/uniq fruit (pummelo-mandarin hybrid)
> ⊯ 1 grapefruit (more acidic)

ORZO *See PASTA, TINY SHAPED*

OUARKA *See BRIK PASTRY*

OVOLO MUSHROOMS/CAESAR'S MUSHROOMS/AMANITA CAESARIS, FRESH – 1 pound
> ⊯ 1 pound fresh chanterelle, cremini, oyster, or hen of the woods mushrooms

OYSTER LIQUOR/JUICE – 1 cup
> ⊯ 1/2 cup each bottled clam juice and water

OYSTER MUSHROOMS/PLEUROTUS/SHIMEJI/HIRATAKE, FRESH – 4 ounces
> ⊯ 4 ounces fresh eringi, enoki, or straw mushrooms
> ⊯ 2 to 3 ounces canned oyster, enoki, or straw mushrooms
> ⊯ 4 ounces fresh shiitake mushroom caps

OYSTER SAUCE (Chinese cooking condiment) – 1 tablespoon
> ⊯ 1 tablespoon Thai oyster sauce/*nam man hoi* (less salty; more oyster flavor)
> ⊯ 1 tablespoon vegetarian oyster-flavored sauce or Lee Kum Kee Vegetarian Stir-Fry Sauce (contains mushrooms and vegetable proteins)
> ⊯ 1 1/2 teaspoons mushroom or dark soy sauce and 1 1/2 teaspoons black bean sauce
> ⊯ 1 teaspoon Asian fish sauce mixed with 2 teaspoons *kecap manis* or Chinese or Thai sweet black soy sauce
> ⊯ 1 tablespoon teriyaki sauce (sweeter)
> ⊯ 1 teaspoon Maggi Seasoning

O

OYSTERS, FRESH – 1 cup shucked
- 1 (10-ounce) jar refrigerated shucked oysters
- 2 (8-ounce) cans whole oysters, drained
- 2 (3 3/4-ounce) cans smoked oysters
- 1 pound fresh mussels

OXTAIL – 1 pound
- 1 pound beef shank from the lower end of the leg

P

PADRÓN PEPPER/PIMIENTO DE PADRÓN, FRESH (small Spanish green pepper) – 3 or 4
- 3 or 4 Japanese shishito peppers
- One Anaheim chile or Cubanelle pepper, cut into quarters lengthwise

PALM FRUIT/PALM NUT/KAONG (Filipino) – 1 pound
- 1 (12-ounce) jar palm fruit in syrup

PALM KERNEL OIL (Southeast Asian mild, light colored oil) – 1 cup
- 1 cup refined melted coconut oil or mild-flavored olive oil

PALM LEAVES (for wrapping) See WRAPPERS FOR FOOD, NONEDIBLE

PALM OIL, RED/ PALM FRUIT OIL/DENDÊ (Brazilian and West African reddish colored oil) – 1 cup
- 1 cup achiote-infused oil (Heat 1 cup corn, coconut, or peanut oil with 1/4 cup achiote seeds until beginning to bubble; cool and strain, discarding the seeds. Alternatively, color the oil with achiote powder, mild paprika, or ground turmeric; let it sit for 30 minutes, then strain off the oil.)
- 1 cup coconut oil (for baking)
- 1 cup strong-flavored olive oil or creamy unsweetened peanut butter (for finishing)

PALM SUGAR, LIGHT/COCONUT PALM SUGAR (Southeast Asian unrefined sugar) –1 (1-inch) piece chopped or shaved See also PILONCILLO
- 2 tablespoons coconut sugar crystals or Sucanat

☞ 1 tablespoon each maple sugar and light brown sugar

☞ 2 tablespoons firmly packed light brown sugar

☞ 4 teaspoons granulated sugar

PALM SUGAR SYRUP, HEAVY – 1 cup

☞ 2 cups light palm sugar, melted over very low heat until liquefied (add a little maple syrup if desired)

☞ 1 cup each shaved palm sugar and water, simmered until thick and syrupy

☞ 1 cup golden syrup, such as Lyle's

PALM SUGAR SYRUP, LIGHT – 1 cup

☞ 1 cup each shaved (or jarred) palm sugar and water heated until sugar is dissolved

☞ 1 cup simple/stock syrup

PALM SYRUP See COCONUT NECTAR

PALM VINEGAR/COCONUT PALM VINEGAR/SIRKA/SUKA NG NIYOG (Indian, Filipino, and Southeast Asian) – 1 tablespoon

☞ 1 tablespoon unseasoned mild rice vinegar, such as Japanese

☞ 2 teaspoons champagne vinegar, coconut vinegar, or white wine vinegar and 1 teaspoon water

☞ 1 1/2 teaspoons each cider vinegar and water

PANANG CURRY PASTE (Thai seasoning) – 1 tablespoon

☞ 1 tablespoon red curry paste (stronger-tasting)

PANCAKE MIX See BAKING MIX/ALL-PURPOSE BISCUIT MIX

PANCAKE SYRUP – 1 cup See also MAPLE SYRUP

☞ 1 cup firmly packed brown sugar, 2/3 cup water plus a pinch of salt, simmered until syrupy, 15 to 20 minutes, stirring occasionally (cool before serving)

- ⇨ 1 cup dark corn syrup, brown rice syrup, barley malt syrup, birch syrup, golden syrup, light or dark agave syrup/nectar, or cane or sorghum syrup, microwaved until warm and pourable
- ⇨ 1 cup jam, jelly, preserves, or fruit spread, melted in the microwave with a little juice or water
- ⇨ 1 1/2 to 2 cups juice from canned fruit, gently boiled until syrupy
- ⇨ 1 1/2 to 2 cups apple cider, gently boiled until syrupy
- ⇨ 2 cups maple sugar and 1 cup water, simmered until the sugar is dissolved and the mixture is syrupy

PANCETTA (Italian salt-cured pork belly) – 1 ounce
- ⇨ 1 ounce guanciale (less salty but fattier), capicola/coppa, prosciutto, or prosciutto end pieces or crumbles
- ⇨ 1 thick strip fresh pork belly, covered in salt, left for 24 hours, then rinsed and dried
- ⇨ 1/2 ounce each boiled ham and salt pork
- ⇨ 1 thick slice slab bacon, blanched in boiling water for 5 to 6 minutes to reduce the smoke flavor
- ⇨ 1 ounce Canadian bacon, blanched in boiling water for 2 or 3 minutes to reduce the smoke flavor
- ⇨ 1 ounce lean salt pork

PANCETTA, SMOKED/PANCETTA AFFUMICATA (Italian smoked bacon) – 1 ounce
- ⇨ 1 ounce regular bacon

PANCH PHORON See BENGALI FIVE-SPICE MIX

PANDAN/PANDANUS FLOWER ESSENCE See KEVDA

PANDAN/PANDANUS LEAF See SCREWPINE LEAF

PANDAN/PANDANUS WATER (Southeast Asian flavoring agent) – 1 tablespoon
- ⇨ 1 or 2 drops pandan essence (or food-grade pure rose extract/essence) and green food coloring

Make Your Own Cut 2 or 3 fresh or frozen pandan leaves into pieces and pulverize in a blender with 1/3 cup water. Strain through a fine sieve, then measure out 1 tablespoon liquid.

PANEER/PANIR (Indian fresh curd cheese) – 4 ounces
- 4 ounces pressed farmer cheese or queso fresco
- 4 ounces drained extra-firm tofu
- 4 ounces halloumi cheese (saltier; reduce the salt in the recipe by 1/2 teaspoon)

PANELA (Mexican fresh crumbly cheese) See QUESO PANELA

PANELA (Latin American loaf sugar) See PILONCILLO

PANKO (Japanese-style crisp, light breadcrumbs) – 1 cup
- 2 ounces sliced white bread, preferably Japanese-style/*shokupan*, crusts removed and dried at room temperature for 24 hours, then briefly pulsed in the food processor until flaky, using the shredding device (or largest grating blade)
- 1 cup crushed crackers, Melba toasts, or low-sodium tortilla chips
- 1 1/2 cups thin, crisp, whole-grain crackers processed using the shredding device (to replace whole-wheat panko)

PAPAYA, GREEN/PAWPAW/MALAKAW – 1 pound
- 1 pound tart green apples, such as Granny Smith or Bramley's Seedling (Prevent discoloring by soaking in acidulated water immediately after cutting.)
- 1 pound chayote or jícama (for cooking; or grated or shredded for salads)

PAPAYA, RIPE HAWAIIAN – 1 pound
- 1 pound fresh Mexican papaya (larger and less flavorful)
- 1 pound fresh or jarred Chilean golden mountain papaya/*ababai/carica* (smaller)

- ⮞ 1 pound fresh Ecuadorian *babaco*/*chamburo* (hybrid of papaya)
- ⮞ 1 pound fresh, frozen, or canned mango (sweeter)
- ⮞ 1 pound fresh cantaloupe, peaches, or nectarines

PAPAYA LEAF/PAPALO/PAPALOQUELITE (Mexican seasoning herb) – 1 small leaf (1 tablespoon minced)

- ⮞ 2 teaspoons finely minced cilantro and 1 teaspoon finely minced watercress
- ⮞ 1 generous tablespoon finely minced *pipicha*

PAPAYA LEAVES See WRAPPERS FOR FOOD, VEGETABLE-BASED

PAPELÓN (Venezuelan unrefined loaf sugar) See PILONCILLO/ PANELA/PANOCHA

PAPRIKA, GENERIC – 1 teaspoon for garnish and color only

- ⮞ 3/4 teaspoon New Mexico chile powder
- ⮞ 1/2 teaspoon ground turmeric, preferably Alleppey, plus a small pinch of ground cayenne pepper
- ⮞ 1 teaspoon dried tomato powder or Australian dried bush tomato/*akudjura* powder
- ⮞ 1 teaspoon Asian fermented black bean powder (darker color)

PAPRIKA, HUNGARIAN HOT – 1 teaspoon

- ⮞ 3/4 teaspoon mild/sweet paprika and 1/4 teaspoon ground cayenne pepper, or other hot chile powder
- ⮞ 1 teaspoon Aleppo or Maras chile powder
- ⮞ 1/2 teaspoon ground cayenne pepper

PAPRIKA, HUNGARIAN MILD/SWEET/KULONLEGES – 1 teaspoon for garnish

- ⮞ 1 teaspoon Spanish unsmoked sweet paprika/*pimentón dulce*, mild Basque chile powder/*piment d'espelette*, or Indian paprika/*Kashmiri mirch*

PAPRIKA OIL (South American seasoning and coloring oil) – 1/4 cup
Make Your Own Heat 1/4 vegetable oil and 4 teaspoons sweet Spanish paprika over medium-low heat until hot, 2 to 3 minutes. Strain through a cheesecloth-lined sieve; discard the solids. (For a zestier oil, add 1/2 teaspoon ground cayenne pepper.)

PAPRIKA PASTE (Hungarian seasoning) – 1 tablespoon
- 1 tablespoon mild red pepper paste (or 2 jarred roasted red piquillo peppers drained and pureed) plus mild/sweet smoked paprika to taste

PAPRIKA, SPANISH HOT SMOKED/PIMENTÓN DE LA VERA PICANTE – 1/2 teaspoon
- 1/4 teaspoon each chipotle chile powder and Hungarian mild/sweet paprika
- 1/2 teaspoon Hungarian hot paprika (replace all or part of the salt in the recipe with smoked salt, if available)
- 1/2 teaspoon Spanish mild/sweet smoked paprika and 1/8 teaspoon ground cayenne pepper
- 1/4 teaspoon ground cayenne pepper or chile de árbol powder

PAPRIKA, SPANISH MILD SMOKED/PIMENTÓN DE LA VERA DULCE – 1/2 teaspoon
- 1/2 teaspoon choricero powder
- 1/4 teaspoon smoked salt and 1/2 teaspoon mild/sweet California, Hungarian, or Indian paprika; reduce the salt in the recipe by 1/4 teaspoon
- Small pinch of ground Lapsang Souchong or Scottish breakfast tea leaves added to Hungarian mild/sweet paprika
- 1 teaspoon mild smoked paprika paste

PAPPADAM/POPPADUM (Indian wafer-thin flatbread)
- Thin, crisp lavash

PARATHA (Indian whole-wheat flatbread) – 1
- ☞ 1 whole-wheat, whole spelt, or multi-grain tortilla

PARDINA LENTILS See LENTILS, SPANISH BROWN

PARMA HAM See PROSCIUTTO DI PARMA

PARMESAN CHEESE (Italian and domestic hard, dry, cow's milk cheese) – 1 ounce
- ☞ 1 ounce Grana Padano, aged Asiago, or Pecorino Romano (sharper-tasting)
- ☞ 1 cup vegan Parmesan cheese, such as Parmela or Parma

PARMESAN CHEESE, VEGAN – 1 cup
- ☞ 3/4 cup raw cashews, 3 tablespoons nutritional yeast, plus half a teaspoon each of sea salt and garlic powder pulsed in a food processor until reduced to a fine meal (store, tightly sealed, in the refrigerator)
- ☞ 1 cup skinned hazelnuts, 1 chopped garlic clove, plus 3/4 teaspoon sea salt pulsed in a food processor until reduced to a fine meal (store, tightly sealed, in the refrigerator)
- ☞ 1 cup nutritional yeast powder or flakes (has a cheesy taste)

PARMIGIANO-REGGIANO (Italian hard aged cow's milk cheese) – 1 ounce
- ☞ 1 ounce Grana Padano (milder, less expensive)
- ☞ 1 ounce Pecorino gran cru, Pecorino Romano, Pecorino Toscano, Kefalotyri Reggianito (sheep's milk cheeses; sharper)
- ☞ 1 ounce aged Asiago, aged Cotija/*queso añejo*, aged Gouda, aged *mizithra*, dry Jack, domestic Parmesan, Romano, or Sbrinz (milder)
- ☞ 1 ounce gluten-free Parmesan, such as Soyco

PARRANO CHEESE (Dutch semifirm Italian-style cheese) – 1 ounce (for grating)
- ☞ 1/2 ounce each grated Parmigiano-Reggiano and aged Gouda

PARSLEY, CURLY (for garnish)
- Feathery carrot tops
- Fennel fronds
- Korean watercress/*minali*
- Parsley root leaves
- Celery or Chinese celery leaves
- Sprigs of basil, chervil, cilantro, lovage, tarragon, or thyme
- Young corn speedwell/*Veronica arvensis* (use the top few inches)

PARSLEY, FLAT-LEAF/ITALIAN PARSLEY – 1 tablespoon chopped
- 4 teaspoons chopped curly-leaf parsley (less flavorful)
- 1 teaspoon dried parsley flakes
- 1/2 to 1 parsley-flavored mini bouillon cube (for soups or stews; reduce the salt in the recipe accordingly)
- 1 or 2 cubes frozen chopped parsley (for cooked dishes; 1 cube equals 2 teaspoons fresh parsley)

PARSLEY ROOT/HAMBURG PARSLEY – 1 pound (3 medium)
- 1 celery root/celeriac plus 1/3 cup parsley leaves
- 1 pound carrots, turnips, or parsnips plus a pinch of celery seed

PARSNIPS – 1 pound
- 1 pound carrots, especially white carrots such as White Satin
- 1 pound turnips (less sweet; more moist)
- 1 pound salsify/white salsify (less sweet)
- 1 pound parsley root/Hamburg parsley (less sweet)
- 1 pound burdock root or wild burdock root/lesser burdock/*Arctium minus*
- 1 pound skirret/*Sium sisarum* (retain the peel but remove the woody core)
- 1 pound dandelion roots (slight dandelion leaf flavor and potato texture)
- 1 pound young evening primrose roots
- 1 pound rampion roots (serve with a sauce)

PASILLA CHILE/PASILLA NEGRO (dried chilaca chile) – 1
- 1 dried ancho, mulato, or New Mexico chile
- 1 tablespoon ancho or New Mexico chile powder
- 1 tablespoon ancho paste
- 1/2 teaspoon ground cayenne pepper

PASILLA DE OAXACA CHILE/PASILLA OAXAQUEÑO, DRIED – 1
- 2 dried mora chiles/*chipotles moras* (purplish-red color)
- 1 teaspoon chipotle chile powder or paste
- 2 canned or jarred chipotles in adobo

PASSATA/SUGOCASA (Italian jarred tomato pulp) – 16 ounces
- 32 ounces whole canned tomatoes, blended or processed, then strained (Alternatively, drain the tomatoes, then puree or crush them.)
- 2 pounds large fresh plum tomatoes, halved, seeded, excess juice expelled, then rubbed against the coarsest holes on a box or sheet grater; skins discarded
- 2 cups thick tomato sauce

PASSION FRUIT/MARACUJÁ DOCE/GRANADILLA – 1 fruit (1 tablespoon pulp with seeds)
- 1/2 large yellow passion fruit (transparent flesh; sweeter)
- 1 tablespoon mango or guava pulp plus a few drops of Key lime juice
- 1 1/2 teaspoons frozen unsweetened passion fruit concentrate or frozen tropical fruit puree (for strained pulp)
- 1 ripe yellow or orange maypop/passionflower fruit (*Passiflora incarnata* and *P. caerulea*)
- 1 or 2 tablespoons passion fruit liqueur/*La Grande Passion* (for flavoring only)

PASSION FRUIT JUICE – 1 cup
- 6 large yellow passion fruits (or 12 purple), pulp removed and pureed in a blender 1 minute, then strained

➼ 3/4 cup plus 2 tablespoons canned passion fruit nectar and 1 or 2 tablespoons lemon or lime juice

➼ 1/2 cup each pineapple juice and lime juice, preferably Key lime

➼ 1 1/3 cups frozen *naranjilla* juice, thawed and strained

PASSION FRUIT PULP – 1 (generous) cup

➼ 6 large yellow, or 12 small purple, passion fruits, halved and pulp removed

➼ 2 cups frozen passion fruit puree, such as Maracuyá

PASTA DOUGH/PASTA ALL'UOVO/LA SFOGLIA, FRESH (Italian egg pasta for ravioli) – 1 pound

➼ 1 pound extra-thin/Hong Kong–style wonton wrappers

➼ 1 pound wheat-flour egg roll skins, cut to size

➼ 1 pound (6-inch) fresh manicotti wrappers, cut to size

PASTA FLOUR (very fine and silky hard durum wheat flour) – 1 cup

➼ 1/2 cup each golden semolina flour and durum wheat flour (best for ravioli)

➼ 1/3 cup each semolina, golden durum, and unbleached all-purpose or whole-wheat flour

➼ 1 cup unbleached all-purpose flour with 10% protein, or equal parts cake and all-purpose flour to approximate 10% (best for delicate stuffed pasta)

PASTA, FREGOLA/FREGOLONE/FREGULA (Sardinian toasted semolina pellets) – 1 cup

➼ 1 cup Italian, Israeli, or Lebanese couscous, toasted before cooking, then prepared following the package directions

➼ 1 cup orzo, toasted before cooking, then prepared following the package directions

PASTA, FRESH – 1 pound

➼ 12 ounces dried pasta (takes a few more minutes to cook)

- 12 ounces dried whole-wheat pasta (firmer; takes a little longer to cook; best for thick sauces)
- 1 pound fresh or thawed frozen gyoza wrappers, lumpia wrappers, wonton wrappers, or wheat-flour egg roll wrappers (for stuffed pasta, soup pasta, or short strand pasta cut as required)

PASTA, GLUTEN-FREE
- Arrowroot vermicelli
- Artichoke pasta (Italian)
- Bifun pasta
- Brown rice fettuccine, lasagna, or other pasta shapes
- Buckwheat noodles made with potato flour and buckwheat (Korean)
- Cornstarch sticks (Filipino)
- Corn noodles, pasta, or spaghetti
- Corn-quinoa linguine and pasta
- Jerusalem artichoke spaghetti and pasta
- Kelp spaghetti, pasta, and ready-to-eat noodles
- Multi-grain blend (corn, quinoa, brown rice, and white rice) pasta and spaghetti
- Mung bean threads/cellophane noodles
- Red lentil penne
- Rice spaghetti or vermicelli, rice sticks, or wide Asian rice noodles
- Rice flour, potato starch, and soy flour pasta
- *Shirataki* fresh precooked angel hair, fettuccine, or spaghetti
- Soba/buckwheat noodles/*tachi soba* (label stating 100% buckwheat or gluten-free)
- Soy pasta (label stating 100% soy)
- Sweet potato vermicelli (Korean)
- Tofu noodles/bean curd strips (fresh, frozen, or dried)

PASTA SAUCE – 1 cup See also PIZZA SAUCE
- 1 cup chunky tomato soup
- 1 cup tomato and roasted red pepper soup

PASTA, STRAND OR RIBBON, DRIED – 8 ounces *See also PASTA, THIN STRAND OR ROD*
- 8 ounces of any of the following: dried *bavette, bavettine,* bucatini (hollow), *ciriole,* fettuccine, fusilli napoletani/lunghi (curled), linguine, mafalde, pappardelle, perciatelli, Shanghai noodles, spaghetti, *spaghetti grossi, spaghetti rigati,* tagliatelle, *tonnarelli, trenette,* or egg noodles (prepare following the package directions)
- 6 ounces fresh precooked *shirataki* fettuccine or spaghetti, rinsed and drained (heat in boiling water for 1 minute)1 to 1 1/2 ounces dried sea palm/*Postelsia palmaeformis* soaked for 15 to 20 minutes, then squeezed dry (resembles spinach pasta; add to the cooked sauce at the last minute)
- 1 to 1 1/2 ounces dried sea spaghetti/thongweed/*Himanthalia elongata,* soaked for 30 minutes, cooked for 10 minutes, then drained and rinsed in cold water (or use jarred thongweed, then just rinse)
- 4 to 5 cups fresh raw zucchini or yellow squash ribbons (Blanch for 1 minute, then rinse in cold water and pat dry; or, to serve raw, lightly salt, let drain in a colander for 15 to 20 minutes, then rinse and pat dry.)
- 3 1/2 to 4 cups fresh raw carrot, parsnip, or broccoli stalk ribbons (Blanch for 1 to 2 minutes to soften, then drain; add to the cooked sauce at the last minute.)

PASTA, STUFFED, FRESH OR FROZEN – 1 pound
- 1 pound fresh or frozen agnolotti, anolini, cappellacci, cappelletti, girasole, lunette, pansotti, ravioli, ravioletti, raviolini, tortelli, tortellini, or tortelloni *See also PASTA DOUGH*

PASTA, THIN STRAND OR ROD, DRIED – 8 ounces
- 8 ounces of any of the following: dried *avgohilos, bavettini, boretti, capelli d'angelo,* capellini (angel hair), *fedelini,* spaghettini, tagliatelle, tagliarini/*tagliolini,* or vermicelli
- 8 ounces dried Asian *ito soba* (40% buckwheat), lo mein, or somen noodles

- 8 ounces adzuki bean spaghetti or edamame and mung bean fettuccine (mild and nutty tasting. Gluten-free, organic and made with nothing but beans)
- 6 ounces precooked angel hair *shirataki*, rinsed and drained (best for Asian dishes)
- 3 to 4 cups fresh baked spaghetti squash strands, drained
- 3 to 4 cups fresh raw zucchini strands, lightly steamed

PASTA, TINY SHAPED/PASTINA, DRIED – *8 ounces*

- 8 ounces of any of the following: dried *alfabeto, amoretti, anelli, anellini, ancini di pepe, coralli, coralline, ditalini, funghini, maccheroni napolitani,* orzo, *pastini, pennette, pipette, quadretti, quadrucci, raviolini, riccilelli, riso, risoni, rosamarina, stellette/stelline, semi di melone, tubetti lisci, tubetti rigati, tubetini,* or *volarelle*
- 8 ounces dried fideos (short threads), broken into pieces
- 8 ounces fresh or dried *kouskousi, kritharaki, manestra,* or *fregula* (barley-shaped pasta)
- 8 ounces dried Israeli/Lebanese couscous (pearl-shaped pasta) or spaetzle (tiny egg dumplings)
- 8 ounces dried pasta shapes or strands, crushed or broken into bits
- 10 ounces *shirataki* orzo, drained, rinsed, and heated briefly (gluten-free)

PASTA, TUBULAR, LARGE DRIED – *1 pound*

- 1 pound of any of the following: dried *cannaroni/zitoni, cannolicchi,* cannelloni, *gramigna, manicotti,* or *paccheri*

PASTA, TUBULAR, SHORT DRIED – *1 pound*

- 1 pound of any of the following: dried *bocconcini, bombolotti, cannolicchi, capricci, caserecci,* cavatappi, *chifferi, chifferotti rigati,* ditali, *elicoidali, garganelli,* macaroni, *maccheroncini, magliette, mezzani, millerighe, mostaccioli, penne lisce* (smooth), *penne rigate* (finely ridged), *pennoni* (large penne), *rigatini,* rigatoni (large rigatini), *rigatoncini* (short rigatoni), *sedani rigati, torchio, tortiglioni, trenne,* ziti, *zitoni* (thick ziti), or *zitoni rigati* (ridged *zitoni*)

PASTA, VARIETY-SHAPED, DRIED – 1 pound

☞ 1 pound of any of the following: dried *aftoudia* (small ears), *anelleti* (little rings), *armoniche* (ridged shells), *canestrini* (little baskets), *calamarata* (wide thick rings), *calamaretti* (small thick rings), *cappelli di pagliaccio* (clowns' hats), *casarecce* (corkscrews), *cavatelli* (short ridged shells), *chiocciole* (snails), *conchiglie* (ridged shells), *corzetti* (large coins), *creste di galli* (cockscombs), *farfalle* (butterflies/bow-ties), *farfallini* (small farfalle), *farfalloni* (large farfalle), *filei* (short twists), *fiochetti* (short curls), *fusilli* (short spirals), *garganelli* (ridged rolls), *gemelli* (double twists), *gnochetti* (ripple-edged shells), *lumache/lumaconi* (snail shells), *lingue di passeri* (sparrows' tongues), *maltagliati* (irregularly cut shapes), *malloreddus* (small ridged curls), *maruzze* (seashells), *nodi marini* (sailor's knots), *orecchiette* (little ears), *radiatore* (little radiators), *riccioli* (fat corkscrews), *rombi* (short ribbons), *rotelle* (wheels), *rotini* (corkscrews), *ruote* (wheels), *strozzapretti* (thin spirals), *torchietti* (corkscrews), *tripolini* (little bow ties), *trofie* (spirals), or *varnishkas* (bow ties)

PASTOÚRMA (Greek salted and spiced veal or pork) – 1 pound

☞ 1 pound Italian bresaola

PASTRY CASES See DESSERT SHELLS

PASTRY CREAM MIX – 4 ounces

☞ 4 ounces vanilla pudding mix, custard powder, or vegan pudding mix, such as Dr. Oetker Organics, prepared following the package directions

PATA NEGRA (Spanish artisanal cured meat) See IBÉRICO HAM

PÂTÉ (French ground-meat preparation)

☞ Braunschweiger or liverwurst

PATIS *See FISH SAUCE; SHRIMP PASTE, FERMENTED*

PAWPAWS *See PAPAYA, GREEN*

PAXIMADIA *See BARLEY RUSKS*

PEACHES – 1 pound
☞ 1 pound nectarines (firmer texture)

PEANUT BUTTER – 1 cup
☞ 1 cup sunflower butter/sunbutter/sunflower seed spread (may turn out green colored from the chlorophyll present)
☞ 1 cup smooth almond butter, cashew butter, hemp butter, or toasted sesame tahini
☞ 1 cup soy nut butter or golden peabutter (legume flavor)
☞ 2 cups dehydrated peanut butter powder mixed with 1 cup water (less calories and fat)

Make Your Own Toast 2 cups skinless peanuts on a baking sheet in a preheated 350°F oven until fragrant, 7 to 10 minutes, stirring half-way through. Transfer to a food processor while warm and process until reduced to a paste, about 15 minutes, scraping down the sides of the bowl as needed. (For chunky butter, stir in 1/4 cup chopped peanuts.) Store up to 3 months in the refrigerator.

PEANUT BUTTER, REGULAR – 1 cup
☞ 1 cup natural peanut butter and 1 tablespoon granulated sugar

PEANUT BUTTER, SALTED – 1 cup
☞ 1 cup unsalted peanut butter and 1 teaspoon salt

PEANUT DIPPING SAUCE (Southeast Asian condiment) – 2/3 cup
Make Your Own Stir together 1/4 cup peanut butter, 1/4 cup warm water, and 1 tablespoon each soy sauce, seasoned rice vinegar, and Chinese chili-garlic sauce.
Or

Heat 1/3 cup smooth peanut butter, 1/3 cup well-shaken canned coconut milk, and 1 teaspoon Sriracha over low heat, stirring until smooth, about 5 minutes.

PEANUT FLOUR (28% fat) – 1 cup
Make Your Own Grind 3/4 cup plus 2 tablespoons raw skinless peanuts in batches in a spice/coffee grinder until powdery. Sift, then regrind any large pieces.

PEANUT OIL, ROASTED – 2 tablespoons
- 2 tablespoons virgin peanut oil (has a roasted flavor)
- 1 tablespoon toasted sesame oil/Chinese sesame oil (has a stronger flavor)
- Cold-pressed peanut oil (has a milder flavor)

PEANUTS – 1 cup
- 1 cup wild jungle peanuts (heirloom variety from the Amazon; does not contain aflatoxin found in American peanuts)

PEANUTS, DRY-ROASTED – 1 cup
- 1 cup raw peanuts roasted on a baking sheet in a preheated 325°F oven until fragrant, 5 to 6 minutes; then rubbed in a cotton kitchen towel to remove the skins

PEARS – 1 pound
- 1 pound Asian pears (crisper; slightly longer cooking time)
- 1 pound apples (crisper texture; longer cooking time)

PEAS, SHELLED, FRESH OR FROZEN – 1 cup
- 1/3 cup dried whole peas, soaked and cooked following the package directions
- 1 cup fresh or frozen shelled lima beans or edamame
- 1 cup fresh or frozen green runner beans, chopped into pea-sized segments
- Green pea flour (for soup)

PEA SHOOTS/LEAVES/TENDRILS/DAU MIU/DOU MIAO (Chinese) – 1 cup
- 1 cup chickweed tips/*Stellaria media*
- 1 cup watercress or garden cress sprigs, thick stems removed
- 1 cup baby arugula or baby spinach, sliced lengthwise
- 1 cup shredded or thinly sliced snow peas or snap peas (about 4 ounces)

PEAS, SPLIT – 1 cup
- 1 cup yellow lentils
- 1/4 cup green pea flour for creamy soup (reduce the cooking time to 3 minutes)

PEA SPROUTS – 1 cup
- 1 cup pea shoots/tendrils, daikon sprouts, sunflower sprouts, or mung bean sprouts
- 1 cup tender chickweed tips/*Stellaria media*

PEA TENDRILS See PEA SHOOTS

PECAN BUTTER – 1 cup
Make Your Own Process 2 cups raw or toasted pecans in a food processor until reduced to a paste, 10 to 15 minutes, scraping down the sides of the bowl as needed. Store, refrigerated, in a lidded jar for up to 1 month.

PECAN FLOUR – 1 cup
Make Your Own Grind 3/4 cup plus 2 tablespoons pecans in batches in a spice/coffee grinder until powdery. Sift, then regrind any large pieces.

PECANS – 1 cup shelled
- 1 cup walnuts

PECORINO ROMANO (Italian sheep's milk hard cheese) – 1 ounce
See also PARMIGIANO-REGGIANO
- ☞ 1 ounce Caprino Romano (sharper), Pecorino campano (milder), Vacchino Romano (milder), or Grana Padano (softer)
- ☞ 1 ounce Fiore Sardo, aged Asiago, dry Jack, extra-aged *kefalotyri*, Parmesan, Romano, or Sbrinz

PECORINO SICILIANO (Italian sheep's milk hard cheese with whole peppercorns) – 1 ounce
- ☞ 1 ounce *Pecorino pepato* (with crushed peppercorns)
- ☞ 1 ounce grated *Pecorino Siciliano bianco/calcagno* (without peppercorns) or Parmesan or Romano plus cracked peppercorns (for cooking)

PECORINO TOSCANO (Italian sheep's milk firm cheese) – 1 ounce
- ☞ 1 ounce Pecorino Crotonese, Fiore Sardo, Manchego, Zamorano, Berkswell, Casciotta, Evora, Spenwood, Toscana, Trade Lake Cedar, or Vermont Shepherd

PECTIN, INSTANT, POWDERED – 0.6 ounce (enough for two 1/2-pint jars)
- ☞ 1 (0.4-ounce) packet regular powdered pectin, 1 1/3 cups sugar, and 1 tablespoon lemon juice; cooked until jam reaches the desired jel (will be sweeter)

PECTIN, REGULAR, POWDERED – 0.4 ounce (enough for two 1/2-pint jars)
- ☞ 1 1/2 ounces regular liquid pectin (Add after the mixture is brought to a full boil, bring again to a full boil, and boil for 1 minute to activate the pectin.)
- ☞ 1 (0.6-ounce) packet instant powdered pectin (Reduce the sugar by half and prepare following the package directions.)
- ☞ 4 teaspoons powdered apple pectin (Add after the mixture is brought to a full boil, bring again to a full boil, and boil for 3 minutes to activate the pectin.)

- 1/4 cup bottled lemon juice, if not already included in the recipe (for jams and preserves; will also reduce the amount of sugar required)
- 1 slightly underripe quince, peeled and chopped (for jams and preserves)
- 1 crab apple or small tart green apple, peeled and grated (for jams and preserves)
- One-quarter of the fruit underripe and three-quarters of the fruit fully ripe (for jams and preserves)
- Increase the cooking time until the jam reaches the desired gel (will result in reduced volume).

PEKMEZ/PETIMEZI (thick Turkish sweetener) *See GRAPE MOLASSES*

PENNYWORT, ASIATIC/GOTU KOLA/GOTUKOLLE/BUA BOK – 1 bunch (4 ounces/1 cup sprigs)
- 1 cup baby arugula leaves, flat-leaf (Italian) parsley, or watercress sprigs

PEPPADEW/PIQUANTÉ PEPPERS, JARRED (South African sweet pickled Juanita peppers)
- Pickled Italian cherry peppers or pepperoncini, plus a little sugar, agave syrup/nectar, or other sweetener added to the brine

PEPPER, BELL (green or yellow) – 1 medium (1 cup chopped)
- 1 fresh Cubanelle, Marconi, green pimiento, or Hungarian wax/banana pepper
- 1 mild Anaheim or Hatch chile
- 1/4 cup dried bell pepper flakes, softened in 1/2 cup water for about 15 minutes
- 1/2 cup freeze-dried pepper,added during the last 5-10 minutes of cooking

PEPPER, BELL (green for stuffing) – 1 pound (3 medium)
- 1 pound Yellow Stuffer heirloom tomatoes or SteakHouse hybrid tomatoes

- 1 pound (about 8) assorted baby bell peppers
- 1 pound (3- to 4-inch-wide) round zucchini/globe squash, such as light green *Ronde de Nice* or dark green Eight-Ball

PEPPER, BELL (red) – 1 medium/1 cup chopped
- 1 fresh black Hungarian pepper or fresh red pimiento
- 2 jarred pimientos or roasted red peppers (or 1/2 cup sliced), drained and rinsed
- 1/4 cup red bell pepper flakes softened in 1/2 cup water, about 15 minutes

PEPPERCORNS, BLACK (Malabar or Tellicherry) – 1 teaspoon/34 to 60 peppercorns
- 1 teaspoon white peppercorns (Muntok or Sarawak), or 1 1/2 teaspoons ground white pepper (for Chinese food, light-colored food, sauces, and soups; less aromatic)
- 1 teaspoon French *mignonette* pepper (a mix of black and white pepper)
- 2 dried Indian/Indonesian long peppers/*pippali* (milder and larger; use whole in cooking)
- 1/8 to 1/4 teaspoon dried Tasmanian pepperberries/mountain pepper (best for slow-cooked dishes; hotter; dark red color)
- 1 teaspoon ground papaya seeds (well-washed and well-dried papaya seeds ground in a pepper mill)
- 1/4 teaspoon ground cayenne pepper (hotter)

PEPPERCORNS, CRACKED – 1 tablespoon
- 1 to 1 1/2 tablespoons whole peppercorns split or cracked into 2 or 3 pieces with a pestle or heavy food can

PEPPERCORNS, CRUSHED – 1 tablespoon
- 1 1/2 tablespoons whole peppercorns crushed coarsely with a pestle; or folded in plastic wrap and crushed with a meat tenderizer, rolling pin, or heavy skillet (sift to remove the pepper dust)

PEPPERCORNS, CUBEB/TAILED PEPPER (Indonesian seasoning) – 1 tablespoon
- 1 tablespoon allspice berries
- 2 teaspoons coarsely crushed black peppercorns mixed with a few toasted crushed Sichuan peppercorns

PEPPERCORNS, GREEN BRINED – 1 tablespoon
- 2 teaspoons air-dried green peppercorns, softened for 30 minutes in 1 tablespoon hot meat stock (or water) and 1 tablespoon distilled white vinegar
- 1 tablespoon rinsed brined capers
- 1 tablespoon dried pink peppercorns

PEPPERCORNS, GREEN, FRESH – 1 tablespoon
- 1 tablespoon freeze-dried green peppercorns (roast to enhance the aroma)
- 1 tablespoon canned or brined green peppercorns, drained and rinsed
- 1 teaspoon black peppercorns (more pungent)

PEPPERCORNS, SZECHUAN See SICHUAN PEPPERCORNS

PEPPER, FRYING See CUBANELLE PEPPER, FRESH

PEPPER, LONG See LONG PEPPER, INDONESIAN

PEPPER, MELEGUETA See GRAINS OF PARADISE

PEPPERMINT, FRESH – 1/4 cup chopped
- 1 tablespoon dried peppermint, or leaves from 2 to 3 peppermint tea bags

PEPPER OIL See CHILI OIL, CHINESE; CHILI OIL, ITALIAN

PEPPERONCINI/TUSCAN PEPPER, DRIED (Italian mild chile) – 1 or 2
 ⊨ 1/2 to 1 teaspoon crushed red chile, such as piquin; or crushed red pepper flakes

PEPPERONCINI/TUSCAN PEPPER, FRESH (Italian mild chile) – 1 or 2
 ⊨ 1 or 2 fresh friggitello, pimiento, Mexi-bell, or Hungarian cherry peppers
 ⊨ 1 or 2 jarred Italian pepperoncini or Greek Salonika peppers, rinsed and blotted dry

PEPPER PASTE See RED PEPPER PASTE, HOT; RED PEPPER PASTE, MILD

PEPPER-PEPPER SAUCE (West African condiment) – 1 tablespoon
 ⊨ 1 teaspoon olive oil added to 2 teaspoons hot pepper sauce, such as Tabasco or Crystal

PEPPER, RED BELL See PEPPER, BELL (red)

PEPPER, ROASTED RED – 1 large (1 cup roasted, peeled, and chopped)
 ⊨ 1 cup jarred pimientos, drained and blotted dry
 ⊨ 2 jarred roasted red peppers (bell, Italian frying, or Hungarian)

PEPPER TREE LEAVES/PRICKLY ASH TREE LEAVES, FRESH See KINOME

PEPPER VINEGAR (Southern U.S. condiment) – 1 cup
Make Your Own Wash and dry 2 to 4 ounces small fresh red or green chiles, such as cayenne, de árbol, Korean finger-hot, serrano, Tabasco, or Thai. Pack into a jar and add 1 cup distilled white vinegar plus a pinch of salt. Cover tightly and keep in a cool cupboard for at least 3 weeks, then strain and refrigerate.

PEQUÍN/PIQUÍN CHILES, DRIED (Mexican) – 3 or 4
 ⊨ 3 or 4 tepín/chiltepín, cayenne, serrano, or de árbol chiles

‣ 1 teaspoon ground cayenne pepper or chiltepín powder

PERILLA LEAF/WILD SESAME LEAF *See SHISO, GREEN*

PERI PERI SEASONING (North African-style hot chile spice blend) – 1 tablespoon
‣ 1 tablespoon berbere or harissa powder
‣ 1 tablespoon ground cayenne pepper

PERUANO/MAYACOBA/CANARIO BEANS, DRIED (Peruvian pale-yellow beans) – 1 pound
‣ 1 pound dried pinto beans

PERSILLADE (French seasoning) – 1/4 cup
‣ 3 tablespoons finely chopped flat-leaf parsley mixed with 2 finely minced garlic cloves

PERSIMMON, DRIED/HOSHIGAKI – 8 ounces
‣ 8 ounces unsulphured dried apricots

PERSIMMON, FUYU, FRESH – 1 pound
‣ 1 pound Israeli Sharon fruit/kaki persimmon

PERSIMMON, HACHIYA, FRESH – 1 pound
‣ 5 ounces Japanese dried persimmon/*hoshigaki*, softened in boiling water for 30 to 45 minutes, or in apple juice 8 to 12 hours
‣ 1 pound ripe plums, mamey sapote, cherimoya, or mango

PERSIMMON PUREE – 1 cup for baking
‣ 1 cup thick applesauce, canned pumpkin, or thawed frozen mango puree

PETIT SUISSE (French double-crème cheese) – 1 ounce
‣ 1 ounce Caprini, Fin de Siècle, Gratte-Paille, Le Coutances, Père Michel, Supreme, or natural cream cheese

PHYLLO/FILO DOUGH (paper-thin sheets of pastry dough) – 1 pound
- ⇨ 1 pound frozen whole-wheat phyllo dough (slightly thicker; easier to handle, and using clarified butter ensures crispiness, as it does for all phyllo dough)
- ⇨ 1 pound frozen Armenian or Turkish *yufka* dough (slightly thicker; comes in 16-inch rounds)
- ⇨ 1 pound country-style phyllo dough/*horiatiko* (thicker and crunchier; easier to work with; use fewer sheets)
- ⇨ 1 pound frozen pre-shredded Greek phyllo dough/*kataifi/kadayfi* (does not roll but is easier to work with for a top and bottom crust; toss with melted butter rather than brushing it on)
- ⇨ 1 pound frozen puff pastry, regular/vegan, or all-butter (thicker)
- ⇨ 1 pound (8- or 10-inch) lumpia wrappers
- ⇨ 1 pound (8 by 8-inch rice-flour spring roll wrappers (for a gluten-free alternative; slightly thicker)

PHYLLO/FILO DOUGH, COUNTRY-STYLE/HORIATIKA (thin sheets of pastry dough) – 1 pound
- ⇨ 1 pound regular phyllo dough (brush unsalted clarified butter between each double layer; and to prevent the edges drying out, brush from outside to center)

PIADINA/PIADA (Italian soft thin bread) – 8 ounces
- ⇨ 8 ounces soft lavash, cut into sections

PICKAPEPPA SAUCE (Caribbean condiment) – 1 tablespoon
- ⇨ 1 tablespoon steak sauce or ketchup plus a dash of Louisiana-style hot sauce, such as Tabasco or Crystal (for the thick sauce)
- ⇨ Tabasco or habañero pepper sauce (for the thin hot sauce)

PICKLE CRISP GRANULES *See CALCIUM CHLORIDE*

PICKLED LEMONS/LAMOUN MAKBOUSS/MAKDOUS (Middle Eastern condiment) *See also PRESERVED LEMON*
Make Your Own Slice lemons, preferably organic, into 1/2-inch slices and freeze overnight. Sprinkle heavily with kosher salt, then let

drain in a colander until softened, about 8 hours. Layer in a glass jar, sprinkling each layer with mild/sweet paprika; cover with olive oil and refrigerate; will keep for at least 5 days.

PICKLED PORK (Creole seasoning) – 8 ounces
☞ 8 ounces ham hocks or pickled pig's feet

PICKLE RELISH – 2 tablespoons
☞ 2 tablespoons finely chopped pickles plus a little pickle brine if necessary

PICKLES, QUICK
Make Your Own Add thinly sliced cucumbers to the boiled leftover brine from a jar of pickles, then refrigerate for 24 hours; they will keep for up to 1 week.

PICO DE GALLO (Mexican relish) – 1 cup
☞ 1 cup chunky bottled salsa

PICO DE GALLO SEASONING (Mexican) – 1 tablespoon
☞ 1 tablespoon chile-lime powder or mild chile powder, such as New Mexico or ancho

PIDE (Turkish flatbread) – 8 ounces
☞ 8 ounces of pita bread split into two halves, small naan, or soft lavash cut into sections

PIGEON See SQUAB

PIGEON PEAS, GREEN/CONGO BEAN/GUNGA PEAS/GANDULES, FRESH OR FROZEN (African and Caribbean) – 1 pound
☞ 1 (15-ounce) can Latin American green pigeon peas, such as Goya brand, drained
☞ 1/3 cup dried Indian split pigeon peas/*toor dahl*, cooked
☞ 1 pound fresh or frozen small crowder or black-eyed peas

PILONCILLO/PANELA/PANOCHA (Mexican and South American unrefined cane sugar) – 1 (8-ounce) cone or 8 (1-ounce) cones See also *JAGGERY*
- 1 1/4 cups Indian palm sugar/jaggery/*gur*
- 1 cup dark brown sugar and 2 tablespoons unsulphured molasses
- 3/4 cup granulated sugar and 5 tablespoons molasses

PIMENT d'ESPELETTE (mild red Basque chile powder) – 1 teaspoon
- 3/4 teaspoon Chilean smoked chile powder/*merquén*
- 1/2 teaspoon Basque chili paste/*crème de piment d'Espelette*
- 1 teaspoon Aleppo, Urfa, ancho, or New Mexico chile powder
- 1 teaspoon medium-hot California, Hungarian, or Spanish paprika/*pimentón*
- 1/2 teaspoon ground cayenne pepper

PIMENTO BERRIES, DRIED See *ALLSPICE, JAMAICAN*

PIMENTÓN See *PAPRIKA, SPANISH HOT SMOKED; PAPRIKA, SPANISH MILD SMOKED*

PIMIENTO, CANNED OR JARRED – 4 ounces (1/2 cup)
- 1 fresh red bell pepper, roasted, peeled, cored, and cut into thin strips
- 2 tablespoons red bell pepper flakes softened in 1/4 cup warm water, about 15 minutes
- 1/2 cup bright red tomato slivers from a peeled and seeded plum tomato (add just before serving)

PINEAPPLE, FRESH – 1 pound
- 1 (12-ounce) can pineapple slices in unsweetened juice

PINEAPPLE VINEGAR – 1 tablespoon
- 2 teaspoons cider vinegar and 1 teaspoon water or rice vinegar

PINEAPPLE, WHOLE FRESH – 2 1/2 pounds
 ☞ 2 (16-ounce) cans pineapple slices in unsweetened juice

PINE NUTS/PIGNOLI/PINYON/PIÑON – 1 cup shelled
 ☞ 1 cup sunflower seed kernels, pumpkin seed kernels/*pepitas*, hemp seeds, or slivered blanched almonds

PINQUITO BEANS, DRIED (small Spanish beans) – 1 pound
 ☞ 1 pound small pink beans
 ☞ 1 pound pinto beans (larger)

PINTO BEANS – 1 pound
 ☞ 1 pound small pink or red beans

PIOPPINI MUSHROOMS See BEECH MUSHROOMS

PIPIÁN (Mexican cooking sauce) – 1 cup
 ☞ 1 ounce pipián powder/*pipián rápido* added to 1 cup chicken broth
 ☞ 1 cup Mexican red chili sauce or enchilada sauce, and 1 1/2 teaspoons smooth peanut butter

PIPICHA (Mexican herb) – 1 tablespoon finely minced leaf
 ☞ 1 tablespoon finely minced cilantro
 ☞ 1 scant tablespoon finely minced papaya leaf/*papalo*

PIPPALI See LONG PEPPER, INDONESIAN

PIQUILLO PEPPERS, FIRE-ROASTED (Spanish deep red sweet peppers) – 2
 ☞ 1 roasted and peeled sweet red pepper, preferably Greek Florina, and a small pinch of mild/sweet smoked paprika
 ☞ 1 roasted and peeled red bell pepper or pimiento chile, and a small pinch of smoked salt (or 1 or 2 drops liquid smoke)
 ☞ 2 jarred roasted red peppers and a small pinch of ancho chile powder

PIRI-PIRI CHILE POWDER – 1 teaspoon
☞ 1 teaspoon cayenne, tepin/chiltepin, Thai, or other hot chile powder

PIRI-PIRI CHILES, DRIED (African and Portuguese) – 3 or 4
☞ 3 or 4 cayenne, bird's eye, pequin/piquin, or tepín/chiltepín chiles
☞ 1/2 to 1 teaspoon piri-piri powder, ground cayenne pepper, or crushed red pepper flakes

PIRI-PIRI SAUCE (African and Portuguese condiment) – 1 cup
☞ 1/2 cup each Sriracha and Louisiana-style hot sauce, such as Tabasco or Crystal

Make Your Own Combine 1 cup heated olive oil, 1/4 cup chopped fresh red chiles, such as piri piri or bird's eye, 2 minced garlic cloves, and 1/2 teaspoon salt. Cover and let sit at room temperature for 24 or more hours. Strain the oil and discard the solids. (Wear plastic gloves when handling the chiles.)

PISELLI SECCHI (Italian large dried green beans) – 1 cup
☞ 1 cup marrowfat peas or other large dried starchy peas

PISTACHIO CREAM/CREMA DI PISTACCHIO (Italian sweetened, enriched pistachio paste) – 1 cup
☞ 1 cup chocolate-hazelnut spread, such as Nutella or Rawtella, or other sweetened spread (different flavor)

PISTACHIO FLOUR – 1 cup
☞ 1 cup almond or chestnut flour

Make Your Own Grind 1 1/2 cups chilled unsalted peeled pistachios, until powdery in a blender, or in small batches in a spice/coffee grinder. Sift and regrind any large pieces.

PISTACHIO OIL – 1 cup
☞ 1 cup almond oil or extra light olive oil

PISTACHIO PASTE/PASTA DI PASTACCHIO (Italian nut paste) – 1 cup

- ☞ 1 1/4 cups raw shelled pistachios and 1/4 cup neutral-tasting vegetable oil, processed in a blender until smooth
- ☞ 1 cup hazelnut paste/*pasta di nocciola*
- ☞ 1 cup smooth-style almond butter; or creamy, unsweetened peanut butter

PISTOU (French pesto) – 2/3 cup

Make Your Own Process 2 cups fresh basil leaves, 2 or 3 garlic cloves, 1/3 cup olive oil, and 1/4 teaspoon kosher salt in a food processor or blender until nearly smooth. (For more color add a few tablespoons fresh parsley to the basil, and for more texture fold in 2 tablespoons Parmesan cheese at the end.)

PITA CHIPS – 4 dozen

Make Your Own Separate 3 (6- or 7-inch) pita breads at the seams, cut each into 8 wedges, and spread in a single layer on a baking sheet. Bake in a preheated 375°F oven until golden, 10 to 15 minutes. (For seasoned chips, coat the rough side with water, oil, or cooking spray and sprinkle with salt, sesame seeds, or seasoning; bake for 8 to 10 minutes.)

PIXIAN CHILI BEAN SAUCE See SICHUAN CHILI BEAN PASTE

PIZZA CHEESE See CHEESE, PIZZA BLEND, SHREDDED

PIZZA CRUST (for baking on a baking/pizza stone or inverted baking sheet at 450 to 500°F)

- ☞ 1 1/2 cups packaged biscuit mix and 1/3 cup boiling water, stirred briskly until the dough holds together, then kneaded or processed until smooth and no longer sticky, 1 to 2 minutes (roll out and bake for 5 minutes before adding the toppings)
- ☞ Refrigerated French bread dough; refrigerated yeast rolls, such as crescent; or biscuit dough (for a thin, crispy Roman-type crust; roll

and stretch the cold dough as thinly as possible and bake immediately)
- Country-style filo/*horiatiko* or refrigerated piecrust (for St. Louis
  or delicate-type pizza; partly bake before adding the toppings)

PIZZA CRUST, GLUTEN-FREE – 1
- 1 prepared pizza crust, such as Udi's or Schar's
- 1 prepared cauliflower pizza crust, such as Amy's or Caulipower
- 2 to 3 cups cups gluten-free pizza crust mix, such as Hodgson
  Farms or Pamela's
- 1 gluten-free or grain-free tortilla wrap
- 1 homemade cauliflower pizza crust using fresh cauliflower

PIZZA CRUST, PREPARED (for baking on a baking/pizza stone at 450°F; or for baking/cooking in a preheated baking sheet or skillet until browned on the bottom then broiling until the top is golden)
- Large whole-wheat pocketless pita bread/*pide*, or large pocket pi-
  tas, separated at the seams
- Middle Eastern whole-grain flatbread, such as soft lavash, cut to size
- Indian flatbread, such as chapati or naan
- Ciabatta or focaccia halved horizontally
- Thin roll halves, such as Sandwich Thins; English muffin halves; or
  thin bagel halves (for individual pizzas)
- 1 (11- to 13-inch) flour tortilla

PIZZA SAUCE – 1 cup
Make Your Own Combine 1 (15-ounce) can crushed tomatoes with
1 1/2 to 2 teaspoons pizza seasoning, or 1 teaspoon Italian seasoning plus 1/8 teaspoon garlic powder. (For a thicker sauce, puree the
mixture until almost smooth, then simmer, uncovered, until thickened, about 30 minutes.)
Or
Drain half of 1 (28-ounce) can whole peeled tomatoes (preferably
San Marzano), then press through a food mill, and combine with 2

to 3 teaspoons olive oil, 1/4 teaspoon each salt and crumbled dried oregano, and 1 minced garlic clove (optional).

PIZZA SEASONING – 1 tablespoon
- 1 teaspoon Italian seasoning
- 1 teaspoon each dried thyme and granulated garlic, and 1/2 teaspoon each ground fennel and dried oregano

PLANTAIN/PLÁTANOS MACHOS/KELA (tropical starchy fruit) – 1 pound
- 1 pound white-fleshed Latin American sweet potatoes/*boniatos/batatas* (cook for a longer time than specified)
- Green, unripe bananas (cook for less time than specified)

PLUM PUDDING (British steamed dessert) – 1 pound
- 1 pound of rich fruitcake, steamed in a pudding basin for 1 to 1 1/2 hours

PLUM SAUCE/DUCK SAUCE/TIM CHEON/SU MUI JEONG (Chinese condiment) – 1/2 cup
- 1/2 cup mango chutney, thinned with a little vinegar
- 1/4 cup apricot or peach jam, 1/4 cup plum jam, 1 tablespoon cider vinegar, and 1/2 teaspoon sugar simmered until slightly thickened, about 5 minutes (the sauce will thicken further as it cools)
- Chinese lemon sauce

PLUM WINE/UMESHU (Japanese) – 1 cup
- 1 cup Chinese plum wine/*mui jow,* or sweet sherry, preferably Oloroso

PLUMS – 1 pound See also PRUNE PLUMS, ITALIAN
- 1 pound plumcots or Pluots (green-yellow or black fruit; cross between plum and apricot)
- 1 pound Pixie Sweets (cross between plum and cherry; labeled Cherrium, Cherub, or Verry Cherry plums)

☞ 1 pound wild plums/*Prunus americana* (red or yellow small tart fruits for jam), or wild sloes of the blackthorn bush/*Prunus spinosa* (small purple sour fruits for jam)

POBLANO CHILE, FRESH – 1

☞ 1 fresh Chilaca, Anaheim/California/Colorado, Hatch, or New Mexico chile
☞ 1 fresh green bell pepper and 1 small jalapeño chile
☞ 1 jarred roasted red pepper and scant 1/8 teaspoon New Mexico chile powder
☞ 1 canned mild green chile, rinsed and drained

POHA, THIN (Indian dried, flattened rice flakes for snack mixes) – 1 cup

☞ 1 cup toasted brown rice flakes
☞ 1/2 cup each toasted rice cereal, such as Rice Krispies, and toasted corn cereal, such as Kix

POLENTA MEAL (Italian stone-ground yellow cornmeal) – 1 cup

☞ 1 cup dry corn kernels (or buckwheat groats), coarsely ground in a grain mill or in batches in a spice/coffee grinder (Dry-roasting the buckwheat groats enhances their aroma and taste; soaking them 8 to 12 hours before cooking makes the polenta creamier and more digestible.)
☞ 1 cup yellow corn grits (coarse-grind degerminated cornmeal) or medium-grind cornmeal
☞ 1 cup quick-cooking polenta (Use 3 1/2 cups water and cook for 8 to 15 minutes, stirring frequently.)
☞ 1 cup instant (precooked) polenta (Use 3 cups water and cook for 2 to 3 minutes.)
☞ 1 cup fine-grind yellow or white cornmeal for creamier polenta/*polentina* (Use 4 cups water and cook for 10 to 15 minutes.)
☞ 1 cup whole-grain teff (Use 3 cups water and cook for 20 minutes.) or whole-grain amaranth (Use 2 cups water and cook for 15 to 20

minutes.) (Both grains can be chilled, baked or pan-fried like po-lenta; they will have slightly stickier consistency.)
☞ 1 cup granulated buckwheat or Cream of Buckwheat (Cook fol-lowing the package directions; makes a polenta-like side dish.)

POLISH MUSHROOMS, DRIED – 1 ounce
☞ 1 ounce dried porcini mushrooms

POLYGONUM See VIETNAMESE MINT

POMEGRANATE CONCENTRATE/ROBB-E ANAR (Middle Eastern souring agent) – 1/4 cup
☞ 3 tablespoons pomegranate molasses
Make Your Own Boil 2 cups fresh or bottled pure unsweetened pomegranate juice gently over medium heat in a wide, uncovered pan, stirring occasionally, until thickened and reduced to 1/4 cup, 20 to 30 minutes.

POMEGRANATE JUICE – 1 cup
☞ 2 cups pomegranate seeds, pureed in a blender, then strained in a cheesecloth-lined fine-mesh sieve, pressing to release the juice
☞ 3 tablespoons pomegranate concentrate combined with enough water to make 8 ounces
☞ 3 tablespoons freeze-dried pomegranate powder combined with 8 ounces water
☞ 1 cup cranberry juice or tart 100% cherry juice

POMEGRANATE JUICE, SOUR (Middle Eastern souring agent) – 1/3 cup
☞ 1/3 cup pure unsweetened pomegranate juice and 1 teaspoon lemon or lime juice
☞ 1 tablespoon pomegranate concentrate added to 4 1/2 table-spoons water
☞ 1/3 cup pure 100% unsweetened cranberry or sour/tart cherry juice

POMEGRANATE MOLASSES/DIBIS ROUMAN/DIBS RUBBA (Middle Eastern seasoning and souring agent) – 1/4 cup

- 2 cups fresh or bottled pure pomegranate juice, 2 tablespoons granulated sugar, and 1 tablespoon lemon juice, gently simmered until syrupy and reduced to 1/4 cup, about 30 minutes
- 3 1/2 tablespoons pomegranate concentrate plus 1 teaspoon fresh lemon juice
- 1/4 cup cherry syrup (for brining)
- 3 tablespoons lemon juice and 1 generous tablespoon unsulphured molasses (or strong flavored honey), warmed in the microwave a few seconds then cooled
- 1 to 2 tablespoons aged balsamic vinegar

POMEGRANATE SEEDS/ARILS, FRESH – 1 tablespoon

- 1 tablespoon fresh papaya seeds (for salad; silvery-black and peppery tasting)
- 1 tablespoon snipped dried barberries or cranberries (for salad or garnish)
- 1 tablespoon pomegranate molasses, applied in tiny drops (for garnish)

POMEGRANATE SEEDS, DRIED SOUR/ANARDANA (Indian and Middle Eastern souring agent) – 1 tablespoon

- 1 tablespoon pomegranate molasses, lemon juice, or lime juice (for souring agent)
- 1 tablespoon snipped dried barberries or cranberries (for garnish)

POMEGRANATE SYRUP See POMEGRANATE MOLASSES

POMEGRANATE VINEGAR – 1 tablespoon

- 1 tablespoon raspberry vinegar, blackcurrant vinegar, or any fruit-flavored vinegar

PONZU SAUCE, QUICK (Japanese citrus shoyu sauce) – 1/3 cup
Make Your Own Stir together 2 tablespoons each Japanese soy sauce, dashi or kombu stock (optional), and yuzu juice (or lemon or

lime juice), and sweeten to taste with mirin (about 1 tablespoon) or sugar.

POPPY SEED OIL (salad oil) – 1 cup
- 1 cup almond oil

POPPY SEEDS, BLUE/BLACK – 1 cup
- 1 cup black amaranth grain, softened in hot water for 8 to 12 hours (for muffins, cakes, and pastries)
- 1 cup packaged ground black poppy seeds or canned poppy seed paste (for pastry filling)
- 1 cup nigella seeds; sesame seeds, preferably black; hulled hemp seeds; chia seeds; dark flaxseeds; salba seeds; or lamb's quarters seeds (as topping for baked goods)

POPPY SEEDS, GROUND – 1 cup
- 1 1/4 cups dark/blue/black poppy seeds, toasted in a dry skillet until fragrant, then ground in a spice/coffee grinder until fine

PORCINI MUSHROOMS/KING BOLETE/PENNY BUN/CÈPE, FRESH – 1 pound
- 1 pound fresh portobello mushrooms, gills removed
- 3 ounces dried porcini/cèpes or dried Polish mushrooms, soaked in warm water until softened, 30 to 40 minutes
- 3 ounces dried shiitake mushrooms, soaked in warm water until softened, 30 to 40 minutes
- 1 (10-ounce) can whole or quartered cèpes

PORCINI POWDER – 1/3 cup See also MUSHROOM POWDER
Make Your Own Break up 1/2 ounce (3 or 4) smooth or cleaned dried porcini mushrooms and grind to a fine powder in a coffee/spice grinder. Sift out large pieces, then regrind and sift again. Store in an airtight container in a cool, dark cupboard. It will keep for up to 3 months.

PORCINI SALT – 1/2 cup
Make Your Own Thoroughly combine 1 tablespoon porcini powder and 1/2 cup kosher salt. Store in an airtight container in a cool, dark cupboard; it will keep for up to 2 months.

PORK BELLY, FRESH, 1 pound
☞ 1 pound unsmoked slab bacon (fresh whole)

POMELO See PUMMELO

PORTOBELLOS/MATURE CREMINI MUSHROOMS, FRESH – 1 pound
☞ 1 pound large fresh cremini, porcini, or matsutake mushrooms
☞ 3 ounces dried porcini mushrooms, soaked in warm water until softened, 30 to 40 minutes
☞ 1 (10-ounce) can whole or sliced mushrooms

PORT, RUBY OR TAWNY (sweet fortified wine) – 2 tablespoons
☞ 2 tablespoons Banyuls, Madeira, Moscatel, or sweet vermouth

PORT-SALUT (French semisoft cheese) – 1 ounce
☞ 1 ounce Belfermiere, Saint-Paulin, Esrom, Gaucho, Havarti, Muenster, Oka, Père Joseph, Port Nicholson, Ridder, or Tilsit

PORTUGUESE ROLLS – 1 pound
☞ 1 pound Cuban bread, kaiser rolls, or ciabatta rolls

POTASSIUM BICARBONATE/BICARBONATE OF POTASH (leavening agent) – 0.1 ounce (1 teaspoon)
☞ 1 teaspoon baking soda (sodium bicarbonate)

POTATOES, BABY – 1 pound
☞ 1 pound small waxy boiling potatoes (red, white, or gold), scrubbed and quartered
☞ 1 pound fingerling potatoes, scrubbed and halved

POTATOES, CUBED (1/2-inch cubes) – 1 pound (3 to 4 cups)
- 1 (16-ounce) package refrigerated precooked diced potatoes
- 3 to 4 cups cauliflower tots

POTATOES, MASHED – 1 pound (2 cups)
- 2 cups frozen mashed potatoes, such as Ore-Ida Steam n'Mash, heated according to microwave instructions
- 1 1/3 cups instant potato flakes, reconstituted following the package directions
- 2 cups creamy mashed cauliflower

POTATOES, SHREDDED – 1 pound (3 to 4 cups)
- 1 (16-ounce) package frozen hash-brown potatoes
- 1 (16-ounce) package refrigerated precooked shredded potatoes
- 3 medium (or 2 large) unpeeled baking potatoes, boiled until tender, but still firm in the center; cooled, then shredded on the large holes of a box grater
- 3 to 4 cups cauliflower hash or fritters

POTATOES, SWEET – 1 pound
- 1 pound deep purple sweet potatoes (richer flavor; denser and drier; longer cooking time)
- 1 pound white sweet potatoes/*Ipomoea batatas* (less sweet; more starchy)
- 1 pound sweet pumpkin, such as sugar or pie pumpkin
- 1 pound winter squash, such as buttercup, butternut, delicata, or sweet dumpling
- 1 (15-ounce) can pure squash puree, or sweet potato chunks

POTATO MILK – 4 cups
- Scant 2/3 cup potato milk powder, such as Darifree, blended with 1 cup hot or cold water, then added to 1 quart additional cold water and blended until smooth

Make Your Own Combine 1 generous cup chopped potatoes with 3 cups mildly salted water and boil until soft. Cool, then add to 1/4 to

1/3 cup soaked sliced almonds and enough cold water to measure 4 cups; blend until smooth, about 5 minutes, then strain in a fine-mesh sieve.

POTATO STARCH/FÉCULE/KATAKURI-KO (for thickening) – 2 teaspoons *See also FLOUR, POTATO*
- ☞ 1 tablespoon cornstarch or glutinous sweet rice flour
- ☞ 4 teaspoons arrowroot powder
- ☞ 2 tablespoons tapioca starch, or 5 teaspoons quick-cooking or small-pearl tapioca, ground until powdery
- ☞ 2 tablespoons all-purpose or quick-mixing flour (cook at least 3 minutes after thickened)

POT CHEESE *See FARMER CHEESE*

POTOLS/PATOLS/POINTED GOURD (Bangladeshi gourd vegetable) – 1 pound
- ☞ 1 pound Mexican squash or small zucchini

POT STICKER DIPPING SAUCE *See ASIAN DIPPING SAUCE*

POULTRY GLAZE/GLACE DE VOLAILLE – 1/4 cup
Make Your Own Boil 2 cups degreased unsalted chicken stock gently, uncovered, in a wide-bottomed pan until syrupy and reduced to 1/4 cup (or 2 tablespoons for a thicker glaze). Cool and store, refrigerated, for up to 1 month, or freeze for longer storage.

POULTRY SEASONING – 1 tablespoon
- ☞ 1 teaspoon each dried sage, thyme, and marjoram, plus a dash of black pepper

POWDERED SUGAR *See SUGAR, CONFECTIONERS'*

POZOLE, BASIC (Mexican nixtamalized corn) – 1 pound
- ☞ 2 (15-ounce) cans whole white hominy, rinsed and drained

PRESERVED LEMON JUICE (Moroccan seasoning) – 1/4 cup
- ⮞ 1/4 cup fresh lemon juice mixed with 1 1/2 teaspoons kosher salt

PRESERVED LEMON/CITRON CONFIT/L'HAMD MARKAD (North African seasoning) – 1
- ⮞ 1 Asian pickled lemon
- ⮞ Lemon zest (use 1 teaspoon minced for each tablespoon minced preserved lemon)

Make Your Own Cut 1 large lemon (well scrubbed; preferably organic) into 12 crosswise slices. Bring to a boil in a small pan with 1/2 cup lemon juice and 1 tablespoon kosher salt, then cover and simmer until the rind is clear and transparent, about 10 minutes. Cool and transfer to a small covered container. Store in the refrigerator for up to 1 week.

Or

Cut 1 large lemon (well scrubbed; preferably organic) into 8 lengthwise wedges. Rub with 1/4 cup kosher salt, then place in a small sealable freezer bag (or a jar with a nonmetal lid) along with the juice from another lemon (about 3 tablespoons). Refrigerate for 6 to 7 days, shaking the bag or jar daily. Store in the refrigerator for up to 6 months.

PRICKLY PEAR/CACTUS PEAR/INDIAN FIG/TUNA (Mexican small cactus fruit) – 1
- ⮞ 2 to 4 tablespoons frozen prickly pear puree
- ⮞ 1 pitaya/dragon fruit or kiwi fruit
- ⮞ 2 to 4 tablespoons pureed watermelon pulp

PRICKLY PEAR PUREE – 1 cup
- ⮞ 5 or 6 medium prickly pears, peeled, chopped, pureed in a blender or food processor, then strained

PRICKLY PEAR, SOUR/TUNA ÁGRIA/XOCONOSTLE (Mexican souring agent) – 1
- ⮞ 1 small fresh underripe plum, such as damson or Italian/prune

PROSCIUTTO DI PARMA (Italian seasoned, air-dried, salt-cured unsmoked ham) – 1 pound
- 1 pound prosciutto di San Daniele (darker in color; slightly sweeter taste)
- 1 pound prosciutto end pieces (less expensive)
- 1 pound domestic prosciutto, such as La Quercia
- 1 pound Spanish Ibérico or Serrano ham
- 1 pound French *jambon de Paris*, Bayonne, or Haute Savoie ham (adds mild smoke flavor)
- 1 pound Virginia or Kentucky dry-cured country-style ham (adds smoke flavor)
- 1 pound good-quality salami

PROVOLONE (Italian stretched-curd cheese) – 1 ounce
- 1 ounce young *caciocavallo*, scamorza, domestic fontina, mozzarella, or asadero/*queso Oaxaca*

PROVOLONE PICANTE (Italian well-aged grating cheese) – 1 ounce
- 1 ounce aged Asiago, Parmesan, Pecorino Romano, Sbrinz, or domestic Romano

PRUNE PLUMS, ITALIAN (small, purple oval plums) – 1 pound
- 1 pound Damson or Mirabelle plums
- 1 pound wild purple beach plums/*Prunus maritime* (smaller; more tart)

PRUNE PUREE/PRUNE BUTTER (butter alternative for lowfat baking) – 3/4 cup
- 3/4 cup baby food prunes

Make Your Own Process 6 ounces pitted prunes (1 cup packed) with 1/2 cup boiling water to a smooth paste in a blender or food processor. Store in the refrigerator for up to 6 months.

PSYLLIUM HUSK FIBER (bulking agent used in gluten-free recipes) – 1 tablespoon
- 2 1/2 teaspoons ground flaxseed or chia seeds

PUDDING MIX, INSTANT – *1 package using 2 cups milk*

☞ 1/4 cup instant dry milk powder, 1/3 cup each instant Clearjel and powdered sugar, plus 1/2 teaspoon fine sea salt (For vanilla add 1 teaspoon vanilla powder; for cocoa add 1/4 cup cocoa powder.)

PUFF PASTRY DOUGH, SHORTENING OR BUTTER-BASED – *1 pound*

☞ 1 pound commercial phyllo/filo dough, or slightly thicker country-style filo/*horiatiko*, brushed with butter or oil

☞ 1 pound commercial *yufka* dough (thicker than regular phyllo and crunchier)

PUFFED WHEAT CEREAL, KHORASAN – *1 cup*

☞ 1 cup puffed brown rice (gluten-free)

PULQUE, PLAIN (*Mexican fermented sap from maguey cactus*) – *1 cup*

☞ 1 cup dry white wine

PUMMELO/POMELO BLOSSOM ESSENCE/KAO PAN (*Thai flavoring agent*) – *1 teaspoon*

☞ 1 teaspoon lemon extract

PUMMELO/POMELO/SHADDOCK/JABONG (*large yellow-green thick-skinned citrus*) – *1*

☞ 1 large Oroblanco citrus (hybrid of pummelo and grapefruit; juicier)

☞ 2 or 3 mondelos/mandalos (sweeter; more seeds)

☞ 2 medium pink grapefruits

PUMPKIN, FRESH – *1 cup chopped fresh*

☞ 1 cup chopped fresh orange-fleshed winter squash (Ambercup, buttercup, butternut, calabaza, Dickinson, Jarrahdale, Hubbard, Queensland blue, or sweet dumpling)

☞ 1 cup chopped fresh sweet potato such as Beauregard, Garnet, or Jewel (takes longer to cook)

PUMPKIN LEAF/GREENS/CUCURBITA MAXIMA (Southeast Asian and African vegetable) – 1 pound
- 1 pound amaranth/Chinese red spinach, spinach beet, Swiss chard, or New Zealand spinach

PUMPKIN PIE SPICE – 1 teaspoon
- 1/2 teaspoon ground cinnamon, 1/4 teaspoon ground ginger, 1/8 teaspoon ground nutmeg, and 1/8 teaspoon ground allspice (or cloves)

PUMPKIN PUREE, CANNED – 1 (29-ounce) can
- 4-pounds fresh Sugar or pie pumpkin, baked, scooped out, seeded, pureed, and then drained in a fine-mesh sieve for at least an hour
- 2 pounds sweet potatoes, such as Garnet or Jewel, baked, peeled, and mashed
- 1 (29-ounce) can yams, drained, mashed, and strained

PUMPKIN SEED MEAL/FLOUR – 1 cup
- 1 1/4 cups pumpkin seeds, ground in batches in a spice/coffee grinder until powdery

PUMPKIN SEED OIL (salad and flavoring oil) – 1 cup
- 1 cup extra-virgin olive oil, preferably deeply colored and flavorful

PUMPKIN SEEDS/PEPITAS – 1 cup
- 1 cup butternut or acorn squash seeds
- 1 cup winter melon seeds
- 1 cup Lady Godiva, Triple Treat, or Hungarian Mammoth squash seeds (hull-less green seeds, three times the size of regular hulled pumpkin seeds)
- 1 cup sunflower seeds

PUMPKIN TIPS (Southeast Asian and African vegetable) – 8 (6-inch) tips
- 1 cup fresh peeled pumpkin, cut into 1/2-inch pieces

PUNTARELLE/ROMAN CHICORY (Italian leggy salad green) – 1 pound

☞ 1 pound dandelion greens
☞ 1 pound curly endive

PURSLANE LEAVES, YOUNG/VERDOLAGAS (small succulent greens) – 8 ounces

☞ 8 ounces golden purslane leaves (grows more upright; pinch off 3-to-4-inch sections of the stem)
☞ 8 ounces baby arugula, watercress, upland cress/creasy greens, garden/pepper cress, nasturtium leaves and stems, or radish sprouts (for salads)
☞ 4 ounces okra (for thickening soups and stews)

Q

QUAIL EGGS, HARD-BOILED – 4
- 4 jarred or canned water-packed hard-boiled quail eggs
- 1 large hen egg, hard boiled, shelled and quartered (or 2 small eggs, halved)

QUAIL/PARTRIDGE – 1
- 1 small squab, young pheasant, or guinea hen

QUARK/QUARGEL (soft, fresh German cheese containing 9 to 10% fat) – 1 cup
- 1 cup Magerquark (low-fat quark), fromage blanc, or plain Greek-style yogurt
- 2/3 cup ricotta and 1/3 cup sour cream blended until smooth (for cream quark/*Sahnequak*)
- 1 cup mascarpone cheese (more expensive; less tangy)

Make Your Own Scald 2 cups whole milk; cool, then whisk in 1/2 cup cultured buttermilk. Lightly cover with a cloth or waxed paper and let sit at room temperature until slightly thickened, 12 to 24 hours. Transfer to a sieve lined with dampened cheesecloth and set over a bowl. Cover the sieve with a plate or plastic wrap, place in the refrigerator, and let drain for 12 hours. It will keep, refrigerated, up to 5 days.

QUATRE-ÉPICES/FRENCH FOUR-SPICE MIX/SPICE PARISIENNE – 1 teaspoon
- 1/2 teaspoon ground white pepper, 1/4 teaspoon grated/ground nutmeg, 1/8 teaspoon ground   cloves, and 1/8 teaspoon dried ginger (For sweet dishes substitute ground cinnamon for ground pepper.)
- 3/4 teaspoon pumpkin or apple pie spice and 1/4 teaspoon ground white pepper

☞ 1/2 teaspoon ground allspice

QUESO AÑEJO/COTIJA/AÑEJADO *See COTIJA/QUESO AÑEJO*

QUESO ASADERO *See ASADERO*

QUESO BLANCO *See QUESO FRESCO*

QUESO CHIHUAHUA *See ASADERO*

QUESO DE MANO *See QUESO FRESCO*

QUESO DE OAXACA *See ASADERO*

QUESO FRESCO/QUESO BLANCO/QUESO RANCHERO (Mexican crumbly fresh cheese) – 1 ounce
- ☞ 1 ounce firm young goat cheese
- ☞ 1 ounce mild young French or Greek feta, preferably sheep's milk, rinsed in cold water to reduce excess saltiness
- ☞ 1 ounce Iranian Tabriz
- ☞ 1 ounce moist-type farmer cheese or dry cottage cheese plus a pinch of salt

Make Your Own Bring 1 quart whole milk to a simmer, then add 1 tablespoon lemon juice and 1/2 teaspoon salt. Stir gently to separate the solids from the whey, then strain in a cloth-lined sieve. Cool, then press or squeeze out any remaining liquid. Form into a ball and flatten slightly; wrap, and refrigerate for at least 4 hours before using. It will make 3 ounces and will keep, refrigerated, for up to 7 days.

QUESO LLANERO (Venezuelan salty white grating cheese) – 1 ounce
- ☞ 1 ounce Mexican cotija, aged Asiago, aged ricotta salata, dry feta, dry Jack, Romano, or domestic Parmesan

QUESO PANELA (Mexican fresh crumbly cheese) – 8 ounces
- ☞ 8 ounces queso fresco, young ricotta salata, hoop cheese, or well-drained farmer cheese

QUESO QUESADILLA *See ASADERO*

QUILLQUIÑA/KILKIÑE (Bolivian seasoning herb) – 1 tablespoon finely chopped
- 1 tablespoon finely chopped Mexican *papaloquelite* or cilantro

QUINCE/CYDONIA OBLONGA (high-pectin, hard yellow fruit) – 1 pound
- 1 pound Japanese flowering quince/*Chaenomeles speciosa* (smaller and more sour)
- 1 pound crab apples or unsprayed hawthorne fruits/thorn apples/ *Crataegus* species (smaller)
- 1 pound tart apples, such as Granny Smith (less sour; reduce the cooking time)

QUINCE PASTE/MEMBRILLO/COTOGNATA/PÂTE DE COINGS (Latin American cheese accompaniment) – 1 ounce
- 1 ounce guava paste, such as Goya, homemade plum paste/ *plumbrillo*, or any tart Mexican fruit paste/*ate*

QUINOA FLOUR *See FLOUR, QUINOA*

QUINOA MILK, UNSWEETENED
- 1 cup cooked white quinoa plus 3 cups filtered water, blended until smooth, then strained in a nutbag or fine-mesh sieve (store in the refrigerator)

QUINOA, LIGHT/TAN/RED – 1 cup
- 1 cup black quinoa (milder flavor; crunchier texture; increase cooking time 15 minutes)
- 1 cup millet (especially foxtail), amaranth, *canahua*, or Arborio rice (white or brown whole-grain)
- 1 cup medium ground bulgur; cracked wheat, preferably No. 1 fine grind; or whole-wheat couscous (All three are chewier and contain gluten)

R

RACLETTE (Swiss semihard melting cheese) – 1 ounce
☞ 1 ounce Emmental, Gruyère, Fontina Val d'Aosta, Jarlsberg, or Appenzeller

RADICCHIO (Italian red-leafed chicory) – 1 pound
☞ 1 pound endigia (cross between Belgian endive and radicchio; its leaves are variegated white and red)
☞ 1 pound purple-or red-tipped endive
☞ 1 pound young Bull's Blood beet greens, lollo rosso/red lollo tops, ruby chard or young Bright Lights chard, young red leaf amaranth, or purple/opal basil (for the color only)
☞ 1 pound Belgian endive/witloof, chicory, curly escarole, or arugula (for the taste, not the color)

RADISH, ASIAN See DAIKON

RADISHES, GLOBE – 1 pound
☞ 1 pound watermelon or China Rose radishes, peeled and cut into pieces (less peppery)
☞ 1 pound White Icicle radishes, cut into pieces (milder; greens are good to eat)
☞ 1 pound black radishes, trimmed and thinly sliced (drier and more pungent)
☞ 1 pound jicama, peeled and cut into pieces (or into little spheres with a melon cutter) and lightly sprinkled with tangy pickle brine or hot paprika
☞ 1 pound baby turnips; or salad turnips, such as Tokyo hakurei, cut in half
☞ 1 pound rampion roots/Campanula rapunculus

RADISH GREENS (peppery radish tops) – 8 ounces
- 8 ounces watercress, curly cress/peppergrass, mustard greens, or garden or wild arugula

RADISH SPROUTS See SPROUTS

RAGI/FINGER MILLET (Shri Lankan flatbread flour) – 1 cup
- 1 cup unbleached whole-wheat flour

RAISINS, HIMALAYAN HUNZA – 1 pound
- 1 pound seedless golden raisins or dried red barberries

RAISINS, SEEDED (Muscatel) – 1 pound
- 1 pound seedless raisins and 1 cup sugar, steeped in 2 cups hot water for 1 hour (drain and pat dry, if necessary)
- Juneberries/serviceberries/*Amelanchier intermedia* dried in a 150°F oven for 8 to 12 hours

RAISINS, SEEDLESS (Thompson dark or golden) – 1 pound
- 1 pound organic sun-dried Black Monukka or Italian Zibibbo raisins (for dark; larger and sweeter)
- 1 pound Himalayan Hunza or Sicilian Sultanina raisins (for golden; larger and moister)
- 1 pound Italian Uvette raisins or dried currants (smaller and sweeter)
- 1 pound dried unsweetened cranberries or barberries (less sweet)
- 1 cup dried cherries, cut in half
- 1 cup dates, figs, or prunes, cut into pieces

RAITA (Indian condiment) – 9 ounces
- 1/3 cup finely chopped fresh mint, or shredded and drained cucumbers, stirred into 1 cup plain yogurt (full fat, lowfat, or nonfat)

RAMBUTAN/HAIRY LYCHEE/MAMON (Southeast Asian small, white-fleshed fruit)
- Fresh, canned, or frozen *pulasans*, longans, or lychees

RAMPS/WILD LEEKS/BARAGNES – 8 ounces (2 bunches) coarsely chopped

- 1 cup coarsely chopped green onions, scallions, or baby leeks (white part only, cut in half lengthwise before chopping), plus a little finely minced garlic
- 1 cup coarsely chopped green garlic/young garlic
- 1 cup coarsely chopped garlic mustard shoots/*Alliaria petiolata*
- 1 cup wild I'iloi onions/*Allium cepa var. aggregarum* (more bulbous base)
- 1/4 cup snipped chives (add at the end of cooking)

RAPADURA (Brazilian evaporated cane sugar) – 1 cup

- 1 cup Sucanat, organic cane sugar, pre-grated *panela*, or finely grated or shaved *piloncillo/panela*

RAPINI See BROCCOLI RABE

RAS EL HANOUT (Moroccan spice blend) – 1 teaspoon

- 1 teaspoon garam masala
- 3/4 teaspoon mild/sweet curry powder
- 1/4 teaspoon each ground allspice, coriander, cumin, and ginger, preferably roasted
- 1/8 to 1/4 teaspoon ground cumin, preferably roasted

RASPBERRIES, RED – 1 cup

- 1 cup black raspberries (drier and seedier)
- 1 cup golden raspberries (sweeter)
- 1 cup small strawberries, such as Alpine/*fraises des bois*, Earliglow, or wild strawberries (sweeter and firmer)
- 1 cup loganberries or moras/*Rubus glaucus* (medium red; less sweet; cross between blackberry and raspberry)
- 1 cup wineberries/*Rubus phoenicolasius* (golden orange or scarlet; larger)
- 1 cup salmonberries/*Rubus spectabilis* (orange or crimson; soft with delicate flavor)

- 1 cup wild thimbleberries/*Rubus parviflorus* (pale or bright red; larger)
- 1 cup cloudberries/*Rubus chamaemorus* (amber; raspberry-size; tart and juicy)

RASPBERRY LIQUEUR/RASPBERRY-FLAVORED SPIRIT (such as Chambord or DeKuyper) – 1 tablespoon for cooking

- 1 tablespoon raspberry brandy/framboise, cranberry liqueur, or raspberry balsamic vinegar
- 1/2 teaspoon raspberry extract plus 2 1/2 teaspoons vodka or water

RASPBERRY VINEGAR – 1 cup

- 1 cup red wine vinegar plus a little raspberry liqueur, such as Chambord
- 1 cup cranberry vinegar or other red fruity vinegar

Make Your Own Lightly mash 1 pint/12 ounces fresh ripe raspberries, combine with 1 cup red wine vinegar, cover and let sit at room temperature for 1 week. Strain in a cloth-lined sieve, then bottle and refrigerate for up to 6 months.

RAYU See JAPANESE CHILI OIL

REBLOCHON (French washed-rind cheese) – 1 ounce

- 1 ounce *Fromage de Savoie*, Pont-d'Eveque, Beaumont, Brie, Camembert, Tamié, Celtic Promise, or Durrus

RED ASIAN MUSTARD See CHINESE MUSTARD CABBAGE

RED FOOD COLORING – 1 bottle (1 fluid ounce/2 tablespoons) See also FOOD COLORING, NATURAL

- 1/3 teaspoon gel food coloring dissolved in 2 tablespoons water

RED KURI SQUASH (reddish orange winter squash) – 1 pound

- 1 pound Baby Hubbard, buttercup, butternut, kabocha, Fairytale pumpkin, or any firm-textured winter squash, peeled

RED PEPPER/CRUSHED RED PEPPER See CAYENNE PEPPER, GROUND

RED PEPPER FLAKES, HOT – 1 teaspoon
- 1/2 teaspoon ground cayenne pepper or very hot crushed red pepper flakes
- 1/4 teaspoon hot pepper sauce, such as Tabasco or Crystal (not for Asian dishes)
- 2 teaspoons Asian chili paste

RED PEPPER PASTE, HOT/ACI BIBER SALÇASI (Turkish condiment) – 1 tablespoon
- 1 tablespoon red pepper paste (or 1 or 2 jarred roasted piquillo peppers, drained and pureed) plus few drops hot peppers sauce
- 1 tablespoon tomato paste plus 1/8 teaspoon ground cayenne peppers
- 1 1/2 teaspoons harissa paste

RED PEPPER PASTE, MILD/SWEET PEPPER PASTE/BIBER SALÇASI (Turkish condiment)
- Jarred roasted red peppers, blotted dry, roughly chopped, then processed in a blender until smooth; season with salt and pepper

RED PEPPERS, ROASTED – 1 (12-ounce) jar
- 2 large red bell peppers, roasted, cored, seeded and peeled (for peppers packed in oil, cut into strips and marinate in olive oil for 1 to 2 days)

RED RICE VINEGAR See CHINESE RED RICE VINEGAR

RED SNAPPER See FISH, LEAN

RED WINE VINEGAR – 1 tablespoon
- 2 teaspoons cider vinegar plus 1 teaspoon red wine
- 1 tablespoon Zinfandel vinegar
- 1 1/2 teaspoons each balsamic vinegar and water

REGAG (Middle Eastern thin flatbread) – 1
⇨ 1 roti (whole-wheat flatbread), toasted briefly over an open flame

RENNET, LIQUID ANIMAL (coagulating enzyme to curdle cheese and junket) – 1 teaspoon
⇨ 1 vegetable rennet tablet (Crush and dissolve in 1/4 cup cool, non-chlorinated water and let sit for 10 to 30 minutes.)
⇨ 1/2 teaspoon double-strength liquid vegetable rennet (Dilute in 1/4 cup cool, nonchlorinated water.)
⇨ 1/8 teaspoon concentrated animal rennet powder (Dissolve in 1/4 cup cool, nonchlorinated water and let sit for 30 to 60 minutes.)

REQUEIJÃO/REQUESON (Brazilian creamy fresh cheese) – 1 cup
⇨ 1 cup dry ricotta or queso fresco
⇨ 1 cup cream cheese thinned with 1 tablespoon sour cream (or 2 tablespoons heavy cream)

RESHAMPATTI CHILE POWDER (Indian seasoning) – 1 teaspoon
⇨ 1 teaspoon ground cayenne pepper

RHUBARB, FRESH OR FROZEN – 1 pound
⇨ 1 pound gooseberries
⇨ 1 pound young Japanese knotweed stems/Polygonum cuspidatum

RICE, ARBORIO SUPERFINE (Italian short-grain, high starch rice) – 1 cup
⇨ 1 cup Italian risotto rice, such as Baldo, Calasperra, Carnaroli superfino, Roma, or Vialone Nano
⇨ 1 cup Australian Risotto Fino
⇨ 1 cup pearl rice, such as Calriso or Calrose, or any short-grain, high-starch rice
⇨ 1 cup English pudding rice

- ⇨ 1 1/4 cups Carolina Gold rice grits
- ⇨ 1 cup whole-grain Arborio brown rice (less creamy; chewy texture)

RICE, BASMATI AGED WHITE (Indian long-grain fragrant Dehra Dun/Dehraduni rice)

- ⇨ 1 cup Daawat, Kohinoor, Pari, or Tilda basmati rice
- ⇨ 1 cup domestic basmati-type rice, such as Calmati, Jasmati, Kasmati, Mahatma, or Texmati
- ⇨ 1 cup baby basmati rice/*Kalijira* or *gobindavog*
- ⇨ 1 cup long-grain brown basmati rice (crunchier texture; double the water and cooking time; or reduce the cooking time by soaking the rice for 6 to 10 hours)
- ⇨ 1 cup white Thai jasmine rice (smaller grain; stickier texture)
- ⇨ 1 cup Patna long-grain Indian rice (less fragrant)
- ⇨ 1 cup white domestic long-grain rice, such as Mahatma
- ⇨ 1 1/3 cups domestic parboiled rice, such as Uncle Ben's converted rice

RICE, BHUTANESE RED (partially milled, medium-grain chewy texture) – 1 cup

- ⇨ 1 cup French Camargue red rice
- ⇨ 1 cup California Calusari red rice
- ⇨ 1 cup Wehani rice
- ⇨ 1 cup long- or medium-grain brown rice

RICE, BLACK JAPONICA (California-grown unmilled medium- or short-grain) – 1 cup

- ⇨ 1 cup medium-grain brown organic rice, such as Golden Rose
- ⇨ 1 cup Wehani rice
- ⇨ 1 cup wild rice

RICE, BOIL-IN-BAG – 3.5 ounces (2 cups cooked)

- ⇨ 2/3 cup long-grain rice added to 1 1/3 cups boiling water and simmered, covered, for 20 minutes

☞ 1/2 cup converted rice added to 1 cup boiling water and simmered, covered, for 15 minutes

RICE, BOMBA EXTRA (Spanish premium Calasparra rice for making paella) – 1 cup
☞ 1 cup Spanish Bahia, Gallaparra, Granza, Montsia Extra, Senia, or Valencia rice
☞ 1 cup Italian superfino-grade Arborio, Baldo, Carnaroli, Roma, or other short-grain risotto rice
☞ 1 cup domestic medium-grain white rice, such as Calriso, Calrose, or Goya

RICE BRAN – 1 ounce
☞ 1 ounce oat bran or wheat bran

RICE BRAN OIL/KOME-NUKA ABURA (Asian cooking oil with a high smoke point) – 1 cup
☞ 1 cup peanut, corn, or canola oil

RICE BRAN, ROASTED/IRI NUKA (Japanese preserving medium for nuka pickles/nukazuke) – 1 pound
☞ 1 pound wheat bran, toasted (Toast in a dry skillet over low heat, stirring frequently, until toasty-smelling, 10 to 12 minutes. Cool completely.)

RICE, BROWN – 1 cup uncooked See also RICE, WHITE
☞ 1 cup brown jasmine, brown basmati, brown Texmati, or Wehani rice (for long-grain)
☞ 1 cup Countrywild rice blend (blend of Wehani, long-grain brown, and black Japonica rice)
☞ 1 cup brown Golden Rose, Italian rosa marchetti, or black Japonica rice (for medium-grain)
☞ 1 cup sprouted brown rice/hatsuga genmai (has more nutrients)
☞ 1 3/4 cups instant/minute brown rice (cooks faster)

☞ 1 1/4 cups whole-wheat couscous (cooks faster)

☞ 2 cups whole-wheat orzo (cooks faster)

RICE, BROWN, INSTANT – 1 cup
☞ 1 cup whole-wheat couscous

RICE, BROWN JASMINE – 1 cup
☞ 1 cup brown basmati rice, brown Texmati rice, Wehani rice, or wild pecan rice

RICE, BROWN, MICROWAVABLE – 1 (8- to 10-ounce) bag
☞ 2 cups cooked brown rice

RICE, BROWN QUICK-COOKING – 1 1/2 cups uncooked
☞ 1 cup plus 2 tablespoons short-grain, regular brown rice soaked in water for at least 4 hours, then drained and cooked in 2 1/2 cups fresh water for 20 minutes

☞ 1 cup long-grain, regular brown rice cooked in 2 to 3 quarts boiling water for 22 to 25 minutes (firmer and fluffier)

☞ 1 cup long-grain regular brown rice, washed, drained, then cooked with 1 1/4 cups fresh water in a pressure cooker for 20 minutes

RICE, BURMESE See RICE, THAI JASMINE WHITE

RICE, CAJUN-STYLE WHITE – 3 cups
☞ 1 cup long-grain white rice, washed in several changes of water before cooking in 1 1/2 cups water

RICE CAKE – 1
☞ 1/2 cup unsalted popped popcorn

RICE, CAMARGUE RED (Provençal hybrid between short-grain and wild red rice) – 1 cup
☞ 1 cup Thai red cargo rice, Bhutanese red rice, Madagascar pink rice, or Wehani (reddish-brown rice)

RICE, CHINESE BLACK/FORBIDDEN (medium-grain unmilled) – 1 cup
- 1 cup Thai long-grain, black sticky rice, or Italian long-grain black rice, such as *Riso Venere*
- 1 cup black barley (chewier)

RICE, CHINESE-TYPE WHITE – 1 cup
- 1 cup long- or medium-grain white rice (cook without salt)
- 1 cup jasmine rice (cook without salt)

RICE, CONVERTED/PARBOILED – 1 cup
- 2/3 cup long-grain white rice (cook following the package directions)

RICE, DAY-OLD FOR FRIED RICE – 1 cup
- 1 cup freshly cooked rice, spread on a rimmed baking sheet and refrigerated at least 1 hour. (Alternatively, place the rice in the freezer for 30 minutes, being careful that it does not freeze.)

RICE, EGYPTIAN (North African medium/short-grain polished rice) *See RICE, ARBORIO SUPERFINE*

RICE, FILIPINO BLACK/PIRURU TONG *See RICE, CHINESE BLACK/ FORBIDDEN*

RICE FLOUR, SWEET/GLUTINOUS RICE FLOUR/SWEET RICE POWDER/MOCHI FLOUR (such as Erawan or Mochiko) *See FLOUR, RICE, BROWN; FLOUR, RICE, WHITE; FLOUR, GLUTINOUS/SWEET RICE*

RICE, FORBIDDEN *See RICE, CHINESE BLACK/FORBIDDEN*

RICE, GREEK/NIHAKI – 1 cup
- 1 cup medium-grain rice (such as Calriso, Calrose, Ichiban Premium)

RICE, GREEN *See RICE, JADE*

RICE GRITS – 1 cup
- 1 1/8 cups Long-grain rice coarsely ground in a blender

RICE, HIMALAYAN RED – 1 cup
- 1 cup Wehani rice
- 1/2 cup each long-grain brown rice and wild rice

RICE, INDIAN/PAKISTANI LONG-GRAIN *See RICE, BASMATI AGED WHITE*

RICE, INDONESIAN LONG-GRAIN (Cianjur) *See RICE, THAI JASMINE*

RICE, INSTANT – 1 cup
- 2/3 cup regular/non-instant rice plus 1 1/3 cups liquid, cooked following the package directions
- 1 cup regular/non-instant rice (to replace instant rice in a recipe; increase the liquid in the recipe to 3 cups, and increase the cooking time by 20 minutes)

RICE, IRANIAN *See RICE, PERSIAN/IRANEAN*

RICE, ITALIAN MEDIUM- TO SHORT-GRAIN (Ambra, Baldo, Calasperra, Carnaroli, Corallo, Lido, Roma, Rosa Marchetti, Vialone Nano) *See RICE, ARBORIO; RICE, RISOTTO*

RICE, JADE (short-grain green rice) – 1 cup
- 1 cup Arborio, Blue rose, Calrose, or other short-grain rice (lacks color)
- 1 cup brown basmati rice (drier; increase the cooking time by 20 minutes)

RICE, JAPANESE SHORT-GRAIN JAPONICA (Akitakomachi, Hitomebore, Sasanisiki, Tamanishiki) – 1 cup
- 1 cup California-grown Japanese-style rice, such as Calrose Asia, Kagayaki, Kahomai, Kokhuto, Koshihikari, Lundberg Sushi, Maruyu, Matsu, Minori, Nishiki, or Shiragiju

- 1 cup short-grain rice, such as Arborio, Blue rose, or Calrose
- 1 cup semi-milled Japanese haiga rice/haigamai (white rice with the rice germ; cross between white and brown rice)
- 1 cup Japanese-style short-grain brown rice/genmai (increase the water to 2 cups and the cooking time to 30 minutes)

RICE, JAPANESE SWEET, STICKY, GLUTINOUS WHITE/MOCHI GOME – 1 cup
- 1 cup Botan rice or other glutinous rice

RICE, JASMINE FRAGRANT See RICE, THAI JASMINE WHITE

RICE, KALIJIRA/BABY BASMATI/GOVINDABHOG (Bangladeshi medium-grain tiny milled rice) See RICE, BASMATI AGED WHITE

RICE, KOREAN/SSAL/HYONMI – 1 cup
- 1 cup short- or medium-grain white rice, such as Blue rose, Calrose, or Calriso
- 1 cup Japanese-style brown rice, such as Lundberg's

RICE MALT SYRUP/STARCH SWEETENER/MIZUAME (Japanese glucose/syrup) – 1/4 cup
- Scant 1/3 cup light-colored (not "lite") corn syrup, brought to a full boil then cooled
- 2 tablespoons pale, mild-tasting honey (such as clover or alfalfa)

RICE MEAL (Indian) – 1 cup
- 3/4 cup plus 2 tablespoons white or brown rice, ground until fine in a blender, or in small batches in a spice/coffee grinder

RICE, MEXICAN/ARROZ – 1 cup
- 1 cup medium-grain white rice, such as Calriso or Calrose

RICE MILK/RICE DRINK – 4 cups (about)
- Powdered rice milk, prepared according to the package instructions

Make Your Own Bring 4 cups water to a boil, stir in 2 cups freshly cooked brown rice (preferably organic), then let sit off the heat for 30 minutes. Process in batches until smooth, 2 to 3 minutes per batch; strain in a fine-mesh sieve, pressing on the pulp to extract the liquid, then cool and refrigerate for up to 4 days. (For thinner milk, increase the amount of water; for sweeter milk add agave syrup/nectar to taste.)

Or

Soak 1 cup raw long-grain brown or white rice in water to cover for 8 to 10 hours. Drain, rinse, then process in a blender or food processor with 4 cups water until the mixture is smooth. Strain in a fine-mesh sieve, pressing on the pulp to extract the liquid; it will keep refrigerated for up to 4 days.

Or

Grind 3/4 cup brown rice flakes in a spice/coffee grinder until powdery, then blend with 4 cups cold water in a blender. Let sit for 5 to 10 minutes, then strain in a cheesecloth-lined sieve, pressing on the pulp to extract all the liquid. It will keep refrigerated for up to 4 days. (For a sweeter milk add brown rice syrup to taste.)

RICE MILK POWDER – 1 cup
- 1 cup soy milk powder

RICE PADDY HERB/NGO OM/MA OM/PHAK KHAYANG (Southeast Asian seasoning) – 4 or 5 sprigs (1 tablespoon chopped)
- 5 or 6 fresh cilantro sprigs (for flavor or for garnish)
- 1/4 teaspoon whole cumin seeds, or 1/8 teaspoon ground cumin (for flavor)

RICE, PAELLA See RICE, BOMBA EXTRA

RICE PAPER WRAPPERS/BANH UOT, FRESH (Vietnamese) – 8 ounces
- 8 ounces dried spring roll wrappers/*Banh Trang,* individually dipped in water to soften
- 8 ounces phyllo dough, cut to size

▷ 8 ounces paper-thin crepes

RICE, PARBOILED (such as Uncle Ben's) See RICE, CONVERTED/
PARBOILED

RICE, PERSIAN/IRANIAN (Darbari, Domsiah, Sandri long-grain) See
RICE, BASMATI AGED WHITE

RICE, PERSIAN/IRANIAN (Gerdeh short-grain) See RICE, SHORT-GRAIN

RICE, PILAF-TYPE (Middle Eastern, Turkish, Greek) – 1 cup
  ▷ 1 cup long-grain rice

**RICE POWDER, ROASTED/KAO KUA PON/THINH/TEPUNG BERTIH
(Southeast Asian thickener) – 1/2 cup**
  ▷ 1/2 cup uncooked sticky rice (or long-grain rice) toasted in a dry
    skillet over medium heat, stirring frequently, until golden, 8 to 10
    minutes; cooled, then ground in small batches in a spice/coffee
    grinder until sandy-textured; store, tightly covered, in the refriger-
    ator (for best flavor store toasted rice and grind just before using).
    For Chinese brown rice powder/*chau mi fen*, use brown rice
  ▷ 1/2 cup toasted chickpea/garbanzo flour

RICE, PUDDING (short-grain used for English rice pudding) See RICE,
SHORT-GRAIN

RICE, PUFFED BASMATI/KURMURA (Indian) – 1 cup
  ▷ 1 cup puffed rice cereal, puffed wheat, or air-puffed millet or sor-
    ghum

RICE, RED (semi-milled, whole-grain) – 1 cup
  ▷ 1 cup Bhutanese red medium-grain, Camargue red medium- to
    short-grain, Himalayan red long-grain, Thai red long-grain or
    short-grain cargo, or Vietnamese red medium-grain cargo

☞ 1 cup domestic short-grain Christmas rice

☞ 1 cup domestic medium-grain Calusari or long-grain Wehani

RICE, RISOTTO (Italian short-grain rice used for risotto) – 1 cup See also RICE, ARBORIO SUPERFINE

☞ 1 cup Italian Ambra, Calasperra, Carnaroli superfino, Corallo, Roma, or Vialone Nano rice

☞ 1 cup Italian Arborio rice (starchier) or Turkish Baldo rice (starchiest)

☞ 1 cup California-grown Japanese-style rice, such as Kagayaki, Kahomai, Kokuho, Maruyu, Matsu, Minori, Nishiki, or Shiragiju

☞ 1 cup pearl barley or semi-pearled farro (more substantial; add extra liquid and increase the cooking time)

RICE, SAKÉ (for saké making) – 2 cups/1 pound

☞ 2 cups short-grain rice or sushi-grade medium-grain rice (double the soaking time)

RICE, SALAD (best for cold dishes) – 1 cup

☞ 1 cup medium-grain rice, such as Valencia, Calrose, or California Pearl

☞ 1 cup domestic long-grain rice (for distinct separate grains)

☞ 3 cups grated raw cauliflower (Use the largest holes on a box grater or pulse a few times in a food processor until the cauliflower resembles rice kernels; serve raw, or lightly sautéed, or steamed for about 5 minutes.)

RICE, SHORT-GRAIN – 1 cup

☞ 1 cup Italian Arborio, Baldo, Carnaroli, Roma, or Vialone Nano rice

☞ 1 cup domestic short-grain rice, such as English pudding rice, Calrose, or California Pearl

☞ 1 cup broken rice/*kakulu-haal* (or long-grain rice crushed briefly in a mortar, or on a cutting board with a rolling pin or mallet)

☞ 1 cup rice flakes, or Indian beaten rice/*chiwda*

☞ 1 cup rice grits, such as Carolina Gold

☞ 1 cup vegetable "rice" (celery root, parsnips, or cauliflower grated into a rice-like texture and cooked for only 60 seconds)

RICE, SPANISH (Bahia, Bomba, Granza, Valencia) See RICE, BOMBA EXTRA (for paella)

RICE STARCH, GLUTINOUS See RICE FLOUR, SWEET

RICE, STICKY/SWEET/GLUTINOUS/MOCHI (Koda, Lundberg Family Farms, Nishiki) – 1 cup
☞ 1 cup Thai black/purple sticky rice (less sticky)
☞ 1 cup Botan rice
☞ 1 cup brown glutinous rice

RICE, SUSHI See RICE, JAPANESE SHORT-GRAIN/JAPONICA

RICE SYRUP See BROWN RICE SYRUP

RICE, THAI JASMINE RED/PURPLE/KHAO HOM MALI (unmilled long-grain) – 1 cup
☞ 1/2 cup each Thai black sticky rice and white jasmine rice cooked together

RICE, THAI JASMINE WHITE/KHAO HOM MALI (aromatic long-grain) – 1 cup
☞ 1 cup domestic jasmine rice, such as Mahatma or Texmati
☞ 1/2 cup brown jasmine rice (chewier texture; increase the cooking time)
☞ 1 cup Indian basmati or Patna rice (less moist; lacks aroma)
☞ 1 cup basmati or long-grain white rice, cooked in jasmine-scented water (Steep 1 or 2 jasmine tea bags, 1 1/2 tablespoons jasmine-tea pearls, or 1 unsprayed jasmine flower in 2 cups boiling water for 5 minutes; remove the tea bags, pearls, or flower and use the water as the cooking liquid for the rice.)

RICE, THAI STICKY BLACK (unmilled, long-grain; chewy when cooked) – 1 cup
- 1 cup Chinese black rice/forbidden rice
- 1 cup Thai sticky white rice (stickier)

RICE, THAI STICKY WHITE/KHAO NEEO (long-grain; sticky when cooked) – 1 cup
- 1 cup Thai sticky unmilled black rice (less sticky, chewier; takes longer to cook)
- 1 cup short- or medium-grain Chinese or Japanese sticky (sweet) rice
- 1 cup broken jasmine rice

RICE, TURKISH BALDO (starchy, milled, short-grain rice) – 1 cup
- 1 cup Egyptian rice, Italian Baldo rice, or other risotto rice
- 1 cup Calriso, or other domestic short- or medium-grain rice

RICE VINEGAR – 1 tablespoon *See also JAPANESE, RICE VINEGAR*
- 1 tablespoon champagne vinegar, cava vinegar, or white wine vinegar
- 2 teaspoons cider vinegar or distilled white vinegar, 1 teaspoon water, and 2 or 3 grains sugar

RICE VINEGAR – 1/2 cup
- 1/3 cup distilled white vinegar and 3 tablespoons water

RICE, WHITE – 1 cup uncooked
- 3/4 cup uncooked brown rice soaked in 1 cup cool water for 5 to 24 hours, then cooked for 30 minutes
- 1 cup broken rice/*kakulu-haal* (available in Asian markets; cooks in 10 minutes)
- 1 1/2 cups uncooked instant white rice (reduce the cooking time to 10 minutes)
- 1 1/2 cups uncooked quick-cooking barley
- 2 cups uncooked white orzo pasta

- ⮞ 1 cup pre-washed, uncooked light quinoa
- ⮞ 1 cup uncooked coarse-ground bulgur (grind #3)
- ⮞ 1 1/4 cups uncooked Israeli or Lebanese couscous (small pearl-shaped pasta)
- ⮞ 2 1/2 to 3 cups grated raw cauliflower (use the largest holes on a box grater or pulse a few times in a food processor until the cauliflower resembles rice)

RICE, WILD *See WILD RICE; WILD RICE, INSTANT*

RICE WINE *See CHINESE YELLOW RICE COOKING WINE; JAPANESE RICE WINE; KOREAN RICE WINE; KOREAN RICE WINE, SWEET COOKING; MIRIN; SAKÉ; SHAOXING*

RICOTTA/SEIRASS (Italian fresh cheese containing 15% fat) – 1 cup
- ⮞ 1 cup Cloumage or *mizithra*
- ⮞ 1 cup hoop cheese, farmer cheese, pot cheese, or Mexican queso fresco (firmer; less moist)
- ⮞ 1 cup small-curd or creamed cottage cheese pressed through a fine-mesh sieve or blended until smooth, then drained if necessary (firmer; less moist)
- ⮞ 1 cup vegan ricotta, such as Tofutti
- ⮞ 1 cup soft or silken tofu pressed through a ricer or crumbled by hand (for cooked dishes with a sauce, such as lasagna or manicotti)

Make Your Own Cook 1 quart whole milk and 1 cup buttermilk over moderate heat, stirring constantly, until curds form, about 185°F. Let sit off the heat for 10 minutes, then spoon into a sieve lined with dampened cheesecloth and drain for 30 to 60 minutes; season with salt, if desired.

RICOTTA, AFFUMICATA (smoked ricotta) – 1 cup
- ⮞ 1/2 cup grated smoked mozzarella/*mozzarella affumicata* combined with 1/2 cup ricotta

RICOTTA IMPASTATA (smooth dry ricotta for baking) – 1 cup
☞ 1 1/2 cups ricotta, drained overnight in a cheesecloth-lined sieve set over a bowl in the refrigerator

RICOTTA, ROMANA/RICOTTA GENTILE (Italian sheep's milk ricotta) – 1 cup
☞ 1 cup cow's milk ricotta plus 1 1/2 teaspoons fresh lemon juice
☞ 1 cup cow's milk ricotta plus 1 tablespoon fresh goat cheese or 2 tablespoons heavy cream
☞ 1 cup fresh goat's milk chèvre

RICOTTA SALATA (salty dry ricotta) – 1 cup
☞ 1 cup ricotta or fresh goat cheese with a little feta cheese mixed in (for fresh)
☞ 1 cup Manouri, or Greek feta rinsed in cold water to reduce saltiness (for fresh)
☞ 1 cup aged Mizithra, Fiore Sardo, Grana Padana, aged Manchego, or Pecorino Romano (for aged)

RIGANI See OREGANO, GREEK

RISOTTO RICE See RICE, RISOTTO

ROASTED BARLEY TEA/MUGICHA/BORICHA See KOREAN ROASTED BARLEY TEA/BORICHA

ROBIOLA LOMBARDIA (Italian semisoft cheese) – 1 ounce
☞ 1 ounce Taleggio, Fontina Val d'Aosta, Reblochon, or Pont-l'Évêque

ROBIOLA PIEMONTE (Italian soft, fresh cheese) – 1 ounce
☞ 1/2 ounce each ricotta and mascarpone
☞ 1 ounce Caprini, Petit Suisse, Fin de Siècle, Père Michel, or natural cream cheese

ROCKET *See ARUGULA*

ROCK SALT *See SALT, ROCK*

ROCK SUGAR *See SUGAR, BROWN ROCK; SUGAR, YELLOW/CLEAR ROCK*

ROCOTILLO/ROCOTO CHILE, FRESH (Peruvian mild chile) – 1
- 1 fresh *aji dulce* or Cuban cachucha chile
- 1 to 2 teaspoons chopped red bell pepper
- 1 to 2 teaspoons rocoto chile paste or milder *pasta de panca* (Peruvian red chile paste)

ROLLED OATS *See OATS, OLD-FASHIONED ROLLED*

ROMANO PEPPER *See PEPPER, BELL (red)*

RONDELÉ *See BOURSIN*

ROOT VEGETABLE CHIPS (beets, parsnips, rutabagas, sweet potatoes, taro, turnips)
Make Your Own Slice the vegetables paper-thin and toss with olive oil (plus salt and seasoning, if desired). Spread in a single layer on parchment-lined baking sheets and bake in a preheated 275°F oven until crisp, 25 to 30 minutes, rotating the pans and flipping the chips halfway through.

ROQUEFORT *See BLUE CHEESE, STRONG*

ROSE EXTRACT/ESSENCE (food flavoring agent) – 1 teaspoon
- 1 1/2 tablespoons rose water (reduce the liquid in the recipe by 1 tablespoon)

ROSE GERANIUM LEAF – 1 fresh or dried leaf
- 1 drop orange flower water

ROSE GERANIUM SYRUP – 1 cup
Make Your Own Add 2 or 3 unsprayed rose geranium sprigs (including leaves) to 1 cup hot simple syrup (*See SYRUP, SIMPLE*). Cool, then remove the sprigs and store, tightly covered, in the refrigerator. It will keep for up to 7 days.

ROSE HIP SYRUP – 1 cup
Make Your Own Halve, seed, and rinse 8 ounces fresh unsprayed rose hips. Simmer, uncovered, with 1 cup water until softened, 20 to 30 minutes. Strain, discard the hips, then boil the liquid with 1 cup sugar until clear, about 2 minutes. Cool and store, refrigerated, in a sterilized jar for up to 6 weeks. (Wear plastic gloves when handling the rose hips, and remove the seeds with a small demitasse spoon.)

ROSEMARY, FRESH – 4-inch sprig (10 leaves/needles/1 tablespoon finely chopped)
- 1 tablespoon frozen rosemary leaves/needles, crushed (frozen sprigs will keep 6 months to a year)
- 1 to 2 teaspoons whole or cracked dried rosemary leaves/needles (crush in a mortar, pepper grinder, or with the back of a spoon)
- 1/2 to 3/4 teaspoon powdered rosemary

ROSEMARY OIL – 1/2 cup
Make Your Own Slowly heat 2 or 3 sprigs fresh rosemary and 1/2 cup olive oil to 190°F. Cool, strain, then store in a sterilized lidded jar for up to 1 week.

ROSE PETALS, WILD FRESH/DOK GULAB (Southeast Asian aromatic garnish) – 1 cup
- 1 cup fresh, pesticide-free Rugosa or pink damask rose petals (cut off the white part at the base of each petal; it is bitter)
- 1 cup fresh, pesticide-free nasturtium petals, or other colorful petals *See FLOWERS/BLOSSOMS/PETALS, FRESH EDIBLE*

ROSE WATER (food flavoring agent) – 1 tablespoon
- 1/2 teaspoon food-grade pure rose extract/essence (reduce the liquid in the recipe by 1 tablespoon)

Make Your Own Simmer 3/4 cup purified water and 1/2 cup trimmed, fresh, pesticide-free rose petals, covered, for 30 minutes. Cool, strain, then add 1 or 2 teaspoons vodka. Store in a sterilized bottle in the refrigerator. Makes 1/3 cup; use 1 tablespoon for each tablespoon in the recipe. Use within 7 days.

ROSELLE See HIBISCUS FLOWERS, DRIED

ROTI (Indian whole-wheat flatbread) – 1
- 1 chapati, paratha, naan, or whole-wheat pita

ROYAL FERN/ZENMAI See FIDDLEHEAD FERNS

ROYAL TRUMPET MUSHROOMS See KING OYSTER/ROYAL TRUMPET MUSHROOMS

RUM – 2 tablespoons for cooking
- 1/2 teaspoon imitation rum extract plus 1 1/2 tablespoons vodka or water
- 2 tablespoons bourbon or brandy
- 1/8 to 1/4 teaspoon butter-rum flavor/extract (if the recipe contains butter)

RUM EXTRACT – 1 teaspoon
- 2 tablespoons rum; omit 2 tablespoons liquid from the recipe

RUSKS See BARLEY RUSKS/PAXIMADIA; BESCHUIT

RUSSIAN DRESSING – 1 cup
- 2/3 cup mayonnaise and 1/3 cup ketchup-based chili sauce

Make Your Own Stir together 1/3 cup each plain yogurt, mayonnaise, and ketchup. Add 1 tablespoon strained bottled horseradish and stir until thoroughly combined.

RUTABAGAS/SWEDES – 1 pound
  ☞ 1 pound parsnips or turnips (drier texture)

RYE CHOPS/CRACKED RYE – 1 cup
  ☞ 1 cup whole-grain rye, chopped in a blender, 15 to 20 seconds, then sieved to remove any fine flour

S

SABAAYAD (Somali and Azerbaijan whole-wheat sourdough flatbread) – 1
- ☞ 1 barbari, sangak, soft lavash, pocketless pita/*pide*, or pita split into 2 halves

SABA/SAPA/MOSTO COTTO (Italian grape must syrup) See GRAPE MOLASSES

SACHA INCHI NUTS, ROASTED (large Peruvian oil-rich nuts) – 1 ounce
- ☞ 1 ounce macadamia nuts

SACHA INCHI OIL (Peruvian oil high in omega-3 fatty acids) – 1 tablespoon
- ☞ 1 tablespoon hemp or flaxseed oil

SAEUJOT/SAEWOO-JEOT See KOREAN SHRIMP, SALTED

SAFFLOWER/SAFFRON THISTLE/FALSE SAFFRON/TURKISH SAFFRON/MEXICAN SAFFRON (coloring agent) – 1 teaspoon dried compressed petals
- ☞ 1 teaspoon pesticide-free dried marigold petals, preferably pot marigold/*Calendula officinalis*, steeped in a little warm water for about 5 minutes (use the liquid for color and discard the petals)
- ☞ 1/2 teaspoon ground annatto seeds
- ☞ 1 teaspoon whole annatto seeds, steeped in a little hot water for about 5 minutes (use the liquid for color and discard the seeds)
- ☞ 1/4 teaspoon sweet California or Hungarian paprika plus 1/2 teaspoon ground turmeric, preferably Madras

SAFFRON/COUPÉ/SARGO – 1/2 teaspoon (10 to 15 threads/pinch)

- ☞ 1/8 teaspoon ground/powdered saffron
- ☞ 2 or 3 drops saffron extract
- ☞ 1 1/2 teaspoons safflower stigmas/Mexican saffron/*azafrán*, soaked in 1 tablespoon warm water for 20 minutes, then added to the dish along with the water (for color)
- ☞ 1 teaspoon pesticide-free dried marigold petals, preferably pot marigold/*Calendula officinalis*, steeped in 1 or 2 tablespoon warm water for 5 minutes (use the liquid for color and discard the petals)
- ☞ 1/2 teaspoon ground annatto seeds (for color)
- ☞ 1 teaspoon whole annatto seeds, steeped in a little hot liquid (use the liquid for color and discard the seeds)
- ☞ 1/4 to 1/2 teaspoon powdered Madras turmeric, or just enough for color

SAGE, COMMON, FRESH – 2 (3-inch) sprigs, or 3 to 5 leaves, or 1 tablespoon chopped

- ☞ 2 or 3 whole dried sage leaves, crushed
- ☞ 1 to 2 teaspoons rubbed sage, or 1/2 teaspoon ground/powdered sage
- ☞ 1 1/2 teaspoons chopped fresh Greek sage, or scant 1/2 scant teaspoon dried (more aromatic)
- ☞ 3/4 teaspoon dried marjoram or summer savory
- ☞ 1 teaspoon poultry seasoning

SAGO PEARLS/BOT BANG/SABUDANA/SAGUDANA – 1 tablespoon

- ☞ 1 tablespoon tapioca pearls, 1/8-inch diameter or smaller (slightly starchier)

SAGO STARCH – 1 tablespoon

- ☞ 1 tablespoon tapioca starch, or 2 1/2 teaspoons quick-cooking tapioca, ground until powdery
- ☞ 2 teaspoons arrowroot powder
- ☞ 1 1/2 teaspoons cornstarch or sweet rice flour/glutinous rice flour/mochiko

☞ 2 tablespoons all-purpose flour or quick-mixing flour, such as Wondra (cook 5 minutes after thickening)

SAHLAB/SALEP (Greek and Turkish ground orchid root thickener) – 1 tablespoon pulverized
☞ 2 teaspoons cornstarch (lacks flavor; for flavor add 1/2 teaspoon rose water, orange blossom water, or even a drop or two of elderflower cordial)

SAINT-PAULIN (French cow's milk semihard cheese) – 1 ounce
☞ 1 ounce Port Salut, Burgues, Chamberat, Esrom, Muenster, Savaron, or Tilsit

SAKÉ/JAPANESE RICE WINE/BEER/SEISHU/FUTSU-SHU – 1/4 cup for cooking
☞ 2 to 3 tablespoons sake-based mirin, such as *aji no haha* or *aske mirin*; reduce the sugar in the recipe accordingly
☞ 1/4 cup Chinese yellow rice wine/Shaoxing
☞ 1/4 cup dry sherry, such as Dry Sack, or dry vermouth
☞ 1/4 cup white wine plus a pinch of brown sugar

SALAD BURNET (cucumber-tasting herb) – 1 tablespoon
☞ 1 tablespoon finely chopped fresh borage

SALAD CREAM (British creamy salad dressing) – 1/2 cup
☞ 1/2 cup honey mustard dressing, or ranch dressing

SALAD DRESSING, CREAMY TYPE – 1/2 cup
☞ 1/4 cup mayonnaise and 1/2 cup sour cream or plain yogurt; thinned with wine vinegar, lemon juice, or pickling liquid from jarred pepperoncini, giardiniera, or pickles

SALAD DRESSING, RUSSIAN *See RUSSIAN DRESSING*

SALAD DRESSING, THOUSAND ISLAND *See THOUSAND ISLAND DRESSING*

SALAD HERBS/LEAVES (wild and cultivated, pesticide-free, salad additions) – 1 cup
- 1 cup or a combination of any of the following: angelica, arugula, basil, chervil, chickweed stem tips/*Stellaria media*, cilantro (use sparingly), curly/yellow dock (use sparingly), miner's lettuce/claytonia, parsley, small lovage leaves (use sparingly), sheep or wood sorrel (use sparingly), shiso leaves, young speedwell tops/*Veronica arvensis*, tarragon, wild fennel (shave or thinly slice), young bok choy leaves, young borage (shred), young daisy leaves/*Bellis perennis*, young dandelion hearts, tender young hawthorn shoots and leaves/*Crataegus monogyna,* young mallow leaf tips/*Malva neglecta*, young primrose leaves, young salad burnet leaves, young sunflower greens, or young winter cress/yellow rocket/creasy greens

SALAD OIL – 1 cup for vinaigrette
- 1 cup oil from jarred marinated artichoke hearts, sun-dried tomatoes, or olives

SALAM LEAF/INDONESIAN BAY LEAF/DAUN SALAM/ (Indonesian seasoning) – 1 (3-inch) dried leaf
- 2 or 3 fresh curry leaves plus a few drops of lime juice

SALEP/SALAP/SAHLAB/ORCHIS MASCULA (Middle Eastern mucilaginous thickening powder for stretchy ice cream) – 1 teaspoon
- 1/2 teaspoon *konjac* flour/*konjac glucomannan* (whisk into cold liquid until thoroughly combined)
- 1 teaspoon locust bean gum or guar gum (for jelling only; not for stretchy properties)
- 1 teaspoon arrowroot powder or cornstarch (for thickening only; not for stretchy properties)

SALICORNIA *See GLASSWORT*

SALMON CAVIAR *See CAVIAR, RED*

SALMON, COOKED FRESH – 1 pound (1 1/2 cups flaked)
- 1 (15-ounce) can red or pink salmon, drained and skin removed
- 2 (6- or 7-ounce) pouches boned, skinned pink salmon
- 3 (5-ounce) cans chunk tuna, drained

SALMON, FRESH – 1 pound
- 2 (6-ounce) cans salmon in water, drained
- 1 pound arctic char or sea trout

SALMON, SALTED, FLAKES/SHIO ZAKE (Japanese) – 1 pound
- 1 pound poached salmon, flaked and lightly sprinkled with salt

SALMON, SMOKED OR CURED – 1 pound
- 1 pound gravlax (dill flavor)
- 1 pound smoked arctic char, bluefish, haddock, mackerel, sable-fish, trout, or whitefish (bones and skin removed as necessary)
- 1 pound vegan smoked salmon, such as Sophie's Kitchen

SALONICA PEPPERS (Greek hot pickled peppers) – 1 cup
- 1 cup jarred Italian pepperoncini

SALSA, FRESH/SALSA CRUDA (Mexican condiment) – 1 cup
- 1 cup canned or jarred salsa freshened with chopped cilantro, chopped white or red onion, and a little lemon or lime juice

SALSA GOLF/MARIE ROSE SAUCE/SALSA ROSADA (Argentine table condiment) – 1 cup
Make Your Own 1/2 cup each ketchup-based chili sauce (or ketchup) and mayonnaise, plus a little lime juice, Worcestershire sauce, or sweet pickle relish

SALSIFY/WHITE SALSIFY/OYSTER PLANT (Greek, Italian, Spanish root vegetable) – 1 pound
  ➼ 1 pound black salsify/scorzonera (milder flavor)
  ➼ 1 pound goatsbeard/wild salsify/*Tragopogon pratensis* (smaller roots)
  ➼ 1 pound parsnips, thin burdock roots, or dandelion roots
  ➼ 1 pound artichoke hearts or Jerusalem artichokes/sunchokes

SALT, BLACK/KALA NAMAK (Indian unrefined pink-colored salt) – 1 tablespoon
  ➼ 1 tablespoon Hawaiian coarse-grain black lava sea salt (slightly smoky flavor)
  ➼ 1 tablespoon Cyprus medium-grain black lava sea salt flakes (for finishing)
  ➼ 4 teaspoons table salt or sea salt (for cooking; lacks sulphuric aroma and flavor)

SALT, CHEESE (coarse non-iodized, additive-free flake salt) – 1 tablespoon
  ➼ 1 tablespoon Diamond Crystal kosher salt

SALT, CHILI – 1 tablespoon
  ➼ 1 teaspoon chili seasoning mixed with 2 teaspoons coarse kosher or sea salt

SALT, CHIPOTLE – 1 tablespoon
  ➼ 1/8 teaspoon chipotle chile powder mixed with 1 tablespoon kosher or sea salt
Make Your Own Toast 1 dried chipotle chile in a dry skillet, 2 to 3 minutes each side. Cut into pieces, then grind in a spice/coffee grinder. Mix with 2 teaspoons kosher or sea salt.

SALT COD/BACALAO/BACCALÀ/BACALHAU/KLIPFISH (Spanish, Italian, Portuguese, and Norwegian salted and dried cod) – 8 ounces
Make Your Own Completely bury 1 pound skinned and boned cod in kosher or sea salt in a small container. Cover tightly and refrigerate

until firm, 6 to 7 days, pouring off any brine that accumulates and adding fresh salt as needed.

SALT, CURING/PINK SALT See *SALTPETER/POTASSIUM NITRATE/ SODIUM NITRATE*

SALT, FLEUR DE SEL See *FLEUR DE SEL DE GUÉRANDE*

SALT, HIMALAYAN PINK (rose-colored, mineral-rich salt) – 1 tablespoon
- 1 tablespoon Bolivian Rose, Hawaiian Haleakala Ruby, Hawaiian Red Alaea Volcanic, Australian Murray River (peach or rose-color), or Peruvian Pink (pinkish-beige color)

SALT, KOSHER/KOSHERING SALT (additive-free salt with irregular coarse grains) – 1 teaspoon Diamond Crystal or 3/4 teaspoon Morton
- 1/2 teaspoon non-iodized table salt
- 1 teaspoon coarse or extra-coarse sea salt (non-iodized and additive-free)
- 3/4 teaspoon pickling, canning, or cheese salt (non-iodized and additive-free)

SALT, LAVENDER (French seasoning) – 1 tablespoon
- 1 teaspoon French dried lavender blossoms and 1 tablespoon coarse sea salt, pulverized until fine, then left several days to develop flavor

SALTPETER/POTASSIUM NITRATE/SODIUM NITRATE (meat curing agent) – 1 ounce
- 1 ounce sodium nitrate–based curing salt, such as DQ Curing Salt #2 or Insta Cure #2, used following the package directions

SALT, PICKLING, GRANULATED (fine-grain non-iodized, additive-free salt) – 1 tablespoon
- 1 1/2 tablespoons flaked pickling salt
- 1 tablespoon non-iodized and additive-free (no anti-caking agent) table salt

☞ 1 1/2 tablespoons Morton kosher salt

☞ 2 tablespoons Diamond Crystal kosher salt (takes longer to dissolve)

SALT, PINK, NATURAL *See SALT, HIMALAYAN PINK*

SALT, POPCORN – 1 cup
☞ 1 1/4 cups kosher or sea salt, ground in a blender or food processor, or in batches in a spice/coffee grinder, until very fine

☞ 1 cup table salt

SALT PORK (fatty, salt-cured flavoring agent) – 4 ounces
☞ 4 ounces thick slice of slab bacon (or fatty end piece of cured ham) soaked in boiling water 2 minutes to reduce smoke flavor

☞ 4 ounces fatback plus salt to taste

☞ 4 ounces pancetta (leaner)

☞ 4 ounces guanciale (less salty)

Make Your Own Completely submerge small, uniform pieces of pork shoulder in pickling or kosher salt in a small container and refrigerate for 2 weeks, adding more salt after 7 days. Rinse, blot dry, and package in plastic wrap. It will keep refrigerated for up to 1 month.

SALT, PRETZEL (large-grain, bright white salt; used for soft pretzels, salt bagels, or focaccia) – 1 cup
☞ 1 cup extra-coarse sea salt; margarita salt; or kosher salt, preferably Diamond Crystal

SALT, ROCK (food-grade coarse salt for an ice cream maker)
☞ Kosher salt, preferably Diamond Crystal, or extra-coarse sea salt

SALT, SEA, FINE-GRAIN – 1 teaspoon *See also SALT, TABLE*
☞ 1 teaspoon table salt

☞ 1 1/2 teaspoons coarse-grain sea salt, pulsed in a spice/coffee mill until fine, then measured (Clean the mill immediately after use to prevent corrosion.)

☞ 1 1/2 teaspoons Morton kosher salt or Morton coarse sea salt

☞ 2 teaspoons Diamond Crystal kosher salt, Morton extra-coarse sea salt, or coarse gray sea salt

SALT, SEASONING – *1 generous tablespoon*

☞ 1 tablespoon kosher salt and 1/8 teaspoon each garlic powder, onion powder, and paprika (or turmeric) plus a few grains of sugar (For a smoky version use smoked paprika or smoked sea salt, or both.)

SALT, SMOKED SEA – *1 cup* See also SALT, CHIPOTLE

☞ 1 cup sea salt and 1/4 to 1/2 teaspoon (or more) hickory smoke powder

☞ 1 cup sea salt and 3 or 4 drops liquid smoke, kneaded together in a sealable plastic bag, then spread out on a baking sheet and dried in an oven with a pilot light, or at warm room temperature for 2 or 3 hours

SALT, SOUR See CITRIC ACID/CITRIC SALT

SALT SUBSTITUTION CONTAINING SODIUM CHLORIDE – *1 teaspoon*

☞ 1 teaspoon Biosalt, LoSalt, or Lite Salt (usually two-thirds potassium chloride with one-third sodium chloride)

☞ 1 teaspoon powdered kelp, or salt substitute containing kelp, such as Herbamare

☞ 1 teaspoon Japanese soy sauce crystals (light, flaky salt crystals)

☞ 2 teaspoons Japanese tamari, or 1 tablespoon soy sauce/*shoyu* (for prepared dishes)

☞ 2 teaspoons Japanese fermented rice/*shio-koji* (for adding an umami taste to dishes)

☞ 1 to 2 tablespoons dark *hatcho* miso containing 12% salt (softened with a little liquid and added to a dish just before removing from heat)

☞ 1 tablespoon Japanese sesame salt/*gomashio* or seaweed *gomashio* containing sesame seeds, dulse, nori, kombu, and sea salt (for lower-sodium finishing salt)

☞ 2 teaspoons dried and ground glasswort/salicornia

SALT SUBSTITUTION, SODIUM-FREE/POTASSIUM CHLORIDE – 1 teaspoon
- 1 or 2 teaspoons salt-free herb-and-spice seasoning blend, such as Mrs. Dash or Vege-Sal
- 1/2 teaspoon lemon juice, unseasoned rice vinegar, or white wine vinegar

SALT, TABLE/GRANULAR, IODIZED AND NON-IODIZED (fine-grained, free-flowing salt with anti-caking additives) – 1 teaspoon
- 1 teaspoon finely ground Baja, Atlantic, or Mediterranean Sea salt (include a few dry rice grains in the salt shaker for the free-flowing feature)
- 1 1/4 teaspoons coarse moist sea salt from Brittany, Baja, Camargue, or Ibiza
- 1 1/2 teaspoons Morton kosher salt
- 2 teaspoons Diamond Crystal kosher salt or Morton extra-coarse sea salt
- 2 teaspoons English Maldon or Welsh Halen Môn crystal-flake sea salt (for finishing)

SALT, TABLE/GRANULAR, IODIZED AND NON-IODIZED – 1 cup
- 1 1/2 cups Morton kosher salt
- 2 cups Diamond Crystal kosher salt

SAMBAL MANIS (Indonesian dipping sauce) – 1 tablespoon
- 1 tablespoon *sambal oelek* (hotter)

SAMBAL OELEK (Indonesian hot chili paste) – 1 tablespoon See also CHILI PASTE, HOT
- 3 stemmed fresh bird's eye chiles (or other small red chiles), simmered in 1/4 cup water for 5 minutes; drained, cooled, and crushed to a coarse paste with a pinch each of salt and brown sugar (Wear plastic gloves when handling the chiles and avoid touching your face.)
- 1 (or more) tablespoons Indonesian dipping sauce/*sambal manis* (milder)

- ⮞ 1 tablespoon harissa, Sriracha, Vietnamese chili sauce/*tuong ot toi*, Chinese hot chili paste/*la jiao jiang*, or Japanese chili yuzu paste/*yuzu koshu*
- ⮞ 1 to 2 teaspoon hot pepper sauce, such as Tabasco, or hot chile powder, such as cayenne

SÂMNA/SAMNEH/SMEN (Middle Eastern and North African preserved butter) – 1 cup
- ⮞ 1 tablespoon toasted sesame seed oil combined with 3/4 cup plus 2 tablespoons room-temperature clarified butter
- ⮞ 1 1/2 teaspoons creamy blue cheese combined with 1 cup room-temperature salted butter (or unsalted butter plus 1/2 teaspoon salt)
- ⮞ 1 cup ghee, clarified butter (preferably tangy, cultured-milk butter), or solidified coconut oil

SAMOSA DOUGH (Indian) – 8 ounces See also WRAPPERS FOR FOOD, PREPARED EDIBLE
- ⮞ 8 ounces egg roll wrappers, Shanghai spring roll skins, or lumpia wrappers, cut to size (for frying)
- ⮞ 8 ounces frozen mini phyllo shells, or phyllo pastry sheets cut to size (for baking)

SANAAM CHILES/LONG CHILES, DRIED (Indian) – 3 or 4
- ⮞ 3 or 4 dried de árbol, cayenne, or Thai red chiles
- ⮞ 1/3 to 1/2 teaspoon ground cayenne pepper, Thai chile powder, or very hot crushed red pepper flakes

SAND GINGER/SAH GEUNG See GALANGAL, GREATER

SANGAK BREAD (Iranian whole-wheat, sourdough flatbread) – 1 pound
- ⮞ 1 pound barbari bread, soft lavash, or pocketless pita bread/*pide*

SANSHO LEAVES/PRICKLY ASH LEAVES/KINOME, FRESH See KINOME

SANSHO POWDER/PRICKLY ASH POWDER/KONA-ZANSHO/SANSYO
(Japanese seasoning) – 1 teaspoon
- 1 teaspoon lemon pepper seasoning; reduce the salt and pepper in the recipe accordingly

SANTAKA CHILE See JAPONÉS CHILE

SARDINES, FRESH – 1 pound
- 2 (3.75-ounce) cans boneless oil-packed sardines or pilchards, drained and rinsed
- 1 pound fresh sprats or fresh small herring or mackerel

SARDINIAN BITTER HONEY See HONEY, BITTER/SAVORY

SATAW/SATO BEANS/LOOK SATAW (Thailand green beans) – 1 cup
- 1 cup young fresh shelled and peeled fava beans
- 1 cup thawed frozen lima beans, peeled
- 1 cup fresh or frozen snap or snow peas

SATAY SAUCE See PEANUT DIPPING SAUCE

SAUCE THICKENER See THICKENER FOR GRAVY OR SAUCE

SAUSAGE, BREAKFAST PORK – 1 pound
Make Your Own Thoroughly combine 1 pound ground pork (25 to 30% fat), 2 tablespoons ice water, and 1 scant tablespoon breakfast sausage seasoning. Cover and refrigerate for 24 hours to develop the flavor. For hot sausage, add 1/2 teaspoon ground cayenne pepper or crushed red pepper flakes.

SAUSAGE, BREAKFAST PORK, SEASONING – 1 scant tablespoon
- 1 teaspoon kosher salt and 1/2 teaspoon each ground white pepper, thyme, and sage
- 1 teaspoon kosher salt and 2 teaspoons poultry seasoning

SAUSAGE, ITALIAN See ITALIAN SAUSAGE, BULK

SAVORY, SUMMER, DRIED – 1 teaspoon
- ⊩ 1/2 teaspoon dried winter savory (spicier and sharper)
- ⊩ 3/4 teaspoon dried thyme and 1/8 teaspoon dried marjoram

SAVORY, SUMMER, FRESH – 1 tablespoon finely chopped leaves
- ⊩ 1 1/2 to 2 teaspoons fresh winter savory (spicier and sharper)
- ⊩ 1 1/2 teaspoons finely chopped fresh thyme and 1/2 teaspoon finely chopped fresh mint

SAVORY, WINTER, FRESH – 1 tablespoon finely chopped leaves
- ⊩ 1 1/2 teaspoon dried winter savory leaves, crumbled
- ⊩ 1 1/2 tablespoons chopped fresh summer savory, or 1 1/2 teaspoons dried summer savory (milder)
- ⊩ 2 teaspoons chopped fresh thyme and 1 teaspoon chopped fresh mint
- ⊩ 1/2 teaspoon dried thyme and 1/4 teaspoon dried marjoram (or sage)
- ⊩ 1/2 teaspoon dried sage or oregano

SAW-LEAF/SAWTOOTH HERB See CULANTRO

SAZÓN (Spanish spice blend) – 1 tablespoon (about)
- ⊩ Scant 1/2 teaspoon each paprika, roasted ground coriander, and ground cumin, plus 1 teaspoon garlic powder and 1 teaspoon salt

SCALLIONS/GREEN ONIONS/SPRING ONIONS – 4 ounces
- ⊩ 4 ounces spring onions, Egyptian onions, Mexican onions, ramp bulbs, onion sprouts, young thin leeks, garlic shoots, or young shallot tops

SCALLOPS, BAY – 1 pound
- ⊩ 1 pound sea scallops, small side muscle removed, and cut into halves or quarters

SCALLOPS, DRY (dry, untreated scallops) – 1 pound
- ⊳ 1 pound white, wet processed scallops, soaked for 30 minutes in 2 cups cold water containing 2 tablespoons lemon juice and 1 tablespoon salt, then blotted dry (Processed scallops have been soaked in a solution of sodium tripolyphosphate to keep them hydrated.)
- ⊳ 1 pound King oyster mushroom stems, sliced 3/4 inch-thick and sautéed on both sides until golden and tender, 3 to 4 minutes
- ⊳ 1 pound vegan scallops, such as Sophie's Kitchen

SCALOPPINI, VEAL See VEAL SCALLOPS

SCAMORZA (Italian stretched-curd cheese) – 1 ounce
- ⊳ 1 ounce *burrata*, young *caciocavallo*, mozzarella, provolone, asadero/*queso Oaxaca*, or string cheese

SCAMORZA, SMOKED – 1 ounce
- ⊳ 1 ounce *mozzarella affumicata* or *provolone affumicata*

SCORZONERA/BLACK SALSIFY See SALSIFY

SCOTCH BONNET CHILE, FRESH (hot Caribbean chile pepper) – 1
- ⊳ 1 fresh Fatalii, Red Savina, or habañero chile
- ⊳ 2 or 3 fresh jalapeño or serrano chiles
- ⊳ 2 tablespoons Scotch bonnet hot pepper sauce

SCREWPINE LEAF/PANDANUS/BAI TOEY/LA DUA/DAUN PANDAN (Southeast Asian flavoring and coloring agent) – 1 fresh, frozen, or dried leaf See also KEWRA
- ⊳ 1/2 teaspoon pandan syrup, powder, or paste
- ⊳ 2 or 3 drops pandan extract or *kewra* essence and 1 small drop green food coloring (optional)

SEA BUCKTHORN JUICE – 1 ounce
- 2 tablespoons orange juice plus a few drops of lemon juice (for flavor, not antioxidant properties)

SEAFOOD COCKTAIL SAUCE See COCKTAIL SAUCE

SEA PALM FRONDS/CALIFORNIA SILKY SEA PALM (crunchy fine-strand seaweed) See SEAWEED/SEA GRASSES

SEASONED SALT See SALT, SEASONING

SEAWEED/SEA GRASSES (edible sea vegetables)
- Alaria, arame, bullwhip kelp, carrageen/Irish moss, dulse, hijiki, kombu/dried kelp, focus/bladderwrack, laver/purple laver/slokum, miyuk/sun-dried kelp, nori/purple laver, sea lettuce/lettuce laver, sea palm, spirulina, or wakame/mekabu
- Fresh or frozen kale, cooked until tender

SEAWEED SEASONING/GARNISH – 1 tablespoon
- 1 tablespoon shredded nori with sesame seeds/*nori komi furikake*
- 1 tablespoon crushed wakame or nori (sheets toasted, then coarsely crushed; or pretoasted nori sheets/*yaki-nori* coarsely crushed)
- 1 tablespoon crumbled seasoned nori strips/*ajitsuke-nori*
- 1 to 2 teaspoons powdered nori/*ao nori/aosa*, or powered sea lettuce/green laver powder

SEED BUTTER See HEMPSEED BUTTER; SUNFLOWER SEED BUTTER

SEITAN, FLAVORED (wheat gluten meat substitute) – 1 pound
- 1 pound tempeh (stronger-tasting)
- 1 pound savory baked tofu (less chewy)
- 1 pound extra-firm tofu, weighted to remove excess water (less flavorful; less chewy)

SELF-RISING CORNMEAL *See CORNMEAL, SELF-RISING*

SELF-RISING FLOUR *See FLOUR, SELF-RISING, UNBLEACHED*

SELF-RISING WHOLE-WHEAT FLOUR *See FLOUR, WHOLE-WHEAT SELF-RISING*

SEMOLINA/FARINA/SEMOLA (coarsely ground durum wheat) – 1 cup *See also FLOUR, SEMOLINA, FINE-GRIND*
- 1 cup dry whole-wheat farina or dry regular Cream of Wheat

SERRA DA ESTRELA (Portuguese soft ewe's milk cheese) – 1 ounce
- 1 ounce fresh mild chèvre (goat cheese)

SERRANO CHILE/CHILE VERDE, FRESH (hot green chile) – 1
- 1 fresh japoné, cayenne, Fresno, or Thai chile
- 1 dried de árbol or cayenne chile
- 1 teaspoon sambal oelek or other hot chili paste; reduce the salt in the recipe accordingly
- 1/2 teaspoon crushed red pepper flakes or ground cayenne pepper

SERRANO HAM/JAMÓN SERRANO (Spanish salted dry-cured ham) – 1 pound
- 1 pound Ibérico ham, Italian proscuitto, Portuguese *presunto*, or French *Haute Savoie*
- 1 pound Iowa organic cured ham, such as La Quercia or Rossa Berkshire proscuitto

SESAME BUTTER *See SESAME PASTE; TAHINI*

SESAME LEAF *See SHISO, GREEN*

SESAME OIL, TOASTED/GOMA ABURA/MA YAU/DAU ME/XIANG YOU (Asian seasoning) – 1 tablespoon
- 1 teaspoon peanut oil mixed with 2 teaspoons ground toasted sesame seeds (or untoasted seeds dry-toasted, then ground)

☞ 1 tablespoon Indian sesame oil/*gingelly/til ka tel*
☞ 1 tablespoon roasted peanut oil

SESAME PASTE/GOMA PASTE/ZHI MA JIANG/NERI-GOMA (Chinese and Japanese seasoning) – 1 tablespoon *See also TAHINI*

☞ 1 tablespoon tahini plus few drops toasted sesame oil
☞ 1 tablespoon smooth unsweetened peanut butter plus few drops light/untoasted sesame oil

Make Your Own Toast 1 tablespoon white unhulled sesame seeds in a dry skillet over medium heat, stirring constantly, until golden, 1 to 2 minutes; then grind it in a spice mill/coffee grinder, with 1 teaspoon sesame oil (or soy oil) and a pinch of salt until reduced to a paste.

SESAME SALT/GOMASHIO (Japanese condiment) – 1/3 cup (about)

☞ 1/3 cup packaged smoked sesame seeds/*shirogoma*

Make Your Own Toast 1/2 cup black sesame seeds in a dry skillet over medium heat, stirring constantly, until fragrant, 3 to 4 minutes (or in a preheated 350°F oven for 5 to 7 minutes). Cool, then coarsely grind it in a spice mill/coffee grinder with 1 tablespoon coarse sea salt (or kosher salt). For 1 teaspoon, grind 1 teaspoon toasted sesame seeds plus few grains of sea salt in a salt mill or mortar.

SESAME SEED FLOUR – 1 cup

☞ 1 1/4 cups hulled/white sesame seeds, ground in a spice/coffee grinder until fine
☞ 1 cup pumpkin seed flour/meal, sunflower seed meal, or hemp-seed meal

SESAME SEEDS, HULLED WHITE/MUKI GOMA (Japanese condiment) – 1 ounce

☞ 1 ounce white poppy seeds, sunflower seed kernels, golden flax-seeds, hulled hemp seeds, salba seeds, or finely chopped blanched almonds

SEVEN-SPICE SEASONING *See JAPANESE SEVEN-SPICE SEASONING*

SEVILLE ORANGE *See ORANGE, SOUR/BITTER/SEVILLE*

SHADO BENI *See CULANTRO*

SHALLOTS, ASIAN/HOM DAENG/BAWANG MERAH/BRAMBANG, FRESH (small, purplish clove) – 1 bunch/3 or 4 small
- ☞ 2 red pearl onions, halved lengthwise
- ☞ 1 medium shallot
- ☞ 1 very small red onion

SHALLOTS, FRESH – 3 to 4 small, or 2 medium, or 1 extra-large
- ☞ 2 to 3 tablespoons freeze-dried shallots, softened in 2 tablespoons warm water for 10 minutes
- ☞ 6 Asian purple shallots (smaller, milder, and less moist) or Egyptian walking onions
- ☞ 1 small-to-medium chopped red onion plus a little minced garlic (more pungent)
- ☞ 1/2 cup chopped young thin leeks, ramp bulbs, green onions, or scallions (white part only)
- ☞ 1/2 to 1 teaspoon shallot salt; reduce the salt in the recipe by 1/2 to 1 teaspoon

SHALLOTS, FRIED, PACKAGED/CHIÊN HAHN HUONG (Vietnamese garnish) – 1 cup
- ☞ 1 cup (2 ounces) packaged fried onions, such as Indonesian *bawang goreng*
- ☞ 1 cup (2 ounces) canned domestic fried onions, such as French's

Make Your Own Thinly slice 5 or 6 shallots, then fry in 1/3 cup hot oil until crisp and golden, about 4 minutes. Drain on paper towels. (For a more pronounced flavor, add the shallots to cold oil and cook on medium heat until golden.)

SHANGHAI BOK CHOY/BOK CHOY SHOOTS – 1 pound
- ☞ 1 pound baby bok choy, or regular bok choy cut into 3-inch pieces

SHANGHAI NOODLES, FRESH – 1 pound *See also PASTA, STRAND OR RIBBON*
- 12 ounces dried bucatini, perciatelli, *spaghetti grossi*, or other thick, oval, white wheat noodles

SHAOXING/SHAO HSING/HUANG JIU (Chinese yellow rice wine, 36% proof) – 1 cup
- 1 cup Shaoxing cooking wine/*liao jiu/chiew* (contains salt)
- 1 cup glutinous yellow rice wine/*gnow mei dew*
- 1 cup medium-dry sherry, such as amontillado
- 1 cup dry vermouth

SHATTA (Sudanese condiment) – 1/3 cup
- 1 crushed garlic clove and 1 tablespoon ground cayenne pepper stirred into 1/3 cup lemon juice
- 1 teaspoon garlic paste stirred into 1/3 cup hot pepper sauce, such as Tabasco or Frank's RedHot Original

SHEMIJI/SHIMIJI MUSHROOMS *See OYSTER MUSHROOMS*

SHEPHERD'S PURSE/NAENGI (salad herb and Asian green vegetable) – 1 pound
- 12 ounces frozen shepherd's purse
- 1 pound mustard greens, green chard, or spinach
- 1 pound pennycress leaves/*Thlaspi arvense*, or wild mustard leaves/*Brassica rapa* or *B. nigra*

SHERIYA (Moroccan noodles) – 1 pound
- 1 pound vermicelli or spaghetti, broken or cut into 1-inch lengths

SHERRY, CREAM (sweet, dark fortified wine) – 2 tablespoons for cooking
- 2 tablespoons dry sherry plus 1/2 teaspoon dark brown sugar
- 2 tablespoons Madeira
- 2 tablespoons apple juice plus a few drops mild vinegar

SHERRY, DRY (fortified wine) – 2 tablespoons for cooking (not cooking sherry, which has salt added)
- 2 tablespoons dry vermouth or saké
- 2 1/2 tablespoons white wine (regular or nonalcoholic) plus few grains light brown sugar
- 2 tablespoons unseasoned rice vinegar

SHERRY PEPPER SAUCE (Caribbean hot pepper sauce) – 1 cup
Make Your Own Put 4 or 5 (or more) small hot dried chiles in a sterilized bottle and add 1 cup dry sherry. Cover and let sit in a cool, dark place for 10 or more days, shaking the bottle occasionally. It will keep for up to 6 months.

SHERRY VINEGAR, AGED/VINAGRE DE JEREZ/XERES (Spanish) – 1 tablespoon
- 1 tablespoon domestic aged sherry vinegar, such as Noble
- 1 1/2 teaspoons each white wine vinegar (or white balsamic vinegar) and dry sherry
- 1 tablespoon balsamic vinegar or red wine vinegar
- 1 tablespoon white wine vinegar or champagne vinegar (milder)

SHICHIMI TOGARASHI See JAPANESE SEVEN-SPICE SEASONING

SHIITAKE MUSHROOMS/GOLDEN OAK/PYOGO, FRESH – 1 pound
- 3 ounces dried shiitake mushrooms, soaked in hot water for 30 minutes, stem sides down and weighted with a saucer, squeezed dry, and stems discarded (The strained soaking water may be reserved for another use. For more deeply flavored mushrooms, soak for 8 to 12 hours in cool water.)
- 3 ounces dried flower mushrooms/*hua gu/hana/donko* (thick variety of shiitake with a more potent flavor; soak for 1 hour in hot water)
- 1 pound fresh cremini or matsutake mushrooms

SHIITAKE POWDER – 1/3 cup (packed)
- 1/2 ounce dried shiitake mushrooms, cleaned and ground in a spice/coffee grinder or blender until fine
- 1/3 cup porcini powder

SHINSHU MISO See MISO, LIGHT

SHISHITO PEPPER/SHISHITO-TOGARASHI, FRESH (small green Japanese pepper) – 3 or 4
- 3 or 4 Japanese green Fushimi peppers/*Fushimi-togarashi*
- 3 or 4 Spanish Padrón peppers
- 1 green Cubanelle pepper, or Italian frying pepper, cut into 1-inch-wide strips
- 1 medium green bell pepper or Anaheim chile, peeled and cut into 1-inch-wide strips

SHISO, GREEN/PERILLA LEAF/OHBO/AOJISO/GAENIP/TULKKAE/LA TIA TO, FRESH (Japanese seasoning and garnish) – 1 leaf
- 1 to 2 fresh wild shiso leaves/*Perilla frutescens* (smaller leaves; more flavorful)
- 1 fresh Vietnamese green/purple perilla/*la tia to* (stronger flavor; less expensive)
- 3 fresh holy basil, Thai basil, lemon basil, or anise basil leaves
- 2 fresh sweet basil leaves (Italian, French, or California) and 2 mint leaves
- 2 to 3 watercress or mint sprigs, baby spinach, baby arugula, or other small fresh leaves (for salad or garnish)
- 1 flat-leaf spinach leaf or palm-size lettuce leaf (for wrapping and shiso rolls)

SHISO, RED/PERILLA LEAF/BEEFSTEAK PLANT/AKAJISO/SHISO ZOJ, FRESH – 1 leaf
- 2 or 3 purple basil leaves, such as Dark Opal, Red Rubin, Purple Delight, or Purple Ruffles added just before cooking ends, or for garnish (loses color when cooked)

S

- ⇒ 1 dried red shiso leaf, or a good pinch of shiso powder (for coloring)

SHITO (GHANAIAN BLACK SAUCE) – 1 tablespoon
- ⇒ 1 tablespoon spicy chili sauce (lacks color and depth of flavor)

SHORTENING, VEGETABLE (100% fat) – 1 cup
- ⇒ 1 cup nonhydrogenated palm fruit oil shortening
- ⇒ 1 cup chilled refined coconut oil or coconut butter
- ⇒ 1 cup plus 2 tablespoons unsalted butter or unsalted stick margarine (if there is liquid in the recipe, reduce the liquid by 2 ounces/4 tablespoons; if the butter is salted, reduce the salt in the recipe by 1/2 teaspoon)
- ⇒ 3/4 cup plus 2 tablespoons rendered leaf lard (for biscuits and pastry crusts)
- ⇒ 7/8 cup strained bacon, poultry, or meat fat/drippings (for biscuits, cornmeal, savory crusts, and frying; not for deep-fat frying)
- ⇒ 3/4 cup vegetable oil (for cookies, quick breads, and pastry; for flaky pastry, mix the oil with 1 1/2 cups flour taken from the recipe; freeze until solid, 1 or 2 hours, then grate or process into the rest of the flour mixture)

SHOYU See SOY SAUCE, JAPANESE

SHRIMP – 1 pound, shelled
- ⇒ 1 pound small shelled prawns
- ⇒ 1 pound crab meat
- ⇒ 1 pound Japanese shrimp surimi
- ⇒ 1 pound vegan shrimp, such as Sophie's Kitchen
- ⇒ 1 pound shrimp-style konnyaku (for cooking)

SHRIMP, DRIED/HAY BEE/HAR MAI/HUNG HAENG/TOM KHO (Asian and Latin American cooking condiment) – 1/4 cup
- ⇒ 1/4 cup dried crayfish
- ⇒ 1/4 cup smoked salted fish, chopped or flaked

- 1/3 pound (27 or 28) small cooked fresh shrimp (used without soaking)
- 1 tablespoon minced anchovies

SHRIMP PASTE, FERMENTED/BAGOONG/BLACHAN/BELACAN / KAPI/MAM TOM/ NGAPI/TRASI/XIA JIANG (Southeast Asian pungent seasoning) – 1/2-inch cube

- 2 teaspoons finely chopped preroasted dried' shrimp paste
- 1 scant tablespoon fermented fish or fish paste, such as pickled gouramy fish (more pungent)
- 1 tablespoon anchovy paste, or 1 1/2 rinsed and mashed salt-packed anchovy fillets
- 1 tablespoon Chinese fermented black beans/*dow see,* Burmese fermented soybean paste/*tua nao,* or Japanese dark miso, such as *inaka* or *hatcho*
- 1 teaspoon Worcestershire sauce plus 1/2 teaspoon red miso/*inaka miso*

SHRIMP POWDER, DRIED/SHRIMP FLOSS/PAZUN CHAUK (Asian flavoring and thickener) – 1/2 cup (packed)

- 1/2 cup toasted chickpea flour plus 1 or 2 teaspoons dark Japanese miso, such as *hatcho,* or Burmese fermented soybean paste/ *tuo nao* (for vegan option)

Make Your Own Toast a scant 1/2 cup dried shrimp in a dry skillet over low heat for 4 to 5 minutes, then grind to a fine powder in a blender or spice/coffee grinder. Store, tightly sealed, in the freezer. Alternatively, soak the shrimp to cover until softened, 20 to 30 minutes; pat dry, then pulse in a food processor until flossy.

SHRIMP SAUCE, FERMENTED/HOM HA/HAE KOH/BALICHAO/MAM RUOC/PETIS (Southeast Asian jarred seasoning) – 1 tablespoon

- 1 tablespoon Chinese jarred fermented shrimp/*xia jiang*
- 2 tablespoons fish sauce, such as *nam pla, nuoc nam, patis* or *shottsuru,* plus a dash of oyster sauce
- 1 tablespoon anchovy paste, anchovy essence/syrup, or 1 1/2 rinsed and mashed salted anchovy fillets, thinned with a little soy sauce

SHRIMP STOCK – 1 cup
- 1 cup quick shrimp stock (Put 1 to 2 cups rinsed shrimp shells and heads in a small saucepan and barely cover with cold water; bring to a gentle boil, and simmer, covered, for 10 to 15 minutes; strain. Alternatively, heat the shells and heads in a dry pan until they turn pink before adding the water.)
- 1/2 to 1 teaspoon shrimp-flavored bouillon powder dissolved in 1 cup hot water

SHUNGIKU See CHRYSANTHEMUM LEAVES, EDIBLE

SICHUAN CHILI BEAN PASTE/PIXIAN CHILI BEAN SAUCE/DOU BAN JIANG/TOBAN JHAN (Chinese condiment) – 1/3 cup
- 1/4 cup fermented black beans/*dow see*, rinsed briefly in a fine sieve, then mashed with 1 1/2 tablespoons Chinese chili sauce or chili-garlic sauce
- 1/3 cup Korean chili bean paste/*gochujang*

SICHUAN PEPPER/ANISE PEPPER/DRIED PRICKLY ASH/SANSHO/ HUĀ JIĀO (Chinese seasoning) – 1 teaspoon ground/powdered
- 1/4 teaspoon each ground anise and allspice
- 1 or 2 teaspoons Sichuan pepper salt/*hu jiao yeni*; reduce salt in the recipe accordingly
- 1/2 teaspoon Chinese five-spice powder (only if it contains ground Sichuan/Sichuan peppercorns, not regular peppercorns)

Make Your Own Toast 1 tablespoon Sichuan/Szechuan peppercorns in a dry skillet over low heat until very fragrant and slightly darkened, 4 to 5 minutes. Crush with a mortar or rolling pin while hot, then sift through a fine-mesh sieve and measure (or cool, grind, sift, and measure). Discard the husks.

SICHUAN PEPPERCORNS/FAGARA – 1 teaspoon
- 1/4 teaspoon sansho powder/*kona-zansho* and 1/4 teaspoon ground black pepper
- 1 teaspoon *timur* (Nepali peppercorns)

- ☞ 1/4 teaspoon crushed dried Tasmanian pepperberries/mountain pepper
- ☞ 1/2 teaspoon black peppercorns and 1/8 teaspoon finely grated lemon zest

SICHUAN PEPPER OIL/HUĀ JIĀO YOU (Chinese seasoning) – 2/3 cup
Make Your Own Heat 1/4 cup toasted Sichuan/Szechuan peppercorns and 1 cup peanut oil over low heat for 10 minutes. Cool, then strain into a sterilized jar or bottle. Store, tightly covered, in the refrigerator. It will keep for up to 6 months. (Toast the peppercorns in a dry skillet over low heat until fragrant, 4 to 5 minutes.)

SICHUAN RED CHILI OIL/HONG YOU (chile and spice-infused oil) – 1 teaspoon
- ☞ 1 teaspoon Chinese savory chili oil/*chiu chow*
- ☞ 1 teaspoon Japanese chili oil/*rayu*

SICHUAN SALT/HUĀ JIĀO YAN (Chinese condiment) – 1/4 cup (about)
Make Your Own Toast 1 tablespoon Sichuan/Szechuan peppercorns and 3 tablespoons coarse sea salt in a dry skillet over low heat until the pepper starts to smoke faintly and the salt is slightly colored, about 5 minutes. Cool, sift, and grind to a powder. (For a coarser texture, toast and grind the peppercorns, then add to the untoasted salt.)

SICHUAN SWEET BEAN PASTE/SAUCE/TIAN MIAN JIANG/ TENMENJAN (Chinese condiment) – 1 tablespoon
- ☞ 2 teaspoons Chinese cooking sauce (*chee hou* sauce or hoisin) and 1 teaspoon rice vinegar

SICILIAN CITRUS FLAVORING/FIORI DI SICILIA – 1 teaspoon
- ☞ 1/8 teaspoon orange citrus oil, such as Boyajian, plus 1/2 teaspoon vanilla extract

SILK BEANS/FRIJOLES ROJOS DE SEDA SALVADOREÑO (small Salvadorian beans) – 1 pound

☞ 1 pound small red beans or red kidney beans (reduce the cooking time by one-third to one-half)

SILVERBEET *See CHARD/SWISS CHARD*

SIMPLE SYRUP *See SYRUP, SIMPLE*

SKYR (Icelandic super thick yogurt) – 1 cup
- ☞ *1 cup fromage blanc*
- ☞ 1 cup quark
- ☞ 1 cup *gvina levana* (Israeli soft white cheese)
- ☞ 1 cup full-fat plain Greek-style yogurt

SMEN *See SÂMNA/SAMNEH/SMEN*

SMETANA/SMATANA/SMITANE (Eastern European fermented cream) – 1 cup
- ☞ 1/2 cup heavy cream and 1/2 cup sour cream, whisked together, lightly covered, and left at room temperature for 2 to 4 hours (Store, tightly covered, in the refrigerator; it will keep for up to 1 week.)
- ☞ 1/2 cup each sour cream and crème fraîche (less fat)
- ☞ 1 cup Mexican sour cream/*crema Mexicana agria* (less fat)

SMOKED CHEESE *See CHEESE, SMOKED*

SMOKE FLAVORING *See LIQUID SMOKE*

SNOW PEAS/CHINESE SNOW PEAS/MANGE-TOUT – 1 pound
- ☞ 1 pound sugar snap peas, strings removed
- ☞ 1 pound Chinese yard-long beans, young green Romano beans, or Spanish Musica beans, trimmed, and cut into segments diagonally (longer cooking time)
- ☞ 1 pound broccoli stalks, peeled and thinly sliced (longer cooking time)

- 1 pound young radish seed pods (from radishes gone to seed or from a podding variety, such as Rat's Tail)

SNOW PEA SHOOTS See *PEA SHOOTS/LEAVES/TENDRILS*

SOBA NOODLES See *JAPANESE NOODLES, BUCKWHEAT*

SOBA SAUCE/KAESHI – 1 scant cup
- 3/4 cup Japanese soy sauce, and 2 tablespoons each mirin and granulated sugar brought to a boil and simmered until sugar dissolves, 2 to 3 minutes; it will keep for up to 3 months refrigerated

SOCCA See *CHICKPEA PANCAKES*

SODA WATER – 1 cup
- 1 cup seltzer, club soda, sparkling mineral water, or carbonated water
- 1 cup tonic water (contains quinine) or quinine water
- 1 cup tap or bottled water, 1 1/2 tablespoons distilled white vinegar, and 3/4 teaspoon baking soda (for batter; use immediately)
- 1 cup sparkling cider (for sweet applications)

SODIUM NITRATE See *SALTPETER*

SODIUM NITRITE (preserving/curing agent for sausage and meat)
- Celery juice powder (for products to be cooked before serving; use following the package directions)
- 1 drop red food coloring, dissolved in liquid from the recipe (for color only; not for preservation)

SOISSONS (French haricot beans) – 1 pound
- 1 pound cannellini beans, white kidney beans, Great Northern beans, navy beans, or yellow French beans/*haricots beurre*

SOJU See *KOREAN RICE WINE, SWEET COOKING*

SOOJI/SUJI/RAWA (Indian course-textured semolina flour) – 1 cup
> ⇨ 1 cup wheat farina or dry regular Cream of Wheat

SOPAIPILLA (Mexican deep-fried pastry) – 2 dozen
> ⇨ 6 unbaked refrigerated biscuits, such as Pillsbury buttermilk, rolled very thin, cut into quarters and deep-fried at 360°F until puffed and hollow, 2 to 4 minutes (drain on paper towels)

SOPRESSATA, SWEET (Italian lightly smoked, spicy dry sausage) – 1 pound
> ⇨ 1 pound Calabrian/Calabrese or Sardinian/Sardo salami (more piquant; contains red pepper)
> ⇨ 1 pound pepperoni, or other firm, spicy salami

SORGHUM/GUINEA CORN/KAFFIR CORN/JOWAR (African and Indian cereal grain) – 1 cup
> ⇨ 1 cup hulled millet (tastes best when lightly toasted in a dry skillet before cooking)

SORGHUM FLOUR – 1 cup
> ⇨ 1 cup light-colored teff flour or superfine brown rice flour
> ⇨ 1 cup whole-wheat pastry flour (contains gluten)

SORGHUM SYRUP/SORGHUM MOLASSES/SWEET SORGHUM (Southern U.S. sweetener with a malty flavor) – 1 tablespoon
> ⇨ 1 tablespoon cane syrup, golden syrup, dark honey, light unsulphured molasses, or maple syrup
> ⇨ 4 teaspoons dark corn syrup

SORREL, COMMON GARDEN/BELLEVILLE – 1 pound
> ⇨ 1 pound French sorrel/Buckler Leaf sorrel (milder and more lemony)
> ⇨ 1 pound wood sorrel/*Oxalis stricta* (smaller leaves; more acidic)
> ⇨ 1 pound young patience/patience dock/*Rumex patientia* (mild acidic taste)
> ⇨ 1 pound curly dock/yellow dock/*Rumex crispus* (thicker leaves; use the tender inner ones, central vein removed if necessary)

- 6 to 8 ounces commercial jarred cooked sorrel
- 1 pound baby arugula, watercress, baby spinach, or Boston lettuce, sprinkled with a little lemon juice just before serving (for salads)
- 1 pound baby spinach or young tender spinach, plus a little fresh lemon juice added just before serving (for soups)

SOUP THICKENER See THICKENER FOR SOUP

SOUP, CANNED CREAM OF See CELERY SOUP, CANNED CREAM OF; CHICKEN SOUP, CANNED CREAM OF; MUSHROOM SOUP, CANNED CREAM OF

SOUR CREAM (18% butterfat) – 1 cup
- 1 cup crème fraîche, Mexican *crema*, or Venezuelan *nata* (higher fat; less sour)
- 1 cup *smetana/smitane* or quark (thinner consistency; lower-fat)
- 1 cup plain full-fat Greek-style yogurt (thicker consistency; more calories)
- 1 tablespoon lemon juice (or distilled white vinegar) stirred into 1 cup heavy cream (or evaporated milk); left at room temperature until slightly thickened, 30 to 40 minutes; and refrigerated for 4 hours before using
- 3/4 cup natural cream cheese, 1/4 cup milk or water, and a dash of lemon juice, blended until smooth and creamy
- 1/2 cup each plain yogurt and creamed cottage cheese, blended until smooth and creamy
- 1 cup (8 ounces) firm or extra-firm silken tofu, 1 to 4 tablespoons canola or olive oil, 2 tablespoons lemon juice, and 1 teaspoon salt, processed in a blender until smooth and creamy
- 1 cup soaked cashews, 1/2 cup water, 2 (or more) tablespoons lemon juice, and 1/4 to 1/2 teaspoon sea salt, processed in a high-speed blender until smooth and creamy
- 1 cup small-curd or creamed cottage cheese, 1/4 cup plain yogurt or buttermilk, and 1 or 2 teaspoons lemon juice (optional), processed until smooth, then drained 2 or 3 hours in a sieve lined

with dampened cheesecloth (Alternatively, use 2 tablespoons milk and 1 teaspoon lemon juice in place of the yogurt or buttermilk.)

SOUR CREAM – 1 cup for baking
- 3/4 cup whole milk and 1/3 cup butter, heated until the butter melts, then mixed with 1 tablespoon lemon juice or distilled white vinegar and left at room temperature until slightly thickened, about 30 minutes
- 1 cup soy sour cream, coconut yogurt, or thick canned coconut milk (dairy- and lactose-free)
- Sour cream powder rehydrated with water following the package directions

SOUR CREAM – 1 cup for cooked sauces See also CRÈME FRAÎCHE
- 1 cup whole-milk goat yogurt (thinner consistency; tangier flavor; does not separate on boiling)
- 1 (3-ounce) package cream cheese, cut up and whisked into the sauce until thoroughly incorporated (if too thick, add a tablespoon or two of milk)
- Sour cream powder, rehydrated with water following the package directions

SOUR CREAM, FAT-FREE OR LOW-FAT – 1 cup
- 1 tablespoon lemon juice or distilled white vinegar, stirred into 1 cup fat-free evaporated milk and left at room temperature until slightly thickened, about 30 minutes (chill for 4 hours before using)
- 1 cup plain nonfat or low-fat quark (richer texture)

SOUR CREAM, MEXICAN See CRÈMA MEXICANA

SOURDOUGH STARTER (tangy leavener for bread and pastries) – 1 cup (8 to 9 ounces)
- 1 teaspoon dry active yeast sprinkled over 1/2 cup lukewarm water and left to dissolve, 3 to 5 minutes, before stirring in 1/2 cup

all-purpose or whole-grain flour (Cover loosely with plastic wrap and leave at room temperature until thick and bubbly, 2 to 3 days.)
- ⇨ 1/8 teaspoon dry powdered/dehydrated sourdough starter (per loaf in the recipe)
- ⇨ 2 to 3 teaspoons instant sourdough flavoring (per cup of flour in the recipe; not for leavening or better keeping qualities)
- ⇨ 1/4 teaspoon citric acid (per each loaf in the recipe; for sour flavor only, not for leavening or better keeping qualities)
- ⇨ 1 cup overnight poolish (for a little sourdough flavor only)
- ⇨ Strained dill pickle brine in place of half the water (for tangy sourdough flavor in rye bread)
- ⇨ Yeasted whole-wheat, no-knead-type dough fermented at room temperature for up to 18 hours (for slightly tangy sourdough flavor only)
- ⇨ Yeasted white bread dough stored for several days in the refrigerator after the first rise and before the second rise (for sourdough flavor only)

SOUR MIX (bottled product for cocktails) – 1 cup
- ⇨ 1/2 cup heavy simple syrup and 1/2 cup fresh lemon juice (or half lemon, half lime)

SOUR PLUM/PRUNE/ALOO BUKHARA (Central Asian souring agent) – 1 medium
- ⇨ 1 umeboshi (Japanese salt-pickled dried plum) or 3 *umeboshi-sa* (tiny plum paste balls)
- ⇨ 2 teaspoons jarred umeboshi puree/sour plum paste/*bainiku/neri-ume*, or pomegranate molasses
- ⇨ 1 regular prune, soaked in white vinegar or umeboshi plum vinegar for 8 to 10 hours

SOUR SALT See CITRIC ACID/CITRIC SALT

SOURSOP/GUANÁBANA (large tropical fruit) – 1 pound
- ⇨ 12 ounces frozen soursop pulp

- 1 pound atemoya, cherimoya, or sweetsop (smaller and sweeter)
- 8 ounces canned soursop nectar/*jugo de guanábana* (for flavor only)

SOYBEAN PASTE, FERMENTED See KOREAN CHILI BEAN PASTE; MISO

SOY BUTTER – 2 cups
Make Your Own Combine 3/4 cup powdered soy milk, 3/4 cup water, 1 teaspoon salt in a double boiler and cook for 25 minutes; gradually whisk in 1 cup canola oil and beat until thick. Store, refrigerated, in a tightly sealed container.

SOY MILK – 2 cups
- 1/2 cup soy powder (powdered soy milk) and 1 3/4 cups water, blended until smooth
- 8 ounces soft silken tofu and 1 cup cold water blended until smooth (For thinner soy milk, increase the amount of water; for sweeter soy milk, add 2 teaspoons rice syrup or light agave syrup.)
- 2/3 cup soy flour and 2 cups water, whisked together; simmered for 30 minutes, stirring occasionally; strained through a fine-mesh sieve; and flavored with sweetener or vanilla, if desired

SOY NUT BUTTER – 8 ounces
Make Your Own Process 8 ounces plain or roasted cooked soybeans, 1/4 teaspoon salt (optional), and 1 to 2 tablespoons vegetable oil in a high-power blender or food processor until reduced to a paste, scraping down the sides of the bowl as needed. Store, refrigerated, in a lidded jar for up to 2 weeks.

SOY PROTEIN CONCENTRATE (sausage-making binder to improve moisture retention) – 14 ounces for 25 pounds meat
- 1 1/2 ounces concentrated carrot fiber binder/C-Binder (per 25 pounds meat)
- 12 ounces nonfat dry milk powder (per 25 pounds meat)

SOY PROTEIN ISOLATE (sausage-making binder to improve moisture retention) – 1 1/4 cups for 10 pounds meat
- 2 cups soy protein concentrate (per 10 pounds meat)

SOY SAUCE (ALL PURPOSE) – 1 tablespoon
- 1 tablespoon reduced-sodium/lower sodium or lite soy sauce (regular or gluten-free)
- 2 teaspoons tamari soy sauce (contains wheat but naturally brewed and without additives)
- 2 teaspoons gluten-free tamari, such as San-J, Crystal, or Westbrae
- 1 tablespoon citrus-seasoned soy sauce, such as Japanese ponzu-seasoned/*ponzu shoyu* or Filipino calamansi-seasoned/*toyo mansi* (for condiments and dressings)
- 1 tablespoon gluten-free liquid aminos, such as Dr. Bronner's or Bragg's
- 1 tablespoon gluten-free and soy-free coconut aminos, such as Coconut Secret, plus a pinch of salt
- 2 to 3 teaspoons Japanese fermented rice/*shio-koji* or miso (thicker consistency; for cooking)
- 1 tablespoon Maggi Seasoning or oyster sauce (for a small amount)
- 2 teaspoons molasses, 1 teaspoon balsamic vinegar, and a few grains of sugar (for a small amount)
- 1 tablespoon Chinese soy sauce powder (for cooking or barbecue dry rubs)

SOY SAUCE, CHINESE DARK/BLACK/TABLE SOY/CHO YO/SEE YAU/ LAO CHOU – 1 tablespoon
- 1 tablespoon Japanese organic tamari (wheat-free, naturally fermented, darker, thicker, more flavorful)
- 1 tablespoon Japanese dark soy sauce (darker, slightly sweeter, less salty)
- 1 tablespoon mushroom soy sauce (richer tasting)
- 2 teaspoons Chinese light soy sauce and 1 teaspoon black/dark/sweet soy sauce (Chinese or Thai)
- 1 tablespoon Chinese light soy sauce plus 1/4 teaspoon molasses

SOY SAUCE, CHINESE DOUBLE DARK/DOUBLE BLACK/SWEET/YEWN SHE JIANG (such as Koon Chun) – 1 tablespoon

- ⇨ 1 tablespoon Malaysian sweet, dark soy sauce/*tim cheong*
- ⇨ 2 teaspoons Chinese dark soy sauce plus 1 teaspoon brown sugar or molasses

SOY SAUCE, CHINESE LIGHT/PALE OR THIN/JIANG JING/JIANG YAO/ SHENG CHOU – 1 tablespoon

- ⇨ 1 tablespoon Japanese all-purpose soy sauce/*shoyu*, such as Kikkoman; or Korean soy sauce/*ganjang* (darker, less salty, and a touch sweeter)
- ⇨ 1 tablespoon Chinese white soy sauce/*yin bai jiang*, or Japanese white soy sauce/*shirojoyu* (a little sweeter, but will not add color)
- ⇨ 1 tablespoon Chinese dark soy sauce/*cho yo* (thicker, stronger, a little sweeter, and less salty)

SOY SAUCE, FILIPINO/TOYO – 1 tablespoon

- ⇨ 1 tablespoon Japanese-style soy sauce/*soyu* (saltier and thinner)

SOY SAUCE, FILIPINO KALAMANSI/TOYOMANSI – 1 tablespoon

- ⇨ 1 tablespoon Lu soy/*lu shiu* (spicy lime soy sauce; contains spices, ginger, sugar)
- ⇨ 1 1/2 teaspoons Filipino soy sauce/*toyo* (or Japanese-style soy sauce) and 1 1/2 teaspoons fresh calamansi juice (or Meyer lemon juice)

SOY SAUCE, INDONESIAN/KECAP ASIN (dark salty soy sauce) – 1 tablespoon

- ⇨ 1 tablespoon Malaysian soy sauce/*kicap pekat*
- ⇨ 1 tablespoon Chinese dark/black soy sauce (thinner and less salty)

SOY SAUCE, INDONESIAN/KECAP MANIS (thick sweet soy sauce)
See KECAP MANIS

SOY SAUCE, JAPANESE ALL-PURPOSE REGULAR DARK/KOIKUCHI SHOYU (such as Kikkoman) – 1 tablespoon
- 1 tablespoon Japanese organic whole soybean soy sauce/*maru-daizu shoyu,* or unpasteurized/raw soy sauce/*nama shoyu* (contains wheat)
- 1 tablespoon Japanese low-salt/reduced-salt soy sauce/*gen'en shoyu* (contains additives)
- 2 1/2 teaspoons Japanese light-colored soy sauce/*usukuchi shoyu* or Chinese regular/light soy sauce (thinner and saltier)
- 1 tablespoon Japanese white soy sauce/*shiro shoyu* (very light colored, mellow, and fairly sweet)
- 1 tablespoon Japanese strong-flavored rich soy sauce/*saishikomi* (dark brown and thick; for sashimi and sushi)

SOY SAUCE, JAPANESE LIGHT-COLORED/USUKUCHI SHOYU (saltier and thinner than all-purpose regular dark soy sauce) – 1 tablespoon
- 1 tablespoon Chinese light/thin regular soy sauce
- 1 tablespoon soy sauce wheat-free replacements, such as Dr. Bronner's or Braggs Liquid Aminos; or wheat- and soy-free replacement, such as Coconut Secret Coconut Aminos
- 2 teaspoon teriyaki sauce and 1 teaspoon water
- 1 teaspoon Maggi Seasoning

SOY SAUCE, KOREAN/GANJANG/KANJANG (medium-bodied) – 1 tablespoon
- 1 tablespoon Japanese-style all-purpose dark soy sauce (saltier)
- 1 tablespoon Chinese light/thin regular soy sauce (saltier and less sweet)

SOY SAUCE, MALAYSIAN/KICAP CAIR (light soy sauce) – 1 tablespoon
- 1 tablespoon Chinese or Japanese all-purpose regular soy sauce

SOY SAUCE, MALAYSIAN/KICAP HITAM (dark sweet soy sauce) – 1 tablespoon
- 1 tablespoon Indonesian thick sweet soy sauce/*kecap manis*

SOY SAUCE, MALAYSIAN/KICAP PEKAT (dark soy sauce) – 1 tablespoon
- 1 tablespoon Indonesian all-purpose soy sauce/*kecap asin*
- 1 tablespoon Chinese dark/black soy sauce (thinner and less salty)

SOY SAUCE, MUSHROOM (dark soy sauce infused with nameko or shiitake mushrooms) – 1 tablespoon
- 1 tablespoon dark soy sauce plus a pinch of sugar or drop of honey

SOY SAUCE, THAI SWEET BLACK/NAM PLA SIIW/SIEW DAM – 1 tablespoon
- 1 tablespoon Indonesian thick sweet soy sauce/*kecap manis* (thicker)
- 1 tablespoon Chinese thick soy sauce/*jee yow* plus a little unsul-phured molasses as sweetener

SOY SAUCE, THAI THIN/SEE EIW/SI-EW – 1 tablespoon
- 1 tablespoon all-purpose Chinese light soy sauce

SOY SAUCE, VIETNAMESE/XI DAU – 1 tablespoon
- 1 tablespoon all-purpose Chinese or Japanese light soy sauce

SOY SAUCE, WHITE/YIN BAI JIANG/SHIROJOYU – 1 tablespoon
- 2 teaspoons all-purpose soy sauce plus 1 teaspoon water

SPAGHETTI See PASTA, STRAND OR RIBBON

SPECK, GERMAN (mildly cured and smoked pork fat) – 1 pound
- 1 pound Italian *lardo*
- 1 pound thinly sliced bacon

SPECK, ITALIAN (cold-smoked seasoned pork product) – 1 pound
- 1 pound Italian or domestic prosciutto (less firm; unsmoked; lacks juniper aroma)
- 1 pound Westphalian ham (hot-smoked; smokier flavor)

➼ 1 pound Serrano ham or Ibérico ham (lacks juniper flavor)

SPELT BERRIES/GROATS – 1 cup
➼ 1 cup pearled spelt or pearl barley (less cooking time)
➼ 1 cup whole-wheat berries or whole-grain/pot barley
➼ 1 cup semi-pearled farro (less cooking time)

SPELT FLOUR See FLOUR, SPELT WHOLE GRAIN

SPELT, PEARLED – 1 cup
➼ 1 cup pearl barley
➼ 1 cup cracked wheat (less cooking time)

SPIGARELLO (heirloom broccoli rabe) – 1 pound
➼ 1 pound broccoli rabe or Chinese broccoli (less leafier and delicate)
➼ 1 1/2 pounds escarole (dark outer leaves) or Chinese mustard greens/*amsoy*

SPINACH, BABY – 6 ounces (6 cups loosely packed)
➼ 6 ounces baby arugula, mâche/lamb's lettuce, amaranth/Chinese spinach, young stemmed mallow leaves, miner's lettuce/claytonia, New Zealand spinach, young orach/mountain spinach, or mizuna

SPINACH, MATURE FLAT-LEAF OR CURLY-LEAF – 1 pound whole spinach (2 bunches)
➼ 1 (8-ounce) bag trimmed fresh leaf spinach
➼ 1 (10-ounce) package frozen leaf or chopped spinach
➼ 10 to 12 ounces Swiss chard, especially Erbette variety, stripped from the stems
➼ 1 to 2 bunches fresh beet greens, young fava greens, Good King Henry, lamb's quarters, Taiwan lettuce/*a choy,* or Texsel greens/Abyssinian mustard
➼ 8 to 12 ounces young stinging nettle shoots and tops/*Urtica dioica* (use gloves when handling raw nettles; cooking and pulverizing removes their sting)

⇨ 8 to 12 ounces wild fresh greens, such as green amaranth/pig-weed/*Amaranthus refroflexus,* mature bishop's weed/*Aegopodium podagraria,* deadnettle/*Lamium purpureum,* or young milk thistle leaves/*Silybum marianum* (smaller leaves; usually milder flavor)

SPINACH, WILD/BOROBORABA (African vegetable) – 1 pound, trimmed
⇨ 1 1/2 pounds curly-leaf/Savoy spinach, trimmed

SPIRALEN (German spiraled pasta) – 1 pound
⇨ 1 pound Italian fusilli, or fusilli lunghi cut or broken into pieces

SPLENDA (sucralose and maltodextrin sweetener) – 1 cup
⇨ 1 cup granulated sugar (has more browning properties)
⇨ 1 cup stevia and maltodextrin sweetener, such as Stevia Extract in the Raw
⇨ 1 1/3 cups erythritol/fermented cane sugar, such as Z-sweet or Organic Zero

SPRING ROLL WRAPPERS – 1 pound
⇨ 1 pound rice paper/wafer paper, cut to size
⇨ 1 pound phyllo dough, cut to size
⇨ 1 pound thin/Hong Kong–style wonton wrappers
⇨ 1 pound lumpia wrappers
⇨ 1 pound regular wonton wrappers or egg roll wrappers (thicker)

SPRINKLES, INDIVIDUAL COLORED – 1 ounce
⇨ 1 ounce white sprinkles shaken with a pinch of powdered food coloring in a tightly closed jar or sealable plastic bag

SPROUTS (tender sprouts of germinated seeds) – 1 ounce
⇨ 1 ounce adzuki/aduki (slightly sweet), alfalfa (mild), amaranth (mild), arugula (peppery), barley (starchy and mild), broccoli (mild), buckwheat (starchy and hearty), cabbage (mild), chickpea

(mild), chive (peppery), clover (mild), daikon (peppery), fenugreek (slightly bitter), kale (mild), kamut (mild), leek (peppery), lentil (mild), millet (mild), mitsuba (peppery), mustard (peppery), mung bean (nutty and crunchy), onion (peppery), pumpkin (nutty and crunchy), quinoa (mild), radish (peppery), red clover (mild), soybean (nutty and crunchy), or sunflower (nutty and crunchy)
- 1 ounce snow peas, cut into narrow strips
- 1 ounce pea shoots, tender chickweed tips/*Stellaria media*, or other plant shoots/microgreens

SPRUCE TIP SYRUP (Norwegian honey-like sweetener) – 1/2 cup (about)
- 1 cup young, tender, unsprayed spruce sprigs/tips/*Picea* species, about 2 inches long (or balsam, Douglas fir, pine, or other fir sprigs), boiled in a simple syrup (1 cup each water and granulated sugar) until thick and syrupy (strain through a fine-mesh sieve and discard the spruce)

SQUAB (young farm-raised pigeon) – 1 (about 1 pound)
- 1 quail, preferably semi-boned (smaller)
- 1 young pheasant (larger)
- 1 small guinea hen/fowl (much larger; gamier tasting)
- 1 Cornish game hen or poussin (larger; fattier; white-colored meat)
- 1 Chicken quarter: leg and thigh (less gamey tasting)

SQUASH, ASIAN (bitter melon, bottle gourd, angled loofah/Chinese okra, fuzzy melon/hairy melon, winter melon/wax gourd) – 1 pound
- 1 pound chayote/mirliton, marrow, large deseeded zucchini, or other summer squash (adjust the cooking time accordingly)

SQUASH BLOSSOMS, SUMMER (edible flowers for stuffing or frying in batter) – 8 ounces
- 8 ounces unsprayed cucumber, melon, or pumpkin blossoms (not as delicate)
- 8 ounces unsprayed winter squash or bottle gourd blossoms (more delicate)

☞ 8 ounces unsprayed daylily blossoms (trim off the fibrous end)

SQUASH, SMALL WINTER (for stuffing) – 1 or 2
☞ 1 or 2 acorn, chayote, delicata, golden nugget, mini pumpkin, pepper squash, small buttercup, or Sweet Dumpling squash

SQUASH, SUMMER See ZUCCHINI

SQUID, FRESH RAW – 1 pound
☞ 1 pound cuttlefish (more tender)
☞ 1 pound baby octopus (less tender)

SQUID INK, CANNED OR FRESH – 1 tablespoon
☞ 1 tablespoon fresh cuttlefish ink

SRIRACHA See THAI HOT CHILI SAUCE

SRIRACHA SALT – 1 cup
Make Your Own Mix 1 cup kosher salt with 1/4 cup Sriracha sauce and spread in a thin layer on a parchment-lined baking sheet. Bake in a preheated 200°F oven until dry, 2 to 3 hours, then cool and pulse in a food processor until finely ground. Store in a tightly sealed container in a cool, dry place; it will keep for several weeks.

STAR ANISE (Chinese seasoning) – 1 whole star (8 points)
☞ 3/4 teaspoon crushed or broken star anise pieces
☞ 1/2 teaspoon ground star anise
☞ 3/4 teaspoon anise seeds (crushed with the side of a knife)
☞ 1/2 teaspoon ground anise or fennel
☞ 1/2 teaspoon Chinese five-spice powder (for savory dishes)

STAR ANISE, GROUND – 1 teaspoon
☞ 2 whole star anise, crushed; or 1 1/2 teaspoons broken pieces
☞ 1 1/2 teaspoons anise or fennel seeds, ground in a pepper mill or spice/coffee grinder

☞ 1 teaspoon ground anise
☞ 1 teaspoon Chinese five-spice powder (for savory dishes)

STARCH SYRUP/SWEETENER *See RICE MALT SYRUP*

STAR FRUIT *See CARAMBOLA*

STEAK, DRY-AGED *See BEEF STEAK, AGED*

STEAK SAUCE *See BROWN SAUCE, BOTTLED*

STEVIA LEAF EXTRACT (liquid herbal sweetener) – 8 ounces (1 cup)
Make Your Own Add 3/4 cup lightly crushed dried stevia leaves/
Stevia rebaudiana to 1 1/2 cups 180° F water; cover and steep for
40 minutes. Strain and transfer to a dark-colored bottle; store in the
refrigerator for up to 2 weeks. (One teaspoon equals 1 tablespoon
granulated sugar.)

STILTON (British blue-veined, creamy white cheese) – 1 ounce *See
also BLUE CHEESE, STRONG*
☞ 1 ounce Blue Cheshire, Cashel Blue, Maytag Blue, Point Reyes Bay
Blue, Fourme d'Ambert, or Shropshire Blue
☞ 1 ounce Gorgonzola, Blu del Moncenisio, or Roquefort (softer;
more pungent)

STOCK, CHICKEN OR MEAT (flavorful cooking liquid) – 1 cup
☞ 1 cup liquid or broth saved from poaching or cooking chicken or
meat (save and freeze the liquid until there is sufficient amount)
☞ 2/3 cup canned reduced-sodium chicken or beef broth (or boxed
no-salt chicken or beef stock) diluted with 1/3 cup water
☞ 1/2 teaspoon chicken or beef instant stock/bouillon granules dissolved in 1 cup hot water
☞ 1/2 teaspoon vegetarian chicken or beef broth/stock powder dissolved in 1 cup hot water
☞ 1/2 cube reduced-sodium chicken, lamb, or beef bouillon dissolved in 1 cup hot water

- ⊵ 1/2 teaspoon concentrated stock base paste, such as Bovril or Better than Bouillon, dissolved in 1 cup hot water
- ⊵ 1/2 teaspoon yeast extract, such as Marmite or Vegemite, dissolved in 1 cup hot water
- ⊵ Seasoning packet from a 3-ounce beef-flavored instant ramen noodle package dissolved in 1 cup hot water
- ⊵ 1 cup mushroom stock made from porcini mushroom–flavored bouillon granules or wild mushroom bouillon granules
- ⊵ 1 cup stout (for full-bodied meat dishes)
- ⊵ 1 cup plain salted water

STOCK, FISH/FUMET – 1 cup

- ⊵ 1 cup hot water plus 1/2 teaspoon instant fish bouillon granules, or 1/2 cube fish or shrimp-flavored bouillon, or 1/2 to 3/4 teaspoon seafood base or fish glaze, or 1/3 (1 1/2-ounce) package concentrated seafood stock
- ⊵ 1 scant teaspoon dried bonito flakes simmered in 1 cup water a few minutes, then strained
- ⊵ 1/2- to 1-inch square kombu/kelp added to 1 cup hot water and gently heated until the water is flavorful, 3 or 4 minutes; remove from heat and remove kombu (do not let boil)
- ⊵ 1/3 cup bottled clam juice diluted with 2/3 cup water, vegetable broth, or dry white wine
- ⊵ 1 cup boxed seafood cooking stock (diluted with water, if desired)
- ⊵ Liquid from water-packed canned fish plus water to make 1 cup

Make Your Own Wash shrimp shells and heads, lobster shells, or fish head and bones (gills removed), well under cold running water, then place in a saucepan and barely cover with water. Bring to a gentle boil and simmer, covered, for 20 to 30 minutes. Cool, strain, then measure 1 cup.

STOCK, HAM *See HAM STOCK; HAM STOCK, SMOKED*

STOCK, KOMBU *See KOMBU STOCK*

STOCK, LOBSTER *See LOBSTER STOCK*

STOCK, SHRIMP *See SHRIMP STOCK*

STOCK SYRUP *See SYRUP, SIMPLE*

STOCK, TRUFFLE *See TRUFFLE STOCK*

STOCK, VEGETABLE – 1 cup
- 1 cup liquid saved from cooked or steamed vegetables (excluding artichoke, broccoli, cabbage, cauliflower, kale, turnip, and other strong smelling or bitter vegetables)
- Well-washed vegetable trimmings (peelings and tough stems) simmered, uncovered, in salted water 30 minutes, then strained without pressing on solids (Save and freeze trimmings until enough is accumulated to make stock; to speed flavor extraction, cut them into small pieces.)
- 1 cup soaking liquid from dried mushrooms (strained to remove grit) or shiitake mushroom stems (removed before serving)
- 1 cup soaking liquid from sun-dried tomatoes
- 1/2 vegetable stock cube, mushroom stock cube, or yeast-free stock cube, such as Kallo, dissolved in 1 cup boiling water (reduce the salt in the recipe by 1 teaspoon)
- 1/2 teaspoon powdered vegetable seasoning, vegetable stock granules, or soup base dissolved in 1 cup hot water
- 1/2 (28-gram) package vegetable stock reduction, such as Knorr Stockpot, dissolved in 1 cup water
- 1 cup water and a piece of Parmesan cheese rind (for bean-based soups; has a rich, smoky flavor; freeze the rind from used cheese and use as needed)

STRACCHINO, FRESH *See CRESCENZA STRACCHINO*

STRACCIATELLA (Italian shredded mozzarella and cream mixture) – 4 ounces
- 4 ounces burrata cheese

STRATTO DI POMODORO (Sicilian tomato paste) – 1 tablespoon
⇨ 1 tablespoon double-concentrated tomato paste (comes in a tube), or tomato extract (comes in a glass jar)

STRAWBERRIES – 1 cup
⇨ 1 cup raspberries (more delicate)
⇨ 1 cup tayberries (a cross between blackberry and red raspberry; bright deep purple)
⇨ 1 cup loganberries (a cross between blackberry and raspberry; reddish purple)
⇨ 1 cup berrylike fruits of strawberry spinach/*Chenopodium capitatum* (for cooking and jellies; bright red)
⇨ 1 cup strawberry guava (smaller and sweeter version of guava; reddish purple)

STRAWBERRY POWDER/DUST – 1 ounce
⇨ 1 ounce freeze-dried strawberries pulsed in a blender or processor until fine

STRAWBERRY SUGAR – 1 cup
⇨ 1 cup freeze-dried strawberries and 3/4 cup granulated sugar processed until combined
⇨ 1 cup granulated sugar and 1/2 teaspoon strawberry extract kneaded together in a plastic bag until evenly distributed; spread on a baking sheet and left at room temperature until the sugar is dry, 30 to 60 minutes

STRAW MUSHROOMS, FRESH – 8 ounces
⇨ 1 (4-ounce) can straw mushrooms
⇨ 8 ounces fresh enoki, oyster, or white button mushrooms

STRIDOLI/STRIGOLI (Italian lemony-tasting wild green) – 1 cup
⇨ 1 cup sorrel or baby spinach

STROOP (Dutch thick sweet syrup) – 1 cup
⇨ 1 cup golden syrup or strong honey

STRUDEL DOUGH – 1 pound
- 1 pound fresh or frozen regular or whole-wheat phyllo/filo dough (thaw overnight if frozen)
- 1 pound frozen Armenian or Turkish *yufka* dough (little thicker; comes in round sheets)
- 1 pound frozen all-butter, ready-to-bake puff pastry (less crisp)

STURGEON, SMOKED – 4 ounces See also CAVIAR, BLACK; CAVIAR RED
- 4 ounces smoked arctic char, bluefish, haddock, mackerel, pollock, sablefish, salmon, trout, or whitefish

SUCANAT (dried sugarcane juice) See SUGAR, GRANULATED

SUCRALOSE See SPLENDA

SUCUK (Turkish spicy cured sausage) – 1 pound
- 1 pound linguiça, chouriço, kielbasa, salami, or other spicy ready-to-eat sausage

SUDACHI (Japanese lime-like citrus; cross between mandarin and ichang papeda) – 1
- 1 kabosu or yuzu (larger; for juice and zest)
- 1 Key lime or small lemon (for juice and zest)
- Fresh or bottled yuzu juice (for juice)

SUET, BEEF – 4 ounces grated (1/2 cup)
- 1/2 cup shredded vegetarian suet, such as Atora light
- 1/2 cup coarsely grated frozen or chilled leaf lard
- 1/2 cup coarsely grated frozen or chilled shortening
- 1/2 cup plus 1 tablespoon finely chopped frozen unsalted butter (if there is liquid in the recipe, reduce the liquid by 2 tablespoons)

SUET, VEGETARIAN – 1/2 cup
- 1/2 cup coarsely grated frozen or chilled nonhydrogenated solid vegetable shortening

SUGAR, BAKER'S See SUGAR, SUPERFINE; SUGAR, GOLDEN BAKER'S

SUGAR, BARBADOS See SUGAR, MUSCOVADO

SUGAR, BLACK See JAPANESE BLACK SUGAR

SUGAR, BRAZILIAN REFINED/ACUCAR See SUGAR, GRANULATED

SUGAR, BROWN See SUGAR, DARK BROWN; SUGAR, LIGHT BROWN/
GOLDEN

SUGAR, BROWN ROCK/SLAB/PIAN TANG/PEEN TONG (Chinese large-crystal sugar) – 1 (5 x 1-inch slab) (3 1/4 ounces coarsely grated or finely chopped)
- 1/2 cup firmly packed dark brown sugar plus 1 teaspoon unsulphured molasses

SUGARCANE, FRESH – 1 (12-inch-long) cane
- 1 (20-ounce) can sugarcane sticks in syrup

SUGAR, CASTOR/CASTER See SUGAR, SUPERFINE

SUGAR, COCONUT PALM See JAGGERY

SUGAR, COLORED/DECORATING – 1 cup
- 1 cup sanding or coarse sugar sprinkled with 6 to 8 drops liquid food coloring (or 1 or 2 drops gel), shaken in a tightly closed jar or kneaded in a sealable plastic bag, then spread on a parchment-lined baking sheet and left at room temperature until the sugar is dry, 2 to 3 hours

SUGAR, CONFECTIONERS'/POWDERED/ICING – 1 cup
- 2/3 cup granulated sugar plus 1/2 teaspoon cornstarch or potato starch (optional), pulverized in a blender or food processor until powdery, 2 to 3 minutes (Let the sugar settle before removing the

cover, then strain, if necessary, to remove any large particles. For glazing sugar, omit the starch.)
☞ 1 cup non-melting confectioners'-type sugar, such as King Arthur topping sugar
☞ 1 cup xylitol, such as Ideal confectioners' sugar

SUGAR, CORN – 3/4 cup
☞ 2/3 cup granulated sugar
☞ 3/4 cup malt powder
☞ 1 1/4 cups dry malt extract

SUGAR, CRYSTALLIZED/CRYSTAL/SPARKLING/DECORATING – 1 cup
☞ 1 cup Swedish pearl sugar
☞ 1 heaping cup white rock sugar or sugar pearls, chopped into small pieces
☞ 1 cup maple sugar/crystals (darker)
☞ 1 cup turbinado or Demerara sugar (darker smaller crystals)

SUGAR, DARK BROWN – 1 cup
☞ 1 1/4 cups light muscovado/Barbados sugar
☞ 1 cup chopped or shaved palm sugar/jaggery, *panela, panocha*, or *piloncillo* (for baking, melt with liquid ingredient)
☞ 1 cup light brown sugar plus 1 tablespoon unsulphured molasses (pulse in a food processor, or add the molasses to the wet ingredients)
☞ 1 cup granulated sugar mixed with 2 tablespoons unsulphured molasses (pulse in a food processor, or add the molasses to the wet ingredients)

SUGAR, DECORATING See SUGAR, COLORED; SUGAR, CRYSTALLIZED

SUGAR, DEMERARA (coarse-grained, pale brown, dry semirefined sugar) – 1 cup
☞ 1 cup turbinado/semirefined sugar, such as Sugar in the Raw
☞ 1 cup pregrated Brazilian semirefined sugar/*rapadura*

☞ 1 cup pregrated Columbian semirefined sugar/*panela*

SUGAR, FLAVORED *See CINNAMON SUGAR; CITRUS SUGAR; LAVENDER SUGAR; LEMON SUGAR; MINT SUGAR; STRAWBERRY SUGAR; VANILLA SUGAR*

SUGAR, FRUCTOSE *See FRUCTOSE/LEVULOSE*

SUGAR, GLAZING *See SUGAR, CONFECTIONERS'*

SUGAR, GOLDEN BAKER'S (British fine-grained unrefined sugar) – 1 cup
- ☞ 1 cup plus 1 tablespoon Demerara or turbinado sugar, pulverized in a blender or food processor until fine-textured, about 20 seconds
- ☞ 1 cup superfine sugar (lacks color and caramel taste)

SUGAR, GRANULATED/WHITE SUGAR – single serving (2 teaspoon/8 g)
- ☞ 1/2 teaspoon (1 packet/tablet) monk fruit extract and erythritol, such as Lakato Monkfruit Sweetener, Health Garden, or Norbu.
- ☞ 2 teaspoons or 1 (0.8 gram) packet Monkfruit in the Raw with maltodextrin
- ☞ 2/3 teaspoon or 1 (3-gram) packet granulated fructose, such as Estee
- ☞ 2/3 teaspoon stevia extract powder and lactose, such as Trader Joe's stevia powder
- ☞ 2/3 teaspoon stevia leaf extract and cane sugar, such as Sugarleaf
- ☞ 3/4 teaspoon stevia leaf extract and erythritol, such as Truvia Natural Sweetener
- ☞ 1 teaspoon crumbled dried stevia leaves, placed in a metal tea or spice infuser
- ☞ 1 teaspoon maple sugar/maple granules
- ☞ 1 teaspoon stevia extract powder and fructo-oligosaccharides, such as New Roots Stevia Sugar
- ☞ 1 1/2 teaspoons honey, maple syrup, agave syrup/nectar, or *yacón* syrup

- 2 packed teaspoons brown sugar or grated palm sugar or jaggery
- 2 teaspoons chicory root sweetener, such as Just Like Sugar Table Top Sweetener
- 2 teaspoons coconut nectar liquid sweetener or granulated coconut crystals
- 2 teaspoons erythritol, stevia leaf extract, and isomaltulose, such as PureVia
- 2 teaspoons erythritol/sugar alcohol, such as Emerald Forest, Z-sweet, or Organic Zero
- 2 teaspoons erythritol and oligosaccharides, such as Swerve
- 2 teaspoons erythritol, inulin, and citrus peel extract, such as All Natural SomerSweet
- 2 teaspoons evaporated cane juice, such as Florida Crystals
- 2 teaspoons granulated sugarcane juice, such as Sucanat
- 2 teaspoons homemade stevia extract *See STEVIA EXTRACT, PURE*
- 2 teaspoons stevia leaf extract and inulin, such as SweetLeaf Stevia Plus, Trader Joe's, or Wholesome Sweeteners Organic Stevia
- 2 teaspoons stevia leaf extract and maltodextrin, such as Stevia in the Raw
- 2 teaspoons sucralose and maltodextrin, such as DiabeticSweet or Granulated Splenda
- 2 teaspoons sugar and stevia leaf extract, such as C&H Light Sugar Blend
- 2 teaspoons turbinado/semirefined sugar, such as Sugar in the Raw
- 2 teaspoons xylitol/birch bark (or corn) sweetener, such as Ideal Granular Blend
- 2 regular sugar cubes, or 4 small (1/2-teaspoon) sugar cubes
- 1 tablespoon birch syrup, brown rice syrup, or prune extract
- 1 tablespoon simple syrup (medium strength)
- 4 teaspoons glucose (loses sweetening powder with heat)
- 4 teaspoons light or dark corn syrup
- 1 (0.8-gram) packet saccharin, such as SugarTwin, Sweet'N Low, or Necta Sweet)
- 1 (1-gram) packet dextrose, maltodextrin, and sucralose, such as Apriva, Equal, Essential Everyday No Calorie Sweetener, Nevella, or Zero Calorie

▻ 1 (1-gram) packet aspartame, dextrose, and maltodextrin, such as AminoSweet, Canderel, Equal, Great Value, NutraSweet, Special Sweet, Sweet Sprinkles, or Zero Calorie

▻ 1 (1-gram) packet dextrose with maltodextrin, aspartame, acesulfame-K (acesulfame potassium), such as Equal original

▻ 1 (1-gram) packet acesulfame-K, such as Sunette, Sweet One, or Swiss Sweet

▻ 1 (1-gram) packet stevia leaf extract and dextrose, such as PureVia Stevia Zero Calorie

▻ (1-gram) packet stevia leaf extract and Frutafit inulin fiber, such as Stevia Plus

▻ 1 (1-gram) packet stevia leaf extract and maltodextrin, such as Nu Naturals or Trader Joe's

▻ 1 (2.5-gram) packet fructose and plant extracts, such as Susta

▻ 1 (3-gram) packet erythritol and stevia leaf extract/rebiana, such as Truvia Natural Sweetener

▻ 1 (4-gram) packet xylitol sweetener, such as XyloSweet

▻ 4 to 6 drops liquid stevia leaf extract, such as Better Stevia, KAL, NuNaturals, Stevia Clear, SweetLeaf, or Trader Joe's

▻ 1 (2- or 3.5-gram) packet or single-serve stick rebiana/rebaudioside-A stevia leaf extract and maltodextrin, such as Better Stevia, Nu Stevia, Pure Via, or Stevia Blend

SUGAR, GRANULATED/WHITE SUGAR (medium-crystal cane or beet sugar) – 1 cup

▻ 1 cup granulated sugarcane juice, such as Sucanat (more granular texture)

▻ 1 cup semi-refined granulated castor sugar or superfine/castor sugar (for cakes, custards, and meringues)

▻ 1 cup firmly packed light or dark brown sugar (For baking with dark brown sugar, add 1/4 teaspoon baking soda, and reduce the oven temperature by 25°F to avoid over-browning.)

▻ 1 3/4 cups unsifted confectioners' sugar (will make cookies less crisp)

▻ 3/4 cup mild-flavored honey (Reduce the oven temperature by 25°F, reduce the liquid in the recipe by 1/4 cup or add 3 extra tablespoons flour, and, unless buttermilk, yogurt, or sour cream is called for in the recipe, add 1/4 teaspoon baking soda.)

- 1 cup sucralose and maltodextrin, such as Splenda Granulated or Essential Everyday No Calorie Sweetener
- 1 cup chicory root dietary fiber/inulin and erythritol, such as All Natural SomerSweet
- 1/2 cup sucralose and sugar, such as Splenda Sugar Blend for Baking; or 1/2 cup stevia leaf extract and sugar, such as Truvia Baking Blend
- 1 cup xylitol sweetener, such as Ideal Granular Blend or XyloSweet (not for yeast bread or hard candies)
- 1 3/4 cups chicory root dietary fiber/inulin, such as Just Like Sugar Baking Sweetener
- 1 1/3 cups erythritol and stevia, such as Z-sweet, Organic Zero, or Emerald Forest
- 1/3 cup homemade stevia leaf extract (for fruit desserts and drinks)
- 2/3 cup granulated fructose (not for baked goods except in pies)
- 2/3 cup light agave syrup/nectar or coconut nectar (for fruit desserts and drinks; reduce the other liquids in the recipe by 1/4 cup)
- Agave nectar: Substitute it for no more than half of the granulated sugar in a recipe. For every cup of sugar, use only 2/3 cup agave nectar, and reduce the other liquids in the recipe by 1/4 cup.
- 8 ounces rock sugar (for glazes and drinks; dissolves rapidly and evenly)

SUGAR, LIGHT BROWN/GOLDEN – 1 cup

- 1/2 cup dark brown sugar mixed with 1/2 cup granulated sugar
- 1 cup granulated sugar mixed with 1 tablespoon unsulphured molasses (combine in a food processor or electric mixer, or add the molasses to the wet ingredients)
- 1 cup light muscovado/Barbados sugar, rapadura, or coconut crystals (air-dried coconut sap)
- 1/2 cup brown sucralose, such as Splenda Brown Sugar Blend

➢ 1 cup white sucralose, such as Splenda or Essential Everyday No Calorie Sweetener, plus 1/4 cup maple syrup (reduce the liquid in the recipe by 2 tablespoons)
➢ 2/3 cup dark agave syrup/nectar (reduce the liquid in the recipe by 1/4 cup, or add 1/3 cup extra flour; reduce the oven temperature by 25°F and increase the baking time slightly)

SUGAR, LUMP – 6 ounces (1 cup)
➢ 3/4 cup granulated sugar

SUGAR, MAPLE (dried crystallized maple syrup) – 1 cup
➢ 2/3 cup Grade A dark, robust maple syrup (reduce the liquid in the recipe by 2 tablespoons or add 2 tablespoons extra flour)
➢ 1 cup light or dark muscovado/Barbados sugar
➢ 1 cup (or more) birch sugar (less sweet)
➢ 1 cup granulated sugar plus 2 teaspoons maple extract, or 2 tablespoons maple syrup

Make Your Own Boil 1 1/2 cups Grade A dark, robust maple syrup to the soft ball stage (240°F), then stir until thick and creamy. Pour into a greased baking dish, let sit until firm, then break up for coarse crystals or pulverize for medium-fine crystals.

SUGAR, MUSCOVADO/BARBADOS, LIGHT OR DARK (moist, fine-textured unrefined sugar) – 1 cup
➢ 1 cup dark brown sugar
➢ 1 cup finely grated *piloncillo/panela* or panocha/*panucha* (Mexican unrefined sugar)

SUGAR, PALM See JAGGERY

SUGAR, PEARL See SUGAR, SANDING

SUGAR, PRESERVING (large-crystal cane or beet white sugar) – 1 cup
➢ 1 cup white granulated sugar

SUGAR, RAW *See JAGGERY; SUGAR, TURBINADO CANE*

SUGAR, ROCK *See SUGAR, BROWN ROCK; SUGAR, YELLOW/CLEAR ROCK*

SUGAR, SANDING/PEARL (extra-large-crystal cane or beet sugar) – 1 ounce
- ☞ 1 ounce Asian rock sugar, coarsely grated or finely chopped
- ☞ 1 ounce sugar pearls or sugar cubes, coarsely crushed
- ☞ 1 tablespoon Turbinado/semirefined sugar

SUGAR, SUPERFINE/ULTRA FINE/BAKER'S/CASTOR/CASTER (fine-crystal cane or beet sugar) – 1 cup
- ☞ 1 cup golden castor sugar/golden baker's sugar
- ☞ 1 cup plus 2 teaspoons granulated sugar, pulverized in a blender or food processor until finely textured, 20 to 30 seconds (let the sugar dust settle before opening lid)
- ☞ 1 cup granulated sugar (takes longer to dissolve)

SUGAR SYRUP *See SYRUP, SIMPLE*

SUGAR, TURBINADO CANE (coarse-grained light-brown unrefined sugar) – 1 cup
- ☞ 1 cup unrefined sugar, such as Sugar in the Raw; or Demerara sugar, such as Florida Crystals
- ☞ 1 packed cup light brown sugar (if sprinkled, press through a sieve)

SUGAR, YELLOW/CLEAR ROCK/BING TANG/DUONG PHEN (large-crystal Asian sugar) – 1-inch crystal piece (scant 1/2-ounce) coarsely grated or finely chopped: *See also SUGAR, BROWN ROCK*
- ☞ 1 tablespoon granulated or turbinado sugar

SULUGUNI (Russian salt-brined cheese) – 1 ounce
- ☞ 1 ounce halloumi or feta cheese

SUMAC LIQUID (Middle Eastern red souring agent) – 1/4 cup

▷ 1/4 cup whole dried sumac berries, soaked in 1/3 cup hot water for 8 to 12 hours (Strain through a fine-mesh sieve, pressing to extract the liquid, then discard the berries.)

▷ 1/2 cup fresh sumac berries, such as Dwarf, Squaw Bush, or Staghorn, lightly crushed and soaked in 1/3 cup cold water until the water turns pink, about 30 minutes (Strain through a fine-mesh sieve, pressing to extract the liquid, then discard the berries.)

▷ 1/4 cup pure pomegranate juice

▷ 1/4 cup verjuice or lemon juice (lacks color)

SUMAC POWDER/DRIED GROUND SUMAC (Middle Eastern tart, red seasoning) – 1 teaspoon

▷ 1 1/2 teaspoons dried European sumac berries/*Rhus coriaria* ground in a spice/coffee grinder with a pinch of salt

▷ 1 1/2 teaspoons ground dried North American wild sumac berries/*Rhus glabra/Rhus typhina/Rhus hirta* (Dry fresh berries for 2 to 3 hours on a parchment-lined baking sheet at 200°F, then cool and grind.)

▷ 1 scant teaspoon sour grape powder, lemon powder (dried and crushed lemon zest), green mango powder (*amchur*), or Indian dried and powdered pomegranate seeds (*anardana*)

▷ 1 teaspoon very finely grated lemon zest plus a tiny pinch of mild paprika or tomato powder spread out to dry slightly (for sprinkling on flatbread or bread salad/*fattoush*)

SUMMER SAVORY See SAVORY, SUMMER

SUMO/DEKOPON (Japanese sweet hybrid orange) – 1

▷ 1 sweet satsuma orange

SUN BUTTER See SUNFLOWER SEED BUTTER

SUNCHOKE/JERUSALEM ARTICHOKE/GIRASOLE/ TOPINAMBOUR (small crunchy tuber) – 1 pound
- 1 pound Chinese artichokes/crosnes, oca, white salsify, water chestnuts, jícama, daikon, or white globe radishes

SUNFLOWER MILK – 4 cups
Make Your Own Soak 1 cup raw unsalted sunflower seeds in water to cover for 4 to 8 hours; drain, rinse, then blend with 4 cups water until smooth, about 3 minutes. Strain in a nutmilk bag or fine-mesh sieve, pressing firmly on the pulp to extract all the liquid. Keep refrigerated and shake before using. It will keep for up to 3 days.

SUNFLOWER OIL – 1 cup
- 1 cup light peanut oil

SUNFLOWER SEED BUTTER – 1 cup
- Golden peabutter (made from brown peas)

Make Your Own Toast 1 1/2 cups sunflower seed kernels in a dry skillet until fragrant, 3 to 4 minutes. Process with 1/4 teaspoon salt (optional) in a blender or food processor until finely ground, then add 2 to 4 tablespoons grapeseed oil, and process to a coarse paste, scraping down the bowl as needed. Store, refrigerated, in a small lidded jar.

SUNFLOWER SEED KERNELS – 1 cup
- 1 cup hulled hemp or pumpkin seeds
- 1 cup pine nuts or slivered almonds
- 1 cup chia or salba seeds

SUNFLOWER SPROUTS – 1 cup See also SPROUTS
- 1 cup daikon sprouts, mung bean sprouts, soybean sprouts, or pea shoots

SUPERFINE SUGAR See SUGAR, SUPERFINE

SURE-JELL See PECTIN, REGULAR, POWDERED

SUSHI DIPPING SAUCE (Japanese condiment) – 1/4 cup
Make Your Own Combine 3 tablespoons water, 3 tablespoons Japanese soy sauce/*shoyu*, and 1 tablespoon mirin in a small saucepan and simmer for 1 minute, then cool to room temperature.

SUSHI GINGER See GINGER, PICKLED

SUSHI MESHI DRESSING (Japanese sushi rice seasoning) – 1/2 cup
  - 1/2 cup Japanese seasoned rice vinegar (for sprinkling on hot rice)
  - 1/2 cup instant powdered sushi vinegar (for sprinkling on hot rice)

SÜZME (Turkish extra-thick yogurt for dips and desserts) – 1 cup
Make Your Own Line a sieve with a double layer of dampened cheesecloth (or 2 basket-type paper coffee filters) and set it over a bowl. Put 2 cups plain full-fat yogurt (without pectin or additives) in the sieve and drain for 8 hours in the refrigerator.

SWAMP CABBAGE See WATER SPINACH

SWEDISH LIGHT SYRUP/LJUS SIRAP See GOLDEN SYRUP/LIGHT TREACLE

SWEET-AND-SOUR SAUCE See CHINESE SWEET-AND-SOUR SAUCE

SWEETENED CONDENSED MILK See CONDENSED MILK, SWEETENED

SWEETENERS See SUGAR, GRANULATED

SWEET POTATO See POTATOES, SWEET

SWEET RICE FLOUR See RICE FLOUR, SWEET/GLUTINOUS

SWEETSOP/SUGAR APPLE/SCALY CUSTARD APPLE (sweet tropical fruit) – 1
- 1 cherimoya, soursop/guanabana, or atemoya

SWISS CHARD See CHARD/SWISS CHARD

SWISS CHEESE/SWISS-TYPE CHEESE See EMMENTAL

SYRUP, FLAVORED – 1 cup See also ALMOND SYRUP; CINNAMON SYRUP; CITRUS SYRUP; COCONUT SYRUP, LIGHT; ROSE GERANIUM SYRUP
- 1 cup heavy simple syrup (*See* SYRUP, SIMPLE) flavored with 1/2 to 1 teaspoon extract (such as vanilla, almond, butterscotch, walnut, coffee, or eggnog in season), or 2 to 4 tablespoons liqueur
- 1 cup sugar-free, calorie-free flavored syrup, such as Torani
- 1 cup syrup from canned fruit packed in heavy syrup

SYRUP, REFINER'S/INVERT – 1 cup
- 1 cup golden syrup, such as Lyle's
- 1 cup light or dark corn syrup

SYRUP, SIMPLE/STOCK SYRUP, REGULAR – 1 cup
- 1/2 cup each honey and boiling water, stirred until combined, then cooled
- 1/2 cup each light agave syrup/nectar and hot water, stirred until combined, then cooled
- 1 cup each superfine sugar and water, shaken in an airtight container until the sugar dissolves

Make Your Own Bring 1 cup granulated sugar and 1 cup water to a gentle simmer over medium heat, then simmer, stirring, until the sugar dissolves, 1 to 2 minutes. Cool and store, refrigerated, for up to 4 weeks. (For light syrup, reduce the sugar to 1/2 cup; for heavy syrup increase the sugar to 1 1/2 cups.)

SYRUP, SIMPLE/STOCK SYRUP, RICH/DOUBLE STRENGTH – 1 tablespoon for drinks

⇨ 1 tablespoon light agave syrup/nectar

Make Your Own Gently simmer 2 cups sugar, 1 tablespoon corn syrup or glucose, and 1 cup water until the sugar dissolves, 2 to 3 minutes. Or omit the corn syrup or glucose and gently simmer, covered, for 10 minutes. Measure out 1 tablespoon.

T

TABASCO CHILES, FRESH – *2 or 3*
- 2 or 3 fresh chiltepin, rocoto/manzano, Thai, or japonés chiles

TABASCO SAUCE – *1 teaspoon* See also HOT PEPPER SAUCE
- 3/4 teaspoon pepper vinegar
- 1/4 teaspoon ground cayenne pepper or crushed red pepper flakes

TABIL/TABBIL (Tunisian spice paste) – *1 generous tablespoon*
- 2 teaspoons each roasted ground coriander and ground caraway, 1 teaspoon ground cayenne pepper, 1/4 teaspoon garlic powder, and enough vegetable oil to make a paste

TACO SAUCE, RED – *1 cup*
- 1 cup canned enchilada sauce
- 1 cup refrigerated or jarred mild salsa, or homemade tomato salsa

TACO SEASONING – *1 tablespoon*
- 2 teaspoons mild chile powder, such as New Mexico or pasilla; 1/2 teaspoon ground cumin; 1/4 teaspoon garlic or onion powder; and salt and pepper to taste

TACO SHELLS/BOWLS (crispy, bowl-shaped tortillas for holding taco ingredients) – *6*
- 6 softened flour tortillas, draped over the oven grates and baked at 400°F for 5 to 7 minutes; will harden when cooled
- 6 warmed soft flour tortillas, pressed into microwave-safe bowls and microwaved, uncovered, on High until dry and light brown, 1 to 2 minutes, rotating the bowls halfway through
- 6 warmed soft flour tortillas, brushed or sprayed each side with oil, then pressed into small Bundt pans or bowls (or over large

custard cups or individual Turks head molds) and baked in a pre 375°F oven until light brown, 8 to 10 minutes

⊯ 6 fried or roasted pappadums, draped over inverted bowls while still hot and soft, then cooled in place to become crispy

⊯ 6 egg roll wrappers, cut into 5 1/2-inch rounds and fried in a taco basket at 350°F until light golden, 10 to 15 seconds (use 3-inch rounds for appetizer-size shells)

TAEYANGCHO RED CHILI POWDER *See KOREAN CHILI FLAKES*

TAEYANGCHO RED PEPPER PASTE *See KOREAN CHILI BEAN PASTE*

TAHINI (Middle Eastern sesame paste) – 1/3 cup *See also SESAME PASTE*
⊯ 1/3 cup roasted tahini (less bitter)
⊯ 1/2 cup powdered tahini, rehydrated with water following the package directions
⊯ 1/4 cup smooth unsweetened almond or peanut butter (or other nut butter) mixed with 4 teaspoons untoasted sesame oil
Make Your Own Combine 1/2 cup hulled (white) sesame seeds and 3 tablespoons vegetable oil, preferably untoasted sesame oil, in a mortar or blender and grind or process until smooth. Transfer to a sterilized lidded jar and store in the refrigerator. It will keep for up to 6 months; stir before using.

TAJIN CLÁSSICO SEASONING (Mexican) – 1 tablespoon (about)
⊯ 2 teaspoons New Mexico chile powder, 1/4 teaspoon fine sea salt, and 1 teaspoon finely grated lime zest
⊯ 1 tablespoon New Mexico chile powder plus a dash of lemon pepper

TAKNOTSUME (Japanese red Hawk claw hot chile) – 2 or 3
⊯ 2 or 3 cayenne or Tabasco chiles

TALAGANI (Greek soft sheep cheese) – 1 ounce
⊯ 1 ounce halloumi or feta cheese

TALEGGIO (Italian semisoft cheese) – 1 ounce
⇨ 1 ounce Fontina Val d'Aosta, Grayson, Robiola Lombardia, Beaumont, or Reblochon

TALO (Basque cornflour flatbread) – 1
⇨ 1 pita bread, piadini, flour tortilla, or light flatbread, such as Flatout

TAMARA/IKURA (roe for cod, carp, or mullet) See BOTTARGA DI MUGGINE; CAVIAR, BLACK; CAVIAR, RED

TAMARI (Japanese naturally fermented/traditionally brewed dense soy sauce) – 1 tablespoon
⇨ 1 tablespoon tamari soy sauce (contains wheat but naturally brewed and without additives)
⇨ 1 tablespoon wheat-free tamari, such as Crystal, Eden, San-J, or Westbrae tamari
⇨ 1 tablespoon Japanese premium whole-bean organic soy sauce/ *marudaizu*, or *marudaizu*-grade soy sauce
⇨ 1 tablespoon gluten-free soy sauce, such as LaChoy or San-J gluten-free
⇨ 1 tablespoon reduced-sodium/lower-sodium tamari or soy sauce
⇨ 1 tablespoon Bragg Liquid Aminos or Raw Coconut Aminos
⇨ 1 1/2 teaspoons Maggi Seasoning
⇨ Small pinch ground dulse seaweed

TAMARILLO/TOMATE DE ÁRBOL, FRESH OR FROZEN (cross between tomato and tomatillo) – 1 pound
⇨ 1 pound (5 to 6) peeled fresh Roma/plum tomatoes plus a little lemon or lime juice

TAMARIND CONCENTRATE/EXTRACT/PASTE/PULP (Asian, Indian, and Latin American souring agent) – 1 tablespoon
⇨ 1 dried tamarind slice/*assam gelugor* (for curries, soups, and stews; discard before serving)
⇨ 1 tablespoon pomegranate molasses

- 1 teaspoon molasses or brown sugar dissolved in 1 1/2 table-spoons lemon or lime juice (or 1 1/2 teaspoons lime juice plus 1/2 teaspoon Worcestershire sauce)
- 2 or 3 chopped pitted prunes, dried apricots, or Medjool dates, pureed with 1 tablespoon lemon juice until smooth

TAMARIND POWDER (Asian, Indian, and Latin American souring agent) – 1 ounce
- 1/3 cup lemon or lime juice

TAMARIND PUREE (Asian, Indian, and Latin souring agent) – 1 cup
- 8 ounces (8 to 10) peeled tamarind pods, soaked in boiling water until softened, 1 to 2 hours; strain pulp and discard solids
- 1/2 cup (3 1/2 ounces) thawed frozen tamarind pulp, blended with 1/2 cup water; strain and discard solids
- 1/4 cup (1 3/4 ounces) tamarind paste/concentrate, blended with 1 cup boiling water until smooth; strain and discard solids

TAMARIND SAUCE (Asian, Indian, and Latin souring agent) – 1/2 cup
- 1 tablespoon tamarind concentrate added to 1/2 cup just-boiled water

TAMARIND SYRUP (Latin American concentrate) – 1 cup
- 3 tablespoons tamarind concentrate/paste, 1/2 cup sugar, and 1/2 cup boiling water, stirred together until the sugar dissolves

TAMARIND WATER (Asian, Indian, and Latin souring agent) – 1 cup medium-strength
- 1 1/2 tablespoons tamarind paste, dissolved in 1 cup hot water

Make Your Own Soak 1 ounce (1 by 1 1/2-inch piece) compressed tamarind (or 6 cracked and peeled tamarind pods) in 1 1/2 cups boiling water until softened, 15 minutes or more. Strain and discard the solids. (For thick tamarind water, simmer the tamarind in the water until reduced by half and then strain.)

TANDOORI COLORING/TANDOORI RANG (Indian seasoning and coloring agent) – 1 teaspoon

- 1 tablespoon mild/sweet Hungarian or Spanish paprika (for coloring only)
- 1 tablespoon ground Madras turmeric, toasted in a dry skillet until fragrant (for coloring only)
- 1 drop red food coloring (for coloring only)

TANDOORI SEASONING (Indian spice blend) – 1 tablespoon

- 1/4 teaspoon each ground cumin (preferably roasted), ground coriander (preferably roasted), ground ginger (preferably roasted), mild paprika, turmeric, and ground cayenne pepper, plus salt to taste (optional)
- 1 tablespoon mild curry powder

TANGERINE/MANDARIN PEEL, DRIED/GOM PEI/TSEN PEI/CHEN PI/ GAW PAE (Chinese and Vietnamese seasoning)

- 1 (2-inch-long) strip orange zest, removed with a vegetable peeler, or 1/4 teaspoon grated fresh orange zest will substitute for 1 (1-inch-wide) piece dried tangerine peel

Make Your Own Arrange tangerine peels (preferably organic) on a rack and set in the sun, covered by a food umbrella or tented cheesecloth, until hard and dry. Alternatively, microwave on High for about 2 minutes, sandwiched between paper towels, or dry on a baking sheet in a preheated 200°F oven for about 1 hour. (If the oven has a top heating unit, place a large baking sheet as close to the heating unit as possible to deflect the heat, then place the baking sheet with the peels on a lower rack.) Store the peels in a small container and grind just before using.

TANGERINE ZEST – 1 teaspoon

- 2 tablespoons tangerine juice; reduce the liquid in the recipe by 2 tablespoons
- 1/2 teaspoon tangerine or orange extract
- 1 teaspoon grated orange zest

▷ 1/8 teaspoon tangerine citrus oil, such as Boyajian

TANSY, FRESH – 3 to 4 sprigs (1 tablespoon chopped)
▷ 1 1/2 tablespoons chopped mint leaves

TAPENADE (French condiment) – 1 cup *See also OLIVE PASTE, BLACK*
Make Your Own Process 1 cup pitted black olives, such as Kalamata or Niçoise; 2 tablespoons rinsed capers; 2 or 3 well-rinsed anchovy fillets; 1 to 2 teaspoons minced garlic; and 1/3 cup (or more) olive oil in a food processor until smooth. Transfer to a small jar, top with a thin layer of olive oil and store, tightly covered, in the refrigerator; it will keep for up to 2 weeks.

TAPIOCA, GRANULAR/QUICK-COOKING – 1 tablespoon for thickening
▷ 2 tablespoons small pearl tapioca, soaked in 1/4 cup milk or water until the liquid is completely absorbed, about 12 hours
▷ 1 1/2 tablespoons tapioca starch
▷ 1 1/2 tablespoons sago starch
▷ 1 1/2 teaspoons sweet rice flour/glutinous rice flour
▷ 2 teaspoon arrowroot powder (separates when frozen)

TAPIOCA PEARLS – 1 tablespoon for cooking
▷ 1 tablespoon sago pearls
▷ 1 1/2 teaspoons quick-cooking tapioca (omit soaking and reduce cooking time)

TAPIOCA STARCH – 1 tablespoon for thickening
▷ 2 1/2 teaspoons quick-cooking tapioca ground in a spice/coffee grinder until powdery
▷ 1 1/2 teaspoons cornstarch or sweet rice flour/glutinous rice flour
▷ 1 1/4 teaspoons potato starch
▷ 2 teaspoons arrowroot powder
▷ 1 tablespoon all-purpose flour (cook for at least 3 minutes after thickening)

TARAMA (salted, dried carp or red mullet roe) *See CAVIAR, RED*

TARBAIS BEANS, DRIED (French white beans) – 1 pound
- 1 pound large cannellini or white kidney beans (smaller)
- 1 pound dried Greek Gigante beans or Italian butter beans

TARÉ (Japanese marinade and glaze) *See TERIYAKI SAUCE*

TARO FLOUR/STARCH (West African, Caribbean, and Polynesian thickening agent) – 1 tablespoon
- 1 tablespoon potato starch

TARO LEAVES *See CALLALOO*

TARO ROOT/COCOYAM/GABI/WOO TAU (Asian, African, and Caribbean starchy vegetable) – 1 pound
- 1 pound eddo/malanga (moister)
- 1 pound yuca root/cassava
- 1 pound Yukon Gold or Yellow Finnish potatoes (for the 7- to 8-inch taro)
- 1 pound small waxy boiling potatoes, such as Red Bliss (for the 2- to 3-inch Japanese baby taro/*gabi*)

TARO STEM/BAC HA/ZUIKI (Vietnamese and Cambodian green crispy vegetable) – 1 cup peeled and sliced
- 1 cup shredded iceburg lettuce

TARRAGON, FRENCH – 1 large branch (4 to 6 sprigs or 1 tablespoon finely chopped leaves)
- 1 teaspoon dried French tarragon, crumbled
- 1 1/4 teaspoons dried Russian tarragon, crumbled
- 2 tablespoons chopped fresh Mexican tarragon/Mexican mint marigold/*Tagetes lucida*
- 2 tablespoons chopped fresh chervil or flat-leaf parsley

☞ 1 1/2 to 2 teaspoons dried chervil, crumbled

☞ 1/8 teaspoon crushed anise or fennel seeds, or 16 whole seeds

☞ 1 to 2 teaspoons anise-flavored spirits, such as pastis or ouzo

TART SHELLS/PASTRY SHELLS *See DESSERT SHELLS*

TARTARIC ACID (tart flavoring and acidifying agent) – 1 teaspoon
See also CITRIC ACID

☞ 1 teaspoon crystallized or powdered citric acid (not for wine making)

☞ 1/4 cup lemon juice (will give a lemon taste; not for wine making)

TARTAR SAUCE – 3/4 cup
Make Your Own Stir together 1/2 cup mayonnaise, 2 to 3 tablespoons finely chopped pickles (or drained pickle relish), 1 to 2 tablespoons finely chopped shallot or onion, and 1 to 2 teaspoons lemon juice or vinegar.

TARTAR SAUCE, QUICK – 1/4 cup

☞ 3 tablespoons mayonnaise plus 1 tablespoon pickle relish

TASAJO (Cuban smoke-dried salted beef) – 1 pound

☞ 1 pound Brazilian dried beef/*carne seca* or sun-dried beef/*carne de sol*

☞ 1 pound Cajun tasso

TASSO/CAJUN HAM (highly seasoned boneless smoked pork shoulder) – 1 pound

☞ 1 pound thick-cut country bacon; smoked ham, such as Black Forest or Westphalian; or country-style cured ham, such as Virginia or Kentucky, rubbed with a little garlic powder and ground cayenne pepper (or Cajun seasoning)

☞ 1 pound Cajun andouille or other fully cooked spicy smoked sausage

TATSOI/SPOON MUSTARD/CHINESE FLAT CABBAGE/TAI GU CHOY – 1 pound

- ⇨ 1 pound baby spinach, baby arugula, young mizuna, young horse-radish leaves, or tender young mustard greens torn into pieces (for salad)
- ⇨ 1 pound curly spinach, green chard, mustard greens with center rib discarded, baby bok choy, or baby Shanghai bok choy (for cooking)

TEA BAG, BLACK OR GREEN – 1

- ⇨ 3/4 tablespoon loose black or green tea (enclose in a reusable muslin tea bag or a metal tea or spice infuser)

TEA, BLACK – 1 cup brewed

- ⇨ 1 cup yerba mate (South American tea; 25 mg less caffeine)
- ⇨ 1/2 cup cassina tea/*Ilex vomitoria* or inkberry tea/*Ilex glabra* (dry the leaves until black; aromatic with significant quantities of caffeine)
- ⇨ 1 cup rooibos/bush tea/*Aspalathus linearis* (South African red-leaf tea; colorful, caffeine-free; low in tannin)
- ⇨ 1 cup Oswego/bee balm tea/*Monarda didyma* (fragrance similar to Earl Grey tea; caffeine-free)
- ⇨ 1 cup brown rice tea/*genmaicha* (Japanese macrobiotic tea; caffeine-free)

TEA, GREEN – 1 cup brewed

- ⇨ 1 cup organic tulsi tea (caffeine-free; higher Orac value: 2,550)
- ⇨ I cup light-roast yaupon tea (less-bitter taste, less tannin, less caffeine)
- ⇨ 1 cup dandelion tea (use dried leaves; caffeine-free)
- ⇨ 1 cup New Jersey Tea/*Ceanothus americanus* (use fresh or dried leaves; resembles green tea in flavor; caffeine-free)

TEFF, IVORY OR BROWN – 1 cup

- ⇨ 1 cup light/tan, red, or black quinoa, prewashed or well rinsed
- ⇨ 1 cup regular or black amaranth

- ⇨ 1 cup Bolivian *canahua*
- ⇨ 1 cup millet toasted before cooking (toast it in a dry skillet for 2 or 3 minutes, stirring constantly)
- ⇨ 1 cup whole-wheat couscous; or fine- or medium-grind bulgur (less cooking time; contains gluten)

TEFF FLOUR *See FLOUR, TEFF*

TEMPEH, FRESH OR FROZEN *(fermented soybean patty) – 1 pound*
- ⇨ 2 (8-ounce) packages Organic Savory Baked Tofu/baked bean curd (spicy or smoked seasoned; softer texture)
- ⇨ 1 pound firm tofu, weighted a few hours, then blotted dry and sliced crosswise (softer texture; less flavorful)
- ⇨ 1 pound seitan (chewier)

TEMPURA BATTER/KOROMO *(Japanese) – 1 cup*
Make Your Own Gently stir together 1 cup tempura flour (or 1 cup rice or cake flour), preferably chilled; 1/2 teaspoon salt; and 1 cup ice-cold sparkling water (or club soda or light beer). (Don't overmix; use immediately.)

TEMPURA DIPPING SAUCE/TENTSUYU *(Japanese) – 1/3 cup*
- ⇨ 1/4 cup dashi (or light vegetable or chicken broth) plus 1 table-spoon each mirin and Japanese soy sauce/*shoyu*, brought to a boil then cooled
- ⇨ 1/4 cup Japanese soy sauce/*shoyu*, 2 tablespoons mild vinegar, 2 teaspoons sugar, and 1 or 2 teaspoons finely grated ginger, stirred until the sugar dissolves
- ⇨ 1 1/2 tablespoons Memmi noodle soup base, such as Kikkoman, mixed with 1/4 cup water

TEMPURA FLOUR/TENPURA KO *(Japanese) – 1 cup*
- ⇨ 3/4 cup plus 2 tablespoons cake flour and 2 tablespoons corn-starch or potato starch

TENTSUYU See TEMPURA DIPPING SAUCE

TERASI/TRASI (Indonesian and Malaysian seasoning) See SHRIMP PASTE, FERMENTED

TERIYAKI SAUCE/TERIYAKI SOSU/TARÉ (Japanese marinade and glaze) – 1/3 cup
Make Your Own Bring 2 tablespoons each Japanese dark soy sauce, mirin, and saké (or dry sherry) to a boil in the microwave, or in a small saucepan over medium heat, then cool. (For a sweeter sauce, add 1 teaspoon sugar; for a thicker sauce add 1 1/2 teaspoons sugar and simmer until syrupy.)
Or
Heat 1/4 cup soy sauce and 2 tablespoons sugar (or honey) in the microwave until the sugar dissolves, 10 to 20 seconds.

TEXSEL GREENS/ABYSSINIAN MUSTARD (mild green cultivar from Ethiopia) – 1 pound
⇨ 1 pound spinach

THAI BASIL See BASIL, THAI

THAI CHILE, FRESH OR DRIED – 1
⇨ 1 fresh or dried de árbol, japonés, small serrano, tien tsin, or cayenne chile
⇨ 1/4 to 1/2 teaspoon Thai red pepper flakes or hot red pepper flakes
⇨ 1/8 teaspoon each ground cayenne pepper and paprika

THAI CHILE FLAKES/POWDER – 1/2 cup
Make Your Own Toast 1 cup dried Thai chiles in a dry skillet over medium heat, stirring frequently, until slightly darker, 2 to 3 minutes (or in a preheated 350°F oven until puffed, about 5 minutes). Cool, remove the stems, then pulse in a food processor into coarse flakes or process to a powder. (For less heat remove the seeds and veins; wear plastic gloves and avoid inhaling the fumes.)

THAI CHILI VINEGAR/NAM SOM – (Pad Thai condiment) – 1/2 cup
- 1/2 cup rice vinegar, 2 to 3 tablespoons sugar, and a few thin slices of serrano chile

THAI CURRY POWDER/PONG GARI – 1 tablespoon
- 1 tablespoon mild Madras curry powder

THAI DIPPING SAUCE/NAM PRIK See NAM PRIK

THAI FISH SAUCE/NAM PLA (salty liquid seasoning) – 1 tablespoon
- 1 tablespoon Vietnamese fish sauce/*nuoc nam/nuoc mam* (slightly stronger), or Vietnamese premium sauce from the first extraction/*nuoc mam nhi* or *nuoc mam cot* (bolder flavor)
- 1 tablespoon Korean fish sauce/*saengseon*, Japanese fish sauce/*shottsuru*, or Filipino fish sauce/*patis*
- 1 tablespoon Vietnamese vegetarian fish sauce/*nuoc mam au chay*
- 1 tablespoon anchovy essence/syrup
- 2 teaspoons anchovy paste mixed with 1/2 teaspoon soy sauce or Maggi Seasoning
- 1 tablespoon Chinese oyster sauce
- 1 scant tablespoon light soy sauce plus a little salt

THAI FISH SAUCE WITH CHILIS/NAM PLA PRIK – 2/3 (scant) cup
Make Your Own Stir 1/4 cup minced fresh Thai chilis (including seeds) into 1/2 cup fish sauce/*nam pla*. Store, tightly covered, in the refrigerator. (Wear plastic gloves when handling the chilis.)

THAI GINGER See GALANGAL, GREATER

THAI HOT CHILI SAUCE/SRIRACHA SAUCE/SOT SI RACHA/TUONG OT SRIRACHA – 1 teaspoon
- 1/2 teaspoon each American-made Sriracha sauce/rooster sauce (thicker, stronger, less sweet) and Thai sweet chili sauce/*nam jim kai*
- 1/2 to 1 teaspoon Sriracha dry seasoning (for pizza or rubs)
- 1 teaspoon sambal oelek sweetened with a little sugar

‣ 2/3 teaspoon ketchup plus 1/3 teaspoon Louisiana-style hot sauce, such as Tabasco or Crystal
‣ 1/4 to 1/2 teaspoon ground cayenne pepper (for cooking)

THAI NOODLES, CLEAR TRANSPARENT/WUN SEN *See NOODLES, CELLOPHANE*

THAI NOODLES, THIN, FLAT RICE/PAD THAI NOODLES, DRIED OR SEMI-DRIED/SEN LEK/BAH PHO/PHAT THAI – 1 pound *See also NOODLES, THIN, FLAT RICE*
‣ 1 pound fresh or 12 ounces dried fettuccine, prepared according to the package directions
‣ 8 to 12 ounces dried, or 1 pound fresh, Vietnamese *banh pho*, Chinese *sha ha fun* or *chow fun*, Filipino *pancit luglug*, or other flat 1/8-inch or 1/4-inch rice noodles
‣ 1 pound fresh or 8 to 12 ounces dried thin, flat brown rice noodles, prepared according to the package directions

THAI NOODLES, THIN RICE, DRIED/KWAY TIO/SEN MEE/KANOM CHINE – 1 pound
‣ 1 pound Thai rice sticks/*sen yai*, Chinese rice vermicelli/*mi fen/so fun*; Japanese *mai fun*; Vietnamese *bun and bahn hoi*; or Filipino *pancit bihon*

THAI NOODLES, WHEAT/BA MEE, FRESH OR FROZEN – 1 pound
‣ 1 pound fresh or 12 ounces dried Chinese egg noodles, or Japanese yakisoba or fresh-frozen ramen noodles

THAI RICE *See RICE, THAI JASMINE RED/PURPLE; RICE, THAI JASMINE WHITE; RICE, THAI STICKY BLACK; RICE, THAI STICKY WHITE*

THAI RICE, GROUND ROASTED *See RICE POWDER, ROASTED*

THAI ROASTED RED CHILI PASTE/CHILI JAM/NAM PRIK PAO – 1 tablespoon
‣ 1 tablespoon chili-garlic sauce

☞ 2 teaspoons vegetable oil, 1 teaspoon granulated sugar, and 1 teaspoon chile powder

THAI SAUCE BASE – 1/4 cup
☞ 3 tablespoons fish sauce/*nam pla*, 1 tablespoon lime juice, 1 tablespoon brown sugar, and 1/8 teaspoon crushed red pepper flakes, stirred until the sugar dissolves

THAI SEVEN-SPICE POWDER – 1 teaspoon
☞ 1 teaspoon Chinese five-spice powder

THAI SHRIMP PASTE/KAPI See SHRIMP PASTE, FERMENTED

THAI SOY SAUCE See SOY SAUCE, THAI THIN

THAI SWEET BLACK SOY SAUCE See SOY SAUCE, THAI SWEET BLACK

THAI SWEET CHILI-GARLIC SAUCE/NAM JIM KRATIEM – 1/2 cup
Make Your Own Cook 1 cup distilled white vinegar, 1/2 cup sugar, and 1 teaspoon salt until syrupy, 10 to 15 minutes. Remove from the heat and add 1 teaspoon minced fresh Thai chile and 1/2 teaspoon minced garlic. Cool and transfer to an airtight container; keep refrigerated. (The sauce will thicken further as it cools.)

THAI YELLOW BEAN PASTE/DAU JIAO/TAO JIAW See VIETNAMESE YELLOW BEAN SAUCE

THICKENER FOR GRAVY OR SAUCE – (per 1 cup gravy/sauce: when using flour/starch, mix with twice the amount of cold liquid, stir immediately before adding to the sauce, then add it in a thin steam while stirring constantly until the sauce thickens)
☞ Gravy and stock-based sauce, gently boiled down until reduced to the desired thickness (season after reducing, not before)
☞ 1 to 3 tablespoons roux (Cook equal parts flour and meat drippings to a paste before adding defatted liquid and cooking until thickened and the flour taste dissipates.)

- 1 to 3 tablespoons beurre manié (Mix equal parts flour and butter to a paste; gradually whisk into the liquid and cook for several minutes to remove the raw flour taste.)
- 2 to 4 tablespoons browned all-purpose flour for gravy (opaque finish)
- 1 to 2 tablespoons reduced-salt gravy granules for gravy (reduce the salt in the recipe accordingly)
- 1 to 2 tablespoons flour: all-purpose, amaranth, cake, pastry, or quick-mixing (opaque finish)
- 1 to 2 tablespoons oat flour, or raw oats ground in a spice/coffee grinder (opaque finish)
- 1 to 3 teaspoons sweet rice flour/glutinous rice flour/mochiko (semi-clear finish; does not separate when frozen)
- 1 to 3 teaspoons cornstarch or potato starch (semi-clear finish)
- 1 to 3 teaspoons water chestnut flour (very clear finish for Asian sauces)
- 2 to 3 teaspoons arrowroot powder (clearest finish, neutral flavor; best for delicate dessert sauces)
- 3 to 4 teaspoons tapioca starch (clear finish, neutral flavor; does not separate when frozen)
- 1 1/2 tablespoons kudzu powder (clear finish, neutral flavor)
- 1 1/2 teaspoons coconut flour (slight sweetish coconut flavor; opaque finish)
- 1 egg yolk beaten with 1 tablespoon wine or cream and added at the end (do not let boil)
- 1 to 2 tablespoons nut butter/paste, such as almond, cashew, or peanut (especially for curries)

THICKENER FOR GREEN SMOOTHIES – (per 8 ounces; to prevent ingredients from separating)
- 1/4 cup purslane leaves, thick stems removed and cut into pieces
- 1/4 cup rolled oats
- 1/4 cup avocado
- 2 tablespoons lecithin granules

THICKENER/EXTENDER FOR MEATLOAF AND MEATBALLS – (per 1 pound of meat)

- 1/4 cup cracker crumbs (regular or non-gluten)
- 2 tablespoons soft breadcrumbs, soaked for 5 minutes in 2 tablespoons milk or stock
- 1/4 cup panko breadcrumbs or regular dried breadcrumbs, soaked for 5 minutes in 2 tablespoons whole milk
- 2 tablespoons instant couscous, soaked for 5 minutes in 2 tablespoons warm water
- 1/4 cup finely grated raw potatoes or instant mashed potato flakes
- 1/4 cup quick-cooking oats

THICKENER FOR SOUP (per 8 ounces of soup)

- 1 to 3 tablespoons grated raw potato, simmered in the soup for 10 to 15 minutes
- 2 to 3 teaspoons instant mashed potato flakes, or one-quarter of a medium cooked and mashed or riced potato, mixed in with a whisk to prevent lumping and added to the soup minutes before serving
- 1 to 3 teaspoons short-grain rice, simmered in the soup for 30 minutes before pureeing
- 1 to 3 teaspoons bean flakes, ground oats, or grits, slowly stirred into the soup and simmered, covered, 8 to 10 minutes
- One-quarter to one-third of the cooked solids taken from the soup, coarsely pureed with a pestle or potato masher (or put through a food mill or sieve), and then stirred back in the soup (Alternatively, leave the solids in the pot and mash them against the sides or bottom, or use an immersion/stick blender.)
- 1/4 to 1/2 teaspoon cornstarch or arrowroot powder, mixed with a little cold liquid (for Chinese clear soup or chicken broth; added at the end and stirred only until thickened for arrowroot powder, or 1 minute after thickening for cornstarch; will not stay thickened upon reheating)
- 2 tablespoons fresh breadcrumbs, or one-half slice white sandwich bread, crust removed and torn into 1-inch pieces (for cream-based and pureed soups)

- 1 tablespoon heavy cream or thick canned coconut milk/or cream added at the last minute, or off the heat (for cream or pureed soups)
- 2 tablespoons avocado (for cold green soups; add to the soup when blending)
- 1 to 2 tablespoons nut puree (1 part soaked cashews or almonds to 3 parts water, ground until smooth and creamy (for cream or pureed soups)
- 2 tablespoons cooked pureed onion (peeled onion microwaved on High for 10 minutes, then blended until smooth)

THOUSAND ISLAND DRESSING – 1 cup
Make Your Own Stir 1/2 cup mayonnaise, 1/4 cup ketchup, and 1/4 cup well-drained pickle relish (or 2 finely minced gherkins) until thoroughly combined; season with salt and thin with cider vinegar, if required.

THYME, GARDEN/COMMON, FRESH – 3 to 5 whole sprigs, or leaves from 6 to 9 sprigs, or 1 tablespoon minced leaves
- 1 teaspoon dried French or English thyme leaves, crumbled
- 1 to 2 teaspoons finely minced fresh Spanish thyme leaves (stronger, slightly bitter)
- 3 to 4 teaspoons minced fresh wild/creeping thyme leaves/*Thymus serpyllum* (less flavorful)
- 1 tablespoon minced fresh summer savory
- 1 teaspoon poultry seasoning
- 1/2 teaspoon each dried marjoram and oregano leaves, crumbled
- 1 teaspoon ajwain/ajowan seeds

THYME, LEMON, FRESH – 3 to 5 whole sprigs, or leaves from 6 to 7 sprigs, or 1 tablespoon finely minced
- 1 teaspoon dried lemon thyme softened in 1 tablespoon warm water for 10 to 15 minutes
- 1 tablespoon minced fresh garden or French thyme plus 1/8 to 1/4 teaspoon grated lemon zest

TILSIT/TILSITER (Dutch, German semisoft to semihard cheese) – 1 ounce
- ⊯ 1 ounce Ansgar, Esrom, Fontal, Fontina Val d'Aosta, Havarti, Kardella, or Monterey Jack

TIPO 00 FLOUR See FLOUR, ITALIAN TIPO 00

TOCINO (Spanish salted pork belly) See PANCETTA

TOFU/BEAN CURD, FRESH – 1 pound
- ⊯ 1 pound tempeh (stronger flavor)
- ⊯ 1 pound Indian paneer/panir or Latin American queso blanco/ fresco (diced for adding to savory dishes)

TOFU, BROILED/YAKIDOFU – 1 pound
- ⊯ 1 pound firm or extra-firm tofu, drained and grilled each side over high heat, preferably charcoal

TOFU, DEEP-FRIED/ABURAGÉ – 1 pound
- ⊯ 1 pound sliced firm tofu, weighted, patted dry, then deep-fried until golden brown, 3 to 4 minutes (drain on paper towels and cool)
- ⊯ 1 pound *atsu-agé* or *nama-agé* (thicker sheets)

TOFU, DRIED/FOO JOOK – 1 pound
- ⊯ 1 pound firm or extra-firm tofu, baked at 375°F until dry, about 25 minutes (or wrapped in a non-terry cotton dishtowel or paper towels and microwaved on High in 30-second increments for about 2 minutes)

TOFU, FERMENTED/DOUFU RU/FUYU/SUFU – 1 pound
- ⊯ 1 pound firm or extra-firm tofu, sliced or cubed, then marinated for 1 to 2 days in miso or soy sauce
- ⊯ 1 pound mild French or Greek feta cheese, crumbled

TOFU, FREEZE-DRIED/KOYADOFU – 1 pound
☞ 1 pound firm or extra-firm tofu, rinsed, weighted for 1 to 2 hours, then frozen in plastic wrap for 8 to 12 hours (rinse in water after thawing)

TOFU, PRESSED/DOUFU-KAN/TAU JUA/TAU KWA – 1 pound
☞ 1 pound extra-firm tofu, placed between 2 folded dishtowels and weighted until dry, 2 to 3 hours (use a heavy skillet or cutting board and canned goods for weights)
☞ 1 pound extra-firm tofu, cut into thin slices, placed on a paper-lined plate, and microwaved on Medium until dry, 4 to 6 minutes

TOFU, SILKEN/KINUGOSHI/SUI –DOUFU – 1 pound
☞ 1 pound soy yogurt

TOGARASHI See JAPANESE HOT RED CHILE

TOLOSA BEANS, DRIED (Spanish small purple-black beans) – 1 pound
☞ 1 pound small dried black turtle beans

TOMATILLOS/MILTOMATES, FRESH (Latin American small husked fruit) – 1 pound (10 to 12 medium)
☞ 1 (11-ounce) can whole tomatillos, rinsed and drained
☞ 1 pound milpero tomatillos (smaller; more intensely flavored)
☞ 1 pound green or unripe tomatoes, plus a little lime juice added to the recipe

TOMATO – 1 medium (peeled, seeded and diced)
☞ 1/2 cup diced canned tomatoes, drained
☞ 1/2 cup tomato sauce (reduce the liquid in the recipe by 1/2 cup)

TOMATOES, CAMPARI – 1 pound
☞ 1 pound small (golf ball–size) vine-ripened or cocktail tomatoes

TOMATOES, CANNED, CHOPPED OR DICED – 1 (14.5 ounce) can
- ⇨ 2 1/2 cups peeled, seeded, and chopped fresh tomatoes, simmered for 10 minutes
- ⇨ 1 (14- or 15-ounce) can whole tomatoes, drained and chopped
- ⇨ 6 to 8 sun-dried tomato halves, softened in hot water for 20 to 40 minutes, then diced (more pungent)

TOMATOES, CANNED, CRUSHED – 1 cup
- ⇨ 1 (14.5-ounce) can diced tomatoes, drained and crushed with a potato masher or pulsed in a food processor to the desired consistency
- ⇨ 3 small-to-medium fresh unpeeled tomatoes, halved vertically and grated on the large holes of a box or flat grater

TOMATOES, CANNED, DICED WITH BASIL, GARLIC, AND OREGANO – 1 (14.5-ounce) can
- ⇨ 1 (14.5-ounce) can diced tomatoes, 1/2 teaspoon each dried basil and oregano, and 1 clove minced garlic (or 1/2 to 1 teaspoon garlic paste or jarred minced garlic)

TOMATOES, CANNED, DICED WITH MILD GREEN CHILES – 1 (10-ounce) can
- ⇨ 1 cup diced canned tomatoes, 3 tablespoons diced canned chiles (or 1 finely chopped seeded jalapeño for more heat), and a sprinkle of garlic powder

TOMATOES, CANNED, STEWED WITH GARLIC AND ONION – 1 (14.5-ounce) can
- ⇨ 1 (14.5-ounce) can stewed tomatoes plus 1/2 teaspoon finely chopped garlic

TOMATOES, FRESH GLOBE – 1 pound (3 medium)
- ⇨ 1 pound fresh Tesoro tomatoes for sandwiches (have seeds but no gel) or Opalka tomatoes (have few seeds but are almost all flesh)

- 1 pound small fresh yellow or golden tomatoes for fruit salad or relish (have a sweeter, less acidic flavor)
- 1 pound Rutgers tomatoes for stuffing and baking (most stable tomato when cooked)
- 1 pound fresh plum tomatoes for sauce (have thick, dry flesh)
- 1 (14.5-ounce) can water-packed plum tomatoes, drained and blotted dry
- 1 (14- or 16-ounce) can no-salt-added diced tomatoes, either with their juice or drained (for cooking)
- 6 or 7 sun-dried tomato halves softened in hot water for 20 to 40 minutes (for cooking; use the soaking liquid in place of water in the recipe, or reserve it for another use)
- 3 tablespoons tomato paste plus 1/3 cup water, or extra liquid (for cooking, if applicable)
- 1 (8-ounce) can tomato sauce (for cooking, if applicable)

TOMATOES, FRESH PLUM – 1 pound (6 to 8)
- 1 pound fresh Datterini, Federle, Olivade, Opalka, Roma, or San Marzano tomatoes
- 1 (14.5- or 15-ounce) can whole San Marzano, Red Gold, or un-salted plum tomatoes in juice

TOMATOES, FRESH YELLOW – 1 pound
- 1 (12-ounce) jar roasted yellow peppers, drained

TOMATOES, SEMI-DRIED/SEMI-CARAMELIZED/MI-CUIT
Make Your Own Halve fresh tomatoes and remove the seeds; place cut-side up in a single layer on a foil-lined baking sheet. Sprinkle with kosher salt, drizzle with olive oil, and bake at 300°F until shriveled, about 3 hours. Let cool, then refrigerate, tightly covered, for up to 1 month or freeze for longer storage. (For extra flavor, add fresh sage, basil, or garlic slivers before baking.)

TOMATOES, SUN-DRIED, ITALIAN – 3 or 4
- 3 or 4 sun-dried wild bush Australian tomatoes/*Solanum centrale*

- 2 to 3 sun-dried, oil-packed tomatoes, drained
- 1 tablespoon sun-dried tomato paste

TOMATOES, SUN-DRIED, OIL-PACKED

- Dry-packed sun-dried tomatoes, softened in hot water to cover for 30 to 60 minutes, drained, blotted dry, and then marinated in olive oil for at least 1 hour (Alternatively, marinate the tomatoes in oil for 12 to 24 hours without prior soaking.)

TOMATO JUICE – 1 cup

- 1/2 cup tomato sauce and 1/2 cup water, whisked together
- 1/4 cup tomato paste, 3/4 cup water, and a dash each salt and sugar, whisked together
- 2 medium fresh tomatoes, peeled, seeded, and blended until smooth; season to taste with salt and lemon juice
- 1 teaspoon tomato bouillon granules, or 1 tomato-flavored mini bouillon cube, added to 1 cup of the water called for in the recipe; reduce the salt by 1/2 teaspoon

TOMATO PASTE – 1 tablespoon

- 1 1/2 teaspoons double-concentrated tomato paste or extra-concentrated tomato extract
- 1 1/2 teaspoons tomato powder and 1 1/2 tablespoons water
- 1 tablespoon sun-dried tomato pesto
- 1 tablespoon ketchup (sweeter)
- 2 oil-packed sun-dried tomato halves, drained and pureed
- 3 tablespoons tomato sauce (Reduce the liquid in the recipe by 2 tablespoons, or gently boil the tomato sauce until reduced to 1 tablespoon.)

TOMATO PASTE – 1/2 cup

- 2 pounds plum tomatoes, peeled, seeded, and coarsely chopped plus 2 tablespoons lemon   juice blended or pulsed until smooth; drain 2 or 3 hours in a fine-mesh sieve, then transfer to a small jar;

top with a thin layer of olive oil and store, tightly covered, in the refrigerator (use the clear tomato juice for a soup base)
- 1 1/2 cups tomato puree, simmered, uncovered, over low heat, stirring occasionally, until reduced to 1/2 cup

TOMATO PASTE, SUN-DRIED – 1 cup
- 2 ounces sun-dried tomatoes, softened in 1 1/2 cups boiling water 20 to 40 minutes, then puréed until smooth (strain if necessary)

TOMATO POWDER – 1 tablespoon
Make Your Own Peel tomatoes, then dry the skins in a food dehydrator, or in a preheated 225°F oven for 45 to 60 minutes. Grind to a powder in a spice/coffee mill. Measure out 1 tablespoon.

TOMATO PUREE OR PULP – 1 cup
- 1 (14.5- to 16-ounce) can whole tomatoes with their juice, pureed in a blender or food processor until smooth (measure out 1 cup, then refrigerate or freeze the rest for another dish)
- 1/3 cup tomato paste and 2/3 cup water
- 1 cup plain tomato sauce

Make Your Own Halve 1 pound tomatoes and then grate on the large holes of a box grater or press through a sieve, discarding the skin and seeds. Cook over high heat until thickened, about 5 minutes. Alternatively, peel and seed the tomatoes and puree them in a blender or food processor until smooth.
Or
Coarsely chop 1 pound plum tomatoes and simmer until softened, 5 to 10 minutes, then press through a sieve or food mill to remove the skins and seeds.

TOMATO SAUCE – 1 cup
- 1 (14.5- to 16-ounce) can tomatoes, drained (reserve the juice) and processed in a blender or food processor until smooth (Measure after blending, then add more juice if needed to make 1 cup. Season with salt if needed.)

- ☞ 2 cups tomato juice, cooked until reduced by half
- ☞ 8 ounces peeled, seeded and chopped plum tomatoes (3 to 4) plus 1 or 2 teaspoons tomato paste
- ☞ 1/2 cup tomato paste and 1/2 cup water (season to taste with salt and sugar, 1/4 to 1/2 teaspoon, to duplicate commercial brands)

TOMATO SAUCE, SPANISH-STYLE – 1 cup
- ☞ 1 cup canned tomato puree
- ☞ 1 cup canned enchilada sauce

TOMATO SOUP – 1 (10 3/4 oz) can for cooking
- ☞ 1 cup tomato sauce plus 1/4 cup water

TONIC WATER – 1 cup
- ☞ 1 cup quinine water
- ☞ 1 cup soda water, seltzer, club soda, sparkling mineral water, or carbonated water (lacks quinine; contains 77 calories)

TONKATSU SAUCE/TON/KATSU SOSHU (Japanese thick sauce for tonkatsu) – 1/3 cup
- ☞ 1/3 cup Hong Kong–style Thick Classic Worcestershire sauce, such as Bull-Dog

Make Your Own Stir 1 tablespoon Worcestershire sauce and 1 teaspoon dark soy sauce into 1/4 cup ketchup until thoroughly combined. (For a more pungent sauce, use 3 tablespoons Worcestershire sauce, 2 tablespoons ketchup, and 1 teaspoon soy sauce.)

TOPFEN (soft, fresh Austrian cheese) See QUARK

TORIGARA BASE (WEIHA) (Japanese chicken stock base) – 1 teaspoon
- ☞ 1 teaspoon reduced-sodium chicken bouillon cube, or 1 envelope instant chicken broth or granules, or 1/2 to 3/4 teaspoon chicken extract or soup base, or 2 teaspoons vegetarian-based chicken broth powder (all substitutions will be saltier)

TORTILLA CHIPS/TOTOPOS/TOSTADITAS – 4 dozen

Make Your Own Brush or rub 6 (6-inch) corn tortillas with vegetable oil (optional); cut into 8 wedges and bake at 375°F until golden, 10 to 15 minutes, stirring halfway through (the chips will continue to crisp as they cool). Alternatively, fry the chips in small batches in 350°F oil until golden, 1 or 2 minutes; drain on paper towels 2 minutes, then shake in a paper bag with seasoned salt, if desired. (For best results, dry the tortillas at room temperature for 30 to 60 minutes before cooking, or use tortillas that are a few days old.)

TORTILLA CRISPS, CINNAMON/BUÑUELOS – 4 to 5 dozen

Make Your Own Brush 6 (6- or 7-inch) whole-grain or plain flour tortillas on both sides with melted butter or oil (or coat with cooking spray), then sprinkle with a mixture of 1/4 cup sugar and 1/2 teaspoon cinnamon. Cut into wedges or strips and bake at 350°F until golden, 8 to 10 minutes, stirring halfway through. Alternatively, cut the tortillas without buttering or sugaring them, then fry in small batches in 350°F oil until golden, 30 to 60 seconds. Toss them with cinnamon sugar while still warm.

TORTILLAS, CORN OR FLOUR (Mexican thin flatbread) – 1 dozen

- 1 dozen brown rice tortillas (gluten-free, suitable for grilling; crispier when heated; not for wraps)
- 1 dozen soft lavash pieces, naan, piadina, roti, or pita bread separated at the seam
- 12 green vegetable leaves or large lettuce leaves (for low-calorie wraps) *See WRAPPERS FOR FOOD, VEGETABLE-BASED*

TORTILLA SHELLS *See TACO BOWLS/SHELLS*

TOSTADA SHELLS (flat, crisp tortillas) – 1 dozen

- 12 white corn tortillas, sprayed with cooking spray and baked on a rack-lined baking sheet at 450°F until crisp, 5 to 7 minutes
- 6 store-bought crisp taco shells, broken in half (for small tostadas)

TOULOUMOTYRI (Greek moist white goat cheese) – 8 ounces
⊳ 8 ounces Cloumage, *mizithra*, or semi-aged feta

TOULOUSE (small French pork sausage) – 1 pound
⊳ 1 pound Spanish fresh/cooking chorizo or Portuguese chouriço
⊳ 1 pound Italian *luganega/lucanica*
⊳ 1 pound mild, flavorful sausage, such as British Cumberland or Italian sweet (larger and milder)

TOYOMANSI See SOY SAUCE, FILIPINO KALAMANSI

TREACLE, DARK (British dark thick syrup) – 1 tablespoon
⊳ 1 tablespoon blackstrap molasses See also MOLASSES, DARK

TREE EAR See CLOUD EAR/BLACK TREE FUNGUS

TRIMOLINE/NULOMOLINE (inverted sugar) – 1 cup
⊳ 1 cup liquid glucose

TRINIDAD MORUGA SCORPION CHILE – 1
⊳ 1 Trinidad Scorpion Butch T chile
⊳ 1 Bhut jolokia/Naga Viper/ghost chile/cobra chile
⊳ 1 Carolina Reaper chile (hotter)
⊳ 1 Dorset Naga
⊳ 1 Infinity chile
⊳ 1 Red Savina, habañero, Scotch bonnet, or goat chile (more fruity tasting)
⊳ 1/4 teaspoon Ghost pepper powder (plain or smoked)
⊳ 1 jarred pickled Ghost pepper/Bhut jolokia rinsed and patted dry (brine contains seasoning)

TRUFFLE, BLACK/FRENCH PÉRIGORD/TUBER MELANOSPORUM, FRESH OR FLASH-FROZEN – 1 ounce
⊳ 1 ounce black summer truffle/*Tuber aestivum* (white and yellow inside; much blander)

- 1 ounce French jarred truffle (slightly smaller)
- 1 ounce Chinese fresh or jarred truffle/*Tuber indicum* or *himalay-ense*
- 1 ounce Syrian, Moroccan, or Lebanese canned or jarred desert truffle/*faqa'a, kamaa, kamaieh, terfezia* (blander)
- 1 ounce jarred black truffle pieces or shavings, canned black truffle peelings in truffle juice, or canned black truffle juice from the preserving process
- 1 to 2 tablespoons black truffle paste or oil (usually synthetic truffle flavoring)
- 1 to 2 ounces Italian hydrated dried cèpes/*Funghi porcini secchi*
- 1 to 2 ounces fresh (or dried rehydrated) black trumpet/horn of plenty mushrooms (for the color only)
- Black truffle butter, if butter is called for in the recipe (add at the last minute)
- Grated truffle cheese, if cheese is called for in the recipe (add at the last minute)
- Black truffle salt, such as Casina Rossa or homemade, if salt is called for in the recipe (reduce the salt in the recipe by 95%)

TRUFFLE BUTTER – 4 ounces (1/2 cup)
Make Your Own Place 1 fresh black truffle and 1 stick unwrapped butter in a glass container, seal tightly, and let sit for 12 to 24 hours (or longer). Wrap the truffle butter in plastic wrap and then foil and keep refrigerated if not using immediately.
Or
Stir 1 to 2 tablespoons minced fresh black truffle (or black truffle paste) into 1/2 cup room-temperature butter until thoroughly incorporated. Season to taste with coarse salt, if desired, then tightly seal and refrigerate for 24 hours before using.

TRUFFLE OIL – 1/2 cup
Make Your Own Add 2 scant teaspoons truffle shavings to 1/2 cup grapeseed or canola oil and heat gently for 1 or 2 minutes. Cool, cover, and leave at room temperature for a few days, then refrigerate or freeze.

TRUFFLE OIL, WHITE – 4 or 5 drops
- 1 scant teaspoon white truffle shavings
- 5 (or more) drops porcini oil

TRUFFLE PASTE, WHITE – 1 tablespoon
- 1/2 to 1 teaspoon white truffle oil

TRUFFLE SALT (flavored finishing salt) – 3 tablespoons
Make Your Own Mix 1 scant teaspoon shaved black truffle with 3 tablespoons coarse sea salt. Tightly seal and leave at room temperature a few days for the salt to absorb the truffle flavor.

TRUFFLE SHAVINGS, BLACK, FRESH OR JARRED – 2 tablespoons
- 1 teaspoon black truffle oil

TRUFFLE STOCK – 1 cup
- 1 cup fresh mushroom stock
- 1 cup wild mushroom stock, prepared from wild mushroom bouillon granules

TRUFFLE, WHITE ITALIAN/PIEDMONTESE/TUBER MAGNATUM, FRESH – 1 ounce *See also TRUFFLE, BLACK FRENCH PÉRIGORD*
- 1 ounce jarred white truffle peelings and pieces (less expensive)
- 1 ounce white Oregon truffle/*Tuber gibbosum/Tuber oregonense* (darker colored; smaller; less aromatic)
- 1 to 2 ounces Italian hydrated dried cèpes/*Funghi porcini secchi*

TRUGOLE (Italian semisoft cheese) – 1 ounce
- 1 ounce fresh Asiago, caciocavallo, domestic fontina, provolone, or scamorza

TSAMPA (Tibetan roasted ground barley) *See BARLEY FLOUR*

TUMBO (tart Peruvian fruit) – 1 scant cup juice
- 8 ounces frozen tumbo juice/*curuba* pulp

- 1/2 cup grapefruit juice, 1/4 cup Key lime juice, and 3 tablespoons passion fruit juice
- 1 cup passion fruit juice (less tart)

TUNA, FRESH – 1 pound
- 1 pound fresh swordfish, shark, or Hawaiian opah
- 14 ounces jarred tuna fillets packed in olive oil/*ventresca*
- 1 (14.7- to 15-ounce) can salmon or mackerel packed in water

TURKISH PEPPER PASTE *See RED PEPPER PASTE, HOT; RED PEPPER PASTE, MILD*

TURKISH VINEGAR/GRAPE VINEGAR – 1 tablespoon
- 1 1/2 teaspoons each red wine vinegar and balsamic vinegar

TURMERIC ROOT, FRESH OR FROZEN (Indian seasoning) – 1-inch piece or 1 tablespoon peeled and finely chopped
- 1 or 2 teaspoons grated dried turmeric rhizome (wear plastic gloves and be careful; turmeric stains are hard to remove)
- 1 tablespoon grated carrot plus 1/2 teaspoon each powdered turmeric and grated fresh ginger
- 2 teaspoons finely chopped fresh ginger
- 1 teaspoon powdered Alleppey turmeric (orange-yellow color; for flavor) or powdered Madras turmeric (bright yellow; for color)
- 1 1/2 teaspoons generic turmeric powder (for color)
- 1/4 teaspoon finely ground annatto seeds, achiote/Bijol powder, or mild yellow curry powder (for color only)

TURMERIC ROOT POWDER/GROUND TURMERIC – 1 teaspoon
- 1 tablespoon packed fresh grated turmeric
- Small pinch of saffron, crushed dried safflower florets, or safflower stigmas/Mexican saffron/*azafrán* (for color)
- 1 teaspoon ground annatto seeds or achiote/Bijol powder (for color)

- 2 teaspoons ground dried marigold petals; or dried petals steeped in a little warm water 5 minutes; use liquid for color and discard petals

TURMERIC, WHITE *See ZEDOARY/WHITE TURMERIC*

TURNIP GREENS – 1 pound
- 1 pound mustard greens, dandelion greens, collard greens, or kohlrabi greens
- 1 pound beet greens, curly green kale, green chard, or young shepherd's purse (milder flavor)

TURNIPS, BABY SCARLET – 1 pound
- 1 pound regular white turnips, peeled and cut into 2-inch pieces

TURNIPS, BABY WHITE – 1 pound
- 1 pound Hakurei or Tokyo Market turnips, trimmed and cut into halves
- 1 pound young sweet turnips, peeled and cut into quarters or into spheres with a melon baller
- 1 pound mild globe radishes
- 1 pound French Breakfast or White Icicle radishes, cut in pieces

TURNIPS, WHITE – 1 pound
- 1 pound golden turnips (sweeter)
- 1 pound parsnips (sweeter)
- 1 pound rutabagas (sweeter; denser; longer cooking time)
- 1 pound green kohlrabi base (sweeter and more delicate)
- 1 pound young evening primrose roots (more peppery)

TURTLE MEAT – 4 ounces
- 4 ounces boneless veal shoulder

TVOROG (Russian-style curd cheese) – 8 ounces *See also COTTAGE CHEESE, DRY*
- ☞ 8 ounces farmer cheese or pot cheese
- ☞ 9 ounces whole-milk ricotta, drained overnight in a cheese-cloth-lined sieve

TXORIZERO PEPPER (Basque dried sweet pepper) – 1
- ☞ 1 dried New Mexico or California chile

U

UDO (Japanese white stalk vegetable) – 1 pound
- ▷ 1 pound fennel (bulb and thick green stalks)
- ▷ 1 pound white asparagus or celery plus a pinch of crushed fennel seeds

UDON See JAPANESE NOODLES, THICK WHEAT

UGLI/UNIQ FRUIT (thick, bumpy-skinned Jamaican citrus) – 1 whole (1 cup segments)
- ▷ 1 honey pummelo/pomelo or red pomelo/shaddock (less sweet and juicy)

UMAMI/FIFTH TASTE/SAVORY FLAVOR (flavor-enhancing foods)
- ▷ Anchovies; Asian fish sauce; kombu/dried kelp; miso; mushrooms, especially morels (always cooked), porcini, portabellos, or shiitakes; Parmigiano-Reggiano or other aged cheese; red wine; smoked or cured fish; soy sauce; or tomatoes, especially vine-ripened or dried

UMAMI DUST (Japanese flavor-enhancing seasoning) – 1 (generous) ounce
- ▷ 1/2 ounce crumbled dried kombu/kelp (1/2 sheet), 1/2 ounce dried shiitake caps (about 5 large), and 3 tablespoons dried bonito flakes, ground until fine

UMEBOSHI (Japanese salt-pickled dried plum) – 1 large (1 tablespoon pitted and mashed)
- ▷ 1 quickly pickled salted plum/*shio-hikaeme umeboshi* (juicier, with less salt)

- 1 Chinese pickled plum/*suan mei* or salted dried plum/*li hing mui/ hua mei*
- 2 teaspoons jarred umeboshi puree/paste/*bainiku/neri-ume*
- 1 1/2 teaspoons umeboshi plum vinegar/*ume su* (much saltier)
- 2 or 3 tiny plum paste balls/*umeboshi-san*

UMEBOSHI PASTE/BAINIKU – 1 ounce
- 1 ounce Japanese dried, salt-pickled plum/*umeboshi* or Chinese pickled plum/*suanmel*, ground with a mortar and pestle until smooth

UMEBOSHI VINEGAR/UME SU – 1 tablespoon
- 1 1/2 teaspoons lemon juice and 1 1/2 teaspoons Japanese soy sauce or tamari
- 1 (scant) tablespoon red rice vinegar or red wine vinegar plus a few drops of soy sauce
- 1 tablespoon cider vinegar plus a pinch of table salt
- 1 tablespoon sherry vinegar

URAD DAL/KALI DAL/DHAL See DAL/DHAL

URAD DAL FLOUR (Indian) – 1 cup
- 1 1/4 cups split and husked black lentils, roasted in a dry skillet until slightly aromatic, 5 to 10 minutes, then finely ground in a food mill, or in batches in a coffee/spice grinder
- 1 cup brown rice flour

URFA PEPPER FLAKES/ISOT PEPPER FLAKES/URFA BIBER (Turkish) – 1 teaspoon
- 1 teaspoon Aleppo or Maras red pepper flakes
- 3/4 teaspoon Aleppo or Urfa chile powder
- 1/2 teaspoon ancho chile powder or smoked Spanish paprika plus 1/4 teaspoon ground cayenne pepper

UTAZI LEAVES (Nigerian leafy vegetable) – 4 ounces
- 4 ounces broccoli rabe leaves, arugula, or any bitter leafy greens

V

VACHERIN FRIBOURGEOIS (Swiss cow's milk cheese) – 1 ounce
- 1 ounce Fontina Val d'Aosta, Vacherin d'Abondance, Appenzeller, or Morbier

VANILLA BEAN, BOURBON/MADAGASCAR OR MEXICAN – 3- to 4-inch section
- 1/4 to 1/2 teaspoon ground whole vanilla bean
- 1 teaspoon pure vanilla extract, vanillin/vanilla powder, vanilla bean paste, vanilla bean crush, vanilla flavoring, or imitation vanilla
- 1 tablespoon vanilla sugar (reduce the sugar in the recipe by 1 tablespoon)
- 4 drops concentrated vanilla essence (add after removing from the heat)

VANILLA BEAN PASTE – 1 teaspoon
- 1 teaspoon vanilla powder
- 4 drops concentrated vanilla essence

Make Your Own Place 1/2 vanilla bean upright in a small container, add 1/2 inch of vodka, and refrigerate until a paste forms, about 2 weeks. Squeeze out the paste and use.

VANILLA BEAN, TAHITIAN – 1 whole bean including scraped seeds
- 2 Bourbon-Madagscar or Mexican vanilla beans
- 1 teaspoon ground whole vanilla beans
- 1 tablespoon vanilla bean paste, pure vanilla extract, vanillin/vanilla powder, or vanilla flavoring (add toward the end of cooking, or after removing from the heat)

VANILLA EXTRACT – 1 teaspoon
- 1 teaspoon vanilla bean paste or vanilla flavoring
- 1/4 to 1/2 teaspoon ground whole vanilla beans
- 1/2 teaspoon double strength vanilla extract
- 1 (2- to 3-inch) piece Bourbon-Madagascar vanilla bean, or 1(1- to 2-inch piece) Tahitian vanilla bean, split and seeds scraped out (add early in the recipe; for puddings, custards, sauces, or ice cream)
- 4 drops concentrated vanilla essence
- 1 teaspoon imitation clear vanilla or vanillin/white vanilla powder (for no color)
- 1 teaspoon alcohol-free vanilla extract, such as Trader Joe's
- 1 tablespoon vanilla sugar (Reduce the sugar in the recipe by 1 tablespoon. Alternatively, grind a piece of vanilla bean with a little sugar, then add it to the granulated sugar before weighing or measuring.)

VANILLA EXTRACT – 8 ounces
Make Your Own Split 1 Bourbon-Madagascar, or cheaper grade B/ extract, vanilla bean lengthwise. Scrape out the seeds and thinly slice the bean. Add the bean and seeds to 1 cup brandy, aged rum, or vodka in a dark-colored 8-ounce bottle; seal tightly and store in a cool, dark cupboard for at least 3 months, shaking the bottle from time to time. (The higher the alcohol proof the better; for wheat-free extract, choose brandy or rum.)

VANILLA EXTRACT, DOUBLE-STRENGTH – 4 ounces
- 1 split and sectioned vanilla bean, gently inserted into a 4-ounce bottle of vanilla extract and left to steep at least 7 days

VANILLA POWDER See VANILLA BEAN PASTE

VANILLA SUGAR – 1 cup
Make Your Own Pulse 1 cup granulated or powdered sugar and 1 teaspoon vanilla powder (or half a vanilla bean cut in half) in a blender or food processor until thoroughly combined and well distributed.

Or

Split 1 vanilla bean lengthwise, then place in a jar with 1 cup granulated or powdered sugar and let sit for 1 to 2 weeks. Replenish the sugar as needed until the bean loses its flavoring capability.

VEAL – 1 pound
⇨ 1 pound beef or lamb fillet

VEAL CUTLETS – 1 pound
⇨ 1 pound turkey cutlets, or turkey breast cut into 1/2-inch slices

VEAL, GROUND – 1 pound
⇨ Ground lamb, pork, or turkey

VEAL SCALLOPS/ESCALOPES (thinly cut veal for making scaloppini) – 1 pound
⇨ 1 1/2 pounds veal chops (eye section cut out and pounded until thin; freeze the bones for stock)
⇨ 1 pound turkey scaloppini/*escalopes*
⇨ 1 pound small, boneless chicken breast halves without tenders, cut in half horizontally (freezing the chicken for 15 minutes makes slicing easier)
⇨ 1 pound pork loin (cut into 1/4-inch slices)
⇨ 5 to 6 (3/8-inch) peeled eggplant slices (for a vegetarian alternative)

VEGETABLES FOR WRAPPING/VEGETABLE WRAPPERS See
WRAPPERS, FOR FOOD, VEGETABLE-BASED

VERBENA See LEMON VERBENA, FRESH

VERDINA BEANS, DRIED (tiny Spanish green beans) – 1 pound
⇨ 1 pound mung beans
⇨ 1 pound small dried flageolets (larger)

VERJUICE/VERJUS/AGRESTO/HOSRUM/KORUK/ABGHOOREH
(unripe grape juice) – 2 tablespoons
- 1/4 to 1/3 cup hard, sour green grapes, pureed and strained to measure 2 tablespoons
- 1 tablespoon each white grape juice and cider vinegar
- 1 tablespoon each white wine and unseasoned rice vinegar
- 1 1/2 tablespoons white wine and 1/2 tablespoon distilled white vinegar or lemon juice
- 1 1/2 teaspoons dried sour grape powder and 2 tablespoons water

VERMICELLI, FRESH OR DRIED – 1 pound See also PASTA, THIN
STRAND OR ROD
- 1 pound fresh or dried angel hair, spaghettini, capellini, fine egg noodles, fideos, or Japanese *ito soba*

VERMICELLI BEAN THREADS See NOODLES, CELLOPHANE

VERMOUTH, DRY/FRENCH (fortified white wine) – 1/4 cup for cooking
- 1/4 cup dry sherry or light, dry/Sercial Madeira
- 1/3 cup dry white wine, saké, or pure Shaoxing yellow rice wine (reduce liquid in the recipe by 1 tablespoon if necessary)

VIETNAMESE BALM/GREEN PERILLA/RAU KINH GIO'I See SHISO,
GREEN

VIETNAMESE BASIL/RAU HUYNG See BASIL, THAI

VIETNAMESE CHILI SAUCE/TUONG OT TOI – 1 tablespoon
- 1 tablespoon sambal oelek, harissa, Sriracha, Szechuan chili sauce, or hot pepper sauce, such as Tabasco or Crystal

VIETNAMESE DIPPING SAUCE/TUONG GUNG – 1/2 cup
- 1/4 cup each Vietnamese fish sauce/*nuoc nam*, fresh lime juice, and superfine sugar mixed together until sugar dissolves

⇨ 2 tablespoons each unseasoned rice vinegar, water, and fresh lime juice; plus 1 teaspoon each chili-garlic paste (or Chinese chili-garlic sauce), sugar, and soy sauce stirred together until sugar dissolves

VIETNAMESE FISH SAUCE/NUOC NAM/NUOC MAM – 1 tablespoon
⇨ 1 tablespoon premium (gluten-free) *nuoc nam* made with the first pressing (*cot, nhi, thuong hang, phu quoc*)
⇨ 1 tablespoon Thai fish sauce/*nam pla*, Korean fish sauce/*saengseon*, Japanese fish sauce/*shottsuru*, or Filipino fish sauce/*patis*
⇨ 1 tablespoon vegetarian fish sauce/*nuoc nam chay*
⇨ 2 teaspoons anchovy essence/syrup mixed with a few drops light soy sauce
⇨ 1/2 teaspoon Worcestershire sauce

VIETNAMESE MINT/LAKSA LEAF/RAU RAM/PHAK PHAI/DAUN KESOM/DAUN LAKSA, FRESH – 1 tablespoon chopped
⇨ 1 1/2 teaspoons each chopped fresh cilantro and spearmint (or peppermint)
⇨ 1 1/2 teaspoons each chopped fresh cilantro and lemon balm leaves (or lemon basil)
⇨ 1 tablespoon chopped domestic garden cilantro going to seed (starting to flower)

VIETNAMESE NOODLES, CELLOPHANE/MUNG BEAN/BEAN THREADS/BUN TAU *See NOODLES, CELLOPHANE*

VIETNAMESE NOODLES, MEDIUM WHITE RICE/BÁNH PHO/NU TIEU – 1 pound
⇨ 1 pound fresh or 8 to 12 ounces dried Chinese, Thai, or other 1/4-inch linguine-type rice noodles

VIETNAMESE PICKLED LEEKS/CU KIEU – 1 cup
⇨ 1 cup Cornichons/gherkins or other mild cucumber pickles

VIETNAMESE SHRIMP PASTE/MAM TOM *See SHRIMP PASTE,*
FERMENTED

VIETNAMESE SOY SAUCE *See SOY SAUCE, VIETNAMESE*

VIETNAMESE SWEET-AND-SOUR DIPPING SAUCE/NUOC CHAM –
scant 1/2 cup
- ➻ 1/4 cup each sugar, Vietnamese fish sauce/*nuoc nam*, and lime
  juice, plus 1 small minced garlic clove, and 1 minced fresh Thai or
  cayenne chile stirred until the sugar dissolves
- ➻ 1/3 cup chili-garlic sauce, 1 tablespoon Vietnamese fish sauce/
  nuoc nam, and 1 tablespoon lime juice stirred until combined (for
  nuoc nam gung, add finely chopped fresh ginger)

VIETNAMESE SWEET CHILI SAUCE/TUONG OT NGOT *– scant 2/3 cup*
- ➻ 2/3 cup Thai sweet chili sauce/dipping sauce for chicken/*nam jim*
  kai
- ➻ 3 tablespoons sambal oelek and 2 tablespoons unseasoned rice
  vinegar stirred into 1/3 cup mild honey

VIETNAMESE YELLOW BEAN SAUCE/TUONG OT/TUONG CU DA *– 1*
tablespoon
- ➻ 1 tablespoon *awase* miso (a mixture of white and red miso)
- ➻ 1 scant tablespoon Chinese yellow/brown soybean paste, or Thai
  yellow bean paste/*tao jiaw* thinned with a little water
- ➻ 1 1/2 teaspoons each Japanese light and dark miso

VIETNAMESE YOGURT/SUA CHUA/DA UA *– 1 cup*
- ➻ 1 (3.5-ounce) can sweetened condensed milk stirred into 3/4 cup
  plain Greek-style yogurt until thoroughly incorporated (store,
  tightly covered, in the refrigerator for up to 2 weeks)

VINAIGRETTE, QUICK *– 1/4 cup*
- ➻ 1 tablespoon olive oil and 3 tablespoons brine from jarred vegetables (olives, pickles, peppers, or other vegetables packed in brine)

☞ 3 tablespoons mild vinegar and 1 tablespoon oil from jarred vegetables (artichokes, sun-dried tomatoes, olives, or other vegetables packed in oil)

☞ 4 tablespoons balsamic vinegar, chopped fresh herbs, and a pinch of xanthan gum (for nonfat dressing)

VIN COTTO (Southern Italian unrefined wine syrup) – 1/3 cup See also GRAPE MOLASSES

☞ 1/3 cup Italian grape syrup/molasses/*saba/mosto cotto*

☞ 1/3 cup Middle Eastern pomegranate syrup/molasses/*dibis rouman/dibs rubba*

☞ 1/3 cup strong-flavored honey

Make Your Own Combine 1 cup fruity red wine and 5 tablespoons sugar and boil gently, stirring constantly and skimming any foam, until syrupy and reduced to 1/3 cup.

VINEGAR (acidifying/souring agent) – 1 tablespoon

☞ 1/16 teaspoon ascorbic acid or 1/4 teaspoon citric acid powder (for acidulated water)

☞ 1 tablespoon lemon or lime juice (for salad dressings, marinades, sauces)

☞ 1 tablespoon sauerkraut juice (for salad dressing; omit the salt)

☞ 1 tablespoon lemon juice, wine, port, or sherry (for deglazing pans)

☞ 1 to 1 1/2 teaspoons green mango powder/*amchur*, ground sumac, or pomegranate seed powder/*anardana* (for chutneys and curries)

☞ 3/4 to 1 teaspoon tamarind paste or concentrate (for chutneys, curries, soups)

VINEGAR, MILD – 1 tablespoon

☞ 1 tablespoon unseasoned rice vinegar, white wine vinegar, or sherry vinegar

☞ 1 1/2 teaspoons each unseasoned rice vinegar and white wine vinegar

☞ 1 1/2 teaspoons each apple cider vinegar and water

VINO SECO (Hispanic Caribbean salted cooking wine) – 2 tablespoons
- 2 tablespoons red or white cooking wine
- 2 tablespoons dry white or red wine; adjust the salt in the recipe as needed

VIN SANTO (Italian amber-colored dessert wine) – 1 cup
- 1 cup sweet Riesling, Manzanilla sherry, White Port, Madeira, or Marsala

VIOLETS, CANDIED/VIOLETTES DE TOULOUSE (French) – 4 ounces
Make Your Own Beat 1 pasteurized egg white with 1 tablespoon water. Brush onto 3 ounces pesticide-free, edible violets, then dredge them in superfine sugar. Place on a rack or parchment-lined baking sheet and dry in a cool place for 24 hours. (To keep the best shape, dry the violets upside down suspended by their stems.)

VITAL WHEAT GLUTEN (high protein flour used to increase gluten content in bread recipes) – 1 tablespoon
- 1 tablespoon whole-grain bread improver blend, such as King Arthur (omit ascorbic acid if called for in the recipe)
- 2 tablespoons high-gluten flour (reduce the flour in the recipe by 1 tablespoon if necessary)

VOLVI (Greek edible hyacinth bulbs) – 1 pound
- 1 pound fresh pearl onions or other small onions

W

WAKAME/HOSHI WAKAME/MIYUK, DRIED (Japanese dark green sea vegetable) – 1 ounce

- 1 ounce freeze-dried, salt-covered wakame/*yutōshi shiozo wakame* (soak in cool water for 10 minutes, then rinse thoroughly to remove excess salt)
- 1 ounce refrigerated finely shredded wakame/*mozuku wakame* (soak in cool water for 10 to 15 minutes, or add directly to soups)
- 1/2 ounce shredded or flaked instant wakame/*katto wakame* (soak in cool water for 1 to 3 minutes, or add directly to soup; swells to several times its original volume: 1 tablespoon makes 1/2 cup/1 1/2 ounces)
- 1 ounce bite-size wakame/*fueru wakame* (soak in cool water for 5 minutes)
- 1 ounce lighter-colored more delicate wakame/*Ito wakame* (soak in cool water for 15 minutes)
- 2/3 ounce dried alaria/winged kelp (saltier and chewier, soak in cool water for 20 to 60 minutes)
- 1 ounce dried arame (long, black delicate strands; milder flavor; rinse, then soak in cool water for 5 to 10 minutes)
- 1 ounce dulse sheets or flakes (saltier; no soaking required)
- 1 ounce dried *nikombu* (kombu for eating; not dashi kombu; stronger flavor; soak in cool water for 5 to 10 minutes)
- 2 cups lightly packed fresh or frozen chopped chard or kale (cook until tender)
- 4 to 5 cups coarsely chopped fresh young spinach leaves (blanch for 1 minute, refresh in ice water, then squeeze out excess water)

WAKAME POWDER (Japanese condiment)
Make Your Own Cut dried wakame into small pieces and toast in a dry skillet, stirring constantly, until very crisp, about 5 minutes. Crumble or grind into a powder (use a mortar and pestle or a rolling pin sleeved in plastic).

WALNUT FLOUR – 1 cup
Make Your Own Grind 1 3/4 to 2 cups shelled walnut halves until powdery in a food processor, or in batches in a spice/coffee grinder.

WALNUT LIQUEUR/WALNUT-FLAVORED SPIRIT (such as Flaschengeist, Lantenhammer, Nocino, or Nux Alpina) – 1 tablespoon for cooking
⮞ 1/4 teaspoon walnut extract and 3/4 tablespoon vodka or water

WALNUT MILK – 4 cups (about)
⮞ 4 cups almond milk or hazelnut milk,
Make Your Own Soak 1 to 1 1/2 cups raw walnut halves in water to cover for 4 to 8 hours; drain, rinse, then process with 4 cups warm water in a blender or food processor until smooth, 2 to 3 minutes. Strain through a nutmilk bag or cheesecloth-lined sieve, pressing firmly on the pulp to extract the liquid. Keep refrigerated and shake before using.

WALNUT OIL – 1/2 cup
⮞ 1/2 cup hazelnut, macadamia nut, or extra-virgin olive oil
Make Your Own Toast 1/2 cup shelled walnuts. Process with 1/2 cup neutral-tasting vegetable oil in a blender or food processor until smooth. Strain and refrigerate for 2 or 3 days to develop the flavor; use immediately or store, tightly covered, in the refrigerator.

WALNUTS, BLACK – 1 cup
⮞ 1 cup English walnuts (thinner; less flavorful)

WALNUTS, ENGLISH – 1 cup
- 1 cup butternuts/*Juglans cinerea* or pecans
- 1 cup hickory nuts (harder shells)
- 1 cup black walnuts (firmer; harder shells; more bitter)

WARKA/WARKHA/WARQA/OUARKA *See BRIK PASTRY*

WASABI/HON WASABI (Japanese horseradish) – 2-ounce root (1 tablespoon freshly grated)
- 1 or more tablespoons wasabi paste/*neriwasabi*
- 1 tablespoon wasabi powder/*konawasabi* stirred into 2 teaspoons cold water and left covered for 5 to 10 minutes to develop the flavor

WASABI, POWDERED – 1 teaspoon
- 1 teaspoon horseradish or mustard powder

WASABI, PREPARED – 1 teaspoon
- 1 teaspoon wasabi powder mixed with 1 scant teaspoon cold water, then left, covered, 10 to 15 minutes to develop the flavor
- 1 teaspoon fresh horseradish (or strained bottled horseradish) plus a touch of green food coloring
- 1 teaspoon mustard powder, 1/2 teaspoon vinegar, 1/4 teaspoon oil, and 1/8 teaspoon salt mixed together until smooth, then left, covered, for 10 to 15 minutes to develop the flavor

WATER CHESTNUT POWDER/MA TIE FUN (Asian thickening agent) – 1 tablespoon
- 1 tablespoon lotus root starch or cornstarch

WATER CHESTNUTS/MAH TAI/HAEW, FRESH (Asian tuber vegetable) – 1 cup
- 1 cup canned water chestnuts, drained and rinsed (or briefly blanched in boiling water)
- 1 cup chopped fresh jícama

- 1 cup chopped cooked (or canned) locust root
- 1 cup chopped cooked burdock root
- 1 cup small cooked sunchokes (or large cooked ones sliced or cubed)

WATERCRESS, CULTIVATED – 1 ounce (1 cup)
- 1 ounce hydroponic-grown cress with roots attached (milder tasting; more tender), or wild watercress (smaller leaves; less tender)
- 1 ounce upland/land cress, or garden/pepper cress (smaller leaves; slightly more pungent)
- 1 ounce young nasturtium leaves and stems, radish sprouts, baby arugula/rocket, or young dandelion greens
- 1 ounce young garland chrysanthemum (for cooking)
- 1 ounce tender wild mugwort/*Artemisia vulgaris*

WATER PURIFICATION TABLETS (product to make questionable water safe to drink, such as Hazalone or Globaline) – 4 tablets
- 5 drops plain chlorine bleach mixed with 1/2 gallon water; let sit, uncovered, for 30 minutes
- 5 drops grapefruit seed extract (GSE) mixed with 1/2 gallon water; let sit for several hours

WATER SPINACH/KANGKONG/PAK BOONG/ONG CHOY/RAU MUONG/ VLITA (Southeast Asian vegetable) – 1 bunch (about 2 pounds)
- 1 bunch sweet potato leaves, including stems (Only sweet potato leaves are edible; regular potato leaves are poisonous.)
- 1 1/2 bunches (about 1 1/2 pounds) regular mature spinach or Taiwan spinach, including stems

WESTPHALIAN HAM (German smoky dry ham) – 1 pound
- 1 pound Italian or domestic prosciutto
- 1 pound Italian or domestic speck
- 1 pound Serrano ham

WHEAT BERRIES, RED WHOLE (whole, unprocessed wheat kernels) – 1 cup (8 ounces)
- 1 cup soft wheat berries (more tender)

- 1 cup whole-grain einkorn/einka berries (small, heirloom wheat berries; reduce cooking time to 25 minutes)
- 1 cup Kamut/khorasan wheat berries, triticale berries, spelt berries, hulled/whole-grain barley, hull-less barley, whole-oat groats, or hulled Job's tears/*hato mugi*
- 1 cup pearled wheat/golden peeled wheat, or pearled farro (reduce the cooking time by half)
- 1 cup cracked wheat plus 1/2 teaspoon wheat bran (no prior soaking required; reduce the cooking time by three-quarters)
- 1 cup coarse bulgur (grind #3 or #4) prepared following the package directions

WHEAT BRAN, UNPROCESSED/MILLERS BRAN
- Whole-wheat flour, sifted through a fine-mesh sieve to extract the bran; use the flour in making country French bread
- Oat bran or rice bran (measure by weight, not volume)

WHEAT, CRACKED – 1 cup
- 1 generous cup hard red wheat berries, chopped to a cracked-wheat stage in a blender, 15 to 20 seconds, or in small batches in a spice/coffee grinder (sift to remove any smaller particles)
- 1 cup cracked rye (rye chops), coarse-ground bulgur (grind #3), or whole-wheat Israeli couscous
- 1 cup buckwheat groats or kasha (for a gluten-free alternative)

WHEAT, FRESH/GREEN ROASTED DURUM/FREEKEH/FARĪK/FRIKEH (Egyptian, Lebanese, and Turkish young green wheat with a smoky flavor) – 1 pound
- 1 pound coarse-ground bulgur (grind #3) or pearl barley, toasted in a dry skillet before cooking

WHEAT GLUTEN See VITAL WHEAT GLUTEN

WHEATGRASS, FRESH (antioxidant-rich food supplement)
- Frozen wheatgrass cubes
- Freeze-dried wheatgrass powder

- Fresh Kamut or barley grass
- Wild grass/*Poa spp.,* or regular perennial lawn grass (not endophyte-enhanced or sprayed with chemical fertilizers)
- Kamut, barley grass, or multi-greens powder
- Chlorella powder or liquid concentrate (more potent)
- Spirulina flakes or powder (more potent)

WHEAT MALT SYRUP (non-diastatic liquid malt) – 1 tablespoon
- 1 tablespoon barley malt syrup
- 1 1/2 teaspoons granulated sugar, or 1 tablespoon light brown sugar

WHEAT STARCH/TANG FLOUR/TANG MIEN FUN/CHENG MIAN FEN (Chinese gluten-free flour and thickener) – 1/4 cup
- 1/4 cup cornstarch

WHEY (the watery part of milk left over from cheese making) – 2 tablespoons
- 2 tablespoons plain yogurt, kefir, or buttermilk (for adding to soaking water for grains)
- 2 tablespoon lemon juice (for adding to soaking water for legumes)
- 1 to 2 teaspoons additional salt (for starter culture for lacto-fermented vegetables)

WHIPPED CREAM STABILIZER See CREAM, WHIPPED, STABILIZER

WHIPPED TOPPING See CREAM, WHIPPED; DAIRY-FREE TOPPING

WHISKEY SAUCE – 1 1/2 cups
- 1/4 cup whiskey, thoroughly stirred into a 14-ounce can warmed sweetened condensed milk (low-fat or regular)

WHITE SAUCE/BÉCHAMEL, MEDIUM – 1 cup for cooking
- 2/3 cup canned cream-style soup, such as celery or mushroom, and 1/3 cup milk, whisked together and heated
- 3 cups canned or homemade coconut milk slowly simmered, uncovered, until reduced to 1 cup (vegan)

☞ 1/3 cup plain macadamia nuts soaked in water to cover for 8 to 12 hours, then drained and processed in a blender with 1 cup water until smooth. Strain through a fine-mesh sieve, then blend again if necessary. (vegan)

WHITE WINE VINEGAR – 1 tablespoon
☞ 1 tablespoon champagne vinegar or unseasoned rice wine vinegar

WHOLE-GRAIN BREAD IMPROVER – 1 tablespoon
☞ 1 tablespoon vital wheat gluten plus scant 1/8 teaspoon ascorbic acid

WILD LIME LEAF See KAFFIR LIME LEAF

WILD PEPPER LEAF/WILD BETAL LEAF/BAI CHA-PLU/BO LA LOT/ DAUN KADOK (Indian and Southeast Asian seasoning and food wrapper)
☞ Chinese broccoli leaves (for seasoning)
☞ Grape leaves, choy sum, large spinach leaves, leafy lettuce leaves, or deveined collard greens cut into 3-inch squares (for wrapping) See also WRAPPERS FOR FOOD, VEGETABLE-BASED

WILD RICE (giant- or long-grain) – 1 cup uncooked
☞ 1 cup sun-dried black raw rice (increase the cooking time by 15 minutes)
☞ 1 cup split or broken wild rice (reduce the cooking time to 30 minutes)
☞ 2 pouches shelf-stable, precooked wild rice (reduce the cooking time to 25 minutes)
☞ 2 (2.75-ounce) packages instant or quick-cooking wild rice (reduce the liquid to 2 1/2 cups and the cooking time to 10 minutes)
☞ 1 cup wild and brown rice mix (parboiled, milder, and more economical; reduce the cooking time to 35 minutes)
☞ 1 cup whole-grain farro, toasted in a dry skillet for 10 minutes, then prepared following the package directions; or precooked farro, such as Arden Farms

- 1 1/3 cups uncooked long-grain brown rice: basmati, jasmine, Texmati, or wild pecan rice (less liquid and cooking time; prepare following the package directions)
- 1 1/4 cups uncooked kasha/roasted buckwheat groats, or coarse-ground bulgur (grind #3) (reduce the water to 2 1/2 cups and the cooking time to 20 minutes)

WILD RICE, INSTANT – 1 cup uncooked
- 2 cups uncooked Minute brown rice prepared following the package directions

WINE – 1/4 cup for deglazing
- 1/4 cup chicken or beef broth plus 1 teaspoon acidic liquid, such as wine vinegar, lemon juice, or verjuice (Use the broth for deglazing, then add the acidic liquid after removing the pan from the heat.)

WINE – 1 cup for marinades
- 1/2 cup vinegar, 1/2 cup water, and 2 tablespoons sugar, heated to dissolve the sugar, then cooled
- 3/4 cup chicken stock plus 1/4 cup vinegar
- 1 tablespoon red wine powder for barbecue spice rubs

WINE – 1 cup for sweet dishes
- 1 cup grape juice made from varietal wine grapes, such as Merlot or Cabernet
- 3/4 cup unsweetened apple juice or cran-apple juice and 1 tablespoon lemon juice or mild vinegar
- 1 cup nonalcoholic fruity wine
- 3/4 cup water and 3 tablespoons lemon juice

WINE, RED – 1 cup for cooking
- 1 cup red vermouth plus a few drops of red wine vinegar or lemon juice
- 1 cup sulfate-free organic red wine, low-alcohol red wine (9% or so), or de-alcoholized red wine (.3 to .5%)
- 1/2 cup each balsamic vinegar and water

- ☞ 1 cup soaking liquid from sun-dried tomatoes or dried mushrooms plus 1 teaspoon cider vinegar (Strain the mushroom liquid through dampened cheesecloth or a paper coffee filter to remove any grit.)
- ☞ 1/2 to 3/4 cup unsweetened red grape juice (not Concord), cranberry juice, or pomegranate juice plus 1 tablespoon white vinegar and enough water to measure 1 cup
- ☞ 1 cup beef or vegetable broth, plus 1 teaspoon red wine vinegar stirred in just before serving; reduce the salt in the recipe accordingly
- ☞ Red wine powder (used dry in cooking or spice rubs)

WINE, SPARKLING *See CHAMPAGNE*

WINE, SWEETENED RICE *See MIRIN*

WINE, WHITE – 1 cup for cooking
- ☞ 3/4 cup dry white vermouth (opened vermouth will last for up to 3 months in the refrigerator)
- ☞ 1 cup white low-alcohol wine (9% or so), or de-alcoholized wine (0.3 to 0.5%)
- ☞ 1 cup pear or apple cider (or unsweetened apple juice plus a few drops of cider vinegar)
- ☞ 1 cup chicken or vegetable broth (or the juice from canned mushrooms), plus 1 teaspoon white wine vinegar or lemon juice, stirred in just before serving (reduce the salt in the recipe accordingly)
- ☞ 1 cup ginger ale, white grape juice, or white cranberry juice drink

WINE, YELLOW RICE *See SHAOXING*

WINGED BEANS/GOA BEANS/ASPARAGUS BEANS/TUA POO/ KECIPIR/SASSAGE (Asian legume) – 1 pound
- ☞ 1 pound snow peas, snap peas, or green beans (less starchy-tasting)

WING SAUCE (condiment for Buffalo chicken wings) – 1/2 cup
Make Your Own Bring 1/4 cup butter, 1/4 cup hot pepper sauce, such as Frank's RedHot, and 1 tablespoon distilled white vinegar to a simmer, then remove from the heat to cool.

WINTER MELON/WAX GOURD/DONG GUA *See SQUASH, ASIAN*

WONTON CRISPS – 2 dozen
Make Your Own Cut 12 wonton wrappers in half diagonally, coat with cooking spray, and spread in a single layer on a baking sheet. Bake in a preheated 375°F oven until golden, 6 to 8 minutes, turning halfway through. Alternatively, fry the cut wrappers in 350°F oil until golden, about 30 seconds, then drain on paper towels. For sweet chips, sprinkle them with cinnamon sugar or plain sugar while still hot.

WONTON WRAPPERS – 1 pound
- 1 pound *siu mai* wrappers (round)
- 1 pound egg roll wrappers, cut into quarters (thicker)
- 1 pound rice paper or spring roll wrappers, cut to size (thinner)
- 1 pound fresh pasta, rolled thin and cut to size
- 1 pound fresh or thawed frozen bean curd skins/*yuba/wu pei/dou fu bao*, cut to size
- 8 to 12 ounces dried bean curd skins/tofu bamboo/tofu leather/*doufu zhu*, soaked in hot water for 1 hour, then cut to size

WOOD EAR FUNGUS *See CLOUD EAR/BLACK TREE FUNGUS*

WORCESTERSHIRE SAUCE – 1 tablespoon
- 1 tablespoon gluten-free Worcestershire sauce, such French's non-gluten; or anchovy-free vegetarian sauce flavored with molasses, soy sauce, and vinegar
- 1/2 tablespoon steak sauce or HP sauce plus 1/2 tablespoon water and a drop or two of lemon juice or vinegar
- 1 scant tablespoon soy sauce, 3 or 4 drops hot pepper sauce, 1/8 teaspoon lemon juice, and a few grains of sugar
- 1 tablespoon mushroom ketchup, 3 drops hot pepper sauce, and 1/8 teaspoon superfine sugar
- 1 tablespoon Worcestershire sauce powder (used dry in cooking or spice rubs)
- 1 tablespoon Bragg Liquid Aminos or Coconut Aminos

WRAPPERS FOR FOOD, NONEDIBLE (soak dried leaves in hot water until softened and pliable, 10 to 60 minutes, then drain and pat dry)

- Agave leaves
- Avocado leaves
- Bamboo leaves, fresh or dried (cut out the dried stem after softening)
- Banana leaves, fresh or thawed frozen, cut into pieces
- Breadfruit leaves
- Corn husks, fresh or dried (use several layers if necessary)
- Lotus leaves
- Maguey leaves
- Plantain leaves, cut into pieces
- Ti leaves, fresh
- Yuka leaves

WRAPPERS FOR FOOD, PREPARED EDIBLE

- Bean curd sheets/tofu skins (fresh, frozen, or dried)
- Bread, thinly sliced lengthwise (homemade or store-bought)
- Crepes, thin pancakes, blintzes, and dosas (homemade or store-bought)
- Dough for bread, pastry, pizza, and biscuits (fresh or frozen)
- Dumpling/gyoza/*jiaozi* wrappers (fresh or frozen)
- Empanada dough disks (frozen)
- Flatbreads: chapati or phulka, soft lavash, naan, paratha, piadini, pita, or roti (fresh or frozen)
- Lumpia wrappers (fresh or frozen)
- Omelets/Japanese egg sheets, paper-thin (homemade)
- Frozen phyllo pastry (fresh or frozen)
- Rice paper, or rice-flour spring-roll skin/wrappers (fresh or frozen)
- Samosa wrappers (fresh or frozen)
- Tortillas: corn, flour, whole spelt, and whole-wheat (fresh or frozen)
- Wonton, *siu mai*, and spring roll wheat flour pastry wrappers (fresh or frozen)

WRAPPERS FOR FOOD, VEGETABLE-BASED *(For thin leaves blanch in boiling water 10 seconds; for thick leaves, 1 to 5 minutes until softened; or microwave, covered, 2 to 3 minutes on High. If necessary, flatten the main rib or shave it to make it the same thickness as the rest of the leaf, or cut it out entirely)*

- Large burdock leaves
- Cabbage leaves: green, napa, or Savoy
- Daikon or butternut squash sheets (peeled, trimmed to create flat edges, then shaved into paper-thin strips)
- Young chaya leaves
- Fava leaves, preferably mature
- Fig leaves, usually Black Mission
- Grape leaves
- Greens: beet, choy sum, collard, kale, kohlrabi, young mallow, mustard, parsnip, Swiss chard, mature spinach, or turnip
- *Hoja santa* leaves
- *La-lot* leaves
- Lettuce leaves (large outer leaves): butterhead, crisphead, iceberg, looseleaf, or romaine (If necessary, soften briefly in the microwave or dip into boiling water.)
- Papaya leaves
- Perilla or shiso leaves
- Radicchio leaves
- Turmeric leaves
- Wild pepper leaves/*la-lot* leaves
- Zucchini slices (Trim large zucchini, cut into paper-thin lengthwise strips, sprinkle with salt, and let soften about 20 minutes. Rinse and pat dry. Alternatively, bake raw slices at 350°F until barely softened.)

X

XANTHAN GUM/POLYSACCHARIDE POWDER (thickening, emulsifying, and stabilizing agent) – 1 teaspoon (4 g)
- 1 1/4 teaspoons guar gum
- 2 teaspoon powdered unflavored gelatin or agar powder (soften in water)
- 2 teaspoon psyllium powder
- 2 tablespoons potato flour

XOCOLATA A LA PEDRA (Catalonian chocolate) See CHOCOLATE, MEXICAN

XO SAUCE (Chinese spicy, dried-seafood-based condiment) – 1 tablespoon
- 1 tablespoon oyster sauce plus a touch of chili oil (or sesame or peanut oil plus cayenne or other hot chile powder)

XTABENTUN (Yucatan anise-flavored spirit) – 2 tablespoons
- 2 tablespoons Absente, anisette, Galliano, Herbsaint, ouzo, Pernod, or another anise-flavored liqueur

XYLITOL (Low-calorie natural sweetener) – 1 tablespoon
- 1 tablespoon sucralose, such as Splenda
- 1 tablespoon Sucanat, granulated sugar, or raw/unrefined sugar (more calories)
- 1 to 4 drops liquid stevia (or to desired sweetness)

Y

YACÓN SLICES, DRIED (South American tuber) – 1 cup
- 1 cup dried apple slices

YACÓN SYRUP (South American thick brown sweetener) – 1 cup
- 1 cup date syrup, palm honey/syrup, blackstrap molasses; amber agave syrup/nectar, coconut nectar, or Swedish dark syrup/*mörk sirap*

YAKISOBA NOODLES, DRIED – 3-ounce packet
- 1 (3-ounce) packet instant ramen noodles (thinner)

YAKISOBA SAUCE (Japanese stir-fry flavoring sauce) – 1 tablespoon
- 1 tablespoon Japanese brown sauce or tonkatsu sauce

YAKITORI SAUCE (Japanese grilling sauce and glaze) – 1 cup *See also TERIYAKI SAUCE*
- 1 cup heavy teriyaki sauce (or 1 1/2 cups thin teriyaki sauce, boiled until reduced to 1 cup)

YAM BEAN (West African and Asian tuberous vegetable) – 1 pound
- 1 pound jícama or hard pears (for cooking, salads or pickling)
- 1 pound water chestnuts, fresh or canned (for cooking or salads; rinse or blanch the canned type)

YAU CHOY/YU CHOY SUM/CAI XIN/PAK KAT/MONG TOI (Chinese vegetable) – 1 pound
- 1 pound Chinese baby broccoli/*gai lan miew*, Chinese broccoli, or bok choy

YAUTIA *See MALANGA/YAUTIA*

YEAST, ACTIVE DRY – 1 teaspoon
- 3/4 teaspoon instant yeast (add dry to ingredients; let the dough rise only once and reduce the rising time by 40 to 50%)
- 2 teaspoons compressed fresh yeast (crumble dry into ingredients)
- 1/2 teaspoon each baking soda and lemon juice stirred together (add to wet and dry ingredients at the end; use for no-rise pizza dough)

YEAST, ACTIVE DRY – 1 packet (1/4 ounce/2 1/4 teaspoons)
- 1 (1/4-ounce) packet instant yeast (add to dry ingredients and reduce the rising time by 40 to 50%; not for refrigerated dough)
- 1 (0.6-ounce) cake (1 tablespoon plus 1 teaspoon) compressed fresh yeast (crumble into dry ingredients)
- 1/2 teaspoon instant yeast (add to dry ingredients; knead the dough half as long, then let rise 2 to 3 times longer than normal, deflating and turning it over every 1 1/2 to 2 hours)

YEAST, ALE, GRANULATED (fermenting agent for homebrew) – 1 packet/2 teaspoons (enough for 5 gallons)
- 3 tablespoons (1 tube or pouch) liquid ale yeast (longer fermentation time)

YEAST, CHAMPAGNE OR WINE, GRANULATED (fermenting agent for homebrew) – 1 teaspoon
- 1 teaspoon granulated ale yeast
- 1 teaspoon active dry bread yeast (for homebrewed sodas; yeastier taste; shorter fermentation time)

YEAST, COMPRESSED FRESH/BAKER'S YEAST – 1 (0.6-ounce) cake
- 1 (1/4-ounce) packet instant yeast (add to dry ingredients; let the dough rise only once and reduce the rising time by 40 to 50%)
- 1 (1/4-ounce) packet active dry yeast (dissolve the yeast in 1/4 cup 110°F water following the package directions)

- 2 cups fermented yeast starter/sponge/sourdough starter (use at room temperature and reduce the liquid in the recipe by 1 cup)
- 1/2 teaspoon active dry yeast (let the dough rise in the refrigerator for 12 to 24 hours, then bring to room temperature and let finish rising before shaping and proofing)

YEAST, COMPRESSED, FRESH/BAKER'S YEAST – 2 ounces
- 3 small (0.6-ounce) cakes fresh compressed yeast
- 1 ounce (3 tablespoons) active dry yeast or 4 (1/4-ounce) packages (dissolve the yeast in 1 cup 110°F water following the package directions)

YEAST, INSTANT/RAPID RISE/FAST RISING/BREAD MACHINE YEAST – 1 teaspoon
- 1 1/4 teaspoons active dry yeast (dissolve the yeast in 1/4 cup 110°F water; let the dough rise twice, and increase the rising time)
- 2 teaspoons compressed fresh yeast (crumble into dry ingredients; let the dough rise twice and increase the rising time)
- 1/2 teaspoon active dry yeast plus 1 1/2 cups pre-ferment starter or sponge (increase the salt in the recipe by 1/4 teaspoon and decrease the water accordingly, by about 1 tablespoon)
- 1/2 teaspoon active dry yeast (let the dough rise in the refrigerator for 12 to 24 hours, then bring to room temperature and, if necessary, let finish rising before shaping and proofing)
- 1/2 teaspoon each baking soda and lemon juice stirred together, then added to the batter at the end (for no-rise pizza dough)

YEAST, LAGER OR SAKE, LIQUID – 1 1/2 tablespoons (1/2 tube)
- 2 teaspoons (1 packet) dry champagne or wine yeast

YEAST, NUTRITIONAL (dietary supplement and vegan cheese flavoring condiment) – 1 tablespoon powdered
- 2 tablespoons nutritional yeast flakes (smoother texture)
- 2 to 3 teaspoons brewer's yeast or debittered brewer's yeast (more bitter)

☞ 2 to 3 teaspoons yeast extract paste, such as Marmite, Vegemite, or Organic Gourmet European Nutritional Yeast Extract Savory Spread (saltier and stronger)

☞ 1 tablespoon finely grated, very sharp Parmesan or Romano cheese (for the cheese flavoring only)

YEAST STARTER, WILD (starter for rye bread)
☞ 1 cup strained brine from a jar of dill pickles or cornichons at room temperature (use as part of the liquid called for in a 4-cup rye bread recipe)

YÉET (Sudanese fermented dried fish)
☞ Southeast Asian-style fish sauce *See FISH SAUCE*

YELLOW BEAN SAUCE *See CHINESE YELLOW/BROWN BEAN SAUCE; VIETNAMESE YELLOW BEAN SAUCE*

YELLOW FOOT MUSHROOMS *See CHANTERELLE MUSHROOMS*

YELLOW SOYBEANS, SALTED FERMENTED (Chinese cooking condiment) – 1 tablespoon
☞ 1 1/2 tablespoons Chinese yellow bean sauce/brown bean paste/ *mien see*, Thai yellow bean sauce/*tao jiew*, or Vietnamese yellow bean sauce/*tuong ot*

☞ 1 or 2 tablespoons Japanese all-purpose light miso (such as *genmai* or *shinshu*)

YERBA BUENA/WILD MINT *See MINT, FRESH*

YERBA MATE (South African tea with 25 mg caffeine per cup) – 1 cup
☞ 1 cup guayusa tea/*Ilex guayusa* (Ecuadorian rainforest tea; less bitter taste; richer in antioxidants)

YOGURT CHEESE – 1 cup (8 ounces) *See also LABNA*
Make Your Own Line a sieve with a double layer of dampened cheesecloth (or 3 basket-type paper coffee filters) and set over a

bowl. Place 3 cups plain full-fat yogurt (or 2 cups plain Greek-style yogurt) in the sieve, cover with plastic wrap or a plate and refrigerate for 24 to 48 hours to drain. (Use yogurt with live cultures and without pectin or other additives/stabilizers.)

YOGURT GARLIC SAUCE *See GARLIC YOGURT SAUCE*

YOGURT, FULL-FAT/WHOLE (3.5 to 5% fat content) – 1 cup
- 2/3 cup 2% Greek-style yogurt and 1/3 cup milk
- 2/3 cup full-fat Greek-style yogurt and 1/3 cup water
- 1 cup nonfat yogurt (lower in calories; higher in sugar and protein)
- 1 cup nondairy yogurt, such as almond, coconut, rice, or soy (lower in protein; higher in sugar)
- 1/2 cup each full-fat Greek-style yogurt and plain nonfat yogurt
- 1 cup low-fat yogurt plus 1 tablespoon heavy cream
- 1 cup goat's milk yogurt (tarter tasting; does not curdle when heated)
- 1 cup sheep's milk yogurt (creamy consistency; higher in calcium and protein)
- 1 cup Bulgarian buttermilk (tarter tasting; thinner consistency)
- 1 cup sour cream, crème fraîche, or Mexican *crèma agria* (for cooking or as a condiment)
- 1 cup fruit puree or thick unsweetened applesauce (for cooking)
- Nonfat yogurt powder (for dressings, sauces, and casseroles)

YOGURT, GREEK-STYLE, FULL-FAT OR 2% – 1 cup
- 1 1/2 to 2 cups plain yogurt (full-fat or low-fat, without pectin or additives) drained for several hours in the refrigerator, in a sieve lined with a double layer of dampened cheesecloth (or a basket-type paper coffee filter)
- 1 cup Icelandic-style skyr yogurt (thicker)
- 1 cup *labna* (richer)
- 1 cup reduced-fat sour cream (for cooking)

YOGURT STARTER/CULTURE – 1 teaspoon Bulgarian 411 powdered culture; or 1 (5-gram) package freeze-dried starter
- 2 tablespoons very fresh room-temperature plain yogurt (full-fat, low-fat, nonfat, or Greek-style) with live active cultures and without additives
- 3 crushed acidophilus tablets (this makes 1 quart when combined with 4 cups pasteurized whole milk, heated and cooled to 115°F, then incubated undisturbed at 100°F to 110°F for 8 to 12 hours)

YOMOGI (Japanese seasoning for soba noodles)
- Fresh mugwort/*ssuk*
- Tender wild mugwort/*Artemisia vulgaris*
- Arugula or watercress leaves (different flavor)

YUCA ROOT/MANIOC, FRESH (African and South American starchy root staple) – 2-pound piece, 2-inches in diameter/3 cups peeled, cored, cut into pieces
- 1 (16-ounce) bag frozen cooked grated yuca, thawed and squeezed
- 1 (24-ounce) bag frozen peeled yuca pieces, fibrous cores removed and cooked for 10 minutes
- 1 (28-ounce) can yuca pieces, drained and rinsed
- 2 pounds fresh taro or yautia, peeled and cooked (wear plastic gloves when peeling taro)
- 1 pound waxy boiling potatoes, such as Red Bliss, peeled or unpeeled and cooked

YU CHOY SUM See YAU CHOY

YUFKA (Turkish flatbread) – 1 (9-inch) round
- 1 *markouk*, folded in half
- 1 (10-inch) thin flour tortilla

YUFKA SHEET (Turkish paper-thin pastry sheet) – 1 large sheet
- 4 sheets thick country-style phyllo dough/*horiatiko*

YUZU/MISHO YUZU (Japanese small tart citrus fruit) – 1
- 1 or 2 *sudachi*
- One-half Meyer lemon (less bitter)

YUZU JUICE, UNSALTED – 1 tablespoon fresh, frozen, or bottled
- 1 tablespoon unsalted *sudachi* juice (slightly more acidic)
- 3/4 teaspoon salted yuzu juice plus 2 1/4 teaspoons fresh lemon juice
- 1 teaspoon each grapefruit, lemon, and lime juice
- 2 1/2 teaspoons fresh lime juice plus 1/2 teaspoon fresh orange juice

YUZU ZEST – 1 teaspoon
- 1/3 teaspoon dried yuzu peel, softened in 2 teaspoons warm water for 15 minutes, then finely chopped
- 3/4 to 1 teaspoon yuzu powder
- 1 to 2 teaspoons lemon zest or fully ripened Key lime zest

Z

ZA'ATAR LEAVES (Middle Eastern seasoning) – 1 sprig
- ᵇ 1 sprig fresh thyme or 1/2 teaspoon dried crushed leaves
- ᵇ 1 sprig fresh Syrian oregano/*Origanum syriacum* or 1/2 teaspoon dried crushed leaves

ZA'ATAR/ZAHTAR/ZATAR SPICE (Middle Eastern seasoning) – 1 tablespoon
- ᵇ 2 teaspoons lightly toasted sesame seeds, 2 teaspoons dried thyme, 1 teaspoon dried sumac berries (or 2 teaspoons lemon zest), and a pinch of salt, coarsely ground with a mortar and pestle or in a spice/coffee grinder

ZAMBO SEEDS/CHILACAYOTE (Ecuadorian seasoning) – 1 ounce
- ᵇ 1/4 cup shelled raw pumpkin seeds

ZEDOARY/WHITE TURMERIC/MANGO GINGER/AMBA HALDI (Indian and Southeast Asian seasoning) – 1 dried slice
- ᵇ 1 slice dried galangal/*galanga* (add directly to a soup or stew without soaking)
- ᵇ 1/4 to 1/2 teaspoon ground *zedoary* powder
- ᵇ 1/8 to 1/4 teaspoon powdered *kencur*, Laos powder, or galangal paste
- ᵇ Tiny pinch ground ginger
- ᵇ 1 small piece fresh or thawed frozen galangal

ZEPPOLI, MINI (Italian holeless doughnuts) – 1 dozen
- ᵇ 1 dozen small Hawaiian *malasadas*

Make Your Own Cut pizza dough into 12 (1-inch) pieces, roll into balls, and fry 3 or 4 at a time in 350°F oil until golden, 2 to 3 minutes on each side. Drain on paper towels and sprinkle with confectioners' sugar.

ZERESHK (Middle Eastern small dried berries) – See BARBERRIES

ZINFANDEL VINEGAR – 1 tablespoon
- ⇨ 1 tablespoon Cabernet Sauvignon vinegar, or other mellow red wine vinegar
- ⇨ 1 tablespoon red wine

ZUCCHINI BLOSSOMS See SQUASH BLOSSOMS, SUMMER

ZUCCHINI/ITALIAN SQUASH/COURGETTES (straightneck, round, and baby/mixed colors) – 1 pound
- ⇨ 1 pound pattypan or scallop, globe, calabacitas, yellow squash (straightneck or crookneck), Tromboncino, young Zuccheta, or Zephyr summer squash
- ⇨ 1 pound young calabash/cucuzza, chayote, or bottle gourd
- ⇨ 1 pound green, immature Potimarron squash (for round French zucchini/Ronde de Nice; more dense)
- ⇨ 1 pound seedless cucumbers, such as Armenian, Asian, Persian, or Kirby (juicier)

Thank you for purchasing this book, lovely reader.
I hope you will find it useful. JBM

BIBLIOGRAPHY

Arasaki, Seibin, and Teruko Arasaki. *Vegetables from the Sea*. Tokyo: Japan Publications, 1983.

Agricultural Research Service, U.S. Department of Agriculture. *Cheeses of the World*. New York: Dover Publications, 1972.

Alford, Jeffrey, and Naomi Duguid. *Beyond the Great Wall: Recipes and Travels in the Other China*. New York: Artisan, 2008.

———. *Seductions of Rice: A Cookbook*. New York: Artisan, 1998.

American Heart Association Low-Salt Cookbook: A Complete Guide to Reducing Sodium and Fat in your Diet. 4th ed. New York: Clarkson Potter, 2011.

America's Test Kitchen eds. *The How Can It Be Gluten Free Cookbook*: *Revolutionary Techniques. Groundbreaking Recipes*. Brookline, MA: America's Test Kitchen, 2014.

Baljekar, Mridula. *Curry Lover's Cookbook*. London: Southwater, 2009.

Barham, Peter. *The Science of Cooking*. New York: Springer-Verlag, 2001.

Bartlett, Jonathan. *The Cook's Dictionary and Culinary Reference: A Comprehensive Definitive Guide to Cooking and Food*. Chicago: Contemporary Books, 1996.

Başan, Ghillie. *The Turkish Kitchen*. London: Southwater, 2010.

Bayless, Rick. *Rick Bayless's Mexican Kitchen*. New York: Scribner, 1996.

Beard, James. *Beard on Food*. New York: Alfred A. Knopf, 1974.

Belleme, Jan, and John Belleme. *Cooking with Japanese Foods*. Garden City Park, NY: Avery, 1993.

Bender, David D. *Dictionary of Food and Nutrition*. 2nd ed. Oxford: Oxford University Press, 2005.

Beranbaum, Rose Levy. *The Bread Bible*. New York: W.W. Norton, 2003.

———. *The Cake Bible*. New York: William Morrow, 1988.

———. *The Pie and Pastry Bible*. New York: Scribner, 1998.

Bladholm, Linda. *The Asian Grocery Store Demystified*. Los Angeles: Renaissance Books, 1999.

——— . *The Indian Grocery Store Demystified*. Los Angeles: Renaissance Books, 2000.

——— . *Latin & Caribbean Grocery Stores Demystified*. Los Angeles: Renaissance Books, 2001.

Booth, Shirley. *Food of Japan*. Brooklyn, NY: Interlink Books, 2002.

Botsacos, Jim. *The New Greek Cuisine*. With Judith Choate. New York: Broadway Books, 2006.

Boxer, Arabella, Jocastas Innes, Charlotte Parry-Crooke, and Lewis Esson. *The Encyclopedia of Herbs, Spices, and Flavorings*. New York: Crescent Books, 1984.

Boyce, Kim. *Good to the Grain: Baking with Whole-Grain Flours*. With Amy Scattergood. New York: Stewart, Tabori & Chang, 2010.

Braker, Flo. *The Simple Art of Perfect Baking*. New York: William Morrow, 1985.

Cancler, Carole. *The Home Preserving Bible*. New York: Alpha Books, 2012.

Carroll, Ricki. *Home Cheese Making: Recipes for 75 Homemade Cheeses*. 3rd ed. North Adams, MA: Storey Publishing, 2002.

——— . "Knotty, Nice." *Los Angeles Times*, October 20, 2011, sec. E.

Chattman, Lauren. *Bread Making: A Home Course*. North Adams, MA: Storey Publishing, 2011.

Child, Julia. *The French Chef Cookbook*. New York: Alfred A. Knopf, 1968.

Claiborne, Craig. *Craig Claiborne's The New York Times Food Encyclopedia*. Compiled by Joan Whiteman. New York: Times Books, 1985.

Compestine, Ying Chang. *Cooking with an Asian Accent: Eastern Wisdom in a Western Kitchen*. New York: Houghton Mifflin Harcourt, 2014.

Conte, Anna del. *Gastronomy of Italy*. London: Pavillion Books, 2001.

Corriher, Shirley O. *BakeWise: The Hows and Whys of Successful Baking with over 200 Magnificent Recipes*. New York: Scribner, 2008.

Cost, Bruce. *Bruce Cost's Asian Ingredients: Buying and Cooking the Staple Foods of China, Japan and Southeast Asia*. New York: William Morrow, 1988.

Cowin, Dana. "Chefs, Can You Please Lighten Your Food?" *Food and Wine*, March 2010, 96.

Cox, Jeff. *The Essential Book of Fermentation: Great Taste and Good Health with Probiotic Foods*. New York, Avery, 2013.

Credicott, Tammy. *The Healthy Gluten-Free Life: 200 Delicious Gluten-Free, Dairy-Free, Soy-Free & Egg-Free Recipes*. Las Vegas, NV: Victory Belt Publishing, 2012.

Cunningham, Marion. *The Fannie Farmer Cookbook*. 13th ed. New York: Alfred A. Knopf, 1996.

Curry, Lynn. *Pure Beef: An Essential Guide to Artisan Meat with Recipes for Every Cut*. Philadelphia: Running Press, 2012.

Cusumano, Camille. *Tofu, Tempeh, and Other Soy Delights*. Emmaus, PA: Rodale Press, 1984.

Dahlen, Martha. *A Cook's Guide to Chinese Vegetables*. Hong Kong: Workman Press, 2000.

Daley, Regan. *In the Sweet Kitchen*. New York: Artisan Workman, 2001.

D'Aprix, David. *The Fearless International Foodie*. New York: Living Language, 2001.

David, Elizabeth. *English Bread and Yeast Cookery*. American Edition. New York: Viking Press, 1997.

Davidson, Alan. *The Oxford Companion to Food*. Oxford: Oxford University Press, 1999.

Davis, Adelle. *Let's Cook It Right*. New York: New American Library, 1974.

De Mers, John. *Authentic Recipes from Jamaica*. Singapore: Periplus Editions, 2005.

DeWitt, Dave, and Nancy Gerlach. *The Spicy Food Lover's Bible*. New York: Stewart, Tabori & Chang, 2005.

——— . *The Whole Chile Pepper Book*. Boston: Little, Brown, 1990.

Duane, Jean. *The Complete Idiot's Guide to Gluten-Free Cooking*. New York: Alpha Books, 2012.

Duea, Angela Williams. *The Complete Guide to Food Preservation: Step-by-Step Instructions on How to Freeze, Dry, Can and Preserve Food*. Ocala, FL: Atlantic Publishing Group, 2011.

Elias, Thomas S., and Peter A. Dykeman. *Edible Wild Plants*. New York: Sterling Publishing, 2009.

Emery, Carla. *The Encyclopedia of Country Living: 40th Anniversary Edition*. Seattle: Sasquatch Books, 2012.

English, Camper. "The New Sweet." *Fine Cooking*, April-May, 2010, 37.

Fearnley-Whittingstall, Hugh, and Nick Fisher. *The River Cottage Fish Book: The Definitive Guide to Sourcing and Cooking Sustainable Fish and Shellfish*. Berkeley, CA: Ten Speed Press, 2012.

Field, Carol. *The Italian Baker*. rev. ed. Berkeley, CA: Ten Speed Press, 2011.

Figoni, Paula. *How Baking Works: Exploring the Fundamentals of Baking Science*. 3rd ed. Hoboken, NJ: John Wiley & Sons, 2011.

Forkish, Ken. *Flour Water Salt Yeast: The Fundamentals of Artisan Bread and Pizza*. Berkeley, CA: Ten Speed Press, 2012.

Gardiner, Anne, and Sue Wilson. *The Inquisitive Cook*. With the Exploratorium. New York: Henry Holt, 1998.

Gibbons, Euell. *Stalking the Good Life: My Love Affair with Nature*. New York: David McKay Co. 1971.

Gigliotti, Lynne. *Mediterranean Cooking at Home with the Culinary Institute of America*. New York: Houghton Mifflin Harcourt, 2013.

Gisslen, Wayne. *Professional Cooking*. 5th ed. New York: John Wiley & Sons, 2003.

Glezer, Maggie. *Artisan Baking*. New York: Artisan, 2005.

Gorsky, Faith. *An Edible Mosaic: Middle Eastern Fare with Extraordinary Flair*. Rutland, VT: Tuttle Publishing, 2012.

Goulding, Sylvia. *Festive Foods: Mexico*. New York: Chelsea Clubhouse, 2008.

Greeley, Alexandra, ed. *Vegetarian Times Complete Cookbook*. Hoboken, NJ: Wiley Publishing, 2005.

Green, Aliza. *Starting with Ingredients*. Philadelphia: Running Press, 2006.

Green, Karen. *Japanese Cooking for the American Table*. Los Angeles: J.P. Tarcher, 1982.

Greene, Janet, Ruth Hertzberg, and Beatrice Vaughan. *Putting Food By*. 5th ed. New York: Penguin, 2010.

Grigson, Jane, and Charlotte Knox. *Exotic Fruits and Vegetables*. New York: Henry Holt, 1986.

Grigson, Sophie. *Gourmet Ingredients*. New York: Van Nostrand Reinhold, 1991.

Gunst, Kathy. *Condiments: The Art of Buying, Making and Using Mustards, Oils, Vinegars, Chutneys, Relishes, Sauces, Savory Jellies and More*. New York: G. P. Putnam's Sons, 1984.

Hachisu, Nancy Singleton. *Japanese Farm Food*. Kansas City, MO: Andrews McMeel Publishing, 2012.

Hachten, Harva. *Best of Regional African Cooking*. New York: Hippocrene Books, 1998.

Harbutt, Juliet. Cheese: *A Complete Guide to Over 300 Cheeses of Distinction*. Minocqua, WI: Willow Creek Press, 1999.

Harlow, Jay. *Cuisines of Southeast Asia: Thai, Vietnamese, Indonesian, Burmese & More*. Santa Rosa, CA: Cole Group, 1987.

Harris, Jessica B. *The African Cookbook: Tastes of a Continent*. New York: Simon & Schuster, 1998.

Hemphill, Ian. *The Spice and Herb Bible*. 2nd. ed. Toronto: Robert Rose, 2006.

Herbst, Sharon Tyler. *The Food Lover's Tiptionary*. New York: Hearst Books, 1994.

Herbst, Sharon Tyler, and Ron Herbst. *The Cheese Lover's Companion*. New York: William Morrow, 2007.

——— . *The New Food Lover's Companion*. 4th ed. Hauppauge, NY: Barron's Educational Series, 2007.

Hibler, Janie. *The Berry Bible with 175 Recipes Using Cultivated and Wild, Fresh and Frozen Berries*. New York: HarperCollins, 2004.

Hill, Tony. *Contemporary Encyclopedia of Herbs and Spices: Seasonings for the Global Kitchen*. Hoboken, NJ: John Wiley & Sons, 2004.

Hilson, Beth. Ask the Chef. *Gluten Free & More*. June/July 2014, 22.

Hocherman, Geila, and Arthur Boehm. *Kosher Revolution: New Techniques and Great Recipes for Unlimited Kosher Cooking*. Lanham, MD: Kyle Books, 2011.

Holzen, Heinz von, and Lothr Arsana. *Authentic Recipes from Indonesia*. Singapore: Periplus, 2006.

Hom, Ken. *Ken Hom's Chinese Kitchen: With a Consumer's Guide to Essential Ingredients*. New York: Hyperion, 1994.

Hosking, Richard. *A Dictionary of Japanese Food Ingredients & Culture*. Rutland, VT: Charles E. Tuttle, 1996.

Hoy, Sharon Wong. *Cuisine of China*. Hawthorne, CA: Benshaw Publications, 1982.

Hoyer, Daniel. *Mayan Cuisine: Recipes from the Yucatan Region*. Layton, UT: Gibbs Smith, 2008.

Hsiung, Deh-Ta. *The Chinese Kitchen*. 1st U.S. ed. New York: St. Martin's Press, 1999.

Hupping, Carol, and the staff of Rodale Food Center. *Stocking Up III*. Emmaus, PA: Rodale Press, 1986.

Hurt, Jeanette. *The Complete Idiot's Guide to Dehydrating Foods*. New York: Alpha Books, 2013.

Imeson, Alan, ed. *Thickening and Gelling Agents for Food*. 2nd. ed. Gaithersburg, MD: Aspen Publishers, 1999.

Jaffrey, Madhur. *At Home with Madhur Jaffrey: Simple, Delectable Dishes from India, Pakistan, Bangladesh, and Sri Lanka*. New York: Alfred A. Knopf, 2010.

——— . *Madhur Jaffrey's A Taste of the Far East*. New York: Carol Southern Books, 1993.

Jenkins, Nancy Harmon. *The Essential Mediterranean*. New York: HarperCollins, 2003.

Jenkins, Steven. *Cheese Primer*. New York: Workman Publishing, 1996.

Joachim, David. *Brilliant Food Tips and Cooking Tricks*. Emmaus, PA: Rodale Press, 2001.

Jordan, Michele Anna. *Salt and Pepper*. New York: Broadway Books, 1999.

Kafka, Barbara. *The Intolerant Gourmet: Glorious Food Without Gluten and Lactose*. New York: Artisan. 2011.

Kallas, John. *Edible Wild Plants: Wild Foods from Dirt to Plate*. Layton, UT: Gibbs Smith, 2010.

Karim, Kay. *The Iraqi Family Cookbook*. New York: Hippocrene Books, 2012.

Karmel, Elizabeth. *Soaked, Slathered, and Seasoned: A Complete Guide to Flavoring Food for the Grill*. Hoboken, NJ: John Wiley & Sons, 2009.

Karoff, Barbara. *South American Cooking: Food and Feasts from the New World*. Berkeley, CA: Aris Books, 1989.

Katz, Sandor Ellix. *The Art of Fermentation: An In-Depth Exploration of Essential Concepts and Processes from around the World*. White River Junction, VT: Chelsea Green Publishing, 2012.

Kazuko, Emi. *Master Class in Japanese Cooking*. London: Pavillion Books, 2002.

Kelley, Laura. *Silk Road Gourmet*. vol. 1. Bloomingdale, IN: iUniverse, 2009.

Kennedy, Diana. *My Mexico: A Culinary Odyssey with More Than 300 Recipes*. New York: Clarkson Potter, 1998.

Keog, Kelly E. *Sugar-Free Gluten-Free Baking and Desserts*. Berkeley, CA: 2009.

Kimball, Christopher, ed. "Cooking Tips." *Cook's Illustrated*, March/April 2010, 17.

King Arthur Flour. *King Arthur Flour Whole Grain Baking*. Woodstock, VT: Countryman Press, 2006.

King Arthur Flour Master Weight Chart www.kingarthurflour.com/recipe/master-weight-chart.

Kingham, Karen. *Eat Well Live Well with Diabetes: Low-GI Recipes and Tips*. North Vancouver, BC: Whitecap Books, 2007.

Kipfer, Barbara Ann. *The Culinarian: A Kitchen Desk Reference*. Hoboken, NJ: John Wiley & Sons, 2011.

Kiwi Magazine editors. *Allergy-Friendly Food for Families*. Kansas City, MO: Andrews McMeel Publishing, 2012.

Kuntz, Bernie. *Whole Foods Kitchen Journal*. Redmond, WA: Elfin Cove Press, 1989.

Lanza, Louis, and Laura Morton. *Totally Dairy-Free Cooking*. New York: William Morrow, 2000.

Lappé, Frances Moore. *Diet for a Small Planet*. rev. ed. New York: Ballantine Books, 1975.

Larkcom, Joy. *Oriental Vegetables: The Complete Guide for the Gardening Cook*. 2nd ed. New York: Kodansha International, 2008.

Lawson, Nigella. *How to Eat*. Hoboken, NJ: John Wiley & Sons, 2000.

Lee, Cecilia Hae-Jin. *Eating Korean*. Hoboken, NJ: John Wiley & Sons, 2005.

Lesem, Jeanne. *Preserving Today*. New York: Owl Books, 1992.

Livingston, A.D. *The Whole Grain Cookbook*. New York: The Lyons Press, 2000.

Longbotham, Lori. *Lemon Zest: More than 175 Recipes with a Twist*. New York: Broadway Books, 2002.

Lucas, Glenis. *The Complete Guide to Gluten-Free and Dairy-Free Cooking*. London: Watkins Publishing, 2008.

Mackey, Leslie, and Sallie Morris. *Illustrated Cook's Book of Ingredients: 2,500 of the World's Best with Classic Recipes*. 1st. U.S. ed. New York: DK Publishing, 2010.

Madadian, Sacha. "Tasting Processed Egg Whites." *Cook's Country*. Feb/March, 2013, 23.

Madison, Deborah. *This Can't Be Tofu: 75 Recipes to Cook Something You Never Thought You Would—and Love Every Bite*. New York: Broadway Books, 2000.

Malgieri, Nick. *Chocolate*. New York: HarperCollins, 1998.

——— . *Nick Malgieri's Bread: Over 60 Breads, Rolls and Cakes Plus Delicious Recipes Using Them*. Lanham, MD: Kyle Books, 2012.

Marks, Gil. *Encyclopedia of Jewish Food*. Hoboken, NJ: John Wiley & Sons, 2010.

McCalman, Max, and David Gibbons. *Cheese: A Connoisseur's Guide to the World's Best*. New York: Clarkson Potter, 2005.

McGee, Harold. *Keys to Good Cooking: A Guide to Making the Best of Food and Recipes*. New York: The Penguin Press, 2010.

Medearis, Angela Shelf. *The New African-American Kitchen*. New York: Lake Isle Press, 2008.

Medrich, Alice. *Bitter Sweet: Recipes and Tales from a Life in Chocolate*. New York: Artisan, 2003.

Mendelson, Anne. *Milk: The Surprising Story of Milk through the Ages*. New York: Alfred A. Knopf, 2008.

Menzel, Peter, and Faith d'Aluisio. *What the World Eats*. Berkeley, CA: Tricycle Press, 2008.

Miller, Mark. *The Great Chile Book*. With John Harrisson. New York: Ten Speed Press, 1991.

Milton, Jane. *Mexican: Healthy Ways with a Favorite Cuisine*. London: Hermes House, 2008.

Mitchell, Paulette. *The Complete Soy Cookbook*. New York: Macmillan, 1998.

Montagné, Prosper, ed. *Larousse Gastronomique*. New York: Clarkson Potter, 2001.

Moonen, Rick, and Roy Finamore. *Fish Without a Doubt: The Cook's Essential Companion*. Boston: Houghton Mifflin, 2008.

Morgan, Lane. *The Ethnic Market Food Guide*. New York: Berkley Books, 1997.

Morimoto, Masaharu. *The New Art of Japanese Cooking*. New York: DK Publishing, 2007.

Morris, Julie. *Superfood Kitchen: Cooking with Nature's Most Amazing Foods*. New York: Sterling Epicure, 2012.

Mouritsen, Ole G. *Seaweeds: Edible, Available & Sustainable*. Chicago: University of Chicago Press, 2013.

Niall, Mäni. *Sweet & Natural Baking: Sugar-Free, Flavorful Recipes from Mäni's Bakery*. San Francisco: Chronicle Books, 1996.

Nilsen, Angela, and Jeni Wright. *21st Century Cook: The Bible of Ingredients, Terms, Tools & Techniques*. London: Cassell Illustrated, 2006.

North, Justin. *French Lessons: Recipes and Techniques for a New Generation of Cooks*. Victoria, Australia: Hardie Grant Books, 2007.

Novas, Himilce, and Rosemary Silva. *Latin American Cooking Across the U.S.A.* New York: Alfred A. Knopf, 1997.

Nyerges, Christopher. *Guide to Wild Foods and Useful Plants*. Chicago: Chicago Review Press, 1999.

Ortiz, Elisabeth Lambert, ed. *The Encyclopedia of Herbs, Spices & Flavorings*. New York: Dorling Kindersley, 1992.

Outlaw, Nathan. *Modern Sea Food*. Guilford, CN: Lyons Press, 2013.

Owen, Sri. *Indonesian Regional Cooking*. New York: St. Martin's Press, 1994.

Paino, Joe, and Lisa Messinger. *The Tofu Book: The New American Cuisine; A Complete Culinary Guide to Using Tofu*. New York: Avery, 1991.

Parks, Simon, and Udit Sarkhel. *The Calcutta Kitchen*. Northampton, MA: Interlink Books, 2007.

Pascal, Cybele. *Allergy-Free and Easy Cooking*. Berkeley, CA: Ten Speed Press, 2012.

——— . *The Allergen-Free Baker's Handbook*. Berkeley, CA: Celestial Arts, 2009.

Pennington, Jean, and Judith Spungen Douglass. *Bowes & Church's Food Values of Portions Commonly Used*. 18th ed. Baltimore: Lippincott Williams & Wilkins, 2005.

Pépin, Jacques. *Jacques Pépin's Simple and Healthy Cooking*. Emmaus, PA: Rodale Press, 1994.

Phan, Charles. *Vietnamese Home Cooking*. New York: Ten Speed Press, 2012.

Phillips, Roger. *Wild Food*. Boston: Little, Brown, 1986.

Pitzer, Sara. *Homegrown Whole Grains: Grow, Harvest & Cook Wheat, Barley, Oats, Rice, Corn & More*. North Adams: Storey Publishing, MA, 2009.

Pleasant, Barbara. "All About Growing the Stevia Plant." *Mother Earth News*, February/March, 2013, 62.

Presilla, Maricel E. *Gran Cocina Latina: The Food of Latin America*. New York: W. W. Norton, 2012.

Quinn, Janie. *Essential Eating: Sprouted Baking with Whole Grain Flours That Digest as Vegetables*. Waverly, PA: Azure Moon Publishing, 2008.

Quinn, Lucinda Scala. *Jamaican Cooking: 140 Roadside and Homestyle Recipes*. New York: Macmillan, 1997.

Raichlen, Steven. *Steven Raichlen's Healthy Latin Cooking: 200 Sizzling Recipes from Mexico, Cuba, Caribbean, Brazil, and Beyond*. Emmaus, PA: Rodale Press, 1998.

Ramineni, Shubhra. *Entice with Spice: Easy Indian Recipes for Busy People*. North Clarendon, VT: Tuttle Publishing, 2010.

Reinhart, Peter. *Peter Reinhart's Whole Grain Breads: New Techniques, Extraordinary Flavor*. Berkeley, CA: Ten Speed Press, 2007.

——— . *The Bread Baker's Apprentice: Mastering the Art of Extraordinary Bread*. Berkeley, CA: Ten Speed Press, 2001.

Resnik, Linda, and Dee Brock. *Food FAQs: Substitutions, Yields & Equivalents*. Tyler, Texas: FAQs Press, 2000.

Riely, Elizabeth. *The Chef's Companion: A Culinary Dictionary*. 3rd ed. Hoboken, NJ: John Wiley & Sons, 2003.

Ringland, Eleanor, and Lucy Ringland Winston. *Fiestas Mexicanas*. 2nd ed. San Antonio, TX: Naylor, 1967.

Rinzler, Carol Ann. *The New Complete Book of Herbs, Spices, and Condiments*. New York: Checkmark Books, 2001.

——— . *What to Use Instead*. New York: Pharos Books, 1987.

Robertson, Robin. *The Laurel's Kitchen Bread Book: A Guide to Whole-Grain Breadmaking*. New York: Random House, 1984.

Roden, Claudia. *The New Book of Middle Eastern Food*. New York: Alfred A. Knopf, 2007.

Rolland, Jacques L, and Carol Sherman. *The Food Encyclopedia*. Toronto: Robert Rose, 2006.

Rombauer, Irma S., Marion Rombauer Becker, and Ethan Becker. *Joy of Cooking: All about Pies and Tarts*. New York: Scribner, 2002.

——— . *Joy of Cooking*. 75th anniv. ed. New York: Scribner, 2006.

Santibañez, Roberto. *Truly Mexican*. With J. J. Goode and Shelley Wiseman. Hoboken, NJ: John Wiley & Sons, 2011.

Sass, Lorna. *Whole Grains: Every Day Every Way*. New York: Clarkson Potter, 2006.

Schneider, Elizabeth. *Uncommon Fruits & Vegetables: A Commonsense Guide*. New York: William Morrow, 1998.

Schmidt, Arno. *Chef's Book of Formulas, Yields, and Sizes*. New York: Van Nostrand Reinhold, 1990.

Scott, Jack Denton. *The Complete Book of Pasta*. New York: Galahad Books, 1968.

Seaver, Barton. *Where There's Smoke: Simple, Sustainable, Delicious Grilling*. New York: Sterling Epicure. 2013.

Selva Rajah, Carol. *Heavenly Fragrance: Cooking with Aromatic Asian Herbs, Fruits, Spices, and Seasonings*. Singapore: Periplus, 2007.

Shafia, Louisa. *Lucid Food: Cooking for an Eco-conscious Life*. Berkeley, CA: Ten Speed Press, 2009.

Shimbo, Hiroko. *Hiroko's American Kitchen Cooking with Japanese Flavors*. Kansas City, MO: Andrews McMeel Publishing. 2012.

Shurtleff, William, and Akiko Aoyagi. *The Book of Miso*. 2nd ed. Berkeley, Ten Speed Press, 2001.

Simmons, Marie. *The Amazing World of Rice*. New York: HarperCollins, 2003.

Sinclair, Charles G. *International Dictionary of Food & Cooking*. Chicago: Fitzroy Dearborn Publishers, 1998.

Skelly, Carole J. *Dictionary of Herbs, Spice, Seasonings, and Natural Flavorings*. New York: Garland Publishing, 1994.

Smith, Barbara. *B. Smith Cooks Southern-Style*. New York: Scribner, 2009.

Solomon, Charmaine. *Encyclopedia of Asian Food*. With Nina Solomon. Sydney, Australia: New Holland Publishers, 2010.

Solomon, Karen. *Can It, Bottle It, Smoke It: And Other Kitchen Projects*. Berkeley, CA: Ten Speed Press, 2011.

——— . *Jam It, Pickle It, Cure It*. Berkeley, CA: Ten Speed Press, 2009.

Song, Young Jin. *The Korean Kitchen*. London: Southwater, 2010.

Sortun, Ana, with Nicole Chaison. *Spice: Flavors of the Eastern Mediterranean*. New York: Regan Books, 2006.

Spieler, Marlena. *Peppers Peppers Peppers*. Buffalo, NY: Firefly Books, 1999.

Stagg, Camille. *The Cook's Advisor*. Brattleboro, VT: Stephen Greene Press, 1982.

Stander-Horel, Lisa, and Tim Horel. *Nosh on This: Gluten-Free Baking from a Jewish-American Kitchen*. New York. The Experiment, 2013.

Steel, Susan, ed. *Home Herbal: Cook, Brew, and Blend Your Own Herbs*. New York: DK Publishing, 2011.

Steinback, Jyl. *The Fat Free Living Super Cookbook*. New York: Warner Books, 1997.

Takahashi, Yoko I. *The Tokyo Diet*. With Bruce Cassiday. New York: William Morrow, 1985.

Techamuanvivit, Pim. *The Foodie Handbook: The (Almost) Definitive Guide to Gastronomy*. San Francisco: Chronicle Books, 2009.

Teubner, Christian. *The Cheese Bible*. New York: Penguin Studio, 1998.

——— . *The Vegetable Bible*. New York: Penguin Studio, 1998.

Teubner, Christian, Eckart Witzigmann, and Tony Khoo. *The Rice Bible*. North Vancouver, BC: Viking Studio, 1999.

Teubner, Christian, Silvio Rizzi, and Tan Lee Leng. *The Pasta Bible*. New York: Penguin Studio, 1996.

The Illustrated Cook's Book of Ingredients: 2,500 of the World's Best with Classic Recipes. 1st. U.S. ed. New York: DK Publishing, 2010.

This, Hervé. *Kitchen Mysteries: Revealing the Science of Cooking.* New York: Columbia University Press, 2007.

Thompson, David. *Classic Thai Cuisine*. Berkeley, CA: Ten Speed Press, 1993.

Time-Life Books. *Preserving: The Good Cook/Techniques & Recipes Series*. Alexandria, VA: Time-Life Books, 1981.

Timperley, Carol, and Cecilia Norman. *A Gourmet's Guide to Cheese.* Los Angeles: HP Books, 1989.

Triêu, Thi Choi, and Marcel Isaak. *The Food of Vietnam: Authentic Recipes from the Heart of Indochina*. Singapore: Periplus, 1997.

Trilling, Susana. *Seasons of My Heart: A Culinary Journey Though Oaxaca, Mexico*. New York: Ballantine Books, 1999.

Tsuji, Shizuo. *Japanese Cooking: A Simple Art*. 25th anniv. ed. With Mary Sutherland. New York: Kodansha International, 2006.

United States Department of the Army. *The Illustrated Guide to Edible Wild Plants*. Guilford, CT: The Lyons Press, 2003.

Van Aken, Norman. *New World Kitchen: Latin American and Caribbean Cuisine*. With Janet Van Aken. New York: HarperCollins, 2003.

Vinton, Sherri Brooks. *Put 'em Up: A Comprehensive Home Preserving Guide for the Creative Cook, from Drying and Freezing to Canning and Pickling*. North Adams, MA: Storey Publishing, 2010.

Virgin Islands Cooperative Extension Service Bulletin No. 1: Native Recipes. St. Croix, U.S. Virgin Islands, 1978.

Ward, Susie, Claire Clifton, and Jenny Stacey. *The Gourmet Atlas*. New York: Macmillan, 1997.

Waters, Alice. *The Art of Simple Food*. New York: Clarkson Potter, 2007.

Weiss, Linda. *Kitchen Magic: Food Substitutions for the Allergic*. New Canaan, CT: Keats Publishing, 1994.

Welanetz, Diana von, and Paul von Welanetz. *The Von Welanetz Guide to Ethnic Ingredients*. Los Angeles: J. P. Tarcher, 1982.

Wickramasinghe, Priya, and Carol Selva Rajah. *The Food of India*. London: Murdock Books, 2002.

Wildsmith, Lindy. *Cured: Salted, Spiced, Dried, Smoked, Potted, Pickled, Raw*. Iola, WI: Krause Publications, 2010.

Wilson, Carol. *Preserving: Self Sufficiency*. New York: Skyhorse Publishing, 2009.

Wolfert, Paula. *Mediterranean Grains and Greens*. New York: HarperCollins, 1998.

——— . *Paula Wolfert's World of Food*. New York: Harper & Row, 1988.

Wong, David. *Authentic Recipes from Thailand*. Singapore: Periplus, 2004.

Wood, Marion N. *Gourmet Food on a Wheat-Free Diet*. Springfield, IL: Charles C. Thomas, 1967.

Wood, Rebecca. *The New Whole Foods Encyclopedia*. New York: Penguin/Arkana, 1999.

Yu, Su-mei. *Cracking the Coconut: Classic Thai Home Cooking*. New York: William Morrow, 2000.

Zane, Eva. *Middle Eastern Cookery*. San Francisco: 101 Productions, 1974.

Zanger, Mark H. *The American Ethnic Cookbook for Students*. Phoenix: Oryx Press, 2001.

Zanini De Vita, Oretta, and Maureen B. Fant. *Sauces & Shapes: Pasta the Italian Way*. New York: W. W. Norton, 2013.

Zibat, Eve. *The Ethnic Food Lover's Companion*. Birmingham, AL: Menasha Ridge Press, 2001.

Also by Jean B. MacLeod

If Id' Only Listened to My Mom, I'd Know How to Do This:
Hundreds of Household Remedies

The Waste-Wise Kitchen Companion; Hundreds of Practical Tips for
Repairing, Reusing, and Repurposing Food

The Waste-Wise Gardener: Tips and Techniques to Save Time, Money, and
Energy While Creating the Garden of Your Dream

The Kitchen Paraphernalia Handbook: Hundreds of Substitutions for
Common (and Not-So-Common) Utensils, Gadgets, Tools, and Techniques

Seasoning Substitutions
Swaps and Stand-ins for Sweet or Savory Condiments and Flavorings

Baking Substitutions
The A-Z of Common, Unique, and Hard-to-Find Ingredients

Asian Ingredient Substitutions: Fish and Fruit, Veggies and Vittles,
Noodles and Noshes, Seasonings and Sauces, and more

Made in United States
North Haven, CT
18 October 2024